London

Here's what the critics say about Frommer's:

"Amazingly easy to use. Very portable, very complete."
—*Booklist*

♦

"Complete, concise, and filled with useful information."
—*New York Daily News*

♦

"Hotel information is close to encyclopedic."
—*Des Moines Sunday Register*

♦

"The only mainstream guide to list specific prices. The Walter Cronkite of guidebooks—with all that implies."
—*Travel & Leisure*

Other Great Guides for Your Trip:

Frommer's London from $70 a Day

Frommer's Born to Shop London

Frommer's Memorable Walks in London

Frommer's Irreverent Guide to London

Frommer's England

Frommer's England from $60 a Day

*Frommer's Complete Hostel Vacation Guide to England,
Scotland & Wales*

Frommer's Driving Tours in Britain

Frommer's Europe

The Complete Idiot's Guide to Planning Your Trip to Europe

Frommer's® 99

London

by Darwin Porter
and Danforth Prince

MACMILLAN • USA

ABOUT THE AUTHORS

Authors Darwin Porter and Danforth Prince share their love of their favorite European city with this guide. Porter, a bureau chief for *The Miami Herald* at 21 who later worked in television advertising, wrote the first-ever book to London for Frommer's. He's joined by Prince, formerly of the Paris bureau of *The New York Times*. Together, they're the authors of several best-selling Frommer's guides, notably to England, France, the Caribbean, Italy, and Germany.

MACMILLAN TRAVEL

A Simon & Schuster Macmillan Company
1633 Broadway
New York, NY 10019

Find us online at **www.frommers.com**

ISBN 0-02-862277-4
ISSN 1096-6439

Editor: Dan Glover
Production Editor: Michael Thomas
Design by Michele Laseau
Digital Cartography by Roberta Stockwell and Ortelius Design
Photo Editor: Richard Fox
Page Creation by Kim Cofer and Heather Pope

SPECIAL SALES

Bulk purchases (10+ copies) of Frommer's and selected Macmillan travel guides are available to corporations, organizations, mail-order catalogs, institutions, and charities at special discounts, and can be customized to suit individual needs. For more information write to Special Sales, Macmillan General Reference, 1633 Broadway, New York, NY 10019.

Manufactured in the United States of America

Contents

List of Maps

An Invitation to the Reader

In researching this book, we discovered many wonderful places—hotels, restaurants, shops, and more. We're sure you'll find others. Please tell us about them, so we can share the information with your fellow travelers in upcoming editions. If you were disappointed with a recommendation, we'd love to know that, too. Please write to:

Frommer's London
Macmillan Travel
1633 Broadway
New York, NY 10019

An Additional Note

Please be advised that travel information is subject to change at any time—and this is especially true of prices. We therefore suggest that you write or call ahead for confirmation when making your travel plans. The authors, editors, and publisher cannot be held responsible for the experiences of readers while traveling. Your safety is important to us, however, so we encourage you to stay alert and be aware of your surroundings. Keep a close eye on cameras, purses, and wallets, all favorite targets of thieves and pickpockets.

What the Symbols Mean

✪ Frommer's Favorites

Our favorite places and experiences—outstanding for quality, value, or both.

The following abbreviations are used for credit cards:

AE	American Express	EURO	Eurocard
CB	Carte Blanche	JCB	Japan Credit Bank
DC	Diners Club	MC	MasterCard
DISC	Discover	V	Visa
ER	EnRoute		

Find Frommer's Online

Arthur Frommer's Outspoken Encyclopedia of Travel (www.frommers.com) offers more than 6,000 pages of up-to-the-minute travel information—including the latest bargains and candid, personal articles updated daily by Arthur Frommer himself. No other Web site offers such comprehensive and timely coverage of the world of travel.

Central London

E-0133

Introducing the City by the Thames

Look out, Paris, and step aside, New York—these days, there's so much fun to be had in London that it's being called the hottest, coolest city in the world.

The very name, LON-DON, still sounds heavy, ponderous, like the ringing of Big Ben in one of those low budget, old black-and-white English mystery films that the Rank group used to churn out. The great clock continues to strike the hour, somberly and consistently, as if setting a dull, gray tone for life in staid old London. But change is now upon us, and some seven million Londoners are marching to a different beat—because Swinging London is back.

A BRITISH RENAISSANCE! LONDON'S GOT ITS GROOVE BACK! These headlines are part of a global media blitz heaped on a British capital that's more eclectic and electric than it's been in years. There's almost a feeding frenzy setting out to prove that London is the most pulsating, vibrant city on the planet, even rivaling New York for sheer energy, outrageous art, trendy restaurants, and a nightlife equal to none. *Newsweek* hailed London as a "hip compromise between the nonstop newness of Los Angeles and the aspic-preserved beauty of Paris—sharpened to New York's edge." *Wine Spectator* proclaims more modestly that "The sun is shining brighter in London these days."

The sounds of Britpop and techno pour out of Victorian pubs, experimental theater is taking over stages that were built for Shakespeare's plays, and upstart chefs are reinventing the bland dishes British mums made for generations into a new and inventive cuisine; for the first time ever, Brits are even running the couture houses of Dior and Givenchy. In food, fashion, film, pop music, the visual arts, and just about everything else, London stands at the cutting edge again, just as it did in the 1960s. But today, instead of names like Mary Quant, Twiggy, and Mick Jagger and Marianne Faithfull ruling the scene, it's such celebrities as the Spice Girls, cow-sawing artist Damien Hirst, and the couple-of-the-moment, actress Patsy Kensit and Liam Gallagher (the lead singer of Oasis, the most beloved band in England since the Beatles), whose names pop up everywhere, from fashion spreads to tabloid headlines. If there's talk of a McCartney today, it's not billionaire Paul, but his daughter Stella, whose street-smart power suits and fitted frock coats are all the rage (of course, she works for the fun of it all, not because she has to—not with all those bags of Beatle billions in her future).

Impressions

I love my city, despite its tattered fabric, its antediluvian public transport system . . . and its unutterable cliquishness and snobbery. I love it for the great, ruckled, grimy surface it presents—a surface that has been distressed by the passage of two thousand years of history.

—Will Self (1996)

When a man is tired of London, he is tired of life, for there is in London all that life can afford.

—Dr. Samuel Johnson (1777)

But if you just don't give a hoot about the new London—if this sea of change worries you more than it appeals to you—rest assured: Staid old London (as we lovingly think of it) still lives, basically intact under the veneer of hip. This ancient city has survived a thousand years of invasion, from the Normans to the Blitz, so a few scenesters moving in isn't going to change anything in the long run—London will forever be one of history's greatest cities. From high tea at Brown's to the changing of the guard at Buckingham Palace, the city still abounds with the tradition, charm, and culture of days gone by.

Discovering London and making it your own can be a bit of a challenge, especially if you have just a little time. Even in the 18th century, Daniel Defoe found London "stretched out in buildings, straggling, confused, out of all shape, uncompact and unequal; neither long nor broad, round nor square." His words still hold true today: London is a city that has never quite made up its mind about its own size. The City of London proper is merely 1 square mile of very expensive real estate around the Bank of England. All the gargantuan rest of the city we think of as London is made up of separate villages, boroughs, and corporations—Westminster, Chelsea, Hampstead, Kensington, and many more—each with its own mayor and administration ready to fight for its independent status at the drop of an ordinance. Together, however, they add up to a mammoth metropolis, once the largest on the globe.

The millions of people who call London home live on a parcel of land that's more than 609 square miles. Luckily, whether you're looking for Dickens's House or the Dr. Marten's Superstore, only a minute fraction of this territory need concern you. The rest is monotonous suburbia, stretching endlessly into the horizon, red-roofed and bristling with TV antennas. But the heart, the brick and mortar core of this behemoth, is one of the most fascinating areas on earth. For about a century, one-quarter of the world was ruled from Central London (comprised by the 1-square-mile City and the conglomeration of villages known as the West End). With almost every step you take, you'll come across some sign of the tremendous influence this city has exerted over our past thoughts and actions—and still wields today.

London is a mass of contradictions. On the one hand, it's a decidedly royal city, studded with palaces, court gardens, coats-of-arms, and other regal paraphernalia. Yet it's also the home of the world's second-oldest parliamentary assembly (Iceland has the oldest); even way back in 1649, when handsome and rash King Charles I tried to defy the members of Parliament, he found himself swept off his throne and onto a scaffold.

Today, London is less English and more international. The gent with the bowler hat has long gone out of fashion; today's Londoner might arrive in a turban. It's becoming easier to find a café au lait and a croissant than a scone and a cup of tea. Increasingly, the city is home to many of the world's immigrants and refugees, both rich and poor, from all reaches of the world.

What's really amazing is that this city—ancient and modern, sprawling and compact, stolidly English and increasingly multicultural—works as well as it does. Come, and discover.

1 Frommer's Favorite London Experiences

- **Watching the Sunset at Waterloo Bridge.** Waterloo Bridge is the ideal place in London to watch the sun set over Westminster, to the west. From here, you can see the last rays of sunlight bounce off the dome of St. Paul's and the City spires in the East End, too.
- **Enjoying a Traditional Afternoon Tea.** Nothing is more typically British. Try the Hotel Goring, dating from 1910. From the lounge, you'll look upon a small garden as you enjoy finger sandwiches (often watercress or cucumber), the hotel's special Ceylon blend tea, scones and clotted cream, and the chef's famous light fruit cake, offered from a trolley.
- **Cruising London's Waterways.** In addition to the Thames, London is riddled with an antique canal system, complete with towpath walks, bridges, and wharves. Replaced by the railroad, the canal system remained forgotten until recently, when it was rediscovered by a new generation. Now, in a process of urban renewal that's been called "industrial archaeology," the old system has been restored, bridges painted and repaired, and towpaths cleaned up. See "Sightseeing & Boat Tours Along the Thames" in chapter 6.
- **Spending Sunday Morning at Speakers' Corner.** At the northeastern corner of Hyde Park, near Marble Arch, a 19th-century British tradition carries on. Speakers sound off on any subject they want, and "in-your-face" hecklers are part of the fun. You might hear everything from denunciations of the monarchy to antigay rhetoric. Anyone can get up and speak. The only rules: You can't blaspheme, be obscene, or incite a riot. The tradition began in 1855—before the legal right to assembly was guaranteed in 1872—when a mob of 150,000 gathered to attack a proposed Sunday Trading Bill. Orators from all over Britain have been taking advantage of this spot ever since.
- **Studying the Turners at the Tate.** Upon his death in 1851, J.M.W. Turner bequeathed his personal collection of 19,000 watercolors and some 300 paintings to the people of Britain. He wanted his finished works, some 100 paintings, displayed under one roof. Today at the Tate, you get not only Turner, but glimpses of the Thames through the museum's windows. How appropriate—the artist lived and died on its banks in Chelsea and painted the river in its many changing moods.
- **Strolling Through Covent Garden.** George Bernard Shaw got his inspiration for *Pygmalion* here, where the character of Eliza Doolittle sold violets to wealthy operagoers and became a household name around the world. The old fruit and vegetable market, with its Cockney cauliflower peddlers and butchers in blood-soaked aprons, is long gone. What's left is just as interesting: Covent Garden today is London's best example of urban renewal and one of its hippest shopping districts. In the footsteps of Chippendale and Dickens, you can wander about and discover colorful street stalls, an array of boutiques, shops selling one-of-a-kind merchandise, and all the while enjoy the city's best sidewalk entertainment. There's an antiques market in the piazza on Monday and a crafts market Tuesday through Saturday. When you're parched, plenty of pubs in the area will quench your thirst, like the Nag's Head, an Edwardian pub that'll serve you a draft Guinness and a plate of pork cooked in cider.

- **Treasure-Hunting for Antiques.** Some 2,000 antiquarians live within the city limits of London. Check with the tourist office to see if a major antiques fair is on at the time of your visit; the Dorchester Fair and Grosvenor House Fair take place in June. If not, head for one of the following antiques centers selling everything from plain old junk (mugs with Prince Philip's face on them) to rare bric-a-brac. The best ones are **Gray's and Gray's** in the Mews, 58 Davies St. (Tube: Bond Street); **Chelsea Antiques Market,** 245A-53 King's Rd. (Tube: Sloane Square); and **Alfie's Antique Market,** 13–25 Church St. (Tube: Edgware Road).

- **Shopping Harrods.** Regardless of how many times you visit London, it's hard to resist a visit to this vast Knightsbridge emporium. Spread across 15 acres, Harrods proclaims as its motto *Omnia Omnibus Ubique* or "everything for everyone, everywhere." They mean it, too: Someone didn't believe the claim, and in 1975 called Harrods at midnight and ordered that a baby elephant be delivered to the home of the governor of California and his First Lady, Mr. and Mrs. Ronald Reagan in Sacramento. The animal arrived safely, albeit a bit bewildered. (Nancy even sent a "thank you" note.) The food halls are our favorite section, with some 500 different cheeses and some 163 brands of whisky among zillions of other goodies. It's estimated that at Christmas, Harrods sells 100 tons of Christmas puddings. You can even arrange your funeral at the store.

- **Rowing on the Serpentine.** When the weather's right, we always like to head to this 41-acre artificial lake dating from 1730. A stream was dammed to create the artificial lake, whose name derives from its winding, snakelike shape. At the Boathouse, you can rent (they call it "hire") a boat by the hour. With the right companion, it's one of the most idyllic ways to spend a sunny London afternoon. Renoir must have agreed; he depicted the custom on canvas.

- **Making a Brass Rubbing.** Re-create all those costumed ladies and knights in armor from England's age of chivalry. One good place to make your very own brass rubbing is the crypt of St. Martin-in-the-Fields in Trafalgar Square; the staff there will be happy to show you how.

- **Getting to Know North London on a Sunday.** Begin by looking for some smart fashion at Camden Market, a Sunday affair in the northern reaches of Camden High Street where stallholders hawk designer jewelry and clothing. Next, walk up to Hampstead Heath off Well Walk and take the right fork, which will lead you to an open field with a panoramic view of London. If you walk long and hard enough, you'll be ready for a traditional Sunday lunch at Jack Straw's Castle at North End Way. Cap your meal with a visit to the Freud Museum, which is open on Sunday until 5pm.

- **Dining at Rules.** Rules, at 35 Maiden Lane (WC2), was first established as an oyster bar in 1798; it may, in fact, be the oldest restaurant in London. Long a venue for the theatrical elite and literary beau monde, it still serves the same dishes that delighted Edward VII and his mistress, Lillie Langtry. They always began with champagne and oysters behind a closed door upstairs. Charles Dickens liked the place so much he had a regular table. Over the years, everyone from William Thackeray to Clark Gable has enjoyed its pheasant and grouse. Where else can you get a good purée of parsnips these days, anyway? If you're looking for unreconstructed British cuisine, finish off with the treacle sponge or apple suet pudding—how English can you get?

- **Spending a Night at the West End Theater.** London is the theatrical capital of the world. The live stage offers a unique combination of variety, accessibility, and economy—and perhaps a look at next year's Broadway hit.

The House of Windsor Online

In the spring of 1997, Elizabeth II made history by launching the first official royal Web site. You can now find more than 150 pages of history, information, and trivia about the Windsors and the British monarchy online at **www.royal.gov.uk**.

* **Crawling the London Pubs.** Americans bar hop, Londoners do a pub crawl. With some 5,000 pubs within the city limits, you would be crawling indeed if you tried to have a drink in each of them. Enough traditional ones remain, especially in central London, to make it worthwhile to go on a crawl. While making the rounds, you can partake of that peculiarly British fare known as "pub grub," which might include everything from a ploughman's lunch (a hunk of bread, cheese, and a pickle) to a plate of shepherd's pie.

    Here's our favorite crawl, which gives you a chance to see several of London's districts: Begin at **Dickens Inn** by the tower on St. Katharine's Way (E1), then go on to **Ye Olde Cheshire Cheese,** Wine Office Court, 145 Fleet St. (EC4), before making your way to **Cittie of Yorke** at 22–23 High Holborn (WC1). Then it's off to **Old Coffee House** at 49 Beak St. (W1) in Soho, before descending on **Red Lion,** 2 Duke of York St. (SW1). If you're still standing, rush to **Shepherd's Tavern,** 50 Hertford St. (W1) in Mayfair, before the publican rings the bell for "final call."

2 On the Cutting Edge: London Today

It's been called the Futura 2000 of cities. With giddy energy and cutting-edge style, London has bounced back to reclaim its position as new wave capital of trendsetting chic.

After mourning the death of Princess Di, Prime Minister Tony Blair set about to create a "New Britain," which might be called a work in progress. Of course, critics have suggested that the new cool Britain is public relations hype, superficial labeling, and cosmetic change. Naturally some of the change occurring is faddish and undoubtedly transitory, but much is real. As Britain's capital, London is still proud of its past (although it's got a lot to be ashamed of, too), but is no longer encumbered by its role as seat of an Empire.

Whatever his critics say, Blair no longer rules over "the sick man of Europe," as England was called when Margaret Thatcher took over in 1979. Today, London presides over Europe's healthiest economy. Consumer-led industries such as music, design, entertainment, and cinema extend its cultural influence around the world. In politics, big changes are ahead: devolving power to disparate entities, especially Scotland and Northern Ireland, and maybe even to regions of England itself. There is big support for the enactment of a bill of rights and a freedom of information act.

The bundle of changes represent a restoration of confidence in London in the wake of 50 years of decline. London now accepts its position as the center of a diminished world power, though some conservative critics are aghast at the change. "Once," an irate MP said, "we ruled a great deal of the world. Now we are in danger of becoming a Disneyland for Americans who will no doubt demand that we parade the Queen out every day for their amusement."

Nothing gauges social change better than the monarchy itself. Following Diana's death, speculation raged that the queen would abdicate and that Prince Charles would never be king. Today Charles seems a liberated single parent and has even been getting

Impressions

If a city makes you arrogant and cruel, then something's happening in it. I'm just old enough to remember the Swinging '60s, when London was like that last. It's getting to be a bit like that now.

—Elvis Costello (1997)

London is not a pleasant place, it is not agreeable, or cheerful, or easy, or exempt from reproach. It is only magnificent.

—Henry James (1870s)

good press for his charitable works. The queen's 50th wedding anniversary was called a "love-in" by the tabloids.

Much of the money sparking London's growth and excitement comes from abroad, particularly from Hong Kong (returned to China in June 1997). Other millions are being earned, and spent, by upstart entrepreneurs—many from working-class backgrounds—who have emerged overnight as icons of pop culture or leaders in the global business market: London currently ranks with New York and Tokyo as one of the world's top nerve centers of financial, business, and banking networks that stretch to virtually every country on the globe. London is awash with *enfants terribles*, even on Savile Row (unthinkable!)—and they're all making a bundle.

The leader of the cutting-edge fashion scene is the outrageous Alexander McQueen, who's been known to wear his own haute couture gowns. But McQueen is often in Paris these days, where he's the chief designer for the House of Givenchy. Even at Dior, the less flamboyant (relatively speaking, that is) John Galliano has taken over and is busy reinventing its look. And the likes of Donna Karan, Calvin Klein, and Tommy Hilfiger have infiltrated Bond Street. In the words of *W,* London is fashion's Boom City.

Not just in fashion, but in almost every field of artistic endeavor, London artists, designers, and chefs are forging ahead. New icons are being created, such as Damien Hirst, who's so well established now that emerging young artists are often referred to as "a young Damien Hirst." Examples of Hirst's works have included cross-sectioned carcasses of mature sheep and cows cut open with chain saws, then immersed in a Plexiglas "sarcophagus" of formaldehyde for the viewing pleasure of millions.

Gentrification continues at a rapid pace. Once-slummish Notting Hill Gate is now the height of fashion, so hipsters are moving on to Clerkenwell, Islington, even West Brompton—these once-anonymous neighborhoods are all up and coming; now, even Alexander McQueen has an atelier on Hoxton Square in Shoreditch. The latest movers and shakers are now supplanting the jellied eel peddlers of the East End. (You have to head much deeper into the anonymous suburbs ringing London to find a true Cockney these days.)

Comparisons to the Swinging '60s are everywhere—but there are differences, big and small, as noted by keen social critics. Although London is more open and dynamic than it's been since 1969, it's not just one giant house party this time. "The Swinging '60s were also the silly '60s," Conservative Member of Parliament (and budding John Major) Jonathan Aitken said in his book, *The Young Meteors.* "What's changed from last time is that [now] it's more hardheaded, less silly. There's a greater understanding that the world is a competitive place." Although seldom mentioned by the press, the horror of AIDS has also served to keep today's London cooled down from a fever pitch. And all the trendy restaurants and pricey boutiques in the world can't change the facts that the dividing line grows between the rich and the poor, and violent crime—almost nonexistent not even all that long ago—increases at the rate of 8% annually.

Despite what the tabloids tell you, not everyone in London is madly obsessed with the cool youth culture, and not everyone spends all nights in techno clubs and hot new dining spots. "The Scene" is largely the province of the privileged—but the spirit of the New London has permeated society at every level. It's the diversity of cultures and tastes that's really making the city so fascinating these days. It seems that half the world is flocking to London, not just from the far-flung colonies of a once-great empire, but from such places as Argentina, Senegal, Algeria, and China. Currently one-fifth of London's population consists of ethnic minorities; based on present trends, those ethnic minorities are projected to rise to one-third of the city's population by the year 2010. The high-speed Eurostar rail link has brought the Continent to London's doorstep, but the invasion is of a kind Brits never expected: Many French (half of whom are under 25) now hop over for a bit of shopping and a good meal—almost unheard of until recently.

There is some bad news. Traffic moves at exactly the same pace it did in the reign of Victoria. And although the Industrial Revolution-era fogs of the "satanic mills" (as William Blake called them) have disappeared, pollution is still strong enough to have caused a rising rate of asthma in children. Unemployment remains at unacceptable rates, and racial tension is all too evident in London today, as is overcrowding.

But the Thames still flows through the city. Melina Mecouri is dead, and the Elgin Marbles from the Parthenon remain in the British Museum in spite of her campaign to return them to Greece. The Queen is still on her throne, although her crown might be a bit shaky these days, and the bobbies and Beefeaters are where you expect them to be. Playgoers flock to the latest productions in the West End just as some 500,000 young clubgoers descend on London's clubland every Saturday night. London's 7,000 pubs are as colorful as ever, and some are serving up better food than you can get at many restaurants. Madame Tussaud's is as gratuitously titillating as it's ever been. And on any night of the week, Londoners and visitors alike can choose from an array of entertainment and diversions almost unmatched by any city in the world. A born-and-bred Londoner recently said, with typical British understatement: "Even the sun itself shines on us now and again—if we're lucky."

3   History 101

The Celts, Romans & Early Middle Ages   London is a very old city by almost any standards. The oldest artifacts ever discovered in London and the first historical reference to the city date from the time of its occupation by the ancient Romans, who adapted a local Celtic name into the Latinized form, Londinium.

Julius Caesar raided England in 55 and 54 B.C., fording the Thames with his armies somewhere downstream from today's London. The bulk of written history dates from about a century later, during the era of Claudius's military campaigns of A.D. 43. Londinium had become a thriving port by A.D. 61. That same year, a union of Celtic tribes, led by Queen Boadicea, attacked the unprotected rear flank of the Roman armies during one of their northern campaigns, and burned the camp of Londinium to the ground.

Dateline

- **55 B.C.** Julius Caesar invades England; he lands just a short distance from present-day London.
- **A.D. 43** Roman armies defeat the Celts and establish a fortified camp called Londinium.
- **61** Celts from East Anglia burn and sack Londinium, but the settlement is repossessed by Romans.
- **410** Romans retreat from London and return to Europe.

continues

- **886** King Alfred, a Saxon, conquers London but rules from his seat at Winchester.
- **1066** Norman invasion of England. William the Conqueror defeats Harold at the Battle of Hastings and is crowned in Westminster Abbey.
- **1100s** London asserts its right for some measure of self-government, establishing the office of Lord Mayor.
- **1400s** Trade flourishes in London.
- **1509–47** Reign of Henry VIII. His feud with Rome over his divorce leads to the English Reformation; church property is confiscated, and the English monarch is declared head of the new Church of England.
- **1558** Elizabeth I ascends throne, solidifying England's position as a Protestant country.
- **1586** William Shakespeare moves to London and buys part of the Globe Theatre.
- **1640s** The Civil War: Much fighting between Cromwellians and Royalists. King Charles I is beheaded at London's Whitehall (1649).
- **1660** Charles II restored to the throne.
- **1665** A plague decimates the population.
- **1666** Great Fire, started in a bakery in Pudding Lane, demolishes much of the city.
- **1710** Wren's St. Paul's Cathedral completed.
- **1710–1820** The arts thrive and London's population increases. Industrial Revolution begins.
- **1837–1901** Reign of Victoria, longest in English history.
- **1851** The Great Exhibition, the brainchild of Victoria's Prince Consort, Albert, is

continues

The Romans erected a much larger camp (excavations reveal that it covered about 11 acres); its grid-work street plan was later altered into a convoluted tangle by medieval Londoners. Before they left, the Romans developed the city, but not to the status of a capital. (The heyday of London's excavations of the Roman occupation coincided with the clearing of World War II's rubble, when a Roman temple and statues dedicated to various Greek deities were revealed.)

The Romans advanced into northern England, as far as the site of Hadrian's Wall, but they faced continuous insurrections. In 410, by which time the seeds of Christianity had been sown in England, the emperor Honorius ordered the Roman legions back to the Continent, leaving England isolated from the European mainland for centuries.

In the 600s, London's first bishop, Mellitus, built a church in honor of St. Paul, but for the most part, London slumbered and stagnated. A hodgepodge of medieval houses arose, some reportedly in the middle of thoroughfares. The irregularity of medieval construction and property lines was reinforced by later generations of Londoners, who were usually required to respect the legal claims of earlier owners and builders. As a result, independent neighborhoods and private enclaves developed.

The Saxons, Danes & Vikings   After the Romans, the next major invaders of London were Teutonic Saxons and Danes, who arrived in about 449. Depending on who was in power, they either embraced or rejected Christianity. Mellitus, the reigning bishop, was banished, and London remained rigidly and lustily pagan.

One ruler who emerged from England's early Middle Ages was Alfred, King of the Saxons, who spent much of his career battling the Norse Vikings. In 886, Alfred strengthened London's fortifications: He appointed his son-in-law as governor, while he continued to rule his growing kingdom from his capital at Winchester. For a century after Alfred's death (around 900), his heirs were occupied almost exclusively with securing and protecting their holdings against the Viking invaders.

1066: The Normans Arrive   Though London was still not officially the island's capital, more and more treaties, rites of succession, and military conferences were hosted within its walls. The last Saxon king was Harold, who chose London as the site of his election. He ruled for only 9 months before the fateful Battle of Hastings in 1066. Here, the politics, bloodlines, language, and destiny of London were to change forever after the victory of the Norman armies, led by William the Conqueror, over the Saxon kingdom.

William the Conqueror was the first ruler to recognize fully the political importance of London. His coronation took place in Westminster Abbey, establishing a precedent that has been observed by almost all British monarchs since. He recognized the capital status of London and the power of the medieval church. Strengthening his political hold in the process, he acquiesced to the Saxon ecclesiastics by granting them many well-defined rights and privileges. He also built the White Tower, a fortification incorporated into the Tower of London by later monarchs.

During the 1100s, London asserted its right to some independence from the rest of England, reinforcing the role of its lord mayor. English monarchs, eager for the support of the country's wealthiest and most influential populace, bid for the fealty and allegiance of Londoners in the hopes that holding London was the key to controlling England.

By the 1400s, the banks of the Thames were lined with buildings, as London-based merchants built massive residences atop or beside their riverfront warehouses. Ferryboats plied the waterway, and life burgeoned on both banks of the river. The city was dotted with ecclesiastical buildings that were later confiscated by Henry VIII during the Reformation but whose neighborhoods and Catholic images (Blackfriars, Greyfriars, and Whitefriars) still remain as part of contemporary London.

The Reformation & Elizabethan London The modern history of London begins with the Tudors. Sadly, Henry VIII's Reformation (1530s) led to the physical destruction of many medieval buildings, and London—as the centerpiece of the country's political and religious conflicts—was sometimes a willing participant in many of the changes. London watched as two of Henry's wives, Anne Boleyn and Catherine Howard, and two of England's most prominent Roman Catholics, Sir Thomas More and Bishop John Fisher, were beheaded.

The wealth of the medieval churches was confiscated and redistributed to a newly appointed aristocracy willing to comply with Henry's wishes. The medieval gardens, convents, and priories of the Catholic church were divested and divided into narrow streets and overcrowded courtyards. The cripples and beggars who had been dependent on the church were unleashed, resourceless, on the population

held at the Crystal Palace in Hyde Park to celebrate Britain's international dominance in trade, science, and industry.

- **1863** The Underground opens.
- **1888** "Jack the Ripper" terrorizes London's East End with the murders of six "women of ill repute."
- **1897** Queen Victoria's Diamond Jubilee. London described as the "centre of an empire on which the sun never sets."
- **1900–05** Four new electric Underground lines rapidly expand the city into sprawling suburbs.
- **1901** Edward VII ascends throne. The end of the Victorian age.
- **1914–18** The devastating Great War.
- **1920–30** Vast new housing estates, funded in part by the "Homes for Heroes" program, quadruple the size of London.
- **1940** The Blitz. London bombed, mainly in the City and East End. St. Paul's stands alone amid the rubble. The city's staunch resistance in the face of destruction is often remembered as London's "finest hour."
- **1945–55** Private and local government redevelopment results in fast modernization.
- **1951** The Festival of Britain celebrates the centennial of the Great Exhibition and gives birth to the South Bank Arts Centre.
- **1953** Elizabeth II ascends throne to begin long reign as head of the scandal-ridden House of Windsor.
- **1955–65** Boom years for property developers, who erect skyscrapers, while the state concentrates on

continues

suburban housing. Mass immigration from the Caribbean, India, Pakistan, and Hong Kong begins, continuing steadily for 15 years.

- **1960–70** "Swinging London." An economic and cultural boom, immigration, and changing values and wealth patterns make London more cosmopolitan.
- **1987** Conservatives under Margaret Thatcher win third term.
- **1990** John Major becomes prime minister.
- **1992** Royals jolted by fire at Windsor Castle and marital troubles of their two sons. Deep recession signals the end of the booming 1980s and the start of a more sober decade.
- **1994** For the first time since the Ice Age, England is linked to the Continent— this time by rail via the Channel Tunnel.
- **1996** The IRA breaks a 17-month cease-fire with a truck bomb at the Docklands that claims two lives. Her Majesty prompts Charles and Di's divorce after the affront of the Princess of Wales's latest tell-all biography; Prince Andrew and Sarah Ferguson's divorce finalized. The government concedes a possible link between "Mad Cow Disease" and a fatal brain ailment afflicting humans.
- **1997** World press hails British Renaissance, as London swings again. Upstart moderate Labour leader Tony Blair becomes the Prime Minister in a landslide, giving Britain its first Labour government in three decades. Death of Princess Di in a car crash in Paris sends Britain into national mourning.

of London. Many recalcitrant nuns and monks, refusing to acknowledge the ecclesiastical leadership of the English monarch, were dragged through the streets to the scaffold, hanged by the neck, and disemboweled.

From the dissent, bloodshed, and strife of Reformation London sprang the creative juices of Elizabethan England, called so for the great queen who reigned from 1558 to 1603. William Shakespeare, arriving in London in 1586, bought part-ownership of the Globe Theatre, which was strategically located a short distance outside the puritanical jurisdiction of incorporated London. Along with the flowering of the arts, England, and especially London, simultaneously entered a period of mercantile and colonial expansion in the Americas, Asia, and Africa.

Plague, Fire & Revolution By the mid-1600s, London was crowded with half-timbered gabled houses topped by tile roofs. Streets were hopelessly narrow, especially those near the river, a result of reliance on the Thames for transport and commerce.

In the 1640s, London saw much fighting between the Puritan troops of Oliver Cromwell and the Royalist followers of Charles I, which culminated with Charles's execution in 1649 on the scaffold at Whitehall, followed by a decade of monarchless Protectorship under Cromwell. Not until 1660, when Charles II ascended to the throne, was the monarchy restored to power.

In 1665, the Great Plague swept through the city's overcrowded slums, claiming an estimated 75,000 lives. A year later, the Great Fire, which began in a bakery on Pudding Lane near London Bridge, destroyed much of the town, including 89 churches and 13,200 homes.

The 18th Century Urban planners, spearheaded by Sir Christopher Wren, used the tragedy of fire as an opportunity to replan and rebuild London. The beauty of Wren's churches remains unequaled in all of Britain. They include St. Mary-le-Bow, one of the most famous, as well as the new St. Paul's Cathedral, both finished by 1710.

By this time, the aristocracy had begun migrating westward toward Covent Garden and Whitehall. The most convenient method of transportation was still via the Thames, while the sedan chair allowed aristocrats to be carried over the filthy streets, where dung, sewage, and refuse littered the undrained cobblestones.

Despite the hardships, the arts and sciences flourished in London. In the second half of the century,

Joshua Reynolds painted his portraits; James Boswell wrote his reminiscences of lexicographer/critic/poet Samuel Johnson; David Garrick performed his famous Shakespearean roles; and some of the best landscape painting in the history of Europe was about to flower.

The spatial proportions of Georgian and (later) Regency architecture changed the facades of thousands of houses throughout London. For a limited number of citizens, the good life was bountiful, and London was the seat of all that was powerful, beautiful, desirable, intelligent, and witty.

The Victorian Age   The most visible progress, as well as the greatest expansion of London, occurred during the Victorian era, when railroad lines and steam engines, sewage systems, cabs, underground trains, and new building techniques transformed London into a modern metropolis and hugely expanded its borders. Massive slums in the city's interior were cleared, but their occupants ended up in newer, more remote slums that remain legendary as examples of the Industrial Revolution's most horrible urban blight. Traffic arteries were rammed through the city's center from west to east. And an unlikely meadow known as Porridge Island was transformed into Trafalgar Square.

Victorian London was the center of the largest empire the world had ever seen. Londoners left their homes to fill military and administrative posts in such faraway dependencies as Calcutta, Kenya, Singapore, and Hong Kong. The art treasures of the world filled London's museums and private houses. In poorer neighborhoods, dyed-in-the-wool Londoners evolved a dialect and attitude later identified as Cockney; its accent and humor filled the city's music halls and vaudeville houses and influenced entertainment from Sydney to San Francisco. London thrived, burgeoning into one of the most complicated and diverse capitals of Europe.

The Dawn of the 20th Century   During the early 1900s, Victoria's successor, Edward VII, brought elaborate pageantry back to affairs of state (and a welcome laissez-faire attitude to affairs of the heart). Buckingham Palace was enlarged and newly sheathed in a honey-colored layer of stone, and a massive statue to Victoria was erected in front of its newly opened processional avenue leading to the Admiralty Arch. The controversial neo-Gothic grandeur of the Albert Memorial helped define the era's architectural style, which permeated vast neighborhoods of London with its eclecticism, ornateness, and high individualism.

The World Wars   World War I sent shock waves through Britain, although George V, who ascended the throne in 1910, ruled steadfastly from his London seat. Even if the damage was relatively minor compared to that later inflicted by World War II, 922 bombs fell on the financial district (the City), causing great damage as well as 2,500 casualties; and almost everyone lost someone near and dear to them at the front. Enraged Londoners poured a collective effort into a conflict that was to be idealistically defined as "the War to End All Wars."

During World War II, however, at least 30,000 people died, and vast tracts of London were destroyed by aerial bombing. Westminster Abbey (parts of which had stood unmolested since the 11th century) and the magnificent bulk of the Houses of Parliament were seriously damaged over two nights in May 1941. During a period remembered for the indomitable spirit of the people, thousands of Londoners systematically moved their mattresses and bedclothes every night to the Underground (the city's subway tunnels), considered safe from Nazi bombing. Amazingly, although the neighborhood that surrounded it was almost completely destroyed, St. Paul's Cathedral escaped with only minor damage, rising majestically above the rubble like a beacon of hope for the sorely tested people of London.

Following World War II, vast rebuilding projects replaced London's bombed-out
rubble. The transportation system was improved. In 1953, the coronation of Elizabeth
II sparked a period of beautification, with myriad houses painted and millions of
flower beds planted.

Swinging London   *Time* magazine once wrote that, in every decade, the attention
of the world often focuses on one city as the place to be—New York in the 1940s,
Rome in the 1950s. In the 1960s, it was London. The pop-culture revolution that was
sweeping the globe seemed to take root here more than anywhere else in the world,
with the possible exception of San Francisco. The sound of the Beatles having "A Hard
Day's Night" was everywhere; no one remembered Elvis anymore. Mary Quant revo-
lutionized fashion, and her Granny Takes a Trip boutiques sprouted up along King's
Road. Young straight men—often wearing lipstick—flocked to Carnaby Street to don
ruffled Edwardian blouses in brilliant chartreuse with orange pants and pink high
heels. The air in the discos was laden with marijuana smoke inhaled by such icons as
Mick Jagger, who, according to the musical *Hair*, every boy secretly wanted to sleep
with. What had happened to staid old London? The horsey set was out, and rail-thin
Twiggy was in. It was the psychedelic 1960s, and the mantra of the day was the late
Timothy Leary's "tune in, turn on, drop out." London did just that, and even lived to
recover from the era of rampant sex, heavy drugs, and rock 'n' roll—but it would never
be the same again.

The 1970s & Beyond   In the 1970s and 1980s, a revitalized economy led to the
revival of some run-down districts (Notting Hill, parts of Chelsea, the Docklands) into
chic and desirable neighborhoods. English wits estimate that at one time or another
since the end of World War II, virtually every corner of London has been covered with
scaffolding, as builders, homeowners, and real-estate moguls add structural support,
modernized comforts, and new life to virtually every building.

Prime Minister Margaret Thatcher's reforms of the 1980s created new and modernized financial institutions, including a computerized London Stock Exchange,
whose presence has reinforced London's traditional role as a financial, shipping, and
insurance center. In 1990, Thatcher was replaced as prime minister by another
member of the Conservative party, the less flamboyant but also controversial John
Major. In 1992, it wasn't the prime minister but the House of Windsor that got the
boldest headlines. In a year that Elizabeth II labeled *annus horribilis*, a fire swept
Windsor Castle; the queen agreed to pay income taxes for the first time; and the marriages of two of her sons crumbled as Princes Charles and Andrew separated from their
wives, Diana and Sarah. Princess Anne, however, remarried.

Although England's (and London's) problems such as unemployment and terrorist
bombings continued to dominate the headlines in 1993, the problems of the royal
family captured the most print and TV time. That year was launched by "Camillagate,"

the release of sexually explicit phone conversations between Prince Charles and his longtime companion, the then-married Camilla Parker-Bowles. British author Anthony Holden wrote that the Crown was dragged "as deep into the mud as at any time in the 500 years since Henry VII found it there at Bosworth Field."

In 1994, talk and speculation continued to focus on the House of Windsor, but it was an engineering feat that captured London's attention even more. Queen Elizabeth II and François Mitterrand of France officially opened the Chunnel under the English Channel, the first link between Britain and France since the Ice Age. Pessimists predicted the "end of London as we know it before the foreign hordes descend."

The so-called fairy-tale marriage of Charles and Diana, which played out around the world, ended like a soap opera with a divorce in 1996. Prince Charles is a little poorer, having dug deep into his pockets for some $26 million in settlement. That money has now been inherited by William and Harry.

In 1997, everyone's attention shifted to the parliamentary election. John Major's support had been steadily eroding since the early '90s, but the public's confidence in him seemed to hit an all-time low with his handling of the mad-cow disease crisis. Although scientists now claim the epidemic will end naturally by 2001, many British voters blamed Major and the Tories for it.

The political limelight shifted to the young Labour leader Tony Blair. From his rock-star acquaintances to his "New Labour" rhetoric, which is chock-full of pop-culture buzzwords, he is a stark contrast to the more staid Major. And his media-savvy personality obviously registered with the British electorate. On May 1, 1997, the Labour Party ended 18 years of Conservative rule with a landslide election victory. Blair became Britain's youngest prime minister in 185 years, following in the wake of the largest Labour triumph since Winston Churchill was swept out of office at the end of World War II. At age 44 and newly installed at 10 Downing St., Blair is Britain's 50th prime minister.

Blair's election had many British entrepreneurs poised and ready to take advantage of what they perceived as enthusiasm for new ideas and ventures just as London was being touted by the press for its renaissance in the realms of art, music, fashion, and dining. Parallels to Harold Macmillan and his reign over the Swinging '60s seem inevitable, and insiders agree that something's in the air.

However, events took a shocking turn in August 1997 when Princess Diana was killed—along with her companion, Harrods heir Dodi al-Fayed—in a high-speed car crash in Paris.

"The People's Princess" still continued to dominate many headlines in 1998 with bizarre conspiracy theories about her death (or "murder," as some tabloids would have). Nevertheless, it isn't the royal family that is the mover and shaker in Britain today, but its relatively young prime minister, Tony Blair, who continues to lead Britain on a program of constitutional reform without parallel in this century. Critics fear that Blair will one day preside over a "disunited" Britain, with Scotland breaking away and Northern Ireland forming a self-government.

In spite of wide criticism of the royal family in the wake of Diana's death, there is little support for doing away with the monarchy in Britain today. If polls are to be believed, some three-quarters of the British populace want the monarchy to continue. At the very least it's good for the tourist trade, on which Britain is increasingly dependent, and what would the tabloids do without it?

4 The Architectural Landscape

Originally, London was a collection of scattered villages and towns that were unified under the pressure of the Industrial Revolution. During the 18th century, when the principles of "picturesque planning" were being evolved for a rapidly expanding London, planners consciously incorporated the best of the greens, riverbank terraces, and small-scale layouts of the original villages. These rural features (rigorously preserved by neighborhood residents today) are now completely enclosed by the bulk and congestion of urban London, but a little of the city's original flavor and feeling remains in such places as Chelsea, Whitechapel, Hammersmith, and Hampstead.

The Birth of English Architecture   Other than the ancient Roman temple of Mithras, excavated in the 1950s on Queen Victoria Street, and the ruins of a fortified wall discovered near Trinity Place, few architectural remnants of the city's Roman colonization exist. London's first major architectural style was imported from northern France. Defined as Norman Gothic, it was solid, majestic, and ideal for such defensive structures as gatehouses and castles. Decoration was blunt and geometric, arches were rounded. The style thrived in Britain until about 1190. It can best be admired today in the Tower of London, St. Bartholomew's, and the Temple Church.

Early English Gothic   As medieval England grew more sophisticated, both structural arches and the frames that surrounded windows were designed with pointed ("broken") tops, and exterior buttresses took on more solidity as the windows became larger. Cathedrals grew taller, with roofs and spires angled more steeply. In London, the Early English Gothic style was manifested in Westminster Abbey's Chapter House.

During the 1300s, the solid rectilinear lines of English cathedrals gave way to increasing ornateness as vaulting grew more complex and windows became ever larger. Eventually, cathedrals were highlighted with huge expanses of glass and fan-shaped vaulting that resembled the trunks and branches of trees gracefully frozen into stone ribbing. The style became known as Gothic Perpendicular. Its best London manifestation is in Henry VII's chapel in Westminster Abbey.

The Tudor to Jacobean Eras   The true surge in London's building didn't begin until the population explosion and outward urban expansion of the Renaissance. Until the early 1500s, London was contained by the original Roman walls and had only 50,000 inhabitants (about 20% more than it had when occupied by the Romans). By 1600, however, the population had passed the quarter-million mark, with only about 75,000 living within the walls.

The main inspirations for Tudor architecture were the Gothic lines and masses that had characterized ecclesiastical building since the 11th century, but this style was now applied to private residences and other structures. London's best examples of this style are St. James's Palace and Hampton Court, the home originally built by Henry VIII's Cardinal Wolsey.

By 1660, the population of London had reached a half-million, many of whom lived in overcrowded and filthy conditions. Their picturesque—but highly flammable—houses had a framework of oak beams whose open spaces were filled with mud, plaster, and chopped straw, and were sometimes whitewashed. More elaborate houses were constructed of brick and tile or slate in a style eventually identified as Jacobean. Low-ceilinged, with dark paneling and leaded-glass windows, they carried Elizabethan motifs to a grander and larger scale and gave off a rich feeling of comfort.

The Masters: Inigo Jones & Christopher Wren   Inigo Jones (1573–1652), the first great modern British architect, introduced the airily and mathematically precise designs promoted by Italian Renaissance architect Andrea Palladio. This style opted for strict spatial ratios of windows to doors, plus a balanced symmetry that often combined the three classic Greek orders (Doric, Ionic, and Corinthian) in gracefully symmetrical neoclassical grandeur. Two of Jones's most famous buildings are the Banqueting House at Whitehall and the Queen's House at Greenwich.

Make Love, Not War: Invasion of the American GIs

In 1943, George Orwell, author of *Animal Farm* and *1984*, wrote: "It is difficult to go anywhere in London without having the feeling that Britain is occupied territory." He wasn't referring to Nazi occupation; that very real threat never materialized. The occupiers Orwell was talking about were of a decidedly different kind: three million "boisterous, materialistic, and decidedly horny" American GIs.

Following the entry of the United States into World War II, Roosevelt, and later Truman, sent three million troops to England. For the most part, U.S. servicemen were hardly eager to rush off to the war-torn British Isles. One Kansas City soldier wrote home that "All of Britain is one gray, dark, muddy swamp."

Even though U.S. troops had arrived to save the English from an attack of Hitler's armies, many Yanks initially found their new hosts "snobbish, cold as their winters, and completely standoffish," according to one report. The British weren't exactly welcoming. The typical wisecrack of the day was: "The Yanks are overpaid, oversexed, overfed, and over here."

The GIs were making themselves quite at home nevertheless. More young male Brits than not were away fighting on foreign soil, leaving their wives and sweethearts behind. As we know from countless wartime memoirs, their hot-blooded American counterparts were more than happy to keep their lovely, lonely women warm at night. As that darling old British actress, Hermione Gingold, star of such films as *Gigi*, once confided to us: "My dear boy, I knew there was a war going on, and that people were dying. But those war years were something special. You Americans made the warmest bedfellows on those cold, rainy English nights."

To the recorded tunes of Glenn Miller's orchestra, thousands of Yanks fell in love with British girls. Black American soldiers felt particularly warmly welcomed; blacks from southern states who didn't dare date a white woman there found themselves swept up in romances with blooming English roses.

Many Brits wondered when the Yanks were ever going to fight. In the view of some, they spent all their time in Britain hanging out, "gum-chewing and jitter-bugging." Of course, D-day and the incredible courage and strength of the American troops would change that skeptical early view.

At the end of the war, however, reality set in, and many English sweethearts were left behind. More than a few, however, married their American servicemen and came to the United States: An unprecedented number of British war brides arrived on American shores in 1945.

For the complete story, read *Rich Relations: The American Occupation of Britain 1942–1945*, by David Reynolds (Random House, 1995), a book that's stirring up many wartime memories—some painful, some wonderful—among older Brits, and letting the next generation in on what happened on the home-front, too.

The Great Fire of 1666, which devastated huge neighborhoods of London, resulted in a revolutionary code of building. Borrowing heavily from construction techniques used in Holland, Sir Christopher Wren did much to replace a city previously built of wood with brick, stone, and (later) stucco. He rebuilt more than 50 churches, dozens of public buildings, and many private homes, making him the most prolific architect in Britain's history. His dignified yet graceful designs have been relentlessly copied

Britspeak

For many Americans, it's a shock to discover that the British speak a very different English language than we do. Believe it or not, there are enough differences between British English and American English to cause a total communication breakdown. Although the British use words and phrases you think you understand, they often have implications quite different from their U.S. equivalents.

When the British call someone "mean," they mean stingy. "Homely," meaning ugly or plain in America, becomes pleasant in England, meaning homey. "Calling" denotes a personal visit, not a phone call; however, a person-to-person phone call is a "personal call." To "queue up" means to form a line, which they do at every bus stop. And whereas a "subway" is an underground pedestrian passage, the actual subway system is called "the Underground" or "the tube." The term "theatre" refers only to the live stage; movie theaters are "cinemas," and the films themselves are "the pictures." And a "bomb," which suggests a disaster in America, means a success in England.

In a grocery store, canned goods become "tins," rutabagas become "swedes," eggplants become "aubergines," and endive is "chicory" (while, conversely, chicory is "endive"). Both cookies and crackers become "biscuits," which can be either "dry" or "sweet"—that is, except for graham crackers, which are "digestives."

The going gets rougher when you're dealing with motor vehicles. When talking about the actual vehicle, very little means the same except for the word "car," unless you mean a truck, which is called a "lorry." In any case, gas is "petrol," the hood is the "bonnet," the windshield is the "windscreen," and bumpers are "fenders." The trunk is the "boot," and what you do on the horn is "hoot."

Most of us already know that an English apartment is a "flat" and that an elevator is a "lift." And you don't rent a room or an apartment, you "let" it. Although the ground floor is the ground floor, the second floor is the "first floor." And once you set up housekeeping, you don't vacuum, you "hoover."

throughout the world. The greatest portion of his work was erected in London, the most famous being St. Paul's Cathedral. Other Wren works include Kensington Palace, the Royal Hospital in Chelsea, and portions of Hampton Court Palace.

Wren had submitted a plan to rebuild London on a French baroque-inspired plan of plazas, traffic circles, and panoramic avenues. Fearing the number of land disputes this would have involved, Charles II rejected the plan, and the city was rebuilt on a less grand and less coherent scale—one that respected the property lines and medieval layouts that had existed prior to the fire.

London, however, was about to embark on one of its greatest expansions. Where the municipal government failed in imposing a logical order on the city's architectural layout, private speculators created developments that usually included a series of almost identical facades opening onto a plaza, square, or garden. Covent Garden (designed by Inigo Jones in 1631) was the first of the monumental squares. Laden with neoclassical details and grand in its proportions, Covent Garden was followed by dozens of imitations, including such famous ones as Portman Square, Soho Square, Grosvenor Square, and Berkeley Square. Later, in the early 19th century, these were copied by private entrepreneurs who created the regular and rhythmic, less monumental neighborhoods

Going clothes shopping? Then you should know that undershirts are called "vests" and undershorts are "pants," while long pants are called "trousers" and their cuffs are called "turn ups." Panties are "knickers" and panty hose are "tights." Pullover sweaters can be called "jumpers," with little girls' jumpers being "pinafores." If you're looking for diapers, ask for "nappies."

The education system offers such varied types of schools, identified by an equally wide variety of terms, that to explain them all to the visitor would be too confusing. Briefly, however, the large English "public schools" (such as Eton) are similar to our large private prep schools (such as Andover). But the English also have other private, or "independent," schools on all levels. And all of the above charge tuition. In addition, there are "state schools," which we would call public schools. These include "primary schools" and secondary "comprehensive schools," "modern schools," and "grammar schools" that are equivalent to our junior and senior high schools.

In school and elsewhere, the letter Z is pronounced "zed," and zero is "nought." And if you want to buy an after-school treat, a Popsicle is called an "iced lolly."

If you really want a challenge in this arena, you can always take on Cockney. The Cockneys are indigenous Londoners, although strictly speaking, the label refers only to people born within the sound of the bells of St. Mary-le-Bow in Cheapside. The exact derivation of the word "Cockney" is lost in the mist of antiquity, but it's supposed to have meant an "odd fellow." And the oddest feature about this fellow is undoubtedly the rhyming slang he has concocted over the centuries, based on the rhyme—or the rhyme of a rhyme—that goes with a particular word or phrase. So take my advice and don't try to delve further, unless you happen to be Professor Higgins—pardon me—"'iggins."

And the British spell many words slightly differently from Americans. Thus, British "colour" equals American "color," "cheque" equals "check," and "centre" equals "center."

of Belgravia, Bloomsbury, Finsbury, and Paddington. The architectural taste of the era (Palladian classical) was endlessly reproduced. This last development partly explains the comparative lack of gargantuan structures in many London neighborhoods, where a sense of privacy and shelter behind walled gardens stems from the British yearning for privacy.

The Victorian Age   The population of London exploded again in the 19th century, so that by 1902 it had reached almost 4½ million inhabitants. The architecture of this period was eclectic and whimsical, with the Gothic tradition as the main inspiration but adapted in idiosyncratic and clever ways. Today, Victorian architecture seems to dominate the city, but the quintessential example is the memorial erected by Queen Victoria to her husband, Albert. Ringed with bronzes of allegorical female figures representing the world's continents, it stands surrounded by greenery in Kensington Gardens.

The English love of gardens, the expansion of London from a series of villages into Europe's biggest metropolis, and the encroachment of urban sprawl on rural areas all helped to form the concept of the city of gardens, of the "corner of the country within the city." In 1898, industrial planner Ebeneser Howard conceived of a low-income garden city: an autonomous urban center that contained within its borders outlets

Impressions

And so the sun sets on the Thames, and all London's children, tucked in with bellies full of black puddings and bubble and squeak, dream dreams of a gleaming tomorrow . . . of a new Tate Gallery where the Bankside power station stands . . . of a new bridge from the Tate to St. Paul's Cathedral . . . of Sir Norman Foster's Millennium Tower pointing 76 stories into the glorious English sky. . . . Take care, Mum and Dad, to have smelling salts ready for the milkman—he won't believe his eyes when he makes his dawn round!

—David Kamp (1997)

both for earning a livelihood and for living within sight of greenery. The first of these developments was Letchworth, a few miles north of London, built in 1903.

The Edwardian Era to Post-1945   During the early 20th century, Edwardian architects (the most celebrated of whom—and deservedly so—was Sir Edwin Lutyens) created the finest examples of domestic architecture in the world. They corrected many of the mistakes of, and improved the designs of, their Victorian predecessors. Often building with earth-colored brick and incorporating elements of Arthurian legend, art nouveau, and the Arts-and-Crafts movement, they added whimsy and great comfort to thousands of buildings, usually siting and landscaping them gracefully. Inside were oversized bathrooms, extra pantries, and reading nooks. Excellent examples of the Edwardian style include most of the grand hotels of London's Park Lane (most notably the Park Lane, the Ritz, and the somewhat newer art deco Dorchester), as well as the Admiralty Arch.

The blitz that Hitler launched on London during World War II destroyed not only much of the city's great architecture but also the East End slums of Whitechapel. This neighborhood—made famous by Charles Dickens and Jack the Ripper—had been London's festering sore, with the worst housing conditions in the Western world. The London City Council rebuilt most of the area into rather drab but infinitely preferable rows of apartment blocks. This postwar building boom may have made London a little less quaint, but it also made it a more healthful place to live.

Modernism & Post Modernism   A consciousness of good modern architecture was much promoted in the 1980s and 1990s by the articulate efforts of Prince Charles. Prodded into a heightened consciousness by his highly publicized comments, London developers have increased their usage of traditional building materials such as concrete, steel, aluminum, and glass in warmly textured, anthropomorphic forms that manage to combine the rectilinear severity of old-fashioned Bauhaus with the organic shapes of Barcelona's Antonio Gaudí. The "New Brutalism" manages to combine a powerfully primitive, even primal kind of appeal to buildings erected in the center of some of the most congested neighborhoods of London. Examples of the style include the Economist building in Haymarket and a housing development in London's East End (the Robin Hood Lane complex), both designed by award-winning London architects Alison and Peter Simpson. The Economist building, painstakingly crafted from Portland stone, retains the honor of being one of London's only buildings erected during the 1970s to be "listed" (legally protected from changes).

London's architecture today is carefully balanced between a new emphasis on historic preservation and dramatic new statements such as those made by iconoclastic visionary Sir Richard Rodgers in his design of the Lloyd's Building. The market floor—called "The Room"—is the core of this building; it's a panoramic atrium with a glass roof the height of St. Paul's Cathedral, linked to a trio of surrounding galleries by illuminated glass-sided escalators. These are serviced by six exterior towers à la Hyatt hotels where "glass bubbles" go up and down.

The main rival to Rogers is Norman Foster, London's second-most-famous architect. Foster has announced his intention to build Europe's tallest building in the midst of the City's financial district, a 76-story Millennium Tower, carrying his signature aerodynamic look. As if to counter his rival, Rogers has become the master planner of the world's fair-like Millennium Festival, which will be constructed in Greenwich on the meridian. In theory at least, the 21st century will begin at this spot.

Even larger—and more far-flung—statements of creativity include such vast commercial developments as Butler's Wharf and Canary Wharf at the Docklands. The Docklands project, conceived by U.S. architectural giant Skidmore, Owings, and Merrill as an alternative financial center to the overburdened facilities in the City, is a 71-acre commercial mini-city beside the Thames, with 12.2 million square feet of offices, at least two high-rise hotels, a battery of shops, swimming pools and health clubs, and work stations for 57,000 people. Final touches on this city within a mega-city are expected by the millennium. Its critics complain about a scale that's so large as to be almost inhuman and an aesthetic whose flashiness sacrificed some of its potential for sensitivity. But its supporters applaud a bold new vision that's managed to carry substantial traffic away from the overburdened heart of merrie olde London and renovate a scandalously decrepit area avoided by tourists and Londoners alike.

These developments, as well as future changes to the capital's periphery, guarantee that the architectural aesthetic of London will continue progressing in creative ways through the 21st century, but without compromising the city's newfound allegiance to its splendid roster of antique buildings.

5 Pies, Puddings & Pints: The Lowdown on British Cuisine

You don't have to travel around England to experience regional English dishes; you'll find them all over London.

WHAT YOU'LL FIND ON THE MENU   On any pub menu you're likely to encounter such dishes as **Cornish pasty** and **shepherd's pie.** The first, traditionally made from Sunday-meal leftovers and taken by West Country fishers for Monday lunch, consists of chopped potatoes, carrots, and onions mixed together with seasoning and put into a pastry envelope. The second is a deep dish of chopped cooked beef mixed with onions and seasoning, covered with a layer of mashed potatoes, and served hot. Another version is **cottage pie,** which is minced beef covered with potatoes, also served hot.

The most common pub meal, though, is the **ploughman's lunch,** traditional farmworker's fare, consisting of a good chunk of local cheese, a hunk of homemade crusty white or brown bread, some butter, and a pickled onion or two, all washed down with ale. You'll now find such variations as pâté and chutney occasionally replacing the onions and cheese. Or you might find **Lancashire hot pot,** a stew of mutton, potatoes, kidneys, and onions (sometimes carrots). This concoction was originally put into a deep dish and set on the edge of the stove to cook slowly while the workers spent the day at the local mill.

Among **appetizers,** called "starters" in England, the most typical are potted shrimp (small buttered shrimp preserved in a jar), prawn cocktail, and smoked salmon. You might also be served pâté or "fish pie," which is very light fish pâté. If you're an oyster

Factoid

The choice to eat or not eat meat in England is (at this point) personal. Certain cuts of meat are easily available in London because they are considered safe and are regularly served in restaurants and sold by butchers with the understanding that most of the diseased animals have been destroyed. However, cuts of meat that are either close to the bone or include any grains of bone meal whatsoever are almost impossible to find because they have been outlawed as too risky for consumption. Some butchers are providing tender cuts that are close to the bone for special customers, but this is only being done behind closed doors.

lover, try some of the famous Colchester variety. Most menus will feature a variety of soups, including cock-a-leekie (chicken soup flavored with leeks), perhaps a game soup that has been flavored with sherry, and many others.

Among the best-known traditional English dishes is, of course, **roast beef and Yorkshire pudding**—the pudding made with a flour base and cooked under the joint, allowing the fat from the meat to drop onto it. The beef could easily be a large sirloin (rolled loin), which, so the story goes, was named by James I (not Henry VIII, as some claim) when he was a guest at Houghton Tower, Lancashire. "Arise, Sir Loin," he cried, as he knighted the joint with his dagger. Another dish that makes similar use of a flour base is toad-in-the-hole, in which sausages are cooked in batter. Game is also a staple on English tables, especially pheasant and grouse.

On any menu you'll find fresh **seafood**—cod, haddock, herring, plaice, or the aristocrat of flat fish, Dover sole. Cod and haddock are the most popular fish used in the making of a British tradition, fish-and-chips (chips, of course, are fried potatoes or thick french fries), which the true Briton covers with salt and vinegar.

The East End of London has quite a few interesting old dishes, among them tripe and onions. Dr. Johnson's favorite tavern, Ye Olde Cheshire Cheese on Fleet Street, still (on most days) offers a beefsteak-kidney-mushroom-and-game pudding in a suet case in winter and a pastry case in summer. East Enders can still be seen on Sunday at the Jellied Eel stall by Petticoat Lane, eating either eel or cockles, mussels, whelks, and winkles—all consumed with a touch of vinegar.

The British call **desserts** "sweets" (although some people still refer to any dessert as "pudding"), with trifle being the most famous. It consists of sponge cake soaked in brandy or sherry, coated with fruit or jam, and topped with a cream custard. A "fool," such as gooseberry fool, is a light cream dessert whipped up from seasonal fruits.

Cheese is traditionally served after dessert as a savory. There are many regional cheeses, the best known being Cheddar, a good, solid, mature cheese, as is Cheshire. Another comes from Wales—Caerphilly, textured semi-smoothly. Stilton, a blue-veined crumbly cheese, is often enriched with a glass of port.

BRITISH FOOD TODAY   The new obsession in England is not sex (that was the 1960s), but food. As long as you stay away from British Beef (see "Health & Insurance" in chapter 2 for the latest on Mad Cow Disease), food is safer. Judge a country's interests by its newspapers: Some Sunday editions carry 20 pages alone dedicated to cuisine, with recipes, wine columns, and reviews of the latest eateries.

There's a lot more to British food today than the Sunday roast. Under the rubric of Modern British cuisine, young upstart chefs are giving traditional dishes very modern twists. Parsnip soup is still served, but now it's likely to be with walnut salsa verde. The new buzz word for British cuisine is magpie—meaning borrowing ideas from global travels, taking them home, but improving on the original. If you want to see what Britain is eating today, just drop in at Harvey Nichols' Fifth Floor in London's Knightsbridge for its dazzling display of produce from all over the globe.

Even in British homes, instead of Sunday's leftover roast disguised as shepherd's pie, you're likely to encounter Indian, Chinese, Thai, or, most likely, Italian. If you slip a look into the larder of your host, you might even encounter Mexican chiles, something almost unheard of a decade ago.

In contemporary London, the chef of the 1990s has taken on celebrity status. The cook creating breast of Gressingham duck topped with deep-fried seaweed and served with a passion-fruit sauce is honored the way the rock star was in the 1970s or the fashion designer in the 1980s. In the late 1990s, this trend is showing early signs of waning, however. These days, some of the most celebrated chefs are getting so many offers for books, TV appearances, or whatever, that they're rarely around tending those pots 'n' pans; thus, it's the restaurant itself that is becoming celebrated, regardless of who's in the kitchen. Some restaurants are so popular that they are demanding reservations 2 weeks in advance, if not more.

WHAT TO WASH IT ALL DOWN WITH   London pubs serve a variety of cocktails, but their stock in trade is beer—brown beer, or bitter; blond beer, or lager; and very dark beer, or stout. The standard English draft beer is much stronger than American beer and is served "with the chill off" because it doesn't taste good cold. Lager is always chilled, whereas stout can be served either way. Beer is always served straight from the tap, in two sizes: half-pint (8 oz.) and pint (16 oz.).

One of the most significant changes in English drinking habits has been the popularity of wine bars, and you will find many to patronize; some turn into dance clubs late at night. Britain isn't known for its wine, although it does produce some medium-sweet fruity whites. Its cider, though, is famous—and very potent in contrast to the American variety.

Whisky (spelled without the *e*) refers to scotch. Canadian and Irish whiskey (spelled with the *e*) are also available, but only the very best-stocked bars have American bourbon and rye. While you're in England, you may want to try the very English drink called Pimm's, a mixture developed by James Pimm, owner of a popular London oyster house in the 1840s. Although it can be consumed on the rocks, it's usually served as a Pimm's Cup—a drink that will have any number and variety of ingredients, depending on which part of the world (or empire) you're in. Here, just for fun, is a typical recipe: Take a very tall glass and fill it with ice. Add a thin slice of lemon (or orange), a cucumber spike (or a curl of cucumber rind), and 2 ounces of Pimm's liquor. Then finish with a splash of either lemon or club soda, 7-Up, or Tom Collins mix.

The English tend to drink everything at a warmer temperature than Americans are used to. So if you like ice in your Coke or Pepsi, be sure to ask for lots of it—or you're likely to end up with a measly melting cube or two.

2 Planning a Trip to London

This chapter tackles the hows of your trip to London—those issues required to get your trip together and take it on the road, whether you're a frequent traveler or a first-timer; a traveler with disabilities; a senior, single, or student traveler; or a family traveling together. In addition to helping you decide when to take your trip, this chapter discusses where to gather information about London, what documents you need to take with you, and how to get there.

1 Visitor Information & Entry Requirements

VISITOR INFORMATION

Before you go, you can get information from the following **British Tourist Authority** offices: 551 Fifth Ave., Suite 701, New York, NY 10176-0799 (☎ **800/462-2748** or 212/986-2200); 111 Avenue Rd., Suite 450, Toronto, ON M5R 3J8, Canada (☎ **888/VISIT-UK** or 416/925-6326); Level 16, Gateway, 1 Macquarie Place, Sydney, NSW 2000, Australia (☎ **02/9377-4400**); and Suite 305, Dilworth Bldg., at Customs and Queen streets, Auckland 1, New Zealand (☎ **09/303-1446**). The British Tourist Authority maintains a Web page at **www.visitbritain.com**.

For a full information pack on London, write to the **London Tourist Board,** Glenn House, Stag Place, London SN1E 5LT, (☎ **0171/932-2000**). You can also call the recorded-message service, **Visitorcall** (☎ **01839/123456**), 24 hours a day. Various topics are listed; calls cost 50p (80¢) per minute.

You can usually pick up a copy of *Time Out,* the most up-to-date source for what's happening in London, at any international newsstand. *Time Out* has joined the Net, so you can also log on for current information; you'll find the weekly magazine at **www.timeout.co.uk**.

London Guide (**www.cs.ucl.ac.uk/misc/uk/london.html**) is run by London's University College and has practical information on cheap dining and accommodations in the Bloomsbury area close to the University. There are also travelogues and tips for theatergoers.

To book accommodations by credit card (MasterCard or VISA), call the **London Tourist Board Booking Office** at ☎ **0171/ 932-2020,** or fax them at 0171/932-2021. They're available to make bookings Monday to Friday from 9:30am to 5:30pm (London time). There is a £5 ($8) fee for booking.

ENTRY REQUIREMENTS
DOCUMENTS
Citizens of the United States, Canada, Australia, New Zealand, and South Africa all require a passport to enter the United Kingdom, but no visa. Irish citizens need only an identity card to enter the U.K. The maximum allowable stay for visitors is 6 months. Some Customs officials will request proof that you have the means to eventually leave the country (usually a round-trip ticket) and visible means of support while you're in Britain. If you're planning to fly to another country from the United Kingdom, it's wise to secure the necessary visa before your arrival in Britain.

Your valid driver's license and at least one year's driving experience is required to drive personal or rented cars.

CUSTOMS
WHAT YOU CAN BRING INTO ENGLAND   For visitors to England, goods fall into two basic categories: goods purchased in a non-European Union (EU) country or bought tax-free within the EU; and goods purchased tax-paid in the EU. In the first category, limits on imports by individuals (17 and older) include 200 cigarettes (or 50 cigars or 250 grams of loose tobacco), 2 liters of still table wine, 1 liter of liquor (over 22% alcohol content) or 2 liters of liquor (under 22%), and 2 fluid ounces of perfume. In the second category, limits are much higher: An individual may import 800 cigarettes bought tax-paid in the EU, 200 cigars, and 1 kilogram of loose tobacco; 90 liters of wine, 10 liters of alcohol (over 22%), and 110 liters of beer; plus unlimited amounts of perfume.

Sorry, but you can't bring your pet to England. Six months' quarantine is required before a pet is allowed into the country. An illegally imported animal is liable to be destroyed.

WHAT YOU CAN BRING HOME   Returning U.S. citizens who have been away for 48 hours or more are allowed to bring back, once every 30 days, $400 worth of merchandise duty-free. You'll be charged a flat rate of 10% duty on the next $1,000 worth of purchases. Be sure to have your receipts handy. On gifts, the duty-free limit is $100. You cannot bring fresh foodstuffs into the United States; tinned foods, however, are allowed. For more information, contact the **U.S. Customs Service,** 1301 Constitution Ave. (P.O. Box 7407), Washington, DC 20044 (☎ **202/927-6724**) and request the free pamphlet *Know Before You Go.* It's on the Web at **www.customs.ustreas.gov/travel/kbygo.htm.** Also see "Taxes" under "Fast Facts: London" in chapter 3 and chapter 8, "Shopping."

For a clear summary of Canadian rules, write for the booklet *I Declare,* issued by **Revenue Canada,** 2265 St. Laurent Blvd., Ottawa, ON K1G 4KE (☎ **613/993-0534** or 800/461-9999). Canada allows its citizens a $500 exemption, and you're allowed to bring back duty-free 200 cigarettes, 2.2 pounds of tobacco, 40 imperial ounces of liquor, and 50 cigars. In addition, you're allowed to mail gifts to Canada from abroad at the rate of C$60 a day, provided they're unsolicited and aren't alcohol or tobacco (write on the package "Unsolicited gift, under $60 value"). All valuables should be declared on the Y-38 form before departure from Canada, including serial numbers of, for example, expensive foreign cameras that you already own. *Note:* The $500 exemption can be used only after an absence of 7 days.

The duty-free allowance in Australia is A$400 or, for those under 18, A$200. Personal property mailed back from England should be marked "Australian goods returned" to avoid payment of duty. Upon returning to Australia, citizens can bring in 250 cigarettes or 250 grams of loose tobacco, and 1.125 liters of alcohol. If you're returning with valuable goods you already own, such as foreign-made cameras, you should file form B263. A helpful brochure, available from Australian consulates or Customs offices, is *Know Before You Go.* For more information, contact **Australian Customs Services,** GPO Box 8, Sydney NSW 2001 (☎ **02/9213-2000**).

The duty-free allowance for New Zealand is NZ$700. Citizens over 17 years of age can bring in 200 cigarettes, or 50 cigars, or 250 grams of tobacco (or a mixture of all three if their combined weight doesn't exceed 250 grams); plus 4.5 liters of wine and beer, or 1.125 liters of liquor. New Zealand currency does not carry import or export restrictions. Fill out a certificate of export, listing the valuables you are taking out of the country; that way, you can bring them back without paying duty. Most questions are answered in a free pamphlet available at New Zealand consulates and Customs offices: *New Zealand Customs Guide for Travellers,* Notice no. 4. For more information, contact **New Zealand Customs,** 50 Anzac Ave., P.O. Box 29, Auckland (☎ **09/359-6655**).

2 Money

CURRENCY

POUNDS & PENCE Britain's decimal monetary system is based on the pound sterling (£), which is made up of 100 pence (written as "p"). There are now £1 coins (called "quid" by Britons), plus coins of 50p, 20p, 10p, 5p, 2p, and 1p. Even though the 0.5p coin has been officially discontinued, it will be around for a while. Banknotes come in denominations of £5, £10, £20, and £50.

As a general guideline, the price conversions in this book have been computed at the rate of £1 = $1.60 (U.S.). Bear in mind, however, that exchange rates fluctuate daily.

GETTING CASH WHILE YOU'RE THERE

ATM NETWORKS Plus, Cirrus, and other networks connecting automated-teller machines (ATMs) are accessible throughout London and at Heathrow and Gatwick airports. By using your bank card to withdraw money you'll debit the amount from your account. When using an ATM abroad, the money will be in local currency; the rate of exchange tends to be as good, more often better, than what you would receive at an airport money counter or a hotel. Note that international withdrawal fees will be higher than domestic—ask your bank for specifics. Always determine the frequency limits for withdrawals and cash advances of your credit card. Also, check to see if your PIN code must be reprogrammed for usage in London. Most ATMs outside the U.S. require a four-digit PIN number.

To receive a directory of **Cirrus** ATMs, call ☎ **800/424-7787;** for **Plus** locations, call ☎ **800/843-7587.** You can also access the VISA/PLUS International ATM Locator Guide via the Internet at **www.visa.com**. If you have a Citibank Visa or MasterCard, you can call their offices in London at ☎ **0171/500-5500** for information on where to get cash from automatic tellers.

CREDIT CARDS The way to get the best rate of exchange is not via money exchange, but to buy whatever you can with credit cards. They virtually always offer a rate of exchange better than any you can get by changing your money, and there's no accompanying service charge. Credit cards are widely accepted in London; American Express, Visa, and Diners Club are the most commonly recognized. A Eurocard or Access sign displayed at an establishment means that it accepts MasterCard.

TRAVELER'S CHECKS Before leaving home, you can purchase traveler's checks and arrange to carry some ready cash (usually about $250, depending on your habits

The U.S. Dollar & the British Pound

Note: The rate of exchange at press time was approximately $1.60 U.S. to £1, and was used to compile this chart. Because rates change almost daily, however, check the current value of the pound in a newspaper or at a bank.

U.S.$	UK £	U.S.$	UK £
0.25	0.16	15	9.45
0.50	0.32	20	12.60
0.75	0.47	25	15.75
1.00	0.63	50	31.50
2.00	1.26	75	47.25
3.00	1.89	100	63.00
4.00	2.52	150	94.50
5.00	3.15	200	126.00
6.00	3.78	250	157.50
7.00	4.41	300	189.00
8.00	5.04	350	220.50
9.00	5.67	400	252.00
10.00	6.30	500	315.00

and needs). You may wish to purchase your checks in pounds to simplify the process and save on exchange rates. In the event of theft, if the checks are properly documented, the value of your checks will be refunded. Most large banks sell traveler's checks, charging fees that average between 1% and 2% of the value of the checks you buy, although some out-of-the-way banks, in rare instances, have charged as much as 7%. If your bank wants more than a 2% commission, it sometimes pays to call the traveler's check issuers directly for the address of outlets where this commission will cost less.

For more information, contact **American Express** (☎ **800/221-7282** in the U.S. and Canada); **Citicorp** (☎ **800/645-6556** in the U.S. and Canada, or 813/623-1709 collect from other parts of the world); **Thomas Cook** (☎ **800/223-7373** in the U.S. or Canada, or 609/987-7300 collect from other parts of the world); or **Interpayment Services** (☎ **800/221-2426** in the U.S. and Canada, or 212/858-8500 collect from other parts of the world).

MONEY EXCHANGE   If you prefer not to use an airport ATM, it's wise to exchange enough money before departure to get from the airport to your hotel. This way, you avoid delays and the lousy rates at the airport exchange booths—and you might make it to the front of the taxi "queue" before everybody who wasn't so smart.

When exchanging money, you're likely to obtain a better rate for traveler's checks than for cash. London banks generally offer the best rates of exchange; they're usually open Monday to Friday from 9:30am to 3:30pm. Many of the "high street" branches are now open until 5pm; a handful of Central London branches are open until noon on Saturday, including **Barclays,** 208 Kensington High St., W8 (☎ **0171/ 441-3200**). Money exchange is now also available at competitive rates at major

What Things Cost in London	U.S. $
Taxi from Heathrow Airport to central London	56.00
Underground from Heathrow Airport to central London	5.30
Local telephone call	.15–.30
Double room at The Dorchester (Very expensive)	456.00
Double room at Tophams Belgravia (Moderate)	150.00
Double room at Edward Lear (Inexpensive)	96.00
Lunch for one at The Ivy (Expensive)	32.00
Lunch for one at Ye Olde Cheshire Cheese (Inexpensive)	18.00
Dinner for one, without wine, at Bibendum/ The Oyster Bar (Expensive)	80.00
Dinner for one, without wine, at Odin's (Moderate)	38.30
Dinner for one, without wine, at Porter's English Restaurant (Inexpensive)	26.00
Pint of beer	3.35
Coca-Cola in a cafe	1.90
Cup of coffee	2.15
Roll of ASA 100 color film, 36 exposures	8.00
Admission to the British Museum	Free
Movie ticket	8.00–14.00
Theater ticket	24.00–96.00

London post offices, with a 1% service charge. Money can be exchanged during off-hours at a variety of bureaux de change throughout the city, found at small shops and in hotels, railway stations (including the international terminal at Waterloo Station), travel agencies, and airports, but their exchange rates are poorer and they charge high service fees. Examine the prices and rates carefully before handing over your dollars, as there's no consumer organization to regulate the activities of privately run bureaux de change.

In a recent *Time Out* survey of various exchange facilities, **American Express** came out on top, with the lowest commission charged on dollar transactions. They're at 6 Haymarket, SW1 (☎ **800/221-7282** or 0171/930-4411) and other locations throughout the city. They charge no commission when cashing traveler's checks. However, a flat rate of £2 ($3.20) is charged when exchanging the dollar to the pound. Most other agencies tend to charge a percentage rate commission (usually 2%) with a £2 to £3 ($3.20 to $4.80) minimum charge. Other reputable firms are **Thomas Cook,** 45 Berkeley St., W1A 1EB (☎ **800/223-7373** or 0171/408-4218), branches of which can also be found at Victoria Station, Marble Arch, and other city locations; and, for 24-hour foreign exchange, **Chequepoint,** at 548 Oxford St., W1N 9HJ (☎ **0171-723-1005**) and other locations throughout London (hours will vary). Try not to change money at your hotel; the rates they offer tend to be horrendous.

MONEYGRAM   If you find yourself out of money, a wire service provided by American Express can help you tap willing friends and family for emergency funds. Through **MoneyGram,** 6200 S. Quebec St., P.O. Box 5118, Englewood, CO 80155 (☎ **800/926-9400**), money can be sent around the world in less than 10 minutes.

Senders should call AMEX to learn the address of the closest outlet that handles MoneyGrams. Cash, credit card, or the occasional personal check (with ID) are acceptable forms of payment. AMEX's fee for the service is $10 for the first $300 with a sliding scale for larger sums. The service includes a short telex message and a 3-minute phone call from sender to recipient. The beneficiary must present a photo ID at the outlet where money is received.

PERSONAL CHECKS   Some British hotels require an advance deposit in pounds to make reservations. An easy way to obtain a check for this is through **Ruesch International,** 700 11th St. NW, 4th Floor, Washington, DC 20001-4507 (☎ **800/ 424-2923** or 202/408-1200; fax 202/408-1211). To place an order, call and tell the staff the amount of the sterling-denominated check you need. Ruesch will quote a U.S. dollar equivalent, adding a $3 service fee per check. After receiving your dollar-denominated personal check, Ruesch will mail you a sterling-denominated bank draft, drawn at a British bank and payable to the party you specify. Ruesch will also convert checks in a foreign currency to U.S. dollars, change currency for more than 120 countries, and sell traveler's checks payable in dollars or six foreign currencies, including pounds. In addition to the Washington office, Ruesch maintains offices in Zurich, London, New York, Los Angeles, Chicago, Atlanta, and Boston. Any of these offices can supply draft and traveler's checks by mail or phone.

3 When to Go

THE CLIMATE

Charles Dudley Warner (in a remark most often attributed to Mark Twain) once said that the trouble with the weather is that everybody talks about it but nobody does anything about it. Well, Londoners talk about weather more than anyone, but they have also done something about it: air-pollution control, which has resulted in the virtual disappearance of the pea-soup fogs that once blanketed the city.

A typical London-area weather forecast for a summer day predicts "scattered clouds with sunny periods and showers, possibly heavy at times." Summer temperatures seldom rise above 78°F, nor do they drop below 35°F in winter. London, being in one of the mildest parts of the country, can be very pleasant in the spring and fall. Yes, it rains, but you'll rarely get a true downpour. It's heaviest in November, when it reaches 2½ inches on average.

The British consider chilliness wholesome and usually try to keep room temperatures about 10°F below the American comfort level.

London's Average Daytime Temperature & Rainfall

	Jan	Feb	Mar	Apr	May	June	July	Aug	Sept	Oct	Nov	Dec
Temp (°F)	40	40	44	49	55	61	64	64	59	52	46	42
Rainfall (")	2.1	1.6	1.5	1.5	1.8	1.8	2.2	2.3	1.9	2.2	2.5	1.9

CURRENT WEATHER CONDITIONS   In the United States, you can dial ☎ **1/900-WEATHER,** then press the first four letters of the desired foreign city—in this case, LOND for London—for the time of day in that city, plus current

Note

The British use the Celsius scale to measure temperature. A quick way to convert to Fahrenheit is to double the Celsius temperature, subtract 10%, and add 32.

temperatures, weather conditions, and forecasts. The cost is 95¢ per minute. Another good way to check conditions before you go is on the Weather Channel's Web site: **www.weather.com**.

HOLIDAYS

In England, public holidays include New Year's Day, Good Friday, Easter Monday, May Day (first Monday in May), spring and summer bank holidays (last Monday in May and August, respectively), Christmas Day, and Boxing Day (December 26).

LONDON CALENDAR OF EVENTS

January
- **London Parade,** from Parliament Square to Berkeley Square in Mayfair. Bands, floats, and carriages. January 1. Procession starts around 2:45pm.
- **January sales.** Most shops offer good reductions. Many sales now start as early as late December to perk up the post-Christmas slump. The most voracious shoppers camp overnight outside Harrods to get in first.
- **London International Boat Show,** Earl's Court Exhibition Centre, Warwick Road. The largest boat show in Europe. Early January. Call ☎ **01784/473377** for details.
- **London Contemporary Art Fair** at the Business Design Centre, Islington Green. Mid-January. Call ☎ **0171/359-3535** for exact dates and details.
- **Charles I Commemoration.** Anniversary of the execution of King Charles I "in the name of freedom and democracy." Hundreds of cavaliers march through central London in 17th-century dress, and prayers are said at the Banqueting House in Whitehall. Free. Last Sunday in January.

February
- **Chinese New Year.** The famous Lion Dancers in Soho. Free. Either in late January or early February (based on the lunar calendar).
- **Great Spitalfields Pancake Race.** Teams of four run in relays, tossing their pancakes. At noon on Shrove Tuesday (last day before Lent) at Old Spitalfields Market, Brushfield Street, E1. To join in, call ☎ **0171/375-0441.**

March
- **St. David's Day.** A member of the Royal Family usually presents the Welsh Guards with the principality's national emblem, a leek; call ☎ **0171/414-3291** for location and further information. March 1 (or nearest Sunday).
- **Chelsea Antiques Fair,** a twice-yearly gathering of England's best dealers, held at Old Town Hall, King's Road, SW3 (☎ **01444/482-514**). Mid-March (and again in mid-September).
- **Oranges and Lemons Service,** at St. Clement Danes, Strand, WC2. Third Thursday in March or the first Thursday in April. As a reminder of the nursery rhyme, children are presented with the fruits during service, and the church bells ring out the rhyme at 9am, noon, 3pm, and 6pm; call ☎ **0171/242-8282** for more information.
- **Abbey Choir** performs at Westminster Abbey on Holy Week Tuesday; call ☎ **0171/222-5152** for information.

April
- **Easter Parade,** around Battersea Park. Brightly colored floats and marching bands; a full day of Easter Sunday activities. Free. Easter Sunday.

- **Harness Horse Parade,** a morning parade of heavy working horses in superb gleaming brass harnesses and plumes, at Battersea Park. Call ☎ **01733/234-451.** Easter Monday.
- **Boat Race, Putney to Mortlake.** Oxford and Cambridge University eights battle upstream with awesome power. Park yourself at one of the Thames-side pubs along the route to see the action. Early April; check *Time Out* for exact dates and times.
- **London Marathon.** 30,000 competitors run from Greenwich Park to Buckingham Palace; call ☎ **0161/703-8161** for information. Mid- to late April.
- **The Queen's Birthday** is celebrated with 21-gun salutes in Hyde Park and on Tower Hill at noon by troops in parade dress. April 21.
- **National Gardens Scheme.** More than 100 private gardens in Greater London are open to the public on set days until October, and tea is sometimes served. Pick up a current copy of the NGS guidebook for £3.50 ($5.60) from most bookstores for schedule information, or contact the National Gardens Scheme Charitable Trust, Hatchlands Park, East Clandon, Guildford, Surrey GU4 7RT (☎ **01483/211-535**). Late April to early May.

May

- **Shakespeare Under the Stars.** If you want to see *Macbeth, Hamlet,* or *Romeo and Juliet* (or any other Shakespeare play), our advice is to bring a blanket and a bottle of wine to watch the Bard's works performed at the Open Air Theatre, Inner Circle, Regent's Park, NW1. Take the tube to Regent's Park or Baker Street. Previews begin in late May and last throughout the summer. Performances are Monday to Saturday at 8pm, Wednesday, Thursday, and Saturday also at 2:30pm. Call ☎ **0171/486-2431** for more information.
- **May Fayre and Puppet Festival,** Covent Garden. Procession at 10am, service at St. Paul's at 11:30am, then Punch and Judy shows until 6pm at the site where Pepys watched England's first show in 1662; call ☎ **0171/375-0441.** Second Sunday in May.
- **FA Cup Final.** England's showpiece soccer match is held at Wembley Stadium in mid-May; for exact date and details, call ☎ **0181/902-8833.**
- The **Royal Windsor Horse Show** is held at Home Park, Windsor Castle (☎ **01753-860633**); you might even spot a royal. Mid-May.
- **Chelsea Flower Show,** Chelsea Royal Hospital. The best of British gardening, with displays of plants and flowers of all seasons. Tickets are available through Ticketmaster (☎ **0171/344-4343**). The show runs from 8am to 8pm on May 20; tickets are £25 ($40). On May 21, the show runs from 8am to 5pm, and tickets are £23 ($36.80). Call ☎ **0171/630-7422** for more information. Ticket sales must be made in advance. There are no event day sales.
- **Glyndebourne Festival Opera Season,** Sussex. Exclusive performances in a beautiful setting, with champagne picnics in between performances. Since the completion of the Glyndebourne opera house, one of the world's best, tickets are a bit easier to come by (☎ **01273/813813**). It runs from mid-May to late August.

June

- **Vodafone Derby Stakes.** Famous horse-racing event at Epsom Racecourse, Epsom, Surrey. It's the best-known event on the British horse-racing calendar and a chance for men to wear top hats and women, including the queen, to put on silly millinery creations. The "darby" (as it's called here) is run June 7 to 9. Grandstand tickets range from £22 to £55 ($35.20 to $88). Call ☎ **01372/470047** for more information.

- **Grosvenor House Art and Antique Fair,** Grosvenor House. A very prestigious antiques fair. Call ☎ 0171/495-8743 for information. Second week of June.
- **Kenwood Lakeside Concerts,** ☎ 0181/348-1286. Annual concerts on the north side of Hampstead Heath. Fireworks displays and laser shows enliven the premier musical performances staged here. Music drifts to the fans from a performance shell across the lake every Saturday in summer from mid-June to early September.
- **Royal Academy's Summer Exhibition.** This institution, founded in 1768 with Sir Joshua Reynolds as president and Thomas Gainsborough as a member, has sponsored summer exhibitions of living painters for some 2 centuries. Visitors can both browse and make art purchases, many of them quite reasonable in price. Exhibitions are presented daily at Burlington House, Piccadilly Circus, W1. Call ☎ 0171/439-7438 for details. From early June to mid-August.
- **Royal Ascot Week.** Ascot Racecourse is open year-round for guided tours, events, exhibitions, and conferences. There are 24 race days throughout the year with the feature race meetings being the Royal Meeting in June, Diamond Day in late July, and the Festival at Ascot in late September. For further information, contact **Ascot Racecourse,** Ascot, Berkshire SL5 7JN (☎ 01344/622211).
- ✪ **Trooping the Colour,** Horse Guards Parade, Whitehall. The official birthday of the queen. Seated in a carriage (no longer on horseback), the royal monarch inspects her regiments and takes their salute as they parade their colors before her. A quintessential British event religiously watched by the populace on TV. The pageantry and pomp are exquisite. Depending on the weather, the young men under the bearskins have been known to pass out from the heat. Held on a designated day in June (not necessarily the queen's actual birthday). Tickets for the parade and two reviews, held on preceding Saturdays, are allocated by ballot. Those interested in attending must write to apply for tickets between January 1 and the end of February, enclosing a stamped, self-addressed envelope or International Reply Coupon—exact dates and ticket prices will be supplied later. The ballot is held in mid-March, and successful applicants *only* are informed in April. For details, write to **HQ Household Division,** Horse Guards, Whitehall, London SW1X 6AA, enclosing a self-addressed envelope with an International Reply Coupon.
- ✪ **Lawn Tennis Championships,** Wimbledon, Southwest London. Ever since the players in flannels and bonnets took to the grass courts at Wimbledon in 1877, this tournament has drawn a socially prominent crowd. Although the courts are now crowded with all kinds of tennis fans, there's still an excited hush at Centre Court and a certain thrill in being here. Savoring the strawberries and cream is part of the experience. Late June to early July. Tickets for Centre and Number One courts are handed out through a lottery; write to **All England Lawn Tennis Club,** P.O. Box 98, Church Road, Wimbledon, London SW19 5AE (☎ 0181/946-2244), between August and December. A certain number of tickets are set aside for visitors from abroad, so you may be able to purchase some in spring for this year's games; call to inquire. Outside court tickets available daily, but be prepared to wait in line.
- **City of London Festival,** annual arts festival throughout the city. Call ☎ 0171/377-0540 for information about the various programs and venues. Held in June and July.

July
- **City of London Festival.** Classical concerts at various venues throughout the City, including St. Paul's Cathedral; for details, call ☎ 0171/377-0540. Early July.

- **Hampton Court Palace Flower Show,** East Molesey, Surrey. This widely acclaimed 5-day international is eclipsing its sister show in Chelsea; here, you can actually purchase the exhibits. Call ☎ **0171/834-4333** for exact dates and details. Early July.
- **Royal Tournament,** Earl's Court Exhibition Centre, Warwick Road. British armed forces put on dazzling displays of athletic and military skills, which have been called "military pomp, show biz, and outright jingoism." For information and details about performance times and tickets, call ☎ **0171/244-0244.** Ticket prices range from £5 ($8) to £25 ($40). July 21 to August 2.
- **The Proms.** "The Proms"—the annual Henry Wood Promenade Concerts at Royal Albert Hall—attract music aficionados from around the world. Staged almost daily (except for a few Sundays) these traditional concerts were launched in 1895 and are the principal summer venue for the BBC Symphony Orchestra. Cheering, clapping, Union Jacks on parade, banners, and balloons create summer fun. Mid-July to mid-September.

August

- **Notting Hill Carnival,** Notting Hill. One of the largest street festivals in Europe, attracting more than a half-million people annually. Live reggae and soul music combine with great Caribbean food. Free. Two days in late August (usually the last Sunday and Monday). Call ☎ **0181/964-0544** for information.

September

- **Chelsea Antiques Fair,** Chelsea Old Town Hall, King's Road, SW3. Mid-September (see March, above, for details).
- **Open House,** a 1-day event during which members of the public have access to normally closed buildings of architectural significance. Mid-September. Call ☎ **0181/341-1371** for schedule and further information.
- **Raising of the Thames Barrier,** Unity Way, SE18. Once a year, a full test is done on this miracle of modern engineering; all 10 of the massive steel gates are raised against the high tide. Call ☎ **0181/854-1373** for exact date and time.

October

- ✪ **Opening of Parliament,** House of Lords, Westminster. Ever since the 17th century, when the English cut off the head of Charles I, the British monarch has had no right to enter the House of Commons. Instead, the monarch opens Parliament in the House of Lords, reading an official speech that is written by the government of the day. The monarch rides from Buckingham Palace to Westminster in a royal coach accompanied by the Yeoman of the Guard and the Household Cavalry. The Strangers' Gallery is open to spectators on a first-come, first-served basis. First Monday in October.
- **Judges Service,** Westminster Abbey. The judiciary attends a service in Westminster Abbey to mark the opening of the law term. Afterward, in full regalia—wigs and all—they form a procession and walk to the House of Lords for their "Annual Breakfast." You'll have a great view of the procession from behind the Abbey. First Monday in October.
- **Horse of the Year Show.** At Wembley Arena, outside London, this event is the premier equestrian highlight on the English calendar. Riders fly in from all continents to join in this festive display of horseflesh (much appreciated by the queen herself). The British press call it "an equine extravaganza." For more information, call ☎ **0181/902-8833.** Early October.
- **Quit Rents Ceremony,** Royal Courts of Justice, WC2. An official receives token rents on behalf of the queen; the ceremony includes splitting sticks and counting horseshoes. Call ☎ **0171/936-6131** for free tickets. Late October.

November
- **Guy Fawkes Night.** Commemorating the anniversary of the Gunpowder Plot, an attempt to blow up King James I and his Parliament. Huge organized bonfires are lit throughout the city, and Guy Fawkes, the plot's most famous conspirator, is burned in effigy. Free. Check *Time Out* for locations. Early November.
- ✪ **Lord Mayor's Procession and Show,** from the Guildhall to the Royal Courts of Justice, in the City of London. This impressive annual event marks the inauguration of the new lord mayor of the City of London. The queen must ask permission to enter the City's square mile—a right that has been jealously guarded by London merchants from the 17th century to this very day. You can watch the procession from the street; the banquet is by invitation only. Second week in November.

December
- **Caroling under the Norwegian Christmas Tree.** There's caroling most evenings beneath the tree in Trafalgar Square. Early December.
- **Harrods After-Christmas Sale,** Knightsbridge. Call ☎ **0171/730-1234** for exact dates and hours. Late December.
- **Watch Night,** St. Paul's Cathedral, where a rather lovely New Year's Eve service takes place on December 31 at 11:30pm; call ☎ **0171/248-2705** for information.

4 Health & Insurance

STAYING HEALTHY

You'll encounter few health problems while traveling in England. The tap water is safe to drink, the milk is pasteurized, and health services are good. You still may want to stay away from British beef because of the Mad Cow crisis. The crisis, in which a probable link was discovered between British beef and versions of a degenerative brain disease, threw Britain into a turmoil and paralyzed the beef industry; even now, the government is still wrestling with the issue. Thus, British beef still appears on menus, and Brits continue to eat it. If you want to play it safe, we suggest that you refrain entirely from ordering beef dishes—or, if you insist on digging into a plate of ye olde roast beef, make sure it's been prepared with non-British beef. Other than that, traveling to London doesn't pose any health risks.

If you need a doctor, your hotel can recommend one, or you can contact your embassy or consulate. Outside London, dial **100** and ask the operator for the local police, who will give you the name, address, and telephone number of a doctor in your area. Also see "Fast Facts: London" in chapter 3. *Note:* U.S. visitors who become ill while they're in England are only eligible for free *emergency* care. For other treatment, including follow-up care, you'll be asked to pay.

Before you leave home you can obtain a list of English doctors from the **International Association for Medical Assistance to Travelers (IAMAT).** Contact IAMAT in the United States at 417 Center St., Lewiston, NY 14092 (☎ **716/754-4883**); in Canada at 40 Regal Rd., Guelph, ON N1K 1B5 (☎ **519/836-0102**).

INSURANCE

Before going out and spending money on various sorts of travel insurance, check your existing policies to see if they'll cover you while you're traveling. Make sure your health insurance will protect you when you're away from home. Some credit and charge cards offer automatic flight insurance when you purchase an airline ticket with that card. These policies insure against death or dismemberment in case of an airplane crash.

Check your homeowner's or renter's insurance to see if it covers off-premises theft and loss wherever it occurs.

If you're traveling on a tour or have prepaid a large chunk of your travel expenses, you might want to ask your travel agent about trip-cancellation insurance.

If you're going to rent a car in England, check to see whether your automobile insurance, automobile club, or charge card covers personal accident insurance (PAI), collision damage waiver (CDW), or other insurance options. You may be able to avoid additional rental charges if you are already covered.

Healthcare Abroad (MEDEX), c/o Wallach & Co., P.O. Box 480 (107 W. Federal St.), Middleburg, VA 20118-0480 (☎ **800/237-6615**), offers coverage for between 10 and 120 days at $4 per day; this policy includes accident and sickness coverage to the tune of $250,000. Medical evacuation is also included, along with a $25,000 accidental death and dismemberment compensation. Provisions for trip cancellation can also be written into this policy at a nominal cost.

Mutual of Omaha (Tele-Trip Company, Inc.), Mutual of Omaha Plaza, Omaha, NE 68175 (☎ **800/228-9792**), offers insurance packages priced from $49 per person for a tour valued at $1,000. Included in these packages are travel-assistance services and financial protection against trip cancellation, trip interruption, flight-and-baggage delays, accident-related medical costs, accidental death and/or dismemberment, and medical evacuation coverages. Tour packages offer the ability to waive pre-existing condition limitations. Application for insurance can be made over the phone by major credit-card holders.

Travel Guard International, 1145 Clark St., Stevens Point, WI 54481 (☎ **800/826-1300** or 715/345-0505), offers a comprehensive travel protection policy that covers lost luggage, emergency assistance, accidental death, trip cancellation, and medical coverage abroad. Package costs start at $40 and are based on your total trip cost. Children under 16 are automatically covered if accompanying adults have purchased a policy.

Travelers Insurance PAK, Travel Insured International, Inc., P.O. Box 280568, East Hartford, CT 06128 (☎ **800/243-3174** or 860/528-7663), offers illness and accident coverage costing from $10 for 6 to 10 days. Trip-cancellation insurance is $5.50 per $100 of coverage to a limit of $10,000 per person.

5 Tips for Travelers with Special Needs

FOR TRAVELERS WITH DISABILITIES

Before you go, there are many agencies to check with about information for persons with disabilities.

One is the **Industrial Rehab Program,** 1200 W. Tabor Rd., Philadelphia, PA 19141, which provides information to telephone callers only at **215/456-9900.**

You can also obtain a copy of *Air Transportation of Handicapped Persons,* published by the U.S. Department of Transportation, by writing for "Free Advisory Circular no. 12032" to Distribution Unit, U.S. Department of Transportation, Publications Division, M-4332, Washington, DC 20590.

One of the best organizations serving the needs of people who use wheelchairs or walkers is **Flying Wheels Travel,** 143 West Bridge St., Owatonna, MN 55060 (☎ **800/535-6790**), which offers various escorted tours and cruises internationally. For names and addresses of other tour operators and additional relevant information, contact the **Society for the Advancement of Travel for the Handicapped,** 347 Fifth Ave., Suite 610, New York, NY 10016 (☎ **212/447-7284;** fax 212/725-8253 or send a stamped, self-addressed envelope). Yearly membership dues are $45, $30 for senior citizens and students.

For people who are blind or have visual impairments, the best source is the **American Foundation for the Blind,** 11 Penn Plaza, Suite 300, New York, NY 10001 (☎ **800/232-5463** or 212/502-7600), which offers information on travel and various requirements for the transport and border formalities for seeing eye dogs. It also issues identification cards to those who are legally blind.

For a $25 annual fee, consider joining **Mobility International USA,** P.O. Box 10767, Eugene, OR 97440 (☎ **541/343-1284;** fax 541/343-6182). It answers questions on various destinations and also offers discounts on videos, publications, and programs it sponsors.

Many London hotels, museums, restaurants, and sightseeing attractions have wheelchair ramps. Persons with disabilities are often granted special discounts at attractions and, in some cases, nightclubs. These are called "concessions" in Britain. It always pays to ask. Free information and advice is available from **Holiday Care Service,** Imperial Building, 2nd Floor, Victoria Road, Horley, Surrey RH6 7PZ (☎ **01293/774535;** fax 01293/784647).

The **British Tourist Authority** sells *London Made Easy* (£2.50 [$4]), a booklet offering advice and describing facilities for travelers with disabilities. Bookstores in London often carry *Access in London* (£4 [$6.40]), an even more helpful publication listing facilities for the disabled, among other things.

The transport system, cinemas, and theaters are still pretty much off-limits, but **London Transport** does publish a leaflet called *Access to the Underground,* which gives details of elevators and ramps at individual Underground stations; call ☎ **0171/918-3312.** And the London Black Cab is perfectly suited for those in wheelchairs; the roomy interiors have plenty of room for maneuvering.

London's most visible organization for information about access to theaters, cinemas, galleries, museums, and restaurants is **Artsline,** 54 Chalton St., London NW1 1HS (☎ **0171/388-2227;** fax 0171/383-2653). It offers free information about wheelchair access, theaters with hearing aids, tourist attractions, and cinemas. Artsline will mail information to North America, but it's even more helpful to contact Artsline once you arrive in London; the line is staffed Monday to Friday from 9:30am to 5:30pm.

An organization that cooperates closely with Artsline is **Tripscope,** The Courtyard, 4 Evelyn Rd., London W4 5JL (☎ **0181/994-9294;** fax 0181/994-3618), which offers advice on travel for persons with disabilities in Britain and elsewhere.

FOR GAY & LESBIAN TRAVELERS

London has one of the most active gay and lesbian scenes in the world; we've recommended a number of the city's best gay clubs (at least as of press time) in chapter 9, "London After Dark." For the gay and lesbian traveler to England, the best guides are *Spartacus Britain and Ireland* ($24.95) and *London Scene* ($11.95). For up-to-the-minute information on activities, we recommend the monthly *Gay Times* (London) for $6.95. These publications and others are available from **Giovanni's Room,** 1145 Pine St., Philadelphia, PA 19107 (☎ **215/923-2960;** fax 215/923-0813).

Our World magazine, 1104 North Nova Rd., Suite 251, Daytona Beach, FL 32117 (☎ **904/441-5367;** fax 904/441-5604; $35 for 10 issues), covers worldwide travel options and bargains for gay and lesbian travelers. *Out and About,* 8 West 19th St., Suite 401, New York, NY 10011 (☎ **800/929-2268** or 212/645-6922; fax 800/929-2215; $49 for 10 information-packed issues), is another great publication on gay travel that profiles the best gay or gay-friendly hotels, gyms, clubs, and other places worldwide.

With some 1,200 member agencies, the **International Gay Travel Association** (IGTA), 4331 N. Federal, Suite 304, Ft. Lauderdale, FL 33308 (☎ **954/776-2626,** or 800/448-8550 for voice mail), specializes in networking travelers with the appropriate gay-friendly service organization or tour specialist. It offers a quarterly newsletter, marketing mailings, and a membership directory.

Our Family Abroad, 40 West 57th St., Suite 430, New York, NY 10019 (☎ **800/999-5500** or 212/459-1800), operates escorted tours for gay men and women to locales around the world, including several to Britain. Guides serve on a volunteer basis—a system that tends to assure the absence of homophobics.

Lesbian and Gay Switchboard (☎ **0171/837-7324**) is open 24 hours a day, providing information about gay-related activities in London, or advice in general. The **Bisexual Helpline** (☎ **0181/569-7500**) offers useful information, but only on Tuesday and Wednesday from 7:30 to 9:30pm, and Saturday between 9:30am and noon. London's best gay-oriented bookstore is **Gay's the Word,** 66 Marchmont St., WC1 (☎ **0171/278-7654;** tube: Russell Square), the largest such store in Britain. It's open Monday to Wednesday, Friday, and Saturday 10am to 6pm, Thursday 10am to 7pm, and Sunday 2 to 6pm.

FOR SENIORS

Many discounts are available to seniors. Be advised, however, that in England you often have to be a member of an association to obtain discounts. Public-transportation reductions, for example, are available only to holders of British Pension books. However, many attractions do offer discounts for senior citizens (women 60 or over and men 65 or over). Even if discounts aren't posted, you might ask if they're available.

If you're over 60, you're eligible for special 10% discounts on **British Airways** through its Privileged Traveler program. You also qualify for reduced restrictions on APEX cancellations. Discounts are also granted for BA tours and for intra-Britain air tickets that are booked in North America.

British Rail offers seniors discounted rates on first-class rail passes for travel around Britain. See the discussion under "Getting There by Train," below.

You can write for a helpful publication, *101 Tips for the Mature Traveler,* available from **Grand Circle Travel,** 347 Congress St., Suite 3A, Boston, MA 02210 (☎ **800/221-2610** or 617/350-7500; fax 617/346-6700); this travel agency also offers escorted tours and cruises for seniors. **SAGA International Holidays,** 222 Berkeley St., Boston, MA 02116 (☎ **800/343-0273**), offers inclusive tours and cruises for those 50 and older.

If you're a member of the **American Association of Retired Persons (AARP),** 601 E St. NW, Washington, DC 20049 (☎ **202/434-AARP**), you may qualify for discounts on car rentals and hotels.

Information on senior travel is also available from the **National Council of Senior Citizens,** 8403 Colesville Rd., Suite 1200, Silver Spring, MD 20910 (☎ **301/578-8800**). A nonprofit organization, the council charges a membership fee of $12 per couple, for which you receive a magazine six times a year and membership benefits, including discounts on hotels and auto rentals, a discount pharmacy program, and accidental death insurance.

Mature Outlook, P.O. Box 9390, Des Moines, IA 50306-9519 (☎ **800/336-6330;** fax 515/252-7855), is a travel organization for people over 50. Members receive a bimonthly magazine and are offered discounts at ITC-member hotels.

Annual membership is $14.95 to $19.95, which also entitles you to discounts—and in some cases free coupons—for discounted merchandise from Sears.

FOR FAMILIES

On airlines, you must request a special menu for children at least 24 hours in advance. Bring your own baby food, though; you can ask a flight attendant to warm it to the right temperature.

Arrange ahead of time for such necessities as a crib, bottle warmer, and car seat (in England, small children aren't allowed to ride in the front seat). If you're staying with friends, you can rent baby equipment from **Chelsea Baby Hire,** 83 Burntwood Lane, SW17 OAJ (☎ **0181/540-8830**). The London Black Cab is a lifesaver for families; the roomy interior allows a stroller to be lifted right into the cab without unstrapping baby.

If you want a night out without the kids, you're in luck: London has its own children's hotel, **Pippa Popins,** 430 Fulham Rd., SW6 1DU (☎ **0171/385-2458**), which accommodates children overnight in a wonderful nursery filled with lots of toys and caring minders. Other recommendable babysitting services are **Babysitters Unlimited** (☎ **0181/892-8888**) and **Childminders** (☎ **0171/935-2049** or 0171/935-3000). Babysitters can also be found for you at most hotels.

Family Travel Times is published quarterly by **TWYCH** (Travel With Your Children) and includes a weekly call-in service for subscribers. Subscriptions ($40 a year) can be ordered from TWYCH, 40 Fifth Ave., New York, NY 10011 (☎ **212/477-5524;** fax 212/477-5173). An information packet, including a sample newsletter, is available for $2.

Families Welcome!, 4711 Hope Valley Rd., Suite 4B, Durham, NC 27707 (☎ **800/326-0724** or 919/489-2555), a travel company specializing in worry-free vacations for families, offers "City Kids" packages to London, featuring accommodations in family-friendly hotels or apartments. Individually designed family packages can include car rentals, train and ferry passes, and special air prices. A welcome kit is available, containing insider advice for families traveling in London, such as reliable babysitters, where to buy Pampers, and a list of family-friendly restaurants.

To find out what's on for kids while you're in London, pick up the leaflet *Where to Take Children,* published by the London Tourist Board. If you have specific questions, ring **Kidsline** (☎ **0171/222-8070**) Monday to Friday 4 to 6pm and summer holidays 9am to 4pm or the **London Tourist Board's** special children's information lines (☎ **0891/505-456** or 089/505-460) for listings of special events and places to visit for children. The number is accessible in London at 50p (80¢) per call.

FOR STUDENTS

Council Travel (a subsidiary of the Council on International Educational Exchange) is America's largest student, youth, and budget travel group, with more than 60 offices worldwide. The main office is at 205 E. 42nd St., New York, NY 10017 (☎ **212/822-2700**). **Council Travel's London Centre** is conveniently located at 28A Poland St., W1V 3DB, just off Oxford Circus (☎ **0171/287-3337** for European destinations, 0171/437-7767 for other destinations). International Student Identity Cards, issuable to all bona fide students for $19, entitle holders to generous travel and other discounts. Discounted international and domestic air tickets are available, and Eurotrain rail passes, YHA passes, weekend packages, overland safaris, and hostel/hotel accommodations are bookable. Council Travel also sells a number of publications for young people about how to work, study, and travel abroad.

For real budget travelers, it's worth joining the **International Youth Hostel Federation.** For information, write **Hostelling International/American Youth Hostels**

(HI-AYH), 733 15th St. NW, no. 840, Washington, DC 20005 (☎ **202/783-6161;** fax 202/783-6171). Membership costs $25 annually; those under age 18 pay $10 and those over 54 pay $15.

STA Travel, 86 Old Brompton Rd., SW7 3LQ (☎ **0171/361-6161;** tube: South Kensington), is the only worldwide company specializing in student- and youth-discounted airfares. It's open Monday to Thursday 9:30am to 6pm, Friday 10am to 6pm, and Saturday 10am to 4pm. Also keep in mind that **British Airways** offers youth fares to anyone 12 to 24.

The International Student House, 229 Great Portland St., W1 (☎ **0171/ 631-3223**), lies at the foot of Regent's Park across from the tube stop for Great Portland Street. It's a beehive of student activity, such as discos and film showings, and rents blandly furnished, very institutional rooms for £27 ($43.20) single, £19.50 ($31.20) per person double, £16 ($25.60) per person triple, and £9.99 ($16) per person in a dorm. English breakfast is included. Laundry facilities are available, and a £10 ($16) key deposit is charged. Reserve way in advance.

University of London Student Union, 1 Malet St., WC1E 7HY (☎ **0171/ 580-9551;** tube: Goodge Street or Russell Square), is the best place to go to learn about student activities in the Greater London area. The Union contains a swimming pool, a fitness center, a gymnasium, a general store, a sports shop, a ticket agency, banks, bars, inexpensive restaurants, venues for live events, an office of STA Travel (see above), and many other facilities. It's open Monday to Thursday 8:30am to 11pm, Friday 8:30am to 1pm, Saturday 9:30am to 2pm, and Sunday 9:30am to 10:30pm. Bulletin boards at the Union provide a rundown on sponsored events, some of which you might be able to attend; others might be "closed door."

6 Getting There

BY PLANE

Most airlines charge different fares according to season. For flights to Europe, the fares are most expensive during midsummer, the peak travel time. Winter offers the least expensive fares. Travel during Christmas and Easter weeks is usually more expensive than in the weeks just before or after those holidays.

If you're concerned about costs, your best strategy is to shop around and, above all, to remain as flexible as you can about dates; prices tend to be higher for weekend travel, so if you want the least expensive fare, book midweek. And keep calling the airlines—if a flight isn't fully booked, an airline might discount tickets in an attempt to achieve a full load, allowing you to buy a lower-priced ticket at the last minute. (This strategy tends to work better in the off-season, when most travelers are heading to warm-weather destinations rather than Europe, and planes tend not to be full; in summer, it's riskier to wait to book a flight—in high season the airlines often charge top-dollar at the last minute.)

Even within the various seasons, most airlines also offer heavily discounted promotional fares available according to the market. *But be warned:* The less expensive your ticket is, the more stringent the restrictions will be. The most common and frequently used such fare is the APEX, or advance-purchase excursion (see below).

FROM NORTH AMERICA

From the United States American Airlines (☎ 800/433-7300; www. americanair.com) offers daily routes to London Heathrow Airport from five U.S. gateways: New York's JFK (six times daily), Chicago's O'Hare and Boston's Logan (twice daily), Miami International, and Los Angeles International (each once daily).

British Airways (☎ 800/247-9297; www.british-airways.com) offers mostly non-stop flights from 18 U.S. cities to Heathrow and Gatwick airports. With more add-on options than any other airline, British Airways can make a visit to Britain cheaper than you might have expected. The 1993 union of some of BA's functions and routings with US Airways has opened additional North American gateways to BA, improved services, and reduced some of its fares. Of particular interest are the "Value Plus," "London on the Town," and "Europe Escorted" packages that include both airfare and discounted accommodations throughout Britain.

Continental Airlines (☎ 800/525-0280; www.flycontinental.com) flies daily to Gatwick Airport from Newark and Houston.

Depending on day and season, **Delta Air Lines** (☎ 800/241-4141; www.delta-air.com) runs either one or two daily nonstop flights between Atlanta and Gatwick, near London. Delta also offers nonstop daily service from Cincinnati.

Northwest Airlines (☎ 800/447-4747; www.nwa.com) flies nonstop from both Minneapolis and Detroit to Gatwick, with connections possible from other cities, such as Boston and New York.

TWA (☎ 800/221-2000; www2.twa.com) flies nonstop to Gatwick every day from its hub in St. Louis. Connections are possible through St. Louis from most of North America.

United Airlines (☎ 800/538-2929; www.ual.com) flies nonstop from New York's JFK and Chicago's O'Hare to Heathrow two or three times a day, depending on the season. United also offers nonstop service twice a day from Dulles Airport, near Washington, D.C., plus once-a-day service from Newark, Los Angeles, and San Francisco to Heathrow.

Virgin Atlantic Airways (☎ 800/862-8621; www.fly.virgin.com) flies daily to either Gatwick or Heathrow from Boston, Newark, New York's JFK, Los Angeles, San Francisco, Washington's Dulles, Miami, and Orlando.

From Canada   For travelers departing from Canada, **Air Canada** (☎ 800/776-3000; www.aircanada.ca) flies daily to London Heathrow nonstop from Vancouver, Montréal, and Toronto. There are also frequent direct flights from Edmonton, Calgary, Winnipeg, Ottawa, Halifax, and St. John's.

FROM AUSTRALIA & SOUTH AFRICA

From Australia   **Qantas** (☎ 131211; www.qantas.com) flies from both Sydney and Melbourne daily. **British Airways** (☎ 02/92583300 or 03/96031133; www.british-airways.com) has five to seven flights weekly from Sydney and Melbourne.

From South Africa   **South African Airways** (☎ 011/978-1111; www.saa.co.za) schedules two daily flights from Johannesburg and three weekly flights from Cape Town. From Johannesburg, both **British Airways** (☎ 0800/011747; www.british-airways.com) and **Virgin Atlantic Airways** (☎ 011/340-3400; www.fly.virgin.com) have daily flights to Heathrow. British Airways flies five times weekly from Cape Town.

LONDON'S AIRPORTS

London Heathrow Airport   Located west of London in Hounslow (☎ 0181/759-4321 for flight information), Heathrow is one of the world's busiest airports, with flights arriving from around the world and throughout Great Britain. It's divided into four terminals, each relatively self-contained. Terminal 4, the most modern, handles the long-haul and transatlantic operations of British Airways. Most transatlantic flights of U.S.-based airlines arrive at Terminal 3. Terminals 1 and 2 receive the intra-European flights of several European airlines.

A New London-Heathrow Link

The newest and fastest way to get from Heathrow to the city is Heathrow Express, a $720 million rail link that rockets between the airport and Paddington Station in just 15 minutes. At press time, one-way fares were expected to range from £10 ($16) to £12.50 ($20). By 1999, full check-ins will exist at Paddington for 29 airlines; currently only carry-on check-in is available

It takes 50 minutes by **Underground** and costs £3.30 ($5.30) to make the 15-mile trip from Heathrow to center city. You can also take the **Airbus,** which gets you into central London in about an hour and costs £6 ($9.60) for adults and £4 ($6.40) for children. A **taxi** is likely to cost at least £35 ($56). For more information about train or bus connections, call ☎ **0171/222-1234.**

Gatwick Airport   While Heathrow still dominates, more and more scheduled flights land at relatively remote Gatwick (☎ **01293/535353** for flight information), located some 25 miles south of London in West Sussex.

From Gatwick, **express trains** leave for Victoria Station in London every 15 minutes during the day and every hour at night. The charge is £9 ($14.40) for adults, half price for children 5 to 15, free for children under 5. There's also an express bus from Gatwick to Victoria, **Flightline Bus 777,** every half-hour from 6:30am to 8pm and every hour from 8 to 11pm; the fare is £7.50 ($12) per person. A **taxi** from Gatwick to central London usually costs £50 to £60 ($80 to $96). However, you must negotiate a fare with the driver before you enter the cab; the meter doesn't apply because Gatwick lies outside the Metropolitan Police District. For further transportation information, call ☎ **0345/484950** in London only.

London Stansted Airport   Located some 50 miles northeast of London's West End, Stansted, in Essex (☎ **01279/680500**), mostly handles flights to and from the European continent. From Stansted, your best bet to reach central London is the **Stansted Express** to Liverpool Street Station, costing £11 ($17.60) for adults and £7.90 ($12.65) for children under 15. Daily service runs every 30 minutes from 5:30am to 11pm. Trip time is 45 minutes.

London City Airport   London City Airport (☎ **0171/474-5555**) receives mainly short-haul flights from Britain and northern Europe, making it popular with business travelers.

From London City Airport, there are three ways to reach the center of London: First, the **blue-and-white bus** charges £3 ($4.80) each way to and from the Liverpool Street Station, where passengers can get rail and Underground transport to almost anywhere in England. The bus runs every 20 minutes Monday to Friday, and every 30 minutes on Saturday and Sunday during open hours of the airport—roughly from 7am to 8:30pm. Second, there's a **shuttle bus to Canary Wharf,** where trains from the Docklands Light Railway make frequent 10-minute runs to the heart of London's financial district, the City. Here, passengers can catch an Underground from the Bank tube stop. Third, **London Transport bus no. 473** goes from the City Airport to East London, where passengers can pick up the Underground at the Plaistow tube stop.

BY TRAIN

Each of London's train stations is connected to the city's vast bus and Underground network, and each has phones, restaurants, pubs, luggage-storage areas, and London Regional Transport Information Centres.

If you're **arriving from France,** the fastest way to get to London is by taking the HoverSpeed connection between Calais and Dover (see "Ferries & Hovercraft" under "By Boat," below), where you can pick up a BritRail train into the city. If you prefer the ease of one-stop travel, you can take the Chunnel train directly from Paris.

Via the Chunnel from the Continent   Queen Elizabeth and President François Mitterrand officially opened the Channel Tunnel in 1994, and the **Eurostar Express** began twice-daily passenger service between London and both Paris and Brussels. The $15-billion tunnel, one of the great engineering feats of all time, is the first link between Britain and the Continent since the Ice Age.

Rail Europe (☎ **800/94-CHUNNEL** for information) sells tickets on the *Eurostar* direct train service between Paris or Brussels and London. A round-trip first-class fare between Paris and London, for example, costs $398 ($278 in second class); but you can cut costs to $182 with a second-class, 14-day advance purchase (nonrefundable) round-trip fare. In London, make reservations for *Eurostar* at ☎ **0345/300003;** in Paris, at ☎ **01-44-51-06-02;** and in the United States, at ☎ **800/EUROSTAR.** *Eurostar* trains arrive and depart from London's Waterloo Station, Paris's Gare du Nord, and Brussel's Central Station.

Via BritRail from Other Parts of Europe   If you're traveling to London from elsewhere in the United Kingdom, consider buying a **BritRail Classic Pass,** which allows unlimited rail travel during a set time period (8 days, 15 days, or 1 month). (Eurailpasses aren't accepted in Britain, although they are in Ireland.) For 8 days, a pass costs $375 in first class, $259 in standard class; for 15 days, it's $575 and $395, respectively; for 22 days, it's $740 and $510; and for 1 month, it's $860 and $590. If a child age 5 to 15 is traveling with a full-fare adult, the fare is half the adult fare. Children under 5 travel free if not occupying a seat. Senior citizens (60 and over) qualify for discounts, but only on first-class travel: It's $319 for an 8-day pass, $489 for a 15-day pass, $630 for a 22-day pass, and $730 for a 1-month pass. Travelers between 16 and 25 can purchase a BritRail Classic Youth Pass, which allows unlimited second-class travel: $205 for 8 days, $318 for 15 days, $410 for 22 days, or $475 for 1 month.

You must purchase your BritRail pass before you leave home. Americans can secure BritRail passes at **BritRail Travel International,** 500 Mamaroneck Ave., Suite 314, Harrison, NY 10528 (☎ **800/677-8585** in the U.S., 800/555-2748 in Canada), or you can get booking information on the internet at **www.raileurope.com**.

Travelers who arrive from France via ferry or hovercraft (see "By Boat" below) and pick up a British Rail train at Dover arrive at **Victoria Station,** in the center of London. Those journeying south by rail from Edinburgh arrive at **King's Cross Station.**

BY BUS

If you're traveling to London from elsewhere in the United Kingdom, consider purchasing a **Britexpress Card,** which entitles you to a 30% discount on National Express (England and Wales) and Caledonian Express (Scotland) buses. Contact a travel agent for details.

Bus connections to Britain from the Continent are generally not very comfortable, although some lines are more convenient than others. One line with a relatively good reputation is **Euroways Eurolines, Ltd.,** 52 Grosvenor Gardens, London SW1W OAU (☎ **0171/730-8235**). They book passage on buses traveling three times a day between London and Paris (9 hours); two times a day from Amsterdam (12 hours); four times a week from Munich (24 hours); and three times a week from Stockholm (44 hours). On the longer routes, which employ two alternating drivers, the bus proceeds almost without interruption, taking occasional breaks for meals.

BY CAR

If you plan to take a rented car across or under the Channel, check carefully with the rental company about license and insurance requirements before you leave.

Ferries from the Continent   There are many "drive-on, drive-off" car-ferry services across the Channel. The most popular ports in France for Channel crossings are Boulogne and Calais, where you can board Stena **Sealink ferries** taking you to the English ports of Dover and Folkestone. For details, see "Ferries & Hovercraft" under "By Boat," below.

Le Shuttle   You can take Le Shuttle (☎ **0990/353535** or 01304/288617) under the English Channel. The tunnel not only accommodates trains but passenger cars, charter buses, taxis, and motorcycles, all taken under the English Channel from Calais, France, to Folkestone, England, or vice versa. It operates 24 hours a day, 365 days a year, running every 15 minutes during peak travel times and at least once an hour at night. With Le Shuttle, gone are weather-related delays, seasickness, and a need for reservations. Motorists drive onto a half-mile-long train and travel though an underground tunnel built beneath the seabed through a layer of impermeable chalk marl and sealed with a reinforced-concrete lining.

Before boarding Le Shuttle, you'll stop at a toll booth to pay, then pass through Immigration for both countries at one time. During the ride, you'll stay in bright, air-conditioned carriages, remaining inside your car or stepping outside to stretch your legs. When the trip is completed, you'll simply drive off toward London. The total travel time between the French and English highway system is about 1 hour.

The cost of moving a car on Le Shuttle varies, according to the season and the day of the week, between £80 and £265 ($128 and $424) each way. Discounts are granted to passengers who return to France with their cars within 5 days of their departure; otherwise, the round-trip fare is twice the price of the one-way fare.

Stores selling duty-free goods, restaurants, and service stations are available to travelers on both sides of the Channel. A bilingual staff is on hand to assist travelers at both the British and French terminals.

Hertz offers **Le Swap,** a service for passengers taking Le Shuttle. At Calais, you can switch cars for either a left-hand- or right-hand-drive vehicle, depending upon which country you're heading for.

Once You've Arrived   Once you arrive on the English side, the M20 takes you directly into London. *Remember to drive on the left.* London is circled by two roadways: the A406 and A205 combination close in and the M25 farther out. Determine which part of the city you wish to enter and follow signposts. We suggest you confine driving in London to the bare minimum, which means arriving and parking.

Parking is scarce and expensive. Before arrival in London, call your hotel and inquire if it has a garage (and what the charges are), or ask the staff to give you the name and address of a garage nearby.

BY BOAT
OCEAN LINER

Cunard Line, 6100 Blue Lagoon Dr., Suite 400, Miami, FL 33126 (☎ **305/ 463-3000** or 800/7-CUNARD), boasts that its flagship, *Queen Elizabeth 2,* is the only five-star-plus luxury ocean liner providing regular transatlantic service—some 18 voyages a year between April and December. Many passengers appreciate its graceful introduction to British mores, as well as the absolute lack of jet lag that an ocean crossing can provide.

Fares vary, based on the season and the cabin grade. During the super-value season (April 12 to May 13 and December 9 to 15), the fares for a 6-day crossing range from $1,300 to $9,200. During peak season (June 2 to October 1), fares for a 6-day crossing range from $2,400 to $12,125. All prices are per person, double occupancy; passengers also pay $193 port and handling charges. Many packages are offered, which include inexpensive airfare from your home city to the point of departure plus a return flight to your home city from London on British Airways.

FERRIES & HOVERCRAFT

For centuries, sailing ships and ferryboats have traversed the English Channel bearing supplies, merchandise, and passengers. Today, the major carriers are P&O Channel Lines, Hoverspeed, and Sealink. Once you arrive in Dover, you can pick up a BritRail train to London (see "By Train," above).

Car & Passenger Ferries   P&O Channel Lines (☎ 0990/980980) operates car and passenger ferries between Portsmouth and Cherbourg, France (three departures a day; 4¼ hours each way, 7 hours at night); between Portsmouth and Le Havre, France (three a day; 5½ hours each way, 7 hours at night); and between Dover and Calais, France (25 a day; 75 minutes each way).

P&O's major competitor is **Stena Sealink** (☎ 01233/615455), which carries both passengers and vehicles. This company is represented in North America by **Rail Europe** (☎ 800/677-8585 or 212/575-2667). Stena Sealink operates conventional ferryboat service between Cherbourg and Southampton (one or two trips a day taking 6 to 8 hours) and between Dieppe and Newhaven (four departures a day taking 4 hours each way). Very popular are Sealink's conventional car ferries between Calais and Dover, which depart 20 times a day in either direction and take 90 minutes for the crossing. Typical one-way fares between France and England are £25 ($40) for adults, £22 ($35.20) for senior citizens, and £12 ($19.20) for children.

Hovercraft & SeaCats   Traveling by Hovercraft or SeaCat cuts your journey time from the Continent to Britain. **HoverSpeed** operates at least 12 daily 35-minute Hovercraft crossings, as well as slightly longer crossings via SeaCat (a catamaran propelled by jet engines; these go four times daily and take about 55 minutes), between Boulogne and Folkestone. A Hovercraft trip is definitely a fun adventure, as the vessel is technically "flying" over the water. SeaCats also travel from the mainland of Britain to the Isle of Wight, Belfast, and the Isle of Man. For reservations and information, call **HoverSpeed** at ☎ 01304/240241. Typical one-way fares are £25 ($40) per person.

Getting to Know London 3

Europe's largest city is like a great wheel, with Piccadilly Circus at the hub and dozens of communities branching out from it. Since London is such a conglomeration of sections, each with its own life and personality, first-time visitors may be intimidated until they get the hang of it. Most visitors spend all their time in the West End, where most of the attractions are located, except for the historic part of London known as the City, where the Tower of London stands.

This chapter will help you get your bearings. It provides a brief orientation and a preview of the city's most important neighborhoods and tells you what you need to know about getting around London by public transportation or on foot. In addition, the "Fast Facts" section covers everything from babysitters to shoe repairs.

1 Orientation

VISITOR INFORMATION

The **British Travel Centre,** Rex House, 4–12 Lower Regent St., London SW1 4PQ (tube: Piccadilly Circus), caters to walk-in visitors who need information about all parts of Britain. Telephone service has been suspended; you must show up in person and wait in an often lengthy line. On the premises you'll find a British Rail ticket office, travel and theater-ticket agencies, a hotel-booking service, a bookshop, and a souvenir shop. It's open Monday to Friday 9am to 6:30pm, Saturday and Sunday 10am to 4pm, with extended hours on Saturday from June to September.

London Tourist Board's **Tourist Information Centre,** Victoria Station Forecourt, SW1 (tube: Victoria Station), can help you with almost anything. The center deals chiefly with accommodations in all sizes and price categories and can handle the whole spectrum of travelers. It also arranges tour-ticket sales, theater reservations, and offers a wide selection of books and souvenirs. From Easter to October, the center is open daily 8am to 7pm; November to Easter, it's open Monday to Saturday 8am to 6pm and Sunday 9am to 4pm.

The tourist board also has offices at **Heathrow** terminals 1, 2, and 3, and on the Underground Concourse at **Liverpool Street Railway Station.**

London's Neighborhoods

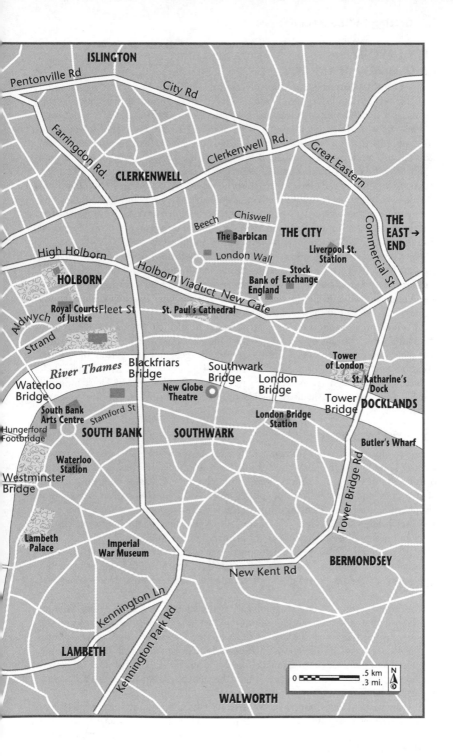

ISLINGTON

Pentonville Rd

City Rd

Farringdon Rd.

Clerkenwell Rd.

Great Eastern

CLERKENWELL

Beech Chiswell

The Barbican

THE CITY

THE EAST →
END

Commercial St

Liverpool St. Station

High Holborn

Holborn Viaduct New Gate

London Wall

Bank of England

Stock Exchange

HOLBORN

Royal Courts of Justice

Fleet St

St. Paul's Cathedral

Aldwych

Strand

River Thames

Blackfriars Bridge

Southwark Bridge

London Bridge

Tower of London

St. Katharine's Dock

Waterloo Bridge

New Globe Theatre

DOCKLANDS

Tower Bridge

South Bank Arts Centre

Stamford St

London Bridge Station

Hungerford Footbridge

SOUTH BANK

SOUTHWARK

Butler's Wharf

Waterloo Station

Westminster Bridge

Lambeth Palace

Imperial War Museum

Tower Bridge Rd

BERMONDSEY

New Kent Rd

Kennington Ln

Kennington Park Rd

LAMBETH

0   .5 km
    .3 mi.

N

WALWORTH

CITY LAYOUT
AN OVERVIEW OF THE CITY

While **Central London** doesn't formally define itself, most Londoners today would probably accept the Underground's Circle Line as a fair boundary. The city center is customarily divided into two areas, the **City** and the **West End.**

The City is where London began; it's the original 1 square mile the Romans called Londinium that still exists as its own self-governing entity. Rich in historical, architectural, and social interest, the City is now one of the world's great financial centers.

The West End, on the other hand, has no precise borders, but is divided by its main thoroughfares into clearly defined neighborhoods—Mayfair, Soho, Kensington, and the like—so by simply crossing the street, it's possible to leave behind a neighborhood of one quite distinct character and enter what seems to be another world. The West End is the area that most Londoners consider the real city center—this is where you find the majority of London's shops, restaurants, and theaters.

The City and the West End are surrounded first by **Inner London** (which includes the East End) and then by the sprawling hinterland of **Outer London.** You'll find the greatest number of hotels in the west, in inner districts such as **Kensington, Chelsea,** and **Victoria,** and in the West End. Even though the City is jeweled with historic sights, it empties out in the evenings and on weekends.

In much the way that the City is a buffer to the east, so is the River Thames to the south. The Barbican Centre in the City and the South Bank Arts Centre across the river were conscious attempts to extend the geographical spread of Central London's nocturnal life, but Central London really fades in the City and only half-heartedly crosses the Thames. Still, the new urban development of Docklands and some up-and-coming residential neighborhoods are infusing energy into the area across the river.

ORIENTING YOURSELF

There is—fortunately—an immense difference between the sprawling vastness of Greater London and the pocket-size chunk north of the River Thames that might be considered Prime Tourist Territory. This London begins at **Chelsea,** on the north bank of the river, and stretches for roughly 5 miles north to **Hampstead.** Its western periphery runs through **Kensington,** whereas the eastern boundary lies 5 miles away at Tower Bridge. Within these 25 square miles, you'll find all the hotels and restaurants and nearly all the sights that are of primary interest to visitors.

Make no mistake: This is still a hefty portion of land to cover, and a really thorough exploration of it would take a couple of years. But it has the advantage of being flat and walkable, besides boasting one of the best public transportation systems ever devised.

The logical (although not geographical) center of this area is **Trafalgar Square,** which we'll take as our orientation point (see "London's Neighborhoods" map on pp. 44–45). If you stand facing the steps of the imposing National Gallery, you're looking northwest. That is the direction of **Piccadilly Circus**—the real core of central London—and the maze of streets that make up **Soho.** Farther north is **Oxford Street,** London's gift to moderate shopping; still farther northwest lies **Regent's Park,** home to the London Zoo.

At your back—that is, south—is **Whitehall,** which houses or skirts nearly every British government building, from the Ministry of Defence to the official residence of the prime minister at No. 10 Downing Street. In the same direction, a bit farther south, stand the Houses of Parliament and Westminster Abbey.

Flowing southwest from Trafalgar Square is the table-smooth **Mall,** flanked by magnificent parks and mansions and leading to Buckingham Palace, residence of the queen. Farther in the same direction lie **Belgravia** and **Knightsbridge,** the city's plushest residential areas, and south of them lie the aforementioned chic **Chelsea** and **King's Road,** the famous shopping boulevard.

Due west of Trafalgar Square stretches the superb and distinctly high-priced shopping area bordered by **Regent Street** and **Piccadilly** (the street, distinct from the Circus). Farther west lie the equally elegant shops and even more elegant homes of **Mayfair.** Then comes ritzy **Park Lane.** On the other side of Park Lane is **Hyde Park,** the biggest park in London and one of the largest in the world.

Charing Cross Road runs north from Trafalgar Square, past **Leicester Square,** and intersects with **Shaftesbury Avenue.** This is London's Theaterland. A bit farther along, Charing Cross Road turns into a browser's paradise, lined with shops selling new and secondhand books.

Finally, Charing Cross Road funnels into **St. Giles Circus;** this is where you enter **Bloomsbury,** site of the University of London, the British Museum, and some of London's best budget hotels, as well as the erstwhile stamping ground of the famed Bloomsbury Group, which included Virginia Woolf, E.M. Forster, and John Maynard Keynes.

Northeast of your position sprawls **Covent Garden,** known for its Royal Opera House and today a major—and very hip—shopping, restaurant, and cafe district.

Following the **Strand** eastward from Trafalgar Square, you'll come into **Fleet Street.** Beginning in the 19th century, this corner of London became the most concentrated newspaper district in the world (most of the papers have fled Fleet Street for the new Docklands development in the last decade or so). Where the Strand becomes Fleet Street stands Temple Bar, and only here do you enter the actual City of London, or **the City.** Its focal point and shrine is the Bank of England on Threadneedle Street, with the Stock Exchange next door and the Royal Exchange across the street. In the midst of all the hustle and bustle rises St. Paul's Cathedral, a monument to beauty and tranquillity. At the far eastern fringe of the City looms the Tower of London, shrouded in legend, blood, and history, and permanently besieged by battalions of visitors.

And this, as far as we're concerned, concludes the London circle.

FINDING YOUR WAY AROUND

It's not easy to find an address in London, as the city's streets—both their naming and house numbering—follow no pattern whatsoever. London is checkered with innumerable squares, mews, closes, and terraces, which jut into, cross, overlap, or interrupt whatever street you're trying to follow. And house numbers run in odds and evens, clockwise and counterclockwise—when they exist at all. Many establishments, such as the Four Seasons Hotel and Langan's Brasserie, don't have numbers, even though the building right next door is numbered.

Face it—you're going to get lost. So if you plan on exploring London in any depth, you'll need a detailed street map with an index, not one of those superficial overviews given away at many hotels or tourist offices. The best ones are published by Falk, and they're available at most newsstands and nearly all bookstores, including **W. & G. Foyle Ltd.,** 113–119 Charing Cross Rd., WC2 (☎ **0171/439-8501;** tube: Leicester Square), which carries a wide range of maps and guides. And no Londoner is without a *London A to Z,* the ultimate street-by-street reference guide, available at bookstores and newsstands everywhere. Also, don't forget to check out the detailed foldout street map included with this book; you may find that it's all you need to find your way around.

Postal Areas

Throughout our book street addresses are followed by designations like SW1 and EC1. These are the postal areas. The original post office was at St. Martin-le-Grand, in the City, so the postal districts are related to where they lie geographically from 'there. For example, Victoria is SW1 since it's the first area southwest of St. Martin-le-Grand; Covent Garden is west (west central), so its postal area is WC1 or WC2; Liverpool Street is east of there, so its postal area is EC1.

LONDON'S NEIGHBORHOODS IN BRIEF

The West End Neighborhoods

Mayfair   Bounded by Piccadilly, Hyde Park, and Oxford and Regent streets, this is the most elegant, fashionable section of London, filled with luxury hotels, Georgian town houses, and swank shops. Grosvenor Square (*Grov*-nor) is nicknamed "Little America" because it's home to the American embassy and a statue of Franklin D. Roosevelt; Berkeley Square (*Bark*-ley) was made famous by the song, whose mythical nightingale sang here. At least once you'll want to dip into this exclusive section. One of the curiosities of Mayfair is **Shepherd Market,** a tiny village of pubs, two-story inns, book and food stalls, and restaurants, all sandwiched within Mayfair's grandness.

Marylebone   Most first-time visitors head to Marylebone to explore Madame Tussaud's waxworks or walk along Baker Street in the make-believe footsteps of Sherlock Holmes. The streets form a near-perfect grid, with the major ones running north–south from Regent's Park toward Oxford Street. Robert Adam laid out Portland Place, one of the most characteristic squares, from 1776 to 1780, and it was at Cavendish Square that Mrs. Horatio Nelson waited—often in vain—for the return of the admiral. Marylebone Lane and High Street still retain some of their former village atmosphere, but this is otherwise a rather anonymous area. Dickens (who seems to have lived everywhere) wrote nearly a dozen books when he resided here. At Regent's Park, you can visit Queen Mary's Gardens or, in summer, see Shakespeare performed in an open-air theater.

St. James's   Often called "Royal London," St. James's basks in its associations with everybody from the "merrie monarch" Charles II to Elizabeth II, who lives at its most famous address, Buckingham Palace. The neighborhood begins at Piccadilly Circus and moves southwest, incorporating Pall Mall, The Mall, St. James's Park, and Green Park; it's "frightfully convenient," as the English say, enclosing such addresses as American Express on Haymarket and many of London's leading department stores. In this bastion of aristocracy and royalty, a certain pomp is still evident—this is where the English gentleman seeks haven at that male-only bastion of English tradition, the gentlemen's club. Be sure to stop in at **Fortnum & Mason,** 181 Piccadilly, the world's most luxurious grocery store. Launched in 1788, the store sent hams to the Duke of Wellington's army, baskets of tinned goodies to Florence Nightingale in the Crimea, and packed a picnic basket for Stanley when he went looking for Livingstone.

Piccadilly Circus & Leicester Square   Piccadilly Circus, with its statue of Eros, is the heart and soul of London. The circus isn't Times Square yet, but its traffic, neon, and jostling crowds don't do anything to make it fashionable. Circus might indeed be an apt word here. Piccadilly, traditionally the western road out of town, was named for the "picadil," a ruffled collar created by Robert Baker, a 17th-century tailor. If you want a little more grandeur, retreat to the Regency promenade of exclusive shops, the **Burlington Arcade,** designed in 1819. The English gentry—tired of being mud-splashed by horses and carriages along Piccadilly—came here to do their shopping. Some 35 shops, housing a treasure trove of goodies, await you. A bit more tawdry is **Leicester Square,** a center of theaters, restaurants, movie palaces, and nightlife. The square is no longer the chic address it was when William Hogarth or Joshua Reynolds lived here, the latter artist painting all of high society in his elegant salon. The square changed forever in the Victorian era, when four towering entertainment halls were opened (even Queen Victoria came to see a circus here on occasion). In time the old palaces changed from stage to screen; three of them are still showing films. The Café de Paris is no longer the chicest cabaret in town—now it's a disco.

Soho   Every city has its low-life area, of course, but few have their red lights woven into a texture of such richness and variety as London's Soho. These densely packed streets in the heart of the West End are famous for their gloriously cosmopolitan mix of people and trades. A decade ago, much was heard about the decline of Soho when the thriving sex industry threatened to engulf it; even the pub where Dylan Thomas used to drink himself into oblivion became a sex cinema. That destruction has now largely been halted. Respectable businesses have returned, and fashionable restaurants and shops prosper; it's now the heart of London's expanding cafe society. But Soho wouldn't be Soho without a scattering of sex shops and porno theaters.

Soho starts at Piccadilly Circus and spreads out, more-or-less bordered by Regent Street, Oxford Street, Charing Cross Road, and the theaters of Shaftesbury Avenue. Carnaby Street, a block from Regent Street, was the center of the universe in the Swinging 1960s, but is now just a schlocky sideshow. Across Shaftesbury Avenue, a busy street lined with theaters, is London's **Chinatown,** centered on Gerrard Street. It's small, authentic, and packed with excellent restaurants. But Soho's heart—with marvelous French and Italian delicatessens, fine butchers, fish stores, and wine merchants—is farther north, on Brewer, Old Compton, and Berwick streets; Berwick is also a wonderful open-air fresh food market. To the north of Old Compton Street, Dean, Frith, and Greek streets have fine little restaurants, pubs, and clubs, like Ronnie Scott's for jazz. The British movie industry is centered in Wardour Street.

Bloomsbury   This district, a world within itself, lies northeast of Piccadilly Circus, beyond Soho. It is, among other things, the academic heart of London; here you'll find the University of London, several other colleges, and many bookstores. Despite its student population, this neighborhood is fairly staid. Its reputation has been fanned by such writers as Virginia Woolf, who lived within its bounds (it figured in her novel *Jacob's Room*). The novelist and her husband, Leonard, were once unofficial leaders of a group of artists and writers known as "the Bloomsbury Group" (nicknamed "Bloomsberries"), which at times included Bertrand Russell.

The heart of Bloomsbury is Russell Square, whose outlying streets are lined with hotels and B&Bs. Most visitors come to the neighborhood to visit the British Museum, one of the world's greatest repositories of treasures. The British Telecom Tower (1964) on Cleveland Street is a familiar landmark.

Nearby is **Fitzrovia,** bounded by Great Portland, Oxford, and Gower streets, and reached by the Goodge Street tube. Goodge Street, with its many shops and pubs, forms the heart of the "village." Once a major haunt of artists and writers—this was the stamping ground of Ezra Pound, Wyndham Lewis, and George Orwell, among others—the bottom end of Fitzrovia is a virtual extension of Soho, with a cluster of Greek restaurants.

Clerkenwell   This was the site of London's first hospital and the home of several early churches before it evolved into a muck-filled 18th-century cattle yard that was home to cheap gin distilleries. By the 1870s, London's new socialist movement centered itself here: Clerkenwell was home to John Stuart Mill's London Patriotic Club in 1872 and William Morris's socialist press of the 1890s; Lenin lived and worked here editing *Iskra*. In later years, the neighborhood dwindled. However, it's recently been reinvented by the moneyed and groovy—a handful of hot new restaurants and clubs have sprouted up, and art galleries now line St. John's Square and the border of Clerkenwell Green. But lorries still rumble into Smithfield Market throughout the night, unloading thousands of beef carcasses for trade, and the church of St. Bartholomew-the-Great, built in 1123, still stands as London's oldest church and the best piece of large-scale Norman building in the city. Farringdon is the central tube stop.

Holborn The old borough of Holborn (*ho*-burn), which abuts the City to the west, takes in the heart of legal London—the city's barristers, solicitors, and law clerks call it home. Still Dickensian in spirit, the area preserves the Victorian author's footsteps in the two Inns of Court and the Bleeding Heart Yard of *Little Dorrit* fame. A 14-year-old Dickens was once employed as a solicitor's clerk at Lincoln's Inn Fields. The Old Bailey has stood for English justice down through the years; Fagin went to the gallows from this site in *Oliver Twist*. Everything in Holborn seems steeped in history. Even as you're quenching your thirst with a half-pint of bitter at the **Viaduct Tavern,** 126 Newgate St. (tube: St. Paul's), you learn the pub was built over the notorious Newgate Prison (which specialized in death by pressing) and was named after the Holborn Viaduct, the world's first overpass.

Covent Garden & the Strand The flower, fruit, and "veg" market is long gone (since 1970), but memories of Professor Higgins and his "squashed cabbage leaf," Eliza Doolittle, linger on. **Covent Garden** now contains the city's liveliest group of restaurants, pubs, and cafes outside Soho, as well as some of the city's hippest shops—including the world's only Dr. Marten's Super Store. The restored marketplace with its glass and iron roofs has been called a magnificent example of urban recycling. Covent Garden is traditionally London's theater area, and Inigo Jones's St. Paul's Covent Garden is known as the actors' church; over the years it has attracted everybody from Ellen Terry to Vivien Leigh and is still attended by actors and artists. The Theatre Royal Drury Lane was where Charles II's mistress Nell Gwynne made her debut in 1665 and the Irish actress Dorothea Jordan first caught the eye of the duke of Clarence, later William IV. (She became not only his mistress, but the mother of 10 of his children.)

Beginning at Trafalgar Square, the **Strand** runs east into Fleet Street and borders Covent Garden to the south. It's flanked with theaters, shops, hotels, and restaurants. Ye Olde Cheshire Cheese pub, Dr. Johnson's House, rooms fragrant with brewing Twinings English tea—all these evoke memories of the rich heyday of this district. The Strand runs parallel to the River Thames, and to walk it is to follow in the footsteps of Charles Lamb, Mark Twain, Henry Fielding, James Boswell, William Thackeray, and Sir Walter Raleigh. The Savoy Theatre helped make Gilbert and Sullivan household names.

Westminster Westminster has been the seat of the British government since the days of Edward the Confessor. Dominated by the Houses of Parliament and Westminster Abbey, the area runs along the Thames to the east of St. James's Park. **Trafalgar Square,** at the area's northern end and one of the city's major landmarks, remains a testament to England's victory over Napoléon in 1805, and the paintings in its landmark National Gallery will restore your soul. Whitehall is the main thoroughfare, linking Trafalgar Square with Parliament Square. You can visit Churchill's Cabinet War Rooms and walk down Downing Street to see No. 10, the world's most famous street address, home to Britain's prime minister. No visit is complete without a call at **Westminster Abbey,** one of the greatest Gothic churches in the world. It has witnessed a parade of English history, beginning when William the Conqueror was crowned here on Christmas Day, 1066.

Westminster also encompasses **Victoria,** an area that takes its unofficial name from bustling Victoria Station, known as "the gateway to the Continent."

The City & Environs

The City   When the Londoners speak of "the City" (EC2, EC3), they don't mean all of London; they mean the original square mile that's now the British version of Wall Street. The buildings of this district are known all over the world: the Bank of England, the London Stock Exchange, and the financially troubled Lloyd's of London. This was the original site of Londinium, as it was called by its Roman conquerors. Despite its age, the City doesn't easily reveal its past; much of it was swept away by the Great Fire of 1666, the bombs of 1940, the IRA bombs of the early 1990s, and the zeal of modern developers. Still, it retains its medieval character, and landmarks include St. Paul's Cathedral, the masterpiece of Sir Christopher Wren, which stood virtually alone among the rubble after the Blitz. Some 2,000 years of history unfold at the Museum of London and the Barbican Centre, opened by Queen Elizabeth in 1982, and hailed by her as a "wonder" of the cultural world. At the Guildhall, the first lord mayor of London was installed in 1192.

Fleet Street was London's journalistic hub since William Caxton printed the first book in English here. *The Daily Consort,* the first daily newspaper printed in England, was launched at Ludgate Circus in 1702. However, most of the London tabloids have abandoned Fleet Street for the Docklands development across the river.

The City of London still prefers to function on its own, separate from the rest of the city; in keeping with its independence, it maintains its own **Information Centre** at St. Paul's Churchyard, EC4 (☎ **0171/332-1456**).

Docklands   In 1981, the London Docklands Development Corporation (LDDC) was formed to redevelop Wapping, the Isle of Dogs, the Royal Docks, and Surrey Docks in the largest, the most ambitious scheme of its kind in Europe. Since then, many businesses have moved to the area—which is bordered roughly by Tower Bridge to the west and London City Airport and the Royal Docks to the east—including most of the Fleet Street newspapers; Thames-side warehouses have been converted to Manhattan-style lofts; and museums, entertainment complexes, shops, and an ever-growing list of restaurants have popped up at this 21st-century river city in the making.

Canary Wharf, on the Isle of Dogs, is the heart of Docklands; this huge 71-acre site is dominated by an 800-foot-high tower, the tallest building in the United Kingdom, designed by Cesar Pelli. The Piazza is lined with shops and restaurants. Across from the country's largest sports complex, London Arena, is the **Docklands Visitor Centre** (☎ **0171/512-3000**). On the south side of the river at Surrey Docks, the Victorian warehouses of **Butler's Wharf** have been converted by Sir Terence Conran into offices, workshops, houses, shops, and restaurants. Butler's Wharf is also home to the Design Museum.

To get to Docklands, take the Underground to Tower Hill and pick up the **Docklands Light Railway** (☎ **0171/538-0311**), which operates Monday to Friday from 5:30am to 12:30am, with selected main routes now offering weekend service from 6:30am to 11:30pm.

The East End   Traditionally, this was one of London's poorest districts, and was nearly bombed out of existence by the Nazis. Hitler, in the words of one commentator at the time, created "instant urban renewal." The East End extends from the City Walls east encompassing Stepney, Bow, Poplar, West Ham, Canning Town, and other districts. The East End has always been filled with legend and lore. It's the home of the Cockney, London's most colorful character. To be a true Cockney, it's said that you must have been born "within the sound of Bow Bells," a reference to a church, St. Mary-le-Bow, rebuilt by Sir Christopher Wren in 1670. Many immigrants to London have found a home here.

South Bank   Although not officially a district like Mayfair, South Bank is the setting today for the **South Bank Arts Centre,** now the largest arts center in Western Europe and still growing. Reached by Waterloo Bridge, it lies across the Thames from the Victoria Embankment. Culture buffs flock to its many galleries and halls, including the National Theatre, Queen Elizabeth Hall, Royal Festival Hall, and the Hayward Gallery. It's also the setting of the National Film Theatre and the Museum of the Moving Image (MOMI). Nearby are such neighborhoods as Elephant and Castle and Southwark, home to grand Southwark Cathedral. To get here, take the tube to Waterloo Station.

Central London Beyond the West End

Knightsbridge   One of London's most fashionable neighborhoods, Knightsbridge is a top residential and shopping district, just south of Hyde Park. **Harrods** on Brompton Road is its chief attraction. Founded in 1901, it's been called "the Notre Dame of department stores"—they'll even arrange your burial. Right nearby, Beauchamp Place (*Bee*-cham) is one of London's most fashionable shopping streets, a Regency-era boutique-lined little street with a scattering of restaurants such as San Lorenzo. Shops include Bruce Oldfield at 27 Beauchamp Place, where the likes of Joan Collins come for evening wear. And, at the end of a shopping day, if Harrods' five restaurants and five bars haven't tempted you, retreat to Bill Bentley's at 31 Beauchamp Place for a dozen oysters, washed down with a few glasses of muscadet.

Belgravia   South of Knightsbridge, this area has long been the aristocratic quarter of London, rivaling Mayfair in grandness and richness. Although it reached its pinnacle of prestige during the reign of Queen Victoria, it's still a chic address; the duke and duchess of Westminster, one of England's richest families, still live at Eaton Square. The area's centerpiece is Belgrave Square (1825–35). When town houses were built there, aristocrats followed—the duke of Connaught, the earl of Essex, even Queen Victoria's mother, the duchess of Kent. Chopin on holiday in 1837 was appropriately impressed: "And the English! And the houses! And the palaces! And the pomp, and the carriages! Everything from soap to the razors is extraordinary."

Chelsea   This stylish Thames-side district lies south of Belgravia. It begins at Sloane Square, with Gilbert Ledward's Venus fountain playing watery music and flower sellers hustling their wares. The area has always been a favorite of writers and artists, including such names as Oscar Wilde (who was arrested here), George Eliot, James Whistler, J.M.W. Turner, Henry James, Augustus John, and Thomas Carlyle (whose former home can be visited). Mick Jagger and Margaret Thatcher (not together) have been more recent residents, and the late Princess Diana and her "Sloane Rangers" of the 1980s gave it even more fame.

Its major boulevard is **King's Road,** where Mary Quant launched the miniskirt in the 1960s and where the English punk look began. King's Road runs the entire length of Chelsea; it's at its liveliest on Saturday. The hip-hop of King's Road isn't typical of otherwise upmarket Chelsea, an elegant village filled with town houses and little mews dwellings that only successful stockbrokers and solicitors can afford to occupy.

On the Chelsea/Fulham border is **Chelsea Harbour,** a luxury development of apartments and restaurants with a private marina. You can spot its tall tower from far away; the golden ball on top moves up and down to indicate tide level. Driving by the Chelsea Harbour Club in the mid-1990s you could often see paparazzi perched on ladders, trying to get a shot of the late Princess Di entering or exiting the exclusive gym.

Kensington This Royal Borough (W8) lies west of Kensington Gardens and Hyde Park and is traversed by two of London's major shopping streets, Kensington High Street and Kensington Church Street. Since 1689, when asthmatic William III fled Whitehall Palace for Nottingham House (where the air was fresher), the district has enjoyed royal associations. In time, Nottingham House became Kensington Palace, and the royals grabbed a chunk of Hyde Park to plant their roses. Queen Victoria was born here. "KP," as the royals say, is still home to Princess Margaret (20 rooms with a view), Prince and Princess Michael of Kent, and the duke and duchess of Gloucester. It was also the residence of the late Princess of Wales. Kensington Gardens is now open to the public, ever since George II decreed that "respectably dressed" people would be permitted in on Saturday—providing that no servants, soldiers, or sailors came. In the footsteps of William III, Kensington Square developed, attracting artists and writers. Thackeray wrote *Vanity Fair* while living here.

Southeast of Kensington Gardens and Earl's Court, primarily residential **South Kensington** is often called "museumland" because it's dominated by a complex of museums and colleges—set upon land bought with the proceeds from Prince Albert's Great Exhibition, held in Hyde Park in 1851—that includes the Natural History Museum, the Victoria and Albert Museum, and the Science Museum; nearby is Royal Albert Hall. South Kensington is also home to some fashionable restaurants and town house hotels. One of the district's chief curiosities is the Albert Memorial, completed in 1872 by Sir George Gilbert Scott; for sheer excess, the Victorian monument is unequaled in the world.

Earl's Court Earl's Court lies below Kensington, bordering the western half of Chelsea. For decades a staid residential district, drawing genteel ladies between the wars who wore pince-nez, Earl's Court now attracts a new and younger crowd (often gay), particularly at night, to its pubs, wine bars, and coffeehouses. It's long been a popular base for budget travelers (particularly Australians, for reasons known only to them), thanks to its wealth of B&Bs and budget hotels, and its convenient access to Central London: A 15-minute tube ride will take you into the heart of Piccadilly.

Once regarded as "the boondocks," nearby **West Brompton** is seen today as an extension of Central London. It lies directly south of Earl's Court (take the tube to West Brompton) and directly southeast of West Kensington. Its focal point is the sprawling Brompton Cemetery, a flower-filled "green lung" and burial place of such famous names as Frederick Leyland, the Pre-Raphaelite patron who died in 1892. It also has many good restaurants, pubs, and taverns, as well as some budget hotels.

Notting Hill Increasingly fashionable Notting Hill is bounded on the east by Bayswater and on the south by Kensington. Hemmed in on the north by West Way and on the west by the Shepherd's Bush ramp leading to the M40, it has many turn-of-the-century mansions and small houses sitting on quiet, leafy streets, plus a growing number of hot restaurants and clubs. Gentrified in recent years, it's becoming an extension of Central London.

On the north end, across Notting Hill Gate and west of Bayswater, is the hip neighborhood known as **Notting Hill Gate.** Portobello Road is home to one of London's most famous street markets. The area tube stops are Notting Hill Gate, Holland Park, or Ladbroke Grove.

Nearby **Holland Park** is a chi-chi residential neighborhood visited chiefly by the chic guests of Halycon Hotel, one of the grandest of London's small hotels.

Paddington & Bayswater   The **Paddington** section centers around Paddington Station, north of Kensington Gardens and Hyde Park. It's one of the major centers in London, attracting budget travelers who fill up the B&Bs in Sussex Gardens and Norfolk Square. After the first railway was introduced in London in 1836, it was followed by a circle of sprawling railway termini, including Paddington Station in 1838, which spurred the growth of this middle-class area, which is now blighted in parts.

Just south of Paddington, north of Hyde Park, and abutting more fashionable Notting Hill to the west is **Bayswater,** a sort of unofficial area also filled with a large number of B&Bs attracting budget travelers. Inspired by Marylebone and elegant Mayfair, a relatively prosperous set of Victorian merchants moved in and built terrace houses around spacious squares.

Nearby is **Maida Vale,** a village that, like St. John's Wood and Camden, has been absorbed by Central London. Maida Vale lies directly west of Regent's Park, north of Paddington, and next to the more prestigious address of **St. John's Wood** (home to the Beatles' Abbey Road Studios). The whole area is very sports oriented; if you take the tube to Maida Vale, you'll find Paddington Recreation Ground, plus a smaller "green lung," Paddington Bowling and Sports Club. It's also home to some of the BBC studios.

FARTHER AFIELD

Greenwich   To the southeast of London, this suburb—ground zero for use in the reckoning of terrestrial longitudes—enjoyed its heyday under the Tudors. Henry VIII and both of his daughters, Mary I and Elizabeth I, were born here. Greenwich Palace, Henry's favorite, is long gone, though; today's visitors come to this lovely port village for nautical sights along the Thames, including visits to the 1869 tea clipper, *Cutty Sark,* and the tiny *Gipsy Moth IV,* a 54-foot ketch in which Sir Francis Chichester sailed solo around the world from 1966 to 1967. Other attractions in the district include the National Maritime Museum.

Hampstead   This residential suburb of north London, beloved by Keats and Hogarth, is a favorite excursion spot for Londoners on the weekend. Everybody from Sigmund Freud to D.H. Lawrence to Anna Pavlova to John Le Carré has lived here, and it's still one of the most desirable districts in the Greater London area to call home. Its centerpiece is Hampstead Heath, nearly 800 acres of rolling meadows and woodland with panoramic views; it still maintains its rural atmosphere even though engulfed by cityscapes on all sides. The hilltop village is filled with cafes, tearooms, and restaurants, and there are pubs galore, some with historic pedigrees. Take the Northern Line to Hampstead Heath station.

Highgate   Along with Hampstead, Highgate in north London is another choice residential area, particularly on or near Pond Square and along Hampstead High Street. Once celebrated for its "sweer salutarie airs," Highgate has long been a desirable place to live, and Londoners used to flock to its taverns and pubs for "exercise and harmless merriment"; some still do. Today, most visitors come to see moody Highgate Cemetery, London's most famous cemetery—it's the final resting place of such famous figures as Karl Marx and George Eliot.

Hammersmith   Sitting on the north bank of the Thames, just to the west of Kensington, Hammersmith will fool you at first into thinking it's an industrial park, thanks to the stretch of factories between Putney and Hammersmith bridges. Actually, it's predominantly residential. Its most attractive feature is its waterfront, filled with boathouses, small businesses, some very good restaurants, and artists' studios. Beyond Hammersmith Bridge the neighborhood blossoms with balconied 18th-century homes behind lime and catalpa trees, more boathouses, and old pubs that use the warm weather as an excuse to spill out onto the riverbank.

Nearby is the delightful old village of **Barnes,** with its ironwork-decorated Barnes Terrace. Hammersmith Terrace, a favorite stamping ground of artists, adds color to the neighborhood, and another stretch of gracious homes lies along Chiswick Mall, curling into Church Street. This area deftly imitates an intimate English village before dumping you back into teeming London along Great West Road.

2 Getting Around

BY PUBLIC TRANSPORTATION

If you know the ropes, transportation in London can be easy and inexpensive. Both the Underground (the subway casually known as the "tube") and bus systems are operated by London Transport.

Travel Information Centres are located in the Underground stations at Hammersmith, King's Cross, Oxford Circus, St. James's Park, Liverpool Street Station, and Piccadilly Circus, as well as in the British Rail stations at Euston and Victoria and in each of the terminals at Heathrow Airport. They take reservations for London Transport's guided tours and offer free Underground and bus maps and other information leaflets. A **24-hour information service** is available (☎ 0171/222-1234). You can get information before you go by writing **London Transport,** Travel Information Service, 55 Broadway, London SW1H 0BD.

Travel Passes   London Transport offers **Travelcards** for use on bus, Underground, and British Rail services in Greater London. Sold in combinations of adjacent zones, Travelcards are available for a minimum of 7 days or for any period from a month to a year. A Travelcard allowing travel in two zones for 1 week costs adults £15.70 ($25), children £5.30 ($8.50). Travelcards must be used in conjunction with a Photocard (a photo ID used for identification by London Transport as well as by several other entities in London). A free Photocard is issued simultaneously with your Travelcard—bring a passport photo from one of the instant photo booths in London's train stations—when you buy your Travelcard at main post offices in the London area, the ticket window of any tube station, or at the Travel Information Centres of London Transport (see above).

For shorter stays in London, consider the **One-Day Off-Peak Travelcard.** This Travelcard can be used on most bus, Underground, and British Rail services throughout Greater London Monday to Friday after 9:30am and at any time on weekends and bank holidays. The Travelcard is available from Underground ticket offices, Travel Information Centres, and some newsstands. For two zones, the cost is £3.50 ($5.60) for adults and £1.80 ($2.90) for children 5 to 15. Children 4 and under travel free.

Visitor Travelcard is worthwhile if you plan to travel a lot within Greater London. This card allows unlimited transport within all six zones of Greater London's Underground and bus network. You'll most likely travel within the first two zones of the network's boundaries, but you're able to travel as far as Heathrow during valid times. However, you must buy this pass in North America; it's not available in England. A pass good for 3 consecutive days of travel is $25 for adults, $11 for children 5 to 15;

Central London Bus Routes

Using the Map
London bus route numbers are shown in circles at places where routes cross. Locate where you are going and then follow the route circles back toward your starting point. This will show if and where you need to change buses and the bus route number or numbers for your trip.

Tube Station ⊖
British Rail Station ⇌

MAJOR ATTRACTIONS
Admiralty Arch **9**
Barbican Centre **25**
British Museum **11**
Buckingham Palace **7**
Downing Street **16**
Harrods **5**
Horse Guards **15**
Houses of Parliament **18**
Imperial War Museum **20**

Law Courts 23
London Transport Museum 12
Madame Tussaud's 1
Marble Arch 3
Museum of London 26
National Gallery 14
Nelson's Column,
  Trafalgar Square 13
Royal Academy of Arts 10
Royal Festival Hall 21

Royal National Theatre &
  Museum of the Moving Image 22
St. James's Palace 8
St. Paul's Cathedral 24
Selfridges 2
Tate Gallery 19
Tower of London 27
Wellington Arch 4
Westminster Abbey 17
Westminster Cathedral 6

Underground Update

Scheduled for completion in late 1999 or early 2000, the **Jubilee Underground** line extension will open south of the river as well as into the East End, thus providing much-needed fast access from central London to both Greenwich and Docklands.

---

for 4 consecutive days of travel, it's $33 for adults, $13 for children; and for 7 consecutive days of travel, it's $53 for adults, $21 for children. Contact **BritRail Travel International,** 500 Mamaroneck Ave., Suite 314, Harrison, NY 10528 (☎ **800/ 677-8585;** 800/555-2748 in Canada).

Another pass is the 1-day **Family Travelcard.** It's a go-as-you-please ticket, allowing as many journeys as you wish on the tube, buses (excluding night buses) displaying the London Transport bus sign, and even the Docklands Light Railway or any rail service within the travel zones designated on your ticket. The family card is valid Monday to Friday after 9:30am and all day on weekends and public holidays. It's available for families as small as two (one adult and one child) to as large as six (two adults and four children). The cost is £3.20 to £4 ($5.10 to $6.40) per adult, 50p (80¢) per child. Yet a final discount pass is the **Weekend Travelcard,** which allows you 2 days of weekend transportation on the Underground or buses. The cost ranges from £4.80 to £6 ($7.70 to $9.60) for adults or £2.50 ($4) for children. These passes are available at all Underground stations.

You can now buy **Carnet** tickets, a booklet of 10 single Underground tickets valid for 12 months from the issue date. Carnet tickets are valid for travel only in Zone 1 (Central London), and cost £10 ($16) for adults and £4.80 ($7.70) for children (up to 15). A book of Carnet tickets gives you a savings of £2 ($3.20) over the cost of 10 separate single tickets.

THE UNDERGROUND

The Underground, or tube, is the fastest and easiest way to get from place to place. All Underground stations are clearly marked with a red circle and blue crossbar. You descend by stairways, escalators, or huge elevators, depending on the depth. Some Underground stations have complete subterranean shopping arcades, and several have push-button information machines.

You pick the station for which you're heading on the large diagram displayed on the wall, which includes an alphabetical index. You note the color of the line (Bakerloo is brown, Central is red, and so on). Then, by merely following the colored band, you can see at a glance whether and where you'll have to change and how many stops are between you and your destination.

If you have British coins, you can get your ticket at a vending machine. Otherwise, buy it at the ticket office. You can transfer as many times as you like as long as you stay in the Underground. The flat fare for one trip within the central zone is £1.30 ($2.10). Trips from the central zone to destinations in the suburbs range from £1.30 to £4.60 ($2.10 to $7.35) in most cases.

Be sure to keep your ticket, as it must be presented when you exit the station at your destination. If you're caught without a valid ticket, you'll be fined £10 ($16) on the spot. If you owe extra money, you'll be asked to pay the difference by the attendant. The tube runs roughly 5am to 11:30pm. After that you must take a taxi or night bus to your destination. For information on the London Tube system, call the **London Underground** at ☎ **0171/222-1234,** but expect to stay on hold for a good while before a live person comes on the line.

BUSES

The first thing you learn about London buses is that nobody just boards them. You "queue up"—that is, form a single-file line at the bus stop.

The comparably priced bus system is almost as good as the Underground and gives you better views of the city. To find out about current routes, pick up a free bus map at one of London Transport's Travel Information Centres, listed above. The map is available in person only, not by mail.

London still has some old-style Routemaster buses, with both driver and conductor: After you've boarded the bus, a conductor will come to your seat; you pay a fare based on your destination and receive a ticket in return. This type of bus is being phased out and replaced with buses that have only a driver; you pay the driver as you enter and you exit via a rear door. As with the Underground, the fares vary according to distance traveled. Generally, bus fares are 50p to £1.20 (80¢ to $1.90)—less than tube fares. If you travel for two or three stops, the cost is 60p (95¢); longer runs within zone 1 cost 90p ($1.45). If you want your stop called out, simply ask the conductor or driver.

Buses generally run between about 5am and 11:30pm. There are a few night buses on special routes, running once an hour or so; most pass through Trafalgar Square. Keep in mind that night buses are often crowded (especially on weekends) and unable to pick up passengers. You may find yourself waiting a long time. Consider taking a taxi. Call the 24-hour **hotline** (☎ **0171/222-1234**) for schedule and fare informtion.

BY TAXI

London cabs are among the most comfortable and best-designed in the world. You can pick one up either by heading for a cab rank or by hailing one in the street (the taxi is available if the yellow taxi sign on the roof is lighted); once they have stopped for you, taxis are obliged to take you anywhere you want to go within 6 miles of the pick-up point, provided it's within the metropolitan area. For a **radio cab**, call ☎ **0171/272-0272** or 0171/253-5000.

The minimum taxi fare is £1.40 ($2.25) for the first third of a mile, with increments of 20p (30¢) thereafter, based on distance or time. Each additional passenger is charged 40p (65¢). Passengers pay 10p (16¢) for each piece of luggage in the driver's compartment and any other item more than 2 feet long. Surcharges are imposed after 8pm and on weekends and public holidays. All these tariffs include VAT. Fares usually increase annually. It's recommended that you tip 10% to 15% of the fare.

If you call for a cab, the meter starts running when the taxi receives instructions from the dispatcher, so you could find £1.40 ($2.25) or more already on the meter when you step inside.

Minicabs are also available, and they're often useful when the regular taxis become scarce or when the tube stops running. These cabs are meterless, so the fare must be negotiated in advance. Unlike regular cabs, minicabs are forbidden by law to cruise for fares. They operate from sidewalk kiosks, such as those around Leicester Square. If you need to call one, try **Abbey Cars** (☎ 0171/727-2637) in west London; **Greater London Hire** (☎ 0181/340-2450) in north London; **London Cabs, Ltd.** (☎ 0181/778-3000) in east London; or **Newname Minicars** (☎ 0181/472-1400) in south London. Minicab kiosks can be found near many tube or Brit Rail stops, especially in outlying areas.

If you have a complaint about taxi service, or if you leave something in a cab, contact the **Public Carriage Office,** 15 Penton St., N1 9PU (tube: Angel Station). If it's a complaint, you must have the cab number, which is displayed in the passenger compartment. Call ☎ **0171/230-1631** with complaints or 0171/833-0996 to locate lost property.

Cab sharing is permitted in London, as British law allows cabbies to carry two to five persons. Taxis accepting such riders display a notice on yellow plastic, with the words "shared taxi." Each of two riders sharing is charged 65% of the fare a lone passenger would be charged. Three persons pay 55%, four pay 45%, and five (the seating capacity of all new London cabs) pay 40% of the single-passenger fare.

BY CAR

Don't drive if you don't have to. London is easy to get around without a car, traffic and parking are nightmares, and—to top it all off—you'll have to drive a car from what you normally consider the passenger seat on the wrong side of the road. It all adds up to a big headache.

Rentals

Car rentals are relatively expensive, and London offers a large array of companies to choose from. Most will accept your U.S. or Canadian driver's license, provided you've held it for more than a year; no special British license is needed. Your passport and driver's license must be presented when you rent a car. There's also an age requirement: 23 for cars rented through Avis, or 25 for cars arranged through Budget Rent-a-Car, British Airways, and Hertz.

Many companies grant discounts to clients who reserve their cars in advance (usually 48 weekday hours) through the toll-free reservations offices in a renter's home country and rent for periods longer than a week. When renting, be sure to ask if the price quoted includes the 17½% value-added tax (VAT), personal accident insurance (PAI), collision damage waiver (CDW), and other insurance options. If not, ask what these will cost because they can make a big difference in your bottom line.

As in the United States, the CDW and some added insurance are offered free by certain credit cards if you use them to rent a car. Check to see if you are covered by the credit card you use, thus avoiding the added expense.

Some of the major agencies—with North American toll-free numbers—are: **Avis** (☎ **800/331-2112;** www.avis.com), whose main office is in Mayfair at 8 Balderton St., London W1 (**0171/917-6700;** tube: Bond Street); **Budget Rent-a-Car** (☎ **800/472-3325;** www.budgetrentacar.com), whose busiest office is at 89 Wigmore St., London W1 (☎ **0171/723-8038;** tube: Marble Arch); and **Hertz** (☎ **800/654-3001;** www.hertz.com), whose main office is at 35 Edgware Rd., Marble Arch, London W1 (☎ **0171/402-4242;** tube: Marble Arch). Two prominent European agencies are **Kemwel Holiday Auto** (☎ **800/678-0678;** www.kemwel.com) and **Auto Europe** (☎ **800/223-5555;** www.autoeurope.com).

British Airways (☎ **800/876-2200** or 800/AIRWAYS; www.british-airways.com) offers a relatively inexpensive way to rent a car in Britain through its reservations service. As the U.K.'s largest car renter, BA can offer discounted rates on Hertz rentals in the U.K. Understandably, these arrangements are offered only to passengers flying into Britain on BA. You must apply at least seven days in advance of your departure from the U.S. or Canada, and have your flight information ready to give the rental agent.

Driving Rules & Requirements

In England, as you probably know, you drive on the left and pass on the right. Road signs are clear and the international symbols unmistakable. The prudent driver will secure a copy of the *British Highway Code,* available from almost any stationer or newsstand. Wearing of seat belts by both front- and rear-seat occupants is mandatory in the British Isles.

Warning: Pedestrian crossings are marked by striped lines (zebra striping) on the road; flashing lights near the curb indicate that drivers must stop and yield the right of way if a pedestrian has stepped into the zebra zone to cross the street.

Parking

Driving around London is tricky business. The city is a warren of one-way streets, and parking spots are at a premium. In addition to strategically placed expensive garages, central London offers metered parking—but be aware that traffic wardens are famous for issuing substantial fines when the meter runs out. The time limit and the cost of metered parking are posted on the meter. Zones marked "Permit Holders Only" are for local residents. If you violate these sacrosanct places, your vehicle is likely to be towed away. A yellow line along the curb indicates "No Parking"; a double yellow line signifies "No Waiting." However, at night (meters indicate exact times), and on Sunday, you're allowed to park along a curb with a single yellow line.

Gasoline (Petrol)

Gasoline, called "petrol" by the British, is usually sold by the liter, with 4.5 liters making an imperial gallon. Prices, incidentally, will be much higher than you're accustomed to paying, and you'll probably have to serve yourself. Many stations are closed on Sunday.

Breakdowns

A membership in one of the two major auto clubs in England can be helpful: the **Automobile Association,** Norfolk House, Priestly Rd., Basingstoke, Hampshire RG24 9NY (☎ **0990/448866** for information, **0800/887766** for 24-hour breakdown service; www.theaa.com), and the **Royal Automobile Club,** P.O. Box 700, Spectrum, Bond St., Bristol, Somerset BS99 1RB (☎ **01454/208000** for information, **0800/828282** for 24-hour breakdown service; www.rac.co.uk). Membership in one of these clubs is usually handled by a car-rental agent; inquire when you book. Members in either club are entitled to free legal and technical advice on motoring matters, as well as a range of discounts on motor-related products and services.

All motorways are provided with special emergency phones connected to police traffic units. The police can also contact an automobile club on your behalf.

BY BICYCLE

You can rent bicycles by the day or week from a number of firms, including **On Your Bike,** 52–54 Tooley St., SE1 (☎ **0171/378-6669;** tube: London Bridge), open Monday to Friday 9am to 6pm, Saturday 9:30am to 5:30pm, and Sunday 11am to 4pm. There's an inventory of some 60 bikes; 10-speed sports bikes, with high seats and low-slung handlebars, cost £8 to £10 ($13 to $16) per day, £25 to £30 ($40 to $48) per week, or £12 to £15 ($19 to $24) for 3-day weekend rates, and require a £50 ($80) deposit. Also popular are 21-gear mountain bikes, with straight handlebars and over-size gears. Designed for rough terrain, they're useful on the roads of backstreet London. These cost £14 ($22) per day, £50 ($80) per week, and require a £200 ($320) deposit. Deposits are payable by MasterCard or Visa.

ON FOOT

London is too vast and sprawling to explore entirely on foot, but if you use public transportation for the long distances and your feet for the narrow crooked lanes, you should do fine. *Remember that cars drive on the left:* Always look both ways before stepping off a curb. Unlike in some countries, vehicles in London have right of way before pedestrians, except in the zebra-striped zones mentioned above.

FAST FACTS: London

American Express   The main AmEx office is at 6 Haymarket, SW1 (☎ **0171/930-4411;** tube: Piccadilly Circus). Full services are available Monday to Friday 9am to 5:30pm and Saturday 9am to 4pm. At other times—Saturday 4pm to 6pm and Sunday 10am to 6pm—only the foreign-exchange bureau is open.

Area Code   London has two telephone area codes: 0171 and 0181. The **0171** area code is for central London within a 4-mile radius of Charing Cross (including the City, Knightsbridge, Oxford Street, and as far south as Brixton). The **0181** area code is for outer London (including Heathrow Airport, Wimbledon, and Greenwich). Within London, you'll need to dial the area code when calling from one section of the city to the other, but not within a section. The country code for England is 44; see "Telephone" below for instructions on how to dial.

Babysitters   Babysitting organizations provide registered nurses and carefully screened mothers, as well as trained nannies, as sitters. One such is **Childminders** (☎ **0171/935-3000** or 0171/935-2049; tube: Baker Street). You pay £5.50 ($8.80) per hour in the daytime and £3.70 to £4.70 ($5.90 to $7.50) per hour at night. There's a 4-hour minimum, and hotel guests pay a £5 ($8) booking fee each time they use a sitter. You must also pay reasonable transportation costs.

Business Hours   Banks are usually open Monday to Friday 9:30am to 3:30pm. Business offices are open Monday to Friday 9am to 5pm; the lunch break lasts an hour, but most places stay open during that time. Pubs and bars are allowed to stay open from 11am to 11pm on Monday to Saturday and from noon to 10:30pm on Sunday. London stores generally open at 9am and close at 5:30pm, staying open until 7pm on Wednesday or Thursday. Most central shops close on Saturday around 1pm. By law, most stores are closed on Sunday. Some service stores such as small groceries might remain open.

Car Rentals   See "Getting Around" earlier in this chapter.

Climate   See "When to Go" in chapter 2.

Currency Exchange   See "Money" in chapter 2.

Dentists   For dental emergencies, call **Eastman Dental Hospital** (☎ **0171/915-1000;** tube: King's Cross).

Doctors   In an emergency, contact **Doctor's Call** (☎ **07000/372255**). Some hotels also have physicians on call. **Medical Express,** 117A Harley St., W1 (☎ **0171/499-1991;** tube: Regent's Park), is a private British clinic; it's not part of the free British medical establishment. For filling the British equivalent of a U.S. prescription, there's sometimes a surcharge of £20 ($32) on top of the cost of the medications. The clinic is open Monday to Friday 9am to 6pm and Saturday 9:30am to 2:30pm.

Documents Required   See "Visitor Information & Entry Requirements" in chapter 2.

Driving Rules   See "Getting Around," earlier in this chapter.

Drugstores   In Britain they're called chemist shops. Every police station in the country has a list of emergency chemists (dial "0" and ask the operator for the local police). One of the most centrally located chemists, keeping long hours, is **Bliss the Chemist,** 5 Marble Arch, W1 (☎ **0171/723-6116;** tube: Marble Arch), open daily 9am to midnight. Every London neighborhood has a branch of **Boots,** Britain's leading pharmacy.

Electricity   British current is 240 volts, AC cycle, roughly twice the voltage of North American current, which is 115–120 volts, AC cycle. You'll probably not be able to plug the flat pins of your appliance's plugs into the holes of British wall outlets without suitable converters or adapters. Some (but not all) hotels will supply them for guests. Experienced travelers bring their own transformers. An electrical supply shop will also have what you need. Be forewarned that you'll destroy the inner workings of your appliance (and possibly start a fire as well) if you plug most American appliances directly into a European electrical outlet without a transformer.

Embassies & High Commissions   We hope you'll not need such services; but in case you lose your passport or have some other emergency, here's a list of addresses and phone numbers:

- **Australia**   The high commission is at **Australia House,** Strand, WC2 (☎ 0171/379-4334; tube: Charing Cross or Aldwych); it's open Monday to Friday from 10am to 4pm.
- **Canada**   The high commission is located at **MacDonald House,** 38 Grosvenor Sq., W1 (☎ 0171/258-6600; tube: Bond Street); it's open Monday to Friday from 8 to 11am.
- **Ireland**   The embassy is at 17 Grosvenor Place, SW1 (☎ 0171/235-2171; tube: Hyde Park Corner); it's open Monday to Friday from 9:30am to 1pm and 2:15 to 5pm.
- **New Zealand**   The high commission is at **New Zealand House,** 80 Haymarket at Pall Mall, SW1 (☎ 0171/930-8422; tube: Charing Cross or Piccadilly Circus); it's open Monday to Friday from 9am to 5pm.
- **The United States**   The embassy is located at 24 Grosvenor Sq., W1 (☎ 0171/499-9000; tube: Bond Street). For passport and visa information go to the **U.S. Passport & Citizenship Unit,** 55–56 Upper Brook St., W1 (☎ 0171/499-9000, ext. 2563 or 2564; tube: Marble Arch or Bond Street). Hours are Monday to Friday from 8:30am to noon and from 2 to 4pm (there are no afternoon hours on Tuesday).

Emergencies   For police, fire, or an ambulance, dial ☎ 999.

Holidays   See "When to Go" in chapter 2.

Hospitals   The following offer emergency care in London 24 hours a day, with the first treatment free under the National Health Service: **Royal Free Hospital,** Pond Street, NW3 (☎ 0171/794-0500; tube: Belsize Park), and **University College Hospital,** Grafton Way, WC1 (☎ 0171/387-9300; tube: Warren Street or Euston Square). Many other London hospitals also have accident and emergency departments.

Hot Lines   For **police or medical emergencies,** dial ☎ 999 (no coins required). If you're in some sort of **legal emergency,** call Release at ☎ 0171/729-9904, 24 hours a day. The **Rape Crisis Line** is ☎ 0171/837-1600, accepting calls after 6pm. **Samaritans,** 46 Marshall St., W1 (☎ 0171/734-2800; tube: Oxford Circus or Piccadilly Circus), maintains a crisis hot line that helps with all kinds of trouble, even threatened suicides, from 9am to 9pm. **Alcoholics Anonymous** (☎ 0171/352-3001) answers its hot line daily from 10am to 10pm. The **AIDS 24-hour hot line** is ☎ 0800/567-123.

Information   See "Visitor Information & Entry Requirements" in chapter 2 and "Orientation" earlier in this chapter.

Libraries   Westminster Reference Library, 35 St. Martin's St., WC2 (☎ 0171/641-2036; tube: Leicester Square), is one of London's best general reference public libraries, specializing in business, art and design, official publications, performing arts, and periodicals. Open Monday to Friday 10am to 7pm and Saturday 10am to 5pm.

Liquor Laws   No alcohol is served to anyone under 18. Children under 16 aren't allowed in pubs, except in certain rooms, and then only when accompanied by a parent or guardian. Don't drink and drive; penalties for drunk driving are stiff, even if you're an overseas visitor. Pubs are open Monday to Saturday from 11am to 11pm and Sunday noon to 10:30pm. Restaurants are allowed to serve liquor during the same hours as pubs; however, only people who are eating a meal on the premises can be served a drink. A meal, incidentally, is defined as "substantial refreshment." And you have to eat and drink sitting down. In hotels, liquor may be served from 11am to 11pm to both residents and nonresidents; after 11pm, only residents may be served.

Mail   An airmail letter to North America costs 43p (70¢) for 10 grams and postcards require a 35p (55¢) stamp; letters generally take 7 to 10 days to arrive from the United States. See "Post Offices" below for locations.

Maps   See "Finding Your Way Around" under "Orientation," earlier in this chapter.

Money   See "Money," in chapter 2.

Newspapers/Magazines   *The Times, Daily Telegraph, Daily Mail,* and *Guardian* are all dailies carrying the latest news. The *International Herald Tribune,* published in Paris, and an international edition of *USA Today,* beamed via satellite, are available daily. Copies of *Time* and *Newsweek* are also sold at most newsstands. Magazines such as *Time Out, City Limits,* and *Where* contain lots of useful information about the latest happenings in London.

Police   In an emergency, dial ☎ **999** (no coins required). You can also go to one of the local police branches in central London, including **New Scotland Yard,** Broadway, SW1 (☎ **0171/230-1212;** tube: St. James's Park).

Post Offices   The **Main Post Office** is at 24 William IV St. (☎ **0171/ 930-9580;** tube: Charing Cross). It operates as three separate businesses: inland and international postal service and banking (open Monday to Saturday 8:30am to 8pm); philatelic postage stamp sales (open Monday to Saturday 8am to 8pm); and the post shop, selling greeting cards and stationery (open Monday to Saturday from 8am to 8pm). Other post offices and sub-post offices are open Monday to Friday 9am to 5:30pm and on Saturday 9am to 12:30pm. Many sub-post offices and some main post offices close for an hour at lunchtime.

Radio   There are 24-hour radio channels operating throughout the United Kingdom, including London. They offer mostly pop music and chat shows at night. Some "pirate" radio stations add more spice. So-called legal FM stations are BBC1 (104.8); BBC2 (89.1); BBC3 (between 90 and 92); and the classical station, BBC4 (95). There is also the BBC Greater London Radio (94.9) station, with lots of rock, plus LBC Crown (97.3), with news and reports of "what's on" in London. Pop/rock U.S. style is heard on Capital FM (95.8), and if you like jazz, reggae, or salsa, tune in to Choice FM (96.9). Jazz FM (102.2) also offers blues and big-band music.

Rest Rooms   They're marked by "public toilets" signs in streets, parks, and tube stations; many are automatic, which are sterilized after each use. The English often call toilets "loos." You'll also find well-maintained lavatories that can be used by anybody in all larger public buildings, such as museums and art galleries, large department stores, and railway stations. It's not really acceptable to use the lavatories in hotels, restaurants, and pubs if you're not a customer, but we can't say that we always stick to this rule. Public lavatories are usually free, but you may need a small coin to get in or to use a proper washroom.

Smoking Most U.S. cigarette brands are available in London. Antismoking laws are tougher than ever: Smoking is strictly forbidden in the Underground (on the cars and the platforms) and on buses, and it's increasingly frowned upon in many other places. But London still isn't a particularly friendly place for the non-smoker. Most restaurants have non-smoking tables, but they're usually separated from the smoking section by only a little bit of space. Non-smoking rooms are available in the bigger hotels. While some of the smaller hotels claim that they have no-smoking rooms, we've often found that this means that the room is smoke-free only during our visit; if you're bothered by the odor, ask to be shown another room.

Taxes To encourage energy conservation, the British government levies a 25% tax on gasoline ("petrol"). There is also a 17.5% national value-added tax (VAT) that is added to all hotel and restaurant bills, and will be included in the price of many items you purchase. This can be refunded if you shop at stores that partic-ipate in the Retail Export Scheme (signs are posted in the window). See the "How to Get Your VAT Refund" box in chapter 8.

In October 1994, Britain imposed a **departure tax:** £5 ($8) for flights within Britain and the European Union or £10 ($16) for passengers flying elsewhere, including to the United States. Your airline ticket may or may not include this tax. Ask in advance to avoid a surprise at the gate.

Taxis See "Getting Around" earlier in this chapter.

Telephone For **directory assistance** in London, dial 142; for the rest of Britain, 192. To call London from the United States, dial 011 (international code), 44 (Britain's country code), 171 or 181 (London's area codes), and the seven-digit local phone number.

There are three types of public pay phones: those taking only coins, those accepting only phonecards (called Cardphones), and those taking both phonecards and credit cards. At coin-operated phones, insert your coins before dialing. The minimum charge is 10p (15¢).

Phonecards are available in four values—£2 ($3.20), £4 ($6.40), £10 ($16), and £20 ($32)—and are reusable until the total value has expired. Cards can be purchased from newsstands and post offices. Finally, the credit-call pay phone operates on credit cards—Access (MasterCard), Visa, American Express, and Diners Club—and is most common at airports and large railway stations.

Phone numbers in Britain outside of the major cities consist of an exchange name plus telephone number. To dial the number, you'll need the code of the exchange being called. Information sheets on call-box walls give the codes in most instances. If your code isn't there, call the operator by dialing 100.

In London, phone numbers consist of the exchange code and number (seven digits or more). These digits are all you need to dial if you are calling from within the same city. If you're calling from elsewhere, you will need to prefix them with the dialing code for the city. Again, you'll find these codes on the call-box infor-mation sheets or by dialing the operator (100).

To make an international call from London, dial the international access code (00), then the country code, then the area code, and finally the local number. Or call through one of the following long-distance access codes: **AT&T USA Direct** (☎ 0800/890011), **Canada Direct** (☎ 0800/890016), **Australia**

(☎ 0800/890061), and **New Zealand** (☎0800/890064). Common country codes are: **USA and Canada,** 1; **Australia,** 61; **New Zealand,** 64; **South Africa,** 27.

Time   England follows Greenwich Mean Time (5 hours ahead of Eastern Standard Time). Most of the year, including the summer, Britain is 5 hours ahead of the time observed on the east coast of the United States. Because the U.S. and Britain observe daylight savings time at slightly different times of year, there's a brief period (about a week) in autumn when Britain is only 4 hours ahead of New York, and a brief period in spring when it's 6 hours ahead of New York.

Tipping   In restaurants, service charges in the 15% to 20% range are usually added to the bill. Sometimes this is clearly marked; at other times it isn't. When in doubt, ask. If service isn't included, it's customary to add 15% to the bill. Sommeliers get about £1 ($1.60) per bottle of wine served. Tipping in pubs isn't common, although in cocktail bars the server usually gets about 75p ($1.20) per round of drinks.

Hotels, like restaurants, often add a service charge of 10% to 15% to most bills. In smaller B&Bs, the tip isn't likely to be included. Therefore, tip for special service, such as for the person who served you breakfast. If several persons have served you in a B&B, many guests ask that 10% or 15% be added to the bill and divided among the staff.

It's standard to tip taxi drivers 10% to 15% of the fare, although a tip for a taxi driver should never be less than 30p (50¢), even for a short run. Barbers and hairdressers expect 10% to 15%. Tour guides expect £2 ($3.20), although it's not mandatory. Gas station attendants are rarely tipped and theater ushers don't expect tips.

Transit Information   Call ☎ 0171/222-1234, 24 hours a day.

Weather   Call ☎ 0171/922-8844 for current weather information, but chances are the line will be busy.

Accommodations 4

As London observer Christopher Reynolds put it, "Looking for a really good price on a hotel room? Try Arizona in August, Alaska in February, or New York in about 1962. But if it's London you want to see, brace yourself."

Face it—you're just going to pay more than you'd like for a hotel room in London. London boasts some of the most famous hotels in the world—such hallowed temples of luxury as Claridge's, the Dorchester, the Park Lane, and the Savoy, as well as recent-vintage rivals like the Four Seasons—and they're all superlative. The problem (and it's a serious one) is that there are too many of them and not enough of the moderately priced options so typical of other European capitals.

Even at the luxury level, you might be surprised at what you *don't* get at a London hotel. Many are stately Victorian and Edwardian gems so steeped in tradition that they still lack most or all of the modern conveniences that come standard in the luxury hotels of, say, New York. Some have gone to no end to modernize, but others have remained at Boer War vintage. London does have some cutting-edge, chintz-free hotels that seem shifted bodily from Los Angeles—complete with high-end sound systems and gadget-filled marble baths—but they're not necessarily superior; what the others lack in streamlining and convenience they frequently make up in personal service and spaciousness. It all depends on what you like.

In the late 1980s and early 1990s, the opening of a number of new boutique hotels generated lots of excitement; each one seemed to out-dazzle the one before. With their charm, intimate scale, and attention to detail, they're an attractive alternative to the larger, stuffier established names. As London faces the millennium, the boutiquing of the hotel scene continues; the city is currently offering more personally run and privately operated boutique hotels than ever before. We've surveyed the best of them for this edition, concentrating on the reasonably priced choices.

If you're looking for reasonably priced options, don't despair. London does have some good value options in the lower price ranges, of which we've included the best. An affordable way to go is to book a **bed-and-breakfast.** At their best, they're clean, comfortable, and friendly. Currently, however, good B&Bs are in short supply in London; don't reserve a room at one without a recommendation you can trust. The following services will arrange a B&B room for you: **Bed & Breakfast** (☎ **800/367-4668** or 423/690-8484), **Worldwide**

Bed & Breakfast Association (☎ 800/852-2632 in the U.S., or 0181/742-9123; fax 0181/749-7084), and **The London Bed and Breakfast Agency Limited** (☎ **0171/586-2768**; fax 0171/586-6567) another reputable agency that can provide inexpensive accommodations in selected private homes. Prices range from £17 to £34 ($27 to $54) per person a night, although some will cost a lot more.

You can almost always get a room at a deluxe hotel if you're willing to pay the price. But during certain peak periods, including the high season (roughly April to October), and during certain trade shows, seasonal events, and royal occasions, rooms in all kinds of hotels may be snatched up early. Book ahead. If you arrive without a reservation, begin your search for a room as early in the day as possible. If you arrive late at night, you may have to take what you can get, often at a much higher price than you'd like to pay.

A Note About Prices   Unless otherwise noted, prices are published rack prices for rooms with private bathroom and include breakfast (often continental instead of English), 17½% VAT, and a 10% to 15% service charge. (VAT and service charges are always included in the prices quoted in this guide, unless otherwise indicated.) Always ask for a better rate, particularly at the first-class and deluxe hotels (B&Bs generally charge a fixed rate). Be aware that you may not get it, particularly in the busy summer season or during certain trade fairs, when practically every room in the city is booked. But it never hurts to ask. You can sometimes negotiate a 20% to 30% discount in winter. The best ways to save money are to call the hotel directly rather than going through an 800 number or travel agent, by booking off-season or weekends, and by same-day booking—provided it's after 8pm. Knowing how hard it is to fill empty rooms at that late hour, you can sometimes negotiate a hefty discount with the reception desk. Parking rates are per night.

Rate Regulations   All hotels, motels, inns, and guesthouses in Britain with four bedrooms or more (including self-catering accommodations) must display notices showing minimum and maximum overnight charges. The notice must be displayed in a prominent position in the reception area or at the entrance. The prices shown must include any service charge and may include VAT, and it must be made clear whether or not these items are included; if VAT isn't included, then it must be shown separately. If meals are provided, this must be made clear, too. If prices aren't standard for all rooms, then only the lowest and highest prices need to be given.

A FEW REMINDERS

- Elevators are called "**lifts.**" Some of them predate Teddy Roosevelt's Rough Riders, and act it. They are, however, regularly inspected and completely safe.
- Hotel rooms are somewhat cooler than elsewhere; it's supposed to be more healthful that way. However, London has had some hot summers in the last few years. If you're coming in the summer months and expect hotter-than-usual weather, don't assume your hotel, even if you're booked at the luxury level, has central air; many have only partial A/C or none at all. Check if this is a concern for you.
- What's termed a **continental breakfast** consists of coffee or tea and some sort of roll or pastry. An **English breakfast** is a fairly lavish, traditionally hearty meal of tea or coffee, cereal, eggs, bacon, ham or sausage, toast, and jam.
- If you want to remain undisturbed, don't forget to hang the "Do Not Disturb" sign on your doorknob. English hotel service personnel—most of whom aren't English—have a disconcerting habit of bursting in simultaneously with their knock.

1 Best Bets

- **Best Historic Hotel:** Founded by the former manservant to Lord Byron, stylish **Brown's Hotel,** 29–34 Albemarle St., W1 (☎ **800/225-5843**), dates back to Victorian times. It's one of London's most genteel hotels, from its legendary afternoon tea to its centenary *Times* clock in the reception area.

- **Best for Business Travelers:** For wheeling and dealing, head to the **Langham Hilton,** 1 Portland Place, W1 (☎ **800/445-8667**), Hilton's flagship hotel in Europe. At times it seems that all the world's business is conducted from this nerve center. It can sound like the Tower of Babel, but it's humming along just fine.

- **Best for a Romantic Getaway: The Gore,** 189 Queen's Gate, SW7 (☎ **800/ 637-7200**), has been sheltering lovers both on and off the record since 1892. The place is eccentric and a lot of fun, and the staff doesn't bother you unless you need something. For nostalgia-accented romance, request the Venus Room—its bed was once owned by Judy Garland.

- **Best Trendy Hotel: The Lanesborough,** 1 Lanesborough Place, Hyde Park Corner, SW1 (☎ **800/999-1828**), is a sumptuous temple of luxury—$1.7 million was spent on each guest room. Not surprisingly, it attracts glitterati galore.

- **Best Lobby for Pretending That You're Rich: The Dorchester,** 53 Park Lane, W1 (☎ **800/727-9820**), has a long Promenade with London's largest floral display and rows of faux-marble columns with ornate gilt capitals. Even if you can't afford to stay at this citadel of luxury, come by for the traditional afternoon tea.

- **Best Lobby for Celebrity Spotting:** If you sit in the lobby long enough at the **Halcyon Hotel,** 81 Holland Park Ave., W11 (☎ **800/595-5416**), you're sure to spot a famous face checking in. It might even be Faye Dunaway—but you might get RuPaul, Snoop Doggy Dogg, or Sting instead. Brad Pitt always stays here when he's in town. The address of this celebrity favorite gets passed around a lot in Hollywood and New York. Many of the rooms are like stage sets for movies, making stars feel quite at home.

- **Best Newcomer of the Year:** Minimalism reigns supreme at the **Metropolitan,** 19 Old Park Lane, W1 (☎ **0171/447-1000**), set smack dab between the London Hilton and the Four Seasons. Functional yet graceful, it attracts a well-heeled young crowd drawn to its sophisticated ambience and relaxing interior. A twin of New York's Nobu restaurant draws the chic set, even those not staying at this citadel of luxury.

- **Best Grande Dame:** The **Park Lane Hotel,** Piccadilly, W1 (☎ **800/325-3535**), is English to the core. It evokes the grand old days of debutante balls; the suites still have their 1920s styling and art deco bathrooms. No wonder the producers of *Brideshead Revisited* filmed part of their series here.

- **Best Shabbily Genteel Hotel:** Not afraid to be old fashioned, the **Wilbraham Hotel,** 1–5 Wilbraham Place, SW1 (☎ **0171/730-8296**), remains true to itself: floral-print wallpaper, old-world English politeness, and stately Victorian style. They're so old-timey here they still call their lounge the "Bar and Buttery."

- **Best for Showing Off:** Anouska Hempel's luxurious **Blake's Hotel,** 33 Roland Gardens, SW7 (☎ **800/926-3173**), is personalized, elegant, and fun, with beautiful bathrooms in marble, opulent accessories, and a restaurant packed with London glitterati. This is the place to show off—and wait until later to worry about how much you spent.

- **Best for Thoroughly British Ambience:** In a gaslit courtyard in back of St. James's Palace, **Dukes Hotel,** 35 St. James's Place, SW1 (☎ **0171/491-4840**), has a nearly unsurpassed dignity. From the bread-and-butter pudding served in the clubby dining room to the impeccable service, it's the epitome of what Britain used to be.

- **Best Re-creation of an English Country House:** Tim and Kit Kemp are hoteliers of charm, taste, and sophistication. They were in top form when they combined two Georgian town houses into the **Dorset Square Hotel,** 39–40 Dorset Sq., NW1 (☎ 800/553 6674). They've made an English country house right in the heart of the city: Gilt-framed paintings, antiques, tapestry cushions, and mahogany bathrooms make you feel warm, cozy, and elegantly refined.

- **Best Service: 22 Jermyn Street,** SW1 (☎ 800/682-7808), does more for its guests than any other hotel in London. The owner, a technology buff, even offers Internet services to his guests. He also diligently informs you of the hottest and newest restaurants, along with old favorites, the best shopping buys, and even what's hot in theater. The staff doesn't deny any reasonable request—they even grant some unreasonable ones.

- **Best Location:** Creaky, quirky **Fielding Hotel,** 4 Broad Court, Bow Street, WC2 (☎ 0171/836-8305), is hardly London's finest hotel, but oh, the location! It's in an alleyway in the dead center of Covent Garden. You're in the heart of the real excitement of London, almost opposite the Royal Opera House, and with pubs, shops, markets, and restaurants, even street entertainment, just outside your door. Stay here, and London is yours.

- **Best Health Club & Pool: The Savoy,** The Strand, WC2 (☎ 800/263-SAVOY), has a unique health club and large swimming pool, built atop the historic Savoy Theatre, overlooking the heart of London. For guests looking to tone up or wind down, it's the best gym in Central London; the views make it extra special. There is also a massage room, plus state-of-the-heart health and beauty treatments.

- **Best Hotel Restaurant: Bracewells,** in the Park Lane Hotel, Piccadilly, W1 (☎ 800/325-3535), is what hotel dining is all about: discreet elegance, top-notch food, and traditional ambience—in this case gilded torchères, armchairs, and Louis XVI paneling removed from the former home of J.P. Morgan. The kitchen is one of London's finest interpreters of classical French and English cuisine, with an increasingly light touch and many innovative dishes. See chapter 5 for a complete review.

- **Best View:** Sometimes the best way to view a great city is from a distance. From the **Sandringham Hotel,** 3 Holford Rd., NW3 (☎ 0171/435-1569), a topnotch little hotel in North London—near the Hampstead Heath so beloved by John Keats— rooms open onto panoramic views of England's capital.

- **Best Boutique Hotel: The Beaufort,** 33 Beaufort Gardens, SW3 (☎ 800/888-1199), is a hotel that's sure to charm. Personal service and rural peace combine to make it a winning choice. And with a location like this—on a tree-lined cul-de-sac 200 yards from Harrods—you'll think you've died and gone to heaven.

- **Best Moderately Priced Hotel:** Tucked away in the Knightsbridge/Belgravia area is the **Diplomat Hotel,** 2 Chesham St., SW1 (☎ 0171/235-1544), a 1892 town house converted into a charming and graceful small hotel that prides itself on the good value it offers. Personal service is one of its hallmarks; you'll even find a box of chocolates waiting in your room.

- **Best Inexpensive Hotel:** Kensington's **Abbey House,** 11 Vicarage Gate, W8 (☎ 0171/727-2594), was built in the 1860s on a Victorian square. It's refurbished annually, and still manages to offer one of the best values in London.

- **Best for Families Who Don't Want to Break the Bank:** Hailed by some as one of the top B&Bs in London, **James House/Cartref House,** 108 and 129 Ebury St. (☎ 0171/730-7338), are two houses filled with charm that face each other across a street in the section of London lying near Victoria Station. Each house deserves its accolades. Some of the large accommodations have bunk beds that make them ideal for families.

- **Best Bed-and-Breakfast:** The **Claverley Hotel,** 13–14 Beaufort Gardens, SW3 (☎ **800/747-0398**), has won awards as the best B&B in London—and they're much deserved. It's tranquil and well located, close to Harrods for that special buy. For breakfast, try the cook's special, the fresh salmon kedgeree.
- **Best Value:** Savvy hotel shoppers seek out **Aston's Budget Studios,** 39 Rosary Gardens, SW7 (☎ **800/525-2810**). The accommodations here range widely in price, and well they should: They vary from basic lodgings to designer suites.

2 West End Hotels

MAYFAIR
VERY EXPENSIVE

✪ **Brown's Hotel.** 29–34 Albemarle St., London W1X 4BP. ☎ **800/225-5843** or 0171/493-6020. Fax 0171/493-9381. www.brownshotel.com. E-mail: brownshotel @ukbusiness.com. 114 units. A/C MINIBAR TV TEL. £235–£265 ($376–$424) double; from £385 ($616) suite. AE, DC, MC, V. Tube: Green Park.

Almost every year a hotel sprouts up trying to evoke an English country house ambience with Chippendale and chintz; this quintessential town-house hotel watches these competitors come and go, and always comes out on top. Brown's was founded by James Brown, a former manservant of Lord Byron's, who knew the tastes of well-bred gentlemen and wanted to create a dignified, clublike place for them. He opened its doors in 1837, the same year Queen Victoria took the throne.

Brown's, which occupies 14 historic houses just off Berkeley Square, is still a thorough realization of its founder's vision. The guest rooms vary considerably and are a tangible record of England's history, showing restrained taste in decoration and appointments; even the washbasins are antiques. In keeping with the atmosphere of the rest of the hotel, the inviting lounges pay homage to the past: They include the **Roosevelt Room** (Theodore Roosevelt spent his honeymoon at Brown's in 1886), the **Rudyard Kipling Room** (the famous author was a frequent visitor), and the paneled **St. George's Bar** for the drinking of spirits.

Dining: The dining room has a quiet dignity and unmatched service. Afternoon tea is served in the **Albemarle Room.** See "Teatime," in chapter 5.

Amenities: 24-hour room service, dry cleaning and laundry service, babysitting, secretarial services, valet, men's hairdresser, tour desk, business center; health club nearby.

Claridge's. Brook St., London W1A 2JQ. ☎ **800/223-6800** or 0171/629-8860. Fax 0171/499-2210. E-mail: info@claridges.co.uk. 187 units. A/C MINIBAR TV TEL. £295–£365 ($472–$584) double; £460 ($736) junior suite, from £690 ($1,104) suite. AE, DC, MC, V. Tube: Bond St.

This is *the* hotel for *Pax Britannia* nostalgists. Although other upper-crust addresses conjure up images of Empire, nobody does it better than Claridge's, which has cocooned royal visitors in an ambience of discreet elegance since the time of the Battle of Waterloo. This is stuffy British formality at its appealing best: As a reviewer once wrote, the "staff here will never try to be your friends"—as they might at, say, the Dorchester.

The hotel took on its present modest exterior in 1898. Inside, an art-deco look was added in the 1930s; much of it still exists agreeably alongside antiques and TVs. The

West End Hotels

Academy Hotel **26**
Avalon Private Hotel **28**
Blooms Hotel **22**
Brown's Hotel **12**
Claridge's **7**
Covent Garden Hotel **19**
Crescent Hotel **29**
The Dorchester **8**
Dukes Hotel **14**
Durrants Hotel **1**
Fielding Hotel **21**
Four Seasons Hotel **9**
Hallam Hotel **4**
Harlingford Hotel **30**
Hazlitt's 1718 **18**
Hotel La Place **2**
Ivanhoe Suites Hotel **6**
Jenkins Hotel **27**
The Langham Hilton **5**
Metropolitan **10**
Park Lane Hotel **11**
Regency Hotel **3**
Regent Palace Hotel **17**
The Ritz **13**
Ruskin Hotel **25**
St. Margaret's Hotel **23**
The Savoy **20**
The Stafford **15**
Thanet Hotel **24**
22 Jermyn St. **16**

guest rooms are spacious, many with generous-size bathrooms complete with dressing rooms and other extras. The emphasis is on old-fashioned room layouts instead of modern comforts, so you may feel embarrassed if you check in without your valet, à la Prince Charles.

Dining: Excellent food is stylishly served in the intimacy of the **Causerie,** renowned for its lunchtime smorgasbord and pretheater suppers, and the more formal **Restaurant,** with English and French specialties. The strains of the Hungarian Quartet, a Claridge's institution since 1902, can be heard in the adjacent foyer during lunch and dinner.

Amenities: 24-hour room service, valet, laundry service, babysitting, on-call physician, concierge, currency exchange, basic secretarial services, salon, travel and theater desk, health club.

✪　**The Dorchester.** 53 Park Lane, London W1A 2HJ. ☎ **800/727-9820** or 0171/629-8888. Fax 0171/409-0114. 244 units. A/C MINIBAR TV TEL. £285–£315 ($456–$504) double; from £400 ($640) suite. AE, DC, MC, V. Tube: Hyde Park Corner or Marble Arch.

This is the best hotel in London today. It has all the elegance of Claridge's, but without the upper-crust attitudes that can verge on snobbery. The Lanesborough is also a premier address, but it doesn't have the time-honored experience of "The Dorch," which has maintained a tradition of fine comfort and cuisine since it opened its doors in 1931.

Breaking from the neoclassical tradition, the most ambitious architects of the era designed a building of reinforced concrete clothed in terrazzo slabs. Within you'll find a 1930s take on Regency motifs: The monumental arrangements of flowers and the elegance of the gilded-cage promenade seem appropriate for a diplomatic reception, yet convey a kind of comfort in which guests from all over the world feel at ease.

The Dorchester boasts guest rooms outfitted with linen sheets, all the electronic gadgetry you'd expect from a world-class hotel, and double- and triple-glazed windows to keep out noise, along with plump armchairs, cherrywood furnishings, and, in many cases, four-poster beds. The bathrooms are equally stylish, with mottled Italian marble and Lalique-style sconces. The best rooms open onto views of Hyde Park.

Dining: The hotel's restaurant, **The Grill Room,** is among the finest dining establishments in London, and the **Dorchester Bar** is a legendary meeting place. The hotel also offers Cantonese cuisine at **The Oriental,** London's most exclusive—and expensive—Chinese restaurant.

Amenities: 24-hour room service, dry cleaning and laundry service, medical service. One of the best-outfitted health clubs in London, the Dorchester Spa; exclusive nightclub; barbershop; hairdresser.

Four Seasons Hotel. Hamilton Place, Park Lane, London W1A 1AZ. ☎ **800/332-3442** or 0171/499-0888. Fax 0171/493-1895. www.fshr.com. 247 units. A/C MINIBAR TV TEL. £295–£305 ($472–$488) double; £400 ($640) conservatory double; from £525 ($840) suite. AE, DC, MC, V. Parking £16.50 ($26). Tube: Hyde Park Corner.

This deluxe hostelry has captured the imagination of glamourmongers the world over ever since it was inaugurated by Princess Alexandra in 1970; its clientele include heads of state, superstars, and top-brass business execs. The hotel sits behind a tastefully modern facade, at a premier location in one of the most exclusive neighborhoods in the world. It's directly opposite its major competitors, the London Hilton and the Inter-Continental—but it has better food, better rooms, more style, and more taste and refinement than either of its rivals. Inside, acres of superbly crafted paneling and opulent but conservative decor create the impression that the hotel is far older than it is. The guest rooms are large and beautifully outfitted with well-chosen chintz, reproductions, plush upholstery, and dozens of well-concealed electronic extras.

Dining: Both restaurants have an alluring atmosphere, particularly the highly acclaimed **Four Seasons,** where fine wines and continental specialties dazzle guests at lunch and at dinner. The less expensive **Lanes Restaurant** is popular with London's business community. Wellington would have felt right at home in the **Cocktail Bar.**

Amenities: 24-hour room service, valet, laundry service, babysitting, quality shops; theater-reservations desk; Conservatory fitness club, with all the latest equipment; garden; car-rental agency; business services available around the clock.

✪ **Metropolitan.** 19 Old Park Lane, London W1Y 4LB. ☎ **1071/447-1000.** Fax 0171/447-1100. www.designhotels.com. 155 units. A/C MINIBAR TV TEL. £245–£285 ($392–$456) double; £305–£325 ($488–$520) studio suite; £325–£385 ($520–$616) city studio suite; £495 ($792) park suite; £750–£850 ($1,200–$1,360) deluxe suite; £1,300 ($2,080) penthouse. AE, DC, DISC, MC, V. Tube: Hyde Park Corner.

Our choice for best newcomer of the year, the Metropolitan, smack dab between the Hilton and the Four Seasons, is the first hotel to open on Park Lane since the heady eighties. Unlike some of its opulent neighbors, minimalism is the word here. Designer Keith Hobbs believes in understatement, a style he perfected at Dublin's Clarence hotel. His staff uniforms are a far cry from the top hats and tails seen at some of the posh nests nearby.

The Metropolitan is graced with hardwood floors, simple marbles, and natural fabrics. Simple elegance is the code word for the bedrooms here, the most desirable of which open onto views of Hyde Park. Bedrooms have moleskin covers and cushions in soothing pastels, and wood furnishings—spare, functional, yet luxurious in a way. Its owner Christina Ong is already a hotel legend in London, having opened, among other properties, the deluxe Halkin in 1991. Her clientele are the young and well-heeled, patrons who value style and a lively atmosphere. The place is a relaxing retreat with wood and leather sofas, a carved stone clock in the pale marble lobby, and cool blue-patterned rugs.

Dining: An all-white skylit breakfast room, open to residents only, sets the tone for the day. The on-site Japanese restaurant and sushi bar, a twin to New York's **Nobu,** is one of the chic dining rendezvous of London. A late-night bar club has a modern-cum-fifties aura with frosted glass and metal tables.

Amenities: In-room fax machines, modern ports; VCRs available on request; 24-hour room service; concierge; dry cleaning and laundry service; massage; babysitting; secretarial services; express checkout.

✪ **Park Lane Hotel.** Piccadilly, London W1Y 8BX. ☎ **800/325-3535** or 0171/499-6321. Fax 0171/499-1965. www.ittsheraton.com. 350 units. MINIBAR TV TEL. £275 ($440) double; from £345 ($552) suite. AE, DC, MC, V. Parking £16 ($26). Tube: Hyde Park Corner or Green Park.

The most traditional of the Park Lane mansions, and once the lone holdout against chain management, the Park Lane Hotel was sold in 1996 (at least 95% of it, anyway) to the Sheraton Corporation, which upgraded it but maintained its quintessential Britishness. Launched in 1913 but kept empty for years, the Park Lane finally opened in 1924 under the leadership of Bracewell Smith, one of London's leading hoteliers. Today, its Silver Entrance remains an art deco marvel that has been used as a backdrop in many films, including the classic BBC miniseries *Brideshead Revisited.*

Designed in a U shape, with a view overlooking Green Park, the hotel offers luxurious accommodations that are a surprisingly good deal—they're among the least expensive on Park Lane. Many of the suites have marble fireplaces and original marble bathrooms. The rooms have benefited from an impressive refurbishment—they're larger, and the decor is lighter in tone. All have double-glazed windows to block out noise.

Dining/Diversions: The hotel's award-winning restaurant, **Bracewell's** (reviewed in chapter 5), adjoins **Bracewell's Bar,** one of London's most charming cocktail lounges, a stylish rendezvous with a talented evening pianist. Less expensive than Bracewell's is the still-very-charming **Brasserie,** serving French cuisine. A harpist plays in the **Palm Court Lounge** every Sunday and tea is served daily (see "Teatime" in chapter 5).

Amenities: 24-hour room service, concierge, valet, dry cleaning and laundry service, babysitting, secretarial services, fitness center, business center, safety-deposit boxes, gift and newspaper shop, barbershop, women's salon, and Daniele Ryman Aromatherapy Shop.

INEXPENSIVE

Ivanhoe Suite Hotel. 1 St. Christopher's Place, Barrett St. Piazza, London W1M 5HB. ☎ **0171/935-1047.** Fax 0171/224-0563. 8 units. MINIBAR TV TEL. £74 ($118) double. Rates include continental breakfast. AE, DC, MC, V. Tube: Bond St.

Born-to-shop buffs flock to this little hidden discovery uniquely located in a part of town off Oxford Street not known for its hotels. Situated above a restaurant on a pedestrian street of boutiques and restaurants and close to the shop-flanked New and Old Bond streets, this town-house hotel has attractively furnished singles and doubles, each with a sitting area. Each stylish room has its own entry, security video, and beverage-making facilities along with a fridge/bar, plus a wide selection of video tapes. Breakfast is served in the downstairs restaurant, and you can stop off for a night cap at the corner pub, a real neighborhood locale. They offer a number of services including room service, babysitting, secretarial service, and laundry.

MARYLEBONE

To locate these hotels, please see "Marylebone, Paddington, Bayswater & Notting Hill Gate Hotels" on pp. 106–107.

VERY EXPENSIVE

○ The Langham Hilton. 1 Portland Place, London W1N 4JA. ☎ **800/445-8667** or 0171/636-1000. Fax 0171/323-2340. www.hilton.com. 379 units. A/C MINIBAR TV TEL. £250–£280 ($400–$448) double; £330 ($528) executive room; from £650 ($1,040) suite. Rates include breakfast for executive room and suite. AE, DC, MC, V. Parking £26 ($42). Tube: Oxford Circus.

When this extremely well-located hotel was inaugurated in 1865 by the Prince of Wales, it was a suitably fashionable address for dozens of aristocratic squires seeking respite from their country estates. After it was bombed in World War II, it languished as dusty office space for the BBC until the early 1990s, when Hilton International took it over. Its restoration was painstaking; today, it's Hilton's European flagship. The Langham's public rooms reflect the power and majesty of the British Empire at its apex. Guest rooms are somewhat less opulent, but they're still attractively furnished and comfortable, featuring French provincial furniture and red oak trim. And the location is still terrific: within easy reach of Mayfair and Soho restaurants and theaters and Oxford and Regent Street shopping; Regent's Park is just blocks away.

Dining/Diversions: Vodka, caviar, and champagne flow liberally at the **Tsar's Russian Bar and Restaurant.** Drinks are served in the **Chukka Bar,** a re-creation of a private polo club. The most upscale restaurant is a high-ceilinged Victorian fantasy called **Memories,** serving patriotic nostalgia and cuisine from the far corners of the British Commonwealth. Afternoon tea is served amid the potted palms of the Edwardian-style **Palm Court.**

Amenities: 24-hour room service, concierge, health club, business center, beauty salon.

Landmark London. 222 Marylebone Rd., London NW1 6JQ. ☎ **800/457-4000** or 0171/631-8000. Fax 0171/631-8080. www.landmarklondon.co.uk. 302 units. A/C MINIBAR TV TEL. £245–£1,083 ($392–$1,733) double. AE, DC, MC, V. Tube: Marylebone or Baker St.

Some hotels in London come with a ghost. This one just has a secret—it's the least expensive luxury hotel in London. Great corporate and promotional rates make it a real find for those in need of five-star luxury (almost nobody pays the rack rates here; ask, and you'll do better). It's also fabulously located, particularly if you're traveling with children: Madame Tussaud's is a half-block away, and the Sherlock Holmes house is just a short walk.

This was the finest Victorian railway hotel in England when it opened in 1899, and millions of dollars of renovations have recently restored it to its former glory. The rooms are some of London's largest, and they come with grand marble bathrooms, blond-wood furnishings, and modern paintings. Half the rooms overlook a soaring eight-story central courtyard known as the Winter Garden, where you can dine amid palm trees.

Dining/Diversions: The cuisine—international, with an emphasis at times on the Mediterranean or Far East—is most recommendable, served rather formally in **The Dining Room** or casually in the **Winter Garden.** You can also come here for afternoon tea: It's not as good as the Ritz, but, chances are, you won't be able to get a reservation at the Ritz anyway. **The Cellar's Bar** is a favorite retreat for a pint.

Amenities: 24-hour room service, concierge, dry cleaning and laundry service, turndown and twice-daily maid service, in-room massage, babysitting, express checkout, valet parking, large health club, indoor pool, access to tennis courts, business center, conference facilities. VCR on request.

EXPENSIVE

✪ **Dorset Square Hotel.** 39–40 Dorset Sq., London NW1 6QN. ☎ **800/553-6674** or 0171/723-7874. Fax 0171/724-3328. E-mail: Dorset@afirmdale.com. 38 units. MINIBAR TV TEL. £125–£185 ($200–$296) double; £195 ($312) junior suite. AE, MC, V. Tube: Baker St. or Marylebone.

Situated in a lovely Regency square steps away from Regent's Park, this is one of London's best and most stylish "house hotels," overlooking Thomas Lord's first cricket pitch. Hot hoteliers Tim and Kit Kemp have furnished the interior of these two Georgian town houses in a comfy mix of antiques, reproductions, and chintz that will make you feel like you're in an elegant private home. All of the impressive guest rooms come with marble baths; about half are air-conditioned. They're all decorated in a personal yet extravagantly beautiful style—the owners are interior decorators known for their taste, which is often bold and daring.

Dining: The menu at the **Potting Shed** changes seasonally and features the best of English cuisine. The restaurant occupies an old servants' hall, with a trompe l'oeil mural of a cricket pitch and a sisal-decked floor.

Amenities: 24-hour room service, babysitting, dry cleaning and laundry service, massage, and secretarial services. You can ride in the owner's chauffeured vintage Bentley for a fee; it'll make you feel like Norma Desmond in *Sunset Boulevard.*

MODERATE

Bryanston Court Hotel. 56–60 Great Cumberland Place, London W1H 7FD. ☎ **0171/262-3141.** Fax 0171/262-7248. 54 units. TV TEL. £110 ($176) double. Rates include continental breakfast. AE, DC, MC, V. Tube: Marble Arch.

This hotel is ideally located in a neighborhood with many lovely squares. Three individual houses were cleverly joined to form the hotel about two centuries ago. Today, it's one of the finest moderately priced hotels in the area, thanks to the refurbishing and maintenance efforts of the Theodore family. Family owned and operated, it offers bedrooms that, although small (the bathrooms are small as well), are comfortably furnished and well-maintained. *Warning:* Don't let them send you down to the basement room, or you'll feel like Cinderella before she met Prince Charming.

On chilly nights, we like to retreat to the bar, in the rear of a comfortable lounge, and relax with a pint in front of the roaring fireplace. Your hosts are happy to arrange theater and tour bookings for you.

✪ **Durrants Hotel.** George St., London W1H 6BJ. ☎ **0171/935-8131.** Fax 0171/487-3510. 99 units. TV TEL. £135–£140 ($216–$224) double; £180 ($288) family room for 3; from £250 ($400) suite. AE, MC, V. Tube: Bond St.

Established in 1789 off Manchester Square, this historic hotel with its Georgian-detailed facade is snug, cozy, and traditional—almost like a poor man's Brown's. We find it to be one of the most quintessentially English of all London hotels and a soothing retreat on a cold, rainy day. In the 100 years that the Miller family has owned the hotel, several neighboring houses have been incorporated into the original structure. A walk through the pine-and-mahogany-paneled public rooms is like stepping back into another time: You'll even find an 18th-century letter-writing room. The rooms are rather bland except for elaborate cove moldings and very comfortable furnishings. They exude an aura of solidity; some are air-conditioned. Alas, all of them are just too small.

The in-house restaurant serves full afternoon tea and a satisfying French or traditional English cuisine in one of the most beautiful Georgian rooms in the neighborhood. The less formal breakfast room is ringed with 19th-century political cartoons by a noted Victorian artist. The pub, a neighborhood favorite, has Windsor chairs, an open fireplace, and decor that hasn't changed much in 2 centuries. Services include 24-hour room service, laundry service, and babysitting.

Hotel La Place. 17 Nottingham Place, London W1M 3FB. ☎ **0171/486-2323.** Fax 0171/486-4335. www.bit-byter.demon.co.uk. 28 units. MINIBAR TV TEL. £98–£150 ($157–$240) double; from £120 ($192) suite. Rates include English breakfast. AE, CB, DC, MC, V. Parking £8.50 ($14). Tube: Baker St.

This elegantly furnished West End hotel gets lots of write-ups as a safe haven for women. Actually, it's a safe haven—and a good bet—for anyone. One of the most desirable hotels north of Oxford Street, in the vicinity of Madame Tussaud's and Baker Street (of Sherlock Holmes fame), this Victorian-era building is similar to many others on its street, a decent street of no particular charm. What makes it exceptional is that it's been completely refurbished inside and is now one of London's better B&Bs for the price. "Discreet and lovely," is how one guest described it, and we agree. Bedrooms are done in Laura Ashley style, with traditional furnishings. Tall windows are opulently swagged and draped. Rooms are moderate in size—not cramped—and each contains such amenities as TV, coffeemaker, orthopedic mattresses, and hair dryers. For such a small hotel, there are a surprising number of services, including concierge, room service, dry cleaning and laundry service, in-room massage, babysitting, and a business center. Instead of a dreary little cafe you get **Jardin,** a chic, intimate wine bar and restaurant with an indoor/outdoor atmosphere and good food and drink.

INEXPENSIVE

Boston Court Hotel. 26 Upper Berkeley St., Marble Arch, London W1H 7PF. ☎ **0171/723-1445.** Fax 0171/262-8823. 13 units (5 with shower only). TV TEL. £49 ($78) double with shower only; £65–£69 ($104–$110) double with bath; £75–£79 ($120–$126) triple with bath. Rates include continental breakfast. MC, V. Tube: Marble Arch.

Upper Berkeley is a classic street of B&Bs; in days of yore, it was a prestigious address, home to Elizabeth Montagu (1720–1800), "queen of the bluestockings," who defended Shakespeare against attacks by Voltaire. Today, it's a good, safe, respectable retreat at an affordable price. This unfrilly hotel offers accommodations in a centrally located Victorian-era building within walking distance of Oxford Street shopping and Hyde Park. The small, basic rooms have been refurbished and redecorated with a no-nonsense decor; now all have private showers, central heating, hair dryers, coffeemakers, and small refrigerators.

Edward Lear Hotel. 28–30 Seymour St., London W1H 5WD. ☎ **0171/402-5401.** Fax 0171/706-3766. 35 units (12 with bathroom). TV TEL. £60 ($96) double without bathroom, £79.50 ($127) double with bathroom; from £85 ($136) suite. Rates include English breakfast. MC, V. Tube: Marble Arch.

This popular hotel 1 block from Marble Arch is made all the more desirable by the bouquets of fresh flowers in the public rooms. It occupies a pair of brick town houses, both of which date from 1780. The western house was the London home of the 19th-century artist and poet Edward Lear, famous for his nonsense verse; his illustrated limericks adorn the walls of one of the sitting rooms. Steep stairs lead up to the cozy rooms, which are fairly small but comfortable. One major drawback: This is an extremely noisy part of London. Rooms in the rear are quieter.

Hallam Hotel. 12 Hallam St., Portland Place, London W1N 5LF. ☎ **0171/580-1166.** Fax 0171/323-4527. 25 units. MINIBAR TV TEL. £92–£97 ($148–$156) double. Rates include English breakfast. AE, DC, MC, V. Tube: Oxford Circus.

This heavily ornamented stone-and-brick Victorian—one of the few on the street to escape the blitz—is just a 10-minute stroll from Oxford Circus. It's the property of the Baker family, brothers Grant and David, who maintain it well. The guest rooms, which were redone in 1991, are comfortably furnished. Some of the singles are so small they're called *cabinettes*. In addition to 24-hour room service, there's a bar where residents gather to swap stories, and a bright breakfast room overlooking the pleasant patio.

Hart House Hotel. 51 Gloucester Place, Portman Sq., London W1H 3PE. ☎ **0171/935-2288.** Fax 0171/935-8516. 16 units (10 with bathroom). TV TEL. £75 ($120) double without bathroom, £93 ($149) double with bathroom; £98 ($157) triple without bathroom, £110 ($176) triple with bathroom; £130 ($208) quad with bathroom. Rates include English breakfast. AE, MC, V. Tube: Marble Arch or Baker Street.

Hart House has been a long-enduring favorite with Frommer's readers. In the heart of the West End, this well-preserved historic building (one of a group of Georgian mansions occupied by exiled French nobles during the French Revolution) lies within easy walking distance of many theaters, as well as some of the most sought-after shopping areas and parks in London. Cozy and convenient, it's run by Andrew Bowden, one of Marylebone's best B&B hosts. The rooms—done in a combination of furnishings, ranging from Portobello antique to modern—are spic-and-span, each one with a different character. Favorites include no. 7, a triple with a big bath and shower. Ask for no. 11, on the top floor, if you'd like a brightly lit eyrie. Guest services include babysitting, dry cleaning and laundry service, and massage service. *Literary buffs, take note:* Poet Elizabeth Barrett resided at no. 99 with her family for many years.

Kenwood House Hotel. 114 Gloucester Place, London W1H 3DB. ☎ **0171/935-3473.** Fax 0171/224-0582. 16 units (9 with bathroom). TV. £44 ($70) double without bathroom, £56 ($90) double with bathroom; £64 ($102) triple without bathroom; £70 ($112) family room for 4 with bathroom. Rates include English breakfast. AE, MC, V. Tube: Baker St.

This 1812 Adam-style town house was a family home until 1942, when the owner's two sons died in the war. Disheartened, the owner sold it to the British army, which used it to billet officers. Now converted into a small hotel (run by English-born Arline Woutersz and her Dutch husband, Bryan), it's a historical landmark; the front balcony is said to be original. Guests gather in the mirrored lounge with its antimacassars in place, just as they were in Victoria's day. Most of the basically furnished bedrooms were upgraded and restored in 1993. Some rooms have en suite bathrooms; spic-and-span modern bathrooms with showers are on every floor. No need to bring your Lysol bottle. Babysitting can be arranged.

Regency Hotel. 19 Nottingham Place, London W1M 3FF. ☎ **0171/486-5347.** Fax 0171/224-6057. 20 units. MINIBAR TV TEL. £85 ($136) double; £99 ($158) family room. AE, CB, DC, MC, V. Tube: Baker St. or Regent's Park.

This centrally located hotel was built, along with most of its neighbors, in the late 1800s. Although it has functioned as some kind of hotel since the 1940s, in 1991 it was gutted and tastefully renovated into its upgraded present format. One of the better hotels on the street, it offers simple, conservatively decorated modern bedrooms scattered over four floors, and a breakfast room set in what used to be the cellar. Each room has a radio, hair dryer, trouser press, and ironing board. Room service is available. The neighborhood is protected as a historic district, and Marble Arch, Regent's Park, and Baker Street all lie within a 12-minute walk. Hotel services include dry cleaning and laundry service, room service, and massage.

ST. JAMES'S
VERY EXPENSIVE

The Ritz. 150 Piccadilly, London W1V 9DG. ☎ **800/525-4800** or 0171/493-8181. Fax 0171/493-2687. www.ritzhotel.com. 130 units. A/C MINIBAR TV TEL. £235–£355 ($376–$568) double; from £385 ($616) suite. Children under 12 stay free in parents' room. AE, DC, MC, V. Parking £43 ($69). Tube: Green Park.

Built in the French-Renaissance style and opened by César Ritz in 1906, this hotel overlooking Green Park is synonymous with luxury: Gold-leafed molding, marble columns, and potted palms abound, and a gold-leafed statue, *La Source,* adorns the fountain of the oval-shaped Palm Court. After a major restoration, this hotel is better than ever: New carpeting and air-conditioning have been installed in the guest rooms, and an overall polishing has recaptured much of the Ritz's original splendor. Still, this Ritz lags far behind the much grander one in Paris (to which this hotel is not affiliated). The belle époque guest rooms, each with its own character, are spacious and comfortable. Many have marble fireplaces, elaborate gilded plasterwork, and a decor of soft pastel hues. All have radios, and in-house movies are available.

Dining: The Ritz is still the most fashionable place in London to meet for afternoon tea at the **Ritz Palm Court** (see "Teatime," in chapter 5). The **Ritz Restaurant,** one of the loveliest dining rooms in the world, has already been faithfully restored to its original splendor. Service is efficient yet unobtrusive, and the tables are spaced to allow the most private of conversations (perhaps the reason Edward and Mrs. Simpson dined here so frequently before they married). The Palm Court also serves coffee and breakfast.

Amenities: 24-hour room service, valet, laundry service, babysitting, concierge, turndown, in-room massage, twice-daily maid service, express checkout, salon fitness center, business center.

✪ **The Stafford.** 16–18 St. James's Place, London SW1A 1NJ. ☎ **800/525-4800** or 0171/493-0111. Fax 0171/493-7121. E-mail: info@thestaffordhotel.co.uk. 80 units. A/C TV

TEL. £220–£260 ($352–$416) double; from £330 ($528) suite. AE, DC, MC, V. Tube: Green Park.

This hotel is famous for its American Bar, its clubby St. James's address, its discretion, and the warmth of its Edwardian decor. The Stafford was built in the late 19th century on a cul-de-sac off one of London's most centrally located and busiest neighborhoods; it's reached via St. James's Place or by a cobble-covered courtyard designed as a mews and known today as the Blue Ball Yard. The recently refurbished hotel has retained a country-house atmosphere, with touches of antique charm and modern amenities. It's not the Ritz, but the Stafford competes well with Dukes and 22 Jermyn Street (both highly recommendable as well) for a tasteful, discerning clientele. All of the guest rooms are individually decorated, reflecting the hotel's origins as a private home. Many singles contain queen-size beds. A handful of the hotel's newest and plushest accommodations in the historically restored stable mews require a walk across the yard.

Dining: Classic international dishes are prepared from select fresh ingredients at the elegant **Stafford Restaurant,** lit with handsome chandeliers and accented with flowers, candles, and white linen. The famous **American Bar,** which brings to mind the memento-packed library of an English country house, is an especially cozy place serving light meals and cocktails.

Amenities: 24-hour room service, babysitting, concierge, secretarial services, laundry service, massage, maid service, privileges at a nearby health club.

EXPENSIVE

✪ **Dukes Hotel.** 35 St. James's Place, London SW1A 1NY. ☎ **800/381-4702** or 0171/491-4840. Fax 0171/493-1264. www.dukeshotel.co.uk. E-mail: dukeshotel@compuserve.com. 76 units. A/C TV TEL. £190–£225 ($304–$360) double; from £250 ($400) suite. AE, MC, V. Parking £35 ($56). Tube: Green Park.

Dukes provides elegance without ostentation in what was presumably someone's Upstairs–Downstairs town house. Along with its nearest competitors, the Stafford and 22 Jermyn Street, it caters to those looking for charm, style, and tradition in a hotel. A hotel since 1908 (and last renovated in 1994), it stands in a quiet courtyard off St. James's Street with turn-of-the-century gas lamps that create the appropriate mood for what's coming once you walk through the front door. Each well-furnished guest room is decorated in the style of a particular English period, ranging from Regency to Edwardian. All rooms are equipped with marble baths, satellite TV, air-conditioning, and private bar. A short walk away are Buckingham Palace, St. James's Palace, and the Houses of Parliament. Shoppers will be near Bond Street and Piccadilly, and literature buffs will be interested to note that Oscar Wilde lived and wrote in St. James's Place for a time.

Dining: Dukes' Restaurant is small, tasteful, and elegant, combining classic British and continental cuisine. The hotel also has a clublike bar, which is known for its rare collection of vintage ports, Armagnacs, and cognacs.

Amenities: Even though it's claustrophobically small—it was once described as England's smallest castle—Dukes offers full hotel services, including 24-hour room service, car-rental and ticket services, and photocopying and typing services, babysitting, dry cleaning and laundry service, access to nearby health club, conference rooms.

✪ **22 Jermyn Street.** 22 Jermyn St., London SW1Y 6HL. ☎ **800/682-7808** or 0171/734-2353. Fax 0171/734-0750. www.22jermyn.com. E-mail: togna@ a22jermyn.com. 18 units. MINIBAR TV TEL. £185 ($296) double; from £240 ($384) suite. AE, DC, MC, V. Valet parking £24 ($38). Tube: Piccadilly Circus.

This is London's premier town house hotel, a gem of elegance and discretion. Set behind a facade of gray stone with neoclassical details, this structure, only 50 yards from Piccadilly, was built in 1870 as an apartment house for English gentlemen doing business in London. Since 1915, it has been administrated by three generations of the Togna family, whose most recent scion closed it for a radical restoration in 1990. Now reveling in its new role as a chic and upscale boutique hotel, 22 Jermyn offers an interior filled with greenery, the kind of art you might find in an elegant private home, and the best "information superhighway services" of any hotel in London. This hotel doesn't have the bar or restaurant facilities of The Stafford or Dukes, but its rooms are even more richly appointed than its main competitors. They're done in traditional English style, with masses of fresh flowers and chintz.

Amenities: 24-hour room service; concierge; babysitting; dry cleaning and laundry service; secretarial services; fax; videophones; video library; CD-ROM library; Internet access; and a weekly newsletter that keeps guests up to date with restaurants, theater, and exhibitions. Access to a nearby health club.

PICCADILLY CIRCUS
INEXPENSIVE

Regent Palace Hotel. 12 Sherwood St., London W1A 4BZ. ☎ **0171/734-7000.** Fax 0171/734-6435. 950 units (none with bathroom). TV TEL. £103 ($165) double. For stays of 2 or more nights, £72–£88 ($115–$141) per person depending on the time of year. Rates include English breakfast. AE, DC, MC, V. Tube: Piccadilly Circus.

The Regent Palace, a major focal point since it was built in 1915 at the edge of Piccadilly Circus, is one of the largest hotels in Europe, a beacon for those who want to be near the bright lights of London's Theaterland. It's certainly a comedown from the deluxe Mayfair palaces recommended above, but you can't expect the same kinds of service, ambience, and amenities at these prices. This hotel is known for staunch loyalty to its original design: None of the simply furnished rooms contains a private bathroom. The shared facilities in the hallways are adequate, though, and each room has a sink with hot and cold running water and coffee- and tea-making facilities.

The hotel's **The Carvery** is a good (and inexpensive) place to dine (see chapter 5); **The Dome** bistro is open for pre-theater meals. Drinks are served in the **Half Sovereign** and the **Planters** bars. Coffee, sandwiches, and snacks are available in **Antonio's Coffee Bar.** There are souvenir and gift shops, a bureau de change, and a theater-booking agency on the premises.

SOHO
MODERATE

✪ **Hazlitt's 1718.** 6 Frith St., London W1V 5TZ. ☎ **0171/434-1771.** Fax 0171/439-1524. 24 units. £148 ($237) double; £205 ($328) suite. AE, DC, MC, V. Tube: Leicester Sq. or Tottenham Court Rd.

This gem, housed in three historic homes on Soho Square—the most fashionable address in London 2 centuries ago—is one of London's best small hotels. Built in 1718, the hotel is named for William Hazlitt, who founded the Unitarian church in Boston and wrote four volumes on the life of his hero, Napoléon; the essayist died here in 1830.

Hazlitt's is a favorite with artists, actors, media people, and models. It's eclectic, filled with odds and ends picked up around the country at estate auctions. Some find the Georgian decor a bit spartan, but the 2,000 original prints hanging on the walls brighten it considerably. Many bedrooms have four-poster beds, and some bathrooms have their original claw-footed tubs (only one unit has a shower). If you can afford it,

---

⊕ Family-Friendly Hotels

Although the bulk of their clients are business travelers staying for short hauls, each of the major international hotel chains does its best to create the impression that they're fully geared for family fun. Look for special summer packages at most hotel chains between June and August. Some of the most consistently generous offers come from the **Forte** (☎ **800/435-4542**) and **Hilton International** (☎ **800/445-8667**) chains, but it all depends on the specific branch. For best results, call the 800 number and ask about special family packages.

London also has some less expensive options that are happy to accommodate traveling families. Also refer to section 1 of this chapter under "Best for Families Who Don't Want to Break the Bank."

- **Hart House Hotel** (Marylebone; *see p. 79*) This small, family-run B&B is right in the center of the West End, near Hyde Park. Many of its rooms are triples; if you need even more room, special family suites, with connecting rooms, can be arranged.

- **Sandringham Hotel** (Hampstead; *see p. 111*) Out in Hampstead, where children have plenty of room to play on the heath, this hotel offers both triple and family rooms that comfortably accommodate four to five people.

---

opt for the elegant Baron Willoughby suite, with its giant four-poster bed and wood-burning fireplace. Some of the floors dip and sway and there's no elevator, but it's all part of the charm. Amenities include a concierge, room service, babysitting, dry cleaning and laundry service, and a discounted rate on a car or limousine. Swinging Soho is at your doorstep; the young, hip staff will be happy to direct you to the local hot spots.

BLOOMSBURY
MODERATE

Academy Hotel. 17–21 Gower St., London WC1E 6HG. ☎ **800/678-3096** or 0171/631-4115. Fax 0171/636-3442. 55 units. A/C TV TEL. £115 ($184) double; £150 ($240) suite. AE, DC, MC, V. Tube: Tottenham Court Rd., Goodge St., or Russell Sq.

Right in the heart of London's publishing district, the Academy attracts budding British John Grishams who haven't hit the big time yet. Although tacky modern design rears its ugly head here and there, many of the original architectural details were preserved when these three 1776 Georgian row houses were joined. The hotel was substantially upgraded in the 1990s, with a bathroom added to every bedroom (whether there was space or not). Grace notes include the glass panels, colonnades, and intricate plasterwork on the facade. Rooms are decorated in a neutral style guaranteed not to offend anybody—except maybe by their blandness—but they're well cared for. The theater district and Covent Garden are within walking distance. Facilities include an elegant bar, a library room, a secluded patio garden, and a restaurant serving modern European food that often attracts businesspeople entertaining their clients.

Blooms Hotel. 7 Montague St., London WC1B 5BP. ☎ **0171/323-1717.** Fax 0171/636-6498. E-mail: blooms@mermaid.co.uk. 27 units. TV TEL. £140–£180 ($224–$288) double. Extra person £40 ($64). Rates include English breakfast. AE, DC, MC, V. Tube: Russell Sq.

This exquisitely restored town house has a pedigree: It stands in what was formerly the grounds of Montague House (now the British Museum). It's had a distinguished, if eccentric, list of former occupants: everybody from Richard Penn, the Whig member of Parliament from Liverpool, to Dr. John Cumming, who firmly believed he'd witness the end of the world (on long winter nights, his ghostly presence—still looking for the world to end, we suppose—has been spotted). Even though it's in the heart of London, the house evokes a country home atmosphere, complete with cozy fireplace, period art, and copies of *Country Life* waiting in the magazine rack. Guests take morning coffee in a walled garden overlooking the British Museum. In summer, light meals are served. Bedrooms are individually designed with traditional elegance, in beautifully muted tones. Services include 24-hour room service, dry cleaning and laundry service, and concierge.

INEXPENSIVE

Avalon Private Hotel. 46–47 Cartwright Gardens, London WC1H 9EL. ☎ 0171/387-2366. Fax 0171/387-5810. E-mail: 100347.447@compuserve.com. 28 units (4 with shower). TV. £52 ($83) double without shower, £65 ($104) double with shower; £70 ($112) triple without shower, £80 ($128) triple with shower; £80 ($128) quad without shower, £90 ($144) quad with shower. Rates include English breakfast. AE, MC, V. Tube: Russell Sq., King's Cross, or Euston.

One guidebook from Victoria's day claimed Bloomsbury attracted "Medical and other students of both sexes and several nationalities, American folk passing through London, literary persons 'up' for a week or two's reading in the British Museum, and Bohemians pure and simple." The same might be said for today's patrons of this hotel, built in 1807 as two Georgian houses in residential Cartwright Gardens. Guests feel privileged because they have use of a semiprivate garden across the street with tennis courts. Top-floor rooms, often filled with students, are reached via impossibly steep stairs, but bedrooms on the lower levels have easier access. The place obviously didn't hire a decorator; everything is wildly mismatched in the bedrooms and the droopy lounge—but the price is right.

Crescent Hotel. 49–50 Cartwright Gardens, London WC1H 9EL. ☎ 0171/387-1515. Fax 0171/383-2054. 24 units, 15 with bathroom (some with shower only, some with tub only). TV TEL. £50 ($80) double without bathroom, £68 ($109) double with bathroom. Rates include English breakfast. MC, V. Tube: Russell Sq., King's Cross, or Euston.

Although Leonard Woolf, Dorothy Sayers, John Ruskin, and Percy Bysshe Shelley no longer pass by the door, the Crescent still stands in the heart of academic London. The private square is owned by the City Guild of Skinners and guarded by the University of London, whose student residential halls are just across the street. You have access to the gardens itself, with its private tennis courts. Mrs. Bessolo and Mrs. Cockle, the managers, are the kindest hosts along the street; they view Crescent as an extension of their private home and welcome you to its comfortably elegant Georgian surroundings, which date from 1810. Some guests have been returning for four decades to enjoy a range of bedrooms, from small singles with shared bathrooms to more spacious twin and double rooms with private plumbing. All rooms have TV and beverage makers; other thoughtful extras include alarm clocks and hair dryers. The good ladies will even let you do your ironing so you'll look sharp when you go out on the town.

Harlingford Hotel. 61–63 Cartwright Gardens, London WC1H 9EL. ☎ 0171/387-1551. Fax 0171/387-4616. 44 units. TV TEL. £75 ($120) double; £85 ($136) triple; £95 ($152) quad. Rates include English breakfast. AE, MC, V. Tube: Russell Sq., King's Cross, or Euston.

This hotel is composed of three once-private town houses built in the 1820s that were joined together around 1900 via a bewildering array of staircases and meandering hallways. Set in the heart of Bloomsbury, it's run by a management that seems genuinely concerned about the welfare of their guests, unlike many of their neighboring rivals.

(In a scene straight from Dickens, they distribute little mincemeat pies to their guests during the Christmas holidays.) Double-glazed windows cut down on the street noise, and all the bedrooms are generally comfortable and inviting, graced with floral prints on the walls. Bathrooms are small, however, since the house wasn't originally designed for them. The most comfortable rooms are on the second and third levels; otherwise, expect to climb some steep English stairs (there's no elevator). Still, say no to the rooms on ground level, as they are darker and have less security. You'll have use of the tennis courts in Cartwright Gardens.

✪ **Jenkins Hotel.** 45 Cartwright Gardens, London WC1H 9EH. ☎ **0171/387-2067.** Fax 0171/383-3139. E-mail: reservations@jenkinshotel.demon.co.uk. 15 units (6 with bathroom). MINIBAR TV TEL. £55 ($88) double without bathroom, £65 ($104) double with bathroom; £76 ($122) triple with bathroom. MC, V. Rates include English breakfast. Tube: Russell Sq., King's Cross, or Euston.

Followers of the Agatha Christie TV series *Poirot* might recognize this Cartwright Gardens residence—it was featured in the series. The antiques are gone and the rooms are small, but some of the original charm of the Georgian house remain—enough so that the London *Mail on Sunday* recently proclaimed it one of the "ten best hotel values" in the city. And the location is great, near the British Museum, London University, theaters, and antiquarian bookshops. There are some drawbacks—no lift and no reception or sitting room, but it's a place where you can settle in and feel at home.

Ruskin Hotel. 23–24 Montague St., London WC1B 5BH. ☎ **0171/636-7388.** Fax 0171/323-1662. 32 units (6 with bathroom). £60 ($96) double without bathroom, £74 ($118) double with bathroom; £75 ($120) triple without bathroom, £85 ($136) triple with bathroom. Rates include English breakfast. AE, DC, MC, V. Tube: Russell Sq. or Holborn.

Although the hotel is named for author John Ruskin, the ghosts of other literary legends who lived nearby may haunt you: Mary Shelley plotting her novel, *Frankenstein;* James Barrie fantasizing about *Peter Pan;* and even the provocative Olive Schreiner (1855–1920), an early feminist who advocated that women should be independent in sexual matters. This hotel has been managed for two decades by a hard-working family who enjoy a repeat clientele. They keep the place spic-and-span—but don't expect a decorator's flair, and the furnishings, though well-polished, are worn. Double-glazing in the front blots out the noise, but we prefer the cozily old-fashioned chambers in the rear, as they open onto a park. Sorry, no elevator. The greenery in the cellar-level breakfast room provides a grace note, and the breakfast is big enough to fortify you for a full day at the British Museum next door. *Insider tip:* Although the private bathrooms are ridiculously small, the shared bathrooms in the hall are generous and well-maintained—and you'll save money by opting for one of the rooms without bathroom.

St. Margaret's Hotel. 26 Bedford Place, London WC1B 5JH. ☎ **0171/636-4277.** Fax 0171/323-3066. 64 units (6 with shower). TV TEL. £54–£66 ($87–$106) double without shower, £70–£72 ($112–$115) double with shower. Rates include English breakfast. No credit cards. Tube: Holborn or Russell Sq.

As you trudge along Bedford Place in the footsteps of Hogarth, Yeats, and Dickens, you'll come across this hotel, composed of four interconnected Georgian town houses. Furnishings are a badly mismatched medley, a bit tattered here and there, but endurable and fine nevertheless. All is forgiven on a spring day when you look out back onto the Duke of Bedford's private gardens in full bloom. Rooms are fairly large, except for a cramped single here or there. Many still retain their original fireplaces, which is how the rooms were once heated. Families should ask for no. 53, with a glassed-in garden along the back. A single who doesn't mind sharing a bathroom will find ample space in no. 24. Only a few rooms have private showers, although several bathrooms and showers are located throughout the building. Guests have use of two lounges, one with a TV. The staff here is so loyal they often work until they retire.

Thanet Hotel. 8 Bedford Place, London WC1B 5JA. ☎ **0171/636-2869.** Fax 0171/323-6676. www.freepages.co.uk/thanet_hotel. 16 units. TV TEL. £75 ($120) double with bathroom; £90 ($144) triple with bathroom; £99 ($158) quad with bathroom. Rates include English breakfast. AE, MC, V. Tube: Russell Sq.

The myriad hotels around Russell Square become peas in a pod at some point, but the Thanet stands out. It no longer charges the same rates it did when it first appeared in *England on $5 a Day*, but it's still a winning choice nonetheless, a fine address and an affordable option for those who want to be close to the British Museum, Theaterland, and Covent Garden. It's a landmark status building on a quiet Georgian terrace between Russell and Bloomsbury squares; although it was restored many times over the years, many original features remain. Third-generation hoteliers, the Orchard family offers small, comfortably furnished and well-decorated rooms—no glaring contrasts in decor here. Amenities include beverage maker, radio, and TV.

COVENT GARDEN
EXPENSIVE

Covent Garden Hotel. 10 Monmouth St., London WC2H 9HB. ☎ **0171/806-1000.** Fax 0171/806-1100. E-mail: covent@firmdale.com. 50 units. A/C MINIBAR TV TEL. £200–£295 ($320–$472) double; £375–£550 ($600–$880) suite. AE, MC, V. Tube: Covent Garden or Leicester Sq.

Constructed as a French-directed hospital around 1850, this building lay derelict for years until it was reconfigured in 1996 by hot hoteliers Tim and Kit Kemp—whose flair for interior design is now legendary—into one of London's most charming boutique hotels, situated in one of the West End's hippest shopping neighborhoods. The Kemps' latest creation epitomizes all that's fine in London town-house hotels—*Travel and Leisure* called it one of 1997's 25 hottest places to stay in the *world*. It remains so today.

Across from Neal's Yard and behind a bottle-green facade reminiscent of a 19th-century storefront, the hotel has a welcoming lobby outfitted with elaborate marquetry furniture and sweeping draperies, plus two charming restaurants. Upstairs, above a dramatic stone staircase, soundproof bedrooms are lushly outfitted in English style with Asian fabrics, many elaborately adorned with hand-embroidered designs, some with crewel work. Their decorative trademark? Each room has a clothier's mannequin—a lithe female form draped in the fabric that's the predominant theme of that particular room. Each comes with VCR, CD player, two phone lines with voice mail, and marble bathrooms with double vanities and deep soaking tubs. The young, well-mannered staff works hard to please, and succeeds—the friendly concierge walked blocks in a downpour to hail us a cab.

Dining: Permeated with a sense of 19th-century nostalgia, **Max's Brasserie** serves up very good French-English bistro fare. With high stools at the bar and crisp table linens, it's a chic place for lunch.

Amenities: 24-hour room service, concierge, valet, secretarial services, office facilities, small gym, small video library.

INEXPENSIVE

○ **Fielding Hotel.** 4 Broad Court, Bow St., London WC2B 5QZ. ☎ **0171/836-8305.** Fax 0171/497-0064. 27 units. £88–£98 ($141–$157) double; £140 ($224) triple; £185 ($296) suite. AE, DC, MC, V. Tube: Covent Garden.

One of London's more eccentric hotels, The Fielding is cramped, quirky, and quaint, but an enduring favorite nonetheless. The hotel—named after novelist Henry Fielding of *Tom Jones* fame, who lived in Broad Court—lies on a pedestrian street still lined with 19th-century gas lamps; the Royal Opera House is across the street, and the pubs, shops, and restaurants of lively Covent Garden are just beyond the front door. Rooms are a little less than small, but they're charmingly old-fashioned and traditional. Bathrooms are minuscule, and very few rooms have anything approaching a view; floors dip and sway, and the furnishings and fabrics have known better times—so be duly warned. But with a location like this, in the very heart of London, The Fielding keeps guests coming back; many love the hotel's rickety charm. There's no room service or restaurant, but breakfast is served. Be sure to introduce yourself to Smokey the African Grey parrot in the bar; he's the hotel's oldest resident.

ALONG THE STRAND
VERY EXPENSIVE

✪ **The Savoy.** The Strand, London WC2R 0EU. ☎ **800/63-SAVOY** or **0171/836-4343.** Fax 0171/240-6040. www.savoy-group.co.uk. E-mail: info@savoy.co.uk. 202 units. A/C MINIBAR TV TEL. £295–£305 ($472–$488) double; from £365 ($584) suite. AE, DC, MC, V. Parking £22 ($35). Tube: Charing Cross or Covent Garden.

Although not as swank as the Dorchester, this London landmark is the premier address if you want to be in the Strand and Covent Garden area. Impresario Richard D'Oyly Carte built the hotel in 1889 as an annex to his nearby Savoy Theatre, where many Gilbert and Sullivan operettas were originally staged. Eight stories of glazed tiles rising in ponderous dignity between the Strand and the Thames, it dwarfs all of its nearby competition, including the Waldorf at Aldwych and the Howard on Temple Place. Each guest room is uniquely decorated with color-coordinated accessories, solid and comfortable furniture, large closets, and an eclectic blend of antiques, such as gilt mirrors, Queen Anne chairs, and Victorian sofas; 48 have their own sitting rooms. The expensive river-view suites are the most sought after, and for good reason—the views are the best in London.

Dining: The world-famous **Savoy Grill** has long been popular with the theater crowd; Sarah Bernhardt was a regular. The even more elegant **River Restaurant** has tables overlooking the Thames; there's dancing to live band music in the evening. The room known as **Upstairs** specializes in champagne, Chablis, and seafood.

Amenities: 24-hour room service, nightly turndown, room service, same-day dry cleaning and laundry service, secretarial service, hairdresser, news kiosk, the city's best health club—the pool has fabulous views. Guests also have temporary membership in the exclusive Wentworth Club, a golf and country club on the outskirts of London (proof of handicap required).

WESTMINSTER/VICTORIA
EXPENSIVE

✪ **Goring Hotel.** 15 Beeston Place, Grosvenor Gardens, London SW1W 0JW. ☎ **0171/396-9000.** Fax 0171/834-4393. www.goringhotel.co.uk. E-mail: reception@goringhotel.co.uk. 76 units. A/C TV TEL. £185–£225 ($296–$360) double; from £250–£275 ($400–$440) suite. AE, DC, MC, V. Parking £17.50 ($28). Tube: Victoria.

For tradition and location, the Goring is our premier choice in the Westminster area—even better than the nearby Stakis London St. Ermins, its closest competitor. Located just behind Buckingham Palace, it lies within easy reach of the royal parks, Victoria Station, Westminster Abbey, and the Houses of Parliament. It also happens to offer the finest personal service of all its nearby competitors.

Built in 1910 by O. R. Goring, this was the first hotel in the world to have central heating and a private bathroom in every room. While no longer on the cutting edge, today's well-furnished guest rooms still offer all the comforts, including refurbished marble bathrooms; many have air-conditioning. The charm of a traditional English country hotel is evoked in the paneled drawing room, where fires crackle in the ornate fireplaces on nippy evenings. The adjoining bar overlooks the rear gardens.

Dining: At the restaurant, the chef uses only the freshest ingredients in his classic English recipes; specialties include medallions of venison with chestnuts, roast breast of pheasant, braised lamb in a rich red wine sauce, and grilled Dover sole. Afternoon tea is served in the lounge.

Amenities: 24-hour room service, valet service, concierge, dry cleaning and laundry service, babysitting, secretarial services, valet, salon, free use of local health club.

MODERATE

Lime Tree Hotel. 135–137 Ebury St., London SW1W 9RA. ☎ **0171/730-8191.** Fax 0171/730-7865. 26 units. TV TEL. £100–£110 ($160–$176) double. Rates include English breakfast. AE, MC, V. Tube: Victoria.

Long-time denizens of London's B&B business, the Wales-born Davies family has transformed what had been a run-down guest house into a cost-conscious but cozy hotel that appeals to budget travelers. The simply furnished bedrooms are scattered over four floors of a brick-fronted town house; each has been recently refitted with new curtains, cupboards, and upholstery. The front rooms have small balconies overlooking Ebury Street; rooms in the back don't have balconies, but are quieter and sport views over the hotel's small rear garden. The rooms tend to be larger than many at similar prices, and the breakfasts are generous. Buckingham Palace, Westminster Abbey, and the House of Parliament are within easy reach, as is Harrods; nearby is the popular Ebury Wine Bar.

Tophams Belgravia. 28 Ebury St., London SW1W 0LU. ☎ **0171/730-8147.** Fax 0171/823-5966. E-mail: 106010.1706@compuserve.com. 43 units (24 with bathroom). TV TEL. £95 ($152) double without bathroom, £115–£135 ($184–$216) double with bathroom; £230 ($368) suite. AE, DC, MC, V. Tube: Victoria.

Tophams came into being in 1937, when five small row houses were interconnected; with its flower-filled window boxes, the place still has a country-house flavor. It was completely renovated in 1997. The petite informal reception rooms are done in flowery chintzes and antiques. All rooms have coffeemakers, hair dryers, and satellite TV; the best of the bunch are comfortably appointed with private bathrooms and four-poster beds. Not all of the rooms have private bathrooms—ask for one when making reservations. The restaurant offers both traditional and modern English cooking for lunch and dinner. And the location is great, especially if you're planning to cover a lot of ground by tube or train: It's only a 3-minute walk to Victoria Station.

INEXPENSIVE

Astors Hotel. 110–112 Ebury St., London SW1W 9QD. ☎ **0171/730-3811.** Fax 0171/823-6728. 22 units (12 with bathroom). TV. £55 ($88) double without bathroom, £64 ($102) double with bathroom; £84 ($134) triple with bathroom. Rates include English breakfast. MC, V. Tube: Victoria.

This well-located choice is a stone's throw from Buckingham Palace and just a 5-minute walk from Victoria's main-line and tube stations. The brick-fronted Victorian was once home to Margaret Oliphant (1828–97), a popular Victorian novelist; Noël Coward was a neighbor for 20 years, and Wells, Yeats, Bennett, and Shaw called down the street at no. 153 when poet, novelist, and racy autobiographer George Moore

Westminster & Victoria Hotels

Astors Hotel **5**
Cartref House **6**
Caswell Hotel **9**
Ebury House **3**
Goring Hotel **1**
James House **4**
Lime Tree Hotel **7**
Tophams Belgravia **2**
Windermere Hotel **8**

Tube Station ⊖

E-0137

89

(1852–1933) was in residence. The guests today don't have such pedigrees, but are frugal travelers looking for a decent, affordable, and respectable address in pricey London. Although more functional than glamorous, the rooms are satisfactory in every way. Since space and furnishings vary greatly, ask to take a little peek before committing yourself to a room. (As the hotel is often full, that won't always be possible.)

Caswell Hotel. 25 Gloucester St., London SW1V 2DB. ☎ **0171/834-6345.** 18 units (7 with bathroom). MINIBAR TV. £54 ($86) double without bathroom, £75 ($120) double with bathroom. Rates include English breakfast. MC, V. Tube: Victoria.

Run with consideration and thoughtfulness by Mr. and Mrs. Hare, Caswell lies on a cul-de-sac that's a calm oasis in an otherwise busy area. The fancy neighbors are all gone—Mozart lived nearby while he completed his first symphony, and that "notorious couple," Harold Nicholson and Victoria Sackville-West, are long departed—but this is still a choice address. Beyond the chintz-filled lobby, the decor is understated: There are four floors of well-furnished but not spectacular bedrooms, each with such amenities as hair dryer and beverage maker. How do they explain the success of the place? One staff member said, "This year's guest is next year's business."

Ebury House. 102 Ebury St., London SW1W 9QD. ☎ **0171/730-1350.** Fax 0171/259-0400. 13 units (none with bathroom). TV. £60 ($96) double; £75 ($120) triple; £85 ($136) family room for 4. Rates include English breakfast. MC, V. Tube: Victoria.

In 1920, Ruth Draper wrote: "I was very lucky in finding a sunny top floor room...a lovely big double room in front and I am so comfortably fixed...for one guinea [£1.05] a week." The first part of her statement could still be true—only the price has gone up a bit. On this highly competitive street, this comfortable guest house stands out, mainly thanks to the welcome you get from its owner-manager, Peter Evans. The bedrooms, while no pacesetters for style, are well-maintained and have sinks and hair dryers. There's one full bath per floor, and a pay phone on one of the stairwells, in case you want to call home for money. "We get just as many Canadians and Aussies as Yanks," one of the staff confided. "They seem to like us." Reserve well in advance in summer. The pine-paneled breakfast room is the morning rendezvous point.

✪ **James House/Cartref House.** 108 and 129 Ebury St., London SW1W 9QD. James House ☎ **0171/730-7338**; Cartref House ☎ **0171/730-6176.** Fax 0171/730-7338. E-mail: jamescartref@compuserve.com. 21 units (9 with bathroom). TV. £65 ($104) double without bathroom, £75 ($120) double with bathroom; £105 ($168) quad with bathroom. Rates include English breakfast. MC, V. Tube: Victoria.

Hailed by many publications, including the *Los Angeles Times,* as one of the top 10 B&B choices in London, James House and Cartref House (across the street), deserve their accolades. Derek and Sharon James seem to have real dedication in their work. They're the finest hosts in the area, and they're constantly refurbishing, so everything looks up to date. Each room is individually designed; some of the large ones have bunk beds that make them suitable for families. The English breakfast is so generous that you might end up skipping lunch. There's no elevator, but the happy guests don't seem to mind. Don't worry about which house you're assigned; each one's a winner.

Windermere Hotel. 142–144 Warwick Way, London SW1V 4JE. ☎ **0171/834-5163.** Fax 0171/630-8831. E-mail: 100773.1171@compuserve.com. 23 units (20 with bathroom). TV TEL. £69 ($110) double without bathroom, £84–£99 ($134–$158) double with bathroom; £106 ($170) triple with bathroom; £112 ($179) quad with bathroom. AE, CB, MC, V. Tube: Victoria.

This award-winning small hotel is an excellent choice for those who want to be near Victoria Station, less than a 10-minute walk away. The Windermere was built in 1857 as a pair of private dwellings on the site of the old Abbot's Lane. The lane linked Westminster Abbey to its abbot's residence—all the kings of medieval England trod here. A fine example of early Victorian classical design, the hotel has lots of English character. All of the refurbished rooms are comfortably furnished and have such amenities as satellite TV, coffeemakers, and hair dryers. They come in a wide range of sizes, some accommodating three or four—but the cheaper ones are somewhat cramped. The ground-floor rooms facing the street tend to be noisy at night. Hotel services include limited room service, dry cleaning, and a car rental and tour desk.

3 In & Around Knightsbridge

VERY EXPENSIVE

The Capital. 22–24 Basil St., London SW3 1AT. ☎ **800/926-3199** in the U.S., or 0171/589-5171. Fax 0171/225-0011. 48 units. A/C MINIBAR TV TEL. £217–£280 ($347–$448) double; from £320 ($512) suite. AE, DC, MC, V. Parking £20 ($32). Tube: Knightsbridge.

One of the most personalized hotels in the West End, this small, modern place is a stone's throw from Harrods. It doesn't have the five-star quality of the nearby Hyatt, but the cuisine is far better than at many of London's more highly rated hotels. With extensive refurbishment, the owner, David Levin, has created a warm town-house ambience. The elegant fin-de-siècle decor is matched by the courtesy and professionalism of the staff. Lined with original oils, the corridors and staircase literally function as an art gallery. The guest rooms are tastefully decorated, often with Ralph Lauren furnishings.

Dining: The Capital Restaurant was refurbished in the early 1990s in a vaguely French style, with David Linley panels for the windows (Linley is Princess Margaret's son). Under the direction of chef Phillip Britton, it's among the finest restaurants in London, specializing in seafood and offering exquisitely prepared French cuisine.

Amenities: 24-hour room service, concierge, dry cleaning and laundry service, babysitting, secretarial service, valet.

Hyatt Carlton Tower. 2 Cadogan Place, London SW1 X9PY. ☎ **800/233-1234** or 0171/235-1234. Fax 0171/235-9129. www.hyatt.com. 220 units. A/C MINIBAR TV TEL. £255 ($408) double; from £425 ($680) suite. AE, DC, MC, V. Parking £30 ($48). Tube: Knightsbridge.

Its location and towering height made this luxurious hotel a landmark even before Hyatt's decorators, painters, and antiques dealers transformed it into the chain's European flagship. It's one of the most plushly decorated and best-maintained hotels in London, with more style, grace, and amenities than Knightsbridge's Sheraton Park Tower. And the setting is lovely—it overlooks one of the city's most civilized gardens and is surrounded by Regency-era town houses. The comfortable and conservative modern guest rooms feature marble baths and artwork; many open onto panoramic views over the rooftops of the neighborhood.

Dining: After the publicity it received from *Time Out* as "Britain's Tea Place of the Year," the hotel has remained one of the most fashionable spots to enjoy a midafternoon pick-me-up. The hotel has a new Northern Italian restaurant, **Grissini London,** a sibling restaurant to the Grissini at the Grand Hyatt Hong Kong. The newer Grissini serves specialties such as ravioli stuffed with lobster, and fried lemon-breaded monkfish medallions.

Amenities: 24-hour room service, valet, laundry service, salon, babysitting, concierge, twice-daily maid service, turndown, express checkout, secretarial service, swimming pool, business center, health club with exercise equipment, aerobics studio, beauty experts, masseurs, sauna, solariums, tennis courts, Jacuzzi, shopping arcade.

Hotels from Knightsbridge to Earl's Court

Aaron House **7**	Avonmore Hotel **4**
Abbey House **2**	Basil Street Hotel **27**
Amber Hotel **3**	The Beaufort **24**
Aster House Hotel **19**	Blair House Hotel **32**
Aston's Budget Studios	Blake's Hotel **12**
& Aston's Designer	The Capital **25**
Studios & Suites **11**	

Claverley Hotel **23**
The Cranley **10**
Diplomat Hotel **30**
5 Sumner Place **18**
Franklin Hotel **21**
The Gallery **15**

The Gore **16**
Harrington Hall **8**
Henley House **6**
Hotel 167 **9**
Hyatt Carlton Tower **29**
Knightsbridge
  Green Hotel **26**

Knightsbridge Hotel **22**
The Lanesborough **28**
Number Sixteen **20**
Pelham Hotel **17**
Regency Hotel **14**

Rushmore Hotel **5**
Swiss House Hotel **13**
Vicarage Private
  Hotel **1**
Wilbraham Hotel **31**

EXPENSIVE

Basil Street Hotel. 8 Basil St., London SW3 1AH. ☎ **0171/581-3311.** Fax 0171/581-3693. E-mail: thebasil@aol.com. 87 units (71 with bathroom). TV TEL. £170 ($272) double without bathroom, £188 ($301) double with bathroom; £240 ($384) family room. AE, DC, MC, V. Parking £22–£27 ($35–$43) at 24-hour lot nearby. Tube: Knightsbridge.

The Basil, an Edwardian charmer totally unmarred by modernization, has long been a favorite for those who make an annual pilgrimage to Harrods—"just 191 steps away"—and the Chelsea Flower Show (Harvey Nichols is also nearby). Several spacious, comfortable lounges are furnished in a fitting style and accented with 18th- and 19th-century accessories; off the many rambling corridors are smaller sitting rooms. Bedrooms are well-maintained but rather standard; some are air-conditioned (a few singles are without bathrooms).

Dining: In the restaurant, candlelight and piano music re-create the atmosphere of a bygone era. **The Parrot Club,** a rendezvous reserved only for women, is ideal for afternoon tea.

Amenities: 24-hour room service, evening maid service, conference facilities, babysitting, dry cleaning and laundry service, shoe cleaning.

✪ **The Beaufort.** 33 Beaufort Gardens, London SW3 1PP. ☎ **800/888-1199** or 0171/584-5252. Fax 0171/589-2834. E-mail: thebeaufort@nol.co.uk. 28 units. TV TEL. £150–£260 ($240–$416) double; £295 ($472) junior suite. Rates include breakfast and afternoon tea. AE, DC, MC, V. Tube: Knightsbridge.

If you'd like to stay at one of London's finest boutique hotels, offering personal service in an elegant, tranquil town-house atmosphere, head to the Beaufort or the Franklin (see below)—they're the market leaders. The Beaufort, only 200 yards from Harrods, sits on a cul-de-sac behind two Victorian porticoes and an iron fence. Owner Diana Wallis, a television producer, combined a pair of adjacent houses from the 1870s, ripped out the old decor, and created a stylish hotel of merit and grace; it has the feeling of a private house in the heart of London. You register at a small desk extending off a bay-windowed parlor, then climb the stairway used by the queen of Sweden during her stay. Each guest room is thoughtfully done in a modern color scheme and adorned with several well-chosen paintings by London artists; they come with earphone radios, hair dryers, flowers, and a selection of books. The all-female staff is exceedingly helpful—a definite plus.

Dining: Light meals are available from room service. There's a 24-hour honor bar.

Amenities: Concierge, theater ticket service, car rental, secretarial services, fax machines, sightseeing, babysitting, massage, room service. Access to nearby health club for a small fee; laundromat nearby.

✪ **Franklin Hotel.** 28 Egerton Gardens, London SW3 2DB. ☎ **0171/584-5533.** Fax 0171/584-5449. E-mail: bookings@thefranklin.force9.co.uk. 44 units. A/C MINIBAR TV TEL. £165–£210 ($264–$336) double; from £225 ($360) suite. AE, DC, MC, V. Tube: Knightsbridge.

This gem immediately attracted an audience when it opened in 1992, even drawing discriminating patrons away from Claridge's and the Dorchester. It's the creation of David Naylor-Leyland, who first attracted attention with another little charmer, the Egerton House, down the street; he also owns Dukes Hotel (see "St. James's," above). The Franklin doesn't offer the services and facilities of those giants, but it's intimate and charming. "Private but not so snobbish" is the motto here.

The hotel lies on a quiet Knightsbridge street halfway between Harrods and the center of South Kensington. A dark red honor bar and a series of parlors constitute the lobby. We prefer the Garden Rooms, which open onto a row of red-brick Victorian town houses across the lawn. The bedrooms have canopy beds, antiques, paintings, and floral prints from Colefax and Fowler. The marble bathrooms include such thoughtful extras as power showers and Floris toiletries; several also have bidets. All are air-conditioned, and many have four-poster beds.

Dining: Breakfast is served in the dining room; the surprisingly varied room-service menu ranges from green Thai curry with coconut and mangos to lamb cutlets with rosemary *jus*, and is served there all day as well.

Amenities: 24-hour room service (limited menu 11pm to 7am), dry cleaning and laundry service, turndown and twice-daily maid service, valet parking; babysitting, massage, and secretarial services can be arranged. Access to a nearby health club with pool.

MODERATE

✪ Claverley Hotel. 13–14 Beaufort Gardens, London SW3 1PS. ☎ **800/747-0398** or 0171/589-8541. Fax 0171/584-3410. 25 units (23 with bathroom), 7 suites. MINIBAR TV TEL. £120–£160 ($192–$256) double with bathroom; from £160 ($256) suite. Rates include English breakfast. AE, DC, MC, V. Tube: Knightsbridge.

Set on a quiet cul-de-sac in Knightsbridge a few blocks from Harrods, this small, cozy place has been called the best B&B in London. Awarded the British Tourist Authority's Certificate of Distinction for Bed-and-Breakfast Hotels in 1988, the Claverley continues to maintain the high standards that garnered it such praise. Renovated in 1995 and 1996, it's tastefully accented with Georgian-era accessories; the appealing lounge has 19th-century oil portraits, a Regency fireplace, and a collection of elegant antiques and leather-covered sofas, much as you'd find in a private country house. Most guest rooms have Victorian-inspired wallpaper, wall-to-wall carpeting, and upholstered armchairs, plus marble bathrooms with power showers and hair dryers (some singles don't have en suite facilities). Amenities include laundry service, room service, and secretarial services. A health club is within walking distance.

The outstanding English breakfast includes bacon, tomato, eggs, Cumberland sausage, homemade waffles with maple syrup, and the cook's specialty, fresh salmon kedgeree. In the lounge, complimentary tea, coffee, hot chocolate, and cookies are available around the clock.

Knightsbridge Green Hotel. 159 Knightsbridge, London SW1X 7PD. ☎ **0171/584-6274.** Fax 0171/225-1635. E-mail: theKGHotel@aol.com. 27 units. A/C MINIBAR TV TEL. £135 ($216) double; £155 ($248) suite. AE, DC, MC, V. Tube: Knightsbridge.

Many return guests from around the world view this dignified 1890s structure as their home away from home. In 1966, when it was converted into a hotel, the developers were careful to retain its wide baseboards, cove moldings, high ceilings, and spacious proportions. Even without kitchens, the well-furnished suites come close to apartment-style living; all have trouser presses and hair dryers. The amenities and decor here don't measure up to the Claverley (see above), but this is still a solid choice, and it's just around the corner from Harrods. Coffee, tea, and pastries are available throughout the day; babysitting, dry cleaning, and laundry service are other perks.

Knightsbridge Hotel. 12 Beaufort Gardens, London SW3 1PT. ☎ **0171/589-9271.** Fax 0171/823-9692. www.knightsbridge.co.uk. 40 units. MINIBAR TV TEL. £135 ($216) double. Rates include English or continental breakfast. AE, MC, V. Parking free on street from 6pm to 8am, or £12 ($19) at a nearby garage. Tube: Knightsbridge.

The Knightsbridge attracts visitors from all over the world seeking a small hotel in a high-rent district. It's fabulously located, sandwiched between fashionable Beauchamp Place and Harrods, and with many of the city's top theaters and museums close at hand, including the Royal Albert Hall and Madame Tussaud's. Built in the early 1800s as a private town house, this family-run place sits on a tranquil, tree-lined square, free from traffic. Small and unpretentious, with a subdued Victorian ambience, it's been recently renovated to a high standard: All the well-furnished rooms have a private bathroom, hair dryer, coffeemaker, trouser press, and safety-deposit box. Amenities include room service, laundry service, and a concierge. There's also a small health club with a steam room and a spa for guests' use.

IN NEARBY BELGRAVIA
VERY EXPENSIVE
✪ The Lanesborough. Hyde Park corner, London SW1X 7TA. ☎ **800/999-1828** or 0171/259-5599. Fax 0171/259-5606. www.roewood-hotels.com. 95 units. A/C MINIBAR TV TEL. £305–£420 ($488–$672) double; from £480 ($768) suite. AE, CB, DC, MC, V. Parking $3.50/hour. Tube: Hyde Park Corner.

One of London's grandest hotels was created from the dreary hospital wards that Florence Nightingale made famous. This Regency-style four-story hotel vies with the Dorchester for sophistication (although it falls short of the Dorch's time-honored experience). When Rosewood Hotels and Resorts (known for managing top hotels like the Bel-Air in Los Angeles and Dallas's Mansion on Turtle Creek) upgraded the building into a luxury hotel, most of the Georgian details were retained. The guest rooms are as opulent and antique-stuffed as the public spaces; each has electronic sensors to alert the staff as to when a resident is in or out, a CD player, VCR, personal safe, fax machine, 24-channel satellite TV, a bathroom with every conceivable amenity, triple glazing on the windows, and the services of a personal butler. Security is tight—there are at least 35 surveillance cameras.

   Dining: The Conservatory is an elegant restaurant with decor inspired by the Chinese, Indian, and Gothic motifs of the Brighton Pavilion. **The Library Bar**—which opens into a Regency-era hideaway, charmingly named "The Withdrawing Room"— re-creates the atmosphere of an elegant private club.

   Amenities: Personal butlers, concierges, room service, dry cleaning and laundry service, massage, babysitting, secretarial services. Car rental, business center, small fitness studio; exercise equipment (Stairmasters, stationary bicycles) can be delivered directly to your room.

MODERATE
✪ Diplomat Hotel. 2 Chesham St., London SW1X 3DT. ☎ **0171/235-1544.** Fax 0171/259-6153. 27 units. TV TEL. £120–£150 ($192–$240) double. Rates include English buffet breakfast. AE, CB, DC, MC, V. Tube: Sloane Sq. or Knightsbridge.

Part of the Diplomat's charm is that it is a small, reasonably priced hotel in an otherwise prohibitively expensive neighborhood filled with privately owned Victorian homes and first-class, high-rise hotels. Only minutes from Harrods, it was built in 1882 as a private residence by the noted architect Thomas Cubbitt. It's very well appointed: The registration desk is framed by the sweep of a partially gilded circular staircase; above it, cherubs gaze down from a Regency-era chandelier. The staff is helpful, well-mannered, and discreet. The high-ceilinged guest rooms are tastefully done in a Victorian style; many were renovated in 1996. Amenities include a massage service, business center, afternoon tea, and a snack menu available daily 1 to 8:30pm. A health club is located nearby. *Note:* Some readers have commented that the hotel is not exactly state-of-the-art. If you're expecting regal accommodations, remember that this is a moderately priced London hotel, and you often get what you pay for.

4 Chelsea

MODERATE

Blair House Hotel. 34 Draycott Place, London SW3 2SA. ☎ **0171/581-2323.** Fax 0171/823-7752. www.demon.co.uk/hotel-net/blair.html. E-mail: 11317.637@compuserve.com. 11 units. TV TEL. £110–£117 ($176–$187) double. Extra bed £18 ($29). Rates include continental breakfast. AE, DC, MC, V. Tube: Sloane Sq.

If you can't afford a luxury hotel, this comfortable B&B-style hotel in the heart of Chelsea near Sloane Square is a good alternative. An older building of some architectural interest, it's been completely refurbished inside. The rooms are individually decorated, but may have too many flowery prints for most tastes. They all come with such amenities as a coffeemaker, hair dryer, and trouser press. Although most singles are small, some rooms are spacious enough to accommodate four. Babysitting and laundry service can be arranged. Only breakfast is served. If you're bothered by noise, ask for a quieter room in the back.

INEXPENSIVE

✪ **Wilbraham Hotel.** 1–5 Wilbraham Place (off Sloane St.), London SW1X 9AE. ☎ **0171/730-8296.** Fax 0171/730-6815. 59 units. TV TEL. £97 ($155) double; from £99 ($158) suite. No credit cards. Parking £17.50 ($28). Tube: Sloane Sq.

This dyed-in-the-wool British hotel is set on a quiet residential street, just a few hundred yards from Sloane Square. Occupying three Victorian town houses, it's a bit faded, but the traditionally furnished, wood-paneled bedrooms are well-maintained and have fireplaces and leaded glass windows. There are even heated towel racks in the bathroom—a lovely comfort on a cold gray London morning. The best double—certainly the most spacious—is no. 1. There's an attractive old-fashioned lounge where you can order drinks, simple lunches, and traditional English dinners. Despite its small size, guest services include room service, babysitting, dry cleaning and laundry service.

5 Kensington & South Kensington

KENSINGTON
INEXPENSIVE

✪ **Abbey House.** 11 Vicarage Gate, London W8 4AG. ☎ **0171/727-2594.** 16 units (none with bathroom). TV. £65 ($104) double; £78 ($125) triple; £90 ($144) quad. Rates include English breakfast. No credit cards. Tube: High St. Kensington.

Some hotel critics have rated this among the best B&Bs in London, and it's recommended by more travel guides than any of its peers. So it must be doing something right—and it is, offering peace, tranquility, and affordability in a very good location, next to Kensington Gardens and the Royal Palace. This is a family-run business, and you can tell: A keen sense of dedication and hospitality abounds. Built about 1860 on a typical Victorian square, Abbey House has been completely modernized. Although rooms are refurbished annually, many original features have been retained. All accommodations are spacious and have central heating and washbasins; two units share a bathroom. Rooms may be too frilly for some, but if you're looking for a small London hotel offering charm, cheery service, and a touch of class, look no further. Complimentary tea and coffee are available around the clock in the tearoom.

Vicarage Private Hotel. 10 Vicarage Gate, London W8 4AG. ☎ **0171/229-4030.** Fax 0171/792-5989. www.deadlock.com/hotels/vicarage. E-mail: reception@londonvicaragehotel. com. 18 units (none with bathroom). £63 ($101) double; £80 ($128) triple; £88 ($141) family room for 4. Rates include English breakfast. No credit cards. Tube: High St. Kensington or Notting Hill Gate.

Eileen and Martin Diviney have a host of admirers on all continents. Their hotel is tops for old-fashioned English charm, affordable prices, and hospitality. Situated on a residential garden square close to Kensington High Street, as well as the Portobello Road Market, this Victorian town house retains many original features. Individually furnished in a country-house style, the bedrooms can accommodate up to four. If you want a little nest to hide away in, opt for the top floor eyrie (no. 19), a private retreat like Noël Coward used to occupy before "I got rich enough to move downstairs." Guests meet in a cozy sitting room for conversation and to watch the telly. As a thoughtful extra, hot drinks are available 24 hours a day. In the morning, a hearty English breakfast awaits.

SOUTH KENSINGTON
VERY EXPENSIVE

○ Blake's Hotel. 33 Roland Gardens, London SW7 3PF. ☎ **800/926-3173** or 0171/370-6701. Fax 0171/373-0442. E-mail: blakes@easynet.co.uk. 51 units. MINIBAR TV TEL. £155–£300 ($248–$480) double; from £475–£695 ($760–$1,112) suite. AE, DC, MC, V. Parking £30 ($48). Tube: South Kensington or Gloucester Rd.

This opulent and highly individual creation of actress Anouska Hempel Weinberg is one of London's best small hotels. No expense was spared in converting this former row of Victorian town houses into one of the city's most original hotels. It's now Oriental nights down in old Kensington: The individually decorated, elaborately appointed rooms contain such treasures and touches as Venetian glassware, cloth-covered walls, swagged draperies, even the Empress Josephine's daybed; the richly appointed lobby boasts British Raj-era furniture from India. Although a formidable rival, the Pelham (see below) doesn't match Blake's in sophistication and style. Go for a deluxe room if you can manage it; the standard singles and doubles are tiny.

Dining: The stylish restaurant is one of the best in town. Neville Campbell's cuisine blends the finest of East and West, ranging from baked sea bass with a crispy fennel skin to chicken and crab shaped like a large delectable Fabergé egg. With cuisine this fabulous, it's no wonder that reservations are strictly observed.

Amenities: 24-hour room service, laundry service, babysitting, secretarial services, and an arrange-anything concierge. Access to a nearby health club for a fee.

EXPENSIVE

The Cranley. 10–12 Bina Gardens, London SW5 0LA. ☎ **800/553-2582** or 0171/373-0123. Fax 0171/373-9497. www.thecranley.co.uk. 37 units. A/C TV TEL. £140–£160 ($224–$256) double; £180–£220 ($288–$352) suite. AE, DC, MC, V. Tube: Gloucester Rd.

A trio of adjacent 1875 town houses became the Cranley Hotel when its Michigan-based owners upgraded the buildings into one of the most charming hotels in South Kensington. All the high-ceilinged guest rooms have enormous windows, much of their original plasterwork, scattered antiques, and plush upholstery, and the public rooms are like a stage set for an English country house. It all adds up to a vivid 19th-century ambience that makes this feel more like a private residence than a hotel. All but one of the guest rooms—which also come with such extras as hair dryers and bathrobes—have tiny kitchenettes. Ground-floor suites open onto a private terrace and have Jacuzzis.

Dining: There's no restaurant, but light meals are served in a small cafe.

Amenities: Room service daily from 7am to 11pm, dry cleaning and laundry service, secretarial services available during office hours. Access to a nearby health club.

✪ **The Gore.** 189 Queen's Gate, London SW7 5EX. ☎ **800/637-7200** or 0171/584-6601. Fax 0171/589-8127. www.gorehotels.co.uk. E-mail: reservations@gorehotels.co.uk. 54 units. MINIBAR TV TEL. £175–£255 ($280–$408) double; £280 ($448) The Tudor Room. AE, DC, MC, V. Tube: Gloucester Rd.

Once owned by the Marquess of Queensberry's family, the Gore has been a hotel since 1892—and it's always been one of our favorites. Victorians would still feel at home here among all the walnut and mahogany, walls covered in antique photos, and Oriental carpets on the floors; throughout the hotel is a collection of some 4,000 English prints. The Gore has always been cited for its eccentricity—the Venus Room, for example, has a bed once owned by Judy Garland. Each room is different, so try to find one that suits your personality. The dark-paneled Tudor Room is the most fascinating, with its gallery and fireplace. Rooms no longer go for the 1892 price of 50p, but they're still a good value.

Dining: It's worth a trip across town to dine at renowned chef Antony Worrall Thompson's **Bistro 190,** especially for the marinated squid, the roast cod with twice-baked endive, and the steamed mussels with green curry.

Amenities: Concierge, room service daily from 7am to 12:20am, dry cleaning and laundry service. Newspaper delivery, babysitting, secretarial services, and express checkout may be arranged. Access to health club next door.

Pelham Hotel. 15 Cromwell Place, London SW7 2LA. ☎ **0171/589-8288.** Fax 0171/ 584-8444. E-mail: pelham@firmdale.com. 52 units. A/C MINIBAR TV TEL. £175–£225 ($280–$360) double; from £350 ($560) suite. AE, MC, V. Tube: South Kensington.

This small hotel is sure to please discerning travelers from all walks of life. Hoteliers extraordinaire Kit and Tim Kemp preside over one of the most stunningly decorated establishments in London, formed from a row of early 19th-century terrace houses with a white portico facade. In the drawing room, 18th-century paneling, high ceilings, and fine moldings create a suitable backdrop for a collection of antiques and Victorian art; needlepoint rugs and cushions evoke a homelike warmth, and an honor bar completes the clublike atmosphere. The sumptuously decorated rooms are outfitted with eiderdown duvets, Oriental carpets, and unique oils; even the smallest room will have a handsome desk. The location is ideal, close to the Victoria and Albert Museum, Hyde Park, and Harrods, and returning guests are welcomed here like part of an extended family.

Dining: Kemps is one of the finest restaurants in South Kensington.

Amenities: 24-hour room service, concierge, babysitting, dry cleaning and laundry service, maid service, business services; a health club is nearby.

MODERATE

✪ **Aster House Hotel.** 3 Sumner Place, London SW7 3EE. ☎ **0171/581-5888.** Fax 0171/584-4925. E-mail: asterhouse@btinternet.com. 12 units. A/C MINIBAR TV TEL. £115–£145 ($184–$232) double. Rates include continental breakfast. MC, V. Tube: South Kensington.

At the end of an early Victorian terrace built in 1848, Aster House is the epitome of discretion; there's not even a sign outside to indicate that this is a hotel. Ring the bell and traverse a pink marble floor, where you'll be greeted by a welcoming staff; the owners, Rachel and Peter Carapiet, will even give you your own front door key. By now they've won so many awards they've lost count—their prizes range from the Spencer Trophy for the best B&B in London to the "London in Bloom" award for their back garden (the only place you're allowed to smoke). Each bedroom is individually decorated in English country-house style, many with four-poster, half-canopied beds and silk wallpaper; although many other hotels do this better, the effect is warm and inviting (the showers are a bit too cozy, however). Breakfasts, served in the glassed-in garden conservatory, are more health-conscious than what you expect from an English B&B. The place is a charmer, especially for the price—similar hotels ask for £250 a night.

○ 5 Sumner Place. 5 Sumner Place, London SW7 3EE. ☎ **0171/584-7586.** Fax 0171/823-9962. www.dspace.dial.pipex.com/town/estate/vz/15. E-mail: no.5@dial.pipex.com. 14 units. MINIBAR TV TEL. £116–£130 ($186–$208) double. Rates include English breakfast. AE, MC, V. Tube: South Kensington.

This little charmer is frequently cited as one of the best B&Bs in the greater Kensington area, and we agree. Completely restored in an elegant, classically English style that captures the flavor of its bygone era, this Victorian terrace house (ca. 1848) now enjoys landmark status. You'll feel the ambience as soon as you enter the reception hall and are welcomed by the graceful staff. After you register, you're given your own front door key—and London is yours. An elevator will take you up to the guest floors, where the well-maintained rooms are tastefully done in traditional period furnishings; all have TV, radio, and phones, and a few have refrigerators. Hotel services include room service, massage, babysitting, dry cleaning and laundry service, and concierge. Breakfast is served in a Victorian-style conservatory.

The Gallery. 8–10 Queensberry Place, London SW7 2EA. ☎ **0171/915-0000.** Fax 0171/915-4400. www.eeh.co.uk. E-mail: gallery@eeh.co.uk. 36 units. TV TEL. £115 ($184) double; £195 ($312) junior suite. Extra bed £20 ($32). Rates include buffet English breakfast. AE, DC, MC, V. Tube: South Kensington.

This is the place for you if you want to stay in an exclusive little town-house hotel, but don't want to pay £300 a night for the privilege. Two splendid Georgian residences have been completely restored and converted into this remarkable hotel (which remains relatively unknown). The location is ideal, near the Victoria and Albert Museum, Royal Albert Hall, Harrods, Knightsbridge, and King's Road. Bedrooms are individually designed and elegantly decorated in Laura Ashley style, with half-canopied beds and luxurious marble-tiled bathrooms with brass fittings. The junior suites have private roof terraces, minibars, Jacuzzis, and air-conditioning. A team of butlers takes care of everything. The lounge, with its rich mahogany paneling and moldings and deep colors, has the ambience of a private club. The drawing room beckons you to a quiet corner. The Gallery Room displays works for sale by known and unknown artists. There's 24-hour room service, use of a nearby fitness center and pool, plus concierge, dry cleaning and laundry service, babysitting, and secretarial services.

Harrington Hall. 5–25 Harrington Gardens, London SW7 4JW. ☎ **800/44-UTELL** or 0171/396-9696. Fax 0171/396-9090. 200 units. A/C MINIBAR TV TEL. £160 ($256) double; £185 ($296) suite. AE, DC, MC, V. Tube: Gloucester Rd.

What a comeback! This six-story terrace house of once-battered apartments has been completely gutted and restored, and it's now one of the most inviting addresses in the Kensington area. One of London's few remaining large, privately owned hotels, it conceals its charm behind an original 1870 facade constructed at the peak of Victoria's reign. Rates are about half of those across the street at the stellar Gloucester—and this hotel is every bit as good. The beautifully designed classical lobby sets the tone for tasteful and stylish bedrooms (some are much more spacious than others); flowery fabrics and patterned carpets create a real English ambience. Perks include 24-hour room service, same-day dry cleaning and laundry service, business center, concierge, and babysitting. There's also a fitness center with gym, saunas, and showers.

The lounge bar, furnished in exotic Burr Vavona and with a marble fireplace, is a good rendezvous point. A classically decorated restaurant serves up better-than-average food and a good-value buffet.

Number Sixteen. 16 Sumner Place, London SW7 3EG. ☎ **800/592-5387** or 0171/589-5232. Fax 0171/584-8615. 36 units (34 with bathroom). MINIBAR TV TEL. £110 ($176) double without bathroom, £157–£189 ($252–$302) double with bathroom; £200 ($320) triple with bathroom. Rates include continental breakfast. AE, DC, MC, V. Parking £20 ($32). Tube: South Kensington.

This is an elegant and luxurious pension, composed of four early-Victorian town houses linked to form a dramatically organized whole. The hotel won four garden awards in 1994 and was named the best B&B in London in 1992. The front and rear gardens are scrupulously maintained, with swaths of greenery that make this one of the most idyllic spots on the street. The rooms are done in an eclectic mix of English antiques and modern paintings, although some look a little faded. There's an honor-system bar in the library. On chilly days, a fire roars in the flowery drawing room's fireplace, although some prefer the more macho library. Breakfast is served in the privacy of your bedroom, and tea and coffee service is available from 7am to 10:30pm. You can also take breakfast in the conservatory or, if the weather's good, in the garden, with its bubbling fountain and fish pond. Guests have access to a nearby health club with pool.

The Regency Hotel. 100 Queen's Gate, London SW7 5AG. ☎ **800/328-9898** or 0171/370-4595. Fax 0171/370-5555. E-mail: regency.london@dial.pipex.com. 209 units. A/C MINIBAR TV TEL. £139 ($222) double; from £199–£235 ($318–$376) suite. AE, DC, MC, V. Tube: South Kensington.

On a street lined with Doric porticoes close to museums, Kensington, and Knightsbridge, six Victorian terrace houses were converted into one stylish, seamless whole by an army of construction engineers and decorators. A Chippendale fireplace, flanked by wing chairs, greets you in the polished reception area. One of the building's main stairwells has what could be London's most unusual lighting fixture: five Empire chandeliers suspended vertically, one on top of the other. The modernized guest rooms are tasteful and elegant.

The **Pavilion** is a glamorous but reasonably priced restaurant specializing in international cuisine (see chapter 5 for a review). Amenities include 24-hour room service; laundry service; babysitting; a health club with steam rooms, saunas, and sensory-deprivation tank; a mini gym; and a business center.

INEXPENSIVE

✪ **Aston's Budget Studios & Aston's Designer Studios and Suites.** 39 Rosary Gardens, London SW7 4NQ. ☎ **800/525-2810** in the U.S., or 0171/370-0737. Fax 0171/835-1419. 76 studios and apts (54 with bathroom). A/C TV TEL. Budget Studios £68 ($109) double; £95 ($152) triple; £115 ($184) quad. Designer Studios £105 ($168) double. Weekly rentals are preferred, but daily rentals are accepted. MC, V. Tube: Gloucester Rd.

This carefully restored row of Victorian town houses offers comfortably furnished studios and suites that are London's best values. Heavy oak doors and 18th-century hunting pictures give the foyer a rich traditional atmosphere. Accommodations range in size and style from budget to designer; every one has a compact but complete kitchenette concealed behind doors. If you go for a budget studio, you'll share a fully serviced bathroom with only a handful of other guests. The air-conditioned designer studios and two-room designer suites are decorated with rich fabrics and furnishings and have their own marble bathrooms. Amenities include laundry service, secretarial services, guests' message line, fax machines, private catering on request, car and limousine service, and daily maid service in the designer studios and suites.

Hotel 167. 167 Old Brompton Rd., London SW5 OAN. ☎ **0171/373-0672.** Fax 0171/ 373-3360. 19 units. MINIBAR TV TEL. £90–£99 ($148–$163) double. Rates include continental breakfast. AE, DC, MC, V. Tube: Gloucester Rd.

Hotel 167 is one of the more fashionable guest houses in the area, attracting a mix of Generation-Xers and young 30-somethings as well as business people and journalists who like its central location; the Manic Street Preachers even wrote a song about it. Occupying a three-story Victorian town house, it's quite stylishly decorated, with Scandinavian modern and Japanese accents: Each room is a comfortable medley of contemporary, antique, and art deco, with big modern paintings decorating the walls. The basement rooms have big windows; being assigned a room in the basement doesn't sound very appealing, but returning guests often end up requesting them because of their cozy feeling. *Tattler* magazine has compared Hotel 167 with Blake's (above) and the Portobello (below) for its amenities, but we wouldn't get that carried away. Owner-manager Frank Cheevers is helpful and friendly and a font of information about London.

Swiss House Hotel. 171 Old Brompton Rd., London SW5 OAN. ☎ **0171/373-2769.** Fax 0171/373-4983. E-mail: recep@swiss-hh.demon.co.uk. 16 units (14 with bath). TV TEL. £75 ($120) double with bathroom; £94 ($150) triple with bathroom; £106 ($170) quad with bathroom. Rates include continental breakfast. AE, CB, DC, MC, V. Tube: Gloucester Rd.

This appealing B&B, in a Victorian row house with a portico festooned with flowers and vines in the heart of South Kensington, is close to the South Kensington museums, Kensington Gardens, and the main exhibition centers of Earl's Court and Olympia. Some of its individually designed country-style guest rooms have fireplaces, and there's enough chintz to please the most avid Anglophile. Try to avoid the rooms along the street, as traffic is heavy; even with double-glazing, they get noisy. Instead, try to book one of the rear bedrooms, which overlook a communal garden and have a view of the London skyline. And there's a luxury that you won't get in most B&Bs: Room service—nothing elaborate, just soups and sandwiches—is available from noon to 9pm. Additional services include babysitting, massage, secretarial services, and laundry service.

IN NEARBY WEST KENSINGTON
INEXPENSIVE

Avonmore Hotel. 66 Avonmore Rd., London W14 8RS. ☎ **0171/603-4296.** Fax 0171/603-4035. 9 units. MINIBAR TV TEL. £70–£80 ($112–$128) double; £80–£90 ($128–$144) triple. Rates include English breakfast. AE, CB, MC, V. Tube: West Kensington.

Avonmore is easily accessible to West End theaters and shops, yet it's located in a quiet neighborhood, only 2 minutes from the West Kensington stop on the Underground's District Line. This privately owned place—a former National Award winner as the best private hotel in London—boasts wall-to-wall carpeting, radio alarms, hair dryers, and central heating in each tastefully decorated room. The owner, Margaret McKenzie, provides lots of personal service, including some secretarial services, room service (until midnight), and laundry service. An English breakfast is served in a cheerful breakfast room, and a wide range of drinks is available in the cozy bar.

6 Earl's Court

MODERATE

Amber Hotel. 101 Lexham Gardens, London W8 6JN. ☎ **0171/373-8666.** Fax 0171/ 835-1194. 40 units. TV TEL. £100–£120 ($160–$192) double. Rates include buffet breakfast. AE, DC, MC, V. Tube: Earl's Court.

This charming, graceful hotel is an inviting oasis in a sea of bad B&Bs. The welcoming staff makes you feel at home at this 1860 house on a terraced street, close to Kensington Gardens, the South Kensington museums, and Holland Park. The majority of the rooms are singles, but there are also 4 twins and 11 double-bedded rooms, along with 2 very attractive executive rooms. The conservatively decorated rooms have such extras as a refreshment tray, radio, satellite TV, and trouser press as well as touches of lavender that can brighten a gray London day, but they're all on the small side; the private bathrooms are cramped but well-maintained. The private garden out back is almost reason enough alone to stay here. Breakfast is served buffet style in the lounge. Basic services include dry cleaning and laundry service, and concierge.

INEXPENSIVE

Aaron House. 17 Courtfield Gardens, London SW5 OPD. ☎ **0171/370-3991.** Fax 0171/373-2303. 23 units (13 with bathroom). £44 ($70) double without bathroom, £53 ($85) double with bathroom; £58 ($93) triple without bathroom, £65 ($104) triple with bathroom; £76 ($122) quad with bathroom. Rates include continental breakfast. MC, V. Tube: Earl's Court.

In the budget district of London known as "Kangaroo Court" because so many Australians stay here, Aaron House stands out. You'll be welcomed with courtesy to this former family home on a Victorian square. Even though it's been considerably modernized and upgraded, many of its original features are intact. Look for the original tile entry and the lacy scrolled staircase leading to the pleasantly comfortable bedrooms, which are small but beautifully kept. Some even have their original fireplaces (no longer in use). The largest rooms overlook the street, which can be noisy at times. If you don't expect miracles, you'll find this an affordable and tasteful place to lay your head.

Henley House. 30 Barkston Gardens, London SW5 0EN. ☎ **0171/370-4111.** Fax 0171/370-0026. 20 units. TV TEL. £97 ($155) double. Rates include continental breakfast. AE, CB, DC, MC, V. Tube: Earl's Court.

This newly refurbished B&B stands out from the dreary pack around Earl's Court— and it's a better value than most. The red-brick Victorian row house sits on a communal fenced-in garden that you can enter by borrowing a key from the reception desk. The helpful staff takes a keen interest in the welfare of their guests and are very happy to take bewildered newcomers under their wing. A ground-floor sitting room overlooks a rear courtyard. The decor is bright and contemporary; a typical room has warmly patterned Anna French wallpaper, chintz fabrics, and solid brass lighting fixtures. Breakfast is a cheerful event around here, served in a room decorated with terracotta accents and pots of dried flowers where guests meet and compare notes. For those who prefer to stay in after dark rather than hitting the area's hot spots (mostly gay bars), there's a shelf of books you're welcome to borrow. Babysitting is available for parents wanting to go to places children can't visit.

Rushmore Hotel. 11 Trebovir Rd., London SW5 9LS. ☎ **0171/370-3839.** Fax 0171/370-0274. 22 units. TV TEL. £79–£85 ($126–$136) double; £89–£95 ($142–$152) triple; £99–£110 ($158–$176) family room for 4 or 5. Rates include buffet breakfast. AE, CB, MC, V. Tube: Earl's Court.

Although it became quite run-down in the early 1970s, this Victorian row house (behind an brick-faced Italianate facade) received a complete overhaul in 1987; today, it's one of the most pleasing hotels in a low-budget neighborhood. Built in 1876, the hotel stands on the former site of the Manor House of Earl's Court Farm; manorial courts were held here until the mid-1850s. As long as you don't require atriums and minibars, the Rushmore proves that it's still possible to get good service and a fine room in London at an affordable price. The multilingual staff works hard to make your visit rewarding. The rooms are individually decorated in a variety of period schemes; those with private bathrooms have such touches as marble tiling and brass fittings. The breakfast room is beautifully outfitted with French limestone floors, unique Murano glass wall- and floor-lighting created by Missoni, wrought-iron furniture from Tuscany, and antique terra-cotta urns holding exotic cacti. Amenities include dry cleaning and laundry service, theater bookings, fax service, security boxes for safeguarding valuables, and babysitting.

7 Notting Hill

MODERATE

The Abbey Court. 20 Pembridge Gardens, London W2 4DU. ☎ **0171/221-7518.** Fax 0171/792-0858. www.lhdr.demon.co.uk. 25 units. TV TEL. £130–£145 ($208–$232) double; £175 ($280) suite with four-poster bed. AE, CB, MC, V. Tube: Notting Hill Gate.

This first-rate hotel is a small white-fronted mid-Victorian town house with a flower-filled patio in front and a conservatory in back. Its recently renovated lobby is graciously decorated and has a sunny bay window, floral draperies, and a comfortable sofa and chairs. You'll always find fresh flowers in the reception area and the hallways. Each room has carefully coordinated fabrics and fine furnishings, mostly 18th- and 19th-century country antiques. Done in Italian marble, bathrooms are equipped with a Jacuzzi bath, shower, and heated towel racks. Light snacks and drinks are available from room service 24 hours a day and breakfast is served in the conservatory. Kensington Gardens is a short walk away, as are the antiques stores along Portobello Road and Kensington Church Street. Other amenities include babysitting, dry cleaning, laundry service, and concierge.

Pembridge Court Hotel. 34 Pembridge Gardens, London W2 4DX. ☎ **0171/229-9977.** Fax 0171/727-4982. 20 units. TV TEL. £135–£170 ($216–$272) double. Rates include English breakfast. AE, DC, MC, V. Tube: Notting Hill Gate.

In an 1852 private Victorian home, this hotel presents an elegant cream-colored neo-classical facade in an increasingly fashionable Notting Hill Gate residential neighborhood. Avid antique hunters like its proximity to Portobello Road. Most guest rooms contain at least one antique, as well as 19th-century engravings and plenty of warm-toned floral fabrics. Some of the largest and most stylish rooms are on the top floor, with bathrooms tiled in Italian marble. Three air-conditioned deluxe rooms, all with VCRs, overlook Portobello Road: The Spencer and Churchill rooms are decorated in blues and yellows, and the Windsor Room has a contrasting array of tartans. Also called Spencer and Churchill are a pair of ginger cats, two of the most adorable in London. Churchill likes the pop stars who stay at the hotel; Spencer tries to avoid them.

Good French, Thai, and English food is served at **Caps,** the hotel restaurant, which also boasts a well-chosen wine list; it's open to guests only from 4 to 11pm. Services include 24-hour room service, same-day dry cleaning and laundry service, and babysitting. A car-rental agency is on the premises, and day membership in a nearby health club is available.

The Portobello Hotel. 22 Stanley Gardens, London W11 2NG. ☎ **0171/727-2777.** Fax 0171/792-9641. 25 units. TV TEL. £135–£140 ($216–$224) double; £175–£210 ($280–$336) suite. Rates include continental breakfast. Tube: Notting Hill Gate.

Mixing an eclectic medley of styles, two six-floor town houses dating from 1850 on an elegant Victorian terrace near the Portobello antiques market were combined to form a quirky property that doesn't please everybody, but has its devotees. We remember these rooms when they looked better, but although they're tattered here and there, they still have plenty of character—whimsy and a fair measure of flamboyance went into their design. Who knows what will show up in what nook? Perhaps a Chippendale, a multi-nozzle clawfoot tub, or a round bed tucked under a gauze canopy. Try for no. 16, with a full-tester bed facing the garden. Some of the cheaper rooms are so tiny they're cabin-like garrets (some consider them romantic). An elevator will take you as far as the third floor; after that, it's the stairs. Some rooms are air-conditioned. Don't expect top-notch service; it's erratic at best. A 24-hour bar and restaurant in the basement is a local favorite, and provides hotel room services.

INEXPENSIVE

The Gate Hotel. 6 Portobello Rd., London W11 3DG. ☎ **0171/221-2403.** Fax 0171/ 221-9128. www.smoothhound.co.uk/hotels/gate.html. 6 units. MINIBAR TV. £65–£72 ($104–$115) double. Rates include continental breakfast. AE, DC, MC, V. Tube: Notting Hill Gate.

This antique-hunters' favorite is the only hotel along the entire length of Portobello Road—and because of rigid zoning restrictions, it will probably remain the only one for many years to come. It was built in the 1820s as housing for the farmhands working the orchards and vegetable plots at the now-defunct Portobello Farms and has functioned as a hotel since 1932. It has two cramped but cozy bedrooms on each of its three floors, plus a renovated breakfast room in the cellar. Be prepared for some *very* steep English stairs. Rooms are color-coordinated, with a bit of style, and have such amenities as a full-length mirror and built-in wardrobe. Especially intriguing are the wall paintings that show what the Portobello Market was in its early days: Every character looks straight from a Dickens novel. The on-site manager can direct you to the antiques markets and the attractions of Notting Hill Gate and nearby Kensington Gardens, both of which lie within a 5-minute walk.

IN NEARBY HOLLAND PARK
VERY EXPENSIVE

✪ **Halcyon Hotel.** 81 Holland Park Ave., London W11 3RZ. ☎ **800/595-5416,** 800/457-4000, or 0171/727-7288. www.halcyon-hotel.co.uk. 63 units. A/C MINIBAR TV TEL. £260 ($416) double; from £295 ($472) suite. AE, DC, MC, V. Tube: Holland Park.

Only a small brass plaque distinguishes the aptly named Halcyon from other buildings on its street. The grandest of London's small hotels, it was formed in 1985 by uniting a pair of Victorian mansions; today, they constitute a hotel of charm, comfort, and urban sophistication. The clientele includes a bevy of international film and recording stars who like the privacy and anonymity it offers. This is where Brad Pitt stays when he's in London. Nearly half the accommodations are suites, lavishly outfitted like an Edwardian country house with a modern twist. Several boast such whimsical touches as tented ceilings; all have been refurbished and are outfitted with all the modern conveniences. The public rooms are inviting oases, with trompe l'oeil paintings against backgrounds of turquoise.

Dining: The hotel's superb French restaurant, **The Room at the Halcyon,** is recommended in chapter 5.

Amenities: 24-hour room service, 1-hour pressing service, message-paging system (for which beepers are provided) extending 20 miles from the hotel, babysitting, night safes, and a theater desk, business center, access to tennis club and health club.

Marylebone, Paddington, Bayswater & Notting Hill Gate Hotels

The Abbey Court 5	Durrants Hotel 24	Kenwood House Hotel 22
Adare House 12	Edward Lear Hotel 18	Landmark London 20
Boston Court Hotel 16	Europa House Hotel 13	Mornington Hotel 10
Bryanston Court Hotel 19	Fairways Hotel 11	Norfolk Court 14
Byron Hotel 7	The Gate Hotel 3	Parkwood Hotel 17
Colonnade Hotel 9	Halycon Hotel 1	Pembridge Court Hotel 4
Darlington Hyde Park 15	Hart House Hotel 23	The Phoenix Hotel 6
Dorset Square Hotel 21	The Hempel 8	Portobello Hotel 2
		St. David's Hotel 14

8 Paddington & Bayswater

VERY EXPENSIVE

✪ The Hempel. 31–35 Craven Hill Gardens, London W2 3EA. ☎ **0171/298-9000.** Fax 0171/402-4666. www.hempelhotel.com. E-mail: the-hempel@easynet.co.uk. 42 units. A/C MINIBAR TV TEL. £200–£225 ($320–$360) double; from £370 ($592) suite. AE, CB, DC, DISC, MC, V. Tube: Lancaster Gate.

Set in a trio of nearly identical 19th-century row houses, this hotel is the newest statement of flamboyant interior designer Anouska Hempel. Don't expect the swags, tassels, and labyrinthine elegance of her better-established hotel, Blake's (see above)—the feeling here is radically different. The Hempel manages to combine a grand Italian sense of proportion with Asian simplicity, all meant for capitalists rich enough to afford it. Its artful simplicity is like that of a Zen temple. Soothing monochromatic tones prevail. The deliberately underfurnished lobby is flanked by symmetrical fireplaces; throughout the hotel are carefully positioned mementos from Asia, including Thai bullock carts that double as coffee tables. Bedrooms continue the minimalist theme, except for their carefully concealed battery of electronic accessories, which includes a VCR, satellite TV control, CD player, twin phone lines, and modem hookup. The hotel mostly caters to business travelers from around the world, most of whom appreciate its tactful service and undeniably snobbish overtones.

Dining: In the cellar is an innovative restaurant and bar, **I-Thai** (see review in chapter 5).

Amenities: 24-hour room service, concierge, dry cleaning and laundry service, turndown and twice-daily maid service, massage, express checkout, limited business services; babysitting can be arranged. Conference rooms, access to nearby health club.

MODERATE

Darlington Hyde Park. 111–117 Sussex Gardens, London W2 2RU. ☎ **0171/460-8800.** Fax 0171/460-8828. www.members.aol.com/darlinghp. E-mail: darlinghp@aol.com. 45 units. TV TEL. £100 ($160) double; £110–£120 ($176–$192) suite. Rates include continental breakfast. AE, DC, MC, V. Tube: Paddington.

Although not flashy and lacking a full range of services, the Darlington Hyde Park is a winning choice and good value for Central London. Rooms are in an updated Victorian style, tasteful and neatly decorated, albeit a bit short of flair. The maintenance is good, however, and a happy blend of business people and vacationers check in here. Five bedrooms are non-smoking. The hotel restaurant serves breakfast only (continental or English).There is no bar but guests are invited to BYOB (bring your own bottle) and drink in the lounge. **La Cuisine,** a nearby modern European restaurant, caters room service for the hotel. Dry cleaning and laundry service are available, and there's a health club nearby.

Mornington Hotel. 12 Lancaster Gate, London W2 3LG. ☎ **800/528-1234** or 0171/ 262-7361. Fax 0171/706-1028. www.mornington.se. E-mail: mornington.hotel-sth@wmhotels.se. 66 units. TV TEL. £99–£140 ($158–$224) double. Rates include Scandinavian buffet breakfast. AE, CB, DC, MC, V. Tube: Lancaster Gate.

Affiliated with Best Western, the Mornington brings a touch of northern European hospitality to the center of London. Just north of Hyde Park and Kensington Gardens, the hotel has a Victorian exterior and a Scandinavian-inspired decor. The area isn't London's most fashionable, but the location is close to Hyde Park and convenient to Marble Arch, Oxford Street shopping, and the ethnic restaurants of Queensway. The recently renovated guest rooms are tasteful and comfortable; all include coffee/tea facilities and pay movies. You can wind down in the library and order snacks or afternoon tea from the well-stocked bar. Every year we get our annual Christmas card from "the gang"—the hotel staff, and what a helpful crew they are. Guest services include babysitting, dry cleaning and laundry service.

INEXPENSIVE

Adare House. 153 Sussex Gardens, London W2 2RY. ☎ **0171/262-0633.** Fax 0171/706-1859. E-mail: c.constantinou@virgin.net. 16 units (10 with shower). TV. £58 ($93) double with shower. Rates include full English breakfast. No credit cards. Tube: Paddington.

This longstanding bed-and-breakfast remains one of the best choices for the budget traveler along B&B-crazed Sussex Gardens; the place still has a little soul, even though so many of its neighbors have lost theirs. You're welcomed by Anne O'Neill, who runs a good ship, and has done so exceedingly well for a quarter of a century. The property is well-maintained and has been gradually improved over the years, with the addition of private bathrooms in admittedly cramped space. The public areas are relatively modest, but smart Regency-era wallpaper and red carpeting give them a touch of class. Many of the homey rooms are quite small, but they're spic-and-span and comfortably furnished. All have beverage-makers, and those with private bathroom have a hair dryer.

The Byron Hotel. 36–38 Queensborough Terrace, London W2 3SH. ☎ **0171/243-0987.** Fax 0171/792-1957. 43 units. TV TEL. £89–£96 ($142–$154) double; £111 ($178) triple; £145 ($232) suite. Rates include English/continental breakfast. AE, DC, MC, V. Tube: Bayswater or Queensway.

A mostly American clientele appreciates this family-run hotel just north of Kensington Gardens for its country-house atmosphere, its helpful staff (who spend extra time with guests hoping to make their stay in London special), and the good value it offers. This is one of the best examples of a Victorian house conversion that we've seen; it was modernized without ruining its traditional appeal. The interior was recently redesigned and refurbished, and the rooms are better than ever, with ample closets, tile bathrooms, good lighting, and extra amenities like trouser presses, coffeemakers, safes, and hair dryers. An elevator services all floors, and breakfast is served in a bright and cheery room.

Europa House Hotel. 151 Sussex Gardens, London W2 2RY. ☎ **0171/402-1923** or 0171/723-7343. Fax 0171/224-9331. www.smoothhound.co.uk/hotels/europa.html. 18 units. TV TEL. £48–£60 ($77–$96) double; £18–£20 ($29–$32) per person family room. Rates include English breakfast. MC, V. Parking £10 ($16). Tube: Paddington.

Another budget find along Sussex Gardens, this family-run hotel attracts those who want a private shower with their room but don't want to pay too much extra for the luxury. Like most along Sussex Gardens, the bedrooms are a bit cramped, but they're well-maintained and often color-coordinated; each has private plumbing and a TV and coffeemaker. Some rooms are custom-built for groups, with three, four, or five beds per unit. A hearty English breakfast awaits you in the bright dining room every morning.

Fairways Hotel. 186 Sussex Gardens, London W2 1TU. ☎ **0171/723-4871.** Fax 0171/723-4871. www.freepages.co.uk/fairwayshotel. 17 units (10 with bathroom). TV. £60 ($96) double without bathroom, £66 ($106) double with bathroom. Rates include English breakfast. MC, V. Tube: Paddington.

Jenny and Steve Adams welcome you into one of the finest B&Bs along Sussex Gardens. Even though it doesn't enjoy the pedigree it used to, this little place near Hyde Park is still a favorite address of bargain-hunters. The black-and-white town house is easily recognizable: Just look for its colonnaded front entrance with a wrought-iron balustrade stretching across the front second-floor windows. Scorning the modern, the Adams family prefers a traditional touch, opting for charm and character whenever possible. They call their breakfast room "homely," which Americans might call home-like instead; it's decorated with photographs of the family and a collection of china. Bedrooms are attractively decorated and comfortably furnished, each with hot and cold running water, intercom, TV, and beverage makers. The breakfast is hearty and home-cooked, fit fortification for a day of sightseeing.

Norfolk Court & St. David's Hotel. 16–20 Norfolk Sq., London W2 1RS. ☎ **0171/ 723-4963.** Fax 0171/402-9061. 70 units (24 with shower). TV. £46 ($74) double without bath, £56 ($90) double with bath or shower; £56 ($90) triple without bath, £66 ($106) triple with shower; £67 ($107) quad without bath, £77 ($123) quad with shower. Rates include full English breakfast. MC, V. Tube: Paddington.

George and Foula Neokledos, two of the more welcoming hosts in this B&B area, manage to run both these properties with a certain style. Lying only a 2-minute walk from Paddington Station, these small and friendly hotels were built when Norfolk Square knew a grander age, attracting such Victorian luminaries as John Addington Symonds (1840–93), the eccentric scholar and literary critic and author of the seven-volume *The Renaissance in Italy.* The bluebloods are long gone, but the area is still safe and recommendable. An interior designer might turn up his nose at the mismatched decor, but each room is well-maintained and comfortably, if not elegantly, furnished. There's a homespun quality here. You get good beds, an affordable price, and, in a few rooms, your own cubicle shower that's not made for lingering, but does the job.

Parkwood Hotel. 4 Stanhope Place, London W2 2HB. ☎ **0171/402-2241.** Fax 0171/ 402-1574. 18 units (12 with bathroom). TV TEL. £59 ($95) double without bathroom, £85 ($136) double with bathroom; £74 ($119) triple without bathroom, £97 ($155) triple with bathroom; £100 ($160) quad with bathroom. Children under 13 sharing parents' room £11.50 ($18) Mon–Fri, free Sat and Sun. Rates include English breakfast. MC, V. Tube: Marble Arch.

Parkwood occupies one of the best locations for a good-value hotel in London: near Oxford Street and Marble Arch and just 50 yards from Hyde Park, in a section known as Connaught Village. The well-maintained, simple bedrooms have coffeemakers and radios. The hotel prides itself on an excellent breakfast; in fact, the menu states that if you're still hungry, you can have another meal—for free.

The Phoenix Hotel. 1–8 Kensington Garden Sq., London W2 4BH. ☎ **800/528-1234** or 0171/229-2494. Fax 0171/727-1419. E-mail: phoenixhotel@dial.pipex.com. 128 units. TV TEL. £92 ($147) double; £120 ($192) family room; £145 ($232) suite. AE, DC, MC, V. Tube: Bayswater.

This hotel occupies the entire south side of one of the most famous garden squares in Europe. Well-situated in what is now an ethnically mixed neighborhood, the Phoenix was created from a series of 1854 town houses. The atmosphere is welcoming and gracious throughout, with a decor done in muted tones and fabrics. The well-furnished bedrooms keep to a smart international standard. Everything is designed for comfort and ease, including the luggage racks. The bar is a good place to unwind; moderately priced meals are served in the downstairs cafe. Our biggest complaint? The public areas are too small for a hotel of this size.

IN NEARBY MAIDA VALE
MODERATE

Colonnade Hotel. 2 Warrington Crescent, London W9 1ER. ☎ **0171/289-2167.** Fax 0171/286-1057. www.colonnade.demon.co.uk. E-mail: louise@colonnade.demon.co.uk. 50 units. TV TEL. £110 ($176) double; £150 ($240) suite. Rates include English breakfast. AE, DC, MC, V. Parking £10 ($16). Tube: Warwick Ave.

The Colonnade, former home of Sigmund Freud, has been a landmark in the neighborhood since 1938. It lies in the fashionable section of Little Venice, about 10 minutes by tube from London's West End. It's been run by the Richards family for about a half-century, and they continue to maintain its charm and special atmosphere. What we like about the place is the variety of rooms—they range from standard singles to suites with four-poster beds. All have private bathrooms and plenty of amenities, including radio, hair dryer, and trouser press (some of the suites even have Jacuzzis). Foam pillows, featherless duvets, cots, and bed boards are also available upon request. Every room and corridor is centrally heated around the clock from the first chilly breeze of autumn until the last retreating wind of winter—a rarity in London—and about half of the rooms are air-conditioned. The hotel also has a highly rated restaurant and bar, **Cascades,** especially known for its winter fondues. Additional services include a concierge desk, dry cleaning and laundry service, and room service from 7am to 11pm; babysitting can be arranged.

9 A Bit Farther Afield: Hampstead

MODERATE

✪ **Sandringham Hotel.** 3 Holford Rd., London NW3 1AD. ☎ **0171/435-1569.** Fax 0171/431-5932. E-mail: pdc@londonnet.co.uk 15 units. TV TEL. £115–£130 ($184–$208) double; £155 ($248) triple. Rates include continental breakfast. MC, V. Free parking. Tube: Hampstead. From the Hampstead tube stop on Heath St., turn right and walk up the hill; at the fourth right, turn into Hampstead Sq., which leads to Holfrod Rd.

If you're looking for something different, take the lead of many savvy Londoners and head for the leafy North London village of Hampstead, one of the city's best neighborhoods. Hampstead is a real retreat: It's well away from the noisy city center, but easily accessible via tube. This large Victorian, set on a residential street, recently underwent extensive refurbishment—which, regrettably, has led to a vast increase in its room rates. But you're paying for a choice location, 2 minutes from the 900-acre heath; another lure is the private walled garden. The rooms are comfortably and beautifully decorated. Breakfast is served in a pretty room with a view of this garden; amenities include laundry service, room service, and access to a nearby health club.

10 Near the Airports

NEAR HEATHROW

EXPENSIVE

Sheraton Skyline. Bath Rd. A4, Hayes, Middlesex UB3 5BP. ☎ **800/325-3535** or 0181/759-2535. Fax 081/750-9150. www.sheraton.com. 356 units. A/C MINIBAR TV TEL. £180 ($288) double; from £400 ($640) suite. AE, DC, MC, V. Parking £4 ($6.40).

Sheraton Skyline—more of a miniature village than a hotel—has consistently been voted the world's best airport hotel. It surrounds an atrium where tropical plants and towering palms thrive beneath a translucent roof; the foundations of a cabana bar are set into the temperature-controlled waters of a pool. Each guest room has the amenities you expect from a Sheraton, including lots of movie channels and a massage-style shower.

Dining: A fireplace flickers late into the night in the **Edwardian Colony Bar** and the adjacent restaurant, the **Colony Room,** where well-prepared food is served beneath massive ceiling timbers and heavy brass chandeliers. A French cafe offers light meals and full buffet breakfasts. **The Sports Bar** serves drinks in a casual atmosphere.

Amenities: 24-hour room service, shuttle service to and from four terminals at Heathrow Airport (running every 5 minutes between 6am and 11pm), and verification and confirmation of departures from Heathrow; babysitting, dry cleaning and laundry service, concierge, and secretarial services. Business center, heated pool, fitness center, car rental desk.

MODERATE

Stanwell Hall. Town Lane, Stanwell, Staines, Middlesex TW19 7PW. ☎ **01784/252292.** Fax 01784/245250. 18 units (17 with bathroom). TV TEL. £100 ($160) double; £130 ($208) suite. Rates include breakfast. AE, DC, MC, V. Free parking.

This sunny Victorian house was purchased in 1951 by the Parke family, who converted it into a comfortable hotel shortly thereafter. The cheery house with its side garden is located in a small village just minutes from Heathrow; it's perfect for business people who are tired of staying in standard airport hotels. About half of the rooms have been fully renovated. The renovated rooms are comfortably furnished, papered in warm shades, and have chintz curtains covering the windows—a dramatic improvement over the washed out pre-renovation rooms. All have coffeemakers. **St. Anne's Restaurant,** located on the ground floor, is small but inviting; the bar, which is popular with locals, serves drinks and snacks at lunchtime. Basic services include dry cleaning and laundry.

INEXPENSIVE

The Swan. The Hythe, Staines, Middlesex TW18 3JB. ☎ **0178/445-2494.** Fax 0178/446-1593. 11 units (5 with bathroom), 1 suite. TV TEL. £59 ($94) double without bathroom, £81 ($130) double with bathroom; £90 ($144) suite. Rates include English breakfast. AE, DC, MC, V. Tube: Heathrow (you must take a taxi from there).

Dating from the days of Samuel Pepys, the Swan is on the south bank of the Thames, beside Staines Bridge and within easy access of Heathrow (15 minutes). Bedrooms have central heating and coffeemakers. The attractive old inn also has a reputation for good food ranging from bar snacks to traditional English fare. The food is served in a gazebo-style dining room, featuring wholesome cooking. If you're just arriving in London, this might be a good introduction to the city's history before you go into the center: Staines was an important Roman settlement, and many surviving buildings in the area date from the 17th century.

NEAR GATWICK

EXPENSIVE

Gatwick Hilton International Hotel. South Terminal, Gatwick Airport, Gatwick, West Sussex RH6 0LL. ☎ **800/HILTONS** or 01293/518080. Fax 01293/528980. www.hilton.com. 572 units. A/C TV TEL. £195–£217 ($312–$347) double; from £250 ($400) suite. AE, DC, MC, V. Parking £5 ($7.90).

This deluxe five-floor hotel—Gatwick's most convenient resting place—is linked to the airport terminal with a covered walkway; an electric buggy service transports people between the hotel and airport. The most impressive part of the hotel is the first-floor lobby; its glass-covered portico rises four floors and contains a scale replica of the de Havilland Gypsy Moth airplane *Jason,* used by Amy Johnson on her solo flight from England to Australia in 1930. The reception area has a lobby bar and lots of greenery. The well-furnished, soundproofed rooms have triple-glazed windows and coffeemakers. Recently, 123 of the rooms were refurbished, in addition to the executive floor and all of their junior suites. Now 300 of the rooms have minibars, stocked upon request.

Dining/Diversions: The American-themed restaurant **Amy's** serves buffet breakfasts, lunches, and dinners. **The Garden Restaurant,** outfitted in a formal English garden theme, serves drinks and full meals. There's also the 24-hour **Lobby Bar,** plus a polo-themed watering hole aptly named the **Jockey Bar.**

Amenities: Same-day dry cleaning and laundry service, up-to-date flight information channel, 24-hour room service, salon, bank, gift shop. Concierge, newspapers, babysitting, health club (sauna, steam room, massage room, swimming pool, gymnasium, Jacuzzi). Conference rooms, business center, shopping arcade.

INEXPENSIVE

Brooklyn Manor Hotel. Bonnetts Lane, Ifield, Crawley, West Sussex RH11 0NY. ☎ **01293/546024.** Fax 01293/510366. 11 units (4 with bathroom). £35 ($56) double without bathroom, £45 ($72) double with bathroom. AE, MC, V. Bus: C5 (Crawley/Ifield).

This old, well-cared-for Victorian house is set on 5 acres of English countryside only 5 minutes from Gatwick. The hotel provides free transportation to and from the airport—just call when you arrive, and someone will come and fetch you. Martin Davis rents rooms with full central heating and beverage makers. Breakfast is available for an extra charge, and light snacks are available in the evening. In addition, a free courtesy service takes guests to and from a nearby restaurant, and there are two pubs within about a 10-minute walk, both of which serve inexpensive meals. The hotel doesn't have a bar, but it is licensed, so drinks can be served in the lounge if you wish. Despite its small size, they offer babysitting and can supply a courtesy car upon request.

5 Dining

George Mikes, Britain's famous Hungarian-born humorist, once wrote about the culinary prowess of his adopted country: "The Continentals have good food. The English have good table manners."

Quite a lot has happened since.

London has emerged as one of the great food capitals of the world. In the last few years, both its veteran and upstart chefs have fanned out around the globe for culinary inspiration, and have returned with innovative dishes, flavors, and ideas that London diners have never seen before—or at least not at such unprecedented rates. These chefs are pioneering a new style of cooking called "Modern British," which is forever changing, forever innovative, yet comfortingly familiar in many ways. They've committed to centering their dishes around local ingredients from field, stream, and air, and have become daringly innovative with traditional recipes—too much so in the view of some critics, who don't like fresh mango over their blood pudding.

Traditional British cooking has made a comeback, too. The dishes that British mums the nation over have been forever feeding their reluctant families are fashionable again. Yes, we're talking British soul food: bangers and mash, Norfolk dumplings, nursery puddings, cottage pie—the works. This may be a rebellion against the excessive minimalism of the nouvelle cuisine that ran rampant over London in the 1980s, but who knows? Maybe it's just plain old nostalgia. Pig's nose with parsley-and-onion sauce may not be your idea of cutting-edge cuisine, but Simpson's-in-the-Strand is serving it for breakfast.

These days, many of the personality chefs spend a lot more time writing cookbooks and performing on TV than they do cooking in their own kitchens. As is so often the case, that chef you've read about in *Condé Nast Traveler* or *Travel & Leisure* may not be in the kitchen when you get here. But never fear: The cuisine isn't suffering. Many an up-and-comer who's even better has taken over. And with many London restaurants becoming so mammoth—with 200+ seats—the identity of the chef presiding over the kitchen is irrelevant as long as he or she can cook. After the wild explosion of openings in 1996 and 1997, the scene has slowed down considerably. In those years some celebrated chefs opened two or even three restaurants a year. But perhaps today's backers are waiting to see if these new ones succeed before pouring money into new ventures.

If you want a lavish meal, London is the place to eat it, with some of the world's top restaurants calling the city home: gourmet havens such as La Tante Claire, Le Gavroche, Chez Nico at Ninety Park Lane, and a half-dozen others you'll find reviewed in the following pages. For those of you who don't want to break the bank, we've included many more affordable restaurants where you can dine really well. You'll find that London's food revolution has infiltrated every level of the dining scene—even the lowly pub has entered London's culinary sweepstakes. Believe the unthinkable: At certain pubs, you can now dine better than in many restaurants. In some, standard pub grub has given way to Modern British and Mediterranean-style fare; in others, oyster bars have taken hold. See "Haute Cuisine Comes to the Lowly Boozer," below, for the best of the bunch.

Some Dining Notes

Hours   Restaurants in London keep varied hours, but in general, lunch is offered from noon to 2pm and dinner is served from 7:30 to 9:30pm—but more and more restaurants are staying open later these days. Sunday is the typical closing day for London restaurants, but there are many exceptions to that rule (many restaurants also close for a few days or a week around Christmas, so call ahead if you're dining during the holiday season). We've listed serving hours in the descriptions below.

Reservations   Nearly all places, except pubs, cafeterias, and fast-food joints, prefer or require reservations. Almost invariably, you get a better table if you book in advance. For a few of the really famous places, you might need to reserve weeks in advance, even before leaving home (such reservations should always be confirmed when you land in London).

Taxes & Tipping   All restaurants and cafés in Britain are required to display the prices of the food and drink they offer in a place visible from outside the establishment. Charges for service, as well as any minimum charge or cover charge, must also be made clear. The prices shown must include 17½% VAT. Most of the restaurants add a 10% to 15% service charge to your bill, but you'll have to check to make sure of that. If nothing has been added to your bill, leave a 12% to 15% tip.

1 Best Bets

- **Best Restaurant for Romance:** The atmosphere is about as romantic as it can get at **Bracewells**, in the Park Lane Hotel, Piccadilly, W1 (☎ **0171/499-6321**). You can enjoy some of the finest hotel dining in London in an intimate, elegant setting of gilded torchères, comfortable armchairs, and candlelight.
- **Best Place for a Business Lunch:** Instead of some noisy City tavern serving up bangers and mash, impress your clients by taking them to **Poons in the City,** 2 Minster Pavement, Minster Court, Mincing Lane, EC3 (☎ **0171/626-0126**). This fabled Chinese restaurant is elegantly outfitted with furniture and accessories from China, and the menu is wide ranging enough to please most clients. After a taste of the finely chopped wind-dried meats or the crispy aromatic duck, it'll be a snap to seal the deal.
- **Best Spot for a Celebration:** There's no spot in all of London that's more fun than **Quaglino's,** 16 Bury St., SW1 (☎ **0171/930-6767**). On some nights, as many as 800 diners show up at Sir Terence Conran's gargantuan Mayfair eatery to dine, laugh, and gossip. It's the best place in London to celebrate almost any occasion— and the food's good, too. There's live jazz on Friday and Saturday nights.
- **Best Wine List:** The renowned wine list at the **Tate Gallery Restaurant,** in the Tate Gallery, Millbank, SW1 (☎ **0171/887-8877**), reads like a who's who of famous French châteaux. So does the one at Le Gavroche—but this one is affordable. The Tate offers the city's best bargains on fine wines; the management keeps the

markups between 40% and 65%, as opposed to the 100% to 200% that most restaurants add to the price of a bottle.

- **Best Newcomer of the Year:** London's most talked-about restaurant, **Vong,** in the Berkeley Hotel, Wilton Place, SW1 (☎ 0171/235-1010), is an offshoot of its famous New York sibling. Just 600 yards from Harrods, the restaurant serves the city's most succulent French and Thai cuisine. Local chefs claim that the availability of superior ingredients in London make this Vong offspring even better than the award-winning restaurant in the Big Apple. Try almost anything here: most definitely the sautéed foie gras with ginger and mango.
- **Best Value:** Cheap and cheerful **Simply Nico,** 48A Rochester Row, SW1 (☎ 0171/630-8061), grand Chef Nico Ladenis' "moment of whimsy," offers some of the best value fixed-price meals in London. This isn't the fabled haute cuisine Nico serves on Park Lane, but quality ingredients are beautifully prepared into some of the best French food in central London. Breast of guinea fowl with lentils and other specialties will keep you coming back for more.
- **Best Traditional British Cuisine:** No restaurant, not even Simpson's-in-the-Strand, is quite as British as **Wiltons,** 55 Jermyn St., SW1 (☎ 0171/629-9955). As other British restaurants loosen up, Wiltons remains fiercely entrenched in tradition—or, as one London diner put it, "Wiltons refuses to unclench its upper-class buttocks." It serves the same menu it did to the 18th-century nobs of St. James's. We're talking grilled plaice, steaks, chops, kidneys, whitebait (a Victorian favorite), and game dishes such as roast widgeon (a wild fish-eating river duck).
- **Best Modern British Cuisine:** In a former smokehouse just north of Smithfield Market, **St. John,** 26 St. John St., EC1 (☎ 0171/251-0848), has a modern interpretation of British cuisine that's like none other in town. The chefs here believe in offals—after all, why use just parts of the animal when you can use it all? Although some diners are a bit squeamish at first, once they get past the first bite, they're usually hooked on the viands—and they keep coming back for more, so book ahead.
- **Best Pub Grub:** Tom Conran, son of über-restaurateur Sir Terence Conran, is attracting all of London to **The Cow,** 89 Westbourne Park Rd., W2 (☎ 0171/221-0021)—even people who haven't been in a pub for years. Leading the revolution in upgrading pub cuisine, The Cow somehow manages to secure the biggest and juiciest oysters in town. Ox tongue poached in milk? Don't knock it 'til you've tried it. Proof that the London pub scene has changed radically: The hip young staff even serves finger bowls to its even hipper clientele.
- **Best Continental Cuisine: Le Gavroche,** 43 Upper Brook St., W1 (☎ 0171/408-0881), was the forerunner of the modern French approach to cuisine in London, and it's lost none of its appeal over the years. If you want to know why, order *pigeonneau de Bresse en vessie aux deux celeris:* The whole bird is presented at your table, enclosed in a pig's bladder; the pigeon is skillfully removed, then carved and served on a bed of braised fennel and celery. Trust us—it's fabulous.
- **Best Indian Cuisine:** London's finest Indian food is served at **Café Spice Namaste,** in a landmark Victorian hall near Tower Bridge, 16 Prescot St., E1 (☎ 0171/488-9242). You'll be tantalized with a bewildering array of spicy southern and northern Indian dishes. What we especially like about this place is its strong Portuguese influence; the chef, Cyrus Todiwala, is a former resident of Goa (a Portuguese territory absorbed by India long ago), where he learned many of his culinary secrets.
- **Best Italian Cuisine: The River Café,** Thames Wharf, Rainville Rd., W6 (☎ 0171/381-6217), is the hottest restaurant in London these days, and for good reason: Foodies flock to this Thameside restaurant (designed by Sir Richard Rogers,

In case you want to see the world.

At American Express, we're here to make your journey a smooth one. So we have over 1,700 travel service locations in over 120 countries ready to help. What else would you expect from the world's largest travel agency?

do more

Travel

In case you want to be welcomed there.

We're here to see that you're always welcomed at establishments everywhere. That's why millions of people carry the American Express® Card—for peace of mind, confidence, and security, around the world or just around the corner.

do more

Cards

In case you're running low.

We're here to help with more than 118,000 Express Cash

locations around the world. In order to enroll, just call

American Express before you start your vacation.

do more

Express Cash

And just in case.

We're here with American Express® Travelers Cheques and Cheques *for Two.*® They're the safest way to carry money on your vacation and the surest way to get a refund, practically anywhere, anytime.

Another way we help you…

do more

Travelers Cheques

who also did the Lloyd's building and Paris's Pompidou Centre) for cuisine that's been likened to that served in the best private homes in Italy. The freshest of ingredients from all over the world are brought here, where waiting chefs transform them into culinary art.

- **Best American Cuisine:** Like a traditionally British gentlemen's club, **Joe Allen,** 13 Exeter St., WC2 (☎ 0171/836-0651), has only a small brass plaque marking its entrance. But the food here will be more familiar: Maryland crab cakes, spinach salad, black-bean soup, chili, Caesar salad, and that famous pecan pie. On our last visit, we spotted movie legend Lauren Bacall digging into a sirloin steak (rare) with sautéed red onions and steak frites—just like she used to cook for Bogie.

- **Best Japanese Cuisine:** Robert de Niro and his gang have arrived with **Nobu,** in the Metropolitan Hotel, 19 Old Park Lane, W1 (☎ 0171/447-4747), and all other Japanese restaurants fear the challenge—rightly so. The kitchen staff here is as brilliant and innovative as at their New York father restaurant. The sushi chefs don't create just sushi but gastronomic pyrotechnics. They do exceedingly well with the other dishes, too.

- **Best Chinese Cuisine:** If you'd like to dine on such dishes as "The Whims and Fancies of the Empress" or "Buddha Jumps Over the Wall," head for **Kay Mayfair,** 65 S. Audley St., W1 (☎ 0171/493-8988). It's one of London's glitziest Chinese restaurants, lying near the American Embassy. Chefs wander the Orient for culinary inspiration, and succeed in serving some of the city's zestiest Chinese fare, like bang-bang chicken in a nut sauce.

- **Best Desserts: Nico Central,** 35 Great Portland St., W1 (☎ 0171/436-8846), is the place to satisfy your sweet tooth. The "puddings" menu is extremely limited, but is it ever choice: The caramelized lemon tart is the best we've ever had in London. The nougat ice cream with a strongly flavored blackberry coulis was worth a return visit, as was the walnut and Armagnac parfait. Other unforgettable desserts accompanying memorable meals here have included a velvety smooth warm chocolate mousse with pear sorbet, and a poached pear sablé made even more delectable with a caramel ginger sauce.

- **Best Late-Night Dining:** Most London restaurants open after 10:30pm aren't worth the trouble. There's one notable exception, however: **Bombay Brasserie,** adjacent to Bailey's Hotel, Courtfield Close, SW7 (☎ 0171/370-4040). Not only is it one of the best Indian restaurants in London (where the competition is stiff), it also serves the same well-prepared dinners at midnight (last order) that it does at 7:30pm.

- **Best People-Watching:** In Karl Marx's former apartment house, **Quo Vadis,** 26–29 Dean St., W1 (☎ 0171/437-9585), is a joint venture of London's *enfant terrible* chef, Marco Pierre White, and Damien Hirst, the artist who wowed the London art world with his cow carcasses in formaldehyde. With a pedigree like this, it's no wonder this is the hottest see-and-be-seen circuit in town. If Goldie Hawn should come to London, this is where you'd find her. And the food's not bad, either.

- **Best Afternoon Tea:** While everyone else is donning their fancy hats and heading for the Ritz (where, chances are, they won't be able to get a table), you should retreat to the **Palm Court at the Waldorf Meridien,** Aldwych, WC2 (☎ 0171/ 836-2400), in the grand 1908 Waldorf Hotel. The Sunday tea dances here are legendary: Originating with the famous "Tango Teas" of the 1920s and 1930s, they've been going strong ever since, interrupted only by war and a few other inconveniences.

- **Best Pre-Theater Menu:** Opposite the Ambassador Theatre, **The Ivy,** 1–5 West St., WC2 (☎ 0171/836-4751), is popular for both pre- and *après*-theater dining. The brasserie-style food reflects both traditional English and modern continental influences. You can try longtime favorites such as potted shrimp or tripe and onions, or more imaginative dishes such as butternut pumpkin salad or a wild mushroom risotto.

- **Best Decor:** There's no more beautiful dining room in all of London than the **Oak Room/Marco Pierre White,** in Le Méridien Piccadilly, 21 Piccadilly, W1 (☎ 0171/734-8000). It's the best of the *fin de siècle* era, with walls of limed oak paneling inlaid with towering gilded mirrors, gargantuan crystal chandeliers hanging from the ornate plaster ceiling, and Chinese vases bursting with flowers. And, best of all, the fabulous French cuisine of Marco Pierre White more than holds its own in the spectacular setting.

- **Best View: Ship Hispaniola,** River Thames, Victoria Embankment, Charing Cross, WC2 (☎ 0171/839-3011), is a ship-turned-restaurant permanently moored to a quay beside the Thames. Tables are set up on two different levels to take full advantage of the grand views. You'll enjoy a seasonal menu as a harpist or pianist sets the mood and the river traffic passes by.

- **Best For Kids:** After you and the kids have visited the Tower of London, take them to **Dickens Inn by the Tower,** St. Katharine's Way, E1 (☎ 0171/488-2208), an old spice warehouse turned three-floor restaurant with sweeping views of the Thames and Tower Bridge. Dickens Inn serves tasty well-stuffed sandwiches, platters of lasagna, and steaming bowls of chili. One whole floor is devoted to serving pizza.

- **Best Fast Food:** Instead of noshing on greasy fish-and-chips while you're exploring the City (or a hamburger with meat from God knows where), take a break from sightseeing at **Poons in the City** (see above). This famous Chinese restaurant serves top-notch Chinese fast food in its bar, the Express. The cookery is homestyle and the recipes original, and the menu still includes Poons's specialty, wind-dried meats.

- **The Best Pizza:** Although many will dispute this accolade, **Pizzeria Condotti,** 4 Mill St., W1 (☎ 0171/499-1308), consistently serves up some of London's most savory pies—with an array of hot, bubbling, and savory toppings. In attractive, rather expensive-looking surroundings, the restaurant serves pizzas on thin, crisp crusts. All are prepared to order and taste fresh from the oven. Each is a meal unto itself.

- **Best Picnic Fare:** If you'd like to prepare a picnic fit for a queen, go to **Fortnum & Mason, Ltd.,** 181 Piccadilly, W1 (☎ 0171/734-8040), the world's most famous grocery store. You'll find a wide array of foodstuffs to take away to your favorite park. (For details, see "The Department Stores," chapter 8).

- **Best Pub Atmosphere:** On leave from fighting Napoléon, the Duke of Wellington's officers downed many a pint of lager at the **Grenadier,** 18 Wilton Row, SW1 (☎ 0171/235-3074). It comes complete with a ghost (allegedly that of an officer flogged to death for cheating at cards) and a very British restaurant. Bloody Marys are a Sunday tradition.

- **Best English Breakfast:** The **Fox and Anchor,** 115 Charterhouse St., EC1 (☎ 0171/253-4838), is a longtime favorite among early-morning pub crawlers and club trawlers who fancy a pint and a bite to get them going for the day. One local called the array of breakfast goodies here "gut-busting"—everything from black pudding to fried bread and baked beans. After the "full house" breakfast at this Smithfield Market pub, you won't be ready to eat again until the following morning.

- **Best Fish 'n' Chips:** The best place to introduce yourself to this trad British dish is **North Sea Fish Restaurant,** 7–8 Leigh St., WC1 (☎ 0171/387-5892). Unlike the overcooked frozen fish served at those joints around Leicester Square, North Sea's fresh cod comes perfectly prepared: crisp batter on the outside, moist and tender fish inside. The haddock is equally delectable—and what a big platter it is.

2 Restaurants by Cuisine

AFTERNOON TEA

The Blue Room (Leicester Square)
Brown's Hotel (Mayfair)
Claridge's (Mayfair)
The Garden Café (Notting Hill)
The Georgian Restaurant
    (Knightsbridge)
Goode's (Mayfair)
The Lanesborough (Belgravia)
MJ Bradley's (Covent Garden)
Oak Room Lounge (St. James's)
The Orangery (Kensington)
Palm Court at the Waldorf Meridien
    (Covent Garden)
Palm Court Lounge (Mayfair)
Richoux (Knightsbridge)
Ritz Palm Court (St. James's)
St. James Restaurant & The Fountain
    Restaurant (St. James's)
The Tearoom at Chelsea Physic
    Garden (Chelsea)

AMERICAN

Chicago Rib Shack (Knightsbridge, *I*)
Christopher's (Covent Garden, *M*)
Hard Rock Café (Mayfair, *I*)
Joe Allen (Covent Garden, *I*)
Pizzeria Condotti (Mayfair, *I*)

BELGIUM

Belgo Centraal (Covent Garden, *M*)

BREAKFAST

Fox and Anchor (The City, *I*)

BRITISH—TRADITIONAL

Bracewells (Mayfair, *M*)
British Museum Restaurant
    (Bloomsbury, *I*)
Butler's Wharf Chop House
    (Docklands, *M*)
The Carvery (Piccadilly Circus, *I*)
Dickens Inn by the Tower
    (Docklands, *I*)

English Garden (Chelsea, *M*)
English House (Chelsea, *M*)
Fifth Floor at Harvey Nichols
    (Knightsbridge, *M*)
The George (The Strand, *I*)
The George & Vulture (The City, *I*)
The Georgian Restaurant
    (Knightsbridge, *E*)
The Granary (Piccadilly, *I*)
The Ivy (Soho, *M*)
Langan's Bistro (Marylebone, *I*)
Langan's Brasserie (Mayfair, *M*)
Maggie Jones (Kensington, *I*)
Plummers Restaurant
    (Leicester Square, *I*)
Porter's English Restaurant
    (Covent Garden, *I*)
Quo Vadis (Soho, *E*)
Rules (Covent Garden, *E*)
Scotts (Mayfair, *M*)
Shepherd's (Westminster, *M*)
Ship Hispaniola (Embankment, *M*)
Simpson's-in-the-Strand
    (The Strand, *E*)
The Stockpot (Leicester Square, *I*)
Tate Gallery Restaurant
    (Westminster, *M*)
Veronica's (Bayswater, *M*)
Wiltons (Piccadilly Circus, *E*)

BRITISH—MODERN

Alastair Little (Soho, *E*)
Atlantic Bar & Grill (Piccadilly
    Circus, *M*)
Bracewells (Mayfair, *M*)
Brinkley's Garden Restaurant &
    Chapter 11 Bar (West Brompton, *I*)
Butler's Wharf Chop House
    (Docklands, *M*)
Clarke's (Notting Hill, *M*)
The Criterion Brasserie—Marco
    Pierre White (Piccadilly Circus, *M*)
English House (Chelsea, *M*)

Key to Abbreviations: *VE* = Very Expensive; *E* = Expensive; *M* = Moderate; *I* = Inexpensive

Fifth Floor at Harvey Nichols
   (Knightsbridge, *M*)
The Georgian Restaurant
   (Knightsbridge, *E*)
Gilbert's (South Kensington, *M*)
Greenhouse (Mayfair, *M*)
Joe's (Kensington, *M*)
Launceston Place (Kensington, *M*)
Museum Street Café (Bloomsbury, *M*)
Nico Central (Fitzrovia, *M*)
Oak Room/Marco Pierre White
   (Mayfair, *VE*)
Plummers Restaurant
   (Leicester Square, *I*)
Quo Vadis (Soho, *E*)
St. John (Clerkenwell, *M*)

CANTONESE
Ming (Soho, *I*)

CHINESE
Chuen Cheng Ku (Soho, *I*)
Dumpling Inn (Soho, *I*)
Kai Mayfair (Mayfair, *M*)
Ken Lo's Memories of China
   (Victoria, *E*)
Poons in the City (The City, *M*)

CONTINENTAL
Blue Bird (Chelsea, *E*)
Hilaire (South Kensington, *E*)
Maison Novelli (Clerkenwell, *E*)
Mezzo (Soho, *E*)
L'Odéon (Piccadilly Circus, *E*)
Quaglino's (Mayfair, *M*)
The Stockpot (Leicester Square, *I*)

FRENCH
Au Jardin des Gourmets (Soho, *M*)
Aubergine (Chelsea, *E*)
Bibendum/The Oyster Bar (South
   Kensington, *E*)
Brasserie St. Quentin (South
   Kensington, *M*)
Bruno Soho (Soho, *E*)
Chez Nico at Ninety Park Lane
   (Mayfair, *VE*)
Gilbert's (South Kensington, *M*)
The Ivy (Soho, *M*)
La Tante Claire (Chelsea, *VE*)
Langan's Bistro (Marylebone, *I*)
Langan's Brasserie (Mayfair, *M*)

Le Gavroche (Mayfair, *VE*)
Magno's (Covent Garden, *M*)
Nico Central (Fitzrovia, *M*)
Pied-à-Terre (Fitzrovia, *E*)
The Room at the Halcyon
   (Notting Hill, *E*)
Ship Hispaniola (Embankment, *M*)
Simply Nico (Victoria, *M*)
Vong (Knightsbridge, *E*)

HUNGARIAN
Gay Hussar (Soho, *E*)

INDIAN
The Bengal Clipper (Butler's
   Wharf, *M*)
Bombay Brasserie (South
   Kensington, *M*)
Café Spice Namaste (The City, *M*)
Chutney Mary (Chelsea, *M*)
Soho Spice (Soho, *M*)
Tamarind (Mayfair, *I*)

INTERNATIONAL
The Canteen (Chelsea Harbour, *M*)
Chelsea Kitchen (Chelsea, *I*)
Coast (Piccadilly Circus, *E*)
Deal's Restaurant and Diner
   (Chelsea Harbour, *I*)
Le Pont de la Tour (Docklands, *E*)
Odin's (Marylebone, *M*)
Pavilion Restaurant (South
   Kensington, *M*)
The Room at the Halcyon
   (Holland Park, *E*)
Turner's (South Kensington, *E*)

ITALIAN
I-Thai (Bayswater, *VE*)
Neal Street Restaurant (Covent
   Garden, *E*)
Pizzeria Condotti (Mayfair, *I*)
The River Café (Hammersmith, *E*)
San Lorenzo (Knightsbridge, *E*)

JAPANESE
Nobu (Mayfair, *E*)
Suntory (St. James's, *VE*)

LEBANESE
Phoenicia (Kensington, *M*)

MEDITERRANEAN
Bibendum/The Oyster Bar (South
 Kensington, *E*)
Bistro 190 (South Kensington, *M*)
dell'Ugo (Soho, *I*)
Mezzo (Soho, *E*)

MOROCCAN/NORTH AFRICAN
Momo (Piccadilly Circus, *M*)

PACIFIC RIM
Sugar Club (Notting Hill, *M*)

PAKISTANI/MUGHLAI
Salloos (Belgravia, *M*)

PEKINESE
Ming (Soho, *I*)

PUBS
Antelope (Belgravia)
Bill Bentley's (Knightsbridge)
The Cow (Westbourne Park)
The Engineer (Camden Town)
The Enterprise (South Kensington)
Front Page (Chelsea)
Grenadier (Belgravia)
King's Head & Eight Bells (Chelsea)
Museum Tavern (Bloomsbury)
Nag's Head (Belgravia)
Nag's Head (Covent Garden)
Old Coffee House (Soho)
Prince Bonaparte (Westbourne Park)
Red Lion (St. James's)
Salisbury (Leicester Square)
Shepherd's Tavern (Mayfair)
Sherlock Holmes (Westminster)
Ye Olde Cheshire Cheese (The City)
Ye Olde Cock Tavern (The City)
Ye Olde Watling (The City)

SEAFOOD
Greens Restaurant & Oyster Bar
 (Piccadilly Circus, *M*)
North Sea Fish Restaurant
 (Holborn, *I*)
Scotts (Mayfair, *M*)

SOUTHEAST ASIAN
Bahn-Thai (Soho, *M*)

SUDANESE
Mondola (Notting Hill, *I*)

SZECHUAN
Zen Central (Mayfair, *M*)

THAI
Bahn-Thai (Soho, *M*)
Blue Elephant (West Brompton, *M*)
Chiang Mai (Soho, *I*)
I-Thai (Bayswater, *VE*)
Vong (Knightsbridge, *E*)

VEGETARIAN
Crank's in London (Mayfair, *I*)

WINE BARS
Boaters Wine Bar (Chelsea Harbour)
Bow Wine Vaults (The City)
Bubbles (St. James's)
Cork & Bottle Wine Bar
 (Leicester Square)
Daniel's Bar/Cafe Royal Grill
 (Piccadilly Circus)
Ebury Wine Bar (Victoria)
Jamaica Wine House (The City)
Le Metro (Knightsbridge)
Shampers (St. James's)

3 West End Restaurants

MAYFAIR
VERY EXPENSIVE

✪ **Chez Nico at Ninety Park Lane.** In Grosvenor House, 90 Park Lane, W1. ☎ **0171/409-1290.** Reservations required (at least 2 days in advance for lunch, 7 days for dinner). Fixed-price lunch £32 ($51) for 3 courses; à la carte dinner £50 ($80) for 2 courses, £62 ($99) for 3 courses. AE, DC, MC, V. Mon–Fri noon–2pm; Mon–Sat 7–11pm. Tube: Marble Arch. FRENCH.

Although the setting is as opulent as the cuisine, nothing takes precedence over food here. It's the work of one of London's supreme culinary artists, the temperamental but always amusing Nico Ladenis. This former oil company executive, self-taught cook, and economist remains one of Britain's most talked about chefs; his food is always impressive, always stylish, and he's constantly reinventing dishes we thought he had already perfected. As starters go, who can top his quail salad with sweetbreads, flavored with an almond vinaigrette? The main courses are a tour de force in the best post-nouvelle tradition, in which the tenets of classical cuisine are creatively and flexibly adapted to local fresh ingredients. With masterful technique, Nico's chefs dazzle with ever-changing fare, including a ravioli of langoustine that's a virtual signature dish. The char-grilled sea bass with basil puree or the Bresse pigeon are rivaled only by the work of Le Gavroche (see below). The only complaint we've ever heard about Chez Nico is that it attracts too many Michelin three-star groupies.

✪ **Le Gavroche.** 43 Upper Brook St., W1. ☎ **0171/408-0881.** Reservations required as far in advance as possible. Main courses £27.60–£70 ($44–$112); fixed-price lunch £40 ($64); menu exceptionnel, for entire table, £85 ($136) per person. AE, MC, V. Mon–Fri noon–2pm and 7–11pm. Tube: Marble Arch. FRENCH.

Le Gavroche has long stood for quality French cuisine, perhaps England's finest, although Michelin gives it only two stars. Though it may have fallen off briefly in the early 1990s, it's fighting its way back to the stellar ranks. There's always something special coming out of the kitchen of Burgundy-born Michel Roux; the service is faultless and the ambience formally chic without being stuffy. The menu changes constantly, depending on the fresh produce that's available and the current inspiration of the chef. But it always remains classically French, although not of the "essentially old-fashioned bourgeois repertoire" that some critics suggest. There are signature dishes that have been honed over years of unswerving practice: Try, if featured, the soufflé Suissesse, *papillote* of smoked salmon, or whole Bresse chicken with truffles and a Madeira cream sauce. Game is often served, depending on availability. Desserts, including the sablé of pears and chocolate, are sublime. The wine cellar is among the most interesting in London, with many quality Burgundies and Bordeaux. The fixed-price dinner has recently been replaced by the *menu exceptionnel,* which is, in essence, a tasting menu for the entire table. The menu usually consists of four to five smaller courses, followed by one or two desserts and coffee. At £85 ($136) per person, this may prove to be a smarter choice as opposed to the à la carte items, given the culinary options and price that the *menu exceptionnel* offers.

✪ **Oak Room/Marco Pierre White,** in Le Méridien Piccadilly, 21 Piccadilly, W1. ☎ **0171/734-8000.** Reservations required as far in advance as possible. Fixed-price lunch £30 ($47); fixed-price menu gourmand £75 ($120). Mon–Fri noon–2:15pm; Mon–Sat 7–11:15pm. Closed Christmas. Tube: Piccadilly Circus. MODERN BRITISH.

Put simply, "MPW" is the best chef in London. The only difference is he has moved from the Hyde Park hotel in Knightsbridge to the glamorous surroundings of Le Méridien Piccadilly. He serves London's finest cuisine in the city's most beautiful dining room, which has been restored to its original oak and gilt splendor and filled with art, including works by Cocteau and Chagall.

Creative, sophisticated and bold, this daring young chef claims he never apprenticed in France, other than 2 weeks of eating in Paris restaurants. Lavish in his choice of ingredients, White explores the depths of flavor in food. As you peruse the dozen or so appetizers, you'll note that most feature foie gras, caviar, and truffles. Afterwards, you can proceed to such main courses as Bressole of Bresse pigeon (with foie gras again), or braised pig's trotter inspired by Pierre Koffmann's masterpiece at La Tante Claire in Chelsea. Platters sometimes appear with brilliant colors, including a gratinée of brill with a soft herb crust, young spinach, and a sabayon of chives. Among all this fancy fare, Marco Pierre White makes the world's greatest mashed potatoes, which one diner claims were "sieved, puréed, and squeezed through silk stockings." White vies with Nico Ladenis as the most temperamental chef in London, but he's clearly a magician. If you can afford it, try to catch his show.

EXPENSIVE

○ **Nobu,** in the Metropolitan Hotel, 19 Old Park Lane, W1. ☎ **0171/447-4747.** Reservations required. Main courses £14.50–£27.50 ($23–$44); sushi and sashimi £2.75–£4.75 ($4.40–$7.60) per piece; fixed-price menu £60 ($96). AE, DC, MC, V. Mon–Fri noon–2:15pm; Mon–Sat 6–10:30pm. Tube: Hyde Park or Green Park. JAPANESE.

Robert de Niro and his restaurant gang of Nobu Matsuhisa and Drew Nieporent have taken their New York hot spot to London, where they offer an intensely innovative and experimental Japanese cuisine. With a beauty like Isabella Rossellini claiming that eating at Nobu keeps her lean and mean, how can you go wrong here?

The kitchen staff is brilliant and as finely tuned as their New York cousins. Sushi chefs don't just create sushi but gastronomic pyrotechnics. Those on the see-and-be-seen circuit don't seem to mind the high prices that go with these incredibly fresh dishes. Elaborate preparations lead to perfectly balanced flavors. Where can you find a good sea urchin tempura these days but at Nobu? Salmon tartare with caviar is a brilliant appetizer, and Madonna agrees. Follow with a perfectly done filet of sea bass in a sour bean paste or soft-shell crab rolls. The squid pasta is sublime, as is the black cod with miso. Cold sake arrives in a green bamboo pitcher. If it's featured, finish with the savory ginger crème brûlée.

MODERATE

○ **Bracewells.** In the Park Lane Hotel, Piccadilly, W1. ☎ **0171/499-6321.** Reservations required. Fixed-price lunch £22.50 ($36) for 2 courses, £27.50 ($44) for 3 courses. Five-course gastronomic menu £45 ($72). AE, DC, MC, V. Mon–Fri 12:30–2:30pm; Mon–Sat 7–10:30pm. Tube: Hyde Park Corner or Green Park. TRADITIONAL BRITISH.

Sheltered by the Park Lane Hotel's fortresslike walls, award-winning Bracewells is one of London's most popular restaurants for truly classic British fare. The cuisine, prepared by Chef David Dent, is among the best in the capital, and the decor and the five-star service are worthy of the distinguished clientele. Amid the gilded torchères and comfortable armchairs of Bracewells Bar, you might begin with a drink and canapés of lobster, foie gras, and caviar. Later, you'll be ushered into an intimately lit room, whose Louis XVI paneling was long ago removed from the London home of the American banker and philanthropist Pierpont Morgan; it was recently restored to its original condition.

The specialties are prepared with the freshest ingredients. The courses are regional English and seasonal specialties ranging from the traditional Dover sole to roasted best-end of lamb. The menu and dining options underwent a series of changes with the arrival of the new chef, and dinner at Bracewells may not be exactly as you had remembered it. Gone is the à la carte menu, but we always felt that the fixed-price menu offered the most outstanding value anyway.

Greenhouse. 27A Hays Mews, W1. ☎ **0771/499-3331.** Reservations essential. Main courses £9.50–£18.50 ($15–$30). AE, DC, MC, V. Mon–Sat noon–2:30pm and 6:30–11pm; Sun 12:30–2:30pm and 6:30–10:30pm. Closed Christmas, bank holidays. Tube: Green Park. MODERN BRITISH.

West End Restaurants

Alastair Little 50
Atlantic Bar & Grill 29
Au Jardin des Gourmets 52
Bahn Thai 46
Belgo Centraal 59
Bracewells 16
British Museum Restaurant 61
Brown's Hotel 20
Bruno Soho 54
Bubbles 3
The Carvery 28
Chez Nico 6
Chiang Mai 49
Christopher's 73
Chuen Cheng Ku 44
Claridge's 4
Coast 21
Cork & Bottle Wine Bar 42
Crank's in London 25
The Criterion Brasserie-Marco Pierre White 39
Daniel's Bar (Cafe Royal Grill) 38

dell'Ugo 53
Dumpling Inn 43
The Fox & Anchor 79
Gay Hussar 57
The George 75
Goode's 9
The Granary 19
Greenhouse 10
Greens Restaurant & Oyster Bar 33
Hard Rock Cafe 15
The Ivy 48
Joe Allen 66
Kai Mayfair 8
L'Odéon 29
Langan's Bistro 1
Langan's Brasserie 17
Le Gavroche 5
The Living Room 51
Magno's 71
Mezzo 55
Ming 47
MJ Bradley's 36
Momo 27
Museum Street Café 72
Museum Tavern 60
Nag's Head 70
Neal Street Restaurant 58
Nico Central 23
Nobu 14
North Sea Fish Restaurant 63
Oak Room 30
Odin's 2
Old Coffee House 26
Palm Court at the Waldorf Meridian 74
Palm Court Lounge 16
Pied-à-Terre 62
Pizzeria Condotti 22
Plummers Restaurant 69
Porter's English Restaurant 60
Quaglino's 34
Quo Vadis 45
Red Lion 37
Ritz Palm Court 18
Rules 67
Salisbury 41
Scotts 7
Shampers 24
Shepherd's Tavern 13
Sherlock Holmes 64
Ship Hispaniola 76
Simpson's-in-the-Strand 65
Soho Spice 56
St. James Restaurant & Fountain Restaurant 32
The Stockpot 40
Suntory 35
Tamarind 12
Wiltons 31
Ye Olde Cheshire Cheese 78
Ye Olde Cock Tavern 77
Zen Central 11

Celebrated TV chef Gary Rhodes may have departed for a lower-profile career in corporate catering, but don't strike the Greenhouse from your list just yet. New head chef Graham Grafton is quite inspired, and seems to spend more time here perfecting dishes than Gary ever did. The modern British cuisine, served in a comfortable room accented with prints and dried flowers, is prepared using only the finest fresh ingredients. Grafton has a winning way with fish, if his poached skate is any example—and his deep-fried cod-and-chips is galaxies beyond what you'd get at the local chippie. But you may prefer the lip-smacking fare from the heart of England, which includes a roast breast of pheasant that Henry VIII would have loved, and grilled farmhouse pork; we're also fond of the wilted greens wrapped in bacon. The menu is backed up by a well-chosen wine list of some 20 selections. Some of the delightfully sticky desserts, including a moist bread-and-butter pudding and a ginger pudding with orange marmalade, would have pleased your Midlands grandmum.

○ **Kai Mayfair.** 65 S. Audley St., W1. ☎ **0171/493-8988.** Reservations recommended. Main courses £9–£12 ($14–$19). AE, DC, MC, V. Mon–Fri noon–2:15pm, Sat–Sun 12:30–3pm; Mon–Sat 6:30–10:45pm, Sun 6:30–10:30pm. Tube: Marble Arch or Hyde Park Corner. CHINESE.

London is filled with sterile Chinese eateries using recipes that didn't transport well from the Far East. An exception is this winning dining room, one of the glitziest Chinese restaurants in town, lying near the American Embassy. The menu promises dishes in such fanciful categories as "The Whims and Fancies of the Emperess" or "Buddha Jumps Over the Wall." The tried-and-true Chinese dishes are here, everything from roast duckling with pineapple to sweet or sour pork. But many other dishes show more imagination and flair, particularly shark's fin and abalone. Bang-bang chicken in a nut sauce packs a powerful taste punch. Children are especially catered to, with dishes prepared just for them.

Langan's Brasserie. Stratton St., W1. ☎ **0171/491-8822.** Reservations recommended. Main courses £12–£14.50 ($19–$23). AE, DC, MC, V. Mon–Fri 12:15–11:45pm; Sat 7pm–11:45pm. Tube: Green Park. TRADITIONAL BRITISH/FRENCH.

Since its heyday in the early 1980s, when it was one of the hippest restaurants in London, this upscale brasserie has welcomed an average of 700 diners a day. The 1976 brainchild of the late restaurateur Peter Langan, in partnership with actor Michael Caine and chef Richard Shepherd, the brasserie sprawls over two noisy, see-and-be-seen floors, each filled with potted plants and spinning ceiling fans that create a 1930s kind of continental feel. The menu is defined as "mostly English with a French influence" and includes a spinach soufflé with anchovy sauce; croustade of quail eggs in a pastry case served with a duxelle of mushrooms and hollandaise sauce; and roast crispy duck with apple sauce and sage-lemon stuffing. There's always a selection of English fare, including bangers and mash and fish 'n' chips.

✪ **Quaglino's.** 16 Bury St., SW1. ☎ **0171/930-6767.** Reservations recommended. Main courses £12–£26 ($19–$42); fixed price 3-course menu (available only for lunch and pre-dinner theater between 5:30 and 6:30pm) £15.50–£19.50 ($25–$31). AE, DC, MC, V. Daily noon–3pm; Mon–Thurs 5:30pm–midnight, Fri–Sat 5:30pm–1am, Sun 5:30–11pm. Tube: Green Park. CONTINENTAL.

It's vast, it's convivial, it's fun, and it was voted the restaurant of 1994 by *Time Out* magazine. It occupies the premises of a restaurant established in 1929 by Giovanni Quaglino, from Italy's Piedmont; personalities who paraded through these premises in ermine and pearls could fill a between-the-wars roster of Who's Who for virtually every country of Europe. In 1993, noted restaurateur and designer Sir Terence Conran brought the place into the postmodern age with a vital new decor that's been likened to a stylishly decorated ocean liner. Eight artists were commissioned to decorate the octet of massive columns supporting the soaring ceiling. A mezzanine with a bar features live jazz every Friday and Saturday night and live piano music the rest of the week, and an "altar" in the back is devoted to what must be the most impressive display of crustaceans and shellfish in Britain.

Everything seems to be served in bowls. Menu items have been criticized for their quick preparation and standardized format—not as marvelously subtle as what you might expect in more manageably sized eateries. But considering that on some nights up to 800 people might show up here for food, laughter, and gossip, the marvel is that the place functions as well as it does. That's not to say there isn't an occasional delay. Come for fun, not culinary finesse. The menu changes often, but your choices might include goat cheese and caramelized onion tart; seared salmon with potato pancakes; crab tartlet with saffron; and roasted cod and ox cheek with char-grilled vegetables.

Scotts. 20 Mount St., W1Y 6HE. ☎ **0171/629-5248.** Reservations required. Fixed-price 2-course lunch £18.75 ($30); fixed-price 3-course lunch or dinner £23–£45 ($37–$72). AE, DC, MC, V. Mon–Fri noon–3pm; Mon–Sat 6–11pm, Sun 7–10pm; Oyster Terrace Mon–Fri noon–11pm; Sat 5–11pm. Tube: Green Park or Bond St. TRADITIONAL BRITISH/SEAFOOD.

In addition to a spacious dining room (refurbished in 1996) and cocktail bar, Scotts has a widely noted raw bar. Its origins were humble, dating back to a fishmonger's in Coventry Street in 1851. However, its fame rests on its heyday, when the proprietors often entertained Edward VII and his guests in private dining rooms.

The chef, who believes in British produce, handles the kitchen with consummate skill and authority. You get top-notch quality and ingredients. Lobster, crab, and oysters are featured along with meat dishes such as cumberland sausage and black pudding or corn-fed chicken with grain mustard. Dover sole is prepared a variety of ways, although the English prefer it "on the bone," considering filet fish for sissies. Starters include mousses of smoked haddock, trout, and mackerel on herb griddle cakes, and oak-smoked salmon with rye bread; Scott's shellfish plate includes oysters, Dublin Bay prawns, mussels, crab, and scallops. More down-to-earth dishes, such as fish cakes, appear regularly on the lunch menu served in the Oyster Terrace.

Zen Central. 20–22 Queen St., W1. ☎ **0171/629-8103.** Reservations recommended. Main courses £10–£15.50 ($16–$25). AE, DC, MC, V. Mon–Sat 12:15–2:30pm and 6:30–11:30pm; Sun 12:15–2:30pm and 6:30–11pm. Tube: Green Park. SZECHUAN.

Movie stars always seem to have an advance scouting party informing them of the best places to dine when they visit a foreign city. When we heard that Eddie Murphy and Tom Cruise were heading for this Szechuan eatery, we followed in their footsteps. Whoever directed them here was right. We didn't spot any stars, but found a designer chic Mayfair restaurant with a cool, dignified decor in minimalist black and white. Mirrors cover much of the place (maybe that's why movie stars like it). Served by a competent staff, the cuisine is first rate. Start with the coriander and crab meat croquettes, or the soft-shelled crabs tenderly cooked in a crust of salt. The steamed sea bass is perfectly cooked and, for extra flavor, served with a black bean sauce. Pork chops with lemon grass has a Thai flavor, and the baked lobster with crushed roast garlic and livers of tangerine peel is worth the walk across Mayfair. Habitués with some justification praise the cold pig's trotter, although this is an acquired taste for some. Vegetarian meals are also available. We find the wine list pricey but the jasmine tea is lovely.

INEXPENSIVE

✪ **Crank's In London.** 8 Marshall St., W1 ☎ **0171/437-9431.** Main courses £5–£6.45 ($8–$10). AE, DC, MC, V. Mon–Tues 8am–8pm; Wed–Fri 8am–9pm. Tube: Oxford Circus. VEGETARIAN.

Located just off Carnaby Street, this is the headquarters of a chain of vegetarian restaurants with seven other branches in London. Outfitted in natural wood, wicker-basket lamps, pinewood tables, and handmade ceramic bowls and plates, Crank's is completely self-service: You carry your own tray to one of the tables. Organic-white and stone-ground flour is used for breads and rolls. The uncooked vegetable salad is especially good, and there's always a hot stew of savory vegetables (with "secret" seasoning), served in a hand-thrown stoneware pot with a salad. Homemade honey cake, cheesecake, tarts, and crumbles are featured. Bakery goods, nuts, and general health-food supplies are sold in an adjoining shop.

Hard Rock Café. 150 Old Park Lane, W1. ☎ **0171/629-0382.** Main courses £8.50–£15 ($14–$24). AE, MC, V. Sun–Thurs 11:30am–12:30am; Fri–Sat 11:30am–1am. Closed Dec. 25–26. Tube: Green Park or Hyde Park Corner. AMERICAN.

This is the original Hard Rock, now a worldwide chain of rock-and-roll-themed southern-cum-midwestern American roadside diners serving up good food and service with a smile. Since it was established on June 14, 1971, more than 12 million people have eaten here. Almost every night there's a line waiting to get in. The portions are generous, and the price of a main dish includes not only a salad but also fries or baked potatoes. The beef-laden menu has forced the restaurateurs to import the meat; the fajitas are always a good choice. The tempting dessert menu offers homemade apple pie and thick, cold shakes. There's also a good selection of beers. The collection of rock memorabilia is worth seeking out if you're a fan.

Pizzeria Condotti. 4 Mill St., W1. ☎ **0171/499-1308.** Reservations not required. Pizzas £5–£7 ($8–$11), pastas £6.30 ($10), salads £6–£8 ($10–$13). AE, DC, MC, V. Mon–Sat 11:30am–midnight; Sun noon–11pm. Tube: Oxford Circus. ITALIAN/AMERICAN.

On pizza there can never be any agreement, but many aficionados come here for what they claim is London's best (frankly, we think dozens of New York dives have it beat). Nevertheless, when you're in London, you can hardly find a better choice for your fix. Tastefully decorated with fresh flowers and local art from the 1970s, this place just off Regent Street looks more costly than it is.

The pizzas are light and crisp, and arrive at your table bubbling hot from the oven. Pies can range from a simple margherita with mozzarella and tomato to the sublime King Edward with potato, four cheeses, and tomato. Dare to try the "American hot," with mozzarella, pepperoni, sausages, and hot peppers. The menu isn't confined to pizzas. The salads are huge and freshly made and the pastas are plentiful; even the wine list is impressive and reasonable in price. Finish off perhaps with a scoop of creamy tartufo ice cream made with chocolate liqueur, a grace note that will evoke a memory of a visit to Rome's Piazza Navona.

Tamarind. 20 Queen St., W1. ☎ **0171/629-3561.** Reservations required. Main courses £6.75–£35 ($11–$56). AE, DC, MC, V. Sun–Fri noon–3pm; Mon–Sat 6–11:30pm, Sun 6–10:30pm. Tube: Green Park. INDIAN.

Currently in favor with food critics as well as the local lunchtime business crowd, Tamarind is the hottest and most fashionable Indian restaurant in Mayfair. A small basement restaurant, it has gold pillars and a "tandoor window" for watching the chefs pull their flavorful, spicy dishes from the ovens. Chef Atul Kochhar leads a culinary brigade direct from Delhi that tries to maintain the style of cooking they knew back home, depending on the availability of spices and produce; only the best and freshest ingredients are selected daily in the markets. The kitchen prides itself on its "nouvelle" dishes, but they also excel at traditional Indian fare—including fabulous breads. The monk fish marinated in saffron and yogurt is especially delectable, as is the mixed kebab platter, cooked in a charcoal-fired tandoor—these chefs are king of the kebabs.

Your best bet for a curry? Opt for the prawns cooked in a five-spice mixture. Vegetarians will find a safe refuge here, especially if they go for the Dal Bukhari, a black-lentil specialty of northwest India.

MARYLEBONE
MODERATE

Odin's. 27 Devonshire St., W1. ☎ **0171/935-7296.** Reservations required. Fixed-price 2-course lunch or dinner £24 ($38); fixed-price 3-course lunch or dinner £26 ($42). AE, DC, MC, V. Mon–Fri 12:30–2:30pm and 6:30–11pm. Tube: Regent's Park. INTERNATIONAL.

This elegant restaurant is one of at least four in London owned by chef Richard Shepherd and actor Michael Caine (whose stable includes Langan's Brasserie). Set adjacent to its slightly less expensive twin, Langan's Bistro (see below), it features ample space between tables and an eclectic decor that includes evocative paintings and deco accessories. The menu changes with the seasons: Typical fare might include forest mushrooms in brioche, braised leeks glazed with mustard and tomato sauce, roast duck with apple sauce and sage and onion stuffing, or roast filet of seabass with a juniper cream sauce.

INEXPENSIVE

Langan's Bistro. 26 Devonshire St., W1. ☎ **0171/935-4531.** Reservations recommended. Fixed-price 2-course lunch or dinner £18 ($29); Fixed-price 3-course lunch or dinner £20 ($32). AE, DC, MC, V. Mon–Fri 12:30–2:30pm; Mon–Sat 6:30–11:30pm. Tube: Regent's Park. TRADITIONAL BRITISH/FRENCH.

This deliberately unpretentious restaurant has been a busy fixture on the London restaurant scene since the mid-1960s, when it was established by the late restaurateur Peter Langan with chef Richard Shepherd and actor Michael Caine. Of the several restaurants within its chain (see Langan's Brasserie and Odin's, above), it's the least expensive (and least spacious), but the most visually appealing. Set behind a brightly colored storefront on a residential street, the dining room's surfaces are richly covered with fanciful clusters of Japanese parasols, rococo mirrors, surrealistic paintings, and old photographs. The menu is defined as "mostly English with a French influence"; it changes with the seasons, but might include salmon and broccoli mousse, snails in a garlic butter sauce, poached salmon in pastry served with a watercress sauce, pan-fried squid, and lamb stew. Chocaholics should finish off with the dessert extravaganza known as "Mrs. Langan's chocolate pudding."

ST. JAMES'S
VERY EXPENSIVE

✪ **Suntory.** 72–73 St. James's St., SW1. ☎ **0171/409-0201.** Reservations required. Main courses £18–£40 ($29–$64); fixed-price lunch £13.50–£38 ($22–$61); fixed-price dinner £50–£69 ($80–$111). AE, DC, MC, V. Mon–Sat noon–2pm and 6–10pm. Tube: Green Park. JAPANESE.

London's longest established and one of its best-known Japanese restaurants, Suntory is still holding its own against increased competition from Nobu. Unlike Nobu, it still leaves out foodstuff deemed unsuitable for Western palates, continuing instead to concentrate on the artistic presentation of the highest quality produce. Prices are as lofty as ever. Owned and operated by Japanese distillers and brewers, Suntory offers a choice of dining rooms in a setting evocative of a Japanese manor house. First-time visitors seem to prefer the tappanyaki dining room downstairs, where iron grills are set on each table and you can watch the mastery of the high-hatted, knife-wielding chef up close. In other rooms you can dine on sukiyaki, tempura, and sushi (especially good is the delicately sliced raw tuna). Waitresses in traditional dress serve you with all the highly refined ritual of Japan. Appetizers are artful and delicate; even the tea is superior.

PICCADILLY CIRCUS & LEICESTER SQUARE
EXPENSIVE

Coast. 26B Albemarle St., W1X 3FA. ☎ **0171/495-5999.** Reservations required. Main courses £10.50–£21.50 ($17–$34). AE, MC, V. Mon–Sat noon–3pm and 6pm–midnight; Sun noon–3:30pm and 6–11pm. Tube: Piccadilly Circus. MODERN INTERNATIONAL.

Coast is so cutting edge, so 21st-century, that you might get the feeling that it strains a bit to maintain its image as one of London's hippest restaurants. Set in a former auto showroom with lots of parquet woodwork, it's painted in colors that resemble, according to your tastes, either spring green or the color of aged bilgewater, and accented with lighting fixtures that protrude like alien bug-eyes from their settings. There's only one piece of art (by the terribly fashionable artist Angela Bulloch), but it's a doozy: a drawing machine that uses a robotic arm to scribble a graph simulating the movement within the room on an electronic screen; like a giant Etch-a-Sketch, it's wiped clean when it becomes unreadable.

With all this forced hipness, we didn't really want to like this place, but it won us over with its surprisingly good food. Innovative chef Stephen Terry is an original (some say too innovative), but we liked his willingness to go where others fear to tread. He handles textures well and brings out the best of the flavors in the light cuisine, particularly the fish dishes. This is no beans-on-toast place. To get you going, Terry tempts with his pressed terrine of quail, pan-fried foie gras, celeriac, and prunes, or his parpadelle pasta with roasted chestnut veloute and Perigord truffles. Then it's on to monkfish tail osso bucco with dried orange zest and roasted mirepoix, or else roast duck breast on Asian greens, a *poppadom millefeuille* of pineapple, and Thai red curry. Finish with the blood-orange trifle.

L'Odéon. 65 Regent St., W1. ☎ **0171/287-1400.** Reservations required. Main courses £14.50–£26 ($23–$42). AE, DC, MC, V. Mon–Sat and Sun noon–2:30pm; Mon–Sat 5:30–11:30pm. Tube: Piccadilly Circus. CONTINENTAL.

When the Michelin-starred chef Bruno Loubet opened this chic 1930s-style brasserie, headlines read "Loubet cooks for the masses." His sous-chef, Anthony Demetre, now carries on following Loubet's departure. But the menu remains rooted in the Loubet repertoire, with innovative additions. Many diners opt for a table opening onto Regent Street, with its bright red double-deckers heading for Piccadilly Circus. In all, some 220 diners can pack this place (and often do).

The white linens and place settings are kept very simple—but not the food. The chef roams the world for inspiration—a bit of the Continent here, a bow to California here, a touch of the Far East, and so on. Starters include a pigeon borscht terrine with dill crème fraîche or roast scallops on black pudding with mashed potatoes and a garlic coulis. For mains, try the roast Hereford duck breast with beetroot and rhubarb marmalade or the firm red mullet with cannelloni, which is bliss on a plate. The hot apple tart with an "alcoholic" Calvados ice cream is a creamy treat.

○ Wiltons. 55 Jermyn St., SW1. ☎ **0171/629-9955.** Reservations required. Jacket and tie required for men. Main courses £15–£25 ($24–$40). AE, DC, MC, V. Mon–Fri and Sun 12:30–2:30pm and 6–10:30pm; closed Sat. Tube: Green Park or Piccadilly Circus. TRADITIONAL BRITISH.

This is one of the top purveyors of traditional British cuisine and our favorite of the current bunch. The thoroughly British menu—it's been called "as British as a nanny"—is known for its fish and game. You might begin with an oyster cocktail and follow with Dover sole, plaice, salmon, or lobster, prepared in any number of ways. In season (from mid-August), there are such delights as roast partridge, pheasant, or grouse; you might even be able to order widgeon, a wild, fish-eating river duck (the chef might ask you if you want it "blue" or "black," a reference to roasting times). Game is often accompanied by bread sauce (milk thickened with bread crumbs). To finish, consider a savory such as Welsh rarebit, soft roes, or anchovies; if that's too much, try the sherry trifle or syllabub.

We consistently find the service, by a bevy of bosomy matrons, to be the most helpful in the West End. Since this is a bastion of traditionalism, however, don't show up in the latest Covent Garden fashions—you might not get in. Instead, don your oldest suit and look like you believe the Empire still exists.

MODERATE

Atlantic Bar & Grill. 20 Glasshouse St., W1. ☎ **0171/734-4888.** Reservations required. Main courses £10.50–£18 ($17–$29); fixed-price lunch £15 ($24), including two glasses of wine. AE, MC, V. Mon–Fri noon–3pm; Mon–Sat 6pm–3am, Sun 6–10:30pm. Tube: Piccadilly Circus. MODERN BRITISH.

A titanic restaurant installed in a former art deco ballroom off Piccadilly Circus, this 160-seat locale draws a trendy crowd to London's tawdry heartland. Hailed as "restaurant of the year" when it opened in the spring of 1994, the Atlantic's business seems to have fallen off a bit recently. Not because the food is bad—it's quite good. But fickle hipsters are beginning to move on, even though on any given night you'll still find yuppies working on a 1980s-style comeback alongside celebrities like Goldie Hawn and Bill Murray; the after-theater crowd also makes a strong showing.

The original chef, Richard Sawyer, is serving his second tour of duty here, in hopes of regaining the restaurant's former grandeur. Even American cuisine comes into focus here, especially the grilled tuna on mashed black beans with seared tomatoes, spiced avocado, and corn chips (the best this side of Santa Fe). The menu changes every 2 months, but is always strong on seafood and meats: The pan-fried skate wing stuffed with black olive purée is a delight. The desserts, however, are purposefully (and inexplicably) unsophisticated: rice pudding, poire Belle Hélène (poached pear). If you're rushed, you can drop into Dick's Bar, where they serve up everything from lamb burgers sparked with yogurt and fresh mint to Cashel blue cheese and pumpkin seeds on ciabatta bread, for a quick bite.

The Criterion Brasserie—Marco Pierre White. 224 Piccadilly, W1. ☎ **0171/930-0488.** Main courses £11.50–£15 ($18–$24); fixed-price 2-course lunch £15 ($24), fixed-price 3-course lunch £18 ($29). AE, MC, V. Daily noon–2:30pm and 6pm–midnight. Tube: Piccadilly Circus. MODERN BRITISH.

Known as the bad boy of British cookery, Michelin-starred Marco Pierre White runs what he calls his "junior" restaurant here. Designed by Thomas Verity in the 1870s, this palatial neo-Byzantine mirrored marble hall is a glamorous backdrop for the master chef's cuisine, served under a golden ceiling, with theatrical peacock-blue draperies. The menu is wide ranging, from Paris brasserie food to "nouvelle-classical," and served by a mainly French staff. The food is excellent, but falls short of sublime. Still, the roast skate wing with deep-fried snails is delectable, as is the roast saddle of lamb stuffed with mushrooms and spinach.

Greens Restaurant & Oyster Bar. 36 Duke St., SW1. ☎ **0171/930-4566.** Reservations recommended. Main courses £9.50–£35 ($15–$56). AE, DC, MC, V. Restaurant daily 12:30–3pm; Mon–Sat 6–11pm; oyster bar Mon–Sat 11:30am–3pm and 5:30–11pm; Sun noon–3pm. Tube: Piccadilly Circus or Green Park. SEAFOOD.

Critics say it's a triumph of tradition over taste but, as far as seafood goes in London, this is a tried-and-true favorite, thanks to an excellent menu, a central location, and a charming staff. This busy place has a cluttered entrance leading to a crowded bar where you can stand to sip fine wines and, from September to April, enjoy oysters. In

ⓘ Family-Friendly Restaurants

- **Pizzeria Condotti** (Mayfair; *see p. 128*) Your kid's pizza fix can be satisfied here better than anywhere else in London. Pies with succulent toppings emerge bubbling hot from the oven. The "American hot" comes with mozzarella, pepperoni, sausages, and hot peppers—and the menu isn't just confined to pizzas.
- **Deal's Restaurant and Diner** (Chelsea; *see p. 157*) After enjoying the boat ride down to Chelsea Harbour, kids will love the burgers and other American fare served here. Reduced-price children's portions are available.
- **Dickens Inn by the Tower** (Docklands; *see p. 148*) Even fussy kids will find something they like at this former old spice warehouse, now a three-story restaurant with sweeping Thames and Tower Bridge views. The fare ranges from parent-pleasing modern British to yummy lasagna and pizza.
- **Ye Olde Cheshire Cheese** (The City; *see p. 173*) Fleet Street's most famous chophouse, established in 1667, is an eternal family favorite. If "ye famous pudding" turns your kid off, the sandwiches and roasts will tempt them into digging in instead.
- **Hard Rock Café** (Mayfair; *see p. 128*) This is a great place for older children. Teenagers like the rock 'n' roll memorabilia as well as the juicy burgers with a heap of fries and a salad doused with Thousand Island dressing.
- **Porter's English Restaurant** (Covent Garden; *see p. 143*) This restaurant serves traditional English meals that most kids love—especially the pies, stews, and steamed "puds." They'll get a real kick out of ordering wonderfully named food like bubble and squeak and mushy peas.

the faux-Dickensian dining room, you can select from a long menu of seafood dishes, ranging from fish cakes with roast pepper and tomato sauce to whole Scottish lobster. For zesty starters, try either the smoked eel filets (Cockney) or the avocado and bacon salad with baby leaf spinach. Desserts include bread and butter pudding.

Momo. 25 Heddon St., W1. ☎ **0171/434-4040.** Reservations required 2 weeks in advance. Main courses £10.50–£15.50 ($17–$25); 2-course fixed-price lunch £12.50 ($20), 3-course fixed-price lunch £15.50 ($25). AE, DC, MC, V. Mon–Fri noon–2:15pm; Mon–Sat 7–11:15pm. Tube: Piccadilly Circus. MOROCCAN/NORTH AFRICAN.

You'll be greeted by a friendly and casual staff member clad in black and white T-shirts and fatigue pants. The setting is like Marrakesh, with stucco walls, a wood and stone floor, patterned wood window shades, burning candles, and cozy banquettes. You can fill up on the freshly baked bread the waiter brings along with appetizers such as garlicky marinated olives and pickled carrots spiced with pepper and cumin. These starters are a "gift" from the chef. Other appetizers, which you'll pay for, are also tantalizing, especially the *briouants,* paper thin and very crisp triangular packets of puffed pastry that are filled with saffron-flavored chicken and other treats. One of the chef's finest specialties is *pastilla au pigeon,* a traditional poultry pie with almonds. Many diners visit for the couscous maison, among the best in London. Served in a decorative pot, this aromatic dish of raisins, meats (including merguez sausage), chicken, lamb, and chick peas is given added flavor with that powerful hot sauce of the Middle East, marissa. After all this, the refreshing cinnamon-flavored orange slices are a tempting treat for dessert.

INEXPENSIVE

✪ **The Carvery.** Regent Palace Hotel, 12 Sherwood St. (entrance on Glasshouse St.), W1. ☎ **0171/488-4600.** Reservations recommended. All-you-can-eat meals £17.50 ($28) or £12.50 ($20) 5:15–7pm, £7.75 ($12) for children 5–16, free for those under 5. AE, DC, MC, V. Mon–Sat 12:15–2:30pm; Mon–Thurs 5:30–10:30pm, Fri–Sat 5:30–midnight, Sun 6–10:30pm. Tube: Piccadilly Circus. TRADITIONAL BRITISH.

Just 20 feet from Piccadilly Circus, you can have all the fabulous roasts you can eat—that's the famous policy of this renowned establishment. There's a wide range of appetizers, and the buffet carving table boasts a roast leg of Southdown lamb with mint sauce and a roast leg of English pork with apple sauce. Your choice of roast will be carved for you by the chef; you'll then serve yourself buttered peas, roast potatoes, new carrots, and gravy. In another area is cold food and assorted salads, whatever's in season. Desserts might include chocolate fudge cake or a sherry trifle. Well-brewed coffee is included in the price.

The Granary. 39 Albemarle St., W1. ☎ **0171/493-2978.** Main courses £7–£8.60 ($11–$14). MC, V. Mon–Fri 11:30am–8pm; Sat–Sun noon–2:30pm. Tube: Green Park. TRADITIONAL BRITISH.

This family-operated country-style restaurant has served a simple but flavorful array of home-cooked dishes, listed daily on a blackboard, since 1974. The daily specials might include lamb casserole with mint and lemon; pan-fried cod; or avocado stuffed with prawns, spinach, and cheese. Vegetarian meals include mushrooms stuffed with mixed vegetables, stuffed eggplant with curry sauce, and vegetarian lasagna. Tempting desserts are bread-and-butter pudding and brown Betty (both served hot). The large portions guarantee that you won't go hungry.

Plummers Restaurant. 33 King St., WC2. ☎ **0171/240-2534.** Reservations recommended. Fixed-price menus £9 ($14) for 1 course, £13 ($21) for 2 courses, £17 ($27) for 3 courses. AE, MC, V. Daily noon–2:30pm; Mon–Sat 5:30–11:30pm. Tube: Covent Garden or Leicester Squre. TRADITIONAL BRITISH.

Year after year, Plummers remains a sturdy and reliable choice. Decorated in an old English style that Laura Ashley might have designed, this informal restaurant is popular with visitors, who find it especially appealing for pre- or post-theater suppers. You can assemble a one-, two-, or three-course dinner according to your tastes from a large menu that changes from time to time, but is likely to include such dishes as apple and stilton soup; parmesan-and-herb-crusted filet of cod with a red pepper and tomato sauce; lamb casserole in a light curry sauce with coconut and lime, served with basmati rice; and char-grilled English lamb steak. Pre-theater menus are abbreviated for the sake of speed and efficiency.

The Stockpot. 40 Panton St. (off Haymarket, opposite the Comedy Theatre), SW1. ☎ **0171/839-5142.** Reservations accepted for dinner. Main courses £2.30–£5.55 ($3.70–$8.90); fixed-price 2-course lunch £3.20 ($5.10); fixed-price 3-course dinner £6 ($10). No credit cards. Mon–Sat 7am–11:30pm; Sun 7am–10pm. Tube: Piccadilly Circus or Leicester Square. TRADITIONAL BRITISH/CONTINENTAL.

Penny for penny, we'd hazard a guess that this cozy little restaurant offers one of the best dining bargains in London. Meals include a bowl of minestrone, spaghetti bolognese (the eternal favorite), a plate of braised lamb, and the apple crumble (or other desserts). At these prices, the food is hardly refined, but filling and satisfying nonetheless. With two levels of dining in a modern room, The Stockpot has a share-the-table policy during peak dining hours.

SOHO
EXPENSIVE

Alastair Little. 49 Frith St., W1. ☎ **0171/734-5183.** Reservations recommended. Fixed-price dinner £30 ($48); fixed-price 3-course lunch £25 ($40). AE, MC, V. Mon–Fri noon–3pm; Mon–Sat 6–11pm. Tube: Leicester Sq. or Tottenham Court Rd. MODERN BRITISH.

In a circa-1830 brick-fronted town house—which for a brief period supposedly housed John Constable's art studio—this informal, cozy restaurant is a pleasant place to enjoy a well-prepared lunch or dinner. Some loyal critics still claim that Alastair Little is the best chef in London, but lately he's been buried under the avalanche of new talent. Actually, Little himself is not often here; he spends a good deal of time at other enterprises and a cooking school in Umbria. The talented Jonathan Ricketts is in charge, and he believes in keeping Modern British dishes simple but flavorful, with exceptional tastes and textures. For inspiration, the kitchen draws upon all corners of the globe, from Japan and Thailand to France and Italy; the menu, which changes twice a day, reflects whatever's good and fresh at the market. You might enjoy a full-flavored roasted sea bass with parsley salad, a tender rack of lamb with rosemary, or Tuscan squab; dessert might be a crème brûlée or tarte tatin with créme fraîche. There's a reasonably priced wine list.

Bruno Soho. 63–64 Frith St., W1. ☎ **0171/734-4545.** Reservations recommended. Main courses £10.50–£18 ($17–$29), 2- and 3-course fixed-price meals £10.50–£15.50 ($17–$25). AE, DC, MC, V. Mon–Fri noon–2:30pm and 6:30–11:30pm; Sat 6–11:30pm. Tube: Tottenham Court Rd. FRENCH.

New in 1997, this dining sensation is daring, innovative, and hot. Kathleen and Pierre Condou and popular London chef James Kirby, the team behind the phenomenally successful L'Odéon, took over both Bistrot and Café Bruno to create this larger 90-seat restaurant, with a spacious bar. The Georgian shop-front facade has been maintained, but the interior is more informal.

Although experimenting initially with the cuisine of the Maghreb, the kitchen has now turned to combining the countryside repertoires of France, creating a broad, exciting palate of flavors. They'll dare to create a zesty concoction from ham hocks or even a poached cod salad, and aren't afraid of earthy, robust flavors, as exemplified by their pan-sautéed skate wings. At times they'll even offer a very British fish-and-chips and most definitely some good steaks, tender and cooked properly—either veal or beef. You might also sample their delectable and tender calf's liver. The wine list is one of London's most eclectic, wandering all the way from South Africa to Chile. Desserts range from apple tart to crème brûlée.

The Gay Hussar. 2 Greek St., W1. ☎ **0171/437-0973.** Reservations recommended. Main courses £20–£25 ($32–$40); fixed-price lunch £16 ($26). AE, DC, MC, V. Mon–Sat 12:15–2:30pm and 5:30–10:45pm. Tube: Tottenham Court Rd. HUNGARIAN.

The Gay Hussar has been called the best Hungarian restaurant in the world. It's an intimate place with undeniably authentic cuisine. You can begin with a chilled wild-cherry soup or smoked Hungarian sausage. Gutsy main courses might include cabbage stuffed with minced veal and rice; half a perfectly done chicken served in mild paprika sauce with cucumber salad and noodles; excellent roast duck with red cabbage and Hungarian-style caraway potatoes; and, of course, veal goulash with egg dumplings. Expect gigantic portions. For dessert, go with either the poppy seed strudel or walnut pancakes.

Mezzo. 100 Wardour St., W1. ☎ **0171/314-4000.** Reservations required for Mezzonine. Mezzo 3-course dinner £35–£40 ($56–$64). £5 ($8) cover at Mezzo Wed–Sat after 10pm.

Mezzonine 3-course dinner £25–£30 ($40–$48). AE, DC, MC, V. Mezzo: daily noon–2:30pm; Mon–Thurs 6pm–midnight, Fri–Sat 6pm–3am, Sun 6–11:30pm. Mezzonine: daily noon–2:30pm; Mon–Thurs and Sun 5:30pm–1am, Fri–Sat 5:30pm–3am. Tube: Tottenham Court Rd. CONTINENTAL/MEDITERRANEAN.

This blockbuster 750-seat Soho restaurant—the latest creation of entrepreneur Sir Terence Conran—may be the biggest in Europe. The mammoth space, on the former site of rock's legendary Marquee club, has been split into several separate restaurants: Mezzonine upstairs, serving a Thai/Asian cuisine with European flair (marinated salmon with ginger, star anise, and shallots; roast marinated lamb with yogurt and cumin on flat bread); the swankier Mezzo downstairs, with an atmosphere that evokes Hollywood in the 1930s (at any minute you expect Marian Davies—drunk or sober—to descend the grand staircase); and Mezzo Café, where you can stop in for a sandwich.

The food is at its most ambitious downstairs, where 100 chefs work behind glass to feed up to 400 diners at a time. This is dinner as theater. Not surprisingly, the modern British cuisine tends to be uneven. We suggest the shoulder of lamb, slow-roasted and enlivened with lemon zest and anchovies, or the roast cod, which was crisp-skinned and cooked to perfection. For dessert, you can't beat the butterscotch ice cream with a pitcher of hot fudge. A live jazz band entertains after 10pm from Wednesday to Saturday, and the world of Marlene Dietrich and Noël Coward comes alive again.

✪ Quo Vadis. 26–29 Dean St., W1. ☎ **0171/437-9585.** Reservations required. Main courses £14–£30 ($22–$48). Fixed-price lunches and pre- and post-theater £15–£18 ($24–$29). AE, MC, V. Mon–Fri noon–3pm; Mon–Sat 6–11pm, Sun 6–10:30pm. Tube: Leicester Sq. or Tottenham Court Rd. MODERN BRITISH.

This hyper-trendy restaurant occupies the former apartment house of Communist patriarch Karl Marx, who would never recognize it. It was a stodgy Italian restaurant from 1926 until the mid-1990s, when its interior was ripped apart and reconfigured into the stylish, postmodern place you'll find today. The stark street-level dining room is a museum-style showcase for dozens of hyper-modern paintings by the controversial Damien Hirst and other contemporary artists. Many bypass the restaurant altogether for the upstairs bar, where Hirst has put a severed cow's head and a severed bull's head on display in separate aquariums. Why? They're catalysts to conversation, satirical odes to the destructive effects of Mad Cow Disease, and perhaps tongue-in-cheek commentaries on the flirtatious games that patrons conduct here.

Quo Vadis is associated with Marco Pierre White, but don't expect to see the temperamental culinary superstar here; as executive chef, he only functions as a consultant. Also, don't expect that the harassed and overburdened staff will have the time to pamper you; they're too preoccupied dealing with the glare of frenetic publicity. And the food? It's appealingly presented and very good, but not nearly as artful or innovative as the setting might lead you to believe. We suggest beginning with the mussel and saffron soup or the terrine of foie gras and duck confit before moving on to the escallop of tuna with tapenade and eggplant caviar (actually eggplant and black olives puréed and seasoned, which gives it the look of caviar) or the sage-scented roast rabbit with a tomato confit and ratatouille.

MODERATE

Au Jardin des Gourmets. 5 Greek St., W1. ☎ **0171/437-1816.** Reservations required. Two courses £25 ($40); three courses £30 ($48); fixed-price 2-course lunch or pre-theater dinner £16.50 ($26). AE, DC, MC, V. Mon–Fri 12:15–2:30pm; Mon–Sat 6:30–11:15pm. Tube: Tottenham Court Rd. FRENCH.

This île-de-France off Soho Square is where devotees of Gallic cuisine have gathered to enjoy traditional specialties since 1931. In recent years, the second-floor Jardin has succeeded in reaching a new level of hospitality. A comprehensive à la carte menu varies with the seasons and may include such specialties as poached salmon with mussels flavored with orange and basil; roast rump of lamb with young herbs on a bed of couscous and Provençale vegetables; and roast saddle of rabbit with bacon and Emmental thyme jus. Vegetarian options are also available. The masterful selection of vintage Bordeaux and Burgundies is expertly served. Reservations require a credit-card guarantee.

Bahn Thai. 21-A Frith St., W1. ☎ **0171/437-8504.** Reservations recommended. Lunch: fixed-price menu £6.75–£8 ($11–$13), main courses £6–£7.50 ($10–$12); dinner fixed-price menu for 2, £37–£51 ($59–$82), main courses £7.25–£12.25 ($12–$20). AE, DC, MC, V. Mon–Sat noon–2:45pm and 6–11:15pm; Sun 12:30–10:30pm. Tube: Leicester Sq. THAI/SOUTHEAST ASIAN.

Located in the heart of Soho, this trendy but somewhat threadbare establishment continues to entertain London diners with a vast menu and dining environment options. Certainly one of the first decisions you'll have to make is where you would like to eat: in the upstairs dining room, or downstairs in the less casual cafe that has more of a Bangkok bistro feel. Perusing the encyclopedic menu is enough work to make you hungry—good luck actually deciding on something. Bear in mind also that if the menu says that the item is spicy, we suggest that you pay heed. Dishes are not cooled down for British palates. Curry comes in four different types, including our favorite, Penang, an aromatic blend of ground peanuts, coconut cream, anise-scented basil, and kafir lime. Chances are you'll wrongly pronounce the name of your order, but the staff is accommodating and the cuisine excellent, helping maintain Bahn Thai's reputation as one of the finest of its kind in London.

۞ The Ivy. 1–5 West St., WC2. ☎ **0171/836-4751.** Reservations required. Main courses £8.50–£16 ($14–$26); Sat–Sun lunch £15.50 ($25). AE, DC, MC, V. Daily noon–3pm and 5:30pm–midnight (last order). Tube: Leicester Sq. TRADITIONAL BRITISH/FRENCH.

Effervescent and sophisticated, The Ivy has been intimately associated with the West End theater district since it opened in 1911. With its ersatz 1930s look and tiny bar near the entrance, this place is fun—and it hums with the energy of London's glamour scene. The menu may seem simple, but the kitchen has a solid appreciation for fresh ingredients and a talent for skillful preparation. Favorite dishes include white asparagus with sea kale and truffle butter; seared scallops with spinach, sorrel, and bacon; and salmon fish cakes. There's also Mediterranean fish soup, a great mixed grill, and such English desserts as sticky toffee and caramelized bread-and-butter pudding. Meals are served quite late to accommodate the post-theater crowd.

INEXPENSIVE

Chiang Mai. 48 Frith St., W1. ☎ **0171/437-7444.** Main courses £6–£9 ($10–$14). AE, MC, V. Mon–Sat noon–3pm and 6–11pm; Sun 6–10:30pm. Tube: Leicester Sq. or Tottenham Court Rd. THAI.

This restaurant in the center of Soho is named after the ancient northern capital of Thailand, a region known for its rich, spicy foods. Try their hot and sour dishes or vegetarian meals. It's located next door to Ronnie Scott's, the most famous jazz club in England, so it's a good stop for an early dinner before a night on the town. Children's specials are available.

Chuen Cheng Ku. 17 Wardour St., W1. ☎ **0171/437-1398.** Reservations recommended on weekend afternoons. Main courses £7.40–£16.80 ($12–$27); fixed-price menus £9.50–£30 ($15–$48) per person. AE, DC, MC, V. Daily 11am–11:45pm. Closed Dec 24–25. Tube: Piccadilly Circus or Leicester Square. CHINESE.

This is one of the finest eateries in Soho's "New China." A large restaurant on several floors, Chuen Cheng Ku is noted for its Cantonese food; it has the longest and most interesting Cantonese menu in London. Specialties of the house are paper-wrapped prawns, rice in lotus leaves, steamed spareribs in black-bean sauce, and shredded pork with cashew nuts—all served in generous portions. Other featured dishes include lobster with ginger and spring onion, sliced duck in chili and black-bean sauce, and Singapore noodles (thin, rich noodles, sometimes mixed with curry and pork or shrimp with red and green pepper). Dim sum is served from 11am to 5:45pm. We must note, however, that we think the standard of service has slipped over the years.

dell'Ugo. 56 Frith St., W1. ☎ **0171/734-8300.** Reservations required. Main courses £6.25–£13.25 ($10–$21). AE, DC, MC, V. Mon–Fri noon–3pm; Mon–Sat 7pm–midnight. Tube: Tottenham Court Rd. MEDITERRANEAN.

This immensely popular multistory restaurant is one of Soho's finest, serving very good food at affordable prices. Critics claim there's too long a wait between courses, and dishes are overly contrived. But we have to agree with its legions of (mostly young) devotees: We've found the robust Mediterranean dishes to be prepared with the finest ingredients and packed with flavor. Most everything tastes fresh and appealing. Both the restaurant and bistro change their menus frequently, but generally feature an array of pasta, meat, fish, and vegetarian dishes. If you can, start with the goat cheese in a spicy tomato vinaigrette, and follow it with the linguini with langoustines or the rosemary-skewered lamb with a charred eggplant. Fish dishes, delectably seasoned and not allowed to dry out on the grill, range from monkfish to sea bass. Not everything works out—some dishes are tough (especially the duck) and lack spice. The crème brûlée (when it *finally* arrived) was excellent. All in all, not the spot for a romantic tête-à-tête, but immensely appealing. The ground-floor "caff" offers snacks all day, from tapas to meze.

Dumpling Inn. 15a Gerrard St., W1. ☎ **0171/437-2567.** Reservations recommended. Main courses £7–£15 ($11–$24); fixed-price lunch or dinner £14–£25 ($22–$40). AE, MC, V. Daily 11:45am–11:45pm. Tube: Piccadilly Circus. CHINESE.

Despite its incongruous name, this is a cool and rather elegant restaurant serving a delectable brand of Peking Mandarin cuisine that dates back almost 3,000 years and owes some of its special piquancy to the inclusion of various Mongolian ingredients; it is best represented by its savory stew called "hot pot." Regulars come here for the shark's-fin soup, the beef in oyster sauce, the seaweed and sesame-seed prawns on toast, duck with chili and black-bean sauce, and the fried sliced fish with sauce. Naturally, the speciality is dumplings; you can make a meal from the dim sum list. Portions aren't large, so you can order a good variety without fear of leftovers. Chinese tea is extra. Service is leisurely, so don't dine here before a theater date.

Ming. 35–36 Greek St., W1. ☎ **0171/734-2721.** Main courses £7.50–£15 ($12–$24); 2-course, fixed-price dinner £15 ($24), 3-course, fixed-price dinner £20 ($32). AE, DC, MC, V. Mon–Sat noon–11:45pm. Tube: Tottenham Court Rd. CANTONESE/PEKINESE.

In bustling Soho, this winning Chinese restaurant lies on Shaftesbury Avenue behind the Palace Theatre. The chefs in the kitchen, Mr. Bib and Mr. Bun (we're not making this up), welcome you to their Far East outpost, gaily decorated in green and pink. This is no chop suey and chow mein menu joint. Many of the recipes have real flair. One is fancifully described on the menu as from an 18th-century recipe from the Emperor Qian Long's head chef. What dazzled the emperor? Lean pieces of tender lamb with a slightly sweetened soy sauce. Fish, especially prawns and squid, are prepared in delectable ways, as are a number of tofu combinations. Cauliflower, sautéed in butter and flavored with bits of chili and slivers of spring onions, is an unusual appetizer. You might follow with spiced and peppered duck breast, or chicken with fresh coriander and lemon zest. White fish rolls are an intriguing choice, wrapped in a bean "skin." Mussels in black bean sauce are worth a return visit, as is a whole sea bass cooked Thai style. However, better skip the "Chiu Yim sliced eel and sea spice shredded pork." We weren't sure what it was!

Soho Spice. 124–126 Wardour St., W1. ☎ **0171/434-0808.** Reservations recommended. Main courses £9.50–£14 ($15–$22); set lunch £9 ($14); set dinner £16 ($26). AE, DC, MC, V. Sun–Wed noon–midnight; Thurs–Sat noon–3:30am. Tube: Tottenham Court Road. SOUTH INDIAN.

One of Central London's most stylish Indian restaurants combines a sense of media and fashion hip with the flavors and scents of Southern India. You might opt for a drink at the cellar-level bar before heading to the large street-level dining room decorated in the saffron, cardamom, bay, and pepper hues prevalent within Soho Spice's piquant cuisine. A staff member dressed in a similarly vivid uniform will propose choices from a wide array of dishes, including a range of slow-cooked Indian *tikkas* that feature combinations of spices with lamb, chicken, fish, or all-vegetarian. The cuisine will satisfy traditionalists, but has a modern, nouveau-Soho flair. The presentation takes it a step above typical Indian restaurants, here or elsewhere.

BLOOMSBURY
MODERATE

✪ **Museum Street Café.** 47 Museum St., WC1. ☎ **0171/405-3211.** Reservations required. Lunch £14.50 ($23) for 2 courses, £17.50 ($28) for 3 courses; dinner £19.50 ($31) for 2 courses, £23.50 ($38) for 3 courses. AE, MC, V. Mon–Fri 12:30–2:15pm (last order); Tues–Fri 6:30–9:15pm (last order). Tube: Tottenham Court Rd. MODERN BRITISH.

A 2-minute walk from the British Museum, this informal restaurant has been transformed from a greasy spoon to a charming dining room. You can sample creative up-to-date dishes impeccably prepared with fresh ingredients, such as salmon and coconut soup with lime, chili, and coriander, or a dill and leek tart with smoked salmon, followed by char-grilled corn-fed chicken with pesto, or else char-grilled quails with a Muscat sauce. Crispy polenta with wilted spinach, baked mushrooms, and a pomegranate balsamic vinaigrette is another winning combination. And who can resist the blood orange sorbet? Frills are few here, but the standard of cooking is quite high. The kitchen is at its best when it's char-grilling. The place has proven so popular that it has recently doubled in size.

INEXPENSIVE

British Museum Restaurant. Great Russell St., WC1. ☎ **0171/323-8256.** Main courses £6–£8 ($10–$13). MC, V. Mon–Sat cold food 11am–4:30pm, hot food 11:45am–3pm; Sun soup and cold food 2:30–5:30pm. Tube: Holborn or Tottenham Court Rd. TRADITIONAL BRITISH.

This is the best place for lunch if you're exploring the wonders of this world-renowned museum. It sits on the lobby level of the West Wing and is decorated with about a dozen full-size copies of the bas-reliefs from a temple in the town of Nereid in ancient Greece. (If you want to compare, you'll find the originals in nearby galleries.) The format is self-service. A few hot specials (including a vegetarian selection) and crisp salads are made fresh every day, and there's always a good selection of fish and cold meat dishes. Desserts include pastries and cakes. On Sunday, the emphasis is on soups, salads, and cold platters. There's also a cafe offering coffee, sandwiches, pastries, and soup.

IN NEARBY FITZROVIA
EXPENSIVE

Pied-à-Terre. 34 Charlotte St., W1. ☎ **0171/636-1178.** Reservations recommended. Fixed-price 3-course lunch £22 ($35); fixed-price 3-course dinner £33–£44 ($53–$70). 7-course tasting menu £52 ($83). AE, DC, MC, V. Mon–Fri 12:15–2:15pm (last order); Mon–Sat 7:15–10:15pm. Closed last week of Dec and first week of Jan and last 2 weeks of Aug. Tube: Goodge St. FRENCH.

This foodie heaven has deliberately understated its decor in favor of a more intense focus on its subtle and very sophisticated cuisine. You'll dine in a strictly (some say rigidly) minimalist room, where gray and pale-pink walls alternate with metal furniture and focused lighting that highlights a prize collection of modern art. France is the inspiration for the wine list and some, but not all, of the cuisine. The menu changes with the seasons, but might include braised snails with celeriac, garlic, and morille creamed sauce; roasted scallops with apple and puréed ginger; halibut filets with queen scallops and caramelized endive; roasted partridge with pear; and the house specialty, ballotine of duck confit. The food is beautifully presented on plates hand painted in lush patterns that offset the stylish starkness of the setting.

MODERATE

✪ **Nico Central.** 35 Great Portland St., W1. ☎ **0171/436-8846.** Reservations required. Fixed-price 2-course lunch £22 ($35); fixed-price 3-course dinner £27 ($43). AE, DC, MC, V. Mon–Fri noon–2:45pm; Mon–Sat 7–11pm. Tube: Oxford Circus. FRENCH/MODERN BRITISH.

This brasserie—founded and inspired by London's legendary chef, Nico Ladenis, who spends most of his time at Chez Nico at Ninety Park Lane—delivers earthy French cuisine that's been called "haute but not haughty" and consistently praised for its "absurdly good value." Of course, everything is handled with considerable culinary urbanity. Guests sit on bentwood chairs at linen-covered tables. Nearly a dozen starters—the pride of the chef—will tempt you. The menu changes seasonally and according to the inspiration of the chef, but might include grilled duck served with risotto with cèpes (flap mushrooms) and parmesan; pan-fried foie gras served with brioche and a caramelized orange; braised knuckle of veal; and baked filet of brill with assorted vegetables. Save room for one of the desserts—they are, in the words of one devotee, "divine."

CLERKENWELL
EXPENSIVE

✪ **Maison Novelli.** 29–31A Clerkenwell Green, EC1. ☎ **0171/251-6606**. Reservations required. Main courses in restaurant £13–£21 ($21–$34); main courses in brasserie £9–£14 ($14–$22). AE, MC, V. Mon–Fri noon–3pm; Mon–Sat 5–11:30pm. Closed two weeks July–Aug. Tube: Farringdon. CONTINENTAL.

You often have to abandon the heart of London these days to experience the city's finest and most imaginative cookery. High rents have driven such stellar chefs as Jean-Christophe Novelli to this up-and-coming area of the city. The cuisine is worth the trouble to get here. Novelli, who oversees the entire operation, is aided by the capable Richard Guest, a devotee of bold flavors, the freshest of ingredients, and imaginative culinary twists.

The ground floor is a brasserie with seats outside in fair weather. More formal service and a more expensive menu are found upstairs. Set within a neighborhood that a decade ago was anything but glamorous, the brasserie and restaurant share a blue-violet decor lined with modern art. The brasserie serves such hearty fare as a mackerel and lemongrass kebab or braised onion filled with cubed lamb. But it is in their restaurant that Guest and Novelli truly shine. The signature dish is a cassoulet terrine that we could dine on every day of the week. But that's only the beginning. Opt for the baby squid and scallop nage, followed by the sublime grilled John Dory (St-Pierre to the French diners). It comes with sliver of foie gras and a green pea-pod emulsion. Stuffed pig's trotters are stunningly rich and appear with mashed almonds for an exquisite flavor.

MODERATE

✪ **St. John.** 26 St. John St., EC1. ☎ **0171/251-0848.** Reservations required. Main courses £8.20–£13.50 ($13–$22). AE, DC, MC, V. Mon–Fri noon–11:30pm; Sat–Sun 6–11pm. Tube: Farringdon. MODERN BRITISH.

Located in a former smokehouse just north of Smithfield Market, this canteen-like dining room is the restaurant of choice for carnivores. This dining oddity is a show-case for the talents of owner-chef Fergus Henderson, a leader in the resurgent offal movement. In true British tradition, he doesn't use just part of the animal, he uses it all—we're talking neck, trotter, tail, liver, heart, the works.

Don't think you'll be served warmed-over haggis: The food is excellent and flavor-packed. In fact, there's a straightforward earthiness and simplicity to this cuisine that's unequaled anywhere in London. Henderson makes the best lambs' brains on toast in the city; both the grilled ox heart with arugula and pickled shallots and the duck neck and gizzard terrine are matchless. Roast bone marrow appears with a parsley salad, and pork chops are called pig chops. It's getting hard these days to find an eel, bacon, and clam stew, but you'll find one here. French wines help to wash it all down. Desserts run to puddings such as vanilla rice, or dates and walnuts with butterscotch. The breads served here can be purchased in an on-site bakery.

HOLBORN
INEXPENSIVE

✪ **North Sea Fish Restaurant.** 7–8 Leigh St., WC1. ☎ **0171/387-5892.** Reservations recommended. Fish platters £6–£13.75 ($10–$22). AE, DC, MC, V. Mon–Sat noon–2pm and 5:30–10pm. Tube: Russell Sq. SEAFOOD.

The fish served in this bright and clean restaurant is purchased fresh every day; the quality is high, and the prices low. In the view of London's most diehard chippie devo-tees, it's the best in town. The fish is most often served battered and deep-fried, but you can also order it grilled. The menu is wisely limited. Students from the Blooms-bury area flock to the place.

COVENT GARDEN & THE STRAND
EXPENSIVE

Neal Street Restaurant. 26 Neal St., WC2. ☎ **0171/836-8368.** Reservations recommended. Main courses £14–£25 ($22–$40). AE, DC, MC, V. Mon–Sat 12:30–2:30pm and 6–11pm. Tube: Covent Garden. ITALIAN.

This hip and stylish restaurant has one of Britain's most extravagant inventories of mushrooms, truffles, and other funghi. It's operated by Turin-born Antonio Carluccio, a noted author on the use of culinary mushrooms from around the world. Surrounded by the brick walls of what was a turn-of-the-century warehouse for the storage and ripening of bananas, the restaurant operates an aperitif bar in the cellar, where prospective diners sometimes wait until a table becomes available. On the walls hang the works of such modern masters as Frank Stella and David Hockney, as well as many lesser luminaries. Available at any time are between 10 and 20 of the world's most exotic mushrooms, including a highly desirable assortment of truffles. Imported according to season from China, Tibet, Japan, France, and California, they pop up in such recipes as the truffled endive salad, wild mushroom soup, pappardelle of venison with funghi, and tagliolini with truffle sauce. Equally appealing—but less expensive because they don't contain the exotics—might be monkfish with saffron and dill sauce, venison and roasted polenta, angolotti Piemontese, or homemade black angel-hair pasta with seafood and bottarga. Service is attentive and polite and the ambience agreeable. Their tiramisu is justifiably popular.

Simpson's-in-the-Strand. 100 The Strand (next to the Savoy Hotel), WC2. ☎ **0171/ 836-9112.** Reservations required. Jacket and tie required for men. Main courses £17.50–£25 ($28–$40); fixed-price 2-course lunch and pre-theater dinner £12.50 ($20); fixed-price breakfast £11.50 ($18). AE, DC, MC, V. Mon–Fri 7am–noon; daily noon–2:30pm and 6–11pm. Tube: Charing Cross or Embankment. TRADITIONAL BRITISH.

Simpson's is more of an institution than a restaurant—it's been in business since 1828. This very Victorian place boasts Adam paneling, crystal, and an army of grandly formal waiters to whom nouvelle cuisine means anything after Henry VIII. But most diners agree that Simpson's serves the best roasts in London, an array that includes roast sirloin of beef, roast saddle of mutton with red-currant jelly, roast Aylesbury duckling, and steak, kidney, and mushroom pie. (Remember to tip the tailcoated carver.) For a pudding, you might order the treacle roll and custard or Stilton with vintage port.

Taking advantage of the recent upsurge in popularity of traditional British cooking, Simpson's now serves the traditional breakfasts. The most popular one, curiously enough, is the one called "the ten deadly sins": a plate of sausage, fried egg, streaky and back bacon, black pudding, lamb's kidneys, fried bread, bubble and squeak, baked beans, lamb's liver, and fried mushrooms and tomatoes. That will certainly fortify you for the day. Simpson's also features late-night jazz.

Rules. 35 Maiden Lane, WC2. ☎ **0171/836-5314.** Reservations recommended. Main courses £14–£17 ($22–$27). AE, DC, MC, V. Daily noon–11:30pm. Tube: Covent Garden. TRADITIONAL BRITISH.

If you're looking for London's most quintessentially British restaurant, eat here or at Wiltons. London's oldest restaurant was established in 1798 as an oyster bar; today, on the site of the original premises, it rambles through a series of antler-encrusted Edwardian dining rooms exuding patriotic nostalgia. You can order such classic dishes as Irish or Scottish oysters, jugged hare, and mussels. Game dishes are offered from mid-August to February or March. There's also wild Scottish salmon or wild sea trout; wild Highland red deer; and game birds like grouse, snipe, partridge, pheasant, and woodcock. As a finale, the "great puddings" continue to impress decade after decade.

MODERATE

Belgo Centraal. 50 Earlham St., WC2. ☎ **0171/813-2233.** Reservations required for the restaurant. Main courses £8–£19 ($13–$31); fixed-price menus £7–£14 ($11–$22). AE, DC, MC, V. Mon–Sat noon–11:30pm; Sun noon–10:30pm. Closed Christmas. Tube: Covent Garden. BELGIAN.

Chaos reigns supreme in this audacious and cavernous basement, where mussels marinière with frites and 100 Belgian beers are the *raison d'être*. You'll take a freight elevator down past the busy kitchen and into a converted cellar, which has been divided into two large eating areas. One is a beer hall seating about 250; the menu here is the same as in the restaurant, but reservations aren't needed. The restaurant side has three nightly seatings: 5:30, 7:30, and 10pm. Between 5:30 and 8pm you can choose one of three fixed-price menus, and you pay based on the time of your order: the earlier you order, the less you pay. Although heaps of fresh mussels are the big attraction here, you can also opt for fresh Scottish salmon, roast chicken, a perfectly done steak, or one of the vegetarian specialties. Gargantuan plates of wild boar sausages arrive with *stoemp*, Belgian mashed spuds and cabbage. Belgian stews called *waterzooi* are also served. With waiters dressed in maroon monk's habits with black aprons and barking orders into headset microphones, it's all a bit bizarre.

Christopher's. 18 Wellington St., WC2. ☎ **0171/240-4222.** Reservations required. Main courses £11–£22 ($18–$35); pre-theater 2-course dinner £12.50 ($20) from 5:30–7:30pm; Sat–Sun brunch £5–£13 ($8–$21). AE, DC, MC, V. Restaurant Mon–Fri noon–2:45pm and 6–11:30pm; Sat noon–11:45pm; Sun noon–4pm. Tube: Covent Garden or Charing Cross. AMERICAN.

Many visitors to Christopher's are tempted to remain at street-level, where oysters, fresh salads, and other dishes are served in a bistro-style setting. Serious drinkers descend into the basement, where a bar awaits. The real showcase, however, is the restaurant, one floor above street level. Beneath a lavishly frescoed ceiling, an elaborate corkscrew-shaped stone staircase ascends to a pair of Italianate dining rooms. Here, flavorful and modern American dishes are served, including smoked tomato soup; roasted red peppers with buffalo mozzarella and basil; roast breast of duck with Kentucky bourbon peaches; and blackened salmon with spinach salad. Pasta is featured daily. Christopher's also serves our favorite Sunday brunch in London.

Magno's. 65a Long Acre, WC2. ☎ **0171/836-6077.** Reservations required. Main courses £10–£14 ($16–$22); fixed-price menu £14–£17 ($22–$27); fixed-price pre-theater supper (5:30–7:15pm) £11 ($18). AE, DC, MC, V. Mon–Fri noon–2:30pm; Mon–Sat 5:30–11:30pm. Tube: Covent Garden. FRENCH.

This well-recommended French restaurant operates in a brasserie-inspired room of green and cream-colored walls, closely spaced tables, and efficient service. The menu is also inspired by traditional French bistro cuisine, and might include such stalwarts as a *feuilleté au Rocquefort* (bleu cheese in puff pastry); duckling with celeriac confit; rack of lamb with ratatouille sauce and couscous; or panfried pork with cracked wheat, apple and cider sauce. The place is especially popular for before- and after-theater meals; make sure you reserve ahead.

INEXPENSIVE

The George. 213 The Strand, WC2. ☎ **0171/427-0941.** Bar platters £3–£6.30 ($4.80–$10). DC, V. Mon–Fri 11am–11pm; Sat 11am–3pm (food served Mon–Sat 11:30am–2:30pm). Tube: Temple. TRADITIONAL BRITISH.

Although its half-timbered facade would have you believe that it's older than it is, this pub was built as a coffeehouse in 1723. Set on the Strand, at the lower end of Fleet Street opposite the Royal Courts of Justice, the George is a favorite of barristers, their clients, and the handful of journalists who haven't yet moved to other parts of London. The pub's illustrious history saw Samuel Johnson having his mail delivered here during his heyday, and Oliver Goldsmith enjoying many tankards of what eventually became draught Bass. Today, the setting seems only slightly changed from those days; much of the original architecture is still intact. Hot and cold platters, including bangers and mash, fish-and-chips, steak-and-kidney pie, and lasagna, are served from a food counter at the back of the pub. Additional seating is available in the basement, where a headless cavalier is said to haunt the same premises where he enjoyed his liquor in an earlier day.

✪ **Joe Allen.** 13 Exeter St., WC2. ☎ **0171/836-0651.** Reservations required. Main courses £6.50–£13.50 ($10–$22); pre-theater dinner £12–£14 ($19–$22); Sun brunch

£13.50–£15.50 ($22–$25). AE, MC, V. Mon–Fri noon–1am; Sat 11:30am–1am; Sun 11:30am–midnight. Tube: Covent Garden or Embankment. AMERICAN.

This fashionable American restaurant near the Savoy attracts primarily theater crowds. Like the New York branch, it's decorated with theater posters. The menu has grown increasingly sophisticated and might include dishes such as grilled corn-fed chicken with sunflower-seed pesto, marinated sweet peppers, and garlic roast new potatoes, as well as specialties like black-bean soup and pecan pie. The Sunday brunch is one of the best in London. You get such main dishes as a mixed grill with lamb chop, calf's liver, and Cumberland sausage, and a choice of a Bloody Mary, Bucks Fizz, or a glass of champagne. The food here has been called "unimaginative." Loyal patrons say, "Who cares?"

✪ Porter's English Restaurant. 17 Henrietta St., WC2. ☎ **0171/836-6466.** Reservations recommended. Main courses £8 ($13); fixed-price menu £16.50 ($26). AE, DC, MC, V. Mon–Sat noon–11:30pm; Sun noon–10:30pm. Tube: Covent Garden or Charing Cross. TRADITIONAL BRITISH.

In 1979 the 7th Earl of Bradford opened this restaurant, stating "it would serve real English food at affordable prices," and he has succeeded notably—and not just because Lady Bradford turned over her carefully guarded recipe for banana and ginger steamed pudding. A comfortable, two-storied restaurant with a friendly, informal, and lively atmosphere, Porter's specializes in classic English pies, including Old English fish pie; lamb and apricot; ham, leek, and cheese; and of course, bangers and mash. Main courses are so generous—and accompanied by vegetables and side dishes—that you hardly need appetizers. They have also added grilled English fare to the menu, with sirloin and lamb steaks, and pork chops. The puddings, including bread-and-butter pudding or steamed syrup sponge, are the real puddings (in the American sense); they're served hot or cold, with whipped cream or custard. The bar does quite a few exotic cocktails, as well as beers, wine, or traditional English mead. A traditional English tea is also served for £3.50 ($5.60) per person. Who knows? You may even bump into his Lordship.

ON THE EMBANKMENT
MODERATE

✪ Ship Hispaniola. River Thames, Victoria Embankment, Charing Cross, WC2. ☎ **0171/839-3011.** Reservations recommended. Main courses £9.50–£19.50 ($15–$31); £15 ($24) minimum per person. AE, DC, MC, V. Mon–Fri noon–2pm; Mon–Sat 6–10:30pm (last order). Closed Dec 24–Jan 4. Tube: Embankment. TRADITIONAL BRITISH/FRENCH.

This large, comfortably outfitted ship was built in 1953 to haul passengers around the islands of Scotland. Stripped of its engine in 1976, the ship is permanently moored to a quay beside the Thames, a few steps from the Embankment Underground station. Good food and spectacular views of the passing river traffic are part of the waterborne experience. The menu changes frequently, but might include such dishes as flambéed Mediterranean prawns with garlic, fried fishcakes with tartar sauce, poached halibut on a bed of creamed spinach, Dover sole meunière, rack of lamb flavored with rosemary and shallots, and several vegetarian dishes. There's live music on most nights.

WESTMINSTER/VICTORIA
EXPENSIVE

Ken Lo's Memories of China. 67–69 Ebury St., SW1. ☎ **0171/730-7734.** Reservations recommended. Main courses £10–£30 ($16–$47); fixed-price lunch £19.50–£22 ($31–$35); fixed-price 3-course dinner £27.50 ($44), fixed-price 5-course dinner £30 ($47), after-theater

3-course dinner £24.50 ($39). AE, DC, MC, V. Mon–Sat noon–2:30pm; daily 7–11:15pm. Tube: Victoria Station. CHINESE.

Many food critics consider this the finest Chinese restaurant in London, although in the past few years the competition has considerably heated up. It was founded by the late Ken Lo, whose grandfather was the Chinese ambassador to the Court of St. James (he was knighted by Queen Victoria in 1880). Mr. Lo wrote more than 30 cookbooks and a well-known autobiography, and once hosted his own TV cooking show. The restaurant, which is impeccably staffed and outfitted in an appealing minimalist decor, has been called "a gastronomic bridge between London and China." The menu spans broadly divergent regions of China, and might include Cantonese quick-fried beef in oyster sauce, lobster with handmade noodles, pomegranate prawn balls, and "bang-bang chicken" (a Szechuan dish), among many others.

MODERATE

Shepherd's. Marsham Court, Marsham St., at the corner of Page St., SW1. ☎ 0171/834-9552. Reservations recommended. Fixed-price meals £22 ($35) for 2 courses, £24 ($38) for 3 courses. AE, DC, MC, V. Mon–Fri 12:30–2:45pm and 6:30–11:30pm (last order at 11pm). Tube: Westminster or Pimlico. TRADITIONAL BRITISH.

Some political observers claim that many of the inner workings of the British government operate from the precincts of this conservative, likable restaurant. Set in the shadow of Big Ben, 2 blocks north of the Tate Gallery, it enjoys a regular clientele of barristers, members of Parliament, and many of their constituents from far-flung districts of the British Isles. Don't imagine that the intrigue here occurs only at lunchtime; evenings seem just as ripe an hour for negotiations, particularly over the restaurant's roast rib of Scottish beef served with (what else?) Yorkshire pudding. (Fears about British beef seem not to have perturbed this ever-loyal crowd.) So synchronized is this place to the goings-on at Parliament that a Division Bell rings in the dining room, calling MPs back to the House of Commons when it's time to vote. Even the decor is designed to make them feel at home, with leather banquettes, sober 19th-century accessories, and a worthy collection of English portraits and landscapes.

The menu reflects many years of British culinary tradition, and dishes are prepared intelligently and with fresh ingredients. In addition to the classic joint, they include a cream-based mussel stew, hot salmon and potato salad with dill dressing, filet of lemon sole, roast leg of lamb with mint sauce, wild rabbit, salmon filet with tarragon and chive butter sauce, and a crème brûlée that this very English restaurant appropriately identifies as "burnt Cambridge cream."

✪ **Simply Nico.** 48A Rochester Row, SW1. ☎ 0171/630-8061. Reservations required. Fixed-price 2-course lunch £22 ($35), fixed-price 3-course lunch £25 ($40); fixed-price 3-course dinner £27 ($43). AE, DC, MC, V. Mon–Fri 12:30–2pm; Mon–Sat 7–11pm. Tube: Victoria or St. James's Park. FRENCH.

This place is the brainchild of Nico Ladenis, of the much grander and more expensive Chez Nico at Ninety Park Lane. Run by his sous-chef, Simply Nico is, in Nico's own words, "cheap and cheerful." We think it's the best value in town. The wood floors reverberate the din of contented diners, who pack in daily at snug tables to enjoy the simply prepared—and invariably French-inspired—food. The fixed-price menu changes frequently, but options might include starters such as poached-egg tartlet with hollandaise and marinated pureed mushrooms, followed by crispy duck with plum sauce.

✪ **Tate Gallery Restaurant.** Millbank, SW1. ☎ 0171/887-8877. Reservations recommended. Main courses £10–£16 ($16–$26); fixed-price 2-course lunch £15.75 ($25); fixed-price, 3-course lunch £18.50 ($30). MC, V. Mon–Sat noon–3pm. Tube: Pimlico. Bus 77 or 88. TRADITIONAL BRITISH.

Westminster & Victoria Restaurants

Ebury Wine Bar ❶
Ken Lo's Memories of China ❷
Shepherd's ❺
Sherlock Holmes ❻
Simply Nico ❸
Tate Gallery Restaurant ❹

⊕ Tube Station

E-0141

145

This restaurant is particularly attractive to wine fanciers; it offers what may be the best bargains for superior wines anywhere in Britain. Bordeaux and Burgundies are in abundance, and the management keeps the markup between 40% and 65%, rather than the 100% to 200% added to the wholesale price in other restaurants. In fact, the prices here are even lower than they are in most retail wine shops. Wine begins at £12.50 ($20) per bottle, or £3 ($4.80) per glass. Oenophiles frequently come just for lunch, heedless of the art. The restaurant specializes in an English menu that changes about every month. Dishes might include pheasant casserole, Oxford sausage with mashed potatoes, pan-fried skate with black butter and capers, and a selection of vegetarian dishes. One critic found the staff and diners as traditional "as a Gainsborough landscape." Access to the restaurant is through the museum's main entrance on Millbank.

4 The City

MODERATE

✪ **Café Spice Namaste.** 16 Prescot St., E1. ☎ **0171/488-9242.** Reservations required. Main courses £8–£10 ($13–$16). AE, DC, MC, V. Mon–Sat noon–3pm and 6–10:30pm. Tube: Tower Hill. INDIAN.

This is our favorite Indian restaurant in London, where the competition is stiff, with Tamarind, Chutney Mary, and Bombay Brasserie also vying for top honors. It's cheerfully housed in a landmark Victorian hall near Tower Bridge. The chef, Cyrus Todiwala, is a Parsi and former resident of Goa, where he learned many of his culinary secrets. He concentrates on spicy southern and northern Indian dishes with a strong Portuguese influence, such as Goa's signature dish, *sorpotel:* diced kidney, liver, and pork slow-cooked and served in a brown-colored stew heavy with onions. Chicken and lamb are prepared a number of ways, from mild to spicy-hot. As a novelty, Todiwala even offers a menu of emu dishes; when marinated, the meat is rich and spicy and evocative of lamb. The homemade chutneys alone are worth the trip; our favorite is made with kiwi. All dishes come with fresh vegetables and Indian bread.

✪ **Poons in the City.** 2 Minster Pavement, Minster Court, Mincing Lane, EC3. ☎ **0171/626-0126.** Reservations recommended for lunch. Fixed-price lunch and dinner £22.50–£32 ($36–$51); main courses £5.15–£7.80 ($8.25–$13). AE, DC, MC, V. Mon–Fri noon–10:30pm. Tube: Tower Hill. CHINESE.

In 1992, Poons opened this branch in the City, less than a 5-minute walk from the Tower of London and close to other City attractions. It's modeled on the Luk Yew Tree House in Hong Kong. Main courses feature crispy, aromatic duck; prawns with cashew nuts; and barbecued pork. Poons's famous *lap yuk soom* (like Cantonese tacos) has finely chopped wind-dried bacon. Special dishes can be ordered on 24-hour notice. At the end of the L-shaped restaurant is an 80-seat fast-food area and take-out counter that's accessible from Mark Lane. The menu changes every 2 weeks, and fixed-price lunches cost £5.15 to £22.50 ($8.25 to $36) per person (minimum of two).

INEXPENSIVE

The George & Vulture. 3 Castle Court, Cornhill, EC3. ☎ **0171/626-9710.** Reservations accepted if you agree to arrive by 12:45pm. Main courses £6.45–£12.45 ($10–$20). AE, DC, MC, V. Mon–Fri noon–2:30pm. Tube: Bank. TRADITIONAL BRITISH.

Dickens enthusiasts should seek out this old Pickwickian place. Founded in 1660, it claims that it's "probably" the world's oldest tavern, and refers to an inn on this spot

Restaurants in & Around the City

N

500 m
550 y

0

Bow Wine Vaults ◆6
Cafe Spice Namaste ◆11
Dickens Inn by the Tower ◆12
The Fox & Anchor ◆4

The George & Vulture ◆9
The Jamaica Wine House ◆8
Maison Novelli ◆3
Poons in the City ◆10

St. John ◆5
Ye Olde Cheshire Cheese ◆2
Ye Olde Cock Tavern ◆1
Ye Old Watling ◆7

Church ✝ Tube Station ⊖ Information①

in 1175. They no longer put up overnight guests here, but English lunches are still served on the tavern's three floors. Besides the daily specials, the menu includes a mixed grill, a loin chop, and fried Dover sole filets with tartar sauce. Potatoes and buttered cabbage are the standard vegetables, and the apple tart is always reliable. The system is to arrive and give your name, then retire to the Jamaican pub opposite for a drink; you're fetched when your table is ready. After, be sure to explore the mazes of pubs, shops, wine houses, and other old buildings near the tavern.

By the way, the Pickwick Club meets in this pub about six times a year for reunion dinners. This literary club is headed by Cedric Dickens, a great-great-grandson of Charles Dickens.

FOR AN ENGLISH BREAKFAST NEAR THE BARBICAN

✪ **Fox & Anchor.** 115 Charterhouse St., EC1. ☎ **0171/253-4838.** Reservations recommended. "Full house" breakfast £7 ($11); steak breakfast £4.50–£9.80 ($7.20–$16). AE, DC, MC, V. Mon–Fri 7–10:30am and noon–2:15pm. Tube: Barbican. BREAKFAST.

For British breakfast at its best, try this place, which has been serving traders from the nearby famous Smithfield meat market since the pub was built in 1898. Breakfasts are gargantuan, especially if you order the "full house"—a plate with at least eight items, including sausage, bacon, kidneys, eggs, beans, black pudding, and a fried slice of bread, along with unlimited tea or coffee, toast, and jam. Add a Black Velvet (champagne with Guinness) and the day is yours. (Of course, in the modern British view, Guinness ruins the champagne, but some people order it anyway—just to be traditional.) More fashionable is a Bucks Fizz, with orange juice and champagne (we usually call it a Mimosa). The Fox and Anchor is noted for its range of fine English ales, all available at breakfast. Butchers from the meat market, spotted with blood, still appear, as do nurses getting off their shifts and clerks and tycoons from the City who've been working at bookkeeping chores (or making millions) all night.

5 On the Thames: Docklands & South Bank

For more Thameside dining in the West End, see **Ship Hispaniola,** p. 143.

ST. KATHARINE'S DOCK
INEXPENSIVE

✪ **Dickens Inn by the Tower.** St. Katharine's Way, E1. ☎ **0171/488-2208.** Reservations recommended. In Pickwick Grill, main courses £10–£22 ($16–$35); in Tavern Room, snacks and platters £3.75–£6 ($6–$10); in pizza restaurant, pizzas £5.75–£23 ($9.20–$37). AE, DC, MC, V. Restaurant daily noon–3pm and 6:30–10:30pm; pizza restaurant daily noon–10pm; bar daily 11am–11pm. Tube: Tower Hill. TRADITIONAL BRITISH.

This three-floor restaurant is in an 1830 brick warehouse initially used to house spices imported from afar. It's deliberately devoid of carpets, curtains, or anything that might conceal its unusual antique trusses, including a set of massive redwood timbers that were part of the original construction. Large windows afford a sweeping view of the nearby Thames and Tower Bridge. On the ground level, you'll find a bar and the **Tavern Room,** serving sandwiches, platters of lasagna, steaming bowls of soup and chili, bar snacks, and other foods kids love. On the floor above is **Pizza on the Dock,** offering four sizes of pizzas that should also make the kids happy when they have a craving for the familiar. Above that, you'll find a relatively formal dining room, **Wheelers Restaurant,** serving more elegant modern British meals; specials include steaks, char-grilled brochette of wild mushrooms, pan-fried calf's kidney with tangy lime and ginger sauce, and baked filet of cod.

(world wonder)

Exploring lost cultures? Take along an **AT&T Direct®** Service wallet guide. It's a list of access numbers you need to call

home fast and clear from around the world, using an AT&T Calling Card or credit card. What an amazing planet we live on.

For a list of **AT&T Access Numbers,** take the attached wallet guide.

I t ' s   a l l   w i t h i n   y o u r   r e a c h .

For Travelers
who want more than
the Official Line

BUTLER'S WHARF
EXPENSIVE

Le Pont de la Tour. 36D Shad Thames, Butler's Wharf, SE1. ☎ **0171/403-8403.** Reservations not accepted in the Bar and Grill; recommended in the restaurant. Bar and Grill main courses £9–£18 ($15–$29); restaurant main courses £16–£24 ($26–$38); fixed-price 3-course lunch £27.50 ($44). AE, DC, MC, V. Restaurant Mon–Fri noon–3pm; Mon–Sat 6–11:30pm; Sun 12:30–3pm and 6–11pm. Bar and Grill daily 11:30am–midnight. Tube: Tower Hill or London Bridge. INTERNATIONAL.

Set at the edge of the Thames near Tower Bridge, the Butler's Wharf complex holds condos, rental apartments, offices, and an assortment of food and wine shops collectively known as the Gastrodome. Built in the mid-19th century as a warehouse, it's now another Terence Conran playland. From its windows, diners and shoppers enjoy sweeping views of some of the densest river traffic in Europe.

Although visual and gastronomic diversions are scattered throughout the complex, many visitors prefer the brash hubbub of the **Bar and Grill.** Live piano music (on evenings and weekends) and a wide choice of wines and cocktails create one of the most lively, convivial ambiences in the area. Although they feature such dishes as ham and foie gras terrine, a half-lobster with roast peppers, olives, and fennel, and langoustines mayonnaise, the culinary star is a heaping platter of fresh shellfish—perfect when shared with a friend, accompanied by a bottle of wine.

In bold contrast is the large, more formal room known simply as **The Restaurant.** Filled with burr oak furniture and decorated with framed lithographs of early-20th-century Parisian cafe society, it offers excellent food and a polite but undeniable English reserve. The menu might offer such temptations as roast squab pigeon with morel and truffle sauce or roast fish with lemon parsley and garlic. One especially winning selection is braised lamb shank with rosemary jus and carrot and parsnip purée. All the fish is excellent, but none is better than the Dover sole, which can be ordered grilled or meunière.

MODERATE

The Bengal Clipper. Shad 10, Butler's Wharf, SE1. ☎ 0171/357-9001. Reservations recommended. Main courses £10–£22 ($16–$35); Sunday buffet £7.35 ($12). AE, DC, MC, V. Daily 11am–3pm and 6–11:30pm. Tube: Tower Hill. INDIAN.

A former spice warehouse by the Thames serves—with much justification—what it calls "India's most remarkable dishes." Set within the dining and entertainment complex of Butler's Wharf, this likable and often animated restaurant is outfitted with cream-colored walls, tall columns, and modern artwork inspired by the Moghul Dynasty's replicas of royal figures, soaring trees, and well-trained elephants. Seven windows afford sweeping views over the industrialized Thameside neighborhood surrounding it. As music from a live pianist emanates from the convivial bar, you can enjoy a cuisine that includes many vegetarian choices derived from the formerly Portuguese colony of Goa and the once-English colony of Bengal. There is a zestiness and spice to the cuisine, but it is never overpowering. The chefs keep the menu fairly short so that all the ingredients can be purchased fresh every day. A tantalizing and tasty specialty is stuffed murgh masala, a tender breast of chicken with potato, onion, apricots, and almonds cooked with yogurt and served with a delectable curry sauce. The hass vindaloo is perfectly cooked duckling (off the bone) in a tangy sauce with a citrus bite. One of the finest dishes we've ever tasted in North India is also served here, and has lost nothing in the transfer: marinated lamb simmered in cream with cashew nuts and seasoned with fresh ginger. One of the best offerings from the Goan repertoire is the karkra chop, a spicy patty of minced crab blended with mashed potatoes and peppered with Goan spices. The poppadums and homemade chutneys add to the savory experience.

Butler's Wharf Chop House. 36E Shad Thames, SE1. ☎ **0171/403-3403.** Reservations recommended. Fixed-price 2-course lunch £18.75 ($30), 3-course, fixed-price lunch £22.75 ($36); dinner main courses £11.50–£28.50 ($18–$46). AE, DC, MC, V. Sun–Fri noon–3pm (last order); Mon–Sat 6–11pm. Tube: Tower Hill. TRADITIONAL BRITISH.

Of the four restaurants housed in Butler's Wharf, this one is the closest to Tower Bridge, and the one that most aggressively retains its commitment to moderate prices. There's an even cheaper restaurant, La Cantina del Ponte, but most diners consider that merely a place for pastas. (The complex's more upscale set of restaurants, Le Pont de la Tour, are recommended above.) The Chop House was modeled after a large boathouse, with russet-colored banquettes, lots of exposed wood, flowers, candles, and big windows overlooking Tower Bridge and the Thames. Lunchtime crowds include workers from the City's nearby financial district; evening crowds are largely made up of friends dining together under less pressing circumstances.

Dishes are largely adaptations of British recipes, some geared for modern tastes: roast rack of lamb with champ (beetroot) and spiced lentils; a warm salad of mushrooms, soft poached egg, and tarragon hollandaise; roast salmon with tarragon and saffron cream sauce; and Dublin bay prawns and salmon wrapped in bacon. To follow, there might be a dark chocolate tart with whisky cream or sticky toffee pudding. The bar offers such stiff-upper-lip choices as Theakston's best bitter, several English wines, and a half-dozen French clarets served by the jug.

6 In & Around Knightsbridge

EXPENSIVE

Georgian Restaurant. On the fourth floor of Harrods, 87–135 Brompton Rd., SW1. ☎ **0171/225-5390** or 0171/225-6800. Reservations recommended for lunch and tea. Main courses £16–£20 ($26–$32); fixed-price lunch £24.50–£28.50 ($38–$46); sandwiches and pastries at teatime £15.50 ($25) per person. AE, DC, MC, V. Mon–Sat noon–3pm; tea Mon–Sat 3:45–5:15pm. Tube: Knightsbridge. TRADITIONAL BRITISH.

The Georgian Restaurant, set under elaborate ceilings and belle-époque skylights atop London's fabled emporium, is one of the neighborhood's most appealing places for lunch and afternoon tea. One of the rooms, big enough for a ball, features a pianist whose music trills among the crystal of the chandeliers. A lunchtime buffet features cold meats and an array of fresh salads. If you want a hot meal, head for the carvery, where a uniformed crew of chefs dishes out such offerings as poultry, fish, and pork.

San Lorenzo. 22 Beauchamp Place, SW3. ☎ **0171/584-1074.** Reservations required. Main courses £14.50–£20 ($23–$32). No credit cards. Mon–Sat 12:30–3pm and 7:30–11:30pm. Tube: Knightsbridge. ITALIAN.

This fashionable restaurant, once a favorite of Princess Di, specializes in regional cuisines from Tuscany and the Piedmont. Frequently mentioned in the London tabloids thanks to its high-profile clients, San Lorenzo is the domain of effervescent owners Lorenzo and Mara Berni. Reliability is the keynote of the seasonal cuisine, which often includes homemade fettuccine with salmon; risotto with fresh asparagus; veal piccata; and partridge in white-wine sauce. Regional offerings might include salt cod with polenta. Though some critics have dismissed this as a once-great place that had its heyday in the 1970s, its continuing popularity is illustrated by how difficult it is to get a table. And while the food is really good, the attitudes and service need improvement. But it's still a great choice, especially if you're doing some upscale shopping along Beauchamp Place.

✪ **Vong.** In the Berkeley Hotel, Wilton Place, SW1. ☎ **0171/235-1010.** Reservations required 7 days in advance. Main courses £12.75–£26.75 ($20–$43); vegetarian main courses £9–£11 ($14–$18); tasting menu £45 ($72); 2-course, fixed-price dinner £27 ($43), 3-course, fixed-price dinner £36.50 ($58); pre- and post-theater dinner £17.50 ($28). AE, DC, MC, V. Mon–Sat noon–2:30pm and 6–11:30pm. Pre- and post-theater dinner available 6–7pm and 10:30–11:30pm. Tube: Knightsbridge. FRENCH/THAI.

Just 600 yards from Harrods, this strikingly modern restaurant on three levels is one of the chic rendezvous of London. Jean-Georges Vongerichten, the darling of New York culinary circles, has brought his award-winning French/Thai menu to London and boldly states that the superior Thai ingredients available in London will make the offspring better than the parent. The results here are subtle, innovative, and inspired.

In a minimalist setting, you can partake of the "black plate," featuring samples of six starters, if you'd like a taste of everything. Other options are a perfectly roasted halibut or a lobster and daikon roll, the latter with a rosemary and ginger sauce. You can virtually eat everything on the menu and be filled with wonder and admiration, especially by the crab spring roll with a vinegary tamarind dipping sauce. The sautéed foie gras with ginger and mango literally melts in the mouth. Squab pigeon breasts on egg-noodle pancakes is well treated. Desserts are equally exotic, especially the salad of banana and passion fruit with white-pepper ice cream (yes, you heard right).

MODERATE

Fifth Floor at Harvey Nichols. 109–125 Knightsbridge, at Sloane St., SW1. ☎ **0171/235-5250.** Reservations recommended. Fixed-price lunch menus £19.50 ($31) for 2 courses, £23.50 ($38) for 3 courses; main courses £12–£30 ($19–$48). À la carte dishes available at dinner only. AE, DC, MC, V. Mon–Fri noon–3pm, Sat and Sun noon–3:30pm; Mon–Sat 6:30–11:30pm (last order). Tube: Knightsbridge. TRADITIONAL BRITISH.

Set on the fifth floor of the Harvey Nichols flagship store, this restaurant is the most carefully orchestrated of any of the large department-store eateries in London. There's a simple cafe near the entrance, which tends to be the domain of package-laden shoppers looking for a quick cup of tea and a salad. Serious diners, many from the upscale neighborhoods nearby, head directly to the high-ceilinged blue-and-white restaurant, where big windows overlook the red-brick Edwardian walls of the Hyde Park Hotel across the street. The menu is appropriately fashionable, and waiters imbue any meal with a polite kind of formality. Starters include goat cheese and lemon risotto with deep-fried baby artichokes, and potted foie gras with orange and onion confit and toasted brioche. Main courses include pan-fried scallops in a bordelaise sauce; shredded duck confit; smoked haddock fish cakes; and a spinach, bacon, and avocado salad.

Although the department store closes at 6pm, a pair of elevators continues to haul patrons to the restaurant. There's a glamorous food emporium (open during store hours) set just outside the restaurant's entrance, where the variety hints at the culinary splendors that await you.

INEXPENSIVE

Chicago Rib Shack. 1 Raphael St., SW7. ☎ **0171/581-5595.** Reservations accepted, except Sat. Main courses £6.45–£15 ($10–$24). AE, CB, MC, V. Daily 11:45am–11:45pm. Tube: Knightsbridge. AMERICAN.

This restaurant, just 100 yards from Harrods, specializes in real American barbecue, cooked in imported smoking ovens and marinated in a sauce made with 15 ingredients. Their decadent onion loaf is a famous treat. Visitors are encouraged to eat with

Restaurants from Knightsbridge to Kensington

Church ✝   Information ⓘ   Tube Station ⊖

Antelope 34	Bombay Brasserie 7	Clarke's 2
Aubergine 12	Brasserie St. Quentin 20	English Garden 36
Bibendum/	Brinkley's Garden	English House 33
The Oyster Bar 16	Restaurant &	The Enterprise 19
Bill Bentley's 22	Chapter 11 Bar 10	Fifth Floor at
Bistro 190 6	Chelsea Kitchen 35	Harvey Nichols 27
Blue Bird 13	Chicago Rib Shack 26	Front Page 40
Blue Elephant 11	Chutney Mary 14	Georgian Restaurant 24

Gilbert's
Grenadier
Hilaire
Joe's
King's Head &
   Eight Bells
The Lanesborough
La Tante Claire

Launceston Place
Le Metro
Maggie Jones
Nag's Head
The Orangery
Pavilion Restaurant
Phoenicia

Richoux
Salloos
San Lorenzo
The Tearoom at the
   Chelsea Physic Garden
Turner's
Vong

their fingers, and bibs and hot towels are provided. A TV screen suspended in the bar shows American sports. The British touch is evident in an overwhelming number of Victorian architectural antiques, which have been salvaged from demolished buildings all over the country. The 45-foot-long ornate mahogany and mirrored bar was once part of a Glasgow pub, and eight massive stained-glass windows came from a chapel in Lancashire.

IN NEARBY BELGRAVIA
MODERATE

Salloos. 62–64 Kinnerton St., SW1. ☎ **0171/235-4444.** Reservations recommended. Main courses £10–£17 ($16–$27); fixed-price 3-course lunch £16 ($26); fixed-price 4-course dinner £25 ($40). MC, V. Mon–Sat noon–2:30pm and 7–11:15pm. Tube: Hyde Park Corner. PAKISTANI/MUGHLAI.

One of London's most elegant Pakistani restaurants is located in one of the city's most fashionable and expensive neighborhoods. This small hideaway has only about 60 seats; the elegant corniced interior is done in pale creamy white with burgundy accents. The lighting is dim and soothing; spotlights focus on Pakistani embroideries. The cosmopolitan clientele comes for such dishes as lamb chops grilled in a tandoori oven, chicken shish kebabs, chicken cooked and served in a karahi (spicy, with curry), chicken korma (moderately spicy and served with yogurt sauce), and a house specialty of *haleem akbari* (shredded lamb cooked in wheat germ with lentils and spices). Most of these specialties were developed during the reign of North India's Moghul emperors. The owner, Muhammad Salahuddin (whose nickname is Salloos), is assisted by his charming and articulate daughters, Farizeh and Nafiseh, who greet customers at the door.

7 Chelsea
VERY EXPENSIVE

✪ **La Tante Claire.** 68–69 Royal Hospital Rd., SW3. ☎ **0171/352-6045.** Reservations required at least 2 weeks in advance. Main courses £26.50–£30 ($42–$48); fixed-price 3-course lunch £28 ($45); minimum charge £50 ($80) per person at dinner. AE, CB, DC, MC, V. Mon–Fri 12:30–2pm and 7–11pm. Tube: Sloane Sq. FRENCH.

This is a culinary monument of the highest order. Thanks to a chef who's far more interested in turning out food of the highest order than he is in creating a media frenzy, the quality of the cuisine is so legendary that "Aunt Claire" is one of London's best—and most popular—French restaurants, even though the setting is far from grand. The ring of a doorbell set discreetly into the Aegean blue-and-white facade prompts an employee to usher you politely inside, where you can settle in and prepare yourself for one of London's finest dining experiences.

Pierre Koffman is the celebrated chef behind such culinary fireworks as ravioli langostine and pigs' trotters stuffed with morels—who would've thought that the lowly pig trotter (long a staple of menus in Paris's Les Halles district) could be transformed into such a sublime creation as this? Other favorites include grilled scallops on squid-ink sauce; baked filet of turbot with mustard-seed sauce on a bed of roasted leeks; and duck in red-wine sauce and confit. The sauces that complement many of Koffman's dishes are exquisite. For dessert, try the caramelized ice cream soufflé with hazelnuts and raspberry coulis, or the pistachio soufflé.

EXPENSIVE

✪ **Aubergine.** 11 Park Walk, SW10. ☎ **0171/352-3449.** Reservations required 2 months in advance. Fixed-price 2-course lunch £24 ($38); fixed-price dinner £45 ($72); menu prestige

£60 ($96). AE, DC, MC, V. Mon–Fri noon–2:15pm; Mon–Sat 7–10:30pm. Tube: South Kensington. FRENCH.

"The Eggplant" is luring savvy diners down to the lower reaches of Chelsea where Gordon Ramsay continues to create excitement and deliver what some food critics (including producer and gourmand Andrew Lloyd Webber) claim is the best food in London. Ramsay trained with some of Europe's greatest chefs, including Marco Pierre White and Joël Robuchon, but here he forges ahead with his own creative statement. Food critic Dominic Bradbury called Ramsay a "Captain Ahab, a dedicated monomaniac, hell-bent on cruising his kitchen until he finds his second Michelin star." Celebrities don't seem to impress him, whether it's Princess Margaret complaining that the air-conditioning is too cold (he lent her his cardigan) or Madonna calling for a late-night booking (she was turned down). Ramsay is a perfectionist, but not pretentious.

The man himself is in the cramped kitchen more and more these days since giving up his Porsche 911 after losing his license for speeding (147 mph). Subtlety and delicacy—without any sacrifice of the food's natural essence—are the keynotes of this grossly talented genius's cuisine: Every dish is satisfyingly flavorsome, including his celebrated cappuccino of white beans with grated truffle. The fish and lighter Mediterranean-style dishes are stunning achievements, as are the Bresse pigeon with a wild-mushroom ravioli and the filet of venison with braised baby turnips. There are only 14 tables, so bookings are imperative.

Blue Bird. 350 King's Rd., SW3. ☎ **0171/559-1142.** Reservations recommended. Set lunch Mon–Fri £12.75–£15.75 ($21–$25); main courses £9.75–£30 ($16–$48). AE, DC, MC, V. Mon–Fri noon–3:30pm and 6–11:30pm; Sat 11am–4pm and 6–11:30pm; Sun 11am–4pm and 6–10:30pm. Tube: Sloane Sq. MODERN CONTINENTAL.

Loyal Rangers from the surrounding neighborhood, as well as members of its French and Australian staff, refer to this 21st-century twist on Bibendum as a *restaurant de gare*—a railway station restaurant. It's an enormous echoing space that resounds every night with clinking silverware and peals of laughter. Although there's a cafe and an upscale delicatessen and housewares store on the street level, the heart and soul of this place is one floor above in the restaurant. Within a cavernous place fit for up to 275 diners at a time, you'll find a color scheme of red and blue canvas cutouts that replicate birds in flight. Tables are close together, but the sheer scale of the place makes dining strangely private and intimate. The massive upscale menu emphasizes savory, cooked-to-the-minute cuisine, some emerging from a wood-burning stove used to roast everything from lobster to game. A breathtakingly immense shellfish bar stocks on ice every crustacean you can think of, and a bar off to one side does a thriving business with the Sloane Square subculture. Perennial favorites include the veal scallopine layered with prosciutto, white beans, and sage, as well as versions of pasta and fresh fish. Prior to its role as a restaurant, the site functioned as a garage that repaired the legendary Bluebird, a very fast English sports car that, alas, is no longer produced.

MODERATE

✪ **Chutney Mary.** 535 King's Rd., SW10. ☎ **0171/351-3113.** Reservations recommended. Main courses £10–£12.50 ($16–$20); fixed-price lunch Mon–Fri £12.50–£14.50 ($20–$23); 3-course brunch Sat–Sun £15 ($24). AE, DC, MC, V. Daily 12:30–3pm and 7–11pm. Tube: Fulham Broadway. INDIAN.

This multiple-award winner is often cited as the best Indian restaurant in England, although we think Café Spice Namaste (see above) wins by a small margin. Originally, Chutney Mary billed itself as "the world's first Anglo-Indian restaurant"; the chefs kept the English palate in mind and didn't go wholeheartedly ethnic. But, realizing that today's patrons are more adventuresome, they've turned the tide and now offer an authentic cuisine, served in a smart setting recalling the days of Raj, that evokes the best of southern and southwestern Indian cooking. Specialties include Mangalore prawn curry, Masala roast lamb shank, and scallop kedgeree with lentils; some dishes, such as green chicken curry, are inspired by the old Portuguese colony of Goa (now part of India). We love the stuffed eggplant in sesame with a tamarind sauce. Of course, the chefs prepare homemade chutneys based on decades-old recipes.

English Garden. 10 Lincoln St., SW3. ☎ **0171/584-7272.** Reservations required. Main courses £9.25–£17.75 ($15–$28); fixed-price lunch £17.75 ($28). AE, CB, DC, MC, V. Mon–Sat 12:30–2:30pm, Sun 12:30–2pm; Mon–Sat 7:30–11:30pm, Sun 7–10:30pm. Tube: Sloane Sq. TRADITIONAL BRITISH.

This is a metropolitan restaurant par excellence. The decor is pretty and lighthearted in the historic town house: The Garden Room is whitewashed brick with a domed conservatory roof; vivid florals, rattan chairs, banks of plants, and candy-pink napery complete the scene. Every component of a meal here is chopped or cooked to the right degree and well proportioned. Launch into a fine repast with a caramelized red onion and cheddar cheesecake or cream of Jerusalem artichoke soup. For a main course, opt for such delights as roast partridge with beetroot and juniper, or roast saddle of hare with black currants. Some of these dishes sound as if they were cloned from an English cookbook of the Middle Ages—and are they ever good. Desserts, especially the rhubarb and cinnamon ice cream or the candied orange tart with orange syrup, would've pleased Miss Marple.

English House. 3 Milner St., SW3. ☎ **0171/584-3002.** Reservations required. Main courses £8–£17 ($13–$27); fixed-price lunch £15.25 ($24); fixed-price dinner (Sun only) £20.75 ($33). AE, DC, MC, V. Mon–Sat 12:30–2:30pm and 7:30–11:15pm; Sun 12:30–2pm and 7:30–9:45pm. Tube: Sloane Sq. TRADITIONAL BRITISH.

Another design creation of Roger Wren (who did the English Garden, above), this tiny restaurant will make you feel like you're a guest in an elegant but cozy Victorian house. The food is British, the menu seasonal, and each dish is given a subtle, modern treatment. Some foodies find the cuisine outdated, but year after year—based on the mail we get—readers find it immensely satisfying. Begin with the pumpkin and rosemary soup (which sounds almost medieval), or grilled pigeon breast with a bean compote. For a main dish, try either the roast chump of lamb with bubble and squeak (cabbage and potatoes), or the braised ham hock with corn and mashed apples. Game is available in season, as is a fresh fish of the day. Summer berries in season predominate on the pudding menu, including fresh berries laced with elderflower syrup. Other offerings include a "Phrase of Apples," the chef's adaptation of a 17th-century recipe for a delectable apple pancake. London is filled with trendy places these days; every time we visit, we're newly pleased that there's still at least one retreat that focuses on rescuing long-forgotten recipes and bringing them to a new audience.

INEXPENSIVE

Chelsea Kitchen. 98 King's Rd., SW3. ☎ **0171/589-1330.** Reservations recommended. Main courses £3–£5.50 ($4.80–$8.80); fixed-price menu £6 ($10). No credit cards. Daily 8am–11:15pm. Tube: Sloane Sq. INTERNATIONAL.

This simple restaurant feeds large numbers of Chelsea residents in a setting that's changed very little since 1961. The food and the clientele move fast, almost guaranteeing that the entire inventory of ingredients is sold out at the end of each day. Menu items usually include leek-and-potato soup, chicken Kiev, chicken parmigiana, steaks, sandwiches, and burgers. The clientele includes a broad cross-section of patrons—all having a good and cost-conscious time.

IN NEARBY CHELSEA HARBOUR
MODERATE

✪ **The Canteen.** Unit G4, Harbour Yard, Chelsea Harbour, SW10. ☎ **0171/351-7330.** Reservations recommended. Cover charge £1 ($1.60) per person. Main courses £13–£20.45 ($21–$33). AE, MC, V. Daily noon–3pm; Mon–Sat 6:30pm–midnight (last order), Sun 7–10:30pm (last order). Tube: Earl's Court, then Chelsea Harbour Hoppa Bus C3; on Sun, take a taxi. INTERNATIONAL.

Some consider this the most viable and popular of the several restaurants in the Chelsea Harbour Complex, the multimillion-dollar development of formerly abandoned piers and wharves southwest of Central London. You'll dine in a whimsical setting influenced by *Alice in Wonderland*—very fantastical and the kind of thing that children as well as adults love. The cuisine is exceptional, too. The menu changes every 2 months, but may include risotto of butternut squash, mascarpone, and coriander; pappardelle with field mushrooms and truffle oil; Roquefort and endive salad with honey-mustard dressing; escalope of calf's liver with Alsace bacon, black pudding, and pomme purée; and monkfish sauté with creamed peas, bacon, and potatoes.

INEXPENSIVE

Deal's Restaurant and Diner. Harbour Yard, Chelsea Harbour, SW10. ☎ **0171/795-1001.** Reservations recommended. Main courses £6.75–£16.50 ($11–$26). AE, DC, MC, V. Mon–Fri noon–3:30pm and 5:30–11pm; Sat noon–11:30pm; Sun noon–10pm. Tube: Earl's Court, then Chelsea Harbour Hoppa Bus C3; on Sun, take a taxi. INTERNATIONAL.

Deal's is co-owned by Princess Margaret's son, Viscount Linley, and Lord Lichfield. As soon as the Queen Mother arrived here on a barge to order a Deal's burger, the success of this place was assured. The early-1900s atmosphere includes ceiling fans and bentwood banquettes. The food is American diner-style, with a strong Eastern influence: Try a teriyaki burger, the prawn curry, spareribs, or a vegetarian dish, and finish with New England-style apple pie.

8 Kensington & South Kensington
KENSINGTON
MODERATE

Launceston Place. 1A Launceston Place, W8. ☎ **0171/937-6912.** Reservations required. Main courses £15–£17 ($24–$27); fixed-price menu £14.50 ($23) for 2 courses, £17.50 ($28) for 3 courses. AE, MC, V. Mon–Fri 12:30–2:30pm, Sun 12:30–3pm; Mon–Sat 7–11:30pm. Tube: Gloucester Rd. or High St. Kensington. MODERN BRITISH.

Launceston Place—sporting a new look as of spring 1996—is situated in an affluent, almost villagelike neighborhood where many Londoners would like to live, if only they could afford it. The stylish restaurant is a series of uncluttered Victorian parlors illuminated by a rear skylight and decorated with Victorian oils and watercolors, plus contemporary paintings. Since its opening in spring 1986, it has been known for its new British cuisine. The menu changes every 6 weeks, but you're likely to be served such appetizers as smoked salmon with horseradish crème fraîche, or seared foie gras with lentils and Madeira sauce. For a main dish, perhaps it'll be bruschetta of monkfish with black bean dressing, or duck confit with chili plum sauce.

✪ **Phoenicia.** 11–13 Abingdon Rd., W8. ☎ **0171/937-0120.** Reservations required. Main courses £9.50–£11 ($15–$18); buffet lunch £10–£12 ($16–$19); fixed-price dinner £15.30–£28.30 ($24–$45). AE, DC, MC, V. Daily noon–midnight; buffet lunch Mon–Sat 12:15–2:30pm, Sun 12:15–3:30pm. Tube: High St. Kensington. LEBANESE.

Phoenicia is highly regarded for the quality of its Lebanese cuisine—outstanding in presentation and freshness—and for its moderate prices. For the best value, go for lunch, when you can enjoy a buffet of more than two dozen *meze* (appetizers), presented in little pottery dishes. Each day at lunch, the chef prepares two or three home-cooked dishes to tempt your tastebuds, including chicken in garlic sauce or stuffed lamb with vegetables. Many Lebanese patrons begin their meal with the *apéritif arak*, a liqueur some have compared to ouzo. To start, you can select from such classic Middle Eastern dishes as hummus or stuffed vine leaves. The chefs bake fresh bread and two types of pizza daily in a clay oven. Minced lamb, spicy and well flavored, is an eternal favorite. Various charcoal-grilled dishes are also offered.

INEXPENSIVE

Maggie Jones. 6 Old Court Place (off Kensington Church St.), W8. ☎ **0171/937-6462.** Reservations required. Main courses £5–£17 ($8-$27). AE, MC, V. Daily 12:30–2:30pm and 6:30–11pm. Tube: High St. Kensington. TRADITIONAL BRITISH.

This whimsical, staunchly English restaurant is a longtime favorite, thanks to its good food and its associations with Princess Margaret (a long-ago frequent client after whom the restaurant was named). There's dining on three floors, but the basement is the most intimate. The furniture is plain pine with candles stuck into bottles, and the allure is that of an old-fashioned English farmhouse. Menu items include grilled leg of lamb chop with rosemary, grilled trout with almonds, and Maggie's famous fish pie. Desserts include treacle tart. Everything is reliably cooked and good, but never thrilling.

SOUTH KENSINGTON

EXPENSIVE

Bibendum/The Oyster Bar. 81 Fulham Rd., SW3. ☎ **0171/581-5817.** Reservations required in Bibendum; not accepted in Oyster Bar. Main courses £17–£23 ($27-$37); fixed-price 3-course lunch £28 ($45); cold seafood platter in Oyster Bar £22 ($35) per person. AE, DC, MC, V. Bibendum Mon–Fri noon–2:30pm and 7–11:15pm; Sat 12:30–3pm and 7–11:15pm; Sun 12:30–3pm and 7–10:15pm. Oyster Bar Mon–Sat noon–11:30pm; Sun noon–3pm and 7–10:30pm. Tube: South Kensington. FRENCH/MEDITERRANEAN.

In trendy Brompton Cross, this still-fashionable restaurant occupies two floors of a garage—the former home of the Michelin tire company—that's an art deco master-piece. Although it's still going strong, Bibendum's heyday was in the early 1990s; it no longer enjoys top berth on the lists of London's food critics. The white-tiled art deco-inspired room, with stained-glass windows, streaming sunlight, and a chic clientele, is an extremely pleasant place to dine. The fabulously eclectic cuisine, known for its freshness and simplicity, is comprised of carefully planned interpretations of what's available seasonally. Dishes might include roast quail flavored with marsala and thyme, braised oxtail with prunes and almonds, and *ris de veau* (sweetbreads) with black butter and capers. Some of the best dishes are for dining *à deux:* Bresse pullet flavored with fresh tarragon, or roast lamb with a soubise sauce and onion rings.

Simpler meals and cocktails are available in the **Oyster Bar** on the building's street level. The bar-style menu stresses fresh shellfish presented in the traditional French style, on ice-covered platters occasionally adorned with strands of seaweed. It's a crustacean-lover's lair.

Hilaire. 68 Old Brompton Rd., SW7. ☎ **0171/584-8993.** Reservations recommended. 2-course fixed-price lunch £19.50 ($31); 3 courses £24 ($38); 3-course fixed-price dinner £30 ($48); 4 courses £36 ($58); dinner main courses £14.50–£19.50 ($23-$31). AE, DC, MC, V. Mon–Fri 12:15–2:30pm; Mon–Sat 6:30–11:30pm. Closed bank holidays. Tube: South Kensington. CONTINENTAL.

After this former Victorian storefront was refurbished following a fire, it became one classy joint, like an elegant restaurant you might find in a town in the heart of France. With its large vases of flowers and shiny mirrors, it's a fitting ambience to enjoy some of South Ken's finest food. Chef Bryan Weber prepares a mixture of classical French and *cuisine moderne*, and does so exceedingly well, always following his own creative impulses and good culinary sense and style. The menu always reflects the best of the season's offerings. A typical lunch might begin with a red-wine risotto with radicchio and sun-dried tomato pesto, followed with sautéed scallops with creamed chicory, and ending with rhubarb sorbet. At dinner, main courses might include rack of lamb with tapenade and wild garlic, saddle of rabbit, or grilled tuna with Provençal vegetables. An aperitif bar, extra tables, and a pair of semi-private alcoves are in the lower dining room.

Turner's. 87–89 Walton St., SW3. ☎ **0171/584-6711.** Reservations required. Fixed-price lunch Mon–Fri £12.50–£15 ($20–$24), Sun £21.50 ($34); fixed-price dinner £35 ($56). AE, DC, MC, V. Mon–Fri and Sun 12:30–2:30pm; Mon–Sat 7:30–11:15pm, Sun 6–8:30pm. Tube: South Kensington. INTERNATIONAL.

This is the domain of Brian J. Turner, a Yorkshire native turned accomplished London chef who gained fame at a number of establishments, including the Capital Hotel, before acquiring his own place in the culinary sun. As one critic aptly put it, his food comes not only fresh from the market each day but also "from the heart." He doesn't imitate anyone, but sets his own goals and standards. The fixed-price menus change every day, and the à la carte listings at least every season, but you might find chicken liver pâté with foie gras, a terrine of fresh salmon with a dill sauce, roast rack of lamb with herb crust, smoked and roasted breast of duck in a port and green peppercorn sauce, or sea bass on a bed of stewed leeks with a bacon dressing.

MODERATE

Bistro 190. In the Gore Hotel, 190 Queen's Gate, SW7. ☎ **0171/581-5666.** Reservations not accepted. Main courses £9–£19.50 ($14–$31). AE, DC, MC, V. Mon–Sat noon–11pm; Sun noon–4pm. Tube: Gloucester Rd. MEDITERRANEAN.

Set in the airy front room of the Gore Hotel (see chapter 4), this restaurant features a light Mediterranean cuisine much appreciated by the hip music and media crowd that keeps the place hopping. In an artfully simple setting of wood floors, potted plants, and framed art accented by a convivial but gossipy roar, you can dine on such dishes as lamb grilled over charcoal and served with deep-fried basil; a cassoulet of fish with chili toast; Mediterranean chowder with pesto toast; and, if available, a rhubarb crumble based loosely on an old-fashioned British dessert. Service isn't particularly fast, and the policy on reservations is confusing: Although membership is required for reservations, nonmembers may leave their name at the door and have a drink at the bar while they wait for a table. In the crush of peak dining hours, your waiter may or may not remember the nuances you expressed while placing your order, but the restaurant is nonetheless memorable. Go down to Downstairs 190 for a seafood or vegetarian meal.

✪ **Bombay Brasserie.** Courtfield Close, adjoining Bailey's Hotel, SW7. ☎ **0171/370-4040.** Reservations required. Main courses £12.50–£21 ($20–$34); buffet lunch £16 ($26). DC, MC, V. Buffet daily 12:30–3pm; daily 7:30pm–midnight. Tube: Gloucester Rd. INDIAN.

This was London's best, most popular, and most talked-about Indian restaurant in the early 1990s, although lately it seems to have fallen off somewhat. It's still an impressive place, if a bit frayed, and most visitors still find the cuisine fabulous. It remains one of the best places in London for late-night dining. Before heading into dinner, you might enjoy a drink amid the wicker of the pink-and-white bar, where the bartender's specialty is a mango Bellini.

The waitstaff is professional and accommodating, each willing to advise you on the spice-laden delicacies. One look at the menu and you're launched on a grand culinary tour of the subcontinent: tandoori trout, fish with mint chutney, chicken tikka, and vegetarian meals. One corner of the menu is reserved for Goan cookery, representing that part of India seized from Portugal in 1961. The cookery of North India is represented by Mughlai specialties, including chicken biryani, the famous Muslim pilaf dish. Under the category "Some Like It Hot," you'll find such main courses as lamb korma, prepared Kashmiri style.

Brasserie St. Quentin. 243 Brompton Rd., SW3. ☎ **0171/581-5131.** Reservations required. Main courses £10–£17 ($16–$27); fixed-price 2-course lunch £12.50 ($20). AE, DC, MC, V. Mon–Sat noon–3pm and 7–11:30pm; Sun noon–3:30pm and 6:30–11pm. Tube: Knightsbridge or South Kensington. FRENCH.

St. Quentin is the most authentic-looking French brasserie in London. Modeled after—but much more intimate than—the famous La Coupole in Paris, it attracts many members of London's French community, all of whom seem to talk at once (which tends to raise the level of noise and conviviality here to a subdued roar). The decor of mirrors and crystal chandeliers reflects a fashion- and trend-conscious clientele who enjoy the social hubbub. The waiters take it all in stride, usually with seemingly effortless Gallic tact. Try the baked sea bass with thyme, the scallops and Bayonne ham, or the duck confit with lentils. Look also for a salad of crab and baby spinach or the artichoke heart with poached egg and mushrooms.

Gilbert's. 2 Exhibition Rd., SW7. ☎ **0171/589-8947.** Reservations recommended. Fixed-price lunch £5.50–£12.50 ($8.80–$20); main courses £9–£18 ($14–$29). AE, DC, MC, V. Mon–Sat noon–3pm and 5:30–10:30pm. Closed Sun in summer. Tube: South Kensington. MODERN BRITISH/FRENCH.

Based on fresh seasonal ingredients, Gilbert's menu changes every 4 weeks. Virtually everything is prepared on the premises of this small restaurant, including homemade bread at dinner and the fudge served with coffee. The cuisine is known as "new English," but much of it is comprised of adaptations of French dishes. The menu is normally limited to six choices per course, and there are often additional specials. Seasonal options may include a beef and vegetable dish or a fish pie. For dessert try, if featured, Mrs. Beeton's lemon tart or chocolate tipsy cake. The wine list changes frequently.

Joe's. 126 Draycott Ave., SW3. ☎ **0171/225-2217.** Reservations required. Main courses £10–£15.50 ($16–$25); Sun brunch £12 ($19). AE, DC, MC, V. Mon–Fri noon–3pm and 7–11pm; Sat 10:30am–4pm and 7–11pm; Sun 10:30am–4pm. Tube: South Kensington. MODERN BRITISH.

This is one of three London restaurants established by fashion designer Joseph Ettedgui. Thanks to its sense of glamour and fun, it's often filled with well-known names from the British fashion, music, and entertainment industries. You can enjoy such dishes as spiced venison strips and vegetables, roast cod in a champagne crab sauce, char-grilled swordfish with cracked wheat and salsa verde (green sauce), or fresh lobster lasagna. It's all safe, but a bit unexciting. No one will mind if your meal is composed exclusively of appetizers. There's a bar near the entrance, a cluster of tables for quick meals near the door, and more leisurely (and gossipy) dining available in an area a few steps up. Brunch is served on Sunday, which is the cheapest way to enjoy this place. The atmosphere remains laidback and unstuffy, just like trendsetters in South Ken prefer it. With a name like Joe's, what else could it be?

Pavilion Restaurant. In the Regency Hotel, 100 Queen's Gate, SW7. ☎ **0171/370-4595.** Reservations recommended. Lunch menu £12.50–£16.50 ($20–$26); dinner menu £19–£25 ($30–$40). AE, DC, MC, V. Mon–Fri noon–2:30pm; daily 5:30–10:15pm. Tube: Gloucester Rd. or South Kensington. INTERNATIONAL.

This is a glamorous but reasonably priced choice if you're staying at one of the many hotels in South Kensington. From the minute you walk in the door and are greeted with the warmth of the maître d', his staff, and the traditional surroundings, you'll know you're in a setting of refined splendor. The chef offers an extensive à la carte menu that ensures that all palates are catered to; there's also a table d'hôte menu that changes weekly. Selections are modern dishes based on prime seasonal produce; they include English lamb cutlets served with tomatoes, mushrooms, and watercress; a cod steak that's lightly grilled and served with anchovy butter; Dover sole that can be grilled or pan-fried at your request; and vegetarian dishes. Care and attention also go into such appetizers as salmon and sole roulade or goat-cheese crostini.

IN NEARBY WEST BROMPTON
MODERATE

Blue Elephant. 4–6 Fulham Broadway, SW6. ☎ **0171/385-6595.** Reservations required. Main courses £8–£20 ($13–$32); Royal Thai banquet £29–£34 ($46–$54); Sun buffet £16.75 ($27). AE, DC, MC, V. Sun–Fri noon–2:30pm; Mon–Sat 7pm–12:30am, Sun 7–10:30pm. Tube: Fulham Broadway. THAI.

This is the counterpart of the famous L'Éléphant Bleu in Brussels. Located in a converted factory building, the Blue Elephant has been all the rage since it opened in 1986. It's become the leading Thai restaurant in London, where the competition seems to grow daily. In an almost magical garden setting of lush tropical foliage, diners are treated to an array of MSG-free Thai dishes. You can begin with a "floating market" (shellfish in clear broth flavored with chili paste and lemongrass), then go on to a splendid and varied selection of main courses, for which many of the ingredients have been flown in from Thailand. We recommend the roasted duck curry served in a clay cooking pot.

INEXPENSIVE

Brinkley's Garden Restaurant & Chapter 11 Bar. 47 Hollywood Rd., SW10. ☎ **0171/351-1683.** Reservations required. Main courses £7–£13.50 ($11–$22). Bar snacks £2.90–£6.50 ($4.65–$10). AE, MC, V. Mon–Sat 7–11:30pm. Closed Dec 23–27. Tube: Earl's Court. MODERN BRITISH.

At one time, the best cuisine you could hope to find in this neighborhood was bangers and mash. But today, shops selling some of the most exclusive and costly goods in town have drawn fashionable young Londoners here. There's a small garden terrace out back and lower-level dining room for bad weather. At the bar (with a happy hour from 6 to 8:30pm), you can get a grilled burger and other bar snacks. The menu in the restaurant is wisely limited to well-prepared dishes based on fresh ingredients. You might begin with Mediterranean fish soup, spinach ravioli with pesto, baked tomatoes pecorino, or goat-cheese soufflé, then follow with Thai prawn curry or a grilled tuna steak.

9 Notting Hill

MODERATE

✪ **Clarke's.** 124 Kensington Church St., W8. ☎ **0171/221-9225.** Reservations recommended. Fixed-price lunches £8–£14 ($13–$22); fixed-price 4-course dinner £40 ($64). AE,

DC, MC, V. Mon–Fri 12:30–2pm and 7–10pm. Tube: Notting Hill Gate or High St. Kensington. MODERN BRITISH.

Sally Clarke is one of the finest chefs in London, and this is one of the hottest restaurants around. Clarke honed her skills at Michael's in Santa Monica and the West Beach Café in Venice (California) before heading back to her native land. In this excellent restaurant, everything is bright and modern, with wood floors, discreet lighting, and additional space in the basement, where tables are more spacious and private. Some people are put off by the fixed-price menu, which offers no choices, but the food is so well prepared that diners rarely object to what ends up in front of them. The menu, which changes daily, emphasizes char-grilled foods with herbs and seasonal veggies. You might begin with an appetizer of salad of blood orange with red onion, watercress, and black olive-anchovy toast, then follow with grilled breast of chicken with black truffle, crisp polenta, and arugula. Desserts are likely to include a warm pear and raisin puff pastry with maple-syrup ice cream. Just put yourself in Clarke's hands—you'll be glad you did.

✪ **Sugar Club.** 33A All Saints Rd., W11. ☎ **0171/221-3844.** Reservations required. Main courses £10–£15 ($16–$24). AE, DC, MC, V. Daily 12:30–3pm and 6:30–10:30pm. Tube: Westbourne Park. PACIFIC RIM.

Homesick Aussies head here for the loin of grilled kangaroo (very tender, with a rich taste, best served with a piquant salsa), but New Zealand-born chef Peter Gordon is far more versatile than that. Since 1995, savvy foodies have been making their way to this Notting Hill Gate bistro with its open kitchen and cramped basement dining room. This food is called "Southern Hemisphere Pacific Rim Modern Mediterranean Cosmopolitan British cookery"—whatever. The menu changes daily, but might include duck leg braised in tamarind and star anise with coconut rice or pan-fried turbot with spinach, sweet potato, a red-curry sauce, and onion raiata. Many of the starters are vegetarian and can be upgraded to a main course; there are also several fresh fish dishes. For dessert, the blood-orange curd tart with crème fraîche is drop-dead delicious.

INEXPENSIVE

Mondola. 139 Westbourne Grove, W11. ☎ **0171/229-4734.** Reservations recommended. Fixed-price meals £7–£10 ($11–$16); vegetarian fixed-price meals £3.50–£8 ($5.60–$13). No credit cards. Daily 11am–11:30pm. Tube: Notting Hill Gate. SUDANESE.

Of all the African restaurants of London, this presumably is the only one that specializes in the spicy cuisine of the Sudan. It may be the only Sudanese restaurant in Europe, although we can't prove that. Very small and intimate, on the fringe of trendy Notting Hill, this bohemian hangout is far from trendy itself. It doesn't have a liquor license, but you're free to brown bag it. A Moorish archway and various photos and artifacts evoke the African milieu.

The food is a blend of various cuisines. The chefs borrow their eclectic and inexpensive fare from various kitchens of North Africa, Ethiopia, and even the Middle East. Begin with the classic soup of the region, made with meat and peanuts. Although the menu is limited, the dishes are well-prepared from fresh ingredients. Opt for lamb, especially the tasty chops marinated in African spices. Ground red chilies add zest to any dish. Lentils with caramelized garlic is another treat, and there's a generous salad bar costing £7.50 ($12) for two persons. Skip the desserts and ask for a traditional African coffee. The place is a dining oddity for London and a bit of a culinary adventure.

IN NEARBY HOLLAND PARK
EXPENSIVE

The Room at the Halcyon. In the Halcyon Hotel, 81 Holland Park Ave., W11. ☎ **0171/ 727-7288.** Reservations required. Fixed-price 2-course lunch £18–£29 ($29–$46); fixed-price 2-course dinner £35 ($56). AE, DC, MC, V. Mon–Fri and Sun noon–2:30pm; Mon–Thurs 7–10:30pm, Fri–Sat 7–11pm, Sun 7–10pm. Tube: Holland Park. INTERNATIONAL.

Dining at this restaurant is a great way to experience the posh life at the Halcyon Hotel (see chapter 4). Located on the hotel's lower level, the restaurant attracts the rich and famous, including royalty. You might enjoy an aperitif in the cream-colored bar before heading to the tastefully uncluttered dining room. Rich tapestried curtains of blue-green and gold enhance a subdued candlelit dining atmosphere.

Of the sophisticated and highly individualized menu, one food critic wrote that it "reads like a United Nations of cuisine." The daily bill of fare is based on the inspiration of the chef and the freshest ingredients available. You might begin with rosette of scallops with fresh pasta or slice of fresh foie gras with poached pears. Main dishes are likely to feature steamed sea bass with fennel cannelloni and basil puree or braised shin of veal with Madeira sauce. There's also a special vegetarian menu. The warm banana pancakes are a luscious way to finish off your meal.

10 Bayswater

VERY EXPENSIVE

✪ **I-Thai.** In The Hempel hotel, Hempel Square, 31–35 Craven Hill Gardens, W2. ☎ **0171/ 298-9000.** Reservations required. Main courses £19–£28 ($30–$45). AE, DC, MC, V. Daily noon–2:30pm and 7–10:30pm. Tube: Lancaster Gate. ITALIAN/THAI.

Part of the aggressively minimalist Hempel hotel (see chapter 4), this newcomer specializes in upscale clients, upscale Thai and Italian food, and upscale prices. The antithesis of the kind of showy, lushly decorated restaurants of the 1980s it was designed to compete with, I-Thai prides itself on a Zen-like calm that permeates the whole place. The sparse but innovative menu is quite expensive—dining here is more fun if you're on an expense account. We suggest beginning with one of the soups, either the spicy squid-ink version with lemongrass and coconut cream or the chicken, coconut, and foie gras soup flavored with Thai basil. Main dishes are prepared exquisitely; we loved the truffle and mascarpone risotto and the stir-fried cellophane noodles with tiger prawns in a black-ink parcel. On our most recent trip, we tried a grilled filet of sea bass with lemongrass and peppercorn, served with coriander-flavored rice. For dessert, try almost anything, especially the steamed Pandan pudding garnished with a warm coconut and blueberry sauce.

MODERATE

✪ **Veronica's.** 3 Hereford Rd., W2. ☎ **0171/229-5079.** Reservations required. Main courses £10.50–£17.50 ($17–$28); fixed-price meals £12.50–£16.50 ($20–$26). AE, DC, MC, V. Mon–Fri noon–3pm; Mon–Sat 6:30pm–midnight. Tube: Bayswater or Queensway. TRADITIONAL BRITISH.

Called the "market leader in cafe salons," Veronica's offers some of the finest traditional fare in London at tabs you won't mind paying. It's a celebration of British cuisine, with some dishes based on medieval and Tudor-age recipes, but all given an imaginative modern twist by owner Veronica Shaw. One month she'll focus on Scotland, another month on Victorian foods, yet another on Wales, and the next on Ireland. Your appetizer might be a salad called salmagundy, made with crunchy pickled

Marylebone, Paddington, Bayswater & Notting Hill Gate Restaurants

Chicago Rib Shack ⑫
Clarke's ⑧
The Cow ③
Fifth Floor at Harvey Nichols ⑬
Garden Cafe ①
Grenadier ⑮
I-Thai ⑪
Lanesborough ⑯
Langan's Bistro ⑱

Maggie Jones ⑨
Mondola ⑤
Odin's ⑰
The Orangery ⑩
Prince Bonaparte ④
Room at the Halcyon ⑦
Sugar Club ②
Veronica's ⑥
Vong ⑭

E-0144

vegetables, that Elizabeth I enjoyed in her day. Another concoction might be Tweed Kettle, a 19th-century recipe to improve the monotonous taste of salmon. Many dishes are vegetarian, and everything tastes better when followed with a British farmhouse cheese or a pudding. The restaurant is brightly and attractively decorated, and the service warm and ingratiating.

11 A Bit Farther Afield: Hammersmith

EXPENSIVE

✪ The River Café. Thames Wharf, Rainville Rd., W6. ☎ **0171/381-6217.** Reservations required. Main courses £16–£25 ($26–$40). AE, DC, MC, V. Mon–Fri 12:30–3pm, Sat–Sun 1–2:45pm; Mon–Thurs 7:30–11pm, Fri–Sat 7:30–11:30pm. Tube: Hammersmith. ITALIAN.

For the best Italian viands in London today, head to this Thames-side bistro operated by Ruth Rogers and Rose Gray. The charmingly contemporary venue with a highly polished steel bar was designed by Ruth's husband, Richard, who also designed the Pompidou Centre in Paris. The cafe attracts a trendy crowd that comes to see and be seen, and to eat fabulous food. The owners' goal was to re-create the kind of cuisine they'd enjoyed in private homes in the Italian countryside, and they've succeeded beautifully. Some chefs can be seen shopping in London's markets—but not these chefs. The market comes to them: first-spring asparagus harvested in Andalusia and arriving in London within the day, live scallops and langoustines taken by divers in the icy North Sea, and, of course, a daily shipment of the finest harvest of Italy, ranging from radicchio to artichokes. Even tiny bulbs of fennel are zipped across the Channel from France. Britain's own rich bounty appears in pheasant and wild salmon. The best dishes are either slowly roasted or quickly seared.

12 Teatime

Everyone should indulge in a formal afternoon tea at least once while they're in London. It's a relaxing, drawn-out, civilized affair that usually consists of three courses, all elegantly served on delicate china: first, dainty finger sandwiches (with the crusts cut off, of course); then fresh-baked scones served with jam and deliciously decadent clotted cream (also known as Devonshire cream); and, lastly, an array of bite-sized sweets. All the while, an indulgent server keeps the pot of tea of your choice fresh at hand. Sometimes, ports and aperitifs are on offer to accompany your final course. It's a quintessential British experience; we've listed our favorites below. We've also included a handful of less formal alternatives, in case high tea just isn't your style.

MAYFAIR

✪ Brown's Hotel. 29–34 Albemarle St., W1. ☎ **0171/493-6020.** Reservations not accepted. Afternoon tea £17 ($27). AE, DC, MC, V. Daily 3–5:45pm. Tube: Green Park.

Along with the Ritz, Brown's ranks as one of the most chic venues for tea in London. Tea is served in the drawing room; done in English antiques, oil paintings, and floral chintz—much like the drawing room of a country estate—it's an appropriate venue for such an affair. Give your name to the concierge upon arrival; he'll seat you at one of the clusters of sofas and settees or at low tables. There's a choice of 10 teas, plus sandwiches, scones, and pastries (all made right in the hotel kitchens) that are rolled around on a trolley for your selection.

Claridge's. Brook St., W1. ☎ **0171/629-8860.** Reservations recommended. Jacket and tie required for men. High tea £17.50 ($28). AE, DC, MC, V. Daily 3–5pm. Tube: Bond St.

Claridge's teatime rituals have managed to persevere through the years with as much pomp and circumstance as the British Empire itself. It's never stuffy, though; you'll feel very welcomed. Tea is served in The Reading Room. A portrait of Lady Claridge gazes benevolently from above as a choice of 17 kinds of tea is served ever so politely. The various courses are served consecutively, including finger sandwiches with cheese savories, apple and raisin scones, and yummy pastries.

✪ **Goode's.** 19 South Audley St., Mayfair Square, W1. ☎ **0171/409-7242.** Fixed-price lunch £30 ($48) for 2 courses, £37.50 ($60) for 3. Afternoon pot of tea £3 ($4.80); high tea £16 ($26), high tea with glass of champagne £23.50 ($38). AE, DC, MC, V. Mon–Fri noon–3pm and 4–6pm (tea). Tube: Bond St. or Green Park.

Few other teatime venues manage to capture as accurately the charm and verve of the Edwardian age. The high-ceilinged gold and blue salon is housed within what used to be a flower shop, on the premises of that prestigious British emporium of fine porcelain, Thomas Goode. The real charm of Goode's, which also serves elegant lunches, emerges during teatime, when any overt reference to the ever-so-polite commerce in the adjoining china shop is swept under the rugs. Indeed, all the trappings of the Empire are present, but with none of the staid cucumber-with-wilted-lettuce sandwiches you'd expect. You'll enjoy about a half-dozen types of tea, sandwiches made with poached chicken with red onion and compote of pear or tuna with sweet corn and arugula, and scones with gingered rhubarb preserves and clotted cream. A hostess and battallion of formally dressed butlers in tails present their fare on Thomas Goode porcelain at lunch (Versailles) and teatime (Pink Carousel).

Palm Court Lounge. In the Park Lane Hotel, Piccadilly, W1. ☎ **0171/499-6321.** Reservations required. Afternoon tea £14 ($22). AE, DC, MC, V. Daily 3:30–6:30pm. Tube: Hyde Park Corner or Green Park.

This is one of the great London favorites for tea. Restored to its former charm, the lounge has an atmosphere straight from 1927, with a domed yellow-and-white-glass ceiling, torchères, and palms in Compton stoneware *jardinières.* A delightful afternoon tea that includes a long list of different teas is served daily. Many guests come here after the theater for a sandwich and drink. A pianist plays every weekday afternoon.

ST. JAMES'S

Oak Room Lounge. In Le Méridien, 21 Piccadilly, W1. ☎ **0171/734-8000.** Reservations not accepted. Afternoon tea £13.50–£19.50 ($22–$31). AE, DC, MC, V. Daily 3:30–6pm. Tube: Piccadilly Circus or Green Park.

Restored to its former Edwardian glory, the Oak Room Lounge is a wonderful place to experience a very traditional afternoon tea. The soothing elegance of this formal but unstuffy oak-paneled room is augmented by comfortable armchairs and background music by a resident harpist. A complete tea includes a selection of sandwiches and tarts, and the menu lists a tempting array of exotic teas.

Ritz Palm Court. In The Ritz Hotel, Piccadilly, W1. ☎ **0171/493-8181.** Reservations required at least 8 weeks in advance. Jeans and sneakers not acceptable. Jacket and tie required for men. Afternoon tea £23.50 ($38). AE, DC, MC, V. Daily 2–6pm. Tube: Green Park.

This is the most fashionable place in London to order afternoon tea—and the hardest to get into without reserving way in advance. Its spectacular setting is straight out of *The Great Gatsby,* complete with marble steps and columns and a baroque fountain. You have your choice of a long list of teas, served with delectable sandwiches and luscious pastries.

The Art of Taking Tea

Tea is serious business in Britain. In a nation where per-capita consumption of tea has risen to five cups a day, the tea-taking ritual is as intricate and powerful in the national psyche as football, rugby, Empire-building, and dishing the Royal Family. Arguments rage regularly (but usually ever-so-politely) about the proper way to prepare a pot of tea, accompanied by debate about how to warm, stir, and flavor it, and what blend of leaves is either the most flavorful, most prestigious, or both. (More reputations were ruined by the tea-drinking ceremony than virtually anything else in the Edwardian social roster.)

The emphasis on midafternoon tea has some illustrious antecedents, as the ceremony developed during an era when the diets of even the richest of Britons were sorely lacking in basic vitamins. Teatime—with its emphasis on caffeine and some kind of sustenance—provided the bursts of energy that helped fuel the expansion of the British Empire. Entire flotillas of clipper ships embarked for India and China to gather leaves, and navies left for to the West Indies to acquire sugar to sweeten the brewed tea and the delectable pastries that sometimes accompany it. (Lest you be led astray by the wide choice of teas, remember that delicate Chinese blends tend to be favored by dowagers and socialites and the robust Indian ones tend to be what construction workers consume on chilly worksites a few hours before breaking off for a round of bitter in a local pub.)

Who are the quintessential arbiters of taste when it comes to pinky elevation and other tea-taking etiquette? The Queen Mother and Noël Coward, who were once spotted sipping Earl Grey together in the lobby of London's Ritz. On that long-ago day, we and our fellow tea drinkers became suspicious that something was up when the hotel's director (a figurehead not usually preoccupied with fine-tuning service) appeared to check the patina on the appallingly valuable antique porcelain and silver (probably the best the Ritz owned) that was laid out at a table adjoining ours. Our suspicions were more than confirmed when in walked the Queen Mother, *sine qua non* figurehead for millions of English-speaking tea-drinkers during the darkest

✪ **St. James Restaurant & The Fozuntain Restaurant.** In Fortnum & Mason, 181 Piccadilly, W1. ☎ **0171/734-8040.** In the St. James, full tea £10.50–£12.25 ($17–$20). In The Fountain, full teas £7–£10 ($11–$16). AE, DC, MC, V. St. James, Mon–Sat 3–5:30pm; The Fountain, Mon–Sat 3–6pm. Tube: Piccadilly Circus.

This pair of tea salons function as a culinary showplace for London's most prestigious grocery store, Fortnum & Mason. As such, the tea-drinking ritual is spiffier than at establishments less dependent on maintaining an impeccable public image. The more formal of the two venues, the St. James, on the venerable store's fourth floor, is a pale green and beige homage to formal Edwardian taste. More rapid, less formal, and better-tuned to the hectic pace of London shoppers and London commuters is The Fountain Restaurant, on the street level, where a sense of tradition and manners is very much a part of the teatime experience, but in a less opulent setting. The quantities of food served in both venues are usually ample enough to be defined as full-fledged early suppers for most theatergoers.

PICCADILLY CIRCUS & LEICESTER SQUARE

The Blue Room. 3 Bateman St., W1. ☎ **0171/437-4827.** Reservations not accepted. Cup of tea £1 ($1.60), cakes and pastries 60p–£2.40 ($1–$4), sandwiches £3–£3.70 ($5–$6). No credit cards. Sun–Thurs 8am–midnight; Fri–Sat 8am–2am. Tube: Leicester Sq.

days of World War II, accompanied by Noël ("a talent to amuse") Coward. Elizabeth *mère* had invited the playwright to tea in order to thank him for the hospitality he had extended to her in Jamaica, where he'd recently served her lunch.

We later learned—through a perfectly acceptable teatime ritual, polite eavesdropping—that the lobster mousse intended for her lunch had melted in the Jamaican heat and that he'd been forced to open a can of split-pea soup instead. That's what one talks about at tea: What you had for lunch. Frilly things like that. Keep it light. Keep it gay.

The tea-drinking ritual is not without its literary precedents. Samuel Pepys, after his first "cuppa" in 1660, found the experience so exhilarating that he devoted an entire diary entry to the experience. The reputation of the Duchess of Bedford was assured forever when, in 1840, she devised a medley of cakes intended for consumption with her brews. And everybody's favorite aesthete, Oscar Wilde, elevated the scathing *bon mot* to an art form over a cup of tea.

"Would you mind pouring the tea, my dear, as I seem to have sprained my wrist," is considered a standard but lethal trap that brides-to-be should avoid whenever meeting their prospective mothers-in-law for the first time. No one could pour tea like a dowager empress of a large country estate, and only the most brazen of social-climbing neophytes ever dared to try.

If you should experience cultural vertigo before the yawning abyss of insecurity induced by such formidable precedents, forego the tea-drinking ritual completely and do instead what the masses do: Elbow up next to a stranger in a local cafe, order a frothy cappuccino, then segue gradually into a bout of lagers-with-lime in a local pub (where, contrary to whatever you might be told, many Brits actually feel more comfortable anyway). At least there, you won't feel compelled to wear a floppy hat, watch your manners, or emulate the Queen Mother—at least in any of the ways required by sit-down tea, of which actress Gladys Cooper once asked, "Is there any other kind?"

Nothing about this place has been patterned on the grand dame tearooms mentioned above, where tea-drinking is presented as an intricate and elaborate social ritual. What you'll find here instead is a cozy, somewhat eccentric enclave lined with the artworks of some of the regular patrons, battered sofas that might've come out of somebody's college dormitory, and a gathering of likable urban hipsters to whom very little is sacred. You can enjoy dozens of varieties of tea, including herbals, served in steaming mugfuls. Lots of arty and eccentric types gather here during the late afternoon, emulating some of the rituals of the old-fashioned tea service but with absolutely none of the hauteur.

COVENT GARDEN & THE STRAND

MJ Bradley's. 9 King St., WC2. ☎ **0171/240-5178.** Cup of tea 95p ($1.50), sandwiches £1.85–£3.50 ($3–$6) each. No credit cards. Mon–Fri 8am–8:30pm; Sat–Sun 11am–8:30pm. Tube: Covent Garden or Charing Cross.

Although it defines itself as a coffeehouse, many of MJ Bradley's fans resolutely drop in for a cup of as many as 20 different kinds of tea, everything from Earl Grey and Assam to such herbal brews as peppermint. Outfitted like a brasserie, it manages to mingle nostalgia with modern wall sculptures. If you're hungry, consider one of the imaginative sandwiches with fillings of herb-flavored cream cheese with sun-dried tomatoes.

✪ Palm Court at the Waldorf Meridien. In the Waldorf Hotel, Aldwych, WC2. ☎ **0171/836-2400.** Reservations required. Jacket and tie required for men at tea dance. Afternoon tea £17–£20 ($27–$32); tea dance £24–£27 ($38–$43). AE, DC, MC, V. Afternoon tea Mon–Fri 3–5:30pm; tea dance Sat 2:30–5:30pm; Sun 4–6:30pm. Tube: Covent Garden.

The Waldorf's Palm Court combines afternoon tea with afternoon dancing (such as the fox-trot, quickstep, and the waltz). The Palm Court is aptly compared to a 1920s movie set (which it has been several times in its long life). You can order tea on a terrace or in a pavilion the size of a ballroom lit by skylights. On tea-dancing days, the orchestra leader will conduct such favorites as "Ain't She Sweet" and "Yes, Sir, That's My Baby," as a butler in a cutaway inquires if you want a cucumber sandwich.

KNIGHTSBRIDGE

✪ The Georgian Restaurant. On the 4th floor of Harrods, 87–135 Brompton Rd., SW1. ☎ **0171/225-6800.** High tea £15.50 ($25) per person. AE, DC, MC, V. Teatime Mon–Sat 3:45–5:30pm (last order). Tube: Knightsbridge.

As long as anyone can remember, teatime at Harrods has been one of the most distinctive features of Europe's most famous department store. A flood of visitors is somehow gracefully herded into a high-volume but nevertheless elegant room. Many come here expressly for the tea ritual, where staff haul silver pots and trolleys laden with pastries and sandwiches through the cavernous dining hall. The list of teas available (at least 50) is sometimes so esoteric that choosing one might remind you of selecting one of the vintages from a sophisticated wine cellar. Most exotic is Betigala, a rare blend from China, similar to Lapsang Souchong.

Richoux. 86 Brompton Rd. (opposite Harrods), Knightsbridge, SW3. ☎ **0171/584-8300.** Full tea £12.50 ($20); English tea £7.50 ($12). AE, DC, MC, V. Jan to mid-May, Mon–Sat 8am–8pm; Sun 10am–9:30pm; mid-May to Dec, Mon–Sat 8am–9:30pm; Sun 10am–9:30pm. Tube: Knightsbridge.

Try the old-fashioned atmosphere of Richoux, established in the 1920s. You can order four hot scones with strawberry jam and whipped cream or choose from a selection of pastries behind a display case. Of course, tea is obligatory; always specify lemon or cream, one lump or two. A full menu, with fresh salads, sandwiches, burgers, and more is served all day. There are three other locations, all open Monday to Saturday 8:30am to 11pm, Sunday 10am to 11:30pm: a branch at the bottom of Bond Street, 172 Piccadilly (☎ **0171/493-2204,** tube: Piccadilly Circus or Green Park); one at 41A S. Audley St. (☎ **0171/629-5228,** tube: Green Park or Hyde Park Corner); and one at 3 Circus Rd. (☎ **0171/483-4001,** tube: St. John's Wood).

BELGRAVIA

The Lanesborough. Hyde Park Corner, SW1. ☎ **0171/259-5599.** Reservations required. High tea £18.50 ($30), high tea with strawberries and champagne £22.50 ($36); pot of tea £3.50 ($5.60). AE, DC, MC, V. Daily 3:30–5:30pm (last order). AE, DC, MC, V. Tube: Hyde Park Corner.

You'll suspect that many of the folks sipping exotic teas here have dropped in to inspect the public areas of one of London's most expensive hotels. The staff here rises to the challenge with aplomb, offering a selection of seven teas that include the Lanesborough special blend, and such herbal esoteria as Rose Cayou. The focal point for this ritual is the Conservatory, a glass-roofed Edwardian fantasy filled with potted plants and a sense of the long-gone majesty of empire. The finger sandwiches, scones, and sweets are all appropriately lavish and endlessly correct.

CHELSEA

The Tearoom at the Chelsea Physic Garden. 66 Royal Hospital Rd., SW3. ☎ **0171/ 352-5646.** Tea with cake £3.50 ($6). MC, V (in shop only). Wed noon–5pm; Sun 2–6pm. Closed Nov–Mar. Tube: Sloane Sq.

It encompasses only 3½ acres, crisscrossed with gravel paths and ringed with a high brick wall that shuts out the roaring traffic of Royal Hospital Road. These few spectacular acres, however, revere the memory of entire industries that were spawned from seeds developed and tested within its walls. Founded in 1673 as a botanical education center, the Chelsea Physic Garden's list of successes include the exportation of rubber from South America to Malaya and tea from China to India.

On the 2 days a week it's open, the tearoom is likely to be filled with botanical enthusiasts merrily sipping cups of tea as fortification for their garden treks. The setting is a rather banal-looking Edwardian building. Since the tearoom is only an adjunct to the glories of the garden itself, don't expect the lavish rituals of teatime venues. But you can carry your cakes and cups of tea outside into a garden that, despite meticulous care, always looks a bit unkempt. (Herbaceous plants within its hallowed precincts are left untrimmed to encourage bird life and seed production.) Botanists and flower lovers in general find the place fascinating.

KENSINGTON

✪ The Orangery. In the gardens of Kensington Palace, W8. ☎ **0171/376-0239.** Reservations not accepted. Pot of tea £1.60 ($3), summer cakes and puddings £1.95–£3.50 ($3–$6), sandwiches £6 ($10). MC, V. Daily 10am–6pm; closing time ½ hour before gates close (usually between 4 and 5pm) in winter. Mar–Oct 10am–6pm; Nov–Mar 10am–4pm. Tube: High St. Kensington or Queensway.

In its way, the Orangery is the most amazing place for midafternoon tea in the world. Set about 50 yards north of Kensington Palace, it occupies a long and narrow garden pavilion built in 1704 by Queen Anne as a site for her tea parties. In homage to that monarch's original intentions, rows of potted orange trees bask in sunlight from soaring windows, and tea is still served amid Corinthian columns, ruddy-colored bricks, and a pair of Grinling Gibbons woodcarvings. To help accessorize the place, there are even some urns and statuary that the Royal Family imported to the site from Windsor Castle. The menu includes lunchtime soups and sandwiches, which come with a salad and a portion of upscale potato chips known as "kettle chips." There's also an array of different teas, served with high style, usually accompanied by freshly baked scones with clotted cream and jam, and Belgian chocolate cake.

NOTTING HILL

The Garden Café. London Lighthouse, 111–117 Lancaster Rd., W11. ☎ **0171/792-1200.** Cup of tea 40p (65¢), platter of food £2.50–£4 ($4–$6). No credit cards. Mon–Fri 9am–7:30pm; Sat–Sun noon–2:30pm. Tube: Ladbroke Grove.

This is the most unusual of the places we recommend, and it also may be one of the most worthwhile. The Garden Café is in The Lighthouse, the largest center in Europe for people affected with HIV and AIDS. The late Princess Diana made the organization one of her projects, and slugged down a cuppa here. The cafeteria is open to the public and is less institutional-looking than you might expect; French doors open onto a spectacular garden with fountains and summertime tables. Tea is available throughout the day, although the midafternoon—between 3:30 and 5:30pm—seems to be the most convivial time. Its Notting Hill location is only a short walk from Portobello Road.

13 Pubs

IN THE WEST END
MAYFAIR

Shepherd's Tavern. 50 Hertford St., W1. ☎ **0171/499-3017.** Reservations recommended. Main courses from £9 ($14). AE, DC, MC, V. Restaurant daily noon–3pm; Mon–Sat 6:30–10pm, Sun 7–9:30pm. Bar Mon–Sat 11am–11pm; Sun noon–10:30pm. Tube: Green Park. BRITISH.

This pub is one of the focal points of the all-pedestrian shopping zone of Shepherd's Market. It's set amid a warren of narrow, cobble-covered streets behind Park Lane, in an 18th-century town house very similar to many of its neighbors. The street-level bar is cramped but congenial, with many luxurious touches, including a collection of memorabilia and antiques. Many of the regulars recall this tavern's popularity with the pilots of the Battle of Britain. Bar snacks include simple platters of shepherd's pie and fish-and-chips. More formal dining is available upstairs in the cozy, cedar-lined Georgian-style restaurant; the classic British menu probably hasn't changed much since the 1950s. If you're a little leery of the roast beef with Yorkshire pudding, go with the Oxford ham instead.

ST. JAMES'S

Red Lion. 2 Duke of York St. (off Jermyn St.), SW1. ☎ **0171/930-2030.** Sandwiches £2.50 ($4), fish-and-chips £8 ($13). No credit cards. Mon–Sat noon–11pm. Tube: Piccadilly Circus. BRITISH.

This little Victorian pub, with its early-1900s decorations and mirrors 150 years old, has been compared in spirit to Édouard Manet's painting *A Bar at the Folies-Bergère* (on display at the Courtauld Institute Galleries). You can order pre-made sandwiches, but once they're gone you're out of luck. On Friday and Saturday, homemade fish-and-chips are also served. Wash down your meal with Ind Coope's fine ales or the house's special beer, Burton's, an unusual brew made of spring water from the Midlands town of Bourton-on-Trent.

LEICESTER SQUARE

Salisbury. 90 St. Martin's Lane, WC2. ☎ **0171/836-5863.** Reservations not accepted. Buffet meal £4–£6.50 ($6–$10). AE, DC, MC, V. Mon–Sat 11am–11pm; Sun noon–10:30pm. Tube: Leicester Sq. BRITISH.

Salisbury's glittering cut-glass mirrors reflect the faces of English stage stars (and hopefuls) sitting around the curved buffet-style bar. A less prominent place to dine is the old-fashioned wall banquette with its copper-topped tables and art-nouveau decor. The pub's specialty—home-cooked pies set out in a buffet cabinet with salads—is really quite good and inexpensive. Hot food is served from noon until 7:30pm, cold sandwiches from noon to 10pm.

SOHO

Old Coffee House. 49 Beak St., W1. ☎ **0171/437-2197.** Main courses £4–£4.50 ($6–$7). No credit cards. Restaurant Mon–Sat noon–3pm; pub Mon–Sat 11am–11pm; Sun noon–3pm and 7–10:30pm. Tube: Oxford Circus or Piccadilly Circus. BRITISH.

Once honored as "Soho Pub of the Year," the Old Coffee House takes its name from the coffeehouse heyday of 18th-century London, when coffee was called "the devil's brew." The pub still serves pots of filtered coffee. The place is heavily decorated with bric-a-brac, including archaic musical instruments and World War I recruiting posters. Have a drink at the long, narrow bar, or retreat to the upstairs restaurant, where you can enjoy good pub food at lunch, including steak-and-kidney pie, one of three vegetarian dishes, scampi-and-chips, or a burger and fries.

BLOOMSBURY

Museum Tavern. 49 Great Russell St., WC1. ☎ **0171/242-8987.** Bar snacks £2–£6 ($3 –$10). AE, DC, MC, V. Mon–Sat 11am–11pm; Sun noon–10:30pm. Tube: Holborn or Tottenham Court Rd. BRITISH.

Across the street from the British Museum, this circa-1703 pub retains most of its antique trappings: velvet, oak paneling, and cut glass. It lies right in the center of the University of London area and is popular with writers, publishers, and researchers from the museum. (Supposedly, Karl Marx wrote over meals in the pub.) Traditional English food is served, with shepherd's pie, sausages cooked in English cider, and chef's specials on the hot-food menu. Cold fare includes turkey-and-ham pie, ploughman's lunch, and salads. Several English ales, cold lagers, cider, Guinness, wines, and spirits are available. Food and coffee are served all day; the pub gets crowded at lunchtime.

COVENT GARDEN

Nag's Head. 10 James St., WC2. ☎ **0171/836-4678.** Reservations not accepted. Sandwich platters with salad £3–£6 ($5–$10), full meal salads £4.75 ($8). AE, DC, MC, V. Mon–Sat 11am–11pm; Sun noon–10:30pm. Tube: Covent Garden. BRITISH.

The Nag's Head is one of London's most famous Edwardian pubs. In days of yore, patrons had to make their way through lorries of fruit and flowers to drink here. But when the market moved, 300 years of British tradition faded away. Today, the pub is patronized mainly by young people. The draft Guinness is very good. Lunch is typical pub grub: sandwiches, salads, pork cooked in cider, and garlic prawns. The sandwich platters mentioned above are served only during the lunch hour (noon to 3:30pm); however, snacks are available in the afternoon.

WESTMINSTER (NEAR TRAFALGAR SQUARE)

Sherlock Holmes. 10 Northumberland St., WC1. ☎ **0171/930-2644.** Reservations recommended for restaurant. Main courses £8–£12.50 ($13–$20); fixed-price menus £11–£16 ($18–$26); ground-floor snacks £3–£7.25 ($5–$12). AE, DC, MC, V. Restaurant Mon–Thurs noon–3pm and 5:30–10:45pm; Fri–Sun noon–10:30pm; pub Mon–Sat 11am–11pm; Sun noon–10:30pm. Tube: Charing Cross or Embankment. BRITISH.

It would be rather strange if the Sherlock Holmes were not the old gathering spot for the Baker Street Irregulars, a once-mighty clan of mystery lovers who met here to honor the genius of Sir Arthur Conan Doyle's most famous fictional character. Upstairs, you'll find a recreation of the living room at 221B Baker Street and such "Holmesiana" as the serpent of *The Speckled Band* and the head of *The Hound of the Baskervilles.* In the upstairs dining room, you can order complete meals with wine. Try "Copper Beeches" (grilled butterfly chicken breasts with lemon and herbs). You select dessert from the trolley. Downstairs is mainly for drinking, but there's a good snack bar with cold meats, salads, cheeses, and wine and ales sold by the glass.

THE CITY

○ **Ye Olde Cheshire Cheese.** Wine Office Court, 145 Fleet St., EC4. ☎ **0171/353-6170.** Main courses £7–£15 ($11–$24). AE, DC, MC, V. Daily noon–9:30pm; Sun noon–2:30pm and 6–9:30pm. Drinks and bar snacks daily 11:30am–11pm. Tube: St. Paul's or Blackfriars. BRITISH.

Set within a recently remodeled, carefully preserved building whose foundation was laid in the 13th century, this is the most famous of the old City chophouses and pubs. Established in 1667, it claims to be the spot where Dr. Samuel Johnson (who lived

Haute Cuisine Comes to the Lowly Boozer

After decades—nay, centuries—of enduring some of the worst food in England, pubbers still can't believe what has happened to their neighborhood boozers (as the locals like to call their favorite pubs): They've become foodie havens. More and more pubs are offering food you can actually eat—not just canned beans on stale toast. Believe it or not, some of the chefs cooking in pubs today could even hold court in top restaurants.

What's brought about such a sea of change in the lowly pub? Many up-and-coming chefs simply can't afford the price tag of opening a restaurant, so they've turned to the pub as an alternative venue. They clean up the decades-old beer and nicotine stains and throw out the smoke-scented draperies hung when Edward VII had his portly butt on the throne—and lo! The place becomes light and airy. A modern kitchen and a new menu follows, and suddenly grandpa's local is a hot new dining destination.

You don't have to be a young fashion victim to enjoy the superb viands served at **The Cow,** 89 Westbourne Park Rd., W2 (☎ 0171/221-0021; tube: Westbourne Grove). Tom Conran (son of restaurateur/entrepreneur Sir Terence Conran) holds forth nightly in this increasingly hip Notting Hill watering hole. It looks like an Irish pub, but the accents you'll hear are trustafarian rather than street-smart Dublin. With a pint of Fuller's or London Pride firmly in hand, you can linger over the modern European menu, which changes daily but is likely to include ox tongue poached in milk; mussels in curry and cream; a mixed grill of lamb chops, calf's liver, and sweetbreads; and steak with onion rings. The seafood selections are especially delectable. "The Cow Special"—a half-dozen Irish rock oysters with a pint of Guinness or a glass of wine for £8 ($13)—is the star of the show. A raw bar downstairs serves an array of fresh choices in addition to oysters. To finish, skip the filtered coffee served upstairs (it's wretched), and opt for an espresso downstairs. Main courses run £8 to £14 ($13 to $22); a fixed-price 2-course dinner costs £35 ($56). Open Monday to Saturday 7 to 11:30pm and Sunday 12:30 to 3:30pm; bar open daily from 11:30am to 11:30pm. MC, V accepted.

Another of our favorites is **The Engineer,** 65 Gloucester Ave., NW1 (☎ 0171/722-0950; tube: Chalk Farm or Camden Town), a stylishly converted pub owned by Abigail Osborne and Tamsin Olivier, daughter of Sir Laurence (or "Larry's daughter," as she's called locally). This citadel of North London chic is named for Victorian bridge, tunnel, and railway builder Isambard Kingdom Brunel; it sits beside Regent's Canal, one of Brunel's creations. The pub is divided into a bar, a dining room, and a garden area that welcomes diners on warm days. The decor is light and modern, enhanced by regular exhibits by local artists. The cuisine is accurately billed as modern British and relies on seasonal produce and organic meat and eggs. Choices include salt beef (corned) with potato latkes and beetroot horseradish; Moroccan-style chicken tagine with couscous; and a warm

nearby) entertained admirers with his acerbic wit. Charles Dickens and other literary lions also patronized the place. Later, many of the ink-stained journalists and scandal-mongers of 19th- and early 20th-century Fleet Street made it their locale. You'll find six bars and two dining rooms here. The house specialties include "ye famous pudding" (steak, kidney, mushrooms, and game) and Scottish roast beef with Yorkshire salad of shiitake mushrooms with celeriac and red-onion confit. A tantalizing appetizer is the deep-fried Camembert with kiwi fruit relish. Desserts change nightly and might include an orange and cardamom pudding. From the tap, go with the Caffrey's or a Guinness. Main courses run £8.50 to £12 ($14 to $19). Open daily noon to midnight, with the bar closing at 11pm. Reservations are required to dine. MC, V accepted.

The poshest pub conversion in town is **The Enterprise,** 35 Walton St., SW3 (☎ **0171/584-3148;** tube: South Kensington). Its proximity to Harrods attracts both regulars and out-of-towners loaded down with packages from the swank department store. Although the joint is cruisy at night (whatever your preference), during the day it attracts the ladies-who-lunch crowd. With banquettes, white linen, and fresh flowers on the tables, you won't mistake it for a lowly boozer. The kitchen serves very respectable traditional English fare prepared with fresh ingredients; featured dishes include fried salmon cakes with perfectly done fries, and grilled sole with new potatoes. They're not so grand that they won't prepare for you an entrecôte with frites if that's what pleases you—actually, the juicy, properly aged, and flavorful thin French-style slice of beef is about the best you can have in London. Main courses cost £8.50 to £12.50 ($14 to $20). Open daily noon to 2:30pm, Monday to Friday 7 to 11pm, and Saturday and Sunday 7 to 10:30pm (the bar is open all day). Reservations are accepted for lunch but not for dinner. AE, MC, V accepted.

The offbeat **Prince Bonaparte,** 80 Chepstow Rd., W2 (☎ **0171/229-5912;** tube: Notting Hill Gate or Westbourne Park), serves great pub grub in what was a grungy boozer in the days before Notting Hill Gate became fashionable. Now pretty young things show up, spilling out onto the sidewalk when the evenings are warm; one patron called it "an ad-man's dream beer shot." The pub is filled with mismatched furniture from schools and churches; jazz and lazy blues fill the air, competing with the babble. It may seem at first that the staff doesn't have its act together, but once the food arrives, you won't care one way or the other: It's very good. The menu roams the world for inspiration: Moroccan chicken with couscous is as good or better than any you'll find in Marrakesh; the seared salmon teriyaki with basmati rice is perfectly prepared, as is the salad of beet root, new potatoes, walnuts, and eggplant. Start with hummus and feta cheese on a grilled slab of grainy bread. Roast lamb, tender and juicy, appears on the traditional Sunday menu. We recommend the London Pride or Grolsch to wash it all down with. Main courses run £7 to £10 ($11 to $16). Open Monday, Wednesday, Thursday, and Friday from noon to 11pm; Tuesday 5 to 11pm; and Sunday noon to 10:30pm. No credit cards.

If this nouvelle trend's got you down, don't worry: You still can dig into traditional pub grub in dozens of genuinely lowly boozers that slept through the revolution. We've recommended a medley of our favorites in these pages.

pudding and horseradish sauce. Sandwiches, salads, and standby favorites like steak-and-kidney pie are also available, as are dishes like Dover sole.

Ye Olde Cock Tavern. 22 Fleet St., EC4. ☎ **0171/353-8570.** Reservations recommended. Main courses £9–£14 ($14–$22); fixed-price 2-course lunch £12 ($19). AE, DC, MC, V. Carvery Mon–Fri noon–3pm; pub Mon–Fri 11am–11pm. Tube: Temple or Chancery Lane. BRITISH.

Dating back to 1549, this tavern boasts a long line of literary patrons: Samuel Pepys mentioned the pub in his diaries; Dickens frequented it; and Tennyson referred to it in one of his poems, a copy of which is framed and proudly displayed near the front entrance. It's one of the few buildings in London to have survived the Great Fire of 1666. At street level, you can order a pint as well as snack-bar food, steak-and-kidney pie, or a cold chicken-and-beef plate with salad. At the Carvery upstairs, a meal includes a choice of appetizers, followed by lamb, pork, beef, or turkey.

Ye Olde Watling. 29 Watling St., EC4. ☎ **0171/653-9971.** Reservations not accepted. Lunch £4–£7 ($6–$11); bar snacks from £2 ($3). AE, MC, V. Restaurant Mon–Fri noon–2:30pm; pub Mon–Fri 10am–10pm. Tube: Mansion House. BRITISH.

Ye Olde Watling was rebuilt after the Great Fire of 1666. On the ground level is a mellow pub; upstairs is an intimate restaurant where, under oak beams and at trestle tables, you can dine on simple English main dishes for lunch. The menu varies daily, with such choices and reliable standbys as fish-and-chips, lamb satay, lasagna, fish cakes, and usually a vegetarian dish. All are served with two vegetables or salad, plus rice or potatoes.

KNIGHTSBRIDGE

Bill Bentley's. 31 Beauchamp Place, SW3. ☎ **0171/589-5080.** Reservations recommended. Main courses £8–£17 ($13–$27). AE, MC, V. Mon–Sat noon–2:30pm and 6–10:30pm. Tube: Knightsbridge. BRITISH.

Bill Bentley's, on fashionable Beauchamp Place, has a varied and reasonable wine list with a good selection of Bordeaux. Many visitors come here just to sample the wines, including some New World choices along with popular French selections. In summer, a garden patio opens to patrons. If you don't prefer the formality of the restaurant, you can order from the wine-bar menu that begins with a half-dozen oysters, or you can enjoy the chef's fish soup with croutons and rouille. Main dishes include the famous salmon cakes, served with tomato sauce, and daily specialties. In keeping with contemporary trends, the restaurant menu has been simplified and is rather less expensive than before. It changes frequently, but typical dishes might include avocado, crab, and prawn salad as an appetizer, followed by suprême of chicken with oyster mushrooms and a madeira jus, or else grilled rainbow trout with a petit garni and lemon sauce. A large selection of bottled beers and spirits is also available.

IN NEARBY BELGRAVIA

Antelope. 22 Eaton Terrace, SW1. ☎ **0171/730-7781.** Reservations recommended for upstairs dining room. Main courses £6–£8 ($10–$13). AE, MC, V. Mon–Sat 11am–11pm; Sun 11am–10:30pm. Tube: Sloane Sq. BRITISH.

Located on the fringe of Belgravia, at the gateway to Chelsea, the Antelope caters to a hodgepodge of clients from all classes, colors, and creeds (including English rugby aficionados). At lunchtime, the ground-floor bar provides hot and cold pub food, but in the evening, only drinks are served there. Upstairs, the lunch menu includes principally English dishes: fish-and-chips, jugged hare, and the like.

✪ **Grenadier.** 18 Wilton Row, SW1. ☎ **0171/235-3074.** Reservations recommended. Main courses £11–£20 ($18–$32). AE, DC, MC, V. Mon–Sat noon–3pm and 6–10pm, Sun noon–3:30pm and 7–10:30pm. Tube: Hyde Park Corner. BRITISH.

Tucked away in a mews, the Grenadier is one of London's reputedly haunted pubs. Aside from the poltergeist, the basement houses the original bar and skittles alley used by the Duke of Wellington's officers on leave from fighting Napoléon. The scarlet front door of the one-time officers' mess is guarded by a scarlet sentry box and shaded by a vine. The bar is nearly always crowded. Lunch and dinner are offered daily—even on Sunday, when it's a tradition to drink Bloody Marys here. In the stalls along the side, you can order good-tasting fare based on seasonal ingredients. Well-prepared dishes include pork Grenadier and chicken and Stilton roulade. Snacks like fish-and-chips are available at the bar.

Nag's Head. 53 Kinnerton St., SW1. ☎ **0171/235-1135.** Main courses £4.50–£5.25 ($7.20–$8.40). No credit cards. Mon–Sat 11am–11pm; Sun noon–10:30pm. Tube: Hyde Park. BRITISH.

The Nag's Head, snuggled on a back street, is a short walk from the Berkeley Hotel. Previously a jail dating from 1780, it's said to be the smallest pub in London, although others claim that distinction. In 1921, it was sold for £12 and 6p. Have a drink up front or wander to the tiny little bar in the rear. For food, you might enjoy "real ale sausage" (made with pork and ale), shepherd's pie, or even the quiche of the day. This warm and cozy pub, with a welcoming staff, is patronized by a cosmopolitan clientele—newspaper people, musicians, and curious tourists. This pub touts itself as an "independent," or able to serve any "real ale" they choose because of their lack of affiliation.

CHELSEA

Front Page. 35 Old Church St., SW3. ☎ **0171/352-0648.** Main courses £3–£8 ($5–$13). AE, MC, V. Restaurant daily noon–2:30pm; Mon–Sat 7–10pm, Sun 7–9:30pm; pub Mon–Sat 11am–11pm; Sun noon–10:30pm. Tube: Sloane Sq. INTERNATIONAL.

Front Page is favored by young professionals who like the mellow atmosphere provided by its wood paneling, wooden tables, and pews and benches. In one section an open fire burns on cold nights. The pub stands in an expensive residential section of Chelsea and is a good place to go for a drink. You can also order bottled Budweiser. Check the chalkboard for the daily specials, which might include hot chicken salad, fish cakes, and smoked salmon and cream cheese on a bagel.

King's Head & Eight Bells. 50 Cheyne Walk, SW3. ☎ **0171/352-1820.** Main courses £5–£6 ($8–$10). MC, V. Mon–Sat 11am–11pm; Sun noon–10:30pm. Tube: Sloane Sq. BRITISH.

Many distinguished personalities once lived near this historic Thameside pub; a short stroll will take you to the former homes of Carlyle, Swinburne, and George Eliot. In other days, press gangs used to roam these parts of Chelsea seeking lone travelers to abduct for a life at sea. Today, it's popular with stage and TV celebrities as well as writers. The best English beers are served here, as well as a good selection of reasonably priced wine. The menu features homemade specials of the day, such as fish-and-chips or sausage and chips, and include at least one vegetable main dish. On Sunday, a roast of the day is served. You can also enjoy live music while you sip your beer.

14 Wine Bars

IN THE WEST END
ST. JAMES'S

Bubbles. 41 N. Audley St., W1. ☎ **0171/491-3237.** Reservations recommended. Main courses £4.50–£12.50 ($7–$20); vegetarian main courses £5.50–£6.25 ($9–$10). AE, DC, MC, V. Daily 11am–11pm. Tube: Marble Arch or Bond St. BRITISH/INTERNATIONAL VEGETARIAN.

This interesting wine bar lies between Upper Brook Street and Oxford Street (in the vicinity of Selfridges). The owners attach equal importance to their food and to their impressive wine list (some wines are sold by the glass). On the ground floor, you can enjoy not only fine wines but also draft beer and liquor, along with a limited but well-chosen selection of bar food, such as smoked salmon on brown bread, or homemade steak burger with fries and salad and cheese. Downstairs, the restaurant serves both English and continental dishes, including an appealing vegetarian selection. You might begin with French onion soup, followed by bangers and mash with onion gravy, Dover sole, or grilled chicken breast with apple rice and creamed leeks.

Shampers. 4 Kingly St. (between Carnaby and Regent sts.), W1. ☎ **0171/437-1692.** Reservations recommended. Main courses £8–£12 ($13–$19). AE, DC, MC, V. Mon–Sat 11am–11pm. Closed Easter and Christmas. Tube: Oxford Circus. CONTINENTAL.

For a number of years now, this has been a favorite of West End wine-bar aficionados. In addition to the street-level wine bar, where platters of food are served, there's a more formal basement-level restaurant. In either section, you can order such main dishes as braised leg and breast of guinea fowl, portions of cured and salted ham with new potatoes, and platters of assorted cheese. Salads are especially popular, including chicken with tarragon-cream dressing and tuna and pasta with a spicy tomato sauce. A platter of Irish mussels cooked in a cream-and-tarragon sauce seems to be everybody's favorite. The restaurant is closed in the evening, but the bar serves an extended menu, incorporating not only the luncheon menu but such dishes as grilled calf's liver, pheasant sausages, pan-fried tiger prawns, free-range chicken, and a variety of fish dishes.

PICCADILLY CIRCUS

Daniel's Bar (Café Royal Grill). 68 Regent St., W1. ☎ **0171/437-9090,** ext. 277. Reservations not required. Main courses £4–£7.75 ($6–$12); menu du jour £9–£12.50 ($14–$20). AE, DC, MC, V. Mon–Sat noon–3pm and 5–11pm (open only for drinks and snacks during evening hours). Tube: Piccadilly Circus. BRITISH.

A deliberately unpretentious annex to the chillingly expensive Café Royal Grill, Daniel's dates from 1865. It's accessible from the grand café's marble-floored lobby, where all the literary greats of 19th-century England have trod, including Oscar Wilde. Despite its opulent decor—art nouveau moldings, oaken half-paneling, abundant framed cartoons and illustrations—the bar is very informal. At lunchtime, order from a long list of platters, sandwiches, and appetizers, or the *menu du jour,* which might include a main course like bangers and mash and bread pudding for dessert. The evening menu is limited to a short list of snacks, including chicken satay, pizza bread, and nachos with guacamole and salsa, as most of the clientele come just to drink.

LEICESTER SQUARE

✪ **Cork & Bottle Wine Bar.** 44-46 Cranbourn St., WC2. ☎ **0171/734-7807.** Reservations recommended. Main courses £7–£9 ($11–$14); glass of wine from £2.50 ($4). AE, DC, MC, V. Mon–Sat 11am–midnight; Sun noon–10:30pm. Tube: Leicester Sq. INTERNATIONAL.

Don Hewitson, a connoisseur of fine wines for more than 30 years, presides over this trove of blissful fermentation. The ever-changing wine list features an excellent selection of Beaujolais crus from Alsace, 30 selections from Australia, 30 champagnes, and a good selection of California labels. If you want something to wash down, the most successful dish is a raised cheese-and-ham pie, with a cream cheese–like filling and crisp well-buttered pastry—not your typical quiche. There's also chicken and apple salad, Lancashire hot pot, Mediterranean prawns with garlic and asparagus, lamb in ale, and tandoori chicken.

VICTORIA

Ebury Wine Bar. 139 Ebury St., SW1. ☎ **0171/730-5447.** Reservations recommended. Average meal £20 ($32). AE, DC, MC, V. Mon–Sat 11am–10:30pm; Sun 6pm–10pm. Tube: Victoria or Sloane Square. INTERNATIONAL.

Older professional people who don't mind smoke and the smell of sizzling steaks close to their tables gravitate here. It's one of the most popular and long-enduring wine bars in the area—all dark and woodsy. In addition to those steaks, the wine-bar menu is surprisingly varied. Some dishes have a Pacific Rim influence, including Thai fish balls. Others are more typically English, as exemplified by roast pork with a crackling and apple sauce.

THE CITY
Bow Wine Vaults. 10 Bow Churchyard, EC4. ☎ **0171/248-1121.** Reservations recommended. Cover £1.40 ($2.25). Main courses £7.50–£10 ($12–$16); 2-course, fixed-price dinner £15.50 ($25). AE, DC, MC, V. The Restaurant and Brasserie Mon–Fri 11am–10pm; pub Mon–Fri 11am–11pm. Tube: Mansion House, Bank or St. Paul's. BRITISH/MODERN EUROPEAN.

Bow Wine Vaults has existed since long before the wine-bar craze began in the 1970s. One of the most famous wine bars of London, it attracts cost-conscious diners and drinkers to its vaulted cellars for such traditional fare as deep-fried Camembert, chicken Kiev, and a mixed grill, along with fish. More elegant meals, served in the street-level dining room, include mussels in cider sauce, English wild mushrooms in puff pastry, beef Wellington, and steak with brown-butter sauce. Adjacent to the restaurant is a cocktail bar that's popular with City employees after work (open weekdays from 11:30am to 8pm).

Jamaica Wine House. St. Michael's Alley off Cornhill, EC3. ☎ **0171/626-9496.** Reservations not accepted. Bar snacks £1–£5 ($2–$8). AE, DC, MC, V. Mon–Fri 11am–9:30pm. Tube: Bank. BRITISH.

Jamaica Wine House was one of the first coffeehouses in England and, reputedly, the Western world. For years, merchants and daring sea captains came here to transact deals over rum and coffee. Nowadays, the two-level house dispenses beer, ale, lager, and fine wines, among them a variety of ports. The oak-paneled bar is on the street level, attracting a jacket-and-tie crowd of investment bankers. You can order standard but filling dishes such as a ploughman's lunch and toasted sandwiches.

KNIGHTSBRIDGE
Le Metro. 28 Basil St., SW3. ☎ **0171/589-6286.** Reservations recommended. Main courses £7.50–£8.50 ($12–$14). AE, DC, MC, V. Mon–Sat 7:30am–10:30pm. Tube: Knightsbridge. INTERNATIONAL.

Located just around the corner from Harrods, Le Metro draws a fashionable crowd to its basement precincts. The place serves good, solid, and reliable food prepared with flair. The menu changes frequently, but try the chicken satays or confit of duck with lentils, garlic, and shallots if you can. You can order special wines by the glass.

CHELSEA HARBOR
Boaters Wine Bar. Harbour Yard, Chelsea Harbour, SW10. ☎ **0171/352-3687.** Main courses £3.75–£5 ($6–$8). MC, V. Mon–Fri noon–10pm. Tube: Earl's Court, then Chelsea Harbour Hoppa Bus C3. BRITISH.

This restaurant occupies the premises of one of London's new "villages," Chelsea Harbour. Well-heeled locals who own the soaringly expensive apartments nearby often come here to drink champagne by the bottle at the long wooden bar; visitors from all over the world pour in here as well. Most of the emphasis at the bar is on an impressive array of bottled beer and beer on tap; an impressive list also offers wine by the glass. Sandwiches, cheese plates, and salads are available throughout the day. For lunch, try some of their homemade pies, chili, and, to the other side of the gastronomic spectrum, vegetarian lasagna.

6 Exploring London

Dr. Samuel Johnson said, "When a man is tired of London, he is tired of life, for there is in London all that life can afford." Indeed, it would take a lifetime to explore every alley, court, street, and square in this vast city (and volumes to discuss them). Since you don't have a lifetime to spend here, we've discussed the best of what London has to offer in this chapter. Still, what's included is more than enough to keep you busy on a dozen trips to the city by the Thames.

For the first-time visitor, the question is never what to do, but what to do *first*. The "Suggested Itineraries" and "The Top Attractions" should help.

A Note about Admission and Open Hours: In the listings below, children's prices generally apply to those 16 and under. To qualify for a senior discount, you must be 60 or older. Students must present a student ID to get discounts, where available. In addition to shutting down on bank holidays, many attractions close around Christmas and New Year's (and, in some cases, early in May), so be sure to call ahead if you're visiting in those seasons.

SUGGESTED ITINERARIES

If You Have 1 Day

Even on the most rushed of itineraries, no first-time visitor should leave London without a visit to Westminster Abbey, with Poet's Corner and its wonderful royal tombs. Afterward, walk over to see Big Ben and the Houses of Parliament. Also see the Changing of the Guard at Buckingham Palace if it's on, and walk over to 10 Downing Street, home of the prime minister. Dine at one of the little restaurants in Covent Garden such as Porter's, owned by the earl of Bradford. Try one of their classic English pies (maybe lamb and apricot). For a nightcap, head over to the ultimate Victorian pub, the Red Lion in Mayfair; it's the kind of place Oscar Wilde might have chosen for a brandy.

If You Have 2 Days

Day 1 Spend day 1 as above.
Day 2 Devote a good part of the second day exploring the British Museum, one of the best museums in the world. Spend the afternoon visiting the Tower of London and seeing the Crown Jewels (expect

slow-moving lines). Later, go to a really local place for dinner, such as Shepherd's in Westminster, where you'll be able to dine alongside MPs from the House of Commons.

If You Have 3 Days

Days 1–2   Spend days 1 and 2 as above.

Day 3   In the morning visit the masterworks in the National Gallery. For a change of pace in the afternoon, head to Madame Tussaud's waxworks. Take a walking tour of St. James's (see chapter 7, "London Walks"). In the evening, take in a West End play or a performance at the South Bank Centre.

If You Have 4 or 5 Days

Days 1–3   Spend days 1, 2, and 3 as above.

Day 4   In the morning, head for the City, London's financial district. Your major sightseeing goal here will be St. Paul's Cathedral, designed by Sir Christopher Wren. Take our walking tour of the City (see chapter 7) and visit such attractions as the Guildhall. In the afternoon, head for King's Road in Chelsea for some boutique hopping and to dine at one of Chelsea's many restaurants. Later that evening, take in a show at a Soho nightclub, such as Ronnie Scott's, which hosts some of the city's best jazz.

Day 5   Explore the Victoria and Albert Museum in the morning, then go to the Tate Gallery for a look at some of its many masterpieces; have lunch at its restaurant, which offers some of the best values on wine in Britain. For a historic glimpse of the dark days of World War II, visit the Cabinet War Rooms at Clive Steps, where Churchill directed British operations in the war against the Nazis. Spend the evening at the theater.

Take in as many West End shows as you can manage in your evenings in London.

1 Sights & Attractions by Neighborhood

BELGRAVIA

Apsley House, the Wellington Museum (p. 207)

BLOOMSBURY

British Library (p. 207)
British Museum (p. 183)
Dickens House (p. 206)
Percival David Foundation of Chinese Art (p. 212)
St. Pancras Station (p. 203)

CAMDEN TOWN

Jewish Museum (p. 209)

CHELSEA

Carlyle's House (p. 205)
Chelsea Physic Garden (p. 215)
Chelsea Royal Hospital (p. 202)
National Army Museum (p. 210)

THE CITY

All Hallows Barking-by-the-Tower (and Brass Rubbing Centre) (p. 198)
Guildhall (p. 202)
London Bridge (p. 217)
Middle Temple Tudor Hall (p. 204)
Museum of London (p. 210)
National Postal Museum (p. 211)
Old Bailey (p. 205)
St. Bride's (p. 198)
St. Giles Cripplegate (p. 199)
St. Mary-le-Bow (p. 200)
St. Paul's Cathedral (p. 190)
Samuel Johnson's House (p. 206)
Temple Church (p. 201)
Temple of Mithras (p. 216)
Tower Bridge (p. 218)
Tower of London (p. 193)

Clerkenwell

St. Etheldreda's (p. 199)

2 The Top Attractions

✪ **British Museum.** Great Russell St., WC1. ☎ **0171/323-8299** or 0171/636-1555 for recorded information. Free admission. Mon–Sat 10am–5pm, Sun 2:30–6pm. Tube: Holborn or Tottenham Court Rd.

Set in scholarly Bloomsbury, this immense museum grew out of a private collection of manuscripts purchased in 1753 with the proceeds of a lottery. It grew and grew, fed by legacies, discoveries, and purchases, until it became one of the most comprehensive collections of art and artifacts in the world. It's utterly impossible to take in this museum in 1 day.

The overall storehouse splits basically into the national collections of antiquities; prints and drawings; coins, medals, and banknotes; and ethnography. Even on a cursory first visit, be sure to see the Asian collections (the finest assembly of Islamic pottery outside the Islamic world), the Chinese porcelain, the Indian sculpture, and the Prehistoric and Romano-British collections. Special treasures you might want to seek out on your first visit include the **Rosetta Stone,** whose discovery led to the deciphering of hieroglyphs, in the Egyptian Room; the **Elgin Marbles,** a priceless series of pediments, metopes, and friezes of the Parthenon in Athens, in the Duveen Gallery; and the legendary **Black Obelisk,** dating from around 860 B.C., in the Nimrud Gallery. Other treasures include the contents of Egyptian royal tombs (including mummies); fabulous arrays of 2,000-year-old jewelry, cosmetics, weapons, furniture, and tools; Babylonian astronomical instruments; and winged lions (in the Assyrian Transept) that once guarded Ashurnasirpal's palace at Numrud. The latest additions include a Mexican gallery, a Hellenistic gallery, and a "History of Money" exhibit. The exhibits change throughout the months, so if your heart is set on seeing a specific treasure, call ahead to make sure it's on display.

Time-Saver

With 2½ miles of galleries, the British Museum is overwhelming. To get a handle on it, we recommend taking a 1½-hour overview tour for £6 ($10) Monday to Saturday at 10:45am, 11:15am, 1:45pm, and 2:15pm, or Sunday at 3pm, 3:20pm, and 3:45pm. After, you can return to the galleries that most interested you. If you have only minutes to spare for the museum, concentrate on the Greek and Roman rooms (1 to 15), which hold the golden hoard of booty both bought and stolen from the Empire's once far-flung colonies.

Central London Sights

E-0145

The year 2000 will see changes to the historic museum. Dubbed the "Great Court" project, the inner courtyard will be canopied by a lightweight, transparent roof transforming the area into a covered square; housing a Centre for Education, exhibition space, bookshops, and restaurants. The center of the Great Court will feature the Round Reading Room restored to its original decorative scheme.

For information on the British Library, see p. 207.

✪ **Buckingham Palace.** At end of The Mall (on the road running from Trafalgar Sq.). ☎ **0171/839-1377.** Palace tours (usually offered in Aug and Sept) £9 ($14) adults, £6.50 ($10) seniors, £5 ($8) children under 17. Changing of the Guard free. Tube: St. James's Park, Green Park, or Victoria.

This massive, graceful building is the official residence of the queen. The red-brick palace was built as a country house for the notoriously rakish duke of Buckingham. In 1762, it was bought by King George III, who needed room for his 15 children. It didn't become the official royal residence, though, until Queen Victoria took the throne; she preferred it over St. James's Palace. From George III's time, the building was continuously expanded and remodeled, faced with Portland stone, and twice bombed (during the blitz). Located in a 40-acre garden, it's 360 feet long and contains 600 rooms. You can tell whether Her Majesty is at home by the Royal Standard flying at the masthead.

For most of the year, you can't visit the palace unless you're officially invited. Since 1993, though, much of it has been open for tours during an 8-week period in August and September, when the Royal Family is usually vacationing outside London. Elizabeth II agreed to allow visitors to tour the State Room, the Grand Staircase, Throne Room, and other areas designed by John Nash for George IV, as well as the huge Picture Gallery, which displays masterpieces by Van Dyck, Rembrandt, Rubens, and others. The admission charges help pay for repairing Windsor Castle, badly damaged by fire in 1992. The queen has decided that the palace will remain open to the public until 2000, at which time a decision to continue will be reviewed.

Buckingham Palace's most famous spectacle is the **Changing of the Guard.** This ceremony begins (when it begins) at 11:30am and lasts for a half-hour. It's been called the finest example of military pageantry extant. The new guard, marching behind a band, comes from either the Wellington or Chelsea Barracks and takes over from the old guard in the forecourt of the palace.

✪ **Houses of Parliament.** Bridge St. and Parliament Sq., SW1. House of Commons ☎ **0171/219-4272;** House of Lords ☎ **0171/219-3107.** Free admission. House of Lords open to public Mon–Wed from 2:30pm, Thurs from 3pm, and some Fridays (check by phone). House of Commons open to public Mon–Tues and Thurs from 3:30pm, Wed and Fri from 9:30am. Join line at St. Stephen's entrance. Tube: Westminster.

The Houses of Parliament, along with their trademark clock tower, are the ultimate symbol of London. They're the stronghold of Britain's democracy, the assemblies that effectively trimmed the sails of royal power. Both the House of Commons and the

---

Insider Tip

You can avoid the long queues at Buckingham Palace by purchasing tickets before you go through **Edwards & Edwards,** 1270 Avenue of the Americas, Suite 2414, New York, NY 10020 (☎ **800/223-6108** or 212/332-2435). Visitors with disabilities can reserve tickets directly through the palace by calling ☎ **0171/930-5526.** You can, however, peep through the railings into the front yard at any time.

Warning

Any schedule announced at Buckingham Palace is not writ in stone. Officials of the ceremony never announce their plans a year in advance, which poses a dilemma for guidebook writers. In theory at least, the guard is changed daily from some time in April to mid-July, at which time it goes on its "winter" schedule—that is, every other day. The cutback is said to be because of budget constraints. In any case, always check locally with the tourist office to see if it's likely to be staged at the time of your visit. The ceremony has been cut at the last minute and on short notice, leaving thousands of tourists angry, feeling they have missed out on a London must-see.

House of Lords are in the former royal Palace of Westminster, the king's residence until Henry VIII moved to Whitehall. The current Gothic Revival buildings date from 1840 and were designed by Charles Barry. (The earlier buildings were destroyed by fire in 1834.) Assisting Barry was Augustus Welby Pugin, who designed the paneled ceilings, tiled floors, stained glass, clocks, fireplaces, umbrella stands, and even the inkwells. There are more than 1,000 rooms and 2 miles of corridors.

The clock tower at the eastern end houses the world's most famous timepiece. **"Big Ben"** refers not to the clock tower itself, but to the largest bell in the chime, which weighs close to 14 tons and is named for the first commissioner of works. At night a light shines in the tower whenever Parliament is in session.

You may observe parliamentary debates from the **Stranger's Galleries** in both houses. Sessions usually begin in mid-October and run to the end of July, with recesses at Christmas and Easter. Although we can't assure you of the oratory of a Charles James Fox or a William Pitt the Elder, the debates in the House of Commons are often lively and controversial (seats are at a premium during crises). The chances of getting into the House of Lords when it's in session are generally better than for the more popular House of Commons, where even the queen isn't allowed. Many political observers maintain that the peerage speak their minds more freely and are less likely to adhere to the party line than their counterparts in the Commons; they do behave, however, in a much more civilized fashion, without the yelling that sometimes accompanies Commons debates.

The general public is admitted to the Strangers' Galleries on "sitting days." You have to join a public line outside the St. Stephen's entrance on the day in question, and there's often considerable delay before the public is admitted. The line forms on the left for the House of Commons, on the right for the Lords. You can speed matters up somewhat by applying at the American Embassy or the Canadian High Commission for a special pass, which should be issued well in advance of your trip, but this is too cumbersome for many people. Besides, the embassy has only four tickets for daily distribution, so you might as well stand in line. It's usually easier to get in after about 5:30pm; debates often continue until about 11pm. To arrange a tour before you leave home, you can write **House of Commons Information Office,** 1 Derby Gate, Westminster, London SW1A 2DG. Tours are usually conducted on Friday.

Impressions

Filled with old doddering peers, cute financial magnates, clever wire-pullers, big brewers with bulbous noses.

—Winston Churchill describing the House of Lords

Kensington Palace. The Broad Walk, Kensington Gardens, W8. ☎ **0171/937-9561.** Admission £7.50 ($12) adults, £5.70 ($9) seniors/students, £5.30 ($9) children. May–Oct 5 daily 10am–6pm by guided tour; last tour leaves at 4:45pm. Closed Oct 6–Apr for ongoing restoration. Tube: Queensway or Bayswater on north side of gardens; High St. Kensington on south side.

Once the residence of British monarchs, Kensington Palace hasn't been the official home of reigning kings since George II. It was acquired in 1689 by William and Mary as an escape from the damp royal rooms along the Thames. Since the end of the 18th century, the palace has been home to various members of the royal family, and the State Apartments are open for tours.

It was here in 1837 that a young Victoria was roused from her sleep with the news that her uncle, William IV, had died and that she was now queen of England. You can view a nostalgic collection of Victoriana, including some of her memorabilia. In the apartments of Queen Mary II, wife of William III, is a striking 17th-century writing cabinet inlaid with tortoiseshell. Paintings from the Royal Collection line the walls of the apartments. A rare 1750 lady's court dress and splendid examples of male court dress from the 18th century are on display in rooms adjacent to the State Apartments.

Kensington Palace is now the London home of Princess Margaret as well as the Duke and Duchess of Kent. Of course, it was once the home of Diana, Princess of Wales, and her two sons (Harry and William now live with their father at St. James's Palace, where Diana's body lay in the Chapel Royal during the week prior to her funeral). The palace is probably best known for the millions and millions of flowers that were placed in front of it during the days following Diana's death. In fact, there's been talk of building here some sort of monument or garden dedicated to Diana, but local residents have objected and the project's fate is uncertain at press time.

Kensington Gardens are open daily to the public for leisurely strolls through the manicured grounds and around the Round Pond. One of the most famous sights here is the controversial Albert Memorial, a lasting tribute not only to Victoria's consort but also to the questionable artistic taste of the Victorian era. There's a wonderful afternoon tea offered in The Orangery; see "Teatime" in chapter 5.

Madame Tussaud's. Marylebone Rd., NW1. ☎ **0171/935-6861.** Admission £9 ($14) adults, £6.75 ($11) seniors, £6 ($10) children under 16, free for children under 5. Combination tickets including the new planetarium £11.20 ($18) adults, £7.10 ($11) children under 16. Mon–Sun 10am–5:30pm. Tube: Baker St.

Madame Tussaud's is not so much a wax museum as an enclosed amusement park. A weird, moving, sometimes terrifying collage of exhibitions, panoramas, and stage settings, it manages to be most things to most people, most of the time.

Madame Tussaud attended the court of Versailles and learned her craft in France. She personally took the death masks from the guillotined heads of Louis XVI and Marie Antoinette (which you'll find among the exhibits). She moved her original museum from Paris to England in 1802. Her exhibition has been imitated in every part of the world, but never with the realism and imagination on hand here. Madame herself molded the features of Benjamin Franklin, whom she met in Paris. All the rest—from George Washington to John F. Kennedy, Mary Queen of Scots to Sylvester Stallone—have been subjects for the same painstaking (and breathtaking) replication.

In the well-known Chamber of Horrors—a kind of underground dungeon—there are all kinds of instruments of death, along with figures of their victims. The shadowy presence of Jack the Ripper lurks in the gloom as you walk through a Victorian London street. Present-day criminals are portrayed within the confines of prison. The latest attraction to open here is "The Spirit of London," a musical ride that depicts

A Little Tussaud Trivia

- Cybill Shepherd was added to the museum's collection in 1997, making her the first American TV star to be displayed.
- Darlene Conley, star of the daytime soap *The Bold and the Beautiful,* was added to the collection later in 1997, making her the first American TV soap star to be displayed. Her figure is now in the Amsterdam branch; though it was supposed to move eventually to the London branch, those plans seem to have been put on hold.
- The royal family are the only exhibits you can't stand alongside for photos. When it was announced that the Prince and Princess of Wales were separating, their mannequins were moved slightly apart. When they were divorced, Diana was moved to the end of the royal line, but since her death she has been brought down from the royal enclosure so people can get closer to her.

400 years of London's history, using special effects that include audio-animatronic figures that move and speak. Visitors take "time-taxis" that allow them to see and hear "Shakespeare" as he writes and speaks lines, be received by Queen Elizabeth I, and feel and smell the Great Fire of 1666 that destroyed London.

✪ **National Gallery.** Northwest side of Trafalgar Sq., WC2. ☎ **0171/737-2885.** Free admission. Mon, Tues, and Thurs–Sat 10am–6pm, Wed 10am–8pm, Sun noon–6pm. Tube: Charing Cross, Embankment, or Leicester Square.

This stately neoclassical building contains an unrivaled collection of Western art that spans 7 centuries—from the late 13th to the early 20th—and covers every great European school. For sheer skill of display and arrangement, it surpasses its counterparts in Paris, New York, Madrid, and Amsterdam.

The largest part of the collection is devoted to the Italians, including the Sienese, Venetian, and Florentine masters. They're now housed in the Sainsbury Wing, which was designed by noted Philadelphia architects Robert Venturi and Denise Scott Brown and opened by Elizabeth II in 1991. On display are such works as Leonardo's *Virgin of the Rocks;* Titian's *Bacchus and Ariadne;* Giorgione's *Adoration of the Magi;* and unforgettable canvases by Bellini, Veronese, Botticelli, and Tintoretto. Botticelli's *Venus and Mars* is eternally enchanting. (The Sainsbury Wing is also used for large temporary exhibits.)

Of the early Gothic works, the *Wilton Diptych* (French or English school, late 14th century) is the rarest treasure; it depicts Richard II being introduced to the Madonna and Child by John the Baptist and the Saxon kings, Edmund and Edward the Confessor.

Then there are the Spanish giants: El Greco's *Agony in the Garden,* and portraits by Goya and Velázquez. The Flemish-Dutch school is represented by Brueghel, Jan van Eyck, Vermeer, Rubens, and de Hooch; the Rembrandts include two of his immortal self-portraits. There's also an immense French impressionist and postimpressionist collection that includes works by Manet, Monet, Degas, Renoir, and Cézanne. Particularly charming is the peep-show cabinet by Hoogstraten in one of the Dutch rooms: It's like spying through a keyhole.

British and modern art are the specialties of the Tate Gallery (see below), but the National Gallery does have some fine 18th-century British masterpieces, including works by Hogarth, Gainsborough, Reynolds, Constable, and Turner.

A collaboration with the Metropolitan Museum of Art in New York and the National Gallery of Art in Washington, D.C. will result in a 1999 exhibition of

---

Insider Tip

The National Gallery has a computer information center where you can design your own personal tour map. The computer room, located in the Micro Gallery, includes a dozen hands-on work stations. The on-line system lists 2,200 paintings and has background notes for each artwork. The program includes four indexes that are cross-referenced for your convenience. Using a touch-screen computer, you design your own personalized tour by selecting a maximum of 10 paintings that you would like to view. Once you have made your choices, you print a personal tour map with your selections; this mapping service is free.

Portraits by Ingres, by the great 19th-century French painter who was made famous by his paintings of sparsely dressed women, notably from the 1850s. One of the finest examples of his genre, *Madame Moitessier,* is a permanent fixture at the museum. Another exhibit highlight in 1999 will be *Signorelli in British Collections* by Italian Renaissance painter Luca Signorelli. Headlining the exhibit will be three large altarpieces, *The Circumcision, The Adoration of the Shepherds,* and *The Virgin and Child with Saints,* along with various frescoes and predellas.

✪ St. Paul's Cathedral. St. Paul's Churchyard, EC4. ☎ **0171/236-4128** or 0171/248-8348. Cathedral £4 ($6.40) adults, £2 ($3.20) children 6–16. Galleries £3.50 ($5.60) adults, £1.50 ($2.40) children. Guided tours £3.50 ($5.60); recorded tours £3 ($4.80). Free for children 5 and under. Sightseeing Mon–Sat 8:30am–4pm; galleries Mon–Sat 9:30am–4pm. No sightseeing Sun (services only). Tube: St. Paul's.

During World War II, newsreel footage reaching America showed St. Paul's Cathedral standing virtually alone among the rubble of the City, its dome lit by fires caused by bombings all around it. That it survived at all is a miracle, since it was badly hit twice during the early years of the Nazi bombardment of London. But St. Paul's is accustomed to calamity, having been burned down three times and destroyed once by invading Norsemen. It was during the Great Fire of 1666 that the old St. Paul's was razed, making way for a new Renaissance structure designed by Sir Christopher Wren and built between 1675 and 1710. It's the architectural genius's ultimate masterpiece.

The classical dome of St. Paul's dominates the City's square mile. The golden cross surmounting it is 365 feet above the ground; the golden ball on which the cross rests measures 6 feet in diameter yet looks like a marble from below. Surrounding the interior of the dome is the Whispering Gallery, an acoustic marvel in which the faintest whisper can be heard clearly on the opposite side—so be careful of what you say. You can climb to the top of the dome for a spectacular 360° view of London.

Although the interior looks almost bare, it houses a vast number of monuments. The Duke of Wellington (of Waterloo fame) is entombed here, as are Lord Nelson and Sir Christopher Wren himself. At the east end of the cathedral is the American Memorial Chapel, honoring the 28,000 U.S. service personnel who lost their lives while stationed in Britain in World War II.

Guided tours last 1½ hours and include parts of the cathedral not open to the general public. They take place Monday to Saturday at 11am, 11:30am, 1:30pm, and 2pm. Recorded tours lasting 45 minutes are available throughout the day.

St. Paul's is an Anglican cathedral with daily services at the following times: matins at 7:30am Monday to Friday, 8:30am on Saturday; Holy Communion Monday to Saturday at 8am and 12:30pm; and evensong Monday to Saturday at 5pm. On Sunday, there's Holy Communion at 8am and again at 11am, matins at 8:45am, and evensong at 3:15pm. Admission charges don't apply if you're attending a service.

E-0143

All Souls' Chapel ❷
American Memorial Chapter ❽
Anglican Martyr's Chapel ❻
Chapel of St. Michael
& St. George ⓮
Dean's Staircase ⓯
Entrance to Crypt
(Wren's grave) ⓫
Font ❺

High Altar ❼
Lady Chapel ❾
Nelson Monument ⓬
Pulpit ❿
St. Dunstan's Chapel ❸
Staircase to Library,
Whispering Gallery & Dome ⓭
Wellington Monument ❹
West Doorway ❶

Insider Tip: One of the most exciting aspects of a spring visit to London is sauntering through the free gardens of St. Paul's when the roses are in bloom.

Tate Gallery. Millbank, SW1. ☎ **0171/887-8000.** Free admission; special exhibitions from £3–£7 ($4.80–$11). Daily 10am–5:50pm. Tube: Pimlico. Bus: 77A, 88, or C10.

Fronting the Thames near Vauxhall Bridge in Pimlico, the Tate looks like a smaller and more graceful relation of the British Museum. The most prestigious gallery in Britain, it houses the national collections, covering British art from the 16th century on, as well as an international array of moderns. The Tate's holdings are split between the traditional and the contemporary. Since only a portion of the collections can be displayed at any one time, the works on view change from time to time. Because it's difficult to take in all the exhibits, we suggest that you try to schedule two visits—the first to see the classic British works, the second to take in the modern collection—or concentrate on whichever section interests you more, if your time is limited.

The older works include some of the best of Gainsborough, Reynolds, Stubbs, Blake, and Constable. William Hogarth is well-represented, particularly by his satirical *O the Roast Beef of Old England* (known as *The Gate of Calais*). The collection of works by J.M.W. Turner is its largest collection of works by a single artist; Turner himself willed most of the paintings and watercolors here to the nation.

Also on display are the works of many major 19th- and 20th-century painters, including Paul Nash. The drawings of William Blake, the incomparable mystical poet and illustrator of such works as *The Book of Job, The Divine Comedy,* and *Paradise Lost,* attract the most attention. In the modern collections are works by Matisse, Dalí,

Trafalgar, London's Most Famous Square

London is a city full of landmark squares. Without a doubt, though, the best-known is Trafalgar Square (Tube: Charing Cross), which honors one of England's great military heroes, Horatio, Viscount Nelson (1758–1805), who died at the Battle of Trafalgar. Although he suffered from seasickness all his life, he went to sea at the age of 12 and was an admiral by the age of 39. Lord Nelson was a hero of the Battle of Calvi in 1794, where he lost an eye; the Battle of Santa Cruz in 1797, where he lost an arm; and the Battle of Trafalgar in 1805, where he lost his life. (For a highly romanticized version of his love affair with Lady Hamilton and his death, seek out the Laurence Olivier/Vivien Leigh film, *That Hamilton Woman;* it runs fairly regularly on American Movie Classics.)

The square today is dominated by the 145-foot granite Nelson's Column, the work of E.H. Baily in 1843. The column looks down Whitehall toward the Old Admiralty, where Lord Nelson's body lay in state. The figure of the naval hero towers 17 feet high—not bad for a man who stood 5'4" in real life. The capital is of bronze cast from cannons recovered from the wreck of the *Royal George.* Queen Victoria's favorite animal painter, Sir Edward Landseer, added the four lions at the base of the column in 1868. The pools and fountains weren't added until 1939, the last work of Sir Edwin Lutyens.

Political demonstrations still take place at the square and around the column, which has the most aggressive pigeons in London. These birds will even land on your head (or perform less-desirable stunts). The birds are part of a long feathery tradition; this site was once used by Edward I (1239–1307) to keep his birds of prey. Called "Longshanks," he came here often before he died of dysentery in 1307. (You'll remember Edward I as the villain king in *Braveheart.*) Richard II, who ruled from 1377 to 1399, kept goshawks and falcons here. By the time of Henry VII, who ruled from 1485 to 1509, the square was used as the site of the royal stables. Sir Charles Barry, who designed the Houses of Parliament, created the present square in the 1830s.

Much of the world focuses on the square via TV cameras on New Year's Eve. It's a wild and raucous time, with crazy revelers jumping into the chilly waters of the fountains. The giant Christmas tree that's installed here every December is an annual gift from Norway to the British people in appreciation for sheltering their royal family during World War II; it's surrounded by carolers most December evenings. Year-round, street performers (now officially licensed) will entertain you in hopes of receiving a token of appreciation for their efforts.

To the southeast of the square, at 36 Craven Street, stands a house occupied by Benjamin Franklin (1757–74) when he was a general of the Philadelphia Academy. On the north side of the square rises the National Gallery, constructed in the 1830s. In front of the building is a copy of a statue of George Washington by J.A. Houdon.

To the left of St. Martin's Place is the National Portrait Gallery, a collection of British portraits—everyone from Chaucer and Shakespeare to Captain Hook and Nell Gwynne to Margaret Thatcher and The Who's Pete Townshend. Also on the square is the towering steeple of St. Martin-in-the-Fields, the final resting place of Sir Joshua Reynolds, William Hogarth, and Thomas Chippendale.

Modigliani, Munch, Bonnard, and Picasso. Truly remarkable are the several enormous abstract canvases by Mark Rothko, the group of paintings and sculptures by Giacometti, and the paintings of one of England's best-known modern artists, the late Francis Bacon. Sculptures by Henry Moore and Barbara Hepworth are also occasionally displayed.

Plans call for the Tate Gallery to split into two separate galleries, the original to be known as the Tate Gallery of British Art. A modern international collection will move across the Thames and will become the new Tate Gallery of Modern Art. The galleries will be linked by a pedestrian bridge across the river. Dates of this transfer and split will be announced further along.

Insider Tip: Spare a little time for the Art Now Gallery, which houses recent works of both new and established artists, some highly controversial. There's always something new, different, and on the cutting edge of the art world here. The average traveler may find it difficult to obtain tickets to a popular exhibit. If you know of an exhibit you'll want to see, we suggest calling **First Call** (☎ **0171/420-0002;** fax 0171/420-0055; P.O. Box 92, London WC2H 9SU), the agency responsible for distributing tickets to said events. A call before your trip, or a call while in London will save you a good bit of time and trouble.

Downstairs is the internationally renowned **Tate Gallery Restaurant** (see chapter 5), with murals by Whistler, as well as a coffee shop.

✪ Tower of London. Tower Hill, EC3. ☎ **0171/709-0765.** Admission £8.50 ($14) adults, £6.40 ($10) students and seniors, £5.60 ($9) children, free for children under 5; £25.40 ($41) family ticket for 5 (but no more than 2 adults). Mar–Oct Mon–Sat 9am–5pm, Sun 10am–5pm; off-season Tues–Sat 9am–4pm, Mon and Sun 10am–4pm. Tube: Tower Hill.

This ancient fortress continues to pack in the crowds, largely because of its macabre associations with all the legendary figures who were imprisoned and/or executed here. James Street once wrote, "There are more spooks to the square foot than in any other building in the whole of haunted Britain. Headless bodies, bodiless heads, phantom soldiers, icy blasts, clanking chains—you name them, the Tower's got them." Even today, centuries after the last head rolled on Tower Hill, a shivery atmosphere of impending doom lingers over the mighty walls. Plan on spending a lot of time here.

The Tower is actually an intricately patterned compound of structures built throughout the ages for varying purposes, mostly as expressions of royal power. The oldest is the **White Tower,** begun by William the Conqueror in 1078 to keep London's native Saxon population in check. Later rulers added other towers, more walls, and fortified gates, until the building became something like a small town within a city. Until the reign of James I, the Tower was also one of the royal residences. But above all, it was a prison for distinguished captives.

Every stone of the Tower tells a story—usually a gory one. In the **Bloody Tower,** according to Shakespeare, the two little princes (the sons of Edward IV) were murdered by henchmen of Richard III. (Modern historians, however, tend to think that Richard may not have been the guilty party.) Here, too, Sir Walter Raleigh spent 13 years before his date with the executioner. On the walls of the **Beauchamp Tower,** you can actually read the last messages scratched by despairing prisoners. Through **Traitors' Gate**

Warning

The White Tower will be closed for refurbishment throughout 1998.

Beauchamp Tower **11**
Bell Tower **3**
Bloody Tower **7**
Bowyer Tower (torture chamber) **14**
Brick Tower **15**
Broad Arrow Tower **18**
Byward Tower **2**
Chapel Royal of St. Peter ad Vincula **8**
Constable Tower **17**
Cradle Tower **21**
Develin Tower **23**
Devereux Tower **12**

Flint Tower **13**
Jewel House (entrance) **9**
Lanthorn Tower **20**
Martin Tower **16**
Middle Tower **1**
Salt Tower **19**
Site of Scaffold **10**
St. Thomas's Tower **5**
Traitor's Gate **4**
Wakefield Tower **6**
Well Tower **22**

passed such ill-fated, romantic figures as Robert Devereux, the second earl of Essex, a favorite of Elizabeth I. A plaque marks the eerie place at **Tower Green** where two wives of Henry VIII, Anne Boleyn and Catherine Howard; Sir Thomas More; and the 4-day queen, Lady Jane Grey, all lost their lives. Lady Jane's husband, Lord Guildford Dudley, was executed across the way at Tower Hill.

The Tower, besides being a royal palace, a fortress, and a prison, was also an armory, a treasury, a menagerie, and in 1675 an astronomical observatory. To reopen in 1999, the White Tower holds the **Armouries,** which date from the reign of Henry VIII, as well as a display of instruments of torture and execution that recalls some of the most ghastly moments in the Tower's history. In the Jewel House, you'll find the tower's greatest attraction, the **Crown Jewels.** Here, some of the world's most precious stones are set into the robes, swords, scepters, and crowns. The Imperial State Crown is the most famous crown on earth; made for Victoria in 1837, it's worn today by Queen Elizabeth when she opens Parliament. Studded with some 3,000 jewels (principally diamonds), it includes the Black Prince's Ruby, worn by Henry V at Agincourt. The 530-carat Star of Africa, a cut diamond on the Royal Sceptre with Cross, would make Harry Winston turn over in his grave. You'll have to stand in long lines to catch just a glimpse of the jewels as you and hundreds of others scroll by on moving sidewalks, but the wait is worth it.

A **palace** once inhabited by King Edward I in the late 1200s stands above Traitors' Gate. It's the only surviving medieval palace in Britain. Guides are dressed in period costumes. Reproductions of furniture and fittings, including Edward's throne, evoke the era, along with burning incense and candles.

Oh, yes—and don't forget to look for the ravens. Six of them (plus two spares) are all registered as official Tower residents. According to a legend, the Tower of London will stand as long as those black, ominous birds remain; so, to be on the safe side, one of the wings of each raven is clipped.

One-hour guided tours of the entire compound are given by the Yeoman Warders (also known as "Beefeaters") every half-hour, starting at 9:25am from the Middle Tower near the main entrance. The last guided walk starts about 3:30pm in summer, 2:30pm in winter, weather permitting, of course.

You can attend the nightly **Ceremony of the Keys,** the ceremonial locking-up of the Tower by the Yeoman Warders. For free tickets, write to the Ceremony of the Keys, Waterloo Block, Tower of London, London EC3N 4AB, and request a specific date, but also list alternate dates. At least 6 weeks' notice is required. All requests must be accompanied by a stamped, self-addressed envelope (British stamps only) or two International Reply Coupons. With ticket in hand, you'll be admitted by a Yeoman Warder at 9:35pm.

Insider Tip: The secret to avoid the Tower's notoriously long lines is to arrive the moment the gates open, before the hordes descend in the afternoon. Choose a day other than Sunday if you can—crowds are at their worst then.

Victoria and Albert Museum. Cromwell Rd., SW7. ☎ **0171/938-8500.** Admission £5 ($8) adults, £3 ($4.80) seniors, free for children under 18 and persons with disabilities. Mon noon–5:50pm, Tues–Sun 10am–5:50pm. Tube: South Kensington. Bus: C1, 14, or 74.

The Victoria and Albert is the greatest museum in the world devoted to the decorative arts. It's also one of the liveliest and most imaginative museums in London—where else would you find the quintessential "little black dress" in the permanent collection?

The medieval holdings include such treasures as the Early English Gloucester Candlestick; the Byzantine Veroli Casket, with its ivory panels based on Greek plays; and the Syon Cope, a highly valued embroidery made in England in the early 14th century. An area devoted to Islamic art houses the Ardabil carpet from 16th-century Persia.

The V&A houses the largest collection of Renaissance sculpture outside Italy, including a Donatello marble relief, *The Ascension;* a small terra-cotta Madonna and Child by Antonio Rossellino; a marble group, *Samson and a Philistine,* by Giovanni Bologna; and a wax model of a slave by Michelangelo. A highlight of the 16th-century collection is the marble group *Neptune with Triton* by Bernini. The cartoons by Raphael, which were conceived as designs for tapestries for the Sistine Chapel, are owned by the queen and on display here. A most unusual, huge, and impressive exhibit is the Cast Courts, life-size plaster models of ancient and medieval statuary and architecture.

The museum has the greatest collection of Indian art outside India, plus Chinese and Japanese galleries as well. In complete contrast are suites of English furniture, metalwork, and ceramics, and a superb collection of portrait miniatures, including the one Hans Holbein the Younger made of Anne of Cleves for the benefit of Henry VIII, who was again casting around for a suitable wife. The Dress Collection includes a collection of corsetry through the ages that's sure to make you wince, and there's also a remarkable collection of musical instruments.

Because of redevelopment, the entire run of British Galleries won't be fully open until 2001. But the museum has a lively program of changing exhibitions and displays, so there's always something new to see. The year 1999 and the turn of the century will see the hosting of *A Grand Design: The Art of the Victoria and Albert Museum,* a celebration of the last 2,000 years of art.

Insider Tip: As incongruous as it sounds, the museum hosts a jazz brunch on Sunday from 11am to 3pm that's worth attending. You'll get some of the hottest jazz in the city, accompanied by a full English breakfast or lunch for only £8 ($12.80). And don't miss the V&A's most bizarre gallery, "Fakes and Forgeries." The impostors here are amazingly authentic—in fact, we'd judge some of them as better than the Old Masters themselves.

✪ **Westminster Abbey.** Broad Sanctuary, SW1. ☎ **0171/222-7110** or 0171/222-5897. Admission £5 ($8) adults, £3 ($4.80) for students and seniors, £1.50 ($2.40) children 11–18, under 11 free. Mon–Fri 9am–3:45pm, Sat 9:15am–1:45pm. Tube: Westminster or St. James's Park.

With its square twin towers and superb archways, this early English Gothic abbey is one of the greatest examples of ecclesiastical architecture on earth. But it's far more than that: It's the shrine of a nation, the symbol of everything Britain has stood for and stands for, the place in which most of its rulers were crowned and where many lie buried.

Nearly every figure in English history has left his or her mark on Westminster Abbey. Edward the Confessor founded the Benedictine abbey in 1065 on this spot, overlooking Parliament Square. The first English king crowned in the abbey was Harold in 1066. The man who defeated him at the Battle of Hastings the next year, William the Conqueror, was also crowned here. The coronation tradition has continued to the present day, broken only twice (Edward V and Edward VIII). The essentially early English Gothic structure existing today owes more to Henry III's plans than to those of any other sovereign, although many architects, including Wren, have contributed to the abbey.

Built on the site of the ancient lady chapel in the early 16th century, the **Henry VII Chapel** is one of the loveliest in Europe, with its fan vaulting, Knights of Bath banners, and Torrigiani-designed tomb of the king himself, over which hangs a 15th-century Vivarini painting, *Madonna and Child.* Also here are the feuding half-sisters, ironically buried in the same tomb, Catholic Mary I and Protestant Elizabeth I (whose archrival, Mary Queen of Scots, is entombed on the other side of the Henry VII Chapel). In one end of the chapel, you can stand on Cromwell's memorial stone and view the **Royal Air Force chapel** and its Battle of Britain memorial window, unveiled in 1947 to honor the RAF.

You can also visit the most hallowed spot in the abbey, the **shrine of Edward the Confessor** (canonized in the 12th century). In the chapel is the Coronation Chair, made at the command of Edward I in 1300 to display the Stone of Scone. Scottish kings were once crowned on it (it has since been returned to Scotland).

When you enter the transept on the south side of the nave and see a statue of the Bard with one arm resting on a stack of books, you've arrived at **Poets' Corner.** Shakespeare himself is buried at Stratford-upon-Avon, but resting here are Dickens, Chaucer, Ben Jonson, John Dryden, William Wordsworth, Milton, Kipling, Shelley, Goldsmith, Thackeray, Hardy, and Alfred, Lord Tennyson; there's even an American, Henry Wadsworth Longfellow, as well as monuments to just about everybody: Chaucer, Shakespeare, "O Rare Ben Johnson" (his name misspelled), Samuel Johnson, the Brontë sisters, George Eliot, Thackeray, Dickens, Tennyson, Kipling. The most stylized monument is Sir Jacob Epstein's sculptured bust of William Blake. More recent tablets commemorate poet Dylan Thomas and Sir Laurence Olivier.

Statesmen and men of science—such as Disraeli, Newton, Charles Darwin—are also interred in the abbey or honored by monuments. Near the west door is the 1965

Westminster Abbey

Bookshop **16**

Chapel of St. John the Baptist **6**

Chapel of St. John the Evangelist **5**

Chapter House **14**

Henry V's Chantry **8**

Poets' Corner **13**

Royal Air Force Chapel **11**

St. Andrew's Chapel **3**

St. Edward's Chapel
(Coronation Chair) **7**

St. George's Chapel **1**

St. Michael's Chapel **4**

Tomb of Mary I &
Elizabeth I **9**

Tomb of Henry VII **10**

Tomb of Mary,
Queen of Scots **12**

Tomb of the Unknown Warrior/
Memorial to Churchill **2**

Undercroft Museum **15**

memorial to Sir Winston Churchill. In the vicinity of this memorial is the tomb of the **Unknown Soldier,** commemorating the British dead in World War I.

Off the Cloisters, the **College Garden** is the oldest garden in England, under cultivation for more than 900 years. Surrounded by high walls, flowering trees dot the lawns and park benches provide comfort where you can hardly hear the roar of passing traffic. It's open only on Tuesday and Thursday. In the Cloisters, you can make a rubbing at the **Brass Rubbing Centre** (☎ **0171/222-2085**).

Insider Tip: Far removed from the pomp and glory is the **Abbey Treasure Museum,** with a bag of oddities. They're displayed in the undercroft or crypt, part of the monastic buildings erected between 1066 and 1100. Here are royal effigies that were used instead of the real corpses for lying-in-state ceremonies because they smelled better. You'll see the almost lifelike effigy of Admiral Nelson (his mistress arranged his hair) and even that of Edward III, his lip warped by the stroke that felled him. Other oddities include a Middle English lease to Chaucer, the much-used sword of Henry VI, and the Essex Ring Elizabeth I gave to her favorite earl when she was feeling good about him.

The only time photography is allowed in the abbey is Wednesday evening from 6 to 7:45pm. On Sunday, the Royal Chapels are closed, but the rest of the church is open unless a service is being conducted. For times of services, phone the **Chapter Office** (☎ **0171/222-5152**). Up to six supertours of the abbey are conducted by the vergers Monday to Saturday, beginning at 10am and costing £7 ($11) per person.

3 More Central London Attractions

CHURCHES & CATHEDRALS

Many of London's churches offer free **lunchtime concerts;** a full list of churches offering them is available from the London Tourist Board. It's customary to leave a small donation.

All Hallows Barking-by-the-Tower. Byward St., EC3. ☎ **0171/481-2928.** Free admission; crypt museum tour £2 ($3.20). Museum Mon–Fri 11am–4pm, Sat 10am–4pm, Sun 1–4pm. Church Mon–Fri 9am–6pm, Sat–Sun 10am–5pm. Tube: Tower Hill.

The brass-rubbing center at this fascinating church, next door to the Tower, has a crypt museum, Roman remains, and traces of early London, including a Saxon arch predating the Tower. Samuel Pepys, the famed diarist, climbed to the spire of this church to watch the raging fire of London in 1666. In 1644, William Penn was baptized here, and in 1797, John Quincy Adams was married here. Bombs destroyed the church in 1940, leaving only the tower and walls standing. Rebuilt from 1949 to 1958, the church is now home to the **London Brass Rubbing Centre.** Materials and instructions are supplied, and the charges range from £1.50 to £11.50 ($2.40 to $18) for the largest.

✪ **Brompton Oratory.** Brompton Rd., SW7. ☎ **0171/589-4811.** Free admission. Daily 6:30am–8pm. Tube: South Kensington.

Converts are supposedly the most zealous adherents of any faith. The Oxford Movement, a group of Victorian intellectuals turned Catholic, certainly didn't go halfway when they created this church in 1884. Done in the Italian Renaissance style, this dramatic Roman Catholic church is famous for its musical services, and its organ with nearly 4,000 pipes. After Westminster Cathedral and York Minster, this is the widest nave in England.

St. Bride's. Fleet St., EC4. ☎ **0171/353-1301.** Free admission. Mon–Fri 8:30am–4:30pm, Sat–Sun 9am–4:30pm. Concerts at 1:15pm. Tube: Blackfriars.

Known as the "the church of the press" thanks to its location at the end of Fleet Street, St. Bride's is a remarkable landmark. The current church is the eighth one that's stood here. After it was bombed in 1940, an archeologist excavated the crypts and was able to confirm much of the site's legendary history: A Roman house was discovered preserved in the crypt, and it was established that St. Brigit of Ireland had founded the first Christian church here. Among the famous parishioners have been writers John Dryden, John Milton, Richard Lovelace, and John Evelyn; the diarist Samuel Pepys was baptized here, and novelist Samuel Richardson and his family are buried here. After the Great Fire destroyed it, the church was rebuilt by Christopher Wren, with a spire that's been described as a "madrigal in stone." This soaring confection (234 feet tall) inspired the wedding cakes of a pastry cook who lived in Fleet Street in the late 17th century, it's said. The crypt was a burial chamber and charnel house for centuries; today, it's a museum. Concerts are given on Tuesday and Friday, and there's an organ recital on Wednesday.

American Connection

The parents of Virginia Dare, the first English child born in America at Roanoke in 1587, were married in St Bride's. An effigy of Virginia can be seen over the baptismal font.

St. Clement Danes. Strand, WC2. ☎ **0171/242-8282.** Free admission. Daily 9am–5pm. Tube: Temple.

It's not known for certain why Danes is part of the church's name, but we do know that there was a wooden Saxon church on this site, which was rebuilt in stone in the late 10th century. Although the church survived the Great Fire, it was declared unsafe, and Christopher Wren was commissioned to rebuild it. The spire was designed by James Gibbs. The interior is decorated with ornate plasterwork. Samuel Johnson attended services regularly, and the wife of poet John Donne is buried here. The Blitz totally gutted the church, and it was reconstructed yet again in the late 1950s. Today, this is the central church of the Royal Air Force, with memorials to the British, Commonwealth, and American airmen who flew in World War II. Among its more famous rectors is William Webb Ellis who, as a schoolboy playing soccer at Rugby, infringed soccer rules when he picked up the ball and ran with it—thereby inventing the game of rugby. Worship is held each Sunday at 11am.

St. Etheldreda's. Ely Place, Holborn Circus, EC1. ☎ **0171/405-1061.** Free admission. Daily 8am–6pm, Sun masses. Tube: Farringdon or Chancery Lane.

The oldest Roman Catholic church in London, St. Etheldreda's stands on Ely Place, off Charterhouse Street at Holborn Circus. Built in 1251, it was mentioned by the Bard in both *Richard II* and *Richard III*. A survivor of the Great Fire of 1666, the church and place were the property of the diocese of Ely, in the days when many bishops had episcopal houses in London as well as in the cathedral cities in which they held their sees. The place is still a private road, with impressive iron gates and a lodge for the gatekeeper, all administered by six elected commissioners.

St. Etheldreda, whose name is sometimes shortened to St. Audrey, was a 7th-century king's daughter who left her husband and turned to religion, establishing an abbey on the Isle of Ely. (The name St. Audrey is the source of the word *tawdry*, from cheap lace sold at the annual fair honoring the saint.) St. Etheldreda's has a distinguished musical tradition, with the 11am mass on Sunday sung in Latin. Other masses are on Sunday at 9am, Monday to Friday at 8am and 1pm, and on Saturday at 9:30am. Lunch, with a varied choice of hot and cold dishes, is served Monday to Friday from 11:30am to 2pm in the Pantry.

St. Giles Cripplegate. At Fore and Wood Sts., London Wall, EC2. ☎ **0171/606-3630.** Free admission. Mon–Sat 10am–5pm, Sun for services. Tube: Moorgate or Barbican.

Named for the patron saint of cripples, St. Giles was founded in the 11th century. The church survived the Great Fire, but the Blitz left only the tower and walls standing. Oliver Cromwell was betrothed to Elizabeth Bourchier here in 1620, and John Milton, author of *Paradise Lost,* was buried here in 1674. More than a century later, someone opened the poet's grave, knocked out his teeth, stole a rib bone, and tore hair from his skull.

St. James's Church. 197 Piccadilly, W1. ☎ **0171/734-4511.** Free admission. Recitals Wed–Fri at 1:10pm. Tube: Piccadilly Circus.

When the aristocratic area known as St. James's was developed in the late 17th century, Sir Christopher Wren was commissioned to build its parish church. Diarist John Evelyn wrote of the interior, "There is no altar anywhere in England, nor has there been any abroad, more handsomely adorned." The reredos, organ case, and font were all carved by Wren's master carver Grinling Gibbons. As might be expected, this church has rich historical associations: The poet William Blake and William Pitt, the first earl of Chatham who became England's youngest prime minister at age 24, were both baptized here; caricaturist James Gillray, auctioneer James Christie, and coffee-house founder Francis White are all buried here. One of the more colorful marriages celebrated here was that of explorer Sir Samuel Baker and the woman he had bought at a slave auction in a Turkish bazaar. St. James's Church is a radical, inclusive Anglican church. It's also the Centre for Health and Healing, and holds seminars on New Age and Creation Spirituality. There's a Bible Garden and a craft market in the courtyard. The Wren Café is open 7 days a week, and lunchtime and evening concerts are held.

St. Martin-in-the-Fields. Trafalgar Sq., WC2. ☎ **0171/930-0089.** Mon–Sat 10am–8pm, Sun noon–8pm. Tube: Charing Cross.

Designed by James Gibbs, a disciple of Christopher Wren, and completed in 1726, this classical temple stands at the northeast corner of Trafalgar Square, opposite the National Gallery. Its spire, added in 1824, towers 185 feet (taller than Nelson's Column, which also rises on the square). The steeple became the paradigm for many churches in colonial America. Since the first year of World War I (1914), the home-less have sought "soup and shelter" at St. Martin, a tradition that continues.

At one time the crypt held the remains of Charles II (he's in Westminster Abbey now), who was christened here, giving St. Martin a claim as a royal parish church. His mistress, Nell Gwynne, was also interred here, as was the notorious highwayman Jack Sheppard (they're both still here). The floors of the crypt are actually gravestones, and the walls date from the 1500s. The little restaurant, **Café in the Crypt,** is still called "Field's" by its devotees. Also in the crypt is London's finest **brass-rubbing center** (☎ **0171/930-9306**), which has 88 exact copies of bronze portraits ready for use. Paper, rubbing materials, and instructions on how to begin are furnished, and there's classical music for you to enjoy as you proceed. The charges range from £2 to £15 ($3.20 to $24), the latter price for the largest, a life-size Crusader knight. There's also a gift shop with brass-rubbing kits for children, budget-priced ready-made rubbings, Celtic jewelry, miniature brasses, and model knights.

In back of the church is a crafts market. Lunchtime and evening concerts are staged Monday, Tuesday, and Friday at 1:05pm, and Thursday to Saturday at 7:30pm. Tickets cost £6 to £15 ($10 to $24).

St. Mary-le-Bow. Cheapside, EC2. ☎ **0171/248-5139.** Free admission. Mon–Thurs 6:30am–6pm, Fri 6:30am–4pm. Tube: St. Paul's or Bank.

A true Cockney is said to be born within hearing distance of this church's famous Bow bells. The church certainly hasn't been blessed by the series of disasters that mark its sometimes gruesome history: In 1091, its roof was ripped off in a storm; the church tower collapsed in 1271 and 20 people were killed; in 1331, Queen Philippa and her ladies-in-waiting fell to the ground when a balcony collapsed during a joust cele-brating the birth of the Black Prince; it was rebuilt by Wren after being engulfed by the Great Fire; and the original "Cockney" Bow bells were destroyed in the Blitz, but have been replaced. The church was rededicated in 1964 after extensive restoration work.

St. Paul's, the Actors Church. Covent Garden, WC2. ☎ **0171/836-5221.** Free admis-sion. Tue–Fri 9:30am–4:30pm, Mon 9:30am–2pm, Sun service 11am. Tube: Covent Garden.

As the Drury Lane Theatre, the Royal Opera House, and many other theaters are all within its parish, St. Paul's has long been associated with the theatrical arts. Inside you'll find scores of memorial plaques dedicated to such luminaries as Vivien Leigh, Laurence Harvey, Boris Karloff, Margaret Rutherford, and Noël Coward, to name only a few. Designed by Inigo Jones in 1631, this church has been substantially altered over the years, but it retains a quiet garden-piazza in the rear. Among the famous who are buried here are woodcarver Grinling Gibbons, writer Samuel Butler, and actress Ellen Terry. Landscape painter J.M.W. Turner and librettist W. S. Gilbert were both baptized here.

Southwark Cathedral. Montague Close, London Bridge, SE1. ☎ **0171/407-3708.** Free admission; suggested donation £2 ($3.20). Daily 8:30am–6pm. Tube: London Bridge.

There's been a church on this site, in the heart of London's first theater district, for more than a thousand years. The present one dates from the 15th century; it was partly rebuilt in 1890. The previous one was the first Gothic church (1106) to be constructed in London. Shakespeare and Chaucer worshipped at services here; a Shakespeare birthday service is held annually, and inside is a memorial to the playwright. A wooden effigy of a knight dates from 1275. In 1424, James I of Scotland married Mary Beaufort here. During the reign of Mary Tudor, Stephen Gardiner, the Bishop of Winchester, held a consistory court in the retro choir that condemned seven of the Marian martyrs to death. Later, the same retro choir was rented to a baker and even used to house pigs. Lunchtime concerts are regularly given on Monday and Tuesday; call for exact times and schedules.

Temple Church. The Temple (within the Inner Temple), EC4. ☎ **0171/353-1736.** Free admission. Wed–Sat 10am–4pm. Tube: Temple.

One of three Norman "round churches" left in England, this one was first completed in the 12th century; not surprisingly, it has been restored. Look for the knightly effigies and the Norman door, and take note of the circle of grotesque portrait heads, including a goat in a mortar board.

On Inner Temple Lane, about where the Strand becomes Fleet Street going east, you'll see the memorial pillar called Temple Bar, which marks the boundary of the City of London.

Wesley's Chapel, House & Museum of Methodism. 49 City Rd., EC1. ☎ **0171/ 253-2262.** Chapel free. House and museum £4 ($6.40) adults, £2 ($3) seniors, students, and children 5–17. House and museum Mon–Sat 10am–4pm (closed Thurs from 12:45–1:30pm). Both free on Sun after service, between noon and 2pm. Tube: Old St. or Moorgate.

John Wesley, the founder of Methodism, established this church in 1778 as his London base. The man who rode on horseback throughout the English countryside and preached in the open air lived at no. 47 next door, and he's buried in a grave behind the chapel. Surviving the Blitz, the church later fell into serious disrepair; major restoration was completed in the 1970s. In the crypt, a museum traces the history of Methodism to today.

Across the road in Bunhill Fields is the **Dissenters Graveyard,** where Daniel Defoe, William Blake, and John Bunyan are buried.

Westminster Cathedral. Ashley Place, SW1. ☎ **0171/798-9055.** Cathedral free, audio tours £2.50 ($4). Tower, £2 ($3.20). Cathedral, daily 7am–7pm. Tower, Apr–Nov daily 9am–1pm and 2–5pm; otherwise Thurs–Sun only. Tube: Victoria.

This spectacular brick-and-stone church (1903) is the headquarters of the Roman Catholic church in Britain. Adorned in high Byzantine style, it's massive: 360 feet long and 156 feet wide. One hundred different marbles compose the richly decorated interior, and eight marble columns support the nave. The huge baldachino over the high altar is lifted by eight yellow marble columns. Mosaics emblazon the chapels and the vaulting of the sanctuary. If you take the elevator to the top of the 273-foot-tall campanile, you're rewarded with sweeping views that take in Buckingham Palace, Westminster Abbey, and St. Paul's Cathedral.

HISTORIC BUILDINGS

Banqueting House. Whitehall Palace, Horse Guards Ave., SW1. ☎ **0171/930-4179.** Admission £3.25 ($5) adults, £2.50 ($4) seniors and students, £2.15 ($3) children. Mon–Sat 10am–5pm (last admission 4:30pm). Tube: Westminster.

The feasting chamber in Whitehall Palace is probably the most sumptuous dining hall on earth. Unfortunately, you can't dine here unless you happen to be a visiting head of state. Designed by Inigo Jones and decorated with, among other things, original ceiling paintings by Rubens, the hall is dazzling enough to make you forget food altogether. Among the historic events that took place here were the beheading of King Charles I (on a scaffold outside) and the restoration ceremony of Charles II, marking the return of monarchy after Cromwell's brief Puritan-republican Commonwealth.

Cabinet War Rooms. Clive Steps, at end of King Charles St. (off Whitehall near Big Ben), SW1. ☎ **0171/930-6961.** Admission £4.60 ($7) adults, £3.40 ($5) seniors and students, £2.30 ($4) children. Apr–Sept daily 9:30am–6pm (last admission at 5:15pm); Oct–Mar daily 10am–5:30pm. Tube: Westminster or St. James's.

This is the bombproof bunker from which Sir Winston Churchill and his government ran the nation during World War II. Many of the rooms are exactly as they were in September 1945: Imperial War Museum curators studied photographs to put notepads, files, typewriters, even pencils, pins, and clips, in their correct places.

Along the tour, you'll have a step-by-step personal sound guide that provides a detailed account of the function and history of each room of this World War II nerve center. They include the Map Room, with its huge wall maps. Next door is Churchill's bedroom-cum-office; it has a very basic bed and a desk with two BBC microphones for those famous broadcasts that stirred the nation. The Transatlantic Telephone Room is little more than a broom closet, but it held the extension linked to the special scrambler phone (called "Sig-Saly"), that allowed Churchill to confer with Roosevelt. (The scrambler equipment itself was actually too large to house in the bunker, so it was placed in the basement of Selfridges department store on Oxford Street.)

Chelsea Royal Hospital. Royal Hospital Rd., SW3. ☎ **0171/730-0161.** If you want a tour, you must apply in writing to Adjutant, Royal Hospital Chelsea, London, SW3 4SR. Guided tours are free, but donations are gratefully accepted. Otherwise, you're welcome to explore on your own. Free admission. Mon–Sat 10am–noon and 2–4pm, Sun 2–4pm. Tube: Sloane Sq.

This dignified institution, founded by Charles II in 1682 as a home for veteran soldiers, was designed and completed by Sir Christopher Wren in 1692. There's been little change to Wren's design, except for minor work done by Robert Adam in the 18th century, and the addition of the stables, designed by Sir John Soane in 1814. The main block containing the hall and chapel is flanked by east and west wings. The Duke of Wellington lay in state in the hall here from November 10 to 17, 1852. So many people thronged here to see him that two were crushed to death.

Guildhall. Off Gresham St., EC2. ☎ **0171/606-3030.** Free admission. Daily 10am–5pm. May be closed for ceremonial occasions, so call ahead. Tube: Bank.

Dating from 1411, Guildhall is the city's most important secular Gothic structure. Twice restored—once after the Great Fire, and again after the Blitz—it's the seat of the City of London's local government, and city council meetings are presided over by the lord mayor, elected once a year by the City's aldermen. These meetings are open to the public; they're held at 1pm on the third Thursday of each month.

The west gallery is guarded at both corners by the statues of Gog and Magog. These giants represent the legendary pre-Christian conflict between ancient Britons and Trojan invaders. In Elizabethan times, the giants were known as Gogmagog and

Corineus, and their images were paraded in midsummer pageants. Placed here in 1708, they were destroyed in the Blitz; but happily, they've been re-created to delight visitors today.

✪ **Horse Guards.** Whitehall, SW1. ☎ **0171/414-2396.**

North of Downing Street, on the west side of Whitehall, is the building of the Horse Guards, designed by William Kent, chief architect to George II, as the headquarters of the British Army (John Vardy took over and completed the structure in 1758). The real draw here is the Horse Guards themselves: Their unit is the Household Cavalry Mounted Regiment, which is a union of the two oldest and most senior regiments in the British Army: The Life Guards and The Blues and Royals. In theory, their duty is to protect the sovereign. "Life Guards" wear red tunics and white plumes and the "Blues and Royals" are attired in blue tunics with red plumes. Two much-photographed mounted members of the Household Cavalry keep watch daily from 10am to 5pm. The mounted sentries change duty every hour as a benefit to the horses. Foot sentries change every 2 hours. The chief guard rather grandly inspects the troops here daily at 4pm. The guard, with flair and fanfare, dismounts at 5pm.

Some visitors prefer the **changing of the guards** here to the more famous ceremony at Buckingham Palace. Beginning around 10:30am Monday to Saturday and 9:30am on Sunday, a new guard leaves the Hyde Park Barracks, rides down Pall Mall, and arrives at the Horse Guards building, all in about 30 minutes. The old guard then returns to the barracks.

If you pass through the arch at Horse Guards, you'll find yourself at the **Horse Guards Parade,** which opens onto St. James's Park. This spacious court provides the best view of the various architectural styles that make up Whitehall. Regrettably, the parade ground itself is now a parking lot.

The military pageant—the most famous in Britain—known as **Trooping the Colour,** which celebrates the queen's birthday, takes place in June at the Horse Guards Parade (see the "London Calendar of Events" in chapter 2). The "Colour" refers to the flag of the regiment. For devotees of pomp and circumstance, "Beating the Retreat" is staged here 3 or 4 evenings a week during the first 2 weeks of June. It's only a dress rehearsal, though, for Trooping the Colour.

Spencer House. 27 St. James's Place, SW1. ☎ **0171/499-8620.** £6 ($10) adults, £5 ($8) children under 16, children under 10 not allowed. Sun 10:30am–5:30pm. Closed Jan and Aug. Tube: Green Park.

This is one of the city's most beautiful buildings. It was built in 1766 for the first Earl Spencer, who intended it as an exuberant shrine to Georgiana Poyntz, his childhood sweetheart whom he'd secretly married the year before. It hasn't been a private residence since 1927, and has had something of a checkered history since then: At various times, it was used by the Ladies' Army and Navy Club, Christies, and British Oxygen Gases, Ltd.; finally, it was restored and opened as a museum in 1990. Rooms are filled with period furniture and art loans, some even from Queen Elizabeth herself as well as from the Tate Gallery and the Victoria & Albert. The most spectacular room is the Palm Room, all in white, gold, and green.

St. Pancras Station. Euston Rd., NW1. Tube: King's Cross/St. Pancras.

The London terminus for the Midland Railway, St. Pancras Station (1863–67) is a masterpiece of Victorian engineering. Designed by W. H. Barlow, the 689-foot-long glass-and-iron train shed spans 240 feet in width and rises to a peak of 100 feet above the rails. The platforms were raised 20 feet above the ground because the tracks ran over the Regent's Canal before entering the station. The pièce de résistance, though, is

Sir George Gilbert Scott's fanciful Midland Grand Hotel. Done in high Gothic style, it's graced with pinnacles, towers, and gables; it now functions as office space. The facade runs 565 feet and is flanked by a clock tower and a west tower.

LEGAL LONDON

The smallest borough in London, bustling **Holborn** (*ho*-burn) is often referred to as "Legal London," as it's home to the majority of the city's barristers, solicitors, and law clerks as well as the ancient **Inns of Court** (Tube: Holborn, Chancery Lane). All barristers must belong to one of these institutions, and many work from their dignified ancient buildings: **Gray's Inn, Lincoln's Inn** (the best preserved of the three), and the **Middle and Inner Temple** (just over the line inside the City). They were severely damaged during World War II, and the razed buildings were replaced with modern offices, but the borough still retains pockets of its former days.

Gray's Inn. Gray's Inn Rd. (north of High Holborn; entrance on Theobald's Rd.), WC1. ☎ **0171/405-8164.** Free admission to squares and gardens. Daily 10am–4pm. Tube: Chancery Lane.

Gray's Inn is the fourth of the ancient Inns of Court still in operation. As you enter, you'll see a late-Georgian terrace lined with buildings that, like many of the other houses in the inns, serve as both residences and offices. Gray's was restored after suffering heavy damage in World War II. It contains a rebuilt Tudor Hall, but its greatest attraction is the tree-shaded lawn and handsome gardens, the best in the inns. The 17th-century atmosphere exists today only in the square. Scientist and philosopher Francis Bacon (1561–1626) was the inn's most eminent tenant.

Law Courts. Strand, WC2. Free admission. No cameras, tape recorders, video cameras, or cellular phones allowed during sessions. Mon–Fri 10am–4:30pm. Tube: Holborn or Temple.

At these 60 or more courts presently in use, all civil and some criminal cases are heard. Designed by G. E. Street, the Neo-Gothic buildings (1874–1882) contain more than 1,000 rooms and 3½ miles of corridors. Sculptures of Christ, King Solomon, and King Alfred grace the front door; Moses is depicted at the back entrance. On the second Saturday in November, the annually elected lord mayor is sworn in by the lord chief justice.

Lincoln's Inn. Carey St., WC1. ☎ **0171/405-1393.** Free admission. Mon–Thurs 9am–5:30pm, Fri 9am–5pm. Tube: Holborn or Chancery Lane.

Lincoln's Inn is the oldest of the four Inns of Court. Between the City and the West End, Lincoln's Inn comprises 11 acres, including lawns, squares, gardens, a 17th-century chapel, a library, and two halls. One of these, Old Hall, dates from 1490 and has remained almost unaltered with its linenfold paneling, stained glass, and wooden screen by Inigo Jones. It was once the home of Sir Thomas More, and it was where barristers met, ate, and debated 150 years before the *Mayflower* sailed on its epic voyage. Old Hall set the scene for the opening chapter of Charles Dickens's *Bleak House*. The other hall, Great Hall, remains one of the finest Tudor Revival buildings in London, and was opened by Queen Victoria in 1843. It's now the center of the inn and is used for the formal ceremony of calling students to the bar.

Middle Temple Tudor Hall. Middle Temple Lane, EC4. ☎ **0171/427-4800.** Free admission. Mon–Fri 10–11:30am and 3–4pm. Tube: Temple.

From the Victoria Embankment, Middle Temple Lane runs between Middle and Inner Temple Gardens to the area known as The Temple, named after the medieval order of the Knights Templar (originally formed by the Crusaders in Jerusalem in the

12th century). It was in the Middle Temple Garden that Henry VI's barons are supposed to have picked the blooms of red and white roses and started the War of the
Roses in 1430; today only members of the Temple and their guests are allowed to enter
the gardens. But the Middle Temple contains a Tudor hall, completed in 1570, that's
open to the public. It's believed that Shakespeare's troupe played *Twelfth Night* here for
the first time in 1602. A table on view is said to have been built from timber from Sir
Francis Drake's *The Golden Hind*.

Old Bailey. Newgate St., EC4. ☎ **0171/248-3277.** Free admission. Court in session
Mon–Fri 10:30am–1pm and 2–4pm. Children under 14 not admitted; those 14–16 must be
accompanied by a responsible adult. No cameras or tape recorders. Tube: St. Paul's. To get
here from the Temple, travel east on Fleet St., which becomes Ludgate Hill; cross Ludgate
Circus and turn left at the Old Bailey, a domed structure with the figure of *Justice* atop it.

This courthouse replaced the infamous Newgate Prison, once the scene of hangings
and other forms of "public entertainment." It's affectionately known as the Old Bailey
after a street that runs nearby. It's fascinating to watch the bewigged barristers presenting their cases to the high court judges. Entry is strictly on a first-arrival basis, and
guests line up outside; security will then direct you to one of the various rooms where
cases are being tried. You enter courts 1 to 4, 17, and 18 from Newgate Street, and the
balance from Old Bailey (the street).

Royal Courts of Justice. The Strand, WC2. ☎ **0171/936-6751.** Free admission. No cameras, video cameras, tape recorders, or cellular phones allowed during sessions. Mon–Fri
10am–4:30pm. Tube: Temple.

Royal Courts of Justice, completed in 1882 but designed in 13th-century style, is the
home of such courts as admiralty, divorce, probate, chancery, appeals, and Queen's
Bench. There's a new exhibition of judicial robes at the Carey Street entrance. Leave
the Royal Courts building by the rear door, and you'll be on Carey Street, not far from
New Square.

Staple Inn. High Holborn, WC1. ☎ **0171/242-5240.** Free admission. Tube: Chancery
Lane.

This half-timbered old inn, near the Chancery Lane tube stop, and eight other former
Inns of Chancery are no longer in use in the legal world. Now lined with shops, it was
built between 1545 and 1589 and has been reconstructed many times. Dr. Johnson
moved here in 1759, the year *Rasselas* was published.

LITERARY LANDMARKS
For more literary sightseeing, see "Hampstead" in "Attractions on the Outskirts,"
below.

Carlyle's House. 24 Cheyne Row, SW3. ☎ **0171/352-7087.** Admission £3.30 ($5) adults,
£1.60 ($3) children. Easter–Oct Wed–Sun 11am–4:30pm. Tube: Sloane Sq. Bus: 11, 19, 22, or
239.

From 1834 to 1881, Thomas Carlyle, author of *The French Revolution,* and Jane Baillie
Welsh Carlyle, his noted letter-writing wife, resided in this modest 1708 terraced
house. Furnished essentially as it was in Carlyle's day, the house is located about three-
quarters of a block from the Thames, near the Chelsea Embankment, along King's
Road. It was described by his wife as being "of most antique physiognomy, quite to
our humour; all wainscotted, carved, and queer-looking, roomy, substantial, com-
modious, with closets to satisfy any Bluebeard." The second floor contains Mrs. Carlyle's drawing room, but the most interesting chamber is the not-so-soundproof
"soundproof" study in the skylit attic. Filled with Carlyle memorabilia—his books, a

---

A Neighborhood of One's Own: The Homes of Virginia Woolf

Born in London in 1882, author and essayist Virginia Woolf used it as the setting of many of her novels, including *Jacob's Room* (1922). The daughter of Sir Leslie Stephen and his wife Julia Duckworth, Virginia spent her formative years at **22 Hyde Park Gate,** off Kensington Road, west of Royal Albert Hall. Her mother died in 1895 and her father in 1904.

After the death of their father, Virginia and her sister Vanessa left Kensington for Bloomsbury, settling near the British Museum. It was an interesting move, as Bloomsbury was a neighborhood that upper-class Victorians didn't view as "respectable." But Virginia would make it her own—and in the process, make the district world-famous as the hub of Literary London. From 1905, the Stephens lived at **46 Gordon Square,** east of Gower Street and University College. It was here that the celebrated literary circle known as the Bloomsbury Group came into being, which would in time embrace Clive Bell and Leonard Woolf, the future husbands of Vanessa and Virginia. Later, Virginia went to live at **29 Fitzroy Square,** west of Tottenham Court Road, in a house once occupied by Bernard Shaw.

During the next two decades, Virginia resided at several more addresses in Bloomsbury, including **Brunswick Square, Tavistock Square,** and **Mecklenburg Square,** in homes that have either disappeared or been altered beyond recognition. During this time, the Bloomsbury Group reached out to include the artists Roger Fry and Duncan Grant, and Virginia became friends with economist John Maynard Keynes and author E. M. Forster (*A Passage to India*). At Tavistock Square (1924–39) and at Mecklenburg Square (1939–40), she operated Hogarth Press with Leonard. She published her own early work here, as well as T. S. Eliot's *The Waste Land.*

To escape urban life, Leonard and Virginia purchased Monk's House, in the village of Rodmell, between Lewes and Newhaven in Sussex. They lived there until 1941, when Virginia drowned herself in the nearby Ouse. Her ashes are buried in the garden at Monk's House.

---

letter from Disraeli, personal effects, a writing chair, even his death mask—this is where the author labored on his *Frederick the Great* manuscript.

Dickens House. 48 Doughty St., WC1. ☎ **0171/405-2127.** Admission £3.50 ($6) adults, £2.50 ($4) students, £1.50 ($2) children, £7 ($11) families. Mon–Sat 10am–5pm. Tube: Russell Sq.

Here in Bloomsbury stands the simple abode in which Charles Dickens wrote *Oliver Twist* and finished *The Pickwick Papers* (his American readers actually waited at the dock for the ship that brought in each new installment). The place is almost a shrine: It contains his study, manuscripts, and personal relics, as well as reconstructed interiors.

Samuel Johnson's House. 17 Gough Sq., EC4. ☎ **0171/353-3745.** Admission £3 ($5) adults, £2 ($3) students and seniors, £1 ($1.60) children, free for children 10 and under. May–Sept Mon–Sat 11am–5:30pm; Oct–Apr Mon–Sat 11am–5pm. Tube: Blackfriars. Walk up New Bridge St. and turn left onto Fleet; Gough Sq. is tiny and hidden, north of Fleet St.

Dr. Johnson and his copyists compiled his famous dictionary in this Queen Anne house, where the lexicographer, poet, essayist, and fiction writer lived from 1748 to 1759. Although Johnson also lived at Staple Inn in Holborn and at a number of other places, the Gough Square house is the only one of his residences remaining in London. The 17th-century building has been painstakingly restored, and it's well worth a visit.

After you're done touring the house, you might want to stop in at **Ye Olde Cheshire Cheese,** Wine Court Office Court, 145 Fleet St. (☎ **0171/353-6170**), Johnson's favorite local. He must have had some lean nights at the pub, because by the time he had compiled his dictionary, he'd already spent his advance of 1,500 guineas. G. K. Chesterton, author of *What's Wrong with the World* (1910) and *The Superstition of Divorce* (1920), was also a familiar patron at the pub.

MUSEUMS & GALLERIES

Apsley House, The Wellington Museum. 149 Piccadilly, Hyde Park Corner, SW1. ☎ **0171/499-5676.** Admission £4 ($6) adults, £3 ($5) seniors and children 12–17, free for children under 12. Tues–Sun 11am–5pm. Tube: Hyde Park Corner.

This was the mansion of the Duke of Wellington, one of Britain's greatest generals. The "Iron Duke" defeated Napoléon at Waterloo, but later, for a short period while prime minister, he had to have iron shutters fitted to his windows to protect him from the mob outraged by his autocratic opposition to reform. (His unpopularity soon passed, however.)

The house is crammed with art treasures, including three original Velázquez paintings, and military mementos that include the duke's medals and battlefield orders. Apsley House also holds some of the finest silver and porcelain pieces in Europe in the Plate and China Room. Grateful to Wellington for saving their thrones, European monarchs endowed him with treasures. The collection includes a Sèvres Egyptian service that was intended as a divorce present from Napoléon to Josephine (but she refused it, foolish woman); Louis XVIII eventually presented it to Wellington. The Portuguese Silver Service, created between 1812 and 1816, has been hailed as the single greatest artifact of Portuguese neoclassical silver.

British Library. 96 Euston Rd., NW1. ☎ **0171/412-7000.** Free admission. Mon–Sat 10am–5pm, Sun 2:30–6pm. Tube: King's Cross/St. Pancras.

One of the world's greatest libraries is no longer at the British Museum but has moved to St. Pancras. Although it will be open in part in 1999, the entire library may not be fully functioning until the dawn of the new millennium. The move began in December 1996, and continues today, as the library moves some 12 million books, manuscripts, and other items. Call ahead if you're looking for a specific exhibition or manuscript; special phone lines are dedicated to providing detailed information about the moves of specific parts of its collection.

Most people visit the library to view its rare books. The fascinating collection includes such items of historical and literary interest as two of the four surviving copies of King John's Magna Carta (1215), the Gutenberg Bible, Nelson's last letter to Lady Hamilton, and the journals of Captain Cook. Almost every major author—Dickens, Jane Austen, Charlotte Brontë, Keats, hundreds of others—is represented in the section devoted to English literature. Beneath Roubiliac's 1758 statue of Shakespeare stands a case of documents relating to the Bard, including a mortgage bearing his signature and a copy of the First Folio of 1623. There's also an unrivaled collection of philatelic items.

Commonwealth Institute. Kensington High St., W8. ☎ **0171/371-3530.** Admission £4.45 ($7) adults, £3.45 ($6) seniors and students, £2.45 ($4) children. Mon–Sat 10am–5pm, Sun 2–5pm. Tube: High St. Kensington. Bus: 9, 9A, 10, 27, 28, 31, 49.

Why come only to London when you can visit the Caribbean, see Canada from a skidoo, climb Mount Kenya, and take a rickshaw across Bangladesh? The history, landscapes, wildlife, and crafts of the Commonwealth of Nations are presented in this tent-shaped building next to Holland Park. Something's always happening here, ranging from special exhibitions to gallery animations. The Commonwealth Shop sells gifts, food, and wine from around the world, and there's a brasserie offering light snacks.

✪ **Courtauld Institute Galleries.** Somerset House, The Strand, WC2. ☎ **0171/ 873-2526.** Admission £4 ($6) adults, £2 ($3) students, free for children under 18. Mon–Sat 10am–6pm, Sun 2–6pm; last admission 5:30pm. Tube: Temple or Covent Garden.

This gallery contains a fabulous wealth of paintings: a great collection of French Impressionist and post-Impressionist paintings, with masterpieces by Monet, Manet, Degas, Renoir, Cézanne, Van Gogh, and Gauguin; a superb collection of old-master paintings and drawings, including works by Rubens, Michelangelo, and Tiepolo; early Italian paintings, ivories, majolica, and other works; the Lee collection of old masters; early 20th-century English and French paintings, as well as 20th-century British paintings.

Insider Tip: Although surprisingly little-known, this gallery contains one of the world's greatest collections of Impressionist works outside of Paris. Like the Frick Collection in New York, it's a superb display in a jewel-like setting—and a visual feast that's hailed as one of the greatest concentrations of Western European art anywhere in the world. We come here at least once every season to revisit one painting in particular: Manet's *A Bar at the Folies-Bergère*—exquisite. Many of the paintings are displayed without glass, giving the gallery a more intimate feeling than most.

Design Museum. Butler's Wharf, Shad Thomas, SE1. ☎ **0171/403-6933.** Admission £5 ($8) adults, £3.75 ($6) children, family ticket £12 ($19). Mon–Fri 11:30am–6pm, Sat–Sun noon–6pm. Tube: Tower Hill or London Bridge.

The Design Museum is a showcase of modern design—kind of like Conran's without the price tags. It's the only museum in Europe that explains why and how massproduced objects work and look the way they do and how design contributes to the quality of our lives. The collection of objects includes cars, furniture, domestic appliances, graphics, and ceramics, as well as changing displays of new products and prototypes from around the world. The cafe offers panoramic views of Tower Bridge and the Thames.

Hayward Gallery. On the South Bank, SE1, ☎ **0171/928-3144,** or 0171/261-0127 for recorded information. Admission £5 ($8) adults, £3.50 ($6) students, seniors, and children, free for children under 12, £12 ($19) family ticket. Fee varies according to exhibitions; children are often half-price. Thurs–Mon 10am–6pm, Tues–Wed 10am–8pm. Tube: Waterloo.

Opened by Elizabeth II in 1968, this gallery presents a changing program of major contemporary and historical exhibits. It's managed by the South Bank Board, which also includes the Royal Festival Hall, the Queen Elizabeth Hall, and the Purcell Room. The gallery closes between exhibitions, so call before crossing the Thames.

Imperial War Museum. Lambeth Rd., SE1. ☎ **0171/416-5000.** Admission £5 ($8) adults, £4 ($6) seniors and students, £2.50 ($4) children; free daily 4:30–6pm. Daily 10am–6pm. Tube: Lambeth North or Elephant and Castle.

One of the few major sights south of the Thames, this museum occupies one city block the size of an army barracks, greeting you with 15-inch guns from the battleships *Resolution* and *Ramillies*. The large domed building, constructed in 1815, was the former Bethlehem Royal Hospital for the insane, known as Bedlam.

A wide range of weapons and equipment is on display, along with models, decorations, uniforms, posters, photographs, and paintings. You can see a Mark V tank, a

Battle of Britain Spitfire, and a German one-man submarine, as well as a rifle carried by Lawrence of Arabia. In the documents room, you can view the self-styled "political testament" that Hitler dictated in the chancellery bunker in the closing days of World War II in Europe, witnessed by henchmen Joseph Goebbels and Martin Bormann, as well as the famous "peace in our time" agreement that Neville Chamberlain brought back from Munich in 1938. (Of his signing the agreement, Hitler later said, "[Chamberlain] was a nice old man, so I decided to give him my autograph.") It's a world of espionage and clandestine warfare in the major new permanent exhibit known as the Secret War Exhibition, where you can discover the truth behind the image of James Bond—and find out why the real secret war is even stranger and more fascinating than fiction. Displays include many items never before seen in public: coded messages, forged documents, secret wirelesses, and equipment used by spies from World War I to the present day.

Public film shows take place on weekends at 3pm and on certain weekdays during school holidays and on public holidays. In 1999 the museum will feature an exhibit by Terence Conran on **Post-War Britain—From the Bomb to the Beatles,** and the turn of the millennium will see the opening of a permanent Holocaust gallery.

Institute of Contemporary Arts. The Mall, SW1. ☎ **0171/930-3647.** Admission £1.50 ($3) Mon–Fri, £2.50 ($4) Sat–Sun adults; £1 ($1.60) Mon–Fri, £1.50 ($3) Sat–Sun students. Galleries Mon–Thurs and Sat–Sun noon–7:30pm, Fri noon–9pm. Bookstore daily noon–9pm. Three film screenings daily. Tube: Piccadilly Circus or Charing Cross.

London's liveliest cultural program takes place in this temple to the avant-garde, launched in 1947. It keeps Londoners and others up-to-date on the latest in the worlds of cinema, theater, photography, painting, sculpture, and other performing and visual arts media. Technically you have to be a member to visit, but membership is immediately granted. Foreign or experimental movies are shown, and special tributes—perhaps a retrospective of the films of Rainer Werner Fassbinder—are often the order of the day. The classics are frequently dusted off, along with cult favorites. On Saturday and Sunday at 3pm, the cinémathèque offers screenings for the kids. Sometimes well-known writers and artists speak here, which makes the low cost of membership even more enticing. Experimental plays are also presented. The American computer company that wrote the computer language that helped spawn the Internet, Sun Microsystems, donated £2 million to build a state-of-the-art New Media Centre in 1998. The photo galleries, showing the latest from British and foreign photographers, wouldn't necessarily win the approval of Jesse Helms.

Jewish Museum. 129–131 Albert St., Camden Town, NW1. ☎ **0171/284-1997.** £3 ($5) adults, £2 ($3) seniors, £1.50 ($3) children. Sun–Thurs 10am–4pm. Closed Fri, Sat, bank holidays, and Jewish festivals. Tube: Camden Town.

This museum tells the story of Jewish life in Britain. Arriving at the time of the Norman Conquest, Jews survived in England until King Edward I forced them out in 1290. From that time, no Jews (or at least no known Jews) lived in Britain until a small community returned in 1656 during the reign of Elizabeth I. On display are silver Torah bells made in London and two loving cups presented by the Spanish and Portuguese Synagogue to the lord mayor in the 18th century. The museum also sponsors walking tours of Jewish London; call for details.

Linley Sambourne House. 18 Stafford Terrace, W8. ☎ **0171/937-0663.** Admission £3 ($4.80) adults, £1.50 ($3) children 15 and under. Mar–Oct Wed 10am–4pm, Sun 2–5pm. Closed Nov–Feb. Tube: High St. Kensington. Bus: 9, 9a, 10, 27, 33, 49.

You'll step back into the days of Queen Victoria when you visit this house, which has remained unchanged for more than a century. Part of a terrace built in the late 1860s, this five-story, Suffolk brick structure was the home of Linley Sambourne, a legendary cartoonist for *Punch*. In the entrance hall, you see a mixture of styles and clutter that typified Victorian decor, with a plush portière, a fireplace valance, stained glass, and a large set of antlers vying for attention. The drawing room alone contains an incredible number of items of Victoriana.

London Transport Museum. The Piazza, Covent Garden, WC2. ☎ **0171/379-6344.** Admission £5 ($8) adults, £3 ($5) children, £13 ($21) family ticket, free for children under 5. Sat–Thurs 10am–6pm, Fri 11am–6pm (last entrance at 5:15pm). Tube: Covent Garden.

A collection of nearly two centuries of historic vehicles is displayed in a splendid Victorian building that formerly housed the Flower Market at Covent Garden. The museum shows how London's transport system evolved, and a representative collection of road vehicles includes a reconstruction of George Shillibeer's omnibus of 1829. A steam locomotive that ran on the world's first underground railway, a knifeboard horse bus, London's first trolleybus, and the Feltham tram are also of particular interest. One of the unique and popular features of the museum is the number of participatory exhibits, which allow you to operate the controls of a tube train, a tram, a bus, and full-size signaling equipment. The shop sells those fabulous "London by Tube" posters you see throughout the Underground. They've recently added "Kidzones"—interactive programs for children so parents can enjoy the museum without having to entertain the kids.

✪ **Museum of London.** 150 London Wall, EC2. ☎ **0171/600-3699.** Admission £4 ($6) adults, £2 ($3) children, students, and seniors, £9.50 ($15) family ticket. Tues–Sat 10am–5:50pm, Sun noon–5:50pm. Tube: St. Paul's or Barbican.

In London's Barbican district near St. Paul's Cathedral, overlooking the city's Roman and medieval walls, the museum traces the history of London from prehistoric times to the 20th century through archeological finds; paintings and prints; social, industrial, and historical artifacts; and costumes, maps, and models. Exhibits are arranged so that you can begin and end your chronological stroll through 250,000 years at the main entrance to the museum. The museum's pièce de résistance is the Lord Mayor's Coach, a gilt-and-scarlet fairy-tale coach built in 1757 and weighing in at 3 tons, but you can also see the Great Fire of London in living color and sound; the death mask of Oliver Cromwell; cell doors from Newgate Prison made famous by Charles Dickens; and most amazing of all, a shop counter with pre-World War II prices.

Museum of the Moving Image. South Bank (underneath Waterloo Bridge), SE1. ☎ **0171/401-2636.** Admission £6 ($10) adults, £4.85 ($8) students, £4 ($6) children and seniors, £16 ($26) family ticket (up to 2 adults and 2 children). Daily 10am–6pm (last admission 5pm). Tube: Waterloo or Embankment.

MOMI, part of the South Bank complex, traces the history of cinema and TV, taking you on an incredible journey from cinema's earliest experiments to modern animation, from Charlie Chaplin to the operation of a TV studio. There are artifacts to handle, buttons to push, and a cast of actors to tell visitors more. Three to four changing exhibitions are presented yearly; it's wise to allow 2 hours for a visit.

National Army Museum. Royal Hospital Rd., SW3. ☎ **0171/730-0717.** Free admission. Daily 10am–5:30pm. Closed Good Friday, first Mon in May, and for some days around Christmas. Tube: Sloane Sq.

The National Army Museum occupies a building adjoining the Royal Hospital, a home for retired soldiers. Whereas the Imperial War Museum is concerned only with wars in the 20th century, the National Army Museum tells the colorful story of British armies from 1485 on. Here you'll find uniforms worn by British soldiers in every corner of the world, plus weapons and other gear, flags, and medals. Even the skeleton of Napoléon's favorite charger is here. Also on display are Florence Nightingale's jewelry, Hitler's telephone exchange (captured in 1945), and Orders and Medals of HRH Duke of Windsor. A more recent gallery, "The Rise of the Redcoats," contains exhibitions detailing the life of the British soldier from 1485 to 1793. Included in the exhibit are displays on the English Civil War and the American War of Independence.

✪ **National Portrait Gallery.** St. Martin's Place, WC2. ☎ **0171/306-0055.** Free admission; fee charged for certain temporary exhibitions. Mon–Sat 10am–5:45pm, Sun noon–5:45pm. Tube: Charing Cross or Leicester Square.

In a gallery of remarkable and unremarkable pictures (they're collected here for their notable subjects rather than their artistic quality), a few paintings tower over the rest, including Sir Joshua Reynolds's first portrait of Samuel Johnson ("a man of most dreadful appearance"). Among the best are Nicholas Hilliard's miniature of a handsome Sir Walter Raleigh and a full-length Elizabeth I, along with the Holbein cartoon of Henry VIII. There's also a portrait of William Shakespeare (with a gold earring, no less) by an unknown artist that bears the claim of being the "most authentic contemporary likeness" of its subject. One of the most famous pictures in the gallery is the group portrait of the Brontë sisters (Charlotte, Emily, and Anne) painted by their brother, Bramwell. An idealized portrait of Lord Byron by Thomas Phillips is also on display.

The galleries of Victorian and early-20th-century portraits were radically redesigned recently. Occupying the whole of the first floor, they display portraits from 1837 (when Victoria took the throne) to present day; later 20th-century portraiture includes major works by such artists as Warhol and Hambling. Some of the more flamboyant personalities of the last two centuries are on show: T. S. Eliot, Disraeli, Macmillan, Iris, Sir Richard Burton, Elizabeth Taylor, Baroness Thatcher, and our two favorites: G. F. Watts' famous portrait of his great actress wife, Ellen Terry, and Vanessa Bell's portrait of her sister, Virginia Woolf. The late Princess Diana is on the Royal Landing, and this portrait seems to attract the most viewers.

National Postal Museum. King Edward Building, King Edward St., EC1. ☎ **0171/776-3636.** Free admission. Mon–Fri 9:30am–4:30pm. Tube: St. Paul's or Barbican.

Actually part of the post office, this museum features permanent exhibitions of the stamps of Great Britain and the world, as well as special displays of postal history, changing every year according to certain themes. On permanent display is the Penny Black, the world's first adhesive postage stamp. Look for the special exhibit of valentines and other greeting cards from the 19th century, which offers a unique perspective on the exquisite artistry of the Victorian era. Also look for the exhibit of early Victorian letter boxes, introduced by the great novelist Anthony Trollope in 1852 (he was also the post office surveyor).

Natural History Museum. Cromwell Rd., SW7. ☎ **0171/938-9123.** Admission £6 ($10) adults, £3.20 ($5) seniors and students, £3 ($5) children 5–17, free for children 4 and under, £16 ($26) family ticket; free to everyone Mon–Fri after 4:30pm and Sat–Sun after 5pm. Mon–Sat 10am–5:50pm, Sun 11am–5:50pm. Tube: South Kensington.

This is the home of the national collections of living and fossil plants, animals, and minerals, with many magnificent specimens on display. Exciting exhibits designed to encourage people of all ages to learn about natural history include "Human Biology— An Exhibition of Ourselves," "Our Place in Evolution," "Origin of the Species," "Creepy Crawlies," and "Discovering Mammals." The Mineral Gallery displays marvelous examples of crystals and gemstones. Also in the museum is the Meteorite

Pavilion, which exhibits fragments of rock that have crashed into the earth, some from the farthest reaches of the galaxy. What attracts the most attention is the huge dinosaur exhibit, displaying 14 complete skeletons. The center of the show depicts a trio of full-size robotic Deinonychus enjoying a freshly killed Tenontosaurus for lunch. The latest addition is "Earth Galleries," an exhibition outlining man's relationship with planet Earth.

Percival David Foundation of Chinese Art. 53 Gordon Sq., WC1. ☎ **0171/387-3909.** Free admission. Donations encouraged; £4 ($6) for a guided tour of 10–20 people. Admission to the library must be arranged with the curator ahead of time. Mon–Fri 10:30am–5pm. Tube: Russell Sq. or Euston Sq. Bus: 7, 8, 10, 14, 18, 19, 24, 25, or 27.

This foundation displays the greatest collection of Chinese ceramics outside of China. Approximately 1,700 ceramic objects reflect Chinese court taste from the 10th to 18th centuries, and include many pieces of exceptional beauty. An extraordinary collection of stoneware from the Song (960–1279) and Yuan (1279–1368) dynasties includes examples of rare Ru and Guan wares. Among the justifiably famous blue and white porcelains are two unique temple vases, dated by inscription to A.D. 1351. A wide variety of polychrome wares is also represented; these include examples of the delicate doucai wares from the Chenghua period (1465–87) as well as a remarkable group of 18th-century porcelains.

Queen's Gallery, Buckingham Palace. Entrance on Buckingham Palace Rd., SW1. ☎ **0171/879-1377** or 0171/839-1377. Admission £4 ($6) adults, £3 ($5) seniors, £2 ($3) children under 17. Daily 9:30am–4:30pm. Closed late Dec to early Mar. Tube: Green Park, St. James's, or Victoria.

Here you can see a sampling of the Royal Family's art collection. We can't predict what works will be on display during your visit, as they change yearly, but we can tell you that the queen's collection contains an unsurpassed range of Royal portraits, including the well-known profile of Henry V; companion portraits of Elizabeth I as a girl and her brother, Edward VI; two portraits of Queen Alexandra from Sandringham; plus paintings of Elizabeth II and other members of the present House of Windsor.

Royal Academy of Arts. Burlington House, Piccadilly, W1. ☎ **0171/300-8000.** Admission varies, depending on the exhibition. Daily 10am–6pm (last admission 5:30pm). Tube: Piccadilly Circus or Green Park.

Established in 1768, this organization included Sir Joshua Reynolds, Thomas Gainsborough, and Benjamin West among its founding members. Since its beginning, each member had to donate a work of art, and so over the years the academy has built up a sizable collection. The outstanding treasure is Michelangelo's beautiful relief of *Madonna and Child.* The annual Summer Exhibition has been held for more than 200 years; see the "London Calendar of Events," in chapter 2 for details.

Royal Mews, Buckingham Palace. Buckingham Palace Rd., SW1. ☎ **0171/839-1377.** Admission £3.20 ($5) adults, £2.60 ($4) seniors, £2.10 ($3) children under 17. Daily noon–4pm (restricted hours in winter). Tube: Green Park, St. James's, or Victoria.

This is where you can get a close look at Her Majesty's State Coach, built in 1761 to the designs of Sir William Chambers and decorated with paintings by Cipriani. Traditionally drawn by eight gray horses, it was formerly used by sovereigns when they traveled to open Parliament and on other state occasions; Queen Elizabeth traveled in it to her 1953 coronation and in 1977 for her Silver Jubilee Procession. The queen's carriage horses are also housed here, as well as other state coaches.

✪ Saatchi Gallery. 98A Boundary Rd., NW8. ☎ **0171/624-8299.** Admission £4 ($6), children under 12 free; free Thurs for all. Thurs–Sun 12–6pm. Tube: St. John's Wood or Swiss Cottage.

In the world of contemporary art, this collection is unparalleled. Charles Saatchi is one of Britain's greatest private collectors, and this personal museum features rotating displays from his vast holdings. Enter through the unmarked metal gateway of a former paint warehouse. The aim, as set forth by Saatchi, is to introduce new and unfamiliar art to a wider audience. The collection comprises more than 1,000 paintings and sculptures. Works which are not on display at the gallery are frequently on loan to museums around the world.

The main focus is works by young British artists, including such controversial ones as Damien Hirst's 14-foot tiger shark preserved in a formaldehyde-filled tank. Also on occasional exhibit is Marc Quinn's frozen "head" cast from nine pints of plasma taken from the artist over several months. Art critics were shocked at Richard Wilson's art when it was introduced: 2,500 gallons of used sump oil which flooded through an entire gallery. Young American and European artists are also represented, their work often controversial as well. Regardless of the exhibition on display at the time of your visit, it's almost guaranteed to be fascinating. And if you've ever wondered what many British people think American tourists look like, catch Duane Hanson's *Tourists II* (1988). It's devastating!

Science Museum. Exhibition Rd., SW7. ☎ **0171/938-8000.** Admission £6 ($10) adults, £3.20 ($5) children 5–17, free for children under 5. Free to all Mon–Fri after 4:30pm and Sat–Sun after 5pm. Daily 10am–6pm. Tube: South Kensington.

This museum traces the development of science and industry and their influence on everyday life. These are among the largest, most comprehensive, and most significant scientific collections anywhere. On display is Stephenson's original Rocket, the tiny prototype railroad engine; you can also see Whittle's original jet engine and the Apollo 10 space module. The King George III Collection of scientific instruments is the highlight of a gallery on science in the 18th century. Health Matters is a permanent gallery on modern medicine. The museum has two hands-on galleries, as well as working models and video displays.

Shakespeare's Globe Theatre & Exhibition. New Globe Walk, Bankside, SE1. ☎ **0171/902-1500.** Exhibition and tour admission £6 ($10) adults, £4 ($6) children 15 and under, £5 ($8) seniors and students. Guided tours £5 ($8) adults, £4 ($6) students and seniors. Daily 10am–5pm (guided tours every 30 minutes or so). Tube: Mansion House.

This is a re-creation of what was probably the most important public theater ever built—on the exact site where many of Shakespeare's plays opened. The late American filmmaker, Sam Wanamaker, worked for some 20 years to raise funds to re-create the theater as it existed in Elizabethan times, thatched roof and all. A fascinating exhibit tells the story of the Globe's re-creation in modern times, using the material (including goat's hair in the plaster), techniques, and craftsmanship of 400 years ago. The new Globe isn't an exact replica: It seats 1,500 patrons, not the 3,000 that regularly squeezed in during the early 1600s; and *this* thatched roof has been specially treated with a fire retardant. Guided tours of the facility are offered throughout the day.

In May 1997, the Globe's company staged its first slate of plays, and has been performing ever since. See "The Play's the Thing: The London Theater Scene" in chapter 9 for details on attending a play here.

Plans also call for an archival library, shops, an auditorium, and an exhibition gallery, but the full complex may not be fully operational until the autumn of 1999.

Sherlock Holmes Museum. 221B Baker St., NW1. ☎ **0171/935-8866.** Admission £5 ($8) adults, £3 ($5) children, under 7 free. Daily 9:30am–6pm. Tube: Baker St.

Where but on Baker Street would there be a museum displaying mementos of this famed fictional detective? Museum officials call it "the world's most famous address" (although 10 Downing Street is a rival for the title); it was here that mystery writer Sir Arthur Conan Doyle created a residence for Sherlock Holmes and his faithful Dr. Watson. These sleuths "lived" here from 1881 to 1904. In Victorian rooms, you can examine a range of exhibits, including published Holmes adventures and letters written to Holmes. This is a very commercial and artificial museum, but Holmes buffs don't seem to mind.

○ **Sir John Soane's Museum.** 13 Lincoln's Inn Fields, WC2. ☎ **0171/430-0175.** Free admission (donations invited). Tues–Sat 10am–5pm; first Tues of each month 6–9pm. Tours given Sat at 2:30pm; £3 ($5) tickets distributed at 2pm on a first-come, first-served basis (group tours by appointment only; call ☎ **0171/405-2107**). Tube: Holborn.

This is the former home of Sir John Soane (1753–1837), an architect who rebuilt the Bank of England (not the present structure). With his multiple levels, fool-the-eye mirrors, flying arches, and domes, Soane was a master of perspective and a genius of interior space (his picture gallery, for example, is filled with three times the number of paintings a room of similar dimensions would be likely to hold). One prize of the collection is William Hogarth's satirical series *The Rake's Progress,* which includes his much-reproduced *Orgy* and *The Election,* a satire on mid-18th-century politics. Soane also filled his house with classical sculpture. The sarcophagus of Pharaoh Seti I was found in a burial chamber in the Valley of the Kings. Also on display are architectural drawings from Soane's collection of 30,000.

Theatre Museum. Russell St., WC2. ☎ **0171/836-7891.** £3.50 ($6) adults, £2 ($3) seniors and children 5–17. Tues–Sun 11am–7pm. Tube: Covent Garden.

This branch of the Victoria and Albert Museum contains the national collections of the performing arts, encompassing theater, ballet, opera, music hall, pantomime, puppets, circus, and rock and pop music. Daily make-up demonstrations and costume workshops are run using costumes from the Royal Shakespeare Company and the Royal National Theatre. The museum also has a major Diaghilev archive.

Insider Tip: The box office inside offers tickets to West End plays—including the hot ones—as well as to concerts, dramas, and musicals, with almost no mark-up in most cases.

Wallace Collection. Manchester Sq., W1. ☎ **0171/935-0687.** Free admission. Mon–Sat 10am–5pm, Sun 2–5pm; Apr–Sept Sun 11am–5pm. Tube: Bond St. or Baker St.

Located in a palatial setting (the modestly described "town house" of the late Lady Wallace), this collection is a contrasting array of art and armaments. The art collection (mostly French) includes works by Watteau, Boucher, Fragonard, and Greuze, as well as such classics as Frans Hals's *Laughing Cavalier* and Rembrandt's portrait of his son Titus. The paintings of the Dutch, English, Spanish, and Italian schools are outstanding. The collection also contains important 18th-century French works of decorative art, including furniture from a number of royal palaces, Sèvres porcelain, and gold boxes. The European and Asian armaments, shown on the ground floor, are works of art in their own right: superb inlaid suits of armor, some obviously more for parade than battle, together with more businesslike swords, halberds, and magnificent Persian scimitars. The Heritage Lottery Fund and Christie's in London have awarded a £7½ million grant to the gallery's Centenary Project for the addition of museum facilities by the summer of 2000.

A BIT FARTHER AFIELD

Royal Air Force Museum. Grahame Park Way, Hendon, NW9. ☎ **0181/205-2266,** or 0181/205-9191 for 24-hour information. Admission £5.85 ($10) adults, £4.40 ($7) seniors,

£3 ($5) children 5–16. Daily 10am–6pm. Tube: Colindale. BritRail: Mill Hill Broadway, then bus no. 303. By car, take A41, A1, and M1 (junction 4).

Britain's national museum of aviation tells the story of flight through the display of more than 60 aircraft, one of the world's finest collections of historic aircraft. The museum stands on 15 acres of the former airfield at Hendon in North London, and its main aircraft hall occupies two large hangars from World War I. Custom-built halls house *The Battle of Britain Experience,* plus a collection of famous bomber aircraft, including "The Friendly Invasion," commemorating the contribution of the U.S. Army and U.S. Army Air Corps to the Allied war effort in World War II. Special features include a flight simulator offering a selection of different flying experiences, film shows, a "sit-in" jet trainer, and guided tours.

PARKS & GARDENS

London's parks are the greatest, most advanced system of "green lungs" of any large city on the globe. Although not as rigidly maintained as those of Paris (Britons traditionally prefer a more natural look), they're cared for with a loving and lavishly artistic hand that puts their American equivalents to shame.

The largest of the central London parks—and one of the biggest in the world—is **Hyde Park** (tube: Marble Arch, Hyde Park Corner, or Lancaster Gate), once a favorite deer-hunting ground of Henry VIII. With the adjoining Kensington Gardens (see below), it covers 615 acres of central London with velvety lawns interspersed with ponds, flowerbeds, and trees. Running through its width is a 41-acre lake known as the Serpentine, where you can row, sail model boats, or swim (provided you don't mind sub-Florida water temperatures). Rotten Row, a 1½-mile sand horseback riding track, attracts some skilled equestrians on Sunday. At the northeastern tip, near Marble Arch, is Speakers' Corner.

Blending with Hyde Park and bordering on the grounds of Kensington Palace, well-manicured **Kensington Gardens** (tube: High Street Kensington or Queensway) contains the famous statue of Peter Pan, with the bronze rabbits that toddlers are always trying to kidnap. It's also home to the Albert Memorial, that Victorian extravaganza. The Orangery is an ideal place to take afternoon tea (see "Teatime" in chapter 5).

East of Hyde Park, across Piccadilly, stretch **Green Park** (tube: Green Park) and **St. James's Park** (tube: St. James's Park), forming an almost unbroken chain of landscaped beauty. This is an ideal area for picnics; you'll find it hard to believe that this was once a festering swamp near a leper hospital. There's a romantic lake stocked with a variety of ducks and some surprising pelicans, descendants of the pair that the Russian ambassador presented to Charles II back in 1662.

Regent's Park (tube: Regent's Park or Baker Street), covers most of the district of that name, north of Baker Street and Marylebone Road. Designed by the 18th-century genius John Nash to surround a palace for the prince regent that never materialized, this is the most classically beautiful of London's parks. Its core is a rose garden planted around a small lake alive with waterfowl and spanned by Japanese bridges; in early summer, the rose perfume in the air is as heady as wine. The park is home to the Open-Air Theatre (see chapter 9) and the London Zoo (see "Especially for Kids," below). As at all the local parks, hundreds of deck chairs are scattered around the lawns, just waiting for sunbathers. The deck-chair attendants, who collect a small fee, are mostly college students on break.

Chelsea Physic Garden, 66 Royal Hospital Rd., SW3 (☎ **0171/352-5646;** tube: Sloane Square), founded in 1673 by the Worshipful Society of Apothecaries, is the second-oldest surviving botanical garden in England. Sir Hans Sloane, doctor to

George II, required the apothecaries of the empire to develop 50 plant species a year for presentation to the Royal Society. The objective was to grow plants for medicinal study; plant specimens and even trees arrived at the gardens by barge. Many plants grew here in English soil for the first time. Cotton seeds from this garden launched an industry in the new colony of Georgia. Some 7,000 plants still grow here, everything from the pomegranate to the willow Pattern tree; there's even exotic cork oak, as well as England's earliest rock garden. The garden is open April to October, Wednesday from noon to 5pm and Sunday from 2 to 6pm. Admission is £3.50 ($5.60) for adults, £1.80 ($2.90) for children 5 to 15 and students. The garden is also the setting for a well-recommended afternoon tea, where you can carry your cuppas on promenades through the garden (see "Teatime," in chapter 5).

Battersea Park, SW11 (☎ 0181/871-7530; tube: Sloane Square), is a vast patch of woodland, lakes, and lawns on the south bank of the Thames, opposite Chelsea Embankment between Albert Bridge and Chelsea Bridge. Formerly known as Battersea Fields, the present park was laid out between 1852 and 1858 on an old dueling ground. (The most famous duel here was between Lord Winchelsea and the Duke of Wellington in 1829.) There's a lake for boating, a deer field with fenced-in deer and wild birds, and areas for tennis and soccer. There's even a children's zoo, open from Easter to late September, daily from 11am to 5pm. Open weekends only in winter. The park's architectural highlight is the Peace Pagoda, built by Japanese craftspeople in cooperation with British architects, the stone and wood pagoda was dedicated in 1986 to the now-defunct Council of Greater London by an order of Japanese monks. The park is open daily from 7:30am to dusk. From the Sloane Square tube stop, it's a brisk 15-minute walk to the park, or you can pick up bus no. 137 (get off at the first stop after the bus crosses the Thames).

The hub of England's—and perhaps the world's—horticulture are the **Royal Botanic Gardens** (also known as Kew Gardens), at **Kew** in Surrey (see "Attractions on the Outskirts," below).

ROMAN LONDON

Rising out of the ground on Victoria Street is London's finest fragment of ancient Rome, the **Temple of Mithras** (tube: Bank or Mansion House). Discovered in 1954 during construction, the remains were transferred from their original location and assembled to form the foundation and lower walls of a Roman temple. Built in A.D. 240, the temple was the worshipping place of an obscure religion, the Cult of Mithras, devoted to the Persian god of heavenly light. The Mithraic religion shared many elements with the fledging Christian religion, including the common idea of a savior who shed his blood for all mankind, and the symbolic ceremonial repast. Many historians claim that early Christians may have borrowed these tenets from the Mithraists. Because of the rivalry between these religions, many sacred relics and shrines to Mithras were destroyed by the Christians. However, some sacred objects were found buried near the temple site, including several idols made of Italian marble and various silver trinkets; they're all on display at the Museum of London (see "Museums & Galleries," above).

4 Sightseeing & Boat Tours Along the Thames

There's a row of fascinating attractions lying on, across, and alongside the River Thames. All of London's history and development is linked with this winding ribbon of water: The Thames connects the city with the sea, from which it drew its wealth and its power, and it was London's chief commercial thoroughfare and royal highway (the only regal one in the days of winding cobblestoned streets). Every royal procession was undertaken on gorgeously painted and gilded barges (which you can still see at the National Maritime Museum in Greenwich; see "Attractions on the Outskirts," below). All important state prisoners were delivered to the Tower of London by water, eliminating the chance of an ambush by their friends in one of those narrow, crooked alleys surrounding the fortress. Much of the commercial traffic disappeared when London's streets were widened enough for horse-drawn coaches to maintain a decent pace.

RIVER CRUISES

A trip up or down the river will give you an entirely different view of London from the one you get from dry land. You'll see exactly how the city grew along and around the Thames and how many of its landmarks turn their faces toward the water. Several companies operate motor launches from the Westminster piers (tube: Westminster), offering panoramic views of one of Europe's most historic waterways en route.

Westminster-Greenwich Thames Passenger Boat Service, Westminster Pier, Victoria Embankment, SW1 (☎ 0171/930-4097), concerns itself only with downriver traffic from Westminster Pier to such destinations as Greenwich (see "Attractions on the Outskirts," below). The most popular excursion departs for Greenwich (a 50-minute ride) at half-hour intervals between 10am and 4pm April to October, and between 10:30am and 5pm from June to August; from November to March, boats depart from Westminster Pier at 40-minute intervals daily from 10:40am to 3:20pm. One-way fares are £5.80 ($9) for adults, £3.10 ($5) for children under 16. Round-trip fares are £7 ($11) for adults, £3.60 ($6) for children. A family ticket for two adults and up to three children under 15 costs £15.70 ($25) one-way, £18.60 ($30) round-trip.

Westminster Passenger Association (Upriver) Ltd., Westminster Pier, Victoria Embankment, SW1 (☎ 0171/930-2062 or 0171/930-4721), offers the only riverboat service upstream from Westminster Bridge to Kew, Richmond, and Hampton Court. There are regular daily sailings from the Monday before Easter until the end of October, on traditional river boats, all with licensed bars. Trip time, one-way, can be as little as 1½ hours to Kew and between 2½ to 4 hours to Hampton Court, depending on the tide. Cruises from Westminster Pier to Hampton Court via Kew Gardens leave daily at 10:30am, 11:15am, and noon. Round-trip tickets are £8 to £12 ($13 to $19) adults, £6 to £10 ($10 to $16) seniors, and £4 to £7 ($6 to $11) children 4 to 14; one child under 4 accompanied by an adult goes free. Evening cruises from May to September are also available departing Westminster Pier at 7:30pm and 8:30pm (9:30pm on demand) for £5 ($8) adults and £3.50 ($6) children.

Pool of London, inaugurated in 1997, allows travelers to visit sites along the Thames River between London Bridge and St. Katharine's Dock by taking a hop-on, hop-off ferry. For only £2 ($3), you can use the ferry as often as you like within a day. The ferry stops at five piers, including Tower Pier, London Bridge Pier, H.M.S. Belfast, Butlers Wharf, and St. Katharine's Dock. The ferry runs between 11am and 5pm until the end of October. From then until the end of March, it operates only on Saturday and Sunday, running every half hour. Beginning in April again, daily service resumes. Tickets are sold on board. For more information, call ☎ 0171/488-0344.

THAMESIDE SIGHTS
THE BRIDGES

Some of the Thames bridges are household names. **London Bridge,** contrary to the nursery rhyme, never fell down, but it has been replaced a number of times. The one that you see is the ugliest of the bunch. The previous one was dismantled and shipped to Lake Havasu, Arizona, in the 1960s.

Its neighbor to the east is the still-standing—and *much* more beautiful—**Tower Bridge,** SE1 (☎ 0171/403-3761; tube: Tower Hill), one of the city's most celebrated landmarks and possibly the most photographed and painted bridge on earth. Its outward appearance is familiar to Londoners and visitors alike. (This is the one that a certain American thought he'd purchased instead of the one farther up the river that really ended up in the middle of the desert.) In spite of its medieval appearance, Tower Bridge was actually built in 1894.

In 1993 an exhibition opened inside the bridge to commemorate its century-old history; it takes you up the north tower to high-level walkways between the two towers with spectacular views of St. Paul's, the Tower of London, and the Houses of Parliament—a photographer's dream. You're then led down the south tower and on to the bridge's original engine room, with its Victorian boilers and steam-pumping engines that used to raise and lower the roadway across the river. Exhibits housed in the bridge's towers use advanced technology, including animatronic characters, video, and computers to illustrate the history of the bridge. Admission to the **Tower Bridge Experience** (☎ 0171/403-3761) is £6 ($10) for adults and £4 ($6) for children 5 to 15, students, and seniors; it's free for children 4 and under. Open April to October daily 10am to 6:30pm, November to March daily 9:30am to 6pm; last entry is 1¼ hours before closing. Closed Good Friday and January 1 to 28 as well as a few days around Christmas.

HMS *Belfast*

An 11,500-ton cruiser, the **HMS** *Belfast* (Morgan's Lane, Tooley Street, SE1; ☎ 0171/407-6434; tube: Monument, Tower Hill, or London Bridge) is a World War II ship now preserved as a floating naval museum. It's moored opposite the Tower of London, between Tower Bridge and London Bridge. During the Russian convoy period and on D-day, the *Belfast* saw distinguished service, and in the Korean War it was known as "that straight shootin' ship." You can explore all the decks of the ship, right down to the engine room; exhibits above and below deck show how sailors have lived and fought over the past 50 years. It's open daily from 10am, with last boarding at 6pm in summer, 5pm in winter. Admission is £4.70 ($8) adults and £2.40 ($4) children; seniors and students pay £3.60 ($6); and family admission (two adults and two children) is £11.50 ($18). A ferry runs from Tower Pier (limited service in winter). The cost of the ferry is 50p (80¢) for adults and 40p (65¢) for children.

DOCKLANDS

What was a dilapidated wasteland in 8 square miles of property surrounded by water—some 55 miles of waterfront acreage within a sailor's cry of London's major attractions—has been reclaimed, restored, and rejuvenated. **London Docklands** is coming into its own as a leisure, residential, and commercial lure.

Next to the Tower of London, **St. Katharine's Dock** was the first of the docks to be given an entirely new role. Originally built from 1827 to 1828, this was for many years one of the leading docks, with the advantage of being closest to the City. Today, as a residential center and yacht marina, St. Katharine's again profits from its proximity to the City. The modern World Trade Centre looks down on the brick-brown sails of sailing barges and gleaming hulls of moored luxury yachts. Blocks of fashionable Manhattan-style loft apartments sit between docks and river.

Canary Wharf, on the Isle of Dogs, is the heart of Docklands; this huge 71-acre site is dominated by a 800-foot-high tower, the tallest building in the United

Kingdom, designed by Cesar Pelli. **The Piazza** is lined with shops and restaurants. A visit to the **Exhibition Centre** on the Isle of Dogs gives you an overview of the Docklands—past, present, and future. Already, the area has given space to the overflow from the City of London's square mile, and its development is more than promising.

On the south side of the river at Surrey Docks, the Victorian warehouses of **Butler's Wharf** have been converted by Sir Terence Conran into offices, workshops, houses, shops, and restaurants; it's also home to the **Design Museum** (see "Museums & Galleries," above).

Docklands can be reached via the **Dockland Light Railway,** which links the Isle of Dogs to London Underground's Tower Hill station. To see the whole complex, take the railway at Tower Gateway near Tower Bridge for a short journey through Wapping and the Isle of Dogs. You can get off at Island Gardens and then cross through the 100-year-old Greenwich Tunnel under the Thames to see the attractions at Greenwich (see "Attractions on the Outskirts," below). For information, call or stop by the **Docklands Visitor Centre** (☎ 0171/512-3000), across from the London Arena at Canary Wharf.

A FAMOUS SHIP AT GREENWICH

Four miles east of London, at Greenwich Pier, now in permanent dry dock, lies the last and ultimate word in sail power: the **Cutty Sark,** King William Walk, Greenwich, SE10 (☎ 0181/858-3445; bus: 177, 180, 188, 199, 286, or 386). Named after the witch in Robert Burns's poem "Tam O'Shanter," it was the greatest of the breed of clipper ships that carried tea from China and wool from Australia in the most exciting ocean races ever sailed. The *Cutty Sark*'s record stood at a then-unsurpassed 363 miles in 24 hours. Launched in Scotland in 1869, the sleek black three-master represented the final fighting run of canvas against steam. Although the age of the clippers was brief, they did outpace the steamers as long as there was wind to fill their billowing mountain of sails. On board the *Cutty Sark* you'll find a museum devoted to clipper lore. Admission is £3.50 ($6) for adults and £2.50 ($4) for children over 5, students, and seniors. It's open Monday to Saturday from 10am to 6pm and Sunday (and Good Friday) from noon to 6pm; it closes at 5pm in winter.

5 Attractions on the Outskirts

These sights are perfect for a morning or afternoon jaunt, and are easily accessible by tube, train, boat, or bus. For information on river launches, see "River Cruises" under "Sightseeing & Boat Tours Along the Thames," above.

HAMPSTEAD

About 4 miles north of the center of London is the lovely village of Hampstead (tube: Hampstead), and scenic Hampstead Heath.

The 800-acre expanse of high heath known as **Hampstead Heath** is a continuous chain of formal parkland, woodland, heath, meadowland, and ponds. On a clear day you can see St. Paul's Cathedral and even the hills of Kent. Londoners would certainly mount the barricades if Hampstead Heath were imperiled; for years, they've come here to sun worship, fly kites, fish the ponds, swim, picnic, and jog. In good weather, it's also the site of big 1-day fairs. At the shore of Kenwood Lake, in the northern section, is a concert platform devoted to symphony performances on summer evenings. In the northeast corner, in Waterlow Park, ballets, operas, and comedies are staged at the Grass Theatre in June and July.

Once the Underground came to **Hampstead Village** in 1907, writers, artists, architects, musicians, and scientists were among those who decamped for the leafy village.

Keats, D. H. Lawrence, Rabindranath Tagore, Shelley, and Robert Louis Stevenson all once lived here, and Kingsley Amis and John Le Carré still do.

The Regency and Georgian houses of the village and the rolling greens of the heath are just 20 minutes by tube from Piccadilly Circus. The village has a quirky mix of historic pubs, toy shops, and chic boutiques along **Flask Walk,** a pedestrian mall. The original village, on the side of a hill, still has old alleys, steps, courts, and groves that are ideal for strolling.

Burgh House. New End Sq., NW3. ☎ **0171/431-0144.** Free admission. House and museum, Wed–Sun noon–5pm. Buttery, Wed–Sun 11am–5:30pm. Tube: Hampstead.

This Queen Anne home (1703) in the center of the village was the residence of the daughter and son-in-law of Rudyard Kipling, who often visited here. It's now used for local art exhibits, concerts, recitals, talks, and public meetings on many subjects, and the house is the home of several local societies, including the Hampstead Music Club and the Hampstead Scientific Society. **Hampstead Museum,** in Burgh House, illustrates the local history of the area. It has a room devoted to reproductions of works by the great artist John Constable, who lived nearby for many years and is buried in the local parish church. There's also a licensed **buttery** (☎ **0171/431-2616**) that's popular for lunch or tea; with the lowest prices in pricey Hampstead, it's a real dining bargain.

Fenton House. Windmill Hill, NW3. ☎ **0171/435-3471.** Admission £4 ($6) adults, £2 ($3) children, £10 ($16) family ticket. Mar Sat–Sun 2–5pm; Apr–Oct Sat–Sun 11am–5pm, Wed–Fri 2–5pm. Closed Good Friday and Nov–Feb. Tube: Hampstead.

This National Trust property is in a village area on the west side of Hampstead Grove, just north of Hampstead Village. Built in 1693, its paneled rooms contain furniture and pictures; 18th-century English, German, and French porcelain; and an outstanding collection of early keyboard musical instruments.

Freud Museum. 20 Maresfield Gardens, NW3. ☎ **0171/435-2002.** Admission £3 ($5) adults, £1.50 ($2) full-time students, free for children under 12. Wed–Sun noon–5pm. Tube: Finchley Rd.

This is the spacious house in which the founder of psychoanalysis lived, worked, and died after escaping with his family and possessions from Nazi-occupied Vienna. The rooms hold his furniture (including the famous couch), letters, photographs, paintings, and personal effects, as well as those of his daughter, Anna Freud, also a noted psychoanalyst. Temporary exhibitions and an archive film program are also offered.

Keats House. Wentworth Place, Keats Grove, NW3. ☎ **0171/435-2062.** Free admission; donations welcome. Apr–Oct Mon–Fri 10am–1pm and 2–6pm, Sat 10am–1pm and 2–5pm, Sun and bank holidays 2–5pm; Nov–Mar Mon–Fri 1–5pm, Sat 10am–1pm and 2–5pm, Sun 2–5pm. Tube: Hampstead.

This was the home of the poet John Keats for only 2 years; but it was here in 1819 that he wrote two of his most famous poems, "Ode to a Nightingale" and "Ode on a Grecian Urn." This Regency house contains some of his manuscripts and letters. Call before coming here, as the house is presently closed for urgent repairs and its reopening hasn't been announced.

Kenwood House. Hampstead Lane, NW3. ☎ **0181/348-1286.** Free admission. Apr–Oct daily 10am–6pm; Nov–Mar daily 10am–4pm. Tube: Golders Green, then bus 210.

This structure was built as a gentleman's country home and later enlarged and decorated by the famous Scottish architect Robert Adam, starting in 1764. The house contains period furniture and paintings by Rembrandt, Vermeer, Gainsborough, and

Hampstead

Abernethy House 9
Admiral's House 12
Benham's Place 6
Burgh House 21
Cannon Hall 17
Church Row 1
Downshire Hill 22
Fenton House 11
Grove Lodge 13
The "Handel Gates" 3
Home of George Romney 10
Home of Lord Alfred Douglas 2

Home of Sir Henry Cole 16
John and Maria
    Constable's Grave 4
John Constable's House 20
Judges' Walk 14
Keats's House 23
The Parish Lock Up 19
"Squires Mount Croft" 18
St. John's Church 5
St. Mary's Church 7
The Watchhouse 8
Whitestone Pond 15

Turner, among others. It's also a venue for special visiting exhibitions and evening concerts (at which time admission is charged).

IN NEARBY HIGHGATE

○ Highgate Cemetery. Swain's Lane, N6. ☎ **0181/340-1834.** Western Cemetery guided tour, £3 ($5) requested donation. Eastern Cemetery, £1 ($1.60) requested donation, £1 ($1.60) camera pass charge. Western Cemetery, Apr–Oct guided tours only Mon–Fri at noon, 2, and 4pm, and Sat–Sun hourly 11am–4pm; Nov and Mar, tours Mon–Fri at noon, 2, and 4pm, and Sat–Sun hourly 11am–3pm; Dec–Feb Sat–Sun hourly 11am–4pm. Eastern Cemetery, Apr–Oct Mon–Fri 10am–5pm, Sat–Sun 11am–5pm; Nov–Mar Mon–Fri 10am–4pm, Sat–Sun 11am–4pm. Both cemeteries closed at Christmas and during funerals. Tube: Archway, then walk through Waterlow Park. Bus: from Archway, 143, 271, or 210.

Described in the British press as everything from "walled romantic rubble" to "an anthology of horror," this 37-acre burial ground is the ideal setting for a fine collection of Victorian sculpture, as well as the graves of Karl Marx and others, including George Eliot, Christina Rossetti, and Elizabeth Siddell, wife of Dante Gabriel Rossetti and the Pre-Raphaelites' favorite model.

GREENWICH

Greenwich Mean Time is the basis of standard time throughout most of the world, and Greenwich has been the zero point used in the reckoning of terrestrial longitudes since 1884. But this lovely village—the center of British seafaring when Britain ruled the seas—is also home of the Royal Naval College, the National Maritime Museum, and the Old Royal Observatory. In dry dock at Greenwich Pier is the clipper ship *Cutty Sark* (see "Sightseeing & Boat Tours Along the Thames," above). Greenwich also has some wonderful shopping, including a famous weekend market (see chapter 8).

Greenwich will be the site of Britain's **Millennium Dome**, which has been billed as "the most spectacular event on earth." At least it will be the largest on earth, a multimedia extravaganza that will mix education and entertainment. A recent poll showed that four out of five Brits oppose the whole project, but work goes on. It's still not known what the dome will contain, only a vague theme called "Time." A live show of some sort will run in the dome's central arena, with a series of themed exhibitions around the edge. A few of the features have already been announced, including a 150-foot androgynous human figure with working arteries and veins. Most of the project's cost, estimated at more than $1 billion U.S. dollars, will come from national lottery revenues.

Getting There   Part of the fun of going to Greenwich, about 4 miles from the City, is getting there. The most appealing way involves boarding any of the frequent ferryboats that cruise along the Thames at intervals that vary from every half-hour (in summer) to every 45 minutes (in winter). Boats that depart from Westminster Pier (tube: Westminster) are maintained by **Westminster Passenger Services, Ltd.** (☎ **0171/930-4097**). Boats that leave from Charing Cross Pier (tube: Embankment) and Tower Pier (tube: Tower Hill) are run by **Catamaran Cruises, Ltd.** (☎ **0171/987-1185**). Depending on the tides and the carrier you select, travel time varies from 50 to 75 minutes each way. Passage is £6.70 to £7.20 ($11 to $12) round-trip for adults, £3.70 to £4.20 ($6 to $7) round-trip for children 5 to 12; it's free for those under 5.

You can also take the train from Charing Cross Station, which, frankly, is a lot more prosaic than the ride along the Thames described above. **Rail Europe** (☎ **0345/484950** in London or 800/848-7245 in the U.S.) trains take about 15 minutes to reach Greenwich from Charing Cross, costing between £2.10 and £3 ($3 to

$5) round-trip, depending on the time of day you travel. A commuter train that can get you here is the **Docklands Light Railway** (☎ **0171/918-4000**), a tourist attraction in its own right: a narrow-gauge railway supported on stilts high above the Docklands. Passengers board the blue-and-white cars at Tower Gateway (tube: Tower Hill) or Bank, passing above the Isle of Dogs before arriving at the train's final stop at Island Gardens, in the Docklands. From here, walk through a pedestrian tunnel that extends below a branch of the Thames to a point in Greenwich a few steps from the *Cutty Sark*. The one-way fare is £1.60 ($3).

Visitor Information The **Greenwich Tourist Information Centre** is at 46 Greenwich Church St. (☎ **0181/858-6376**). From April to October, it's open daily 10am to 5pm; November to March, Monday to Thursday 11:15am to 4:30pm, Friday to Sunday 10am to 5pm. The Tourist Information Centre conducts **walking tours** of Greenwich's major sights. The tours, which cost £4 ($6), depart daily at 12:15 and 2:15pm and last 1½ to 2 hours. Advance reservations aren't required, but it's a good idea to phone in advance to find out if there have been any last-minute schedule changes. Those who take a walking tour get a 50% reduction in admission to the National Maritime Museum, Old Royal Observatory, and Queen's House.

SEEING THE SIGHTS

One ticket will admit you to Greenwich's three greatest attractions, **National Maritime Museum, the Old Royal Observatory,** and **Queen's House.** The three attractions stand together in a beautiful royal park, high on a hill overlooking the Thames. You buy your combination ticket at your first stop. Ticket prices are £5 ($8) adults, £4 ($6) seniors and students, £2.50 ($4) children 5 to 16, free for those 5 and under; a family ticket, for two adults and up to three children, is £16 ($26). A reconstruction of the core of the museum will result in a large number of new galleries opening Easter 1999 as part of the museum's aim to be ready with a much improved attraction at the dawn of the millennium celebrations in Greenwich. All three attractions are open daily from 10am to 5pm. For more information, call ☎ **0181/858-4422.**

From the days of early seafarers to 20th-century sea power, the **National Maritime Museum** illustrates the glory that was Britain at sea. The cannon, relics, ship models, and paintings tell the story of a thousand naval battles and a thousand victories, as well as the price of those battles. Look for some oddities here—everything from the dreaded cat-o'-nine-tails used to flog sailors until 1879 to Nelson's Trafalgar coat, with the fatal bullet hole in the left shoulder clearly visible. Many galleries will be closed intermittently through 1999 to allow for massive renovations.

Old Royal Observatory is the original home of Greenwich Mean Time. It has the largest refracting telescope in the United Kingdom, and a collection of historic timekeepers and astronomical instruments. You can stand astride the meridian and set your watch precisely by the falling time-ball. Wren designed the Octagon Room. Here, the first royal astronomer, Flamsteed, made his 30,000 observations that formed the basis of his *Historia Coelestis Britannica.* Edmond Halley, who discovered Halley's Comet, succeeded him. In 1833, the ball on the tower was hung to enable shipmasters to set their chronometers accurately.

Designed by Inigo Jones, **Queen's House** (1616) is a fine example of this architect's innovative style. It's most famous for the cantilevered tulip staircase, the first of its kind. Carefully restored, the house contains a collection of royal and marine paintings and other objets d'art.

Nearby is the **Royal Naval College,** King William Walk (off Romney Road; ☎ **0181/858-2154**). Designed by Sir Christopher Wren in 1696, it occupies 4 blocks named after King Charles, Queen Anne, King William, and Queen Mary. Formerly,

Greenwich Palace stood here from 1422 to 1640. It's worth stopping in to see the magnificent Painted Hall by Thornhill, where the body of Nelson lay in state in 1805, and the Georgian chapel of St. Peter and St. Paul. Open daily 2:30 to 5pm; admission is free.

SHOPPING

The **Linen & Lace Company,** 7 Greenwich Market, SE10 (☎ 0181/293-9407), is the domain of Elizabeth Dashwood, who produces her own line of original bed and table linens. Merchandise ranges from pillow shams to duvets and from throws to patchwork bedspreads, in both cotton and linen. She also sells restored antique beds and night wear for both children and adults. You won't find any of her goods in London's department stores. And if you come to Greenwich on Saturday or Sunday, we suggest that you make time for the fun **Greenwich Antiques Market,** Greenwich High Road. The market has everything—books, furniture, crafts, and bric-a-brac galore, and has been a trading area in London since the rule of Henry VIII.

KEW

Nine miles southwest of central London near Richmond, Kew is home to the best-known botanic gardens in Europe, maybe even the world. It's also the site of **Kew Palace,** former residence of George III and Queen Charlotte, which is closed until spring 1999. We suggest you come anyway, as the gardens are the big attraction. The most convenient way to get to Kew is to take the **District line** tube to the Kew Gardens stop, on the south bank of the Thames.

✪ **Royal Botanic (Kew) Gardens.** Kew. ☎ 0181/940-1171. Admission £4.50 ($7) adults, £3 ($5) students and seniors, £2.50 ($4) children, family ticket £12 ($19). Mon–Sat 9:30am–3:30pm (to 6:30pm Apr–Oct); Sun and holidays 9:30am–8pm. Tube: Kew Gardens.

These world-famous gardens offer thousands of varieties of plants. But Kew is no mere pleasure garden—it's essentially a vast scientific research center that happens to be beautiful. The gardens, on a 300-acre site, encompass lakes, greenhouses, walks, pavilions, and museums, along with fine examples of the architecture of Sir William Chambers. Among the 50,000 plant species are notable collections of ferns, orchids, aquatic plants, cacti, mountain plants, palms, and tropical water lilies.

No matter what season you visit Kew, there's always something to see, from the first spring flowers through winter. Gigantic hothouses grow species of shrubs, blooms, and trees from every part of the globe, from the Arctic Circle to tropical rain forests. Attractions include a newly restored Japanese Gateway in traditional landscaping, as well as exhibitions that vary with the season. The newest greenhouse, the Princess of Wales Conservatory (beyond the rock garden), encompasses 10 climatic zones, from arid to tropical; it has London's most thrilling collection of miniature orchids. The Marianne North Gallery (1882) is an absolute gem, paneled with 246 different types of wood that the intrepid Victorian artist collected on her world journeys; she also collected 832 paintings of exotic and tropical flora, all of which are displayed on the walls. Afternoon tea is offered at the Orangery; there's no better place in the gardens. The Visitor Centre at Victoria Gate houses an exhibit telling the story of Kew, as well as a bookshop.

Afternoon Tea   Across the street from the Royal Botanic Gardens is one of the finest tearooms in the area, the **Original Maids of Honour Tearooms,** 288 Kew Rd. (☎ 0181/940-2752). Its oak paneling and old leaded glass windows give the place a cozy warmth. The homemade cakes are delectable, as are the delightfully light scones. The Maids of Honour is their pastry specialty, originally baked for Henry VIII, who liked it so much its secret recipe has been passed along through the centuries. After-noon tea is £4.50 ($7). The tearoom is open Monday 9am to 2pm and Tuesday to Sat-urday 9am to 5pm, and tea is served from 3:30 to 5:30pm.

HAMPTON COURT

Hampton Court, on the north side of the Thames, 13 miles west of London in East Molesey, Surrey, is easily accessible. Frequent **trains** (☎ **0345/484950** in the U.K. only or 01603/764776) run from Waterloo Station (Network Southeast) to Hampton Court Station. **London Transport** (☎ **0171/730-3466** or 0990/808080) buses no. 111, 131, 216, 267, and 461 make the trip from Victoria Coach Station on Buck-ingham Palace Road (just southwest of Victoria Station). Boat service is offered to and from Kingston, Richmond, and Westminster (see "Sightseeing & Boat Tours Along the Thames," above). If you're **driving** from London, take A308 to the junction with A309 on the north side of Kingston Bridge over the Thames.

✪ **Hampton Court Palace.** ☎ **0181/781-9500.** Admission £9.25 ($15) adults, £7 ($11) students and seniors, £6 ($10) children 5–15, free for children under 5. Gardens open year-round daily 7am–dusk (no later than 9pm), free admission to all except Privy Garden (admis-sion £2 without palace ticket). Cloisters, courtyards, state apartments, great kitchen, cellars, and Hampton Court exhibition open mid-Mar–mid-Oct daily 9:30am–6pm; mid-Oct–mid-Mar Mon 10:15am–6pm, Tues–Sun 9:30am–6pm. Tudor tennis court open mid-Mar–mid-Oct.

Cardinal Wolsey's 16th-century Hampton Court Palace can teach us a lesson: Don't try to outdo your boss—particularly if he happens to be Henry VIII. The rich cardinal did just that, and he eventually lost his fortune, power, and prestige and ended up giving his lavish palace to the Tudor monarch.

Today, you can parade through the apartments, filled with porcelain, furniture, paintings, and tapestries. You see that Henry even outdid Wolsey when he took over the palace. Tudor additions included the **Anne Boleyn Gateway,** with its 16th-century astronomical clock that even tells the high-water mark at London Bridge. From **Clock Court,** you can see one of Henry's major contributions, the aptly named **Great Hall,** with its hammerbeam ceiling. Henry cavorted through the various apart-ments with his wife of the moment, from Anne Boleyn to Catherine Parr (the latter reversed things and lived to bury her erstwhile spouse). Later, Charles I was impris-oned here at one time, and temporarily managed to escape his jailers.

Although the palace enjoyed prestige and pomp in Elizabethan days, it owes much of its present look to William and Mary—or, rather, to Sir Christopher Wren, who designed and had built the northern or **Lion Gates,** intended to be the main entrance to the new parts of the palace. **The King's Dressing Room** is graced with some of the best art, mainly paintings by old masters on loan from Queen Elizabeth II. Be sure to inspect the **royal chapel**—Wolsey wouldn't recognize it. To confound yourself totally, you may want to get lost in the serpentine shrubbery **maze** in the garden, also the work of Sir Christopher Wren. The fine wrought-iron screen at the south end of the south gardens was made by Jean Tijou around 1694 for William and Mary. There's a cafe and restaurant in the Tiltyard Gardens.

6 Especially for Kids

The attractions that follow are fun places for kids of all ages. In addition to what's listed below, kids also love **Madame Tussaud's,** the **Science Museum,** the **London Transport Museum,** the **Natural History Museum,** the **Tower of London,** the **Commonwealth Institute,** and the **National Maritime Museum** in Greenwich, all discussed above.

Kidsline (☎ 0171/222-8070) offers computerized information about current events that might interest kids. The line is open from 4 to 6pm during school term time, 9am to 4pm on holidays. Only problem is, every parent in London is calling for information; it's almost impossible to get through.

Bethnal Green Museum of Childhood. Cambridge Heath Rd., E2. ☎ **0181/980-2415.** Free admission. Mon–Thurs and Sat 10am–5:50pm, Sun 2:30–5:50pm. Tube: Bethnal Green.

This branch of the Victoria and Albert specializes in toys from past and present. The variety of dolls alone is staggering; some have such elaborate period costumes that you don't even want to think of the price tags they must've carried. With the dolls go doll-houses, from simple cottages to miniature mansions, complete with fireplaces, grand pianos, kitchen utensils, household pets, and carriages. There are also optical toys, marionettes, puppets, a considerable exhibit of soldiers and war toys from both World War eras, trains and aircraft, and a display of clothing and furniture relating to the social history of childhood.

Little Angel Theatre. 14 Dagmar Passage, N1. ☎ **0171/226-1787.** Admission £5.50–£6.50 ($9–$11) adults, £4.50–£5 ($7–$8) children. Show times Sat–Sun 11am and 3pm, some weekdays. Tube: Angel or Highbury & Islington.

This theater, constructed for the presentation of puppetry in all its forms, gives between 400 and 500 performances a year. The Little Angel presents homegrown shows that tour nationally and internationally as well as the work of a wide variety of visiting companies. The range of puppetry is also wide, from marionettes (string puppets) to rod and glove puppets. A large percentage of the work is targeted at children; age limits are stated for every show presented (for example, "no under-3s allowed"). It has a coffee bar and is accessible to people with disabilities. There's also an adjacent workshop where the puppets, sets, and costumes are made. One show per season is adult-oriented, call for information.

London Dungeon. 28–34 Tooley St., SE1. ☎ **0171/403-0606.** Admission £9 ($14) adults, £8 ($13) students and seniors, £6.50 ($11) children under 15. Admission includes 2 shows. Apr–Sept daily 10am–5:30pm; Oct–Mar daily 10am–4:30pm. Tube: London Bridge.

This ghoulish place was deliberately designed to chill the blood while reproducing the conditions of the Middle Ages. Set under the arches of London Bridge Station, the dungeon is a series of tableaux that are more grisly than the ones in Madame Tussaud's. The rumble of trains overhead adds to the horror of the place, and tolling bells bring a constant note of melancholy to the background; dripping water and caged rats make for even more atmosphere. The murder of Thomas à Becket in Canterbury Cathedral is depicted, among others: Naturally, there's a burning at the stake, as well as a torture chamber with racking, branding, and fingernail extraction. For the first time in a British attraction, you can now experience special effects originally conceived for major film and TV productions. The "Jack the Ripper Experience" is spine-chilling! They've recently added a new show called "Judgment Day." Performed by actors, you will be sentenced to death and taken on a boat ride to meet your fate. If you survive, there's a Pizza Hut on premises (for a little taste of home), and a souvenir shop selling certificates that testify that you made it through the works.

London Planetarium. Marylebone Rd., NW1. ☎ **0171/935-6861.** £5.65 ($9) adults, £4.45 ($7) seniors, £3.70 ($6) children 5–17. Weekdays daily from 10am, Sat–Sun 9:30am with shows beginning at 12:20pm (10:20am on weekends) and last show at 5pm. Tube: Baker St.

Next door to Madame Tussaud's, the planetarium explores the mysteries of the stars and the night sky. The most recent star show starts with a spaceship of travelers forced to desert their planet when a neighboring star explodes; accompanying them on their journey, the audience travels through the solar system, visiting its major landmarks and witnessing spectacular cosmic activity. There are also several hands-on exhibits that relate to planets and space; for example, you can see what shape or weight you'd be on other planets. You can also hear Stephen Hawking talk about mysterious black holes.

London Zoo. Regent's Park, NW1. ☎ **0171/722-3333.** Admission £8.50 ($14) adults, £6 ($10) children, free for children under 4. Mar–Sept daily 10am–5:30pm; Oct–Feb daily 10am–4pm. Tube: Regent's Park or Camden Town, then bus Z1 or 274.

One of the greatest zoos in the world, the London Zoo is more than a century and a half old. This 36-acre garden houses about 8,000 animals, including some of the rarest species on earth. Separate houses are reserved for various species: the insect house (incredible bird-eating spiders, a cross-sectioned ant colony); the reptile house (huge dragonlike monitor lizards and a fantastic 15-foot python); and others, such as the Sobell Pavilion for Apes and Monkeys and the Lion Terraces. In the Moonlight World, special lighting effects simulate night for the nocturnal beasties, while rendering them clearly visible to onlookers, so you can see all the night rovers in action.

Many families budget almost an entire day here, watching the penguins being fed, enjoying an animal ride in summer, and meeting elephants on their walks around the zoo.

Rock Circus. London Pavilion, Piccadilly Circus, W1. ☎ **0171/734-7203.** £8 ($13) adults, £7 ($11) seniors and students, £6.50 ($10) children under 16, £20 ($32) family ticket. Sun–Mon and Wed–Thurs 11am–9pm, Tues noon–9pm, Fri–Sat 11am–10pm; summer, daily 10am–10pm (except Tues noon–9pm). Tube: Piccadilly Circus.

This outpost of Madame Tussaud's presents the history of rock and pop music from Bill Haley and the Beatles to Sting and Madonna through wax and audio-animatronic figures, which move and perform golden oldies and more recent chart-toppers in an eerily lifelike way. Authentic memorabilia, videos, and personal stereo sound surround you.

Unicorn Theatre for Children. The Arts Theatre, 6–7 Great Newport St., WC2. ☎ **0171/379-3280;** box office 0171/836-3334. Admission £8.75 ($14), £7 ($11), £5 ($8) depending on seat locations. Show times Sept–June daily 11am and 2:30pm. Tube: Leicester Sq.

Situated in the heart of London's West End theater district, the Unicorn is its only children's theater. Founded in 1947 and going stronger than ever, it presents a season of plays for 4- to 12-year-olds from September to June. The schedule includes specially commissioned plays and adaptations of old favorites, all performed by adult actors. You can also become a temporary member while you're in London and join in an exciting program of weekend workshops.

7 Organized Tours

ORIENTATION TOURS
BY BUS

For the first-timer, the quickest and most economical way to bring the big city into focus is to take a bus tour. One of the most popular is **The Original London Sightseeing Tour,** which passes by all the major sights in just about 1½ hours. The tour, which uses a traditional double-decker bus with live commentary by a guide, costs £12 ($19) for adults, £6 ($10) for children under 16, free for those under 5. The popular London Plus Hop On/Hop Off ticket has been discontinued and is now incorporated into the sightseeing tour, allowing you to hop off or hop on the bus at any point in the tour at no extra charge. The tour plus admission to Madame Tussaud's is £21 ($34) for adults, £12 ($19) for children; with a River Thames trip, the tour costs £16.50 ($26) for adults and £8.50 ($14) for children.

Departures are from convenient points within the city; you can choose your departure point when you purchase your ticket. Tickets can be purchased on the bus or at a discount from any London Transport or London Tourist Board Information Centre. Most hotel concierges also sell tickets. For information or phone purchases, call ☎ 0181/877-1722. It's also possible to write for tickets: **London Coaches,** Jews Row, London SW18 1TB.

A double-decker air-conditioned coach in the distinctive green-and-gold livery of **Harrods,** 87–135 Brompton Rd. (☎ 0171/581-3603; tube: Knightsbridge), offers sightseeing tours around London. The first departure from Door 8 of Harrods is at 10:30am; afternoon tours begin at 1:30 and 4pm. Tea, coffee, and orange juice are served on board. It's £18 ($29) for adults, £10 ($16) for children under 14, free for those under 5. All-day excursions to Blenheim Palace, Windsor, Stratford-upon-Avon, and outlying areas of London are available. You can purchase tickets at Harrods, Sightseeing Department, lower ground floor.

Big Bus Company Ltd., Waterside Way, London SW17 (☎ 0181/944-7810), operates a 2-hour tour in summer, departing every 5 to 15 minutes from 9am to 6pm daily (in winter, every 10 to 15 minutes from 9am to 6pm daily) from Marble Arch by Speakers Corner, Green Park by the Ritz Hotel, and Victoria Station (Buckingham Palace Road by the Royal Westminster Hotel). Tours cover the highlights—18 in all—ranging from the Houses of Parliament and Westminster Abbey to the Tower of London and Buckingham Palace (exterior looks only), accompanied by live commentary. The cost is £12 ($19) for adults, £6 ($10) for children. There's also a 1-hour tour that follows the same route, but covers only 13 sights. Tickets are valid all day; you can hop on and off the bus as you wish.

WALKING TOURS

John Wittich, 88 Woodlawn St., Whitstable, Kent, CT5 1HH (☎ 0122/777-2619), started offering walks around London in 1960. A Freeman of the City of London and a member of two of London's ancient guilds, he is the author of several books on London walks. All the tours are conducted by Mr. Wittich himself; you'll search out the unusual, the beautiful, and the historic. He'll also arrange personal tours for families and groups in advance. The cost for a walking tour of up to 2 hours is £20 ($32) for one or two adults, with £12.50 ($20) per hour assessed for extended walks. A whole-day guided tour costs £75 ($120).

Of the companies operating a daily program of regularly scheduled public walks, **The Original London Walks,** 87 Messina Ave. (P.O. Box 1708), London NW6 4LW (☎ 0171/624-3978), is the best, hands down. The oldest established walking-tour company in London, it's run by an Anglo-American couple, David and Mary Tucker (he's an American journalist, she's an English actress). Their hallmarks are a variety of routes, reliability, reasonably sized groups, and—above all—superb guides, including renowned crime historian Donald Rumbelow (internationally recognized as the leading authority on Jack the Ripper), a distinguished BBC producer, the foremost authority on the Regent's Canal, the author of the classic guidebook *London Walks,* a London Historical Society officer, and several prominent actors and actresses (including classical actor Edward Petherbridge). They offer more than 100 walks a week, year-round. Their repertory ranges from Greenwich to Ghost Walks; Beatles to Bloomsbury; Dickens to Docklands; Hampstead to Hidden London; Old Westminster to the Old Jewish Quarter; Legal London to Little Venice to the London Nobody

Knows; Covent Garden to Camden Town; Shakespeare to Soho; the Famous Square Mile to the Footsteps of Sherlock Holmes; the Undiscovered City to the Secret Village; and Aristocratic London to Along the Thames. Walks cost £4.50 ($7) for adults, £3.50 ($6) for students and seniors, and children under 15 go free. Call for schedule; no reservations needed.

CANAL TOURS

London's canals were once the city's major highways. Since the Festival of Britain in 1951, some of the traditional painted canal boats have been resurrected for Venetian-style trips through the waterways. One of them is *Jason,* which takes you on a 90-minute trip from Bloomfield Road in Little Venice through the long Maida Hill tunnel under Edgware Road; through Regent's Park, passing the Mosque, the London Zoo, and Lord Snowdon's Aviary; past the Pirate's Castle to Camden Lock; and finally back to Little Venice. Passengers making the 45-minute one-way journey disembark at Camden Lock.

The season runs from March 28 to October, with trips at 10:30am, 12:30, and 2:30pm. In June, July, and August, an additional trip on weekends and bank holidays leaves at 4:30pm. A canalside seafood specialty restaurant/cafe at *Jason's* moorings offers lunches, dinners, and teas, all freshly made. Advance notice must be made for lunch service on the boat. The round-trip fare is £6 ($10) for adults and £4.50 ($7) for children and seniors. One-way fares are £5 ($8) for adults and £3.75 ($6) for children and seniors. Family tickets cost £17.50 ($28). For reservations, contact **Jason's Trip,** Jason's Wharf, opposite 60 Blomfield Rd., Little Venice, London W9 (☎ **0171/286-3428;** tube: Warwick Avenue).

8 Staying Active

Call **Sportsline** (☎ **0171/222-8000**) Monday to Friday from 10am to 6pm with any questions you may have about participatory sports in London.

Bicycling   The asphalt pavements and dense traffic of London make biking a challenge. But that doesn't deter dozens of hardy souls from taking two wheels onto the streets. **On Your Bike** rents 3-speed bikes for £12 ($19) a day. You'll find them at 52–54 Toley St., SE1 (☎ **0171/378-6669;** tube: London Bridge), and in Covent Garden at 14 Southampton St., WC2 (☎ **0171/497-2299;** tube: Covent Garden). Hours are Monday to Friday 9am to 6pm, Saturday 9:30am to 5:30pm. **The Mountain Bike and Ski Co.,** 18 Gillingham St., SW1 (☎ **0171/834-8933;** tube: Pimlico), rents both 18- and 21-speed bikes starting at £7 ($11) per day. The **London Cycling Campaign,** 3 Stamford St., SE1 (☎ **0171/928-7220;** tube: Waterloo), offers a *Cyclist's Route Map.*

Boating   You can rent a paddleboat or a rowboat from the boathouse (open March to October) on the north side of **Hyde Park's Serpentine.** Rowboats and sailing dinghies are also available in **Regent's Park** (☎ **0171/486-4759**) and at the **Royal Victoria Dock Project** (Royal Victoria Dock, Tidal Basin Rd., E16 (☎ **0171/ 511-2326**).

Health & Fitness Centers   If your hotel doesn't have or provide access to a gym, try one of the following facilities:

Jubilee Hall Sports Centre, 30 The Piazza, Covent Garden, WC2 (☎ **0171/ 836-4835;** tube: Covent Garden), is one of London's best and most centrally located sports centers, with the capital's largest weight room and an avid corps of body-building regulars. It also offers badminton, basketball, aerobics, gymnastics, martial arts, and soccer. Open Monday to Friday 7am to 10pm, Saturday and Sunday 10am to 5pm. Admission is £6.30 ($10) for use of the weight room, £5.30 ($9) for an aerobics class; both prices include use of sauna and showers.

If you're into a casual workout, try **Lambton Place Health Club,** Lambton Place, Westbourne Grove, W11 (☎ **0171/229-2291;** tube: Notting Hill Gate). For everything from a beauty studio to a sauna with a TV, go to **The Peak,** Hyatt Carlton Tower, 2 Cadogan Place, SW1 (☎ **0171/235-1234;** tube: Knightsbridge). An exclusive, women-only club is **The Sanctuary,** 12 Floral St., WC2 (☎ **0171/420-5151;** tube: Covent Garden). Another excellent facility is **The Savoy Fitness Gallery,** The Savoy, Strand, WC2 (☎ **0171/836-4343;** tube: Charing Cross). If you just want the basics in a pleasant gym, try the **Aquilla Health Club,** which looks like a Roman bath, 11 Thurloe Place, SW7 (☎ **0171/225-0225;** tube: South Kensington).

If you prefer to get fit through dancing, try **Danceworks,** 16 Balderton St., W1 (☎ **0171/629-6183;** tube: Marble Arch), which offers a wide-range of dance and fitness classes. **The Life Centre,** 15 Edge St., W8 (☎ **0171/221-4602;** tube: Notting Hill Gate), conducts yoga classes at all levels. For a small membership fee, plus class fees, you can take dance classes daily at the **Pineapple Dance Studio,** 7 Langley St., WC2 (☎ **0171/836-4004;** tube: Covent Garden), or at the **Pineapple Kensington,** 38–42 Harrington Rd., SW7 (☎ **0171/581-0466;** tube: Gloucester Road).

London has some good options for swimmers. The small but modern **Brittania Leisure Centre,** 40 Hyde Rd., N1 (☎ **0171/729-4485;** tube: Old Street) has a swimming pool with a wave machine, fountains, badminton-and-squash courts, and soccer-and-volleyball fields. Admission is £2.50 ($4) for adults, £1.50 ($2) for children. The complex is open Monday to Friday from 9am to 10pm and on Saturday and Sunday from 9am to 5:45pm. Other indoor pools with facilities are at **Chelsea Sports Centre,** Chelsea Manor Street, SW3 (☎ **0171/352-6985;** tube: Sloane Square); **Fulham Pools,** Normand Park, Lillie Road, SW6 (☎ **0171/385-7628;** tube: West Kensington); and **Golden Lane Pool,** Golden Lane, EC1 (☎ **0171/250-1464;** tube: Old Street).

Horseback Riding The **Ross Nyde Riding School,** 8 Bathurst Mews, W2 (☎ **0171/262-3791;** tube: Lancaster Gate), is a public stable in Hyde Park. The school has 16 horses that are reliable and not easily spooked by traffic or other disruptions. It's recommended that you go riding early in the morning to avoid crowds in the park. On weekdays (except Monday), the stable opens at 7am, with rides leaving each hour during the week until dark. On the weekend, scheduled rides are Saturday and Sunday at 10 and 11am, Saturday at 2 and 3pm, and Sunday at 1:30 and 2:30pm. A group lesson is £25 ($40), a private lesson £30 ($48). The **Stag Lodge Stables,** Robin Hood Gate, Richmond Park, SW15 (☎ **0181/974-6066**), provides a more pastoral setting. They also have a pony club for children, the Red Riders, that meets on Saturday.

In-Line Skating In-line skating is very popular are in London, whose parks are great places to skate. Rental skates are available at **The London Blade Skate Centre,** 229 Brompton Rd., SW3 (☎ **0171/581-2039;** tube: Knightsbridge), and at **Road Runner,** Lancaster Rd. at Portobello Rd., W11 (☎ **0171/792-0584;** tube: Ladbroke Grove).

Running Some of the more scenic routes for joggers and runners are in London's Royal Parks, including Green Park, Hyde Park, Regent's Park, and St. James's Park. The most bucolic routes are in Hampstead Heath, Hyde Park, and Regent's Park. Most of the routes are about 2 miles in length and can be extended to 4 miles by combining two routes. They're not only scenic, but also fairly free of traffic; some pass historic sites such as Buckingham Palace, as well as some less-noted but still splendid residences. One of the more scenic routes in all of London is the loop that borders the Grand Union Canal. This path, which is for the exclusive use of joggers, runs between Regent's Park and Little Venice and takes you through St. John's Wood.

Of course, as in most places today, it's best not to jog after dark. For information on where to jog, call **London Hash House Harriers** (☎ **0181/995-7879**). For a small fee, they'll arrange hour-long runs through interesting parts of town.

Tennis   There are two places where outdoor courts are available to the public: **Holland Park,** Holland Park, W8 (☎ **0171/602-2226;** tube: Holland Park), has six outdoor courts; you must book in person, as priority is given to local residents. **Regent's Park Tennis,** Outer Circle, Regent's Park, NW1 (☎ **0171/724-0643;** tube: Regent's Park), has one floodlit court.

9 Spectator Sports

Sportsline (☎ **0171/222-8000**) can answer questions about spectator sports Monday to Friday from 10am to 6pm. Check the papers or call the venues listed below for schedules and ticket information.

Cricket   In summer, attention turns to cricket, played either at **Lord's,** St. John's Wood Road, NW8 (☎ **0171/289-1611;** tube: St. John's Wood), in north London; or at the somewhat less prestigious **Oval Cricket Ground,** The Oval, Kennington, London SE11 (☎ **0171/582-6660;** tube: The Oval), in south London. During the international test matches between Britain and Australia, the West Indies, India, or New Zealand (as important as the World Series in the United States), Britons go into a collective trance, with everyone glued to the nearest radio or TV.

Football (Soccer)   England's soccer (called "football") season runs from August to April and attracts fiercely loyal fans. Games usually start at 3pm and are great to watch, but the stands can get very rowdy, so think about reserving seats. Centrally located first-division football clubs include **Arsenal,** Arsenal Stadium, Avenell Road, N5 (☎ **0171/704-4000,** box office 0171/704-4040; tube: Arsenal); **Tottenham Hotspur,** 748 High Rd., N17 (☎ **0181/365-5000,** box office 0171/420-0234; tube: Seven Sisters); and **Chelsea,** Stamford Bridge, Fulham Road, SW6 (☎ **0171/385-5545,** box office 0891/121-011; tube: Fulham Broadway). Tickets cost £22 to £50 ($35 to $80). The country's most visible site of world-class soccer matches is **Wembley Stadium,** Wembley, Middlesex (☎ **0181/902-8833;** tube: Wembley Park), about 6 miles north of London's center.

Horse Racing   Within easy reach of central London are horse-racing tracks at Kempton Park, Sandown Park, and the most famous of them all, Epsom, where the Derby is the main feature of the meeting in early June. Racing takes place both midweek and on weekends, but not continuously. Contact **United Racecourses Ltd.** (☎ **01372/470047**) for information on the next races on one of these tracks.

Tennis   Fans from around the world focus on **Wimbledon** (tube: Southfields) for 2 weeks (usually late June to early July). At the All England Lawn Tennis & Croquet Club, you'll see some of the world's greatest tennis players in action. The famous annual championships span roughly the last week in June to the first week in July, with matches lasting from about 2pm until dark. (The gates open at 10:30am.) Tickets usually range in price from £8 to £54 ($13 to $86). Center court seats are sold by lottery. A limited number of tickets for the outside courts are available at the gate. For recorded ticket information, call ☎ **0181/946-2244,** or send a self-addressed stamped envelope (only from August to December) to the **All England Lawn Tennis & Croquet Club,** P.O. Box 98, Church Road, Wimbledon, SW19 5AE.

The Royal Tournament   It's hard to find a comprehensive tag for the Royal Tournament, which some viewers describe as a series of indoor parades paying homage to the traditions and majesty of the British armed forces. Performed every year in late July, usually for 12 days, this long-running spectacle attracts an enthusiastic audience. The show includes massed bands presenting stirring music, the Royal Navy field-gun competition, the Royal Air Force with their dogs, the Royal Marines in action, the King's Troop Royal Horse Artillery, the Household Cavalry, and a series of visiting military-style exhibitions from throughout the British Commonwealth. There are two performances Tuesday to Saturday, at 2 and 7:30pm, except Sunday evening and Monday afternoon, at the Earl's Court Exhibition Centre, Warwick Road, SW5 (tube: Earl's Court). Seats cost from £5 to £25 ($8 to $40), with discounts of around 20% for children 5 to 14 and seniors 60 and over. For tickets and other information, contact the **Royal Tournament Exhibition Centre,** Warwick Road, London SW5 9TA (☎ 0171/370-8206; tube: Earl's Court).

London Walks

The best way to discover London is on foot. A jumble of ancient mews and antique-filled alleyways, it's a city that's easy and fun to get lost in. Since many of the major sights are concentrated in specific areas of the city—official London in Westminster and Whitehall, gentlemanly London in St. James's, and so on—walking is a good way to take in a number of London sights at one time.

For additional information on many of the sights mentioned below, see chapter 6.

WALKING TOUR 1
Where London Was Born: The City

Start: The southern terminus of London Bridge. Tube: London Bridge or Monument.
Finish: St. Paul's Cathedral. Tube: St. Paul's.
Time: About 3 hours, excluding interior visits.
Best Times: Weekday mornings, when the financial district is functioning but churches aren't crowded.
Worst Times: Weekends, when the district is almost deserted.

Encompassing but a small patch of urban real estate, the area known as the City—the original one-square mile that the Romans called "Londinium"—offers the densest concentration of historic and cultural monuments in Britain. It's also one of the financial capitals of the world—Britain's Wall Street, as it were.

Our tour begins on the southern edge of the Thames, directly to the west of London Bridge, one of the world's most famous bridges. Facing the Thames rises the bulk of:

1. **Southwark Cathedral.** When built in the 1200s, it was an outpost of the faraway diocese of Winchester. Deconsecrated after Henry VIII's Reformation, it later housed bakeries and pigpens. Much of what you see is a result of a sorely needed 19th-century rebuilding, but its Gothic interior, with its multiple commemorative plaques, gives an idea of the religious power of the medieval church.

After your visit, walk across the famous:

2. **London Bridge.** Originally designed by Henry de Colechurch under the patronage of Henry II in 1176 but replaced several times since, it's the most famous bridge in the world. Until 1729,

it was the only bridge across the Thames. During the Middle Ages the bridge was lined with shops; houses crowded its edges. The bridge served as the showplace of the severed heads—preserved in tar—of enemies of the British monarchs. (The most famous of these was the head of Sir Thomas More, the highly vocal lord chancellor, beheaded in 1535.) The bridge built from 1825 to 1831 was moved to the United States; it's now a tourist attraction in Lake Havasu, Arizona. The current bridge was completed in 1973.

After crossing the river, head east along Monument Street, the steep cobbled street that descends to the right. Detour down it a short distance to read the commemorative plaques attached to the:

3. **Monument.** Commemorating the Great Fire of 1666, this soaring Doric column is appropriately capped with a carved version of a flaming urn. The disaster it memorializes started in a bakery in nearby Pudding Lane; the fire raged for 4 days and nights, and destroyed 80% of the City. A cramped and foreboding set of stairs spirals up to the top. It's a tough climb, but the view of the cityscape, so heavily influenced after the fire by architect Sir Christopher Wren (who also designed the Monument itself), is worth it.

Retrace your steps toward London Bridge, but this time head northwest along King William Street until you reach the Bank underground station, within a stone's throw of some of England's most powerful financial institutions. As you reach Mansion House Place, make a left, looking right to:

4. **Mansion House,** the official residence of the Lord Mayor, built between 1739 and 1752 and designed by George Dance the Elder. A rather optimistic pediment frieze depicts London defeating *Envy* and ushering in *Plenty.* The mansion's architectural showcase is the Egyptian Hall. Official banquets are staged here, but unless you get an invitation, you'll have to confine your viewing to the exterior.

From the mansion, proceed into a small passageway, St. Stephen's Row, and at the end make a left into Walbrook, the site of a polluted brook that was paved over in medieval times. On the left is the entrance to:

5. **St. Stephen Walbrook.** One of Sir Christopher Wren's finest works, the splendid dome of this church served as a model for St. Paul's Cathedral. The British sculptor Henry Moore carved the travertine altar under the dome in 1986.

Now walk across Walbrook and head into Bucklersbury, continuing until you reach Queen Victoria Street. Turn left, walk one block, make another left and climb the steps outside the major entrance to Temple Court. Here on your left you can peer over the railings at:

6. **The Temple of Mithras,** Queen Victoria St., London's archeological jewel. Although shaped like a miniature Christian church, the temple was held sacred by the Mithraic cult, which had its origins in Iran and reached the Roman empire prior to Christianity. For more details, see "Roman London" in "More Central London Attractions," in chapter 6.

After you've looked around, walk back to the Bank underground. Here, head east along Cornhill, which becomes Leadenhall Street. Just after the intersection with Gracechurch Street, behind Lloyd's of London, you'll come upon:

7. **Leadenhall Market,** the City's central and conspicuously non-financial market. Horace Jones designed these curved arcades in 1881, which have been home ever since to a colorful collection of butchers, fishmongers, cheesemongers, and flowermongers, as well as pubs and restaurants.

Once you're finished buying or browsing, return to Gracechurch Street and walk north, then right (east) on Leadenhall Street. Take the second right (south) on Lime Street, where you can admire the soaring and iconoclastically modern:

1. Southwark Cathedral
2. London Bridge
3. Monument
4. Mansion House
5. Church of St. Stephen Walbrook
6. The Temple of Mithras
7. Leadenhall Market
8. Lloyd's of London Building
9. St. Helen Bishopsgate
10. NatWest Tower
11. London Stock Exchange
12. Royal Exchange
13. Bank of England
14. St. Margaret, Lothbury
15. Guildhall
16. Museum of London
17. St. Paul's Cathedral

☕ "Take a Break" Stop
Church ⬛   Tube Station ⊖

8. **Lloyd's of London Building.** Designed by Richard Rogers in 1986, this striking glass, steel, and concrete structure in the heart of ancient Roman London is the most recent home of Lloyd's of London, founded in the 1680s as a marine insurer. Today it is perhaps the most famous—and financially troubled—insurer in the world. Immense underwriting losses in the early 1990s threatened the company's survival. The viewing gallery and exhibit on the role of Lloyd's past and present have been closed since a massive IRA bomb went off in Bishopsgate in 1992.

Nearby are the London Metal Exchange, the London Futures and Options Exchange, and other financial institutions whose clout is felt around the world.

Next follow Lime Street back onto Leadenhall and turn left. Take the first right on Bishopsgate, then the second right, and turn into an alleyway known as Great St. Helen's. Toward the end, you'll find the largest surviving medieval church in London:

9. **St. Helen Bishopsgate,** built in the 1400s and dedicated to St. Helen, the legendary British mother of the Roman emperor Constantine. Fashionable during the Elizabethan and Jacobean periods, its interior monuments, memorials, and grave markers are of special interest.

Exit back onto Bishopsgate and turn right (north). Two blocks later, turn left onto Wormwood Street. Then take the first left, Old Broad Street. Towering above you rises the modern bulk of the tallest building in Britain and the second-highest in Europe, the:

10. **NatWest Tower.** Richard Seifert designed these headquarters of National Westminster Bank in 1981. Its massive concrete foundations are built on top of mostly impervious clay, allowing the building to sway gently in the wind. Unfortunately, since it has no observation tower open to the public, you'll have to admire it from afar.

Continue south along Old Broad Street, noticing on your right the imposing headquarters of the:

11. **London Stock Exchange.** Built in the early 1960s to replace its outmoded original quarters, this institution has become much less boisterous since most of the City's financial operations went modern in 1986, from face-to-face agreements between brokers to computerized dealmaking, with the exchange functioning as an electronic clearinghouse.

TAKE A BREAK Continue southwest along Old Broad Street until it merges with Threadneedle Street. Cross Threadneedle Street, walk a few paces to your left, and head south along the narrow confines of Finch Lane. Cross busy Cornhill to the south side of the street. Follow it east to St. Michael's Alley to **Jamaica Wine House,** St. Michael's Alley, EC3 (☎ **0171/626-9496**), one of Europe's oldest coffeehouses. Once a favorite hangout of London merchants and the sea captains who imported their goods, today it also dispenses ale, lager, wine, and bar snacks.

After tippling, take time to explore the medieval maze of narrow alleyways that provide shelter from roaring weekday traffic. Then head back to the major boulevard, Cornhill, just north of your refueling stop. Here, near the junction of five major streets, rises the:

12. **Royal Exchange.** Designed by William Tite in the early 1840s, its imposing neoclassical pediment is inset with Richard Westmacott's sculpture of *Commerce*.

Launched by a partnership of merchants and financiers during the Elizabethan Age, the Royal Exchange was a direct attempt to lure European banking and trading functions from Antwerp (then the financial capital of northern Europe) to London. Frenzied trading and auctioning of raw materials continued here until 1982, when the building became the headquarters of the London International Financial Futures Exchange (LIFFE).

On the opposite side of Threadneedle Street rises the massive bulk of the:

13. **Bank of England.** Originally established "for the Publick Good and Benefit of Our People" in a charter granted in 1694 by William and Mary, it's a treasure trove of gold bullion, British banknotes, and historical archives. The only part of this massive building open to the public is the **Bank of England Museum,** whose entrance is on a narrow side street, Bartholomew Lane (☎ 0171/ 601-4878; open Monday through Friday from 10am to 5pm; free admission).

From the Bank of England, walk northwest along Prince's Street to Lothbury. On the northeast corner of the intersection rises yet another church by Sir Christopher Wren, this one completed in 1690:

14. **St. Margaret Lothbury.** Filled with statues of frolicking cupids, elaborately carved screens, and a soaring eagle near the altar, the interior is well worth a visit.

Now walk west on Lothbury, which will become Gresham Street. After passing a handful of alleyways, on your right you'll see the gardens and the grand historical facade of the:

15. **Guildhall.** The power base for the Lord Mayor of London since the 12th century (continually rebuilt and enlarged since), Guildhall was the site of endless power negotiations throughout the Middle Ages between the English kings (headquartered outside the City at Westminster) and the guilds, associations, and brotherhoods of the City's merchants and financiers. Today, the rituals associated with the Lord Mayor are almost as elaborate as those of the monarchy itself. The Guildhall's medieval crypt is the largest in London; its east facade was rebuilt by Sir Christopher Wren after the Great Fire of 1666.

Continue westward on Gresham and turn right onto Wood Street. Walk north to London Wall, then left for about a block. On the right you'll see the modern:

16. **Museum of London.** Located in new quarters built in 1975, it contains London memorabilia gathered from several earlier museums, as well as one of the best collections of period costumes in the world. Built on top of the western gate of the ancient Roman colony of Londinium, the museum has a strong collection of archeological remnants unearthed during centuries of city construction projects, as well as dioramas portraying the Great Fire and Victorian prison cells.

Now head south on Aldersgate, which quickly becomes St. Martins-le-Grand. After you merge with Newgate Street, the enormous stately dome of one of Europe's most important churches slowly appears in front of you:

17. **St. Paul's Cathedral.** Sir Christopher Wren's undisputed masterpiece is known to many as the site of the ill-fated wedding of Prince Charles and Princess Diana. St. Paul's also held the state funerals of Nelson, Wellington, and Churchill, and it served as an inspiration to a generation of Londoners who survived the bombings of World War II. The only cathedral in England to be constructed with a dome and the country's only church built in the English baroque style, St. Paul's was also the first English cathedral designed and built by a single architect.

From St. Paul's, you can catch the Underground's Central Line to your next destination.

WALKING TOUR 2
Official London: Westminster & Whitehall

Start: Entrance of the Tate Gallery. Tube: Pimlico.
Finish: National Portrait Gallery, Trafalgar Square. Tube: Charing Cross or Leicester Square.
Time: About 3 hours, excluding interior visits.
Best Times: Monday through Thursday, when Parliament is in session.
Worst Times: Evenings and Sunday, when the district becomes almost deserted except for fast-moving traffic.

This tour will take you on a route parallel to the Thames, immersing you in some of the most visible symbols of England's historic democracy and monarchy.

After leaving the Pimlico Station, continue east along Bessborough Street, which becomes Bessborough Gardens as it leads toward the Thames and the Vauxhall Bridge. Once you reach Millbank, fronting the Thames, head north (left) along this major artery. On your left you can begin your tour in front of the grand Palladian entrance to one of the finest art museums in the world, the:

1. **Tate Gallery.** Built in 1897 and donated to London by the scion of a sugar baron, it's packed with the works of virtually every great painter in British history. You'll want to return to enjoy the collection at your leisure, but for the moment, walk north along the west bank of the Thames (known at this point as Millbank), with the Houses of Parliament looming ahead of you. Just past Lambeth Bridge, turn inland onto Dean Stanley Street and after 1 block you'll arrive at:

2. **Smith Square** and its centerpiece **St. John's Church.** Built in a highly personal neoclassical style by Thomas Archer in 1728, the church was heavily damaged by bombing in 1941. Since rebuilt, it now serves as a concert venue for some of the world's most renowned musicians.

Retrace your steps to the Thames and turn left (north) in the direction of the Houses of Parliament. Enter the verdant triangular-shaped park at the southern entrance, a tranquil oasis rich with sculpture, the:

3. **Victoria Tower Gardens.** Here you'll find a 1915 replica of Auguste Rodin's 1895 masterpiece *The Burghers of Calais,* and A. G. Walker's monument to Emmeline Pankhurst, an early-20th-century champion of British suffragists who was frequently imprisoned for her politics.

Near the northern perimeter of the garden, detour inland by turning left on Great College Street for about a block and on your right notice:

4. **Abbey Garden.** Associated with nearby Westminster Abbey and continuously cultivated over the past 900 years, it's the oldest garden in England, rich with lavender and ecclesiastical ruins. Even if the gate is locked, parts of this charming historic oddity are visible from the street outside.

Retrace your steps along Great College Street to Millbank (which on some maps might be referred to as Abingdon Street) and turn left (north), remaining on the side of Millbank opposite the Houses of Parliament. The tower on your left, completed in 1366 by Edward III for storing treasures, is the:

5. **Jewel Tower.** This is all that remains of the domestic portions of the once-mighty Palace of Westminster. A small museum details the construction of the Houses of Parliament.

Now continue north along Millbank (or Abingdon Street) for 2 blocks, passing on your left the semicircular apse of the rear side of one of Britain's most densely packed artistic and cultural highlights:

Walking Tour—Westminster & Whitehall

1. Tate Gallery
2. Smith Square, St. John's Church
3. Victoria Tower Gardens
4. Abbey Garden
5. Jewel Tower
6. Westminster Abbey
7. Sanctuary
8. St. Margaret's Church
9. Houses of Parliament
10. Big Ben
11. Westminster Bridge
12. Cabinet War Rooms
13. Downing Street
14. Horse Guards
15. Banqueting House
16. Old Admirality Building
17. Statue of Charles I
18. Trafalgar Square
19. National Gallery
20. St. Martin-in-the-Fields
21. National Portrait Gallery

✝ Church
⊖ Tube Station
🔵 "Take a Break" Stop

E-0151

6. **Westminster Abbey,** one of the most majestic and frequently visited sights in Europe. Completed in 1245, it's the spiritual heart of London, steeped in enough tradition, majesty, sorrow, and blood to merit a volume of its own. Turn left, skirting the building's northern flank, and enter through its western facade.

   After your visit, leave the abbey through the Cloisters, emerging into Dean's Yard, site of Westminster School. Look for an arch straight ahead on the right, which leads to the west door of the abbey and the:

7. **Sanctuary.** Consisting of two streets, called Broad Sanctuary and Little Sanctuary, the Sanctuary in medieval days was a jumble of buildings and narrow winding lanes. Enclosed by the precinct wall of Westminster, the complex offered safe haven for the downtrodden and occasional political refugees. Over time, the Sanctuary gained a reputation for sheltering a "mire of cutthroats, whores, pickpockets, and murderers." It became so disease-ridden and crime-infested that James I ordered it closed. Although slums existed here for centuries, urban renewal has successfully removed all remnants of its more notorious days.

   After a walk around, look to your right, just beyond the abbey's north transept, to see the much-restored:

8. **St. Margaret's Church.** Built between 1504 and 1523, it is the parish church for the House of Commons. It contains a noteworthy collection of stained-glass windows as well as the body of Sir Walter Raleigh (who was beheaded just outside its front entrance). Both John Milton (1656) and Winston Churchill (1908) were married here.

   Exiting from St. Margaret's, you'll see the Neo-Gothic grandeur of the:

9. **Houses of Parliament.** The mother of all Parliaments was built between 1840 and 1860 by architects Sir Charles Barry and Augustus Pugin (both of whom are said to have suffered several nervous breakdowns and early deaths as a result of the overwork and stress involved in its building). The Houses cover 8 acres and proudly display perhaps the greatest volume of ornate stonework in the world. Your tour of the interior (which you might choose to reserve for another day) begins at the base of:

10. **Big Ben.** The tall clocktower of the Houses of Parliament is located near the building's northwest corner (not that you could miss it!). Just as the Eiffel Tower is the symbol of Paris, Big Ben is the international icon of London. Completed in 1858–59, the 316-foot clock tower takes its name from Sir Benjamin Hall, the first commissioner of public works and evidently a gentleman of considerable proportions. Perhaps not inappropriately, the clock mechanism in this tower alone weighs 5 tons. Big Ben kept time for 117 years before succumbing to "metal fatigue" in 1976, at which time major repairs were needed to keep it running. When the House of Commons is in session, the light above the clock is lit.

    One of the best views of the Houses of Parliament can be enjoyed from:

11. **Westminster Bridge,** built in 1862 in cast iron and one of the most ornate bridges in London. To reach the bridge from Big Ben, turn right on Bridge Street. The western base of the bridge, aptly named Westminster Pier, is the departure point for many boat trips down the Thames; see "Sightseeing & Boat Tours Along the Thames" in chapter 6.

    Now retrace your footsteps along Bridge Street, passing Big Ben, and take the second right along the busy thoroughfare of Parliament Street. Take the first left along King Charles Street where, at Clive Steps on the left, you'll reach the:

12. **Cabinet War Rooms.** This unpretentious handful of rooms served as the meeting place for Churchill's cabinet during World War II, the site where many

of the statesman's most stirring speeches were crafted. The rooms were built 17 feet underground for protection from Nazi air raids; a half-dozen of them are open to visitors.

Retrace your steps back to Parliament Street, turning left (north) and left again at:

13. Downing Street. Although security might prevent you from getting a close look, no. 10 is the famed official residence of the British prime minister; no. 11, the residence of the chancellor of the exchequer; and no. 12, the office of the chief government whip—the member of Parliament responsible for maintaining discipline and cooperation among party members in the House of Commons.

Continue north along Parliament Street, which becomes Whitehall near Downing Street. Here both sides of the street reflect the administrative soul of Britain; meetings and negotiations inside these majestic buildings influence politics around the world. One of the most noteworthy of these is the:

14. Horse Guards. Completed in 1760 and designed by William Kent, it's one of the most symmetrical and imposing of the many buildings along Whitehall. The ceremonial Mounting of the Guard is held here (the first step of an equestrian ceremony that ends with the Changing of the Guard in front of Buckingham Palace; see chapter 6 for details).

Across the avenue rise the pure proportions of one of London's most superlative examples of Palladian architecture, the:

15. Banqueting House. Commissioned by James I and designed by Inigo Jones in the early 1600s, it's one of the most aesthetically perfect buildings in England. Its facade was the backdrop for one of the blackest events in British history: the beheading of Charles I by members of Parliament. The ceilings in the magnificent dining hall were painted by Peter Paul Rubens.

Continuing north 1 block along Whitehall, you'll come to a great place for a breather:

> 🗩 **TAKE A BREAK   The Clarence Pub,** 53 Whitehall, W1 (☎ **0171/930-4808**). One of London's most famous pubs, beloved by Parliamentarians throughout England. Opened in the 18th century, it has been quenching the thirsts of government administrators ever since. With oak ceiling beams and battered wooden tables ringed by churchlike pews, at least a half-dozen real ales are on tap, complemented by the usual pub grub. A restaurant serves hardier fare.

After drinks with perhaps a few members of Parliament, notice the building almost directly across Whitehall, the:

16. Old Admiralty Building, Spring Gardens. Designed in 1725 by Sir Thomas Ripley (and strictly off-limits except for official business), it served for almost two centuries as the administrative headquarters of the British Navy until it was replaced by new quarters between the wars.

Continue north until you see what may be the finest and most emotive equestrian statue in London, the:

17. Statue of Charles I. On an island in the middle of speeding traffic, it commemorates the tragic fate of this British king and signals the beginning of:

18. Trafalgar Square. The grandest plaza in London, it is centered around a soaring monument to Lord Nelson, the hero of the Battle of Trafalgar who defeated Napoléon's navy off the coast of Spain in 1805. Against the square's northern perimeter rises the grand neoclassical:

19. National Gallery. The collection—one of the finest in the world of Western art—definitely merits a detailed tour of its own.

The church that flanks the eastern edge of Trafalgar Square is one of London's most famous:

20. St. Martin-in-the-Fields. Designed in the style of Sir Christopher Wren in 1726 by James Gibbs, it has a Corinthian portico and a steeple whose form inspired the architects of many American churches. The christening place of Charles II and the burial place of his infamous but fun-loving mistress, Nell Gwynne, the church also boasts a noted orchestra.

Finally, for an overview of the faces instrumental in British and world history, walk to the right (eastern) side of the National Gallery, where the greatest repository of portraits in Europe awaits your inspection at the:

21. National Portrait Gallery, 2 St. Martin's Place. They're all here: kings, cardinals, mistresses, playwrights, poets, coquettes, dilettantes, and other names rich in historical connotations (and modern ones—look for the likes of Paul McCartney, Sir Richard Attenborough, and others on the first floor). The museum celebrates the portraits' subjects more than their authors. An hour or two here is a great way to wind up your tour.

WALKING TOUR 3
Aristocratic St. James's

Start: Admiralty Arch. Tube: Charing Cross.
Finish: Buckingham Palace. Tube: St. James's Park or Green Park.
Time: About 2 hours, not including stops.
Best Time: Before 3pm.
Worst Time: After dark.

Incorporating neighborhoods reserved almost since their development for the British aristocracy, this walking tour includes many of the grandest sights of the 18th- and 19th-century imperial England.

After leaving Charing Cross Station, walk left (west) along the Strand toward the Mall, Trafalgar Square on your right, and look straight ahead for the monumental eastern entrance of the:

1. Admiralty Arch. Commissioned by Queen Victoria's son, King Edward VII (who died before it was completed), it was designed in 1911 by Sir Aston Webb. Piercing its center are a quintet of arches faced with Portland stone, marking the first (and widest) stage of a majestic processional route leading from Buckingham Palace eastward to St. Paul's Cathedral. The centermost of the five arches is opened only for ceremonial occasions; the two side arches are for vehicular traffic, and the two smallest arches for pedestrians.

Pass beneath the arch and enter the wide panoramic thoroughfare, which will eventually lead to Buckingham Palace. With your back to the Admiralty Arch, stretching out before you is:

2. The Mall. Lined with even rows of plane trees, The Mall was originally the garden of nearby St. James's Palace and host to aristocratic games of *paille maille* (a precursor of croquet) by the courtiers of Charles II. The present planned avenue was designed by Sir Aston Webb as a memorial to the recently departed Queen Victoria and was opened in 1911. The Mall is often closed to traffic on Sundays, when it becomes a pedestrian extension of adjacent St. James's Park.

Walking Tour—St. James's

Charing Cross Station

Hungerford Footbridge

Thames

Victoria Embankment

Westminster Bridge

start here

Trafalgar Sq.

Northumberland Ave.

Whitehall

Horse Guards Ave.

Richmond Terr.

Downing St.

Parliament St.

King Charles St.

St. Margaret

Parliament Square

National Gallery

Admiralty Arch

Horse Guards Rd.

Cockspur St.

St. Albans St.

Haymarket

Charles St.

Lower Regent St.

Pall Mall

Carlton House Terr.

The Mall

Carlton House Terr.

St. James's Park

Old Queen St.

Queen St.

Tothill St.

St. James's Park

Jermyn St.

Sackville St.

Piccadilly

Duke St.

Bury St. St.

King St. St.

St. James's St.

Marlborough Rd.

Cleveland Row

Marlborough Row

Stable Yard Row

On Anne's Gate

Birdcage Walk

Petty France

Vigo St.

Old Bond St.

Albemarle St.

Dover St.

Berkeley St.

Stratton St.

Piccadilly

Green Park

Green Park

Queen's Walk

Queen's Gardens

Queen Victoria Memorial

Constitution Hill

The Spur

The Mall

finish here

Palace Rd.

E-0152

1 Admiralty Arch
2 The Mall
3 New and Old Admiralties
4 Carlton House Terrace
5 The Duke of York Steps and the Duke of York Monument
6 Waterloo Place
7 Statue of Edward VII
8 No. 4 Carlton House Gardens
9 Pall Mall
10 St. James's Square
11 Jermyn Street
12 St. James's Street, White's
13 St. James's Palace
14 Clarence House
15 Lancaster House
16 Buckingham Palace

"Take a Break" Stop
Tube Station
Information

200 m
220 y
0

N

The Mall's expanse is a favorite exercise area for London's equestrians and their mounts.

Immediately to your left (with your back to the Admiralty Arch) are the interconnected buildings of the:

3. **New and Old Admiralties.** Important nerve centers of the British military, they have seen their share of drama since the early 18th century.

As you stroll southwest down The Mall, on your right will be one of the most regal ensembles of town houses in London:

4. **Carlton House Terrace.** These buildings replaced the once-palatial home of the 18th-century prince regent, who later became George III. He built, and subsequently demolished at staggering expense, the most beautiful private home in Britain. Only the columns were saved, which were later recycled into the portico of Trafalgar Square's National Gallery. The resulting row of ivory-colored neoclassical town houses was one of architect John Nash's last works before he died, much maligned from financial scandal in 1835. Today, in addition to art galleries and cultural institutions, Carlton House Terrace houses the headquarters of one of the most highly reputed scientific bodies in the world, the Royal Society.

Midway along the length of Carlton House Terrace, its pristine neoclassical expanse is pierced by:

5. **The Duke of York Column and Steps.** Built in honor of the second son of George III, this massive sculpture was funded by withholding 1 day's pay from every soldier in the British Empire. The resulting column was chiseled from pink granite, and the statue created by Sir Richard Westmacott in 1834. Contemporary wits, aware that the duke died massively in debt, joked that placing his effigy on a column was the only way to keep him out of his creditors' grasp. The soaring column and monument (the statue weighs 7 tons) dominates the square it prefaces:

6. **Waterloo Place.** One of the most prestigious examples of urban planning in London, it symbolizes both aristocratic elegance and nostalgia for England's great military victories over Napoléon. No. 107 (designed in 1830 and one of the finest examples of early-19th-century neoclassical architecture in London) is headquarters for one of the most distinguished gentlemen's clubs in Britain, the Athenaeum Club.

Notice, within Waterloo Place, the:

7. **Statue of Edward VII.** Crafted in 1921 by Sir Bertram Mackennal, it honors the man who ushered in the Edwardian Age and was responsible for much of the grand neighborhood northeast of Buckingham Palace. The son of long-lived Victoria, he ascended the throne at the age of 60, only 9 years before his death. As if to create a sense of historical perspective, a statue dedicated to the victims of the Crimean War, part of which honors Florence Nightingale, stands at the opposite end of Waterloo Place.

History buffs especially will appreciate Carlton House Gardens, which runs into Carlton House Terrace's western end. Devotees of French history in particular should read the plaques that identify:

8. **No. 4 Carlton House Gardens,** the World War II London headquarters of Charles de Gaulle's French government in exile and the site of many of his French-language radio broadcasts to the French underground. (A second facade of this same building faces The Mall, on the opposite side of the block.)

One of the streets intersecting Waterloo Place is an avenue replete with exclusive private clubs. Not to be confused with the longer and broader expanse of The Mall, this is:

9. Pall Mall. Note that Londoners usually say "pell mell" (rather than "paul mawl"). Membership in many of the clubs here is very prestigious and sought-after; wait lists of up to a decade for membership to the most exclusive of them are not uncommon (and many on these lists will never get in).

Walk west for a block along Pall Mall (beware of the dangerously fast one-way traffic) and take the first right (north) into the elegant 18th-century precincts of:

10. St. James's Square. Laid out in the 1660s, it was built on land donated by the first earl of St. Albans, Henry Jermyn, a friend of the widow of Charles I and the future king Charles II. Magnificent private houses, occupied by noble families wishing to live near the seat of royal power at nearby St. James's Palace, originally lined the square on all sides. Of special interest are no. 10 (Chatham House), the private residence of three British prime ministers, the last of whom was Queen Victoria's nemesis, William Gladstone. At no. 32, General Eisenhower and his subordinates planned the 1942 invasion of North Africa and the 1944 Allied invasion of Normandy. At no. 16, a blood-stained officer delivered the announcement of Wellington's climactic defeat of Napoléon's forces at Waterloo (along with the captured eagle-shaped symbols of Napoléon's army).

After you circumnavigate the square, exit at its northern edge via Duke of York Street. One block later, turn left onto the most prestigious shopping street in London:

11. Jermyn Street. Expensive, upscale, and politely attended shops here are the best of British tradition and luxury goods.

Follow Jermyn to Duke Street, where you can:

🍽 **TAKE A BREAK   Green's Champagne and Oyster Bar,** 36 Duke St., SW1 (☎ **0171/930-4566**). Its facade and paneled decor might call to mind gentlemen's clubs you've already passed in the neighborhood. This one, however, welcomes non-members, and many clients are female. From the battered bar you can order spirits and wine, as well as platters of oysters, caviar, shrimp, and crab (to take at the bar or a table) and a wide variety of English appetizers and main courses. The place is especially popular at lunchtime.

Exit from Duke Street onto Jermyn Street, turn right (west) and continue along the shops. Two blocks later, turn left onto:

12. St. James's Street. It too contains its share of private clubs, the most fashionable of which is arguably **White's,** at no. 37, designed in 1788 by James Wyatt. Prince Charles' friends held his stag party here the night before his marriage to Lady Diana. Past members have included Evelyn Waugh (who took refuge here from his literary "hounds of modernity"). Even should you be recommended for membership (which is unlikely), the wait list is 8 years.

At the bottom (southern end) of St. James's Street is one of the most historic buildings in London:

13. St. James's Palace. Birthplace of many British monarchs, it served as the principal royal residence from 1698 (when Whitehall Palace burned down) until the ascent of Victoria—who preferred Buckingham Palace—in 1837. Originally enlarged from a Tudor core built by Henry VIII for one of his ill-fated queens, it was altered by Sir Christopher Wren in 1703. The palace, rich in history, gave its name to the entire neighborhood.

All the world seemingly viewed this palace on TV during the late summer funeral of Princess Diana in 1997. The cortege began at her former residence, Kensington Palace, but stopped at St. James's Palace, the present residence of

Charles. At St. James's, the cortege picked up not only Charles, but the young princes Harry and William, along with Prince Philip and Diana's brother, Earl Spencer.

After your visit, walk southwest along Cleveland Row, then turn left (southeast) onto Stable Yard Row. On your left rises the side of:

14. **Clarence House.** Designed in 1829 by John Nash, it's the official London home of the Queen Mother. On the opposite side of Stable Yard Row rises the side of the decidedly formal:

15. **Lancaster House.** Designed in 1827 by Benjamin Wyatt, it has been known variously as York House and Stafford House. Chopin performed his ballads and nocturnes for Victoria here. Edward VIII lived here during the renunciation of his throne (required as a precondition for his marriage to the notorious Mrs. Simpson). Heavily damaged by World War II bombings, it has since been gracefully restored and furnished in the French Louis XV style, and it serves as a setting for state receptions and dinners.

Within a few steps you arrive at the multiple plane trees of The Mall; here, turn right for a view of the front of fabled:

16. **Buckingham Palace.** Known the world over, the official London residence of every British monarch since Victoria is many things: regal, mysterious, magical and, yes, vital. Its present occupant, of course, is Elizabeth II. Tours are offered in the summer months; see chapter 6.

WALKING TOUR 4
Chelsea, London's Quintessential Village

Start: Sloane Square. Tube: Sloane Square.
Finish: National Army Museum. Tube: Sloane Square.
Time: About 2 hours, not counting stops.
Best Times: Wednesday through Saturday from 10am to 4pm when most attractions are open. Saturday morning is best for shopping along King's Road.
Worst Times: After 5pm and on Sunday when shops and most interiors are closed (although on Sunday there is less traffic).

Historically, Chelsea has been one of the most artistic districts of London. Today, it is home to some of the most prosperous residents of the capital and one of the most complete and attractively scaled "villages" within the city. Its residents have included Henry VIII, Henry James, J.M.W. Turner, John Singer Sargent, Thomas Carlyle, Oscar Wilde, Mick Jagger, and Baroness Margaret Thatcher.

From Sloane Square station, you'll be facing:

1. **Sloane Square.** This northernmost gateway to Chelsea was laid out in 1780 on land belonging to Sir Hans Sloane (1660–1753), whose collection of minerals, fossils, and plant specimens formed the core of the British Museum. A few steps to the right of the tube station is the **Royal Court Theatre,** which opened in 1888. The theater became famous for staging plays by George Bernard Shaw, including the first performance of *Candida* (1904). Since the 1956 premier of John Osborne's *Look Back in Anger,* it has been known for producing new and often adventurous plays.

Walk back past the tube station straight ahead (south) along:

2. **Sloane Gardens.** Honoring Sir Hans Sloane, former president of the Royal Society, are gardens flanked by splendid red-brick houses. Curiously enough, the

Chelsea Bridge

Chelsea Embankment

Ebury Sq.

Semley Pl.
Eaton Terr.
Ebury St.
Ebury Bridge Rd.

Ranelagh Gardens

T h a m e s

C h e l s e a   R e a c h

Battersea Park

Sloane Square

Holbein Pl.

start here

finish here

Holbein Mews
Lower Sloane St.
Sloane Gdns.

Turk's Row

Franklin's Row

West Rd.

Royal Hospital Rd.

Chelsea Bridge Road

Pimlico Rd.
St. Barnabas St.
Bourne St.

Cadogan Gdns

Cheltenham Terr.

Wellington Sq.

Markham Sq.

Draycott Ave.

Cadogan St.
Rawlings St.
Denyer St.
Draycott Ave.
Sloane Ave.

Whitehead's Grove
Elystan Pl.
Tryon St.
Bury Walk
Smith St.
St. Leonard's Terr.
Tedworth Sq.
Ormonde
Christchurch St.
St. Loo Ave.
Cheyne Gdns.

Cheyne Walk

Albert Bridge

Markham St.
Godfrey St.
Astell St.
Flood St.
Chelsea Manor St.

Shawfield St.
Redesdale St.
Tite St.

Paradise Walk
Dilke St.

Chelsea Embankment

Elystan St.
Ixworth St.
St. Luke's St.
Britten St.
Cale St.

Pond Pl.
Sydney St.
King's Rd.
Manresa Rd.
Oakley St.
Glebe Pl.
Margaretta Terr.
Upper Cheyne Row
Cheyne Row

Battersea Bridge

Pelham St.
Pelham Crescent
Fulham Rd.
Old Brompton Rd.
Harrington Rd.
Queen's Gate
Onslow Gardens
Summer Pl.
Cranley Pl.
Selwood Terr.
Cranley Gardens

Onslow Sq.

Chelsea Sq.

Carlyle Sq.

Paultons Sq.

Foulis Terr.

Elm Park Gardens
Fulham Rd.

Old Church St.
Mallord St.
The Vale
Mulberry Walk

Paultons St.
Danvers St.
Milman's St.
Cheyne Walk
Beaufort St.
Park Walk
Chelsea Park Gdns.
King's Rd.

Evelyn Gardens

South Parade

E-0153

1. Sloane Square
2. Sloane Gardens
3. The Old Burial Ground
4. Ranelagh Gardens
5. Chelsea Royal Hospital
6. The Duke of York's Headquarters
7. St. Leonard's Terrace
8. King's Road
9. Antiquarius
10. Chelsea's Old Town Hall
11. Thomas Carlyle's House
12. 48 Cheyne Walk
13. Chelsea Old Church
14. Crosby Hall
15. Battersea Bridge
16. Turner's House
17. Lindsey House
18. Albert Bridge
19. Chelsea Physic Garden
20. Swan Walk
21. Home of Oscar Wilde
22. National Army Museum

developer, William Willett, invented Daylight Saving Time, a concept that wasn't terribly popular with workers in 1889. Chelsea has counted a great many prominent names among its residents, including Sir Philip Gibbs (1877–1962), the novelist, journalist, historian, and political analyst who lived at 8 Sloane Gardens; and Egerton Castle (1858–1920), the novelist and dramatist who resided at 49 Sloane Gardens in his later years.

When you reach the end of Sloane Gardens, take a left onto Lower Sloane Street and proceed 2 blocks, crossing the street to:

3. **The Old Burial Ground.** Adjoining Chelsea Royal Hospital, it's estimated that some 10,000 soldiers were interred here, though few gravestones remain. One local newspaper reported that in the 1700s a 123-year-old man was buried here. Although you can't go inside to visit the burial grounds, you can get a good view through the railings.

Next take a right onto Royal Hospital Road (the burial ground will be on your left). After about 100 yards, go left through:

4. **Ranelagh Gardens.** Informal and undulating, this was once the 1690 house and gardens of Lord Ranelagh, paymaster general to the British Armed Forces. At one time this was one of the most fashionable pleasure gardens of London, attracting the *beau monde*. Gibbon called it "the most convenient place for courtships of every kind," while Goldsmith loved the "fashionable frivolity" of the place. Only the Chelsea Royal Hospital remains in the park; all other buildings were demolished.

Head right after leaving the gardens and backtrack through London Gate, taking another left into the driveway. From here, continue straight through the wooden doors leading in the foreground of:

5. **Chelsea Royal Hospital.** Designed in 1682 in the aftermath of the Great Fire of London, this is Sir Christopher Wren's second-greatest masterpiece (after St. Paul's Cathedral). The hospital was inspired by Louis XIV's Hôtel des Invalides in Paris; both were planned as homes for wounded or aging soldiers, and both are grandiose. The hospital is home to more than 400 Chelsea war veteran pensioners who, in their blue or scarlet uniforms and three-cornered hats worn on special occasions, show visitors about.

Exit on Royal Hospital Road, take a pedestrian-only walkway to Franklin's Row, and continue in a northwesterly direction to:

6. **The Duke of York's Headquarters.** The Duke of York, second son of George III, founded this school, constructed in 1801 for the children of soldiers. The duke had been a military reformer, protesting against the selling of commissions until a scandal revealed that his own mistress was involved in hawking these commissions; the reformer resigned in disgrace. Today England's National Guard inhabits the grounds, and the headquarters are off-limits.

After viewing the well-kept grounds, take a left and head west along:

7. **St. Leonard's Terrace.** One of London's most delightful residential streets. No. 7 was the former residence of Sir Lawrence Olivier (1907–1989) in the late 1970s. Bram Stoker (1847–1912), the creator of Count Dracula, lived on the terrace in 1896. The Irish author published his famous novel a year after moving here. The terrace boasts some of London's most beautiful homes: see nos. 19, 21, 22, and especially no. 26, one of the oldest houses in the row.

Backtrack a bit to Olivier's former abode, turning left onto Royal Avenue, filled with stately red-brick Victorian homes. The street itself is much older, having been first laid out in 1682 by Sir Christopher Wren. At the end of the avenue, turn left onto dynamic:

8. King's Road. Jammed with antiques stores, booksellers, restaurants, coffee-houses, tearooms, and designer boutiques, and peopled with hip "Sloane Rangers," it's a delightful area in which to observe the human comedy. Today it hardly recalls its origins; it was named King's Road because it was designed for Charles II as his route between his London palace and Hampton Court Palace.

☕ **TAKE A BREAK   Henry J. Bean's Bar & Grill,** 195–197 King's Rd. (☎ **0171/352-9255**). This "Cheers"-style bar lures the homesick Yankee with big burgers, meaty hotdogs, and other Americana. In summer, you can eat and drink in the rose garden in the back. Happy hour with reduced drink prices is daily from 6 to 8pm (except Sunday).

After relaxing, continue walking southwest along King's Road. Midway between Shawfield Street and Flood Street is a warren of antiques sellers, clustered together into a complex known as:

9. Antiquarius, 135–141 King's Rd., SW3. Browse at will—maybe you'll find a near-heirloom you can't live without.

As you continue down King's Road, oval-shaped blue-and-white plaques identify buildings of particular interest. One that you should watch for is:

10. Chelsea's Old Town Hall. On the south side of King's Road, midway between Chelsea Manor and Oakley Street, it's the favorite hangout of everyone from punkers with nowhere else to go to soon-to-be-married couples applying for a marriage license. Many wedding parties stage photographs in front of its Georgian grandeur.

Continue to Oakley Street and head south until you come to Upper Cheyne Row. Follow it to Cheyne Row and the address at no. 24 that was:

11. Thomas Carlyle's House. One of the most interesting houses in London, particularly to literary enthusiasts, it's also one of the neighborhood's few houses open to the public. The former home of "the sage of Chelsea" and his wife Jane offers fascinating insight into Victorian life. Notice the small gravestone in the garden marking the burial place of the author's favorite dog.

After leaving the author's house, continue south to the Thames and Cheyne Walk, one of London's most famous streets, filled with expensive and chic town houses. Occupants of these elegantly proportioned buildings have included some very famous people, including Mick Jagger of the Rolling Stones. Pause a moment at:

12. No. 48 Cheyne Walk, where Jagger lived for a while, alongside neighbors like bandmate Keith Richards, publishing magnate Lord Weidenfeld, and the grandson of oil industry giant J. Paul Getty. Artistic denizens of an earlier age included George Eliot, who lived part of her flamboyant life (and later died) at no. 41. The star of the Pre-Raphaelite movement, Dante Gabriel Rossetti, lived in perhaps the street's finest building, no. 16.

If you head west toward Battersea Bridge, you'll come to Old Church Street, containing the parish church of St. Thomas More:

13. Chelsea Old Church (All Saints). Its graceful beauty survived the heavy damages inflicted on it and the surrounding neighborhood by Nazi bombing during World War II. Lovingly repaired, it contains a chapel partly designed by Hans Holbein; an urn holding the earthly remains of the man who owned most of Chelsea during the 1700s, Sir Hans Sloane; and a plaque commemorating the American novelist Henry James, a longtime Chelsea resident who died nearby in 1916. The building's Lawrence Chapel is reputed to have been the scene of

Henry VIII's secret marriage to Jane Seymour several days before their official marriage in 1536.

Midway between heavily trafficked Beauford Street and quieter Danvers Street (both opening onto Cheyne Walk) is:

14. Crosby Hall. Unmarked by a street number, its chapel-like original brick-and-stone wing was built in the early 1400s and owned by both Richard III and Sir Thomas More. It was transported stone-by-stone from Bishopsgate in the early 1900s, partly under the financial incentive of American-born Lady Nancy Astor. With a modern wing of gray stone added in the 1950s, today it provides apartments and dining facilities for the British Federation of University Women. Sections of its interior (containing paintings by Holbein, a trussed roof, and some Jacobean furniture) are open free to the public (Monday through Saturday from 10am to noon and 2:15pm to 5pm).

Back on Cheyne Walk, you can continue west, passing on your left:

15. Battersea Bridge. Although not the most famous bridge in London, it will help orient you and provide a clue to Chelsea's vital link to the Thames.

Next go westward to 119 Cheyne Walk, which is:

16. Turner's House. Its tall and narrow premises sheltered one of England's greatest painters, J.M.W. Turner (1775–1851), during the last years of his life. His canvases, although predating those of the French Impressionists, shimmer with color (you'll find a wonderful array at the Tate Gallery). When he died in this house, his very appropriate final words were, "God is Light."

Just to the east, at nos. 96–100, is one of Chelsea's most beautiful buildings, completed in the 1670s:

17. Lindsey House. Built around 1674 by the Swiss-born physician to two British kings (James I and Charles II), this house became the British headquarters of the Moravian Church around 1750. Later divided and sold as four separate residences, it housed the American-born painter James Whistler (at no. 96) between 1866 and 1879. Britain's most celebrated Edwardian architect, Sir Edwin Lutyens (1869–1944), designed the gardens of nos. 99 and 100.

At this point, retrace your steps eastward to Battersea Bridge. Here begins a beautiful walk eastward along Cheyne Walk through a historic neighborhood, marred only by the roar of the riverside traffic. Across the water is Battersea, a rapidly gentrifying neighborhood. Looming in the distance is:

18. Albert Bridge. Rivaled only by Tower Bridge and Westminster Bridge, this might be the most-photographed bridge in London. It was designed in 1873—at the height of the Victorian fascination with cast iron—by R. M. Ordish.

Continue past the Albert Bridge along Cheyne Walk until you reach Royal Hospital Road. The turf at this intersection (its entrance is at 66 Royal Hospital Rd.) belongs to the oldest surviving botanic garden in Britain, the:

19. Chelsea Physic Garden (also known as Chelsea Botanic Garden). In 1673 the Worshipful Society of Apothecaries founded these gardens for the collection, study, and dissemination of plants with medicinal value. Sir Hans Sloane, a botanist and physician to George II, provided permanent funding for them in 1722. Its 4 acres continue to serve as a research and educational facility. The exotic trees and shrubs, aromatic herbs, rock garden, tranquil pond, and greenhouses, make this a delightful place in which to stroll and take tea.

Now, continue your walk northeast along Royal Hospital Road, and turn right at the first cross-street onto:

20. **Swan Walk,** a charming and obscure part of Chelsea worth a look for its wonderful 18th-century rowhouses. Walk down it, making the first left onto Dilke Street and at the dead end, turn left again onto Tite Street. At 34 Tite St., you'll see a plaque commemorating the:

21. **Home of Oscar Wilde.** Here, Wilde wrote many of his most charming plays, including *The Importance of Being Earnest* and *Lady Windermere's Fan.* After Wilde was arrested and imprisoned following the most famous trial for homosexuality in British history, the house was sold to pay his debts. The plaque was presented in 1954, a century after Wilde's birthday.

A few steps away on the same street are houses that once belonged to two of America's most famous expatriate painters: No. 31 was the home of John Singer Sargent (and the studio where he painted many of his most famous portraits); James McNeill Whistler lived at no. 35.

At the end of Tite Street, turn right onto Royal Hospital Road. Within a block are the fortresslike premises of the:

22. **National Army Museum.** Its premises contain galleries devoted to weapons, uniforms, and art, with dioramas of famous battles and such memorabilia as the skeleton of Napoléon's favorite horse.

Next door to the museum, a short distance to the northeast, is the building where the annual Chelsea Flower Show is held each May (see the "London Calendar of Events" in chapter 2).

To get back to the Sloane Square tube station, continue east along Royal Hospital Road until you come to Holbein Place, then cut left (north) to Sloane Square.

8 | Shopping

When Prussian Field Marshal Blücher, Wellington's stout ally at Waterloo, first laid eyes on London, he allegedly slapped his thigh and exclaimed, "Herr Gott, what a city to plunder!" He was gazing at what, for the early 19th century, was a phenomenal mass of shops and stores—overwhelming to Herr Blücher's unsophisticated eyes. Since those days, other cities may have equaled London as a shopping mecca, but none have surpassed it.

1 Shopping London

Although London is one of the world's best shopping cities, it often seems made for visitors from Arabian kingdoms who sleep by a pot of gold at the end of the rainbow; locals are far more careful with their hard-earned pounds. To find real values, you'll have to do what most Londoners do: wait for sales or search out specialty finds.

American-style shopping has taken Britain by storm, both in concept—warehouse stores and outlet malls—and in actual name: One block from Hamley's, you'll find the Disney Store. The Gap is everywhere; Tiffany sells more wedding gifts than Aspery these days. Your best bet is to ignore anything American and to concentrate on British goods. You can also do well with French products; values are almost as good as what you'd find in Paris.

TAXES & SHIPPING

Value-Added Tax (VAT) is the British version of sales tax. VAT is a whopping 17.5% on most goods, but it's already included in the price, so the number you see on the price tag is exactly what you'll pay at the register. Non-EU residents can get back much of the tax they pay by applying for a VAT refund.

One of the first secrets of shopping in London is that the minimum expenditure needed to qualify for a refund on Value-Added Tax is a mere £50. Not every single store honors this minimum (it's £100 at Harrods; £75 at Selfridges; £62 at Hermès), but it's far easier to qualify for a tax refund in Britain than almost any other country in the European Union.

Vendors at flea markets might not be equipped to provide the paperwork for a refund, so if you're contemplating a major purchase and really want that refund, ask before you buy. Be suspicious of any dealer who tells you there's no VAT on antiques. There wasn't before,

---

How to Get Your VAT Refund

To receive back a portion of the tax paid on purchases made in Britain, first ask the store if they do VAT refunds and what their minimum purchase is. Once you've achieved this minimum, ask for the paperwork; the retailer will have to fill out a portion themselves. Several readers have reported that merchants have told them that they can get refund forms at the airport on their way out of the country. *This is not true.* You must get a refund form from the retailer (don't leave the store without one), and it must be completed by the retailer on the spot.

Fill out your portion of the form and then present it—along with the goods—at the Customs office in the airport. Allow a half-hour to stand in line. Remember: You're required to show the goods at your time of departure, so don't pack them in your luggage and check it; put them in your carry-on instead.

Once you have the paperwork stamped by the officials, you have two choices: You can mail the papers and receive your refund in either a British check (no!) or a credit-card refund (yes!), or you can go directly to the Cash VAT Refund desk at the airport and get your refund in cash. The bad news: If you accept cash other than sterling, you will lose money on the conversion rate. (If you plan on mailing your paperwork, try to remember to bring a stamp with you to the airport; if you forget, you can usually get stamps from stamp machines and/or the convenience stores in the terminal.)

Be advised that many stores charge a flat fee for processing your refund, so £3 to £5 may be automatically deducted from the total refund you receive. But since the VAT in Britain is 17.5%, if you get back 15%, you're doing fine.

Note: If you're traveling to other countries within the European Union, you don't go through any of this in Britain. At your final destination, prior to departure from the EU, you file for all your VAT refunds at one time.

---

but there is now—the European Union has made the British add VAT to antiques. Since dealers still have mixed stock, pricing should reflect this fact. So ask if it's included—before you bargain on a price. Get to the price you're comfortable with first, then ask for the VAT refund.

VAT is not charged on goods shipped out of the country, whether you spend £50 or not. Many London shops will help you beat the VAT rap by shipping for you. But watch out: Shipping can double the cost of your purchase. Also expect to pay U.S. duties when the goods get to you at home.

You may want to consider paying for excess baggage (rates vary with the airline), or else have your packages shipped independently. Independent operators are generally less expensive than the airlines. Try **London Baggage,** London Air Terminal, Victoria Place, SW1 (☎ 0171/828-2400; tube: Victoria), or **Burns International Facilities,** at Heathrow Airport Terminal 1 (☎ 0181/745-5301) and Terminal 4 (☎ 0181/745-7460).

But remember, you can only avoid the VAT up front if you have the store ship directly for you. If you ship via excess baggage or London Baggage, you'll still have to pay the VAT up front, and apply for a refund.

HOURS

London keeps fairly uniform store hours, mostly shorter than American equivalents. The norm is 10am opening and 5:30pm closing, with a late Wednesday or Thursday night, until 7pm, maybe 8pm. Some stores in districts such as Chelsea and Covent Garden tend to keep slightly later hours.

Sunday shopping is now legal. Stores may be open for six hours; usually they choose 11am to 5pm. Stores in designated tourist areas and flea markets are exempt from this law and may stay open all day on Sunday. Thus, Covent Garden, Greenwich, and Hampstead are big Sunday destinations for shoppers.

2 London's Best Buys

Bargain hunters should zero in on goods that are manufactured in England and are liable to cost much more when exported. These are—above all—anything from **The Body Shop, Filofax,** or **Dr. Martens;** many woolens and some cashmeres; most English brands of bone china; antiques; used silver; and rare books.

Antiques   Whether you're looking for museum-quality antiques or simply fun junk, London has the stores, the resources, the stalls, and the markets. While it might not be 1969 any more (you won't find priceless majolica for £20), there are still plenty of great finds along Portobello Road and the myriad other markets.

Aromatherapy   The British must have invented aromatherapy—just about every store sells gels, creams, lotions, and potions made with the right herbs and essential oils to cure whatever ails you, including jetlag. Whether it all works or not is secondary to the fact that most of the British brands are half the U.S. price when bought on home soil. **The Body Shop** becomes the best store in the world at prices like these. Check out drugstore brands as well, especially The Body Shop knock-offs that **Boots The Chemist** makes, as well as their own line (sold in another part of the store) of healing foot gels.

Bone China   Savings actually depend on the brand, but can be as much as 50% off U.S. prices. Shipping and U.S. duties may wipe out any savings, so know what you're doing before you buy.

Cashmere   Some shoppers may be shocked at the price of cashmere, even on sale. While sale prices on Scottish cashmere are generally fair, most American shoppers are used to prices on Chinese cashmere, which is cheaper and of much lesser quality. It's rare to even find Chinese cashmere in the better stores in London, so before you throw down a piece in horror, check the quality. On an oranges-for-oranges basis, Scottish cashmere when on sale in London can be an excellent buy.

Designer Wear   Designer clothing from any of the international makers may be less in London than in the United States or Paris—but know your prices. Often, the only differential is the VAT refund, which at 15% to 17.5% is substantial. This game is also highly dependent on the value of the dollar.

While you won't get a VAT refund on used designer clothing, London has the best prices on used Chanel (and similar) clothing of any major shopping city.

Royal Souvenirs   Forget about investing in Diana memorabilia; word is that it won't appreciate significantly because there is so much of it. Still, royal collectibles can be cheap kitsch bought in street markets or serious pieces from coronations long past found in specialty shops. If you're buying new for investment purposes, it must be kept in mint condition.

Teen Fashions   Street fashion, punk, grunge, whatever you want to call it—it's alive and well, with several areas in town, including Carnaby Street, Covent Garden, and Kensington High Street, catering to the young mod squad.

Also in the Cheap Thrills Department   Dime-store brands of makeup cost less than they do in the United States. The French line **Bourjois** (made in the same factories that make Chanel makeup) sells for less in London than in Paris and isn't sold in the United States; **Boots** makes its own Chanel knockoff line, No. 7.

SALES

Traditionally, stores in Britain only held two sale periods: January and July. Now, whenever they need cash, they have a sale. July sales begin in June—or earlier—and promotions are commonplace. Still, the January sale is the big event of the year. Though a few stores hold their after-Christmas sale on December 27, the really famous sales usually start after the first week in January, when round-trip airfares are in the low range, and savings on sale items might earn your travel money back if you find enough bargains.

Discounts can range from 25% to 50% at leading department stores, such as Harrods and Selfridges. Harrods produces this event, with special buyers and bins of imports. The best buys are on Harrods logo souvenirs, English china (seconds are trucked in from factories in Stoke-on-Trent), and English designer brands like Jaeger. But while the Harrods sale is the most famous in London, it's not the only game in town. Just about every other store—save Boots—also has a big sale at that time. Beware, though: There's a huge difference in the quality of the finds bought in genuine sales, where the stores are actually clearing the shelves, and the goods bought at "produced" sales, where special merchandise has been hauled in just for the sale.

DUTY-FREE AIRPORT SHOPPING

Shopping at airports is big business, so big business has taken over the management of some of Britain's airports to ensure that those in transit are enticed to buy. Whereas Terminal 4 at Heathrow is a virtual shopping mall, each terminal has a good bit of shopping, with not a lot of cross-over between brands.

Prices at the airport for items like souvenirs and candy bars are actually higher than on the streets of London, but duty-free prices on luxury goods are usually fair. There are often promotions and coupons that allow for pounds off at the time of the purchase. Don't save all your shopping until you get to the airport, but do know prices on hand so you know when to pounce.

3 The Top Shopping Streets & Neighborhoods

Thankfully for those with too little time to shop, there are several key streets that offer some of London's best retail stores—or simply one of everything—compactly located in a niche or neighborhood so you can just stroll and shop.

THE WEST END

As a neighborhood, the West End includes the tony Mayfair district and is home to the core of London's big-name shopping. Most of the department stores, designer shops, and multiples (chain stores) have their flagships in this area.

The key streets are **Oxford Street** for affordable shopping (start at Marble Arch tube station if you're ambitious, or Bond Street station if you just want to see some of it); and **Regent Street,** which intersects Oxford Street at Oxford Circus (tube: Oxford Circus). The Oxford Street flagship (at Marble Arch) of the private-label department store **Marks & Spencer** is worth visiting for high-quality goods. Regent Street has fancier shops—more upscale department stores (including the famed **Liberty of London**), multiples (**Laura Ashley**), and specialty dealers—and leads all the way to Piccadilly.

Parallel to Regent Street, **Bond Street** (tube: Bond Street) connects Piccadilly with Oxford Street and is synonymous with the luxury trade. Divided into New and Old, it has experienced a recent revival and is the hot address for all the international designers; **Donna Karan** has not one but two shops here. A slew of international hot-shots from **Chanel** to **Ferragamo** to **Versace** have digs nearby.

Burlington Arcade (tube: Piccadilly Circus), the famous glass-roofed, Regency-style passage leading off Piccadilly, looks like a period exhibition and is lined with intriguing shops and boutiques. Lit by wrought-iron lamps and decorated with clusters of ferns and flowers, its small, smart stores specialize in fashion, jewelry, Irish linen, cashmere, and more. If you linger there until 5:30pm, you can watch the beadles, those ever-present attendants in their black-and-yellow livery and top hats, ceremoniously put in place the iron grills that block off the arcade until 9am the next morning, at which time they just as ceremoniously remove them to mark the start of a new business day. (There are only three beadles remaining; they're the last London representatives of Britain's oldest police force.) Also at 5:30pm, a hand bell called the Burlington Bell is sounded, signaling the end of trading.

Tucked right behind Regent Street is **Carnaby Street** (tube: Oxford Circus). While it no longer dominates the world of pacesetting fashion as it did in the 1960s, it's become a comeback street for cheap souvenirs, a purple wig, or a little something in leather. There's also a convenient branch of **Boots** here.

For a total contrast, check out **Jermyn Street** (tube: Piccadilly Circus), on the far side of Piccadilly, a tiny 2-block-long street devoted to high-end men's haberdasher's and toiletries shops; many have been doing business for centuries. Several hold royal warrants, including **Turnbull & Asser,** where HRH Prince Charles has his pjs made.

The West End theater district borders two more shopping areas: the still-not-ready-for-prime-time **Soho** (tube: Tottenham Court Road), where the sex shops are slowly converting into cutting-edge designer shops; and **Covent Garden** (tube: Covent Garden) which is a masterpiece unto itself. The original marketplace has overflowed its boundaries and eaten up the surrounding neighborhood; it's fun to wander the narrow streets and shop. Covent Garden is especially mobbed on Sundays.

KNIGHTSBRIDGE & CHELSEA

The home of **Harrods, Knightsbridge** (tube: Knightsbridge) is the second-most famous of London's retail districts. (Oxford Street edges it out.) Nearby **Sloane Street** is chock-a-block with designer shops; in the opposite direction, **Cheval Place** is lined with designer resale shops.

Walk toward Museum Row and you'll soon find **Beauchamp** (*Bee*-cham) **Place**. It's only 1 block long, but it's very "Sloane Ranger," featuring the kinds of shops where young British aristos buy their clothing for "The Season."

King's Road (tube: Sloane Square), the main street of Chelsea, will forever remain a symbol of the Swinging Sixties. Today, it's still popular with the young crowd, but there are fewer Mohawk haircuts, Bovver boots, and Edwardian ballgowns than before. More and more in the 1990s, King's Road is a lineup of markets and "multistores," large or small conglomerations of indoor stands, stalls, and booths within one building or enclosure. About a third of King's Road is devoted to these kinds of antiques markets; another third houses design trade showrooms and stores of household wares for British Yuppies; and the remaining third is faithful to the area's teeny-bopper roots.

If you walk west from Harrods along Brompton Road you connect to **Brompton Cross,** another hip area for designer shops made popular when Michelin House was rehabbed by Sir Terence Conran for **The Conran Shop.**

Also seek out **Walton Street,** a tiny little snake of a street running from Brompton Cross back toward the museums. Most of the street is devoted to fairytale shops for m'lady where you can buy aromatherapy from **Jo Malone,** needlepoint, or costume jewelry.

Finally, don't forget all those museums in nearby South Kensington—they all have great gift shops.

KENSINGTON, NOTTING HILL & BAYSWATER

Kensington High Street (tube: High Street Kensington) is the hangout of the classier breed of teen, one who has graduated from Carnaby Street and is ready for street chic. While there are a few staples of basic British fashion on this strip, most of the stores feature items that stretch, are very, very short, very, very tight, and very, very black.

From Kensington High Street, you can walk up **Kensington Church Street,** which, like Portobello Road, is one of the city's main shopping avenues for antiques, selling everything from antique furniture to impressionist paintings.

Kensington Church Street dead-ends at the Notting Hill Gate tube station, jumping-off point for **Portobello Road;** the dealers and weekend market are 2 blocks beyond.

Not far from Notting Hill Gate is **Whiteleys of Bayswater,** Queensway, W2 (☎ **0171/229-8844;** tube: Bayswater or Queensway), an Edwardian mall whose chief tenant is Marks & Spencer. There are also 75 to 85 shops (the number varies from year to year), mostly specialty outlets, and an array of restaurants, cafes, and bars as well as an eight-screen movie theater.

4 Street & Flea Markets

If Mayfair stores are not your cup of tea, don't worry; you'll have more fun, and find a better bargain, at any of the city's street and flea markets.

THE WEST END

Covent Garden Market (☎ **0171/836-9136;** tube: Covent Garden), the most famous market in all of England—possibly all of Europe—offers several different markets daily from 9am to 5pm (we think it's most fun to come on Sunday). It can be a little confusing until you dive in and explore it all. **Apple Market** is the fun, bustling market in the courtyard, where traders sell...well, everything. Many of the items are what the English call collectible nostalgia; they include a wide array of glassware and ceramics, leather goods, toys, clothes, hats, and jewelry. Some of the merchandise is truly unusual. Many items are handmade, with some of the craftspeople selling their own wares—except on Mondays, when antiques dealers take over. Out back is **Jubilee Market** (☎ **0171/836-2139**), also an antiques market on Mondays. Every other day, it's sort of a fancy hippie-ish market with cheap clothes and books. Out front there are a few tents of cheap stuff, except again on Monday.

The market itself (in the superbly restored hall) is one of the best shopping opportunities in London. Specialty shops sell fashions and herbs, gifts and toys, books and personalized dollhouses, hand-rolled cigars, automata, and much, much more. There are bookshops and branches of famous stores (**Hamley's, The Body Shop**), and prices are kept moderate.

Sheltered in a rambling old building, **Chelsea Antiques Market,** 245A–253 King's Rd., SW3 (☎ **0171/352-5686;** tube: Sloane Square), offers endless browsing possibilities for the curio addict. About one-third of the market is given over to old or rare books. You're also likely to run across Staffordshire dogs, shaving mugs, Edwardian buckles and clasps, ivory-handled razors, old velours, lace gowns, wooden tea caddies, antique pocket watches, wormy Tudoresque chests, silver snuff boxes, grandfather clocks, and jewelry of all periods. Of note are the Optical Department, featuring surgeon's tools, microscopes, sextants, and compasses, and Harrington Brothers' selections of antiquarian children's and travel books. Closed Sunday.

St. Martin-in-the-Fields Market (tube: Charing Cross) is good for teens and hipsters who don't want to trek all the way to Camden Market (see "North London," below) and can make due with imports from India and South America, crafts, and some local football souvenirs. Located near Trafalgar Square and Covent Garden; hours are Monday to Saturday 11am to 5pm, and Sundays noon to 5pm.

Berwick Street Market (tube: Oxford Circus or Tottenham Court Road) may be the only street market in the world that's flanked by two rows of strip clubs, porno stores, and adult-movie dens. Don't let that put you off, however. Humming 6 days a week in the scarlet heart of Soho, this array of stalls and booths sells probably the best and cheapest fruit and vegetables in town. It also hawks ancient records, tapes, books, and old magazines, all which may turn out to be collectors' items one day. It's open Monday to Saturday from 8am to 5pm.

On Sunday mornings along **Bayswater Road,** artists hang pictures, collages, and crafts on the railings along the edge of Hyde Park and Kensington Gardens for more than a mile. If the weather's right, start at Marble Arch and walk. You'll see much of the same thing by walking along the railings of **Green Park** along Piccadilly on Saturday afternoon.

NOTTING HILL

Portobello Market (tube: Notting Hill Gate) is a magnet for collectors of virtually anything. It's mainly a Saturday happening, from 6am to 5pm. You needn't be here at the crack of dawn; 9am is fine. Once known mainly for fruit and vegetables (still sold here throughout the week), in the past 4 decades Portobello has become synonymous with antiques. But don't take the stallholder's word for it that the fiddle he's holding is a genuine Stradivarius left to him in the will of his Italian great-uncle; it might just as well have been "nicked" from an East End pawnshop.

The market is divided into three major sections. The most crowded is the antique section, running between Colville Road and Chepstow Villas to the south. (*Warning:* There's a great concentration of pickpockets in this area.) The second section (and the oldest part) is the "fruit and veg" market, lying between Westway and Colville Road. In the third and final section there's a flea market, where Londoners sell bric-a-brac and lots of secondhand goods they didn't really want in the first place. But looking around still makes for interesting fun.

The serious collector can pick up a copy of a helpful official guide, *Saturday Antique Market: Portobello Road & Westbourne Grove,* published by the Portobello Antique Dealers Association. It lists where to find what, ranging from music boxes to militaria, lace to 19th-century photographs.

Note: Some 90 antiques and art shops along Portobello Road are open during the week when the street market is closed. This is actually a better time for the serious collector to shop, because you'll get more attention from dealers and you won't be distracted by the organ grinder.

SOUTH BANK

Open on Fridays only, **New Caledonian Market** is commonly known as the Bermondsey Market, because of its location on the corner of Long Lane and Bermondsey Street (tube: London Bridge, then bus 78 or walk down Bermondsey

---

A Great Way to Spend a Sunday: Shopping Greenwich

Even though many shops throughout London are now open on Sundays, the best Sunday shopping is still in the stalls of the flea and craft markets in the royal city of Greenwich, now officially a London suburb.

While sometime in the next 10 years a new tube stop will open here, the best way to enjoy the trip is to float downstream on a boat from Charing Cross or Westminster pier (service begins at 10:30am on Sundays; see "Sightseeing & Boat Tours Along the Thames" in chapter 6 for details). The trip takes about a half-hour, but you'll get commentary on the Docklands development and the history of the river, and see The Tower and much of London from the water along the way.

The boat leaves you right in the heart of Greenwich, so you're minutes from the **craft market,** held on Saturday and Sunday. Follow the signs...or the crowd. After you're done here, head for the streets (again, follow the crowd) to Greenwich's several antiques markets. First is **Canopy Market,** which isn't under a canopy at all, but sprawls through several parking lots of junk and old books and then onto **High Street,** where the fancier flea market is held. It's possible that there's yet another antiques market at **Town Hall,** across the street, but these are usually shows which charge an admission fee.

You're only a half-block from the Greenwich BritRail station now; there's a train back to London every half-hour.

Street). The market is at the extreme east end, beginning at Tower Bridge Road. It's one of Europe's outstanding street markets for the number and quality of the antiques and other goods. The stalls are well-known, and many dealers come into London from the country. Prices are generally lower here than at Portobello and the other markets. It gets under way at 5am—with the bargains gone by 9am—and closes at noon. Bring a "torch" (flashlight) if you go in the wee hours.

NORTH LONDON

If it's Wednesday, it's time for **Camden Passage** (☎ 0171/359-9969; tube: Angel) in Islington, where each Wednesday and Saturday there's a very upscale antiques market. It starts in Camden Passage and then sprawls into the streets behind. It's on Wednesdays from 7am to 2pm, and Saturdays from 9am to 3:30pm.

Don't confuse Camden Passage with Camden Market (very, very downtown). **Camden Market** (tube: Camden Town) is for teens and others into body piercing, blue hair (yes, still), and vintage clothing. Serious collectors of vintage may want to explore during the week, when the teen scene isn't quite so overwhelming. Market hours are 9:30am to 5:30pm daily, with some parts opening at 10am.

5 The Department Stores

Contrary to popular belief, Harrods is not the only department store in London. The British invented the department store, and they have lots of them—mostly in Mayfair, and each with its own customer profile.

Daks Simpson Piccadilly. 203 Piccadilly, W1. ☎ **0171/734-2002.** Tube: Piccadilly Circus.

Opened in 1936 as the home of DAKS clothing, Simpson's has been going strong ever since. It's known for menswear—its basement-level men's shoe department is a model of the way quality shoes should be fitted—as well as women's fashions, perfume, jewelry, and lingerie. Many of the clothes are lighthearted, carefully made, and well suited to casual elegance. Its Simpson Collection rubs shoulders with international designer names such as Armani and Yves Saint Laurent.

Fenwick of Bond Street. 63 New Bond St., W1. ☎ 0171/629-9161. Tube: Bond St.

Fenwick (*Fen*-ick), dating from 1891, is a stylish fashion store that offers an excellent collection of designer womenswear, ranging from moderately priced ready-to-wear items to more expensive designer fashions. A wide range of lingerie in all price ranges is also sold.

✪ **Fortnum & Mason, Ltd.** 181 Piccadilly, W1. ☎ 0171/734-8040. Tube: Piccadilly Circus.

The world's most elegant grocery store is a British tradition dating back to 1707. Down the street from the Ritz, it draws the carriage trade, those from Mayfair to Belgravia who come seeking such tinned treasures as pâté de foie gras or a boar's head. This store exemplifies the elegance and style you would expect from an establishment with two royal warrants. Enter and be transported to another world of deep-red carpets, crystal chandeliers, spiraling wooden staircases, and unobtrusive, tailcoated assistants.

The grocery department is renowned for its impressive selection of the finest foods from around the world—the best champagne, the most scrumptious Belgian chocolates, and succulent Scottish smoked salmon. You can wander through the four floors and inspect the bone china and crystal cut glass, find the perfect gift in the leather or stationery departments, or reflect on the changing history of furniture and ornaments in the antiques department. Dining choices include the **Patio & Buttery, St. James Restaurant,** and **The Fountain Restaurant** (for details on taking afternoon tea here, see "Teatime" in chapter 5).

✪ **Harrods.** 87–135 Brompton Rd., Knightsbridge, SW1. ☎ 0171/730-1234. Tube: Knightsbridge.

Harrods is an institution. As firmly entrenched in English life as Buckingham Palace and the Ascot Races, it's an elaborate emporium, at times as fascinating as a museum. Some of the goods displayed for sale are works of art, and so are the 300 departments displaying them. The sheer range, variety, and quality of merchandise is dazzling. The motto remains, "If you can eat or drink it, you'll find it at Harrods."

The whole fifth floor is devoted to sports and leisure, with a wide range of equipment and attire. Toy Kingdom is on the fourth floor, along with children's wear. The Egyptian Hall, on the ground floor, sells crystal from Lalique and Baccarat, plus porcelain. There's also a men's grooming room, an enormous jewelry department, and a fashion-forward department for younger customers. Along with the beauty of the bounty, check out the tiles and architectural touches. When you're ready for a break, you have a choice of 18 restaurants and bars. Best of all are the Food Halls, stocked with a huge variety of foods and several cafes. Harrods began as a grocer in 1849, and that's still the heart of the business.

In the basement you'll find a bank, a theater-booking service, and a travel bureau. Harrods Shop for logo gifts is on the ground floor.

Harvey Nichols. 109–125 Knightsbridge, SW1. ☎ 0171/235-5000. Tube: Knightsbridge.

Locals call it Harvey Nicks. Once a favorite of the late Princess Di, the store is large, but doesn't compete with Harrods because it has a much more upmarket, fashionable image. Harvey Nicks has its own gourmet food hall and fancy restaurant, The Fifth

Floor (see chapter 5), and a huge store crammed with the best designer home furnishings, gifts, and fashions for all, although women's clothing is the largest segment of its business. The store carries many American designer brands; avoid them, as they're more expensive in London.

Liberty. 214–220 Regent St., W1. ☎ **0171/734-1234.** Tube: Oxford Circus.

This major British department store is celebrated for its Liberty Prints, top-echelon, carriage-trade fabrics, often in floral patterns, that are prized by decorators for the way they add a sense of English tradition to a room. The front part of the store on Regent Street isn't particularly distinctive, but don't be fooled: Some parts of the place have been restored to Tudor-style splendor that includes half-timbering and lots of interior paneling. There are six floors of fashion, china, and home furnishings, as well as the famous Liberty Print fashion fabrics, upholstery fabrics, scarves, ties, luggage, and gifts.

Peter Jones. Sloane Sq., SW1. ☎ **0171/730-3434.** Tube: Sloane Sq.

Founded in 1877 and rebuilt in 1936, Peter Jones is known for household goods, household fabrics and trims, china, glass, soft furnishings, and linens. The linen department is one of the best in London.

Selfridges. 400 Oxford St., W1. ☎ **0171/629-1234.** Tube: Bond St. or Marble Arch.

One of the largest department stores in Europe, Selfridges has more than 500 divisions selling everything from artificial flowers to groceries. The store has recently been redone to become more upscale and to attract shoppers who are interested in the top designer brands. Yet the size of the store also allows them to feature the less expensive, mass-marketed lines as well.

Enter through the cosmetics department; the flagship Miss Selfridge boutique is located on one side of the store. While there are freestanding Miss Selfridge shops all over the United Kingdom, this one is the best. It features teen fashions, hotshot clothes, accessories, makeup, and the best of a slew of English and European designers who specialize in moderately priced cutting-edge fashions. Note the cafe tucked into this side of the store.

6 Goods A to Z

ANTIQUES
Alfie's Antique Market. 13–25 Church St., NW8. ☎ **0171/723-6066.** Tube: Marylebone or Edgware Rd.

This is the biggest and one of the best-stocked conglomerates of antiques dealers in London, all crammed into the premises of what was built before 1880 as a department store. It has more than 370 stalls, showrooms, and workshops scattered over 35,000 square feet of floor space. You'll find the biggest Susie Cooper collection in Europe here (Susie Cooper was a well-known designer of tableware and ceramics for Wedgwood). A whole antique district has grown up around Alfie's along Church Street.

Antiquarius. 131–141 King's Rd., SW3. ☎ **0171/351-5353.** Tube: Sloane Square.

Antiquarius echoes the artistic diversity of King's Road. More than 120 dealers offer specialized merchandise, usually of the small, domestic variety, such as antique and period jewelry, porcelain, silver, first-edition books, boxes, clocks, prints, and paintings, with an occasional piece of antique furniture. You'll also find a lot of items from the 1950s.

Bond Street Antiques Centre. 124 New Bond St., W1. ☎ **0171/351-5353.** Tube: Bond St. or Green Park.

This place, in the heart of London's finest shopping district, enjoys a reputation for being London's finest center for antique jewelry, silver, watches, porcelain, glass, and Asian antiques and paintings.

Grays & Grays in the Mews. 58 Davies St., and 1–7 Davies Mews, W1. ☎ **0171/629-7034.** Tube: Bond St.

These antiques markets have been converted into walk-in stands with independent dealers. The term "antique" here covers items from oil paintings to, say, the 1894 edition of the *Encyclopaedia Britannica*. Also sold here are exquisite antique jewelry; silver; gold; maps and prints; bronzes and ivories; arms and armor; Victorian and Edwardian toys; furniture; art-nouveau and art-deco items; antique lace; scientific instruments; craft tools; and Asian, Persian, and Islamic pottery, porcelain, miniatures, and antiquities. There's a cafe in each building.

The Mall at Camden Passage. Islington, N1. ☎ **0171/351-535?.** Tube: Angel.

This mall contains one of Britain's greatest concentrations of antiques dealers. In individual shop units, you'll find some 35 dealers specializing in fine furniture, porcelain, and silver. This area expands into a street market on Wednesday and Saturday.

ART & CRAFTS

ACAVA (☎ **0171/603-3039**) represents about 250 artists located in West London. Call for individual open-studio schedules, as well as dates for the annual Open Studios weekend.

Cecilia Colman Gallery. 67 St. John's Wood High St., NW8. ☎ **0171/722-0686.** Tube: St. John's Wood.

One of London's most established crafts galleries features decorative ceramics, studio glass, jewelry, and metalwork. Among the offerings are glass sculptures by Lucien Simon, jewelry by Caroline Taylor, and pottery by Simon Rich. There's also a large selection of mirrors and original-design perfume bottles.

Contemporary Applied Arts. 2 Percy St., W1. ☎ **0171/436-2344.** Tube: Goodge St.

This association encourages both traditional and progressive contemporary artwork. Many of Britain's best-established craftspeople, as well as lesser-known but promising talents, are represented in galleries that house a diverse retail display of glass, ceramics, textiles, wood, furniture, jewelry, and metalwork—all by outstanding artisans currently producing in the country, ranging in price from £10 to £10,000 ($16 to $16,000). A program of special exhibitions, including solo and small-group shows, focuses on innovations in craftwork.

Crafts Council Gallery. 44A Pentonville Rd., Islington, N1. ☎ **0171/278-7700.** Tube: Angel.

The largest crafts gallery is run by the Crafts Council, the national body for promoting contemporary crafts. You'll discover some of today's most creative work here. There's also a shop specializing in craft objects and publications, a picture library, a reference library, and a cafe.

Delfina Studio Trust. 50 Bermondsey St., SE1. ☎ **0171/357-6600.** Tube: London Bridge.

This registered charity provides studio space for 35 painters, photographers, and sculptors from Britain and abroad. The gallery doesn't have a fixed schedule; rather, exhibits are hung periodically, at which times the gallery keeps weekend hours. There's also a biannual open house. Call for a list of visiting artists, exhibition schedules, and sales information. All art is for sale, with prices generally starting at £250 ($400). The Trust takes no commission.

England & Co. 216 Westbourne Grove, W11. ☎ **0171/221-0417.** Tube: Notting Hill Gate.

Under the guidance of the energetic Jane England, this gallery specializes in Outsider Art (by untrained artists) and Art in Boxes, which incorporates a box structure into the composition or frame of a three-dimensional work, while focusing attention on neglected post-war British artists such as Tony Stubbings and Ralph Romney. One-person and group shows are mounted frequently, and many young artists get early exposure here.

✪ **Whitechapel Open Studios.** Whitechapel High St., E1. ☎ **0171/522-7878.** Tube: Aldgate East.

Since it opened its art nouveau doors in 1901, savvy collectors have been heading to this East End gallery to find out what's hot and happening in the art world. It still maintains its cutting edge; to some, it's the incubation chamber for some of the most talented of East London's artists. The collections are fun, hip, often sexy, and definitely in your face.

BATH & BODY

✪ **The Body Shop.** 375 Oxford St., W1. ☎ **0171/409-7868.** Tube: Bond St. Other locations throughout London.

There's a branch of The Body Shop in every trading area and tourist zone in London. Some stores are bigger than others, but all are filled with politically and environmentally correct beauty, bath, and aromatherapy products. Prices are drastically lower in the United Kingdom than they are in the United States. There's an entire children's line, a men's line, and lots of travel sizes and travel products. You won't have as much fun in a candy store.

✪ **Boots The Chemist.** 72 Brompton Rd., SW3. ☎ **0171/589-6557.** Tube: Knightsbridge. Other locations throughout London.

This store has a million branches; we like the one across the street from Harrods for convenience and size. The house brands of beauty products are usually the best, be they Boots products (try the cucumber facial scrub), Boot's versions of The Body Shop (two lines, Global and Naturalistic), or Boot's versions of Chanel makeup (called No. 7). They also sell film, pantyhose (called tights), sandwiches, and all of life's little necessities.

Culpeper the Herbalist. 8 The Market, Covent Garden, WC2. ☎ **0171/379-6698.** Tube: Covent Garden.

This store has another shop in Mayfair (21 Bruton St., W1; ☎ **0171/629-4559**) but the hours are better at Covent Garden, so you'll have to put up with the cramped space here to check out all the food, bath, and aromatherapy products. You can stock up on essential oils, or go for the dream pillows, candles, sachets, and many a shopper's fave: the aromatherapy fan.

✪ **Floris.** 89 Jermyn St., SW1. ☎ **0171/930-2885.** Tube: Piccadilly Circus.

A variety of toilet articles and fragrances fill Floris's floor-to-ceiling mahogany cabinets, which are architectural curiosities in their own right. They were installed relatively late in the establishment's history—that is, 1851—long after the shop had received its Royal Warrants as suppliers of toilet articles to the king and queen.

Neal's Yard Remedies. 15 Neal's Yard, WC2. ☎ **0171/379-7222.** Tube: Covent Garden.

Noted the world over for their cobalt-blue bottles, these chi-chi bath, beauty, and aromatherapy products are must-haves for those who pooh pooh The Body Shop as too common. Prices are much higher in the United States, so stock up here.

✪ **Penhaligon's.** 41 Wellington St., WC2. ☎ **0171/836-2150,** or 800/588-1992 in the U.S. for mail order. Tube: Covent Garden.

This Victorian perfumery, established in 1870, holds Royal Warrants to HRH Duke of Edinburgh and HRH Prince of Wales. All items sold are exclusive to Penhaligon's. It offers a large selection of perfumes, aftershaves, soaps, and bath oils for women and men. Gifts include antique silver scent bottles, grooming accessories, and leather traveling requisites. Penhaligon's is now in more than 20 Saks Fifth Avenue stores across the U.S., allowing you to sneak a peek at their collection before you shop in London.

BOOKS, MAPS, & ENGRAVINGS

In addition to the specialty bookstores listed below, you'll also find well-stocked branches of the **Dillon's** chain around town, including one at 82 Gower St. (tube: Euston Square).

Children's Book Centre. 237 Kensington High St., W8. ☎ **0171/937-7497.** Tube: High St. Kensington.

With thousands of titles, this is the best place to go for children's books. Fiction is arranged according to age, up to 16. There are also videos and toys for kids.

Gay's The Word. 66 Marchmont St., WC1. ☎ **0171/278-7654.** Tube: Russell Sq.

London's leading gay and lesbian bookstore offers a large collection as well as a selection of magazines, cards, and guides. There's also a used-books section.

Hatchards. 187 Piccadilly, W1. ☎ **0171/439-9921.** Tube: Piccadilly Circus or Green Park.

On the south side of Piccadilly, Hatchards offers a wide range of books in all subjects and is particularly renowned in the areas of fiction, biography, travel, cookery, gardening, and art, plus history and finance. In addition, Hatchards is second to none in its range of books on royalty.

Map House. 54 Beauchamp Place, SW3. ☎ **0171/589-4325.** Tube: Knightsbridge.

This is an ideal place to find an offbeat souvenir. Map House sells antique maps and engravings and a vast selection of old prints of London and England, both original and reproduction. A century-old original engraving can cost as little as £5 ($8).

Murder One. 71–73 Charing Cross Rd., WC2. ☎ **0171/734-3485.** Tube: Leicester Sq.

Maxim Jakubowski's bookshop is dedicated to the genres of crime, romance, science fiction, and horror. Crime and science fiction magazines, some of them obscure, are also available.

Silver Moon Women's Bookshop. 64–68 Charing Cross Rd., WC2. ☎ **0171/836-7906.** Tube: Leicester Sq.

This place stocks thousands of titles by and about women, plus videos, jewelry, and a large selection of lesbian books.

Stanfords. 12–14 Long Acre, WC2. ☎ **0171/836-1321.** Tube: Leicester Sq. or Covent Garden.

Established in 1852, Stanfords is the world's largest map shop. Many of its maps, which include worldwide touring and survey maps, are unavailable elsewhere. It's also London's best travel bookstore (with a complete selection of Frommer's guides!).

W & G Foyle, Ltd. 113–119 Charing Cross Rd., WC2. ☎ **0171/439-8501.** Tube: Tottenham Court Rd.

Claiming to be the world's largest bookstore, W & G Foyle has an impressive array of hardcovers and paperbacks, as well as travel maps, records, videotapes, and sheet music.

CASHMERES & WOOLENS

British Designer Knitwear Group. 2–6 Quadrant Arcade, 80 Regent St., W1. ☎ **0171/734-5786.** Tube: Piccadilly Circus.

Here you'll find woolens from all over the British Islands, including the Scottish Shetlands. Some of the woolens are handmade; often, many of the designers are well known. Some have a tweedy English look, while others are more high fashion.

Scotch House. 84–86 Regent St., W1. ☎ **0171/734-5966.** Tube: Piccadilly Circus.

For top-quality woolen fabrics and garments, go to Scotch House, renowned worldwide for its comprehensive selection of cashmere and wool knitwear for men, women, and children. Also available is a wide range of tartan garments and accessories, as well as Scottish tweed classics.

Westaway & Westaway. 62–65 and 92–93 Great Russell St. (opposite the British Museum), WC1. ☎ **0171/405-4479.** Tube: Tottenham Court Rd.

Stopping in here is a substitute for a shopping trip to Scotland. You'll find a large range of kilts, scarves, waistcoats, capes, dressing gowns, and rugs in authentic clan tartans. The staff is knowledgeable about the intricate clan symbols. They also sell cashmere, camel-hair, and Shetland knitwear, plus Harris tweed jackets, Burberry raincoats, and cashmere overcoats for men.

CHINA, GLASS & SILVER

The Glasshouse. 21 St. Albans Place, N1. ☎ **0171/359-8162.** Tube: Angel.

Not only can you buy beautiful glass here, but you can also watch the craftspeople producing glass works of art in the workshop. Glass can even be made to your own designs.

✪ **Lawleys.** 154 Regent St., W1. ☎ **0171/734-3184.** Tube: Piccadilly Circus or Oxford Circus.

Founded in the 1930s, this store has one of the largest inventories of china in Britain. A wide range of English bone china, as well as crystal and giftware, is sold. The firm specializes in Royal Doulton, Minton, Royal Crown Derby, Wedgwood, Spode, and Aynsley china; Lladró figures; David Winter Cottages; Border Fine Arts; and other famous names. Lawleys also sells cutlery. The January and July sales are excellent.

London Silver Vaults. Chancery House, 53–63 Chancery Lane, WC2. ☎ **0171/242-3844.** Tube: Chancery Lane.

Don't let the slightly out-of-the-way location, or the facade's lack of charm, slow you down. Downstairs, you go into real vaults—40 in all—that are filled with tons of silver and silverplate, plus a collection of jewelry. It's a staggering selection of old to new, with excellent prices and friendly dealers.

Reject China Shop. 183 Brompton Rd., SW3. ☎ **0171/581-0739.** Tube: Knightsbridge. Other locations throughout London.

Don't expect too many rejects or too many bargains, despite the name. This shop sells seconds (sometimes) along with first-quality pieces of china with such names as Royal Doulton, Spode, and Wedgwood. You also can find a variety of crystal, glassware, and flatware. If you'd like to have your purchases shipped home for you, the shop can do it for a fee.

Thomas Goode. 19 S. Audley St., W1. ☎ **0171/499-2823.** Tube: Bond St. or Green Park.

This is one of the most famous emporiums in Britain; it's worth visiting for its architectural interest and nostalgic allure alone. Originally built in 1876, Goode's has 14 rooms loaded with porcelain, gifts, candles, silver, tablewares, and even a private museum. There's also a tearoom-cum-restaurant tucked into the corner (see "Teatime" in chapter 5 for details).

EYEGLASSES

Cutler & Gross. 16 Knightsbridge Green, SW1. ☎ **0171/581-2250.** Tube: Knightsbridge.

This is London's best optometry shop. Hand-crafted frames run £87 to £110 ($139 to $176); there's also a wide range of tints for prescription lenses. Orders usually require a 5-day waiting period. Eye exams and repair services are also available.

FASHION
THE TRUE BRIT

Whereas every internationally known designer worth his or her weight in shantung has a boutique in London, the best buys are on the sturdy English styles that last forever.

Aquascutum. 100 Regent St., W1. ☎ **0171/734-6090.** Tube: Piccadilly Circus.

It is about as quintessentially British as you'll get this side of Savile Row, and it's a popular stop-off for American tourists wanting to look more British than the Brits. On four floors, this classic shop offers only high-quality British and imported clothing (including leisurewear) for men and women.

Austin Reed. 103–113 Regent St., W1. ☎ **0171/734-6789.** Tube: Piccadilly Circus.

Austin Reed has long stood for superior-quality clothing and excellent tailoring. The suits of Chester Barrie, for example, are said to fit like bespoke (custom-made) clothing. The polite employees are unusually honest about telling you what looks good. The store always has a wide variety of top-notch jackets and suits, and men can outfit themselves from dressing gowns to overcoats. For women, there are carefully selected suits, separates, coats, shirts, knitwear, and accessories.

Berk. 46 Burlington Arcade, Piccadilly, W1. ☎ **0171/493-0028.** Tube: Piccadilly Circus or Green Park.

This store boasts one of the largest collections of cashmere sweaters in London—at least the top brands. The outlet also carries capes, stoles, scarves, and camel-hair sweaters.

✪ Burberry. 18–22 Haymarket, SW1. ☎ **0171/930-3343.** Tube: Piccadilly Circus.

The name has been synonymous with raincoats ever since Edward VII publicly ordered his valet to "bring my Burberry" when the skies threatened. An impeccably trained staff sells the famous raincoats, plus excellent men's shirts, sportswear, knitwear, and accessories. Raincoats are available in women's sizes and styles as well. Prices are high, but you get quality and prestige.

Dr. Marten's Department Store. 1–4 King St., WC2. ☎ **0171/497-1460.** Tube: Covent Garden.

Dr. Marten (called Doc Marten) makes a brand of shoe that has become so popular—internationally—that now there's an entire department store selling them in a huge variety of styles, plus accessories, gifts, and even clothes. Teens come to worship here because ugly is beautiful, and because the prices are far better than they are in the United States or elsewhere in Europe.

Gieves & Hawkes. 1 Savile Row, W1. ☎ **0171/434-2001.** Tube: Piccadilly Circus or Green Park.

This place has a prestigious address and a list of clients that includes the Prince of Wales, yet its prices aren't as lethal as others on this street. They're high, but you get good quality. Cotton shirts, silk ties, Shetland sweaters, and exceptional ready-to-wear and tailor-made (bespoke) suits are sold.

Hilditch & Key. 37 and 73 Jermyn St., SW1. ☎ **0171/734-4707.** Tube: Piccadilly Circus or Green Park.

The finest name in men's shirts, Hilditch & Key has been in business since 1899. The two shops on this street both offer men's clothing (including a bespoke shirt service) and women's ready-made shirts. There's also an outstanding tie collection. Shirts go for half-price during the twice-yearly sales; men fly in from all over the world for them.

Jigsaw. 21 Long Acre, WC2. ☎ **0171/240-3855.** Tube: Covent Garden. Also at 9–10 Floral St., WC2 (☎ **0171/240/5651**) and other locations throughout London.

Branches of this fashion chain are too numerous to mention here, but the Long Acre shop features safely trendy, middle-market womenswear and children's clothing. Much of the rather hip clothing is for Goldie Hawn types, not the Queen at Ascot. Around the corner, the Floral Street shop carries menswear, including a wide range of colored moleskin items.

Laura Ashley. 256–258 Regent St., W1. ☎ **0171/437-9760.** Tube: Oxford Circus. Other locations around London.

This is the flagship store of the company whose design ethos embodies the English country look. The store carries a wide choice of women's clothing and home furnishings. Prices are lower than in the United States.

Next. 20 Long Acre, WC2. ☎ **0171/836-1516.** Tube: Covent Garden. Other locations throughout London.

This chain of "affordable fashion" stores knew its heyday when it became celebrated in the 1980s for its main-street fashion revolution. No longer at its peak, it still merits a stopover. The look is still very contemporary, with a continental flair worn not only by men and women but kids too.

✪ Thomas Pink. 85 Jermyn St., SW1. ☎ **0171/930-6364.** Tube: Green Park.

This Jermyn Street shirtmaker, named after an 18th-century Mayfair tailor, gave the world the phrases "hunting pink" and "in the pink." It has a prestigious reputation for well-made cotton shirts, for both men and women, made from Egyptian and Sea Island cotton. The shirts are created from the finest two-fold pure-cotton poplin, coming in a wide range of patterns, stripes, and checks, as well as in plain colors. Some patterns are classic, others new and unusual. All are generously cut, with extra-long tails and finished with a choice of double cuffs or single-button cuffs. A small pink square in the tail tells all.

Turnbull & Asser. 71–72 Jermyn St., SW1. ☎ **0171/930-0502.** Tube: Piccadilly Circus.

Over the years, everyone from David Bowie to Ronald Reagan has been seen in a custom-made shirt from Turnbull & Asser. Excellent craftsmanship and simple lines— even bold colors—distinguish these shirts. The outlet also sells shirts and blouses to women, a clientele that has ranged from Jacqueline Bisset to Candice Bergen. Note that T&A shirts come in only one sleeve length and are then altered to fit. The sales department will inform you that its made-to-measure service takes 10 to 12 weeks, and you must order at least a half-dozen. Of course, the monograms are included.

THE CUTTING EDGE

Anya Hindmarch. 91 Walton St., SW3. ☎ **0171/584-7644.** Tube: South Kensington.

Although her fashionable bags are sold at Harvey Nichols, Liberty, Harrods, and in the United States and Europe, this is the only place to see the complete range of Anya Hindmarch's designs. Featuring handbags, wash bags, wallets, purses, and key holders, smaller items range in price from £38 ($61) whereas handbag prices stretch from £150 ($240) and up, with alligator being the most expensive. There's a limited bespoke service, and you may bring in your fabric to be matched.

✪ **Browns.** 23–27 S. Molton St., W1. ☎ **0171/491-7833.** Tube: Bond St.

This is the only place in London to find the designs of Alexander McQueen, now head of the House of Givenchy in Paris, and one of the fashion industry's major stars. Producing his own cottons, silks, and plastics, McQueen creates revealing and feminine women's couture and ready-to-wear, and has recently started marketing a well-received menswear line. McQueen made his reputation creating shock-value apparel more eagerly photographed than worn. But recently his outfits have been called more "consumer friendly" by fashion critics.

Egg. 36 Kinnerton St., SW1. ☎ **0171/235-9315.** Tube: Hyde Park Corner or Knightsbridge.

This shop is hot, hot, hot with fashionistas. It features imaginatively designed, contemporary clothing by Indian textile designer Asha Sarabhai and knitwear by Eskandar. Designs created from handmade textiles from a workshop in India range from everyday dresses and coats to hand-embroidered silk coats. Prices begin at £60 ($96). Crafts and ceramics are also available.

Hennes. 261 Regent St., W1. ☎ **0171/493-4004.** Tube: Oxford Circus.

Here are copies of hot-off-the-catwalk fashions at affordable prices. While the quality isn't much to brag about, the prices are. For disposable cutting-edge fashion, you can't beat it.

Hype DF. 48–52 Kensington High St., W8. ☎ **0171/937-3100.** Tube: High St. Kensington.

This retailer has been showcasing young designers since 1983, but in a different location that was known as Hyper-Hyper. Designs for men and women range from sports to evening wear, with plenty of accessories, including shoes. There's a wide range of prices; some of this stuff isn't cheap, but some styles are very affordable. Hype DF will definitely intrigue.

Joseph. 23 Old Bond St., W1. ☎ **0171/629-3713.** Tube: Green Park. Also at 16 Sloane St., SW1 (☎ 0171/235-1991; tube: Sloane Sq.); 26 Sloane St., SW1 (☎ 0171/235-5470; tube: Sloane Sq.); and 77 Fulham Rd., SW3 (☎ 0171/823-9500; tube: South Kensington). **Joseph's Own APC, Inc.** is at 124 Draycott Ave., SW3 (☎ 0171/225-0364; tube: South Kensington).

Joseph Ettedgui, a fashion retailer born in Casablanca, is a maverick in the fashion world—he's known for his daring designs and his ability to attract some of the most talented designers in the business to work with him. This is the flagship store among five London branches, and it carries the Ettedgui collection of suits, knitwear, suede, and leather clothing for men and women. The stretch jeans with flair ankles are the label's best-selling items.

The 16 Sloane St. branch carries only the label's womenswear; the 26 Sloane St. shop displays all Joseph products and stocks the complete menswear line. Joseph's Own APC also features womenswear, and across the street, the Fulham Road store showcases mens- and womenswear collections by other designers, including Prada, Gucci, Marni, Misoni, and Anne Deimunister.

Katharine Hamnett. 20 Sloane St., SW1. ☎ **0171/823-1002.** Tube: Knightsbridge.

One of Britain's big-name designers—her so-called "slut dresses" earned her the title of the bad girl of Brit fashion—Katharine Hamnett is best known for her slogan T-shirts. Recent collections, although greeted with a media feeding frenzy, continue to mixed reviews. You can judge for yourself while browsing through her complete line of men's and women's day and evening wear. She's also a strong environmental activist and is known for using "nature friendly" fabrics.

✪ **Vivienne Westwood.** 6 Davies St., W1. ☎ **0171/629-3757.** Tube: Bond St. Branches: World's End, 430 King's Rd., SW3 (☎ 0171/352-6551; tube: Sloane Sq.); and Vivienne Westwood, 43 Conduit St., W1 (☎ 0171/439-1109; tube: Oxford Circus).

No one in British fashion is hotter than the unstoppable Vivienne Westwood. While it's possible to purchase select Westwood pieces around the world, her U.K. shops are the best places to find her full range of fashion designs. The flagship location concentrates on her couture line, or The Gold Label, as it's known. Using a wide range of uniquely British resources, Westwood creates jackets, skirts, trousers, blouses, dresses, and evening dresses. Her latest line features taffeta ballgowns, made-to-measure tailored shirts, even some Highland plaids. If all this weren't enough, she came out with her own perfume in 1997 (who hasn't?).

The World's End branch carries casual designs, including T-shirts, jeans, and other sportswear. The sale shop on Conduit Street has a bit of everything: The Gold Label; her second women's line, The Red Label; and The Man Label, her menswear collection. Accessories available include women's and men's shoes, belts, and jewelry.

VINTAGE & SECONDHAND

Note that there's no VAT refund on used clothing.

Annie's Vintage Costume and Textiles. 10 Camden Passage, N1. ☎ **0171/359-0796.** Tube: Angel.

The shop concentrates on carefully preserved dresses from the 1920s and 1930s, but has a range of clothing and textiles from the 1880s through the 1960s. A 1920s fully beaded dress will run you about £400 ($640), but there are scarves for £10 ($16), camisoles for £18 ($29), and a range of exceptional pieces priced between £50 and £60 ($80 and $96). Clothing is located on the main floor; textiles, including old lace, bed linens, and tapestries, are upstairs.

Old Hat. 62 and 66 Fulham High St., SW6. ☎ **0171/736-5446.** Tube: Putney Bridge.

This large dealer of secondhand menswear is the place to find Savile Row suits, Jermyn Street silk ties, Burberry's raincoats, and Turnbull and Asser shirts for a fraction of their original cost. There's a variety of styles from the last 80 years on hand, and everything's in good condition. Prices range from £5 to £100 ($8 to $160); tailoring is available for about £5 to £30 ($8 to $48). Be sure to check out the window displays, which regularly feature such incongruities as a pair of BSA Bantam motorcycles (also available for purchase).

Pandora. 16–22 Cheval Place, SW7. ☎ **0171/589-5289.** Tube: Knightsbridge.

A London institution since the 1940s, Pandora stands in fashionable Knightsbridge, a stone's throw from Harrods. Several times a week, chauffeurs will drive up with bundles packed anonymously by England's gentry. One woman voted best-dressed at Ascot several years ago was wearing a secondhand dress acquired here. Prices are generally one-third to one-half the retail value. Chanel and Anne Klein are among the designers represented. Outfits are usually no more than two seasons old.

Pop Boutique. 6 Monmouth St., WC2. ☎ **0171/497-5262.** Tube: Covent Garden.

For the best in original streetwear from the 1950s, 1960s, and 1970s, this clothing store is tops. Right next to the chic Covent Garden Hotel, it has fabulous vintage wear at affordable prices: Leather jackets that would run $250 or $300 in the vintage shops of downtown New York go for as little as £40 ($64) here.

Steinberg & Tolkien. 193 King's Rd., SW3. ☎ **0171/376-3660.** Tube: Sloane Sq.

This place is London's leading dealer in vintage costume jewelry and clothing. There's also some used designer clothing that isn't old enough to be vintage but is prime for collectors; other pieces are merely secondhand designer thrills.

FILOFAX

All major department stores sell Filofax supplies, but the full range is carried in their own stores. They also have good sales; calendars for the next year go on sale very early the previous year (about 10 months in advance), so you can stock up and save.

The Filofax Centre. 21 Conduit St., W1. ☎ **0171/499-0457.** Tube: Oxford Circus. Also at 69 Neal St., WC2 (☎ 0171/836-1977; tube: Covent Garden).

Get to the West End shop if you can; it's larger and fancier than the Covent Garden address, with the entire range of inserts and books, and prices that will floor you, at least half the U.S. going rate.

FOOD

English food has come a long way lately; it's worth enjoying and bringing home. Don't pass up the Food Halls in Harrods; consider the Fifth Floor at Harvey Nicks if Harrods is crammed with too many tourists—it isn't the same, but it'll do. Also, **Fortnum & Mason** is internationally famous as a food emporium. See "The Department Stores," above.

Charbonnel et Walker. 1 The Royal Arcade, 28 Old Bond St., W1. ☎ **0171/491-0939.** Tube: Green Park.

Charbonnel et Walker is famous for its hot chocolate in winter (buy it by the tin) and their strawberries-and-cream chocolates during "The Season." The firm will send messages of thanks or love spelled out on the chocolates themselves. Ready-made presentation boxes are also available.

Neal's Yard Dairy. 17 Shorts Gardens, WC2. ☎ **0171/379-7646.** Tube: Covent Garden.

The front is actually a photo-op; please take note. Then enjoy the cheeses as well as foodstuffs, snack items, and picnic supplies. It could be the highlight of a Sunday afternoon in Covent Garden.

GIFTS & SOUVENIRS

Asprey & Company. 165–169 New Bond St., W1. ☎ **0171/493-6767.** Tube: Green Park.

This is as well-entrenched a name in luxury gift-giving as anything you're likely to find in Britain, with a clientele that includes the likes of the Sultan of Brunei and Queen

Elizabeth (some of her jewelry comes from here). Scattered over four floors of a dignified Victorian building you'll find antiques, porcelain, leather goods, crystal, clocks, and enough unusual objects of dignified elegance to stock an English country house.

The Irish Shop. 14 King St., WC2. ☎ **0171/379-3625.** Tube: Covent Garden.

This family business has been selling a wide variety of articles shipped directly from Ireland since 1964. You'll find a wide selection of colorful knitwear, traditional Irish linens, hand-knitted Aran fisherman's sweaters, and Celtic jewelry. There's a little bit of everything here—even Guinness paraphernalia.

HANDBAGS

Bill Amberg's. 10 Chepstow Rd., W2. ☎ **0171/727-3560.** Tube: Notting Hill Gate.

Most famous for his logo-free handbags, Amberg has opened his own shop and expanded his line to include luggage, picture frames, and furniture. Supporters of Amberg's designs include Donna Karan, Romeo Gigli, Jerry Hall, and Christy Turlington. Given that, fashion-conscious shoppers may consider the £65 to £265 ($104 to $424) price range of most items a steal.

HOME DESIGN & HOUSEWARES

The Conran Shop. Michelin House, 81 Fulham Rd., SW3. ☎ **0171/589-7401.** Tube: South Kensington.

You'll find high style at reasonable prices from the man who invented it all for Britain: Sir Terance Conran. It's great for gifts, home furnishings, and table top—or just for gawking.

✪ Designers Guild. 267–271 and 275–277 King's Rd., SW3. ☎ **0171/351-5775.** Tube: Sloane Sq.

Often copied but never outdone—after more than 26 years in business, creative director Tricia Guild and her young designers still lead the pack in all that's bright and whimsical. There's an exclusive line of handmade furniture and accessories at the no. 267–271 location, and wallpaper and more than 2,000 fabrics at the neighboring no. 275–277 shop. The colors remain forever vivid, and the designs always irreverent. Also available are children's accessories, toys, crockery, and cutlery.

Purves & Purves. 80–81 and 83 Tottenham Court Rd., W1. ☎ **0171/580-8223.** Tube: Tottenham Court Rd.

This store has a varied collection of modern furniture from Britain and the continent. Many pieces are individually made by the designers themselves. The light and airy interior holds an eye-catching display of furniture, lighting, fabrics, rugs, and beds. Two doors up is an accessory shop with everything from clocks to cufflinks.

JEWELRY

Garrard & Co. 112 Regent St., W1. ☎ **0171/734-7020.** Tube: Piccadilly Circus.

Behind the neoclassical facade is London's largest showroom, specializing in antique and modern jewelry and silverware. The in-house designers also produce pieces to order and do repairs. You can have a pair of pearl earrings or silver cufflinks for a mere £60 ($96)—but the prices go nowhere but up from there.

Lesley Craze Gallery/Craze 2/C2 Plus. 33–35 Clerkenwell Green, EC1. ☎ **0171/608-0393** (Gallery), 0171/251-0381 (Craze 2), 0171/251-9200 (C2 Plus). Tube: Farringdon.

This complex has developed a reputation as a showcase of the best contemporary British jewelry and textile design. The gallery shop focuses on precious metals, and includes pieces by such renowned designers as Wendy Ramshaw. Prices start at £50

($80). Craze 2 features costume jewelry in materials ranging from bronze to paper, with prices starting at £12 ($19). C2 Plus features contemporary textile designs, including wall hangings, scarves, and ties by artists such as Jo Barker, Dawn DuPree, and Victoria Richards. C2 Plus has recently added a hanging gallery to display their textiles and wall hangings. The store is now billing itelf as "London's only contemporary textile gallery."

Sanford Brothers Ltd. Old Elizabeth Houses, 3 Holborn Bars, EC1. ☎ **0171/405-2352.** Tube: Chancery Lane.

In business since 1923, this family firm sells all styles of jewelry, both modern and Victorian, silver of all kinds, and a fine selection of clocks and watches.

LINENS
Irish Linen Company. 35–36 Burlington Arcade, W1. ☎ **0171/493-8949.** Tube: Green Park or Piccadilly Circus.

This Royal Warrant boutique carries items crafted of Irish linen, including hand-embroidered handkerchiefs and bed and table linens.

LINGERIE
Bradley's. 57 Knightsbridge, SW1. ☎ **0171/235-2902.** Tube: Knightsbridge or Hyde Park Corner.

Bradley's is the best-known lingerie specialty store in London; members of the royal family shop here. Established in the 1950s and very fashionable today, Bradley's fits "all sizes" in silk, cotton, lace, poly-cotton, or whatever.

LUGGAGE
Mulberry Company. 11–12 Gees Court, W1. ☎ **0171/493-2546.** Tube: Bond St.

This flagship store offers the complete line of the town's most cutting-edge designer luggage. The company's signature grosgrain and leather luggage begins at £150 ($240). Mulberry is also earning a name in fashion for its English country-style ready-to-wear for both men and women; it also carries a fashionable display of furnishings and accessories for the home, including throws and cushions in chenille and damask.

MUSEUM SHOPS
London Transport Museum Shop. Covent Garden, WC2. ☎ **0171/379-6344.** Tube: Covent Garden.

This museum shop carries a wide range of reasonably priced repro and antique travel posters as well as tons of fun gifts and souvenirs. Those great London Underground maps that you see at every tube station can be purchased here.

Victoria & Albert Gift Shop. Cromwell Rd., SW7. ☎ **0171/938-8500.** Tube: South Kensington.

Run by the Craft Council, this is the best museum shop in London—indeed, one of the best in the world. It sells cards, a fabulous selection of art books, and the usual items, along with reproductions from the museum archives.

MUSIC
Collectors should browse Notting Hill; there's a handful of good shops near the Notting Hill Gate tube stop. Also browse Soho in the Wardour Street area, near the Tottenham Court Road tube stop. Sometimes dealers show up at Covent Garden on the weekends.

Note

Americans should beware of buying videotapes in the United Kingdom; the British standard is PAL, which is incompatible with the U.S. standard, NTSC. Even if a tape says VHS, it won't play in your machine at home.

In addition to the two listed below, also worth checking out is the ubiquitous **Our Price** chain, which offers only the current chart-toppers, but usually at great prices.

Tower Records. 1 Piccadilly Circus, W1. ☎ **0171/439-2500.** Tube: Piccadilly Circus. Other locations throughout London.

Attracting the throngs from a neighborhood whose pedestrian traffic is almost overwhelming, this is one of the largest record and CD stores in Europe. Sprawling over four floors, it's practically a tourist attraction in its own right. In addition to a huge selection of most of the musical styles ever recorded, there's everything on the cutting edge of technology, including interactive hardware and software, CD-ROMs, and laser discs.

Virgin Megastore. 14–16 Oxford St., W1. ☎ **0171/631-1234.** Tube: Tottenham Court Rd. Also at 527 Oxford St., W1 (☎ 0171/491-8582; tube: Oxford Circus).

If a record has just been released—and if it's worth hearing in the first place—chances are this store carries it. It's like a giant musical grocery store, and you get to hear the release on headphones at listening stations before making a purchase. Even visiting rock stars come here to pick up new releases. A large selection of classical and jazz recordings is sold, as are computer software and video games. In between selecting your favorites, you can enjoy a coffee at the cafe, or purchase an airline ticket from the Virgin Atlantic office.

SHOES
Also see **Dr. Marten's Department Store** in "Fashion," above.

Church's. 13 New Bond St., W1. ☎ **0171/493-1474.** Tube: Bond St.

Well-made shoes, the status symbol of well-heeled executives in financial districts around the world, have been turned out by Church's since 1873. These are said to be recognizable to all the maîtres d'hôtel in London, who have always been suspected of appraising the wealth of their clients by their footwear.

Lilley & Skinners. 360 Oxford St., W1. ☎ **0171/560-2000.** Tube: Bond St.

This is the largest shoe store in Europe, displaying many different brands over three floors staffed by an army of salespeople. It specializes in not particularly glamorous names, but offers good value and a wide selection of difficult-to-find sizes.

Natural Shoe Store. 21 Neal St., WC2. ☎ **0171/836-5254.** Tube: Covent Garden.

Shoes for both men and women are stocked in this shop, which also does repairs. The selection includes all comfort and quality footwear, from Birkenstock to the best of the British classics.

Shelly's. 266 Regent St., W1. ☎ **0171/287-0939.** Tube: Oxford Circus. Other locations throughout London.

This is the flagship of the mother of all London shoe shops, where they sell everything from tiny-tot hip shoes to grown-up hip shoes and boots at affordable prices. They're famous for their Dr. Martens, but there's much more—and none of it traditional.

SPORTING GOODS

❂ **Lillywhites Ltd.** 24–36 Lower Regent St., Piccadilly Circus, SW1. ☎ **0171/915-4000.** Tube: Piccadilly Circus.

Europe's biggest and most famous sports store has floor after floor of sports clothing, equipment, and footwear. It also offers collections of fashionable leisurewear for men and women.

STATIONERY & PAPER GOODS

Paperchase. 213 Tottenham Court Rd., W1. ☎ **0171/580-8496.** Tube: Goodge St. or Tottenham Court Rd. Other locations throughout London.

This flagship store offers three floors of paper products including storage boxes, handmade paper, wrapping paper, ribbons, picture frames, and a huge selection of offbeat greeting cards. It's the best of its kind in London.

TEAS

Of course, don't forget to visit Fortnum & Mason as well (see "The Department Stores," above).

The Tea House. 15A Neal St., WC2. ☎ **0171/240-7539.** Tube: Covent Garden.

This shop sells everything associated with tea, tea drinking, and teatime. It boasts more than 70 quality teas and tisanes, including whole-fruit blends, the best tea of China (Gunpowder, jasmine with flowers), India (Assam leaf, choice Darjeeling), Japan (Genmaicha green), and Sri Lanka (pure Ceylon), plus such longtime favorite English blended teas as Earl Grey. The shop also offers novelty teapots and mugs, among other items.

TOYS

❂ **Hamleys.** 188–196 Regent St., W1. ☎ **0171/734-3161.** Tube: Oxford Circus. Also at Covent Garden and Heathrow Airport.

This flagship is the finest toy shop in the world—more than 35,000 toys and games on seven floors of fun and magic. The huge selection includes soft, cuddly stuffed animals as well as dolls, radio-controlled cars, train sets, model kits, board games, outdoor toys, and computer games.

TRAVEL SERVICES

British Airways Travel Department Store. 156 Regent St., W1. ☎ **0171/434-4700.** Tube: Piccadilly Circus or Oxford Circus.

The retail flagship of British Airways offers not only worldwide travel and ticketing, but also a wide range of services and shops, including a clinic for immunization, a pharmacy, a bureau de change, a passport and visa service, and a theater-booking desk. The ground floor sells luggage, guidebooks, maps, and other goods. Passengers with hand baggage only can check in here for a BA flight. Travel insurance, hotel reservations, and car rentals can also be arranged.

London's pulsating scene is the most vibrant in Europe. Although pubs still close at 11pm, the city is staying up later. More and more clubs extend partying into the wee hours.

London is on a real high right now, especially in terms of music and dance; much of the current techno and electronica (including the hip hop, tribal, and drum-and-bass styles being appropriated by aging rockers like Bowie and U2) originated in London clubs. Sounds made hip by Tricky and Aphex Twin reverberate not only throughout the city, but across the Continent and the Atlantic as well. Youth culture prevails; downtown denizens flock to the latest clubs where pop culture superstars are routinely spotted, from Noel Gallagher (of Oasis fame) to Damien Hirst (known for suspending dead animals in formaldehyde and calling it Art).

London nightlife is always in a state of constant flux. What's hot today probably just opened and many clubs have the lifespan of fruit flies. **Groucho,** at 44 Dean St., W1 (☎ **0171/439-4685**) is still the *in* club, though it is still members-only. The Marquee, the legendary live-music venue where the Rolling Stones played when they were still bad boys, has regrettably shut its doors. But a few perennials, like Ronnie Scott's, are still around.

London nightlife, however, is not just music and dance clubs. The city abounds with what's the world's best live theater scene, pubs oozing historic charm, and many more options for a night out.

HOW TO FIND OUT WHAT'S GOING ON

Weekly publications such as *Time Out* and *Where* provide the most complete up-to-the-minute entertainment listings. They contain information on live music and dance clubs as well as London's diverse theater scene, which includes everything from big-budget West End shows to fringe productions. Daily newspapers, notably *The Times* and the *Daily Telegraph,* also provide listings. The arts section of the weekend *Independent* is also a good reference.

If you really want to take full advantage of London's arts scene, your best bet is to do a bit of research before you leave home—even a few months in advance. To get a good idea of what's going on, check out *Time Out's* **World Wide Web page** at www.timeout.co.uk. If you're not online, *Time Out* is available at many international newsstands in the United States and Canada. In London, it can be picked up almost anywhere.

1 The Play's the Thing: The London Theater Scene

Even more so than New York, London is the theater capital of the world; the number and variety of productions, as well as high standards of acting and directing, are unrivaled. The London stage accommodates both the traditional and the avant-garde and is uniquely accessible and affordable.

The city's first permanent theater, in the Fields at Shoreditch, opened in 1576 under the patronage of Queen Elizabeth I. The following year saw the debut of the Curtain theater, and in 1598, the most fabled of all: the Globe. This was Shakespeare's and Marlowe's stage, and as long as Queen Bess ruled, legitimate theater held its own against rival attractions like bearbaiting, cockfighting, and public executions—no small feat.

After its Elizabethan heyday, English drama suffered periodic declines that nearly brought it to extinction; the first was an outgrowth of Cromwell's official Puritanism, which banned *all* stage performances (along with the celebration of Christmas) as "heathenish and un-Godly."

In more recent times, decline came out of the social and moral rigidity Britain acquired along with its Empire. Theater came largely from real life. It tended to reflect little more than the vanities of upper-middle class theater-goers who admired their own petrified reflection in a polite but distorted mirror.

Attempts at creating an earthier theater were stomped out by an official known as the Lord Chamberlain, who wielded unlimited powers of censorship. Yet this mandarin figure was indirectly responsible for London's theater clubs, which—being private rather than public stages—lay outside his jurisdiction. One theater club was founded expressly to stage Arthur Miller's *A View from the Bridge* for English audiences, who would have been otherwise deprived of this masterpiece.

The Great Thaw in London theater occurred sometime during the mid-1950s. In truth, the theater's recovery was more like a volcanic eruption. The pressures of repressed talent and creativity—which had been building since World War II—broke loose in a stream of stage and film productions that swept away London's dusty theatrical mores and swung open the gates of a second Elizabethan dramatic era.

Britain hasn't looked back since, and London theater is still a wellspring of originality. The greatest theatrical excitement in the city today is being stirred up by the new Globe Theatre. Since the Globe is also a sightseeing attraction, it's previewed in chapter 6 (see "Shakespeare's Globe Theatre & Exhibition").

Few things in London are as entertaining and rewarding as the theater. A trip to London could be nothing more than a splendid orgy of drama and musicals.

GETTING TICKETS

Prices for London shows usually vary from £16 to £55 ($26 to $88), depending on the theater and the seat. Matinees, performed Tuesday to Saturday, are cheaper than evening performances. Evening performances begin between 7:30 and 8:30pm, midweek matinees at 2:30 or 3pm, and Saturday matinees at 5:45pm. West End theaters are closed Sundays. Many theaters offer the bonus of licensed bars on the premises and coffee at intermissions (which Londoners call "intervals").

Many theaters accept telephone bookings at regular prices with a credit card. They'll hold your tickets for you at the box office, where you pick them up at show time with a credit card.

Central London Theaters

E-0154

277

Warning

Beware of unlicensed ticket agencies in London. You could end up paying £28 ($45) for a ticket worth only £16 ($26). According to law, the face value of a ticket sold at a premium should be declared to the consumer at the time of sale. However, this code appears to be unenforceable. The **Society of London Theatre (☎ 0171/ 557-6700)** reports that it receives complaints of overcharging on a frequent basis. The society advises that you book your ticket at the theater box office by telephone or in person.

Beware also of scalpers who hang out in front of hit shows at London theaters. Even if the tickets they're selling are valid—there are many reports of forged tickets—scalpers charge very high prices.

TICKET AGENCIES

If you've got your heart set on seeing a specific show, particularly one of the big hits, you'll have to reserve in advance through one of the many London ticket agencies. For tickets and information before you go, on just about any show and entertainment option in London, try **Edwards & Edwards,** 1270 Ave. of the Americas, Suite 2414, New York, NY 10020 (☎ **800/223-6108** or 914/328-2150; fax 914/328-2752). They also have offices in London at the **Palace Theatre,** Shaftesbury Avenue, W1 8AY (☎ **0171/734-4555**) or at the **Harrods** ticket desk, 87–135 Brompton Rd. (☎ **0171/589-9109**), located on the Lower Ground floor opposite the British Airways desk. A personal visit isn't necessary; they'll mail tickets to your home, fax you a confirmation, or leave your tickets at the box office. Instant confirmations are available with special "overseas" rates for most shows. A booking and handling fee of up to 20% is added to the ticket price.

You might also try calling **Keith Prowse/First Call** (☎ **0171/836-9001;** fax 212/302-4251). This agency also has an office in the United States that allows you to reserve months in advance for hit shows: Suite 1000, 234 W. 44th St., New York, NY 10036 (☎ **800/669-8687** or 212/398-1430). Various locations exist in London. The fee for booking a ticket is 25% in London and 35% in the United States.

Another option is **Theatre Direct International (TDI)** (☎ **800/334-8457,** U.S. only). TDI specializes in providing London theater and fringe production tickets, but also has tickets to most London productions, including the Royal National Theatre and Barbican. The service allows you to arrive in London with your tickets or have them held for you at the box office.

GALLERY & DISCOUNT TICKETS

London theater tickets are quite reasonable compared to those in the United States. Sometimes gallery seats (the cheapest) are sold only on the day of the performance; you'll need to head to the box office early in the day and, since these are not reserved seats, return an hour before the performance to queue up.

Many major theaters offer reduced-price tickets to students on a standby basis. When available, these tickets are sold 30 minutes prior to curtain. Line up early for popular shows, as standby tickets get snapped up. Of course, you'll need a valid student ID.

The **Society of London Theatre** (☎ **0171/557-6700**) operates a **discount ticket booth** in Leicester Square, where tickets for many shows are available at half price, plus a £2 ($3) service charge. Tickets (limited to four per person) are sold only on the day of performance. You cannot return tickets, and credit cards are not accepted.

False Discounts

Many less-than-scrupulous agents near Leicester Square offer "discounted" tickets that are nothing of the kind. Out-of-towners could pay $30 to $35 for a "discount" ticket only to find them available at the box office for $25. If you believe you've been ripped off, you can complain directly to the theater or call **0171/798-1111**.

Hours are daily from 12:30 to 6:30pm, except on days with scheduled matinees, when the booth opens from noon to 6:30pm.

MAJOR THEATERS & COMPANIES

Barbican Theatre—Royal Shakespeare Company. In the Barbican Centre, Silk St., Barbican, EC2. ☎ **0171/638-8891.** Barbican Theatre £5–£26 ($8–$42). The Pit £12–£18 ($19–$29) matinees and evening performances. Box office daily 9am–8pm. Tube: Barbican or Moorgate.

The Barbican is the London home of the Royal Shakespeare Company, one of the world's finest theater companies. The core of its repertoire remains, of course, the plays of William Shakespeare. It also presents a wide-ranging program of three different productions each week in the Barbican Theatre—a 2,000-seat main auditorium with excellent sight lines throughout, thanks to a raked orchestra—and in The Pit, a small studio space where much of the company's new writing is presented. The Royal Shakespeare Company is in residence in London during the winter months; it spends the summer touring in England and abroad.

Old Vic. Waterloo Rd., SE1. ☎ **0171/928-7616** or 0171/928-2651 (box office). Musicals £6–£22 ($10–$35). Plays £7–£24 ($11–$38). Tube: Waterloo.

The Old Vic, a repertory theater, is a 180-year-old theater whose facade and much of the interior have been restored to their original early-19th-century style, but most of the modernization is behind the scenes. The proscenium arch has been moved back, the stage has tripled in size, and more seats and stage boxes have been added. This fabled theater was where Sir John Gielgud made his debut in 1921 and Lord Olivier directed the National Theatre. But it was announced in 1997 that the theater would be put up for sale. What will eventually happen to this theater seems to be anybody's guess. According to London city codes, it could even be turned into a disco.

Open-Air Theatre. Inner Circle, Regent's Park, NW1. ☎ **0171/935-5884.** Tickets £8–£20 ($13–$32). Tube: Baker St.

This outdoor theater is in Regent's Park; the setting is idyllic, and both seating and acoustics are excellent. Presentations are mainly Shakespeare, usually in period costume. Its theater bar, the longest in London, serves both drink and food. In the case of a rained-out performance, tickets are given for another date. The season runs from the end of May to mid-September, Monday to Saturday at 8pm, plus Wednesday, Thursday, and Saturday matinees at 2:30pm.

✪ **Royal National Theatre.** South Bank, SE1. ☎ **0171/452-3540.** Tickets £10–£25 ($16–$40); midweek matinees, Sat matinees, and previews cost less. Tube: Waterloo, Embankment, or Charing Cross.

Home to one of the world's greatest stage companies, the Royal National Theatre is not one but three theaters—the Olivier, reminiscent of a Greek amphitheater with its open stage; the more traditional Lyttelton; and the Cottesloe, with its flexible stage and seating. The National presents the finest in world theater, from classic drama to award-winning new plays, including comedies, musicals, and shows for young people.

The theater offers a choice of at least six plays at any one time. It's also a full-time theater center, featuring an amazing selection of bars, cafes, restaurants, free foyer music and exhibitions, short early-evening performances, bookshops, backstage tours, riverside walks, and terraces. Eating options abound: You can have a three-course meal in Mezzanine, the National's restaurant; enjoy a light meal in the brasserie-style Terrace Café; or have a snack in one of the coffee bars.

Shakespeare's Globe Theatre. New Globe Walk, Bankside, SE1. ☎ **0171/928-6406.** Box office: 0171/401-9919. Tickets £5 ($8) for groundlings, £5–£20 ($8–$32) for gallery seats. Tube: Mansion House.

In May 1997, the new Globe Theatre—a replica of the Elizabethan original, thatched roof and all—staged its first slate of plays (*Henry V* and *A Winter's Tale*) on the exact site of the 16th-century theater where the Bard originally staged his work.

Productions vary in style and setting; not all are performed in Elizabethan costume. In keeping with the historic setting, there's no lighting focused just on the stage, but floodlighting is used during evening performances to replicate daylight in theater. Theatergoers sit on wooden benches of yore—in thatch-roofed galleries, no less—but these days you can rent a cushion to make yourself more comfortable. About 500 "groundlings" can stand in the uncovered yard around the stage, just like they did when the Bard was here. Mark Rylane, the artistic director of the Globe, told the press he'd be delighted if the audience threw fruit at the actors, as they did in Shakespeare's time. A spokesperson coyly told us that they wish for the theatergoing experience to be "as authentic as possible." Occasionally, you'll hear a comment, hopefully witty, from the audience (perhaps delivered in iambic pentameter).

From May to October, the company intends to hold performances Tuesday to Saturday at 2pm and 7:30pm, and Sunday at 4pm. There will be a limited winter schedule. In any season, the schedule may be affected by the weather, since this is an outdoor theater. Performances last 2½ to 4 hours, depending on the play.

Also in the works is a second theater, the **Inigo Jones Theatre,** based on the architect's designs from the 1600s, where plays will be staged year-round. For details on the exhibition that tells the story of the painstaking re-creation of the Globe, as well as guided tours of the theatre, see "More Central London Attractions" in chapter 6.

Theatre Royal Drury Lane. Catherine St., Covent Garden, WC2. ☎ **0171/494-5060.** Tickets £5.75–£32.50 ($9–$52). Box office Mon–Sat 10am–8pm. Evening performances Mon–Sat 7:45pm; matinees Wed and Sat 3pm. Tube: Covent Garden.

Drury Lane is one of London's oldest and most prestigious theaters, crammed with tradition—not all of it respectable. This, the fourth theater on this site, dates from 1812; the first was built in 1663. Nell Gwynne, the rough-tongued cockney lass who became Charles II's mistress, used to sell oranges under the long colonnade in front. Nearly every star of London theater has taken the stage here at some time. It has a wide-open repertoire but leans toward musicals, especially long-running hits. Guided tours of the backstage area and the front of the house are given Monday, Tuesday, and Thursday at 10:30am and 1, 2:30, and 5:30pm. Occasional tours are given at 10:30am on Wednesday and Saturday. Call ☎ **0171/494-5091** for more information.

FRINGE THEATER

Some of the best theater in London is performed on the "fringe"—at the dozens of so-called fringe theaters devoted to alternative plays, revivals, contemporary dramas, and musicals. These shows are usually more adventurous than established West End productions; they are also consistently lower in price. Expect to pay from £4 to £20 ($6 to $32). Most theaters offer discounted seats to students and seniors.

Fringe theaters are scattered around London. Check the weekly listings in *Time Out* for schedules and show times. Some of the more popular and centrally located theaters are listed below; call for details on current productions.

✪ Almeida Theatre. Almeida St., N1. ☎ **0171/359-4404.** Tickets £6.50–£19.50 ($10–$31). Box office Mon–Sat 9:30am–6pm. Tube: Angel or Highbury & Islington.

Home to the annual Festival of Contemporary Music (also called the Almeida Opera) from mid-June to mid-July, the Almeida is also known for its adventurous stagings of new and classic plays. The theater's legendary status is validated by consistently good productions at lower-than-average prices. Among the more recent celebrated productions have been *Hamlet* with Ralph Fiennes, and *Medea* with Dame Diana Rigg, both of which went to Broadway. Performances are usually held Monday to Saturday.

The Gate. In the Prince Albert Pub, 11 Pembridge Rd., Notting Hill, W11. ☎ **0171/ 229-0706.** Tickets £10 ($16) regular admission, £6 ($10) for students and senior citizens. MC, V. Box office Mon–Fri 10am–7pm. Tube: Notting Hill Gate.

This tiny room above a Notting Hill pub is one of the best alternative stages in London. Popular with local cognoscenti, the theater specializes in translated works by foreign playwrights. Performances are held Monday to Saturday at 7 or 7:30pm. Call for shows and times.

ICA Theatre. The Mall, SW1. ☎ **0171/930-3647.** Average tickets £7–£10 ($11–$16). Box office daily noon–9pm. Tube: Charing Cross or Piccadilly Circus.

In addition to a cinema, cafe, bar, bookshop, and two galleries, the Institute of Contemporary Arts (ICA) has one of London's top theaters for experimental work. ICA's government subsidies usually produce high-quality performances. Bar hours are Tuesday to Saturday from noon to 1am, Sunday noon to 9pm; galleries are open daily from noon to 7:30pm; and cinema showtimes are daily at 5, 7, and 9pm.

The King's Head. 115 Upper St., N1. ☎ **0171/226-1916.** Tickets £10–£11 ($16–$18). Box office Mon–Fri 10:30am–8pm, Sat 10am–8pm, Sun 10am–4pm. Tube: Angel.

Arguably London's most famous fringe locale, the King's Head is also the city's oldest pub-theater. Despite its tiny stage, the popular theater is heavy on musicals; several that opened here have gone on to become successful West End productions.

Matinee performances are held on Saturday and Sunday at 3:30pm. Evening performances Tuesday to Saturday at 8pm.

Young Vic. 66 The Cut, Waterloo, SE1. ☎ **0171/928-6363.** Tickets £7–£20 ($11–$32) adults, £7–£10 ($11–$16) students and children. Performances Mon–Sat 7 or 7:30pm; matinee Sat 2pm. Tube: Waterloo.

Young Vic presents classical and modern plays in the round for theatergoers of all ages and backgrounds, but primarily focuses on young adults. Recent productions have included Shakespeare, Ibsen, Arthur Miller, and specially commissioned plays for children. Call for specific times, as they can fluctuate.

2 The Rest of the Performing Arts Scene

Currently, London supports five major orchestras—the **London Symphony,** the **Royal Philharmonic,** the **Philharmonia Orchestra,** the **BBC Symphony,** and the **BBC Philharmonic**—several choirs, and many smaller chamber groups and historic instrument ensembles. Look for the **London Sinfonietta,** the **English Chamber Orchestra,** and of course the **Academy of St. Martin in the Fields.** Performances are in the South Banks Arts Centre and the Barbican. For smaller recitals, there's Wigmore Hall and St. John's Smith Square.

British Music Information Centre, 10 Stratford Place, W1 (☎ 0171/499-8567), is the city's clearinghouse and resource center for serious music. The center is open Monday to Friday noon to 5pm, and provides free telephone and walk-in information on current and upcoming events. Recitals featuring 20th-century British classical compositions cost up to £5 ($8) and are offered here weekly, usually on Tuesday and Thursday at 7:30pm; call ahead for day and time. Since capacity is limited to 40, you may want to check early. Take the tube to Bond Street.

○ **Barbican Centre—London Symphony Orchestra (& more).** Silk St., the City, EC2. ☎ 0171/638-8891. Tickets £6–£30 ($10–$48). Box office daily 9am–8pm. Tube: Barbican or Moorgate.

The largest art and exhibition center in Western Europe, the roomy and comfortable Barbican is a perfect setting for enjoying music and theater. Barbican Theatre is the London home of the **Royal Shakespeare Company** (see "Major Theaters & Companies," above), while Barbican Hall is the permanent home address of the **London Symphony Orchestra** and host to visiting orchestras and performers, from classical to jazz, folk, and world music.

In addition to the hall and theater, the Barbican Centre includes: The Pit, a studio theater; the Barbican Art Gallery, a showcase for visual arts; the Concourse Gallery and foyer exhibition spaces; Cinemas One and Two, which show recently released mainstream films and film series; the Barbican Library, a general lending library that places a strong emphasis on the arts; the Conservatory, one of London's largest plant houses; and three restaurants, cafes, and bars.

Contemporary Dance. At The Place, 17 Duke's Rd., WC1. ☎ 0171/387-0031. Tickets £7–£11 ($11–$18). Box office Mon–Fri (and Sat performance days) 10:30am–6pm. Tube: Euston.

This showplace usually offers good performances and cheap tickets. The space is small; the mirrors and bars you'll see give an indication of the theater's day job as a dance school.

Dance Umbrella. 20 Chancellor's St., W6. ☎ 0181/741-4040. Tickets £10–£15 ($16–$24). Tube: Hammersmith.

This company's fall season showcase became *the* contemporary dance event in London. During its 6-week season, new works by up-and-coming choreographers are featured. Performances are held at a variety of theaters.

English National Opera. London Coliseum, St. Martin's Lane, WC2. ☎ 0171/632-8300. Tickets £5–£10 ($8–$16) balcony, £12.50–£55 ($20–$88) Upper or Dress Circle or stalls; about 100 discount balcony tickets sold on the day of performance from 10am during the season. Tube: Charing Cross or Leicester Sq.

Built in 1904 as a variety theater and converted into an opera house in 1968, the London Coliseum is the city's largest theater. One of two national opera companies, the English National Opera performs a wide range of works from classics to Gilbert and Sullivan to new and experimental works, each staged with flair and imagination. All performances are in English. A repertory of 18 to 20 productions is presented 5 or 6 nights a week for 11 months of the year (dark in July). Although balcony seats are cheaper, many visitors seem to prefer the Upper Circle or Dress Circle.

Royal Albert Hall. Kensington Gore, SW7. ☎ 0171/589-8212. Tickets £8–£130 ($13–$208), depending on the event. Box office daily 9am–9pm. Tube: South Kensington.

Opened in 1871 and dedicated to the memory of Victoria's consort, Prince Albert, the building encircles one of the world's most famous auditoriums. With a seating capacity of 5,200, it's a popular place to hear music by stars like Eric Clapton and Shirley Bassey, or even the latest in rock and pop. Occasional sporting events (especially boxing) figure strongly here, too.

Since 1941, the hall has been the setting for the BBC Henry Wood Promenade Concerts, known as **"The Proms,"** a concert series that lasts for 8 weeks between mid-July and mid-September. The Proms have been a British tradition since 1895. Although most of the audience occupies reserved seats, true aficionados usually opt for standing room in the orchestra pit, which affords close-up views of the musicians performing on stage. Newly commissioned works are often given their maiden performances here. The final evening of The Proms is the most traditional; the rousing favorites "Jerusalem" or "Land of Hope and Glory" echo through the hall. For tickets, call Ticketmaster (☎ 0171/379-4444) directly.

○ **Royal Festival Hall.** On the South Bank, SE1. ☎ **0171/960-4242.** Tickets £5–£90 ($8–$144). Box office daily 10am–9pm. Tube: Waterloo or Embankment.

In the aftermath of World War II, the principal site of London's music scene shifted to a specialized complex of buildings erected between 1951 and 1964 on the site of a bombed-out 18th-century brewery. In the midst of industrial wastelands on the rarely visited south side of the Thames arose three of the most comfortable and acoustically perfect concert halls in the world. They include Royal Festival Hall, Queen Elizabeth Hall, and the Purcell Room. Together they hold more than 1,200 performances a year, including classical music, ballet, jazz, popular music, and contemporary dance. Also here is the internationally renowned **Hayward Gallery** (see chapter 6).

Royal Festival Hall, which opens daily at 10am, offers an extensive array of things to see and do, including free exhibitions in the foyers and free lunchtime music at 12:30pm. The Poetry Library is open from 11am to 8pm, and shops display a wide selection of books, records, and crafts. **The Festival Buffet** has a wide variety of food at reasonable prices, and bars dot the foyers. **The People's Palace** offers lunch and dinner with a panoramic view of the River Thames. Reservations are recommended by calling ☎ 0171/928-9999.

○ **The Royal Opera House—The Royal Ballet & The Royal Opera.** Bow St., Covent Garden, WC2. Closed for redevelopment. For information on Royal Opera and Royal Ballet performances, in other venues, call **0171/212-9123.**

The nation's most elite opera company (**The Royal Opera**) and leading ballet company (**The Royal Ballet**) have been temporarily dislodged from the Royal Opera House, their Covent Garden home, because of its ongoing renovation. They'll be back on their home stage in the autumn of 1999. In the meantime, they will be appearing at a number of venues within London and abroad, including the Barbican, Royal Albert Hall, and a West End theater. The Royal Ballet also has seasons at the Labatts Apollo in Hammersmith, the Royal Festival Hall, and the London Coliseum. Performances of the Royal Opera are usually sung in the original language, but supertitles are projected, translating the libretto for the audience.

The Royal Ballet performs a repertory with a tilt toward the classics, including works by its earlier choreographer-directors Sir Frederick Ashton and Sir Kenneth MacMillan.

Sadler's Wells Theatre. Rosebery Ave., EC1. ☎ **0171/314-8800.** Tickets £7.50–£35 ($12–$56). Performances usually 8pm. Box office Mon–Sat 10am–8pm. Tube: Angel.

This is London's premier venue for dance. It occupies the site of a theater that was built in 1683, on the location of a well that was once prized for the healing powers of its waters. In the early 1990s, the old-fashioned, turn-of-the-century theater was demolished, and construction began on an innovative new design that was scheduled for completion sometime during the lifetime of this edition, in late 1998 or perhaps 1999. In the interim, performances are presented in the Peacock, on Portugal Street, WC2 (same phone; tube: Holborn).

The new theater will offer both traditional and experimental dance within two theaters. They will include the new, state-of-the-art theater on the original site as well as offshoot productions within the Peacock, which the Sadler's Wells Trust will continue to rent until sometime after the millennium.

Wigmore Hall. 36 Wigmore St., W1. ☎ **0171/935-2141.** Tickets £5–£35 ($8–$56). Performances nightly, plus Sun Morning Coffee Concerts and Sun concerts at 4 or 7pm. Tube: Bond St. or Oxford Circus.

An intimate auditorium, Wigmore Hall offers an excellent regular series of song recitals, piano and chamber music, early and baroque music, jazz, and concerts featuring particular composers or themes. A free list of the month's programs is available from Wigmore. A cafe-bar and restaurant are on the premises; a cold supper can be pre-ordered if you are attending a concert.

ON THE OUTSKIRTS

Kenwood Lakeside Concerts. Kenwood, Hampstead Lane, Hampstead Heath, London NW3 7JR (☎ **0181/348-1286**). Tickets for adults £9–£12 ($14–$19) for seats on the grass lawn, £11–£16 ($18–$26) for reserved deck chairs. Reductions of 25% for students and persons over 60. Every summer Saturday at 7:30pm from mid-June to early Sept. Tube: Golders Green or Archway, then bus no. 210.

Presented on the north side of Hampstead Heath, these band and orchestral concerts have been a British tradition for some 50 years. In recent years, laser shows and fireworks have added to a repertoire that includes everything from rousing versions of the *1812 Overture* to jazz, and such operas as *Carmen.* The final concert of the season always features some of the Pomp and Circumstance Marches of Sir Edward Elgar, everyone's favorite imperial composer. Music drifts across the lake to serenade wine-and-cheese parties on the grass.

3 The Club & Music Scene

It's the nature of live music and dance clubs to come and go with alarming speed, or shift violently from one trend to another. *Time Out* is the best way to keep current.

COMEDY & CABARET

Comedy Spot. The Spot, Maiden Lane, WC2. ☎ **0171/379-5900.** Cover Fri and Sat £4 ($6) after 8pm. Mon–Thurs noon–midnight, Fri–Sat noon–1am, Sun noon–10:30pm.

This bar-restaurant has DJs Tuesday to Saturday; singers on Sunday; and "spotlight comedy" on Monday nights, with a host and three comedians, mixing beginners with old pros. If you're into stand-up comedy, English-style, this is one of the best places in town.

The Comedy Store. 1A Oxendon St., off Piccadilly Circus, SW1. ☎ **0142/691-4433.** Cover £10 ($16) Tues–Thurs, £11–£12 ($18–$19) Fri–Sun. Daily from 6:30pm. Tube: Leicester Sq. or Piccadilly Circus.

In the heart of the city's nighttime district, this is London's most visible showcase for established and rising comic talent. Inspired by comedy clubs in the United States, this London club has given many comics their starts. Today a number of them are established TV personalities. Even if their names are unfamiliar, you'll enjoy the spontaneity of live comedy performed before a British audience. Visitors must be 18 and older; dress is casual. Reserve through Ticketmaster (☎ **0171/344-4444**); the club opens 1½ hours before each show. *Insider's Tip:* Go on Tuesday when the humor is more cutting edge and topical.

Tiddy Dols. 55 Shepherd Market, Mayfair, W1. ☎ **0171/499-2357.** No cover. Mon–Sat 6–11:30pm, Sun 6–11pm. Tube: Green Park.

Encompassing nine small and atmospheric Georgian houses built around 1741, Tiddy Dols is named after a famous eccentric gingerbread baker. Diners are entertained with madrigals, Noël Coward, Gilbert and Sullivan tunes, vaudeville, and music-hall songs. You'll get an insight into the sort of vaudeville that spurred the Doughboys of World War I across the Atlantic. Enjoy rack of lamb, cock-a-leekie, plum pudding, and the original gingerbread of Tiddy Dol. In summer, a large street cafe with parasols provides a view of the "village" of Shepherd Market; in winter there are open fires. Main courses range in price from £11.50 to £15.25 ($18 to $24); set dinners, £22 ($35).

BOUZOUKI

Elysée. 13 Percy St., W1. ☎ **0171/636-4804.** Cover Mon–Thurs £3 ($5), Fri–Sat £4 ($6). Meals Mon–Fri noon–3pm, Mon–Sat 7:30pm–4am. Tube: Goodge St. or Tottenham Court Rd.

Elysée is for *Never on Sunday* devotees who like the reverberations of bouzouki and the smashing of plates. The Karegeorgis brothers—Michael, Ulysses, and the incomparable George—offer hearty fun at moderate tabs. You can dance nightly to music by Greek musicians. Two different cabaret shows are presented (the last one at 1am), highlighted by brother George's amusing art of balancing wine glasses. You can book a table on either the ground floor or the second floor, but the Roof Garden is the place to be in summer. The food is good, too, especially the house specialty, the classic moussaka, and kebabs from the charcoal grill.

LIVE MUSIC

The Rock Garden. 6–7 The Piazza, Covent Garden, WC2. ☎ **0171/836-4052.** Cover £5–£12 ($8–$19); diners enter free. Mon–Thurs 5pm–3am, Fri 5pm–4am, Sat 4pm–4am, Sun 7:30–11pm. Bus: Any of the night buses that depart from Trafalgar Square. Tube: Covent Garden.

A long-established performance site for a wide array of bands, The Rock Garden maintains a bar and a stage in the cellar, and a restaurant on the street level. The cellar, known as The Venue, has hosted such acts as Dire Straits, Police, and U2 before their rises to stardom. Today bands vary widely, from promising up-and-comers to some who'll never be heard from again. Simple American-style fare is served in the restaurant.

Wag Club. 35 Wardour St., W1. ☎ **071/437-5534.** Cover £3–£10 ($5–$16). Tues–Fri 10pm–4am, Sat 10pm–5am, Sun 10pm–3am. No credit cards. Tube: Leicester Sq. or Piccadilly Circus.

The split-level Wag Club is one of the more stylish live-music places in town. The downstairs stage usually attracts newly signed, cutting-edge rock bands, while a DJ spins dance records upstairs. Door policy can be selective.

ON THE OUTSKIRTS

Several of London's best music venues are in Camden Town and adjacent Kentish Town, just east of Regent's Park.

The Bull & Gate. 389 Kentish Town Rd., NW5. ☎ **0171/485-5358.** Cover £2–£4 ($3–$6). Tube: Kentish Town.

Smaller, cheaper, and often more animated and less touristed than many of its competitors, The Bull & Gate is the unofficial headquarters of London's pub rock scene. Indie and relatively unknown rock bands are often served up back-to-back by the half dozen in this somewhat battered Victorian pub. If you like spilled beer, this is off-the-beaten-track London at its most authentic. Bands that played here and later ascended to Europe's clubby scene have included Madness, Blur, Pulp, and that 1980s music video oddity, Sigue-Sigue-Sputnik. The place operates pub hours, with music nightly from 8 to 11pm.

FOLK

Cecil Sharpe House. 2 Regent's Park Rd., NW1. ☎ **0171/485-2206.** No cover. Tube: Camden Town.

CSH was the focal point of the folk revival in the 1960s, and it continues to treasure and nurture the style. Here you'll find a whole range of traditional English music and dance. Call to see what's happening.

JAZZ & BLUES

Ain't Nothing But Blues Bar. 20 Kingly St., W1. ☎ **0171/287-0514.** Cover Fri–Sat £3–£5 ($5–$8); free before 9:30pm. Mon–Thurs 5:30–1am, Fri–Sat 6pm–3am, Sun 7:30pm–midnight. Tube: Oxford Circus.

The club, which bills itself as the only true blues venue in town, features local acts and occasional touring American bands. On weekends prepare to queue. From the Oxford Circus tube, walk south on Regent Street, turn left on Great Marlborough Street, and then make a quick right on Kingly Street.

The Blue Note. 1 Hoxton Sq., N1. ☎ **0171/729-8440.** Cover £5–£12 ($8–$19). Mon–Sat noon–6pm, Thurs 10pm–3am, Fri–Sat 10pm–5am, Sun 1–6pm and 7pm–midnight. Tube: Old St.

Owned by the Acid Jazz Record label, this is a cafe-bar by day and live-music club by night. It became famous on the London nightlife circuit in its former incarnation as the Bass Clef. Acid Jazz took it over, saved the building from demolition, and now books bands ranging from hip-hop and drum and bass to jazz, funk, and soul. Sundays feature soul music upstairs and hot jazz in the basement.

Bull's Head. 373 Lonsdale Rd., Barnes, SW13. ☎ **0181/876-5241.** Cover £3–£8 ($5–$13). Mon–Sat 11am–11pm, Sun noon–10:30pm. Tube: Hammersmith, then bus 9A to Barnes Bridge, then retrace the path of the bus for some 200 yards on foot; or take Hounslow Look train from Waterloo Station and get off at Barnes Bridge Station, then walk 5 minutes to the club.

This club has showcased live modern jazz every night of the week for more than 30 years. One of the oldest hostelries in the area, it was a mid-19th-century staging post where travelers on their way to Hampton Court could eat, drink, and rest while coach horses were changed. Today the bar features jazz by musicians from all over the world. Live jazz on Sunday from noon to 10:30pm; Monday to Saturday, from 8 to 11pm. You can order lunch at the Carvery in the Saloon Bar or dinner in the 17th-century Stable Restaurant.

Jazz Café. 5 Parkway, NW1. ☎ **0171/916-6060.** Cover £9.50–£14 ($15–$22); £12 ($19) per person to book a table. Tube: Parkway.

Afro-Latin jazz fans are hip to this club hosting combos from around the globe. The weekends, described by one patron as "bumpy jazzy-funk nights," are the best time to decide for yourself what that means. Call ahead for listings, cover, and table reservations (when necessary); opening times can vary.

100 Club. 100 Oxford St., W1. ☎ **0171/636-0933.** Cover Fri £8 ($13) members and non-members, Sat £8 ($13) members, £9 ($14) nonmembers, Sun £6 ($10) members and non-members. Mon–Fri 8:30pm–3am, Sat 7:30pm–1am, Sun 7:30–11:30pm. Tube: Tottenham Court Rd. or Oxford Circus.

Although less plush and expensive than some jazz clubs, 100 Club is a serious contender. Its cavalcade of bands includes the best British jazz musicians and some of their Yankee brethren. Rock, R&B, and blues are also on tap.

✪ Pizza Express. 10 Dean St., W1. ☎ **0171/439-8722.** Cover £8–£15 ($13–$24). Mon–Fri 7:45pm–midnight, Sat–Sun 9pm–midnight. Tube: Tottenham Court Rd.

Don't let the name fool you: This restaurant-bar serves up some of the best jazz in London by mainstream artists. While enjoying a thin-crust Italian pizza, check out a local band or a visiting group, often from the United States. Although the club has been enlarged, it's important to reserve ahead of time.

✪ Ronnie Scott's Club. 47 Frith St., W1. ☎ **0171/439-0747.** Cover non-member £15 ($24), member £4–£8 ($6–$13). Mon–Sat 8:30pm–3am. Tube: Leicester Sq. or Piccadilly Circus.

Inquire about jazz in London and people immediately think of Ronnie Scott's, long the European vanguard for modern jazz. Only the best English and American combos, often fronted by a top-notch vocalist, are booked here. The programs inevitably make for an entire evening of cool jazz. In the heart of Soho, Ronnie Scott's is a 10-minute walk from Piccadilly Circus along Shaftesbury Avenue. In the Main Room you can watch the show from the bar or sit at a table, from which you can order dinner. The Downstairs Bar is more intimate; among the regulars at your elbow may be some of the world's most talented musicians. On weekends, the separate Upstairs Room has a disco called Club Latino.

606 Club. 90 Lots Rd., SW10. ☎ **0171/352-5953.** Cover Sun–Thurs £4.75 ($8), Fri–Sat £6 ($10). Mon–Sat 8:30pm–2am, Sun 8:30pm–midnight. Bus: 11, 19, 22, 31, 39, or C3. Tube: Earl's Court.

Located in a discreet basement site in Chelsea, the 606 presents live music nightly. Predominantly a venue for modern jazz, style ranges from traditional to contemporary. Local musicians and some very big names play here, whether planned gigs or informal jam sessions after their shows elsewhere in town. This is actually a jazz supper club in the boondocks of Fulham; because of license requirements, patrons can only order alcohol with food.

DANCE, DISCO & ECLECTIC

Bar Rumba. 26 Shaftesbury Ave., W1. ☎ **0171/287-2715.** Cover £3–£12 ($5–$19). Mon–Thurs 5pm–3:30am, Fri 5pm–4:30am, Sat 6pm–6am, Sun 8pm–1:30am. Tube: Piccadilly Circus.

Despite its location on Shaftesbury Avenue, this Latin bar and club could be featured in a book of "Underground London." A hush-hush address, it leans toward radical jazz fusion on some nights, phat funk on other occasions. Boasting two full bars and a different musical theme every night, Tuesday and Wednesday are the only nights you probably won't have to queue at the door. Monday's "That's How It Is" showcase features jazz, hip hop, and drum and bass; Friday's "KAT Klub" grooves with soul, R&B, and swing; and Saturday's "Garage City" buzzes with house and garage. On weeknights you have to be 18 and up; the age limit is 21 on Saturday and Sunday.

Camden Palace. 1A Camden High St., NW1. ☎ **0171/387-0428.** Cover Tues–Wed £5 ($8), Fri–Sat £7–£20 ($11–$32). Tues–Wed 9pm–2am, Fri 9pm–6am, and Sat 9pm–8am. Tube: Camden Town or Mornington Crescent.

Housed in a former theater built around 1910, Camden Palace draws an over-18 crowd that flocks here in trendy downtown costumes. Energy levels vary according to the night of the week, as does the music, so call in advance to see if that evening's musical program appeals to your taste. A live band performs only on Tuesday. There's a restaurant if you get the munchies.

The Cross. The Arches, Kings Cross Goods Yard, York Way, N1. ☎ **0171/837-0828.** Cover £10–£15 ($16–$24). Fri 10pm–4:30am, Sat 10:30pm–6am. Tube: Kings Cross.

In the backwaters of Kings Cross, this club has stayed hot since 1993. London hipsters come here for private parties thrown by Rough Trade Records or Red Or Dead, or just to dance in the space's cozy brick-lined vaults. It's always party time here. Call to find out who's performing.

Diva. 43 Thurloe St., SW7. ☎ **0171/584-2000.** Cover £1.50 ($3). Mon–Sat 7:30pm–3am, July–Sept also Sun 12:30pm–3am. Tube: South Kensington.

Diva combines a first-class Italian restaurant with a dance club. So get down with your manicotti! Meals, from £20 ($32), are mostly Neapolitan-inspired. Only restaurant patrons are allowed into the disco (where recorded music is played).

Equinox. Leicester Sq., WC2. ☎ **0171/437-1446.** Cover £5–£12 ($8–$19), depending on the night of the week. Mon–Thurs 9pm–3am, Fri–Sat 9pm–4am. Tube: Leicester Sq.

Built in 1992 on the site of the London Empire, a dance emporium that has witnessed the changing styles of social dancing since the 1700s, the Equinox has established itself as a perennial favorite. It contains nine bars, the largest dance floor in London, and a restaurant modeled after a 1950s American diner. With the exception of rave, virtually every kind of dance music is featured here, including dance hall, pop, rock, and Latin. The setting is lavishly illuminated with one of Europe's largest lighting rigs, and the crowd is as varied as London itself.

Equinox has been quite busy lately, hosting some of the U.K.'s hottest talents. Most recently, the Equinox featured those international sex symbols, the Spice Girls, Prince Harry's favorite group. Summer visitors can enjoy their theme nights, which are geared to entertaining a world-wide audience, including a once a week "Ibiza" foam party—you'll actually boogie the night away on a foam covered floor. Happy hour drinks are £1 ($1.60) from 5 to 7pm.

Hanover Grand. 6 Hanover St., W1. ☎ **0171/499-7977.** Cover £5–£15 ($8–$24). Mon–Sat 10pm–4am. Tube: Oxford Circus.

Thursdays are funky and down and dirty. Fridays and Saturdays the crowd dresses up in their disco-finery, clingy and form-fitting or politicized and punk. Dance floors are always crowded, and masses seem to surge back-and-forth between the two levels. Age and gender is sometimes hard to make out at this cutting-edge club.

Hippodrome. Corner of Cranbourn St. and Charing Cross Rd., WC2. ☎ **0171/437-4311.** Cover £4–£12 ($6–$19). Mon–Sat 9pm–3am. Tube: Leicester Sq.

Located near Leicester Square, the popular Hippodrome is London's grand old daddy of discos, a cavernous place with a great sound system and lights to match. It was Lady Di's favorite scene in her bar-hopping days. Tacky and touristy, the 'drome is packed on weekends.

Iceni. 11 White Horse St., W1. ☎ **0171/495-5333.** Cover Fri £12 ($19), Sat £10 ($16). Fri 11pm–3am, Sat 10pm–3am. Tube: Queen's Park.

Attracting an older 20-something crowd on Fridays, and 18-to-25ers on Saturdays, this funky three-story nightclub features films, board games, tarot readings, and dancing to swing, soul, hip hop, and R&B. You can even get a manicure. Leave your name at the door and make a love connection courtesy of Flipside Dating Service.

Limelight. 136 Shaftesbury Ave., WC2. ☎ **0171/434-0572.** Cover £4–£8 ($6–$13) before 10pm, £8–£12 ($13–$19) thereafter. Mon–Sat 9pm–3am, Sat 10pm–3am, Sun 6–11pm. Tube: Leicester Sq.

Although opened in 1985, this large dance club—located inside a former Welsh chapel that dates to 1754—has only recently come into its own. The dance floors and bars share space with plenty of cool Gothic nooks and crannies. DJs spin the latest house music.

✪ **Ministry of Sound.** 103 Gaunt St., SE1. ☎ **0171/378-6528.** Cover £12–£20 ($19–$32). Fri and Sat midnight–9am. Tube: Elephant & Castle.

Removed from the city center, this club-of-the-hour is relatively devoid of tourists. With a large bar and an even bigger sound system, it blasts garage and house music to energetic crowds that pack the two dance floors. If the stimulants in the rest of the club have gone to your head, you can chill in the cinema room. *Note:* the club's cover charge is stiff, and bouncers decide who is cool enough to enter.

The Office. 3–5 Rathbone Place, W1. ☎ **0171/636-1598.** Cover £5 ($8). Mon–Sat noon–3am. Tube: Tottenham Court Rd.

An eclectic club with a bureaucratic name, one of The Office's most popular nights is Wednesday's "Double Six Club," featuring easy listening and board games from 6pm to 2am. Other nights are more traditional recorded pop, rock, soul, and disco. Ambience wins out over decor.

Smollensky's on The Strand. 105 The Strand, WC2. ☎ **0171/497-2101.** Cover £4–£6 ($6–$10) for live music. Mon–Sat noon–12:30am, Sun 6:30–10:30pm. Tube: Charing Cross or Embankment.

This American eatery and drinking bar is a cousin to Smollensky's Dover Street. At the Strand location, dance from Thursday to Saturday nights. Sunday night features a special live jazz session. Meals average £24 ($38).

Stringfellows. 16–19 Upper St. Martin's Lane, WC2. ☎ **0171/240-5534.** Cover £10–£15 ($16–$24). Mon–Thurs 7:30pm–3:30am, Fri and Sat 8pm–3:30am, Sun 9pm–3:30am. Reservations recommended for restaurant. Tube: Leicester Sq.

This would-be glam club has a varied clientele and lots of velvet and gloss. In theory, it's members-only, but—at the discretion of management—non-members may be admitted. The disco has a glass dance floor and a dazzling sound-and-light system. A restaurant feeds late-night diners, and there's no charge for admission to the club if you dine in the restaurant.

Subterania. 12 Acklam Rd., W10. ☎ **0181/960-4590.** Cover £8–£10 ($13–$16). Fri–Sat 10:30pm–3am, other nights vary. Tube: Ladbroke Grove.

Affordable, unpretentious, and informal, the feel of this club changes according to the style of the live band that happens to be available at the time. Call ahead. The place has a busy street-level dance floor and a mezzanine-style bar upstairs. The decor is energetic orange, purple, and blue; if those colors work for you, there are also sofas covered in downtown *faux* leopardskin. More or less constant is the Friday music card of soul, funk, hip-hop, and swing, and Saturday's house music. Other nights of the week, it's pot luck.

The Velvet Room (formerly The Velvet Underground). 143 Charing Cross Rd., WC2. ☎ **0171/439-4655.** Cover £4–£10 ($6–$16). Mon–Thurs 10pm–3am, Fri–Sat 10:30pm–4am. Tube: Tottenham Court Rd.

The World's Greatest Pub Crawl

Dropping into the local pub for a pint of real ale or bitter is about the best way to soak up the character of the different villages that make up London. You'll hear the accents and slang and see first-hand how far removed uppercrust Kensington is from blue-collar Wapping. Catch the local gossip or football talk—and of course, enjoy some of the finest ales, stouts, ciders, and malt whiskies in the world.

The Heart of the City   Central London is awash with wonderful historic pubs as rich and varied as the city itself.

    Cittie of Yorke, 22 High Holborn, WC1 (☎ 0171/242-7670; tube: Holborn Chancery Lane), boasts the longest bar in all of Britain, rafters ascending to the heavens, and a long row of immense wine vats, all of which give it the air of a great medieval hall—appropriate since a pub has existed at this location since 1430. Samuel Smiths is on tap, and the bar offers novelties such as chocolate-orange flavored vodka.

    Dickens once hung out in the **Lamb & Flag,** 33 Rose St., off Garrick Street, WC2 (☎ 0171/497-9504; tube: Leicester Square), and the room itself is little changed from the days when he prowled this neighborhood. The pub has an amazing and somewhat scandalous history. Dryden was almost killed by a band of thugs outside its doors in December 1679; the pub gained the nickname the "Bucket of Blood" during the Regency era (1811–20) because of the routine bare-knuckled prizefights that broke out here. Tap beers include Courage Best and Directors, Old Speckled Hen, John Smiths, and Wadworths 6X.

    Olde Mitre, Ely Place, EC1 (☎ 0171/405-4751; tube: Chancery Lane), is the namesake of a working-class inn built here in 1547, when the Bishops of Ely controlled the district. It's a small pub with an odd assortment of customers. Friary Meux, Ind Coope Burton, and Tetleys are on tap.

    Seven Stars, 53 Carey St., WC2 (☎ 0171/242-8521; tube: Holborn), is tiny and modest except for its collection of toby mugs and law-related art, the latter a tribute to the pub's location at the back of the Law Courts and the large clientele of barristers who drink here. It's a great place to pick up some British legal jargon. Courage Best and Directors are on tap, as well as a selection of single malts.

    Black Friar, 174 Queen Victoria St., EC4 (☎ 0171/236-5650; tube: Black-friars), will transport you to the Edwardian era. The wedge-shaped pub reeks of marble and bronze art-nouveau, featuring bas-reliefs of mad monks, a low-vaulted mosaic ceiling, and seating carved out of gold marble recesses. It's espe-cially popular with the City's after-work crowd, and it features Adams, Wadsworth 6X, Tetleys, and Brakspears on tap.

South London   In South London you can follow in the footsteps of Shake-speare and Dickens by quenching your thirst at the **Anchor,** 34 Park St., Bank-side, SE1 (☎ 0181/876-5241; tube: Barnes Bridge). If literary heroes are not your bag, then perhaps you'll enjoy knowing that Tom Cruise had a pint or two here during the filming of *Mission Impossible*. Rebuilt in the mid-18th century to replace a pub that withstood the Great Fire of 1666, the rooms are worn and comfortable, and you can choose from among Greenalls Best and Youngs Special on tap.

    For even greater antiquarian ambience, retreat to the **Cutty Sark,** Ballast Quay, off Lassell Street, SE10 (☎ 0181/858-3146; train: Maze Hill), located inside a

16th-century dwelling with flagstones, barrel tables, open fires, and rough-hewn brick walls. The pub has such an old London feel that you may find yourself seeing Dickensian riffraff after a few pints of Bass or Worthington's Best.

Another historic option is the **George,** off 77 Borough High St., SE1 (☎ 0171/407-2056; tube: Borough, London Bridge). Preserved by the National Trust, the existing structure was built to replace the original pub, destroyed in the Great Fire. The pub's accolades date to 1598, when it was reviewed as a "faire inn for the receipt of travellers." No longer an inn, it's still a great place to enjoy Flowers Original, Boddingtons, and Whitbread Castle Eden on tap.

West London   Heading to the western part of town, you can relax by the Thames at the **Dove,** 19 Upper Mall, W6 (☎ 0181/748-5405; tube: Ravenscourt Park), the place where James Thomson composed "Rule Britannia" and part of his lesser-known "The Seasons." For toasting the old empire, you can hoist a Fullers London Pride or ESB, and then move on to the **Churchill Arms,** 119 Kensington Church St., W8 (☎ 0171/727-4242; tube: Notting Hill Gate or High St. Kensington), for a nod to the empire's end. Loaded with Churchill memorabilia, the pub hosts an entire week of celebration leading up to his birthday on November 30th. Show up then and you may get recruited to help decorate the place; visitors are often welcomed like regulars here. Decorations and festivities are featured at Halloween, Christmas, and St. Paddy's Day as well, helping to create the most homey, village feel you're likely to find in London.

Ladbroke Arms, 54 Ladbroke Rd., W11 (☎ 0171/727-6648; tube: Holland Park), previously honored as London's *Dining Pub of the Year,* is that rare pub known for its food. A changing menu includes chicken breast stuffed with avocado and garlic steak in pink peppercorn sauce. With background jazz and rotating art prints, the place strays a bit from a traditional pub environment, but it makes for a pleasant stop and a good meal. The excellent Eldridge Pope Royal is on tap, as well as John Smiths and Courage Directors, and several malt whiskies.

North London   Continuing clockwise around London, settle in for a touch of the Victorian and Edwardian eras, respectively, at the **Olde White Bear,** Well Rd., NW 31 (☎ 0171/435-3758; tube: Hampstead), and the **Holly Bush,** Holly Mount, NW3 (☎ 0171/435-2892; tube: Hampstead). The former is a friendly place for regulars decorated with Victorian prints, cartoons, and furnishings. Tap offerings include Greene King Abbott and Youngs Bitter. The Holly Bush is the real thing: authentic Edwardian gas lamps, open fires, private booths, and a tap selection of Benskins, Eldridge Pope, and Ind Coope Burton.

East London   Finally arriving in Cockney territory, head to **Grapes,** 76 Narrow St., E14 (☎ 0171/987-4396; tube: Shadwell), a rustic 16th-century pub that served as Dickens' inspiration for "Six Jolly Fellowship Porters" in *Our Mutual Friend.* Whistler came here, too, inspired by the view of the river. Taps include Friary Meux and Tetleys, with several malt whiskies to choose from as well.

The **Town of Ramsgate,** 62 Wapping High St., E1 (☎ 0171/264-0001; tube: Wapping), is another old-world pub, overlooking King Edward's Stairs and the Thames. Here you can enjoy Bass and Fullers London Pride on tap.

The Velvet Underground was a London staple for years. Times changed and the clientele grew up—hence The Velvet Room, a more mature setting that is luxurious but not stuffy. DJs Carl Cox and others spin favorite dance hits—more laid back to better represent the new theme. The Velvet Room hasn't sacrificed a shred of cool, and still sets a standard for the next generation of Soho bar life.

✪ **Venom Club/The Zoo Bar.** 13–18 Bear St., WC2. ☎ **0171/839-4188.** Cover £3–£5 ($5–$8) after 10pm. Zoo Bar daily 4pm–2am; Venom Club daily 9:30pm–3am. Tube: Leicester Sq.

The owners spent millions of pounds outfitting this club in the slickest, flashiest, and most psychedelic decor in London. If you're looking for a true Euro nightlife experience replete with gorgeous *au pairs* and trendy Europeans, this is it. Zoo Bar upstairs is a menagerie of mosaic animals beneath a glassed-in ceiling dome. Downstairs, the music is intrusive enough to make conversation futile. Clients range from 18 to 35; androgyny is the look of choice. The first Wednesday of every month is devoted to the sugar pop of Boy George, whose groupies cavort here in hopes of glimpsing the campy star.

LATIN RHYTHMS

Cuba. 11 Kensington High St., W8. ☎ **0171/938-4137.** Cover £3–£5 ($5–$8) after 10pm. Mon–Sat noon–2am, Sun 2–11pm. Tube: High St. Kensington.

This Spanish/Cuban-style bar-restaurant, which has a music club downstairs, features live music acts from Cuba, Brazil, Spain, and the rest of Latin America. Odd as it may seem, the crowd is equal parts restaurant diners, after-work drinkers, Latinophiles, and dancers. Salsa dance classes are offered Monday, Tuesday, and Wednesday from 8:30 to 9:30pm for £3 ($4.80). Happy hour is Monday to Saturday, noon to 8:30pm.

Salsa. 96 Charing Cross Rd., WC2. ☎ **0171/379-3277.** Cover Fri–Sat £7 ($11) after 9pm. Mon–Sat 5:30pm–2am. Tube: Leicester Sq.

This lively bar-restaurant and music club for Latin music aficionados features mostly bands from Central and South America. Dance lessons are available nightly starting at 6:30pm; live music starts at 9pm. Some of the best dancers in London strut their stuff here.

GAMING CLUBS

Long before Monte Carlo or Las Vegas was a glint in a slot machine's eye, London was a gambler's town. However, Queen Victoria's reign squelched games of chance to such an extent that no bartender dared to keep a dice cup on the counter. Only in 1960, with the institution of the Betting and Gaming Act, did gambling become permitted in bona fide gaming clubs.

In the West End alone are at least 25 gambling clubs, with many more scattered throughout the London periphery. But under British law, casinos may not advertise. Hence, if you wish to gamble away your beer money while in London, your best bet is to ask a knowledgeable concierge. You'll be required to become a member and wait 24 hours before you can play at the tables. Games are cash-only and commonly include roulette, blackjack, Punto Banco, and Baccarat.

Men must wear a jacket and tie in all of the establishments below; hours for each club are from 2pm to 4am daily.

Some of the more popular clubs include **Crockford's,** a 150-year-old club with a large international clientele, located at 30 Curzon St., W1 (☎ **0171/493-7777;** tube: Green Park). Offered here are American roulette, Punto Banco, and blackjack. Another favorite is the **Golden Nugget,** 22 Shaftesbury Ave., W1 (☎ **0171/ 439-0099;** tube: Piccadilly Circus), where gamblers go to play blackjack, Punto

Banco, and roulette. A final choice is **Sportsman Club,** 3 Tottenham Court Rd., W1 (☎ 0171/637-5464; tube: Tottenham Court Road), featuring a dice table along with American roulette, blackjack, and Punto Banco.

4 Cocktail Bars

For a complete selection of pubs and wine bars, see chapter 5 and the description of "The World's Greatest Pub Crawl," above.

American Bar. In The Savoy, The Strand, WC2. ☎ 0171/836-4343. Jacket and tie required for men. Tube: Charing Cross, Covent Garden, or Embankment.

This is still one of the most sophisticated gathering places in London. The bartender is known for his special concoctions, "Savoy Affair" and "Prince of Wales," as well as what is reputedly the best martini in town. Monday to Saturday evenings, jazz piano is featured from 7 to 11pm. Near many West End theaters, the location is ideal for a pre- or post-theater drink.

Beach Blanket Babylon. 45 Ledbury Rd., W11. ☎ 0171/229-2907. No cover. Tube: Notting Hill Gate.

Go here if you're looking for one of the hot singles bars of London, attracting a crowd in their 20s and 30s. This Portobello joint—named after a kitschy musical revue in San Francisco—is very cruisy. The decor is a bit wacky, no doubt designed by an aspiring Salvador Dalí, who decided to make it a fairy-tale grotto (or did he mean a medieval dungeon?). It's close to the Portobello Market. Saturday and Sunday nights are the hot, crowded times to show up for bacchanalian revelry.

Bracewells Bar. In the Park Lane Hotel, Piccadilly, W1. ☎ 0171/499-6321. Tube: Green Park or Hyde Park.

Chic, nostalgic, and elegant, Bracewells is the kind of bar where Edward VII and his stylish companion Mrs. Langtry might have felt at home. With its plush decor of Chinese lacquer, comfortable sofas, and soft lighting, the bar seems like an elegant private club. The bar adjoins the Bracewells restaurant, one of the finest hotel dining experiences in London. Complimentary hors d'oeuvres are offered in the evenings.

The Dorchester Bar. In the Dorchester, Park Lane. ☎ 0171/629-8888. Tube: Hyde Park Corner or Marble Arch.

This sophisticated and modern bar is on the lobby level of one of the most lavishly decorated hotels in the world. You'll find an international clientele confident of its good taste and privilege. The bartender knows his stuff. The bar serves Italian snacks, lunch, and dinner. A pianist performs every evening after 7pm; he is joined by a jazz trio Wednesday to Saturday.

The Library. In the Lanesborough Hotel, 1 Lanesborough Place, SW1. ☎ 0171/259-5599. Tube: Hyde Park Corner.

For one of London's poshest drinking retreats, head for this deluxe hotel with its high ceilings, leather chesterfields, respectable oil paintings, and grand windows. Its collection of ancient cognacs is unparalleled in London.

Lillie Langtry Bar. In the Cadogan Hotel, Sloane St., SW1. ☎ 0171/235-7141. Tube: Sloane Sq. or Knightsbridge.

Next door to Langtry's Restaurant, this 1920s-style bar epitomizes the charm and elegance of the Edwardian era. Lillie Langtry, the turn-of-the-century actress and society beauty (notorious as the mistress of Edward VII), once lived here. Oscar Wilde—

arrested in this very hotel bar—is honored on the drinks menu by his favorite libation, the Hock and Seltzer. Sir John Betjeman's poem "The Arrest of Oscar Wilde at the Cadogan Hotel" tells the story. The Cadogan Cooler seems to be the most popular drink here. An international menu is also served in the adjoining restaurant.

Smollensky's Dover Street. 1 Dover St., W1. ☎ **0171/491-1199.** Tube: Green Park.

This American bar and restaurant is packed during happy hour (Monday to Friday from 5 to 7pm) with Mayfair office workers on their way home. You'll find a 1930s piano-bar atmosphere, with polished wood and a mirrored ceiling. Standard American-style fare is served, including well-prepared vegetarian dishes.

5 The Gay & Lesbian Scene

The most reliable source of information on gay clubs and activities is the **Lesbian and Gay Switchboard** (☎ 0171/837-7324). The staff runs a 24-hour service for information on gay-friendly places and activities. *Time Out* also carries listings on such clubs.

The Box. 32–34 Monmouth St. (at Seven Dials), WC2. ☎ **0171/240-5828.** Mon–Sat 11am–11pm, Sun noon–6pm, 7–10:30 (women only). Tube: Covent Garden.

Adjacent to one of Covent Garden's best-known junctions, Seven Dials, this sophisticated Mediterranean-style bar attracts more lesbians than many of its competitors. This is especially the case on women-only Sunday nights, cutely labeled "Girl Bar at the Box." The rest of the week, men slightly outnumber women. In the afternoon, this is primarily a restaurant, serving meal-sized salads, club sandwiches, and soups. Food service ends abruptly at 5:30pm, after which the place reveals its core: a cheerful, popular place of rendezvous for London's gay and countercultural crowds. The Box considers itself a "summer bar," throwing open doors and windows to a cluster of outdoor tables that attracts a crowd at the slightest hint of sunshine.

Comptons of Soho. 53 Old Compton St., W1. ☎ **0171/437-4445.** Mon–Sat noon–11pm, Sun noon–10:30pm. Tube: Leicester Sq.

This gay bar is so firmly entrenched as a London institution that it's sometimes referred to as the official gay bar of Soho. It's also a network of information about what's new and hot on the London gay scene. Stop off here early in the evening just to find out what the latest gay event is around town. Shaved heads and leather bomber jackets aren't at all out of place here. All ages are attracted to this joint, and it's very cruisy—an evening testosterone fest, in fact.

The Edge. 11 Soho Square, W1. ☎ **0171/439-1313.** Mon–Sat noon–1am, Sun noon–10:30pm. No cover. Tube: Tottenham Court Rd.

Few bars in London can rival the tolerance, humor, and sexual sophistication found here. The first two floors are done up with accessories that, like an English garden, change with the seasons. Dance music can be found on the high-energy and crowded lower floors, while the upper floors are best if you're looking for intimate conversation. Three menus are featured: a funky daytime menu, a cafe menu, and a late-night menu. Dancers hit the floors starting around 7:30pm. Clientele ranges from the flamboyantly gay to hetero pub crawlers out for a night of slumming.

First Out. 52 St. Giles High St., W1 ☎ **0171/240-8042.** Mon–Sat 10am–11pm, Sun noon–10:30pm. Tube: Tottenham Court Rd.

First Out prides itself on being London's first (est. 1986) all-gay coffee shop. Set in a 19th-century building whose wood panels have been painted the colors of the gay liberation rainbow, the bar is intimate (that is, not particularly cruisy) and offers an exclusively vegetarian menu, with most items priced at £3.50 ($6). Cappuccino and whisky are the preferred libations; curry dishes, potted pies in phyllo pastries, and salads are the foods of choice. Don't expect a raucous atmosphere—some clients come here with their grandmothers. Look for the bulletin board with leaflets and business cards of gay and gay-friendly entrepreneurs.

The Fridge. Town Hall Parade, Brixton Hill, SW2. ☎ **0171/326-5100.** Cover £10 ($16). Fri–Sat 10pm–6am. Tube: Brixton.

A 15-minute tube ride southwest from Piccadilly and Leicester Square, this club occupies what was originally a 1920s movie theater. Open just 2 nights a week, The Fridge caters to the young and trendy. The club features a good sound system and the latest tunes. On the premises are two bars (one on street level, another on a balcony upstairs) and a restaurant. On Friday it's the straight-oriented "Trance and Techno" night, but Saturday is way gay.

The Gardening Club. 6–7 The Piazza, Covent Garden. ☎ **0171/836-4052.** Cover £5–£13 ($8–$21). Sun–Thurs, 11pm–3am, Fri and Sat 11pm–6am. Tube: Covent Garden.

Associated with the Venue, a cutting-edge concert hall next door, this nightclub often sports a spill-over crowd of rowdy music lovers looking to continue the mayhem. Originally conceived as a food warehouse, it is now a mainstream Tex-Mex restaurant from noon until midnight. Beginning every night at 11, however, a colorful mix of gays and straights groove to house, garage, and other sounds in an adjacent room— where counterculture fashions also predominate. Thursday is gay night; you'll see a flamboyant costume or two. Cover charge on Thursday is £6 ($10). Don't expect anything approaching coherent advance scheduling here: DJs alternate with live bands in a happily haphazard schedule.

Halfway to Heaven. 7 Duncannon St., WC2. ☎ **0171/321-2791.** Mon–Sat noon–11pm, Sun noon–10:30pm. Tube: Charing Cross or Embankment.

A century-old structure with a beamed ceiling, this is the least frenetic gay bar in the Trafalgar Square neighborhood. The quiet, snug downstairs saloon and the upstairs bar attract a young but still cruisy clientele.

Heaven. The Arches, Villiers and Craven sts., WC2. ☎ **0171/930-2020.** Cover £5–£8 ($8–$13). Tues–Sat 10:30pm–3am. Tube: Charing Cross or Embankment.

This club in the vaulted cellars of Charing Cross Railway Station is a London landmark. Owned by the same investors who brought the world Virgin Atlantic Airways, Heaven is one of the biggest and best-established gay venues in Britain. Painted black inside, and reminiscent of an air-raid shelter, the club is divided into at least four distinct areas connected by a labyrinth of catwalk stairs and hallways. Each area has a different activity going on. Heaven also has theme nights, which depending on the night are frequented by gays, lesbians, or a mostly heterosexual crowd. Thursday in particular seems open to anything. Call before you go.

The Leisure Lounge. 121 Holborn, EC1. ☎ **0171/242-1345.** Cover Fri £6–£7 ($10–$11), Sat £8–£10 ($13–$16). Fri 10pm–5am, Sat 10pm–4:30am. Tube: Chancery Lane.

This large, spacious club attracts a gay crowd for Friday's "Pop Starz," when DJs mix indie and Britpop, and Saturday's "Cookies and Cream," which boasts the most cutting edge music in London. There are two dance floors, three bars, and a VIP area. The decor features huge backlit photos and projected slides. No food is served.

Madame Jo Jo's. 8 Brewer St., W1. ☎ **0171/734-2473.** Cover £12.50–£22.50 ($20–$36). Mon–Sat 10pm–3am. Tube: Piccadilly Circus.

Tucked alongside Soho's most explicit girlie shows, Madame Jo Jo's also presents "girls"—more accurately described as drag queens. London's most popular transvestite showplace—an eye-popper with decadent art nouveau interior—has attracted film directors such as Stanley Kubrick, who filmed scenes from *Eyes Wide Shut,* starring Tom Cruise, here. Other celebrities, including Hugh Grant and Mick Jagger, have dropped in to check out Jo Jo's drag cabaret. Drag shows are Thursday to Saturday nights, with outside promoters organizing entertainment on other nights.

Mars. 12 Sutton Row, W1. ☎ **0171/439-4655.** Cover £5–£10 ($8–$16). Thurs 10pm–2am, Fri–Sat 11pm–5am. Tube: Tottenham Court Rd.

This large, stark dance club frequently goes gay and lesbian. Regardless of sexual preference, Mars is a hot planet for London's dance crowd. Thursday's "Speed" night is heavy on drum and bass; "Kitty Lips" transforms the club into London's hottest lesbian bar on Friday; and Saturday's "Naked" features house music. Occasionally there is a live band.

Royal Vauxhall Tavern. 372 Kennington Lane, SE11. ☎ **0171/582-0833.** Cover Sat and Sun £2–£3 ($3.20–$4.80). Mon–Sat 9pm–2am, Sun noon–midnight. Tube: Vauxhall.

Originally an 1880s vaudevillian pub frequented by London's East End working class, this place has long been a bastion of campy humor and wit. It has been a gay pub since the end of World War II. The tavern received a jolt of fame when—as legend has it—Queen Elizabeth's carriage broke down, and the monarch stopped in for a cup of tea. Since then, "Royal" has been gleefully affixed to the name, no doubt suiting the regular queens found here. Charington, one of the largest breweries in England, recently acquired this unabashedly gay pub.

Shaped like an amphitheater, the bar has a large stage area and gay themes on weekends. Friday nights are reserved for women only. Saturday is camp night, when the pub overflows with gay men fawning over their favorite cabaret acts.

Side Trips from London 10

There's much more to England than London. But you could spend the best part of a year—or a lifetime—exploring *only* London, without risking either boredom or repetition. Still, we advise you to tear yourself away from Big Ben for at least a day or two, as the capital city is surrounded by some of the most memorable spots on earth.

1 Windsor & Eton

21 miles W of London

Windsor—the site of England's best-known and greatest castle and its most famous boys' school, Eton—would still be a captivating Thames town to visit, were it not for its association with the royal Windsors. Instead, it's overrun in summer by tourists, who tend to obscure its charm.

The good news is that, after the disastrous fire of 1992, things are on the mend at Windsor Castle. But not without controversy—some of the new designs unveiled have been called a "Gothic shocker" and "ghastly." After an inspection, you'll have a chance to decide for yourself.

ESSENTIALS
Getting There The train from Waterloo or Paddington Station in London makes the trip in 30 minutes, involving a transfer at Slough to the Slough–Windsor shuttle train. There are more than a dozen trains per day, and fares start at £6.20 ($10). For information call ☎ **0345/484950** (in the U.K. only) or 01603/764776.

Green Line coaches (☎ **0181/668-7261**) no. 700 and 702 from Hyde Park Corner in London take about 1½ hours. A same-day round-trip costs £6.50 ($10). The bus will drop you near the Town Guildhall, to which Wren applied the finishing touches. It's only a short walk up Castle Hill to the top sights.

If you're traveling by car, take M4 west from London.

Visitor Information A **Tourist Information Centre** is located across from Windsor Castle on High Street (☎ **01753/743900**). There's also an information booth in the tourist center at Windsor Coach Park. Both are open daily from 10am to 4pm, Saturday and Sunday 10am to 5pm.

CASTLE HILL SIGHTS

✪ **Windsor Castle.** Castle Hill. ☎ **01753/868286.** Admission £9.50 ($15) adults; £7 ($11) students and senior citizens; £5 ($8) children 16 and under; £21.50 ($34) family of 4, £17 ($27) on Sun, when St. George's Chapel is closed to sightseers. Mar–Oct daily 10am–5pm; Nov–Feb daily 10am–4pm. Last admissions are 1 hour before closing. Closed periods in Apr, June, and Dec when the royal family is in residence.

When William the Conqueror ordered Windsor Castle to be built, he established a base for English sovereignty that has known many vicissitudes: King John cooled his heels at Windsor while waiting to put his signature on the Magna Carta at nearby Runnymede; Charles I was imprisoned here before losing his head; Queen Bess renovated; Victoria mourned her beloved Albert, who died at the castle; the royal family rode out much of World War II behind its sheltering walls.

With 1,000 rooms, Windsor is the world's largest inhabited castle. Today, when Queen Elizabeth II is in residence, the royal standard flies. On display are many works of art, porcelain, armor, furniture, three Verrio ceilings, and several 17th-century Gibbons carvings. Several works by Rubens adorn the King's Drawing Room; in the relatively small King's Dressing Room is a Dürer, along with Rembrandt's portrait of his mother, and Van Dyck's triple portrait of Charles I. Of the apartments, the grand reception room, with its Gobelin tapestries, is the most spectacular.

In November 1992, a fire swept through part of Windsor Castle, severely damaging it. The castle has since reopened, and all the rooms that were once open to the public should be available for viewing in 1999. However, St. George's Hall and the Grand Reception Room are currently open.

In our opinion, the Windsor **changing of the guard** is a much more exciting and moving experience than the London exercises. The guard marches through the town whether the court is in residence or not, stopping the traffic as it wheels into the castle to the tune of a full regimental band; when the queen is not here, a drum-and-pipe band is mustered. From May to August, the ceremony takes place Monday to Saturday at 11am. In winter, the guard is changed every 48 hours Monday to Saturday. It's best to call ☎ **01753/868286** to find out which days the ceremony will take place.

Queen Mary's Doll's House. Windsor Castle. ☎ **01753/831118.** Castle tickets include admission here. Open same days and hours as Windsor Castle (see above).

A palace in perfect miniature, the Doll's House was given to Queen Mary in 1923 as a symbol of national goodwill. The house, designed by Sir Edwin Lutyens, was created on a scale of 1 to 12. It took 3 years to complete and involved the work of 1,500 tradesmen and artists. Every item is a miniature masterpiece; each room is exquisitely furnished, and every item is made exactly to scale. Working elevators stop on every floor, all five bathrooms have running water, and electric lighting brightens the house.

✪ **St. George's Chapel.** The Cloisters, Windsor Castle. ☎ **01753/865538.** Admission included in admission to Windsor Castle. Mon–Sat 10am–4pm. Sunday services open to public, but closed for sightseeing tours. Closed during services, Jan, and a few days in mid-June.

Along with Westminster Abbey, this Perpendicular-style chapel shares the distinction of being a pantheon of English monarchs. The present St. George's was founded in the late 15th century by Edward IV on the site of the original Chapel of the Order of the Garter. Monarchs entombed here include George V, George VI, and Edward IV. History's path forked at Princess Charlotte's memorial; had she survived childbirth in 1817, she—and not her cousin Victoria—would have ruled the British Empire. At the chapel's center is a flat tomb containing the vault of the beheaded Charles I, along with Henry VIII and his third wife, Jane Seymour.

A Weekend Trip to Paris

Regardless of how much you love London, too long a stint within the great grey capital of the British Empire might make you itch to experience the allures of Paris, at least for a weekend. So, if like the randy, good-natured son of Queen Victoria, Edward VII, you yearn for a dose of Gallic charm and French *laissez-faire,* know that transit between London and Paris is easier than ever.

A giant boost for cross-Channel commerce occurred in 1994, when Queen Elizabeth II and former French President François Mitterand jointly inaugurated the Channel Tunnel (Chunnel), whose debut had been dreamed about since the military campaigns of Napoleon. Now the Eurostar train roars at high speeds through its innards, reducing the travel time between London and Paris to a breathtakingly brief three hours, at prices that rival conventional train and ferryboat fares, and at a level of convenience (direct transit between Paris's Gare du Nord and London's Waterloo Station) never before imagined. One-way fares, with some restrictions, begin at $99 second-class and $139 first-class, with discounts for Eurail or Britrail passholders. Additional discounts are offered to youths under 18 and bona-fide students. If you're willing to pay for it, you can opt for ultra-upscale service, enhanced cuisine, and such perks as limousine service to and from the Gare du Nord and your hotel for a maximum of $299 each way, tax included.

Where should you lay your weary head for the two or three nights you spend in Paris? The folks at Eurostar can even set that up for you as part of a rail-and-hotel package at a highly discounted rate. For as little as $319 per person, with a $30 per person supplement on Fridays and Saturdays, you can buy a package that includes rail transport, two nights (double occupancy) in a simple but clean and safe hotel, and an inner-city sightseeing tour. The price is hard to beat and the sheer convenience of the routing makes the plan easier and faster than flying.

From North America, these packages can most easily be arranged by calling the **EuroStar** division of RailEurope (☎ **800/EUROSTAR**). For details about hotel packages, contact **EuroVacations** (☎ **888/281-EURO**). Citizens of Australia, New Zealand, and South Africa should contact a local travel agent. If you're already in London, contact any travel agency or talk to your hotel concierge, who should be able to arrange the same basic package, depending on seasonal promotions.

EXPLORING THE TOWN

Windsor is a largely Victorian town of brick buildings, with a few remnants of Georgian architecture. Near the castle, antiques shops, silversmiths, and pubs line cobblestoned **Church and Market streets.** Nell Gwynne supposedly occupied a shop on Church Street, which allowed her to be within shouting distance of Charles II's chambers. After lunch or tea, you may want to stroll along the aptly named 3-mile **Long Walk.**

On Sundays in **Windsor Great Park** and at **Ham Common,** you may see Prince Charles playing polo and Prince Philip serving as umpire while the queen watches. The park is also the site of the queen's occasional equestrian jaunts. On Sunday she attends a little church near the Royal Lodge. Traditionally, she prefers to drive herself there, later returning to the castle for Sunday lunch. For more information, call the **Tourist Information Center** (☎ **01753/743900**).

NEARBY ETON

From Windsor, Eton is just an easy stroll across the Thames Bridge. Follow Eton High Street to the college.

Eton College (☎ **01753/671177**) was founded by the adolescent Henry VI in 1440. Some of England's greatest men, notably the Duke of Wellington, have played on these fields. Twenty prime ministers were educated here, as well as such literary figures as George Orwell, Aldous Huxley, Ian Fleming, and Percy Bysshe Shelley—who, during his years at Eton (from 1804 to 1810), was called "Mad Shelley" by his fellow pupils.

The history of Eton College since its inception is depicted in the **Museum of Eton Life,** located in vaulted wine cellars under College Hall. The displays include a turn-of-the-century boy's room, schoolbooks, sports trophies, canes used by senior boys to apply punishment to their juniors, and birch sticks used by masters for the same purpose. Also on display are letters written home by students describing day-to-day life at the school, as well as samples of the numerous magazines produced by students over the centuries. Many of the items on display were provided by Old Etonians. If it's open, take a look at the **Perpendicular Chapel's** 15th-century paintings and reconstructed fan vaulting.

Admission to the school and museum costs £2.50 ($4) for adults. You can also take guided tours for £3.70 ($6). Eton College is open from March 19 to April 14 and June 27 to September 3, daily from 10:30am to 4:30pm; April 15 to June 26 and September 2 to October 4, daily from 2 to 4:30pm. Call in advance; Eton may close for special occasions.

ORGANIZED TOURS OF WINDSOR & ETON

Horse-Drawn Carriage Rides   You can also take a **horse-drawn carriage** for a half-hour promenade up the sycamore-lined length of Windsor Castle's Long Walk. Horses with carriages and drivers line up beside the castle waiting for fares, which run about £20 ($32) for up to four passengers.

Boat Tours   Tours depart from The Promenade, Barry Avenue, for a 35-minute ride to Boveney Lock. There's also a 35-minute tour from Runnymede on board the *Lucy Fisher,* a replica of a Victorian paddle steamer. The boat passes Magna Carta Island, among other places. Both tours cost £3.20 ($5) for adults, half price for children. A 2-hour tour through the Boveney Lock and up past stately private riverside homes, the Bray Film Studios, Queens Eyot, and Monkey Island, is £5.40 ($9) for adults, half-price for children. In addition, longer tours between Maidenhead and Hampton Court are offered. The boats offer light refreshments and have a well-stocked bar, and the decks are covered in case of an unexpected shower. Contact **French Brothers, Ltd.,** Clewer Boathouse, Clewer Court Rd., Windsor (☎ **01753/851900**).

WHERE TO DINE
WINDSOR

The Orangerie. In Sir Christopher Wren's House Hotel, Thames St. ☎ **01753/861354.** Main courses £11–£18 ($18–$29). AE, DC, MC, V. Daily 12:30–2:30pm and 6:30–10pm. CONTINENTAL.

A 3-minute walk from the castle, this restaurant is the most elegant and charming restaurant in Windsor, with garden terraces and a conservatory. The dining room is designed a bit like a greenhouse, and a pianist entertains at dinner. Although it has a good range of starters, including blue-cheese beignets, main courses are limited. Count on typical English dishes such as lemon sole, Welsh lamb, and venison steak.

The traditionally roasted half duckling with a light orange and brandy sauce is quite delectable.

ETON

Eton Wine Bar. 82–83 High St. ☎ **01753/854921.** Reservations recommended. Main courses £6.25–£12 ($10–$19). AE, DC, MC, V. Mon–Fri noon–2:30pm and 6–11pm; Sat and Sun 11am–11pm. FRENCH/ENGLISH/CONTINENTAL.

Just across the bridge from Windsor, this graceful dinner bar is set among the antiques shops on Eton's main street. Inside are pinewood tables and old church pews and chairs, and there's a glassed-in conservatory out back. A brigade of eight chefs turns out a fine array of modern British cookery. Appetizers usually include several well-prepared soups and a roasted sweet pepper tart. Main dishes include pine-nut and spinach risotto topped with peccorino cheese, and roast lamb filet served with boulangère potatoes and vegetables. For dessert, try the tarte tatim, a tasty and creative upside-down apple pie.

House on the Bridge. 71 High St. ☎ **01753/860914.** Reservations recommended. Main courses from £13 ($21); fixed-price meal £20 ($32) at lunch, £30 ($48) at dinner; Sun lunch £25 ($40). AE, DC, MC, V. Daily noon–2:30pm and 6–11pm. ENGLISH/INTERNATIONAL.

This charming restaurant is housed in a lovely red-brick and terra-cotta Victorian building, adjacent to the bridge at the edge of Eton. Near the handful of outdoor tables is a precipitous garden whose plants cascade into the Thames. Among the well-prepared main dishes are crispy duckling with Calvados and Seville oranges, and chicken flavored with tarragon and served with mushrooms. Some specialties, such as roast rack of herb-flavored lamb, are served only for two. Although traditionally based, the preparations have many modern touches, and the chefs always use good fresh ingredients. Desserts include flambés and crêpes suzette.

2 Oxford, City of Dreaming Spires

54 miles NW of London

A walk down the long sweep of The High, one of the most striking streets in England; a mug of cider in one of the old student pubs; the sound of May Day dawn when choristers sing in Latin from Magdalen Tower; the Great Tom bell from Tom Tower, whose 101 peals traditionally signal the closing of the college gates; towers and spires piercing the clouds; the barges on the upper reaches of the Thames; nude swimming at Parson's Pleasure; the roar of a cannon launching the bumping races; a tiny, dusty bookstall where you can pick up a valuable first edition—all coincide in Oxford, home of one of the greatest universities in the world.

Romantic Oxford still exists, but to get to it, you'll have to navigate the bustling and crowded city that has grown about it. A never-ending stream of polluting buses and the fast-flowing pedestrian traffic can make the city core feel more like London than an ancient university town.

At any time of the year, you can enjoy a tour of the colleges, many of which are the loveliest England has to offer. The **Oxford Tourist Information Centre** (see below) conducts daily walking tours throughout the year. Just don't mention the other place (Cambridge), and you shouldn't have any trouble. The city predates the university—it emerged as a Saxon town in the early part of the 10th century. By the 12th century, Oxford was growing in reputation as a seat of learning at Paris's expense. When the first colleges emerged in the 13th century, Oxford began to churn out powerful and distinguished alumni, among them Roger Bacon, Sir Walter Raleigh, John Donne, Sir

Christopher Wren, Samuel Johnson, Edward Gibbon, William Penn, John Wesley, Lewis Carroll, T.E. Lawrence, and W.H. Auden.

ESSENTIALS

Getting There   Trains from Paddington Station (☎ **0345/484950** (U.K. only) or 01603/764776) reach Oxford in 1¼ hours. Service is every hour. A cheap, same-day round-trip ticket costs £12.40 ($20).

The **X90 London Express** departs from Victoria Station (☎ **0990/808080**) for the Oxford Bus Station daily. Coaches usually leave about every 20 minutes during the day, taking 1¾ hours. A same-day round-trip ticket costs £7 ($11).

Or take the **Oxford Tube,** an express coach that takes you from Oxford to London in 90 minutes. Coaches operate every 20 minutes, 24 hours a day. Single fares are £5.70 ($9) and £6 ($10) for a 24-hour round-trip return. For schedules call ☎ **01865/772250.**

By car, take M40 west from London and follow the signs. Note, however, that parking is a nightmare in Oxford. There are four well-marked "Park and Ride" parking lots on the north, south, east, and west of the city's ring road. Parking is free, but from 9:30am on, and all day Saturday, you pay 75p ($1) for a bus ride into the city, which drops you off at St. Aldate's Cornmarket or Queen Street. The buses run every 8 to 10 minutes in each direction from Monday to Saturday. The parking lots are on the Woodstock road near the Peartree traffic circle, on the Botley road toward Farringdon, on the Abingdon road in the southeast, and on A40 toward London.

Visitor Information   Oxford Tourist Information Centre is at the Old School Gloucester Green, opposite the bus station (☎ **01865/726871**). The center sells a comprehensive range of maps and brochures, as well as the famous Oxford University T-shirt, and provides hotel booking services for £2.50 ($4). Open Monday to Saturday from 9:30am to 5pm and Sunday in summer and bank holidays from 10am to 3pm.

EXPLORING OXFORD UNIVERSITY

Many Americans arriving at Oxford ask: "Where's the campus?" If a local chortles when answering, it's because Oxford University is made up of 35 widely dispersed colleges. To tour all of these would be a formidable task. It's best to focus on just a handful of the better known colleges.

The **Oxford Story,** 6 Broad St. (☎ **01865/790055**), has packaged Oxford's complexities into a concise and entertaining audiovisual ride through the campus. The exhibition reviews some of the architectural and historical features that hurried visitors might miss. The exhibition includes a trip through a three-level former warehouse and takes you through more than 800 years of history. You're also filled in on the backgrounds of the colleges and those who have passed through their portals. The audiovisual presentation runs daily from 9:30am to 5:30pm. Tickets are £5 ($8) for adults and £4 ($6) for children. A family ticket for two adults and two children is £15 ($24).

GUIDED TOURS

The best way to get a running commentary on the important sights is to take a 2-hour walking tour through the city and the major colleges. The tours leave daily from the Oxford Tourist Information Centre at 11am and 2pm. Tours costs £4 ($6) for adults and £2.50 ($4) for children; they do not include New College or Christ Church.

For a good orientation, **Guide Friday** (office at the railway station, ☎ **01865/790522**) offers hour-long, open-top bus tours around Oxford. In winter, buses leave every half hour beginning at 10:10am on weekdays, and every 20 minutes

Oxford

0 ——————— 400 m
—————— 440 y
N

To Woodstock &
Stratford-upon-Avon

To Coventry

University Parks

To Woodstock & ↑
To Coventry
Keble Rd.
Woodstock Rd.
Banbury Rd.
Blackhall Rd.
Walton Cres.
Wellington Sq.
Richmond Rd.
Wor- cester Pl.
Walton St.
St. John's St.
Alfred Lane
Pusey St.
St. Giles St.
Museum Rd.
South Parks Rd.
St. Cross Rd.
River Cherwell
Beaumont St.
Gloucester St.
Green St.
Bus Station
Magdalen St.
Parks Rd.
Mansfield Rd.
Manor Rd.
George St.
Broad St.
Catte St.
Jowett Walk
St. Cross Rd.
Path along River Cherwell
St. Michael's St.
Ship St.
Holywell St.
New Inn Hall St.
Commarket St.
Market St.
Radcliffe Sq.
Queen's Lane
Longwall St.
To Station
Castle St.
St. Ebbes St.
Queen St.
Turl St.
King Edward St.
Alfred St.
Oriel St.
High St.
Deer Park
Church St.
Pembroke St.
Blue Boar St.
Magpie Lane
Merton St.
Old Grey Friars St.
Littlegate St.
Brewer St.
Rose Lane
Botanic Garden
Norfolk St.
Speedwell St.
St. Aldates St.
Merton Field
To London →
To Cowley →
To Reading →
River Thames
Christ Church Meadow
To Abingdon, Reading, London ↓

E-0155

All Souls College **1**	Magdalen College **6**	Somerville College **27**
Ashmolean Museum **25**	Manchester College **33**	St. Catherine's College **5**
Balliol College **22**	Mansfield College **31**	St. Hilda's College **7**
Brasenose College **20**	Merton College **8**	St. John's College **24**
Carfax Tower **16**	Museum of Modern Art **15**	St. Peter's College **17**
Christ Church College **12**	New College **3**	Town Hall **35**
Corpus Christi College **11**	Oriel College **10**	Trinity College **23**
Exeter College **21**	Pembroke College **14**	University College **9**
Hertford College **2**	Queen's College **4**	University Museum **29**
Jesus College **18**	Regent's Park College **26**	Wadham College **32**
Keble College **28**	Rhodes House **30**	Worcester College **13**
Lincoln College **19**	Sheldonian Theatre **34**	Information ⓘ

303

A Word of Warning

To avoid distraction for students, Oxford has restricted visiting to certain hours and to groups of six or fewer. Furthermore, there are areas where visitors aren't allowed at all. The tourist office will be happy to advise you when and where you may take in the sights of this great institution.

Saturday and Sunday at 9:30am. In summer, buses depart every 10 minutes beginning at 9:10am. Tickets are good for the day and can be purchased from the driver. The cost is £8 ($13) adults, £6.50 ($10) students and seniors, and £2.50 ($4) children.

A BIRD'S-EYE VIEW FROM CARFAX TOWER

For a bird's-eye view of the colleges, climb Carfax Tower, located in the center of the city. Carfax Tower is all that remains from St. Martin's Church, where William Shakespeare once stood as godfather for the playwright William Davenant. The tower used to be higher, but after 1340 it was lowered following complaints that townspeople threw stones and fired arrows at students during town-and-gown disputes. Admission is £1.20 ($2) for adults, 60p ($1) for children. From November to March 31, hours are daily from 10:30am to 3:30pm. Rest of year hours are daily from 10am to 5:30pm. The tower is closed from Christmas Eve until January 2. For information, call ☎ 01865/792653.

THE MAJOR COLLEGES

✪ **Christ Church**   Begun by Cardinal Wolsey as Cardinal College in 1525, Christ Church (☎ 01865/276499)—known as the House—was renamed by Henry VIII in 1546. Facing St. Aldate's Street, Christ Church has the largest quadrangle of any college in Oxford.

Tom Tower houses Great Tom, the 18,000-pound bell that rings nightly at 9:05pm, signaling the closing of the college gates. The 101 times it peals signifies the number of students in residence at the time of the founding of Christ Church. Although the student body has grown significantly, Oxford traditions live on forever. In the 16th-century great hall hang several notable portraits, including works by Gainsborough and Reynolds. The walls are thick with prime ministers, since Christ Church was the training ground for 13 of them. The college also hosts a separate portrait gallery.

The **college chapel** was constructed over several hundred years, beginning in the 12th century. (Incidentally, it's not only the college chapel, but also the cathedral of the diocese of Oxford.) The chapel's most impressive features are its 15th-century Norman pillars and the vaulting of the choir. Outside, in the center of the great quadrangle is a statue of Mercury mounted in the center of a fish pond. The college and chapel are open from 9am to 5:30pm. The entrance fee is £3 ($5) for adults and £2 ($3) for children. A family ticket costs £6 ($10).

Magdalen College   Magdalen (*Maud*-lin) College, High Street (☎ 01865/276000), was founded in 1458. Its alumni range from Wolsey to Wilde. Opposite the **botanic garden** (the oldest in England), is the **bell tower,** where the choristers sing in Latin at dawn on May Day. This 15th-century tower reflects mightily in the waters of the Cherwell below. Visit the equally old **chapel,** which feels ancient despite many of its latter-day trappings. Ask when the hall and other places of special interest are open. The grounds of Magdalen are the most extensive of any Oxford college; there's even a deer park. You can visit from Easter to September, daily from noon to 6pm; off-season, daily from 2 to 6pm. Admission is £2 ($3) adults; £1 ($1.60) children.

Merton College   Founded in 1264, Merton College (☎ **01865/276310**) is among the three oldest colleges at the university. It stands near Corpus Christi College on Merton Street, the sole survivor of Oxford's medieval cobbled streets. Merton College is noted for its **library,** built between 1371 and 1379 and said to be the oldest college library in England. One of the treasures is an astrolabe (an astronomical instrument used for measuring the altitude of the sun and stars) thought to have belonged to Chaucer. It costs £1 ($1.60) to visit the ancient library, including admission to the **Max Beerbohm Room,** honoring the satirical English caricaturist who died in 1956. The library and college are open Monday to Friday from 2 to 4pm and Saturday and Sunday from 10am to 4pm. Merton College is closed for 1 week at Easter and at Christmas.

A favorite pastime is to take **Addison's Walk** through the water meadows. The stroll is so named after a former alumnus, Joseph Addison, the 18th-century essayist and playwright noted for his contributions to *The Spectator* and *The Tatler.*

University College   University College, High Street (☎ **01865/276602**), is the oldest college at Oxford and dates back to 1249, when an ecclesiastic, William of Durham, donated money for its foundation (the old claim that the real founder was Alfred the Great is fanciful). All the original structures have disappeared; the architecture of the 17th century predominates today, with subsequent additions in Victoria's day as well as in more recent times. The college's most famous alumnus, Shelley, was "sent down" for his part in collaborating on a pamphlet on atheism. But with poetical success, all was forgiven, as evidenced by a memorial to Shelley erected in 1894, a mere 72 years after his death. The hall and chapel of University College are open daily during vacations from 2 to 4pm for a charge of £1.50 ($2) for adults, 60p ($1) for children. Chapel services take place daily at 4 and 6pm.

New College   New College, New College Lane, off Queen's Lane (☎ **01865/279555**), was founded in 1379. The **first quadrangle,** dating from before the end of the 14th century, was the initial quadrangle to be built in Oxford and formed the architectural boilerplate for many other colleges. In the **antechapel** is Sir Jacob Epstein's remarkable modern sculpture of Lazarus and a fine El Greco study of St. James. One of the treasures of the college is a crosier (pastoral staff of a bishop) belonging to the founding father. In the **garden,** you can stroll among the remains of the old city wall and the mound. The college (entered at New College Lane) can be visited Easter to September, daily from 11am to 5pm; off-season, daily from 2 to 4pm. Admission is free.

PUNTING THE RIVER CHERWELL

Punting on the River Cherwell remains the favorite outdoor pastime in Oxford. At **Punt Station,** Cherwell Boathouse, Bardwell Road (☎ **01865/515978**), you can rent a punt (flat-bottom boat maneuvered by a long pole and a small oar) for £8 to £10 ($13 to $16) per hour, plus a £40 to £50 ($64 to $80) deposit. A punt can take up to six people. Magdalen Bridge Boathouse charges similar rates. Punts are available for rent from March to mid-June and late August to October, daily from 10am to dusk; a larger inventory of punts is available from mid-June to late August daily from 10am to 10pm. Hours of operation seem to be rather informal; you're not always guaranteed that someone will be here to rent you a boat, even if a punt is tied to the dock.

WHERE TO STAY

The **Oxford Tourist Information Centre,** Gloucester Green, opposite the bus station (☎ **01865/726871**), operates a year-round room-booking service for a fee of £2.50

($4), plus a refundable deposit. If you'd like to seek lodgings on your own, the center has a list of accommodations, maps, and guidebooks.

EXPENSIVE

✪ Old Parsonage Hotel. 1 Banbury Rd., Oxford OX2 6NN. ☎ **01865/310210.** Fax 01865/311262. E-mail: oldparsonage@dial.pipex.com. 30 units. MINIBAR TV TEL. £145–£170 ($232–$272) double; £205 ($328) suite. Rates include English breakfast. AE, DC, MC, V.

This extensively renovated hotel near St. Giles Church and Keble College is so old (1660) that it looks like an extension of one of the ancient colleges. Once a 13th-century hospital, it was restored in the early 17th century. Oscar Wilde lived here for a time; this is where he said, "Either this wallpaper goes, or I do." In the 20th century, a modern wing was added, and in 1991 it was completely renovated and made into a first-rate hotel. The bedrooms are not large, but they're individually designed and have such amenities as satellite TV, hair dryers, and even phones in the bathrooms. All suites and some doubles have sofa beds, and all open onto the private gardens. The Parsonage Bar serves everything from cappuccino to mixed drinks. You can order from a well-prepared menu of continental and English food from 7am until "late at night." There's also 24-hour room service.

MODERATE

Dial House. 25 London Rd., Headington, Oxford, Oxfordshire OX3 7RE. ☎ and fax **01865/769944.** www.oxlink.co.uk/oxford/hotels.house.html. 8 units. TV. £50–£60 ($80–$96) double. No credit cards. Bus: 7, 7A, 20, 21, or 22.

This country house, built between 1924 and 1927, rests beside the highway to London, 2 miles east of the heart of Oxford. Graced with mock-Tudor half-timbering and a prominent blue-faced sundial (from which it derives its name), it has roomy, recently renovated bedrooms, each equipped with tea-making facilities and hair dryers. No smoking is permitted in the house. The owners, Julie and Tony Lamb, serve breakfast only in their bright dining room.

Eastgate Hotel. 23 Merton St., The High, Oxford, Oxfordshire OX1 4BE. ☎ **01865/248244.** Fax 01865/791681. 64 units. TV TEL. £110 ($176) double; £150 ($240) suite. AE, DC, MC, V.

Eastgate, built on the site of a 17th-century structure, stands opposite the ancient Examination Halls, next to Magdalen Bridge, and within walking distance of the city center. It offers recently refurbished facilities but retains most of the atmosphere of an English country house. All of the comfortably furnished rooms have radios and coffeemakers. The Shires Restaurant serves roasts and traditional English fare; the bar is popular with Oxford undergrads.

River Hotel. 17 Botley Rd., Oxford OX2 0AA. ☎ **01865/243475.** Fax 01865/724306. 21 units (19 with bathroom). TV TEL. £67.50 ($108) double with bathroom. Rates include breakfast. MC, V. Bus: 4C or 52.

This hotel lies within a quarter-mile west of Oxford's commercial core, and charges less than many of its competitors that are just a bit more central. It was built around 1900 by a respected local craftsman whose casement windows and flower boxes are still in place. About a quarter of the accommodations lie across the street, within a comfortable stone-sided annex, whose architectural details more or less match those of the main house. There's a bar on the premises, a simple restaurant, and cozy furnishings within the bedrooms. Three singles without bathroom rent for £45 ($72). Each contains a tea-making facility.

Tilbury Lodge Private Hotel. 5 Tilbury Lane, Eynsham Rd., Botley, Oxford, Oxfordshire OX2 9NB. ☎ **01865/862138.** Fax 01865/863700. www.oxlink.co.uk/oxford/hotels. tilbury.html. 9 units. TV TEL. £56–£66 ($90–$106) double, £75 ($120) double with four-poster. Rates include English breakfast. MC, V. Bus: 42, 45, 45A, 45B, or 109.

This small hotel lies on a quiet country lane 2 miles west of the center of Oxford, less than a mile from the railway station. Eddie and Eileen Trafford house guests in well-furnished and comfortable bedrooms. (The most expensive room has a four-poster bed.) The hotel also has a Jacuzzi and welcomes children. If you don't arrive by car, Eddie can pick you up at the train station; a bus also stops nearby.

WHERE TO DINE
MODERATE

Bath Place Hotel. 4–5 Bath Place (at Holywell St.), Oxford OX1 3SU. ☎ **01865/791812.** Fax 01865/791834. www.oxlink.co.uk/oxford/hotels.bath.html. Reservations recommended. Main courses £18–£23 ($29–$37); fixed-price 6-course dinner £28 ($45). AE, MC, V. Wed–Sat noon–2pm, Sun 12:30–2:30pm; Sun–Thurs 7–10pm, Fri–Sat 7–10:30pm. Bus: 7. ANGLO/FRENCH.

Composed of four interconnected 17th-century cottages, this place has been well known since 1989 as a haven for sophisticated cuisine. Since it also houses 10 cozy bedrooms upstairs, it operates something like a non-smoking French *restaurant avec chambres*, where diners can head directly upstairs after an evening meal. The menu, which usually changes every month, includes vegetarian selections and a pleasing mix-ture of English cuisines, with heavy emphasis on French. Choices might include baked young English partridge, boned and encased in a puff pastry served with red wine jus and seasonal vegetables; a filet of Scottish beef, roasted and served in a chive and herb sauce with wild mushrooms and baby vegetables; and a steamed filet of Cornish sea bass with diced vegetables in a "mouclade" sauce with homemade linguini.

Each of the non-smoking upstairs bedrooms features a TV and telephone. Including continental breakfast, doubles cost £90 to £127.50 ($144 to $204) per night.

Cherwell Boathouse Restaurant. Bardwell Rd. ☎ **01865/552746.** Reservations recom-mended. Main courses £9–£14 ($14–$22); fixed-price dinner from £18.50 ($30); fixed-price lunch £17.50 ($28). AE, DC, MC, V. Tues 6–11:30pm; Wed–Sat noon–2pm and 6–11:30pm; Sun noon–2pm. Closed Dec 24–30. Bus: Banbury Rd. Bus: 7. MODERN ENGLISH/FRENCH.

This landmark on the River Cherwell is owned by Anthony Verdin, who offers a fixed-price menu that changes every 2 weeks to take advantage of the availability of fresh vegetables, fish, and meat. On any given night, you might try starters such as game terrine with Cumberland sauce or a warm salad of black pudding and bacon with a damson dressing. For a main course, you might opt for breast of guinea fowl with tapenade or, for vegetarians, an eggplant gratin with saffron custard and a mixed-bean ragout. For dessert, few have resisted the "fallen" chocolate soufflé with "drunken" prunes and sour cream. The restaurant also has an exciting, reasonable wine list. In summer, dinner is served on the terrace. Before dinner, you can try punting; there's a rental agency on the other side of the boat house (see "Punting the River Cherwell," above).

Elizabeth. 82 St. Aldate's St. ☎ **01865/242230.** Reservations recommended. Main courses £13.25–£17.75 ($21–$28); lunch £15 ($24). AE, DC, MC, V. Tues–Sat 12:30–2:30pm and 6:30–11pm; Sun 7–10:30pm. Closed Easter weekend and Christmas week. Bus: 7. FRENCH.

Despite the portraits of Elizabeth II that hang near the entrance, this restaurant is named after a less-than-royal owner, a matriarch who founded the place in this stone-sided house in the 1930s opposite Christ Church College. Today, you'll find a well-trained staff from Spain, who serve beautifully presented dishes in the French style. The larger of the two dining rooms exudes a restrained dignity; the smaller is devoted to *Alice in Wonderland* designs inspired by Lewis Carroll. Some of the kitchen's best dishes include a range of Scottish steaks; grilled salmon, Dover sole, and sea bass in white-wine or lemon-butter sauce; duck with orange sauce; and roast rack of lamb with *gratin dauphinois.*

INEXPENSIVE

Al-Shami. 25 Walton Crescent. ☎ **01865/310066.** Reservations recommended. Main courses £7.50–£12 ($12–$19); fixed-price menu £15 ($24). MC, V. Daily noon–midnight. Bus: 7. LEBANESE.

Ideal for meals all afternoon and late into the evening, this Lebanese restaurant has awakened Oxford's sleepy taste buds. Many diners don't go beyond the appetizers, more than 35 delectable hot-and-cold selections—everything from falafel to a lamb's-brain salad. Charcoal-grilled chopped lamb, chicken, or beef constitute most of the main-dish selections. In between, guests nibble on uncut raw vegetables; afterwards they choose desserts from the trolley. Al-Shami also serves vegetarian meals.

✪ **Munchy Munchy.** 6 Park End St. ☎ **01865/245710.** Reservations recommended. Main courses £5.50–£9.75 ($8.80–$16). MC, V. Tues–Sat noon–2pm and 5:30–10pm. Closed 2 weeks in Sept and 3 weeks in Dec. Bus: 52. SOUTHEAST ASIAN/INDONESIAN.

Some Oxford students think that this place offers the best food value in the city. The menu depends on what's available in the marketplace; Ethel Ow is adept at herbs and seasoning, and often uses fresh fruit creatively, as reflected in such dishes as king prawns sautéed with turmeric, coriander, and a puree of apricots or a spicy lamb with eggplant, Szechuan red pepper, star anise, and crushed yellow bean sauce. At times, long lines form at the door, especially on Fridays and Saturdays. Children 5 and under are not permitted Friday and Saturday evenings.

PUBS

The Bear Inn. Alfred St. ☎ **01865/721783.** Snacks and bar meals £2.50–£6 ($4–$10). No credit cards. Mon–Sat noon–11pm; Sun noon–3pm and 7–10:30pm. Bus: 2A or 2B. ENGLISH.

A short block from The High, overlooking the north side of Christ Church College, this village pub is an Oxford tradition. Its swinging inn sign depicts the bear and ragged staff, the old insignia of the earls of Warwick, who were among its early patrons. Many famous Oxford students and residents have caroused within the pub's walls since the 13th century, earning it a well-worn place in English literature. The Bear has served a useful purpose in breaking down social barriers, bringing a wide variety of people together in a relaxed way. You might converse with a raja from India, a university don, a titled gentleman, or the latest in a line of owners that goes back more than 700 years. Some past owners developed a prankish and astonishing habit: clipping neckties. Around the lounge bar you'll see the remains of thousands of ties, all labeled with their owners' names. For those who seek to join this legacy of sartorial abuse, the bar patrons will cut a thin strip from the bottom of your tie (with your per-mission, of course). After this initiation, you may want to take part in some of the informal songfests of the undergraduates.

The Turf Tavern. 4 Bath Place (off Holywell St.). ☎ **01865/243235.** Main courses £3–£5 ($4.70–$8). MC, V. Mon–Sat 11am–11pm; Sun noon–3pm and 7–10:30pm. Bus: 52. ENGLISH.

This 13th-century tavern, the oldest in Oxford, stands on a very narrow passageway near the Bodleian Library. Thomas Hardy used it as a setting in *Jude the Obscure,* and it was "the local" of Burton and Taylor when they were in Oxford many years ago making a film; today's patrons include a healthy sampling of the university's students and faculty. During his student days at Oxford, Bill Clinton was a frequent visitor here. During warm weather you can choose a table in one of the three separate gardens that radiate outward from the pub's core. For wintertime warmth, braziers are lighted in the courtyard and in the gardens.

A separate food counter, set behind a glass case, displays the day's fare. To eat, present yourself to the employee behind the case, and carry your food back to your table. Menu choices include salads, soups, sandwiches, and platters of such traditional dishes as English beef pie, chili con carne, pork and cider, and chicken Kiev. Local ales (including a vicious brew named Headbanger) are served, as well as a range of wines. Food is served Monday to Saturday only from noon to 2:30pm. The pub is reached via St. Helen's Passage, which stretches between Holywell Street and New College Lane. (You'll probably get lost, but any student worth his beer can direct you.)

3 Town & Gown: Cambridge

55 miles N of London, 80 miles NE of Oxford

The university town of Cambridge is a collage of images: the Bridge of Sighs; spires and turrets; willows; dusty secondhand bookshops; the lilt of Elizabethan madrigals; lanes where Darwin, Newton, and Cromwell walked; the grassy "Backs" of the colleges, sweeping down to the banks of the Cam; punters; the tattered robes of hurried upperclassmen flying in the wind.

Along with Oxford, Cambridge is one of Britain's ancient seats of knowledge. In many ways their stories are similar—particularly the age-old conflict between town and gown. But beyond the campus, Cambridge has a thriving, high-tech industry. Yes, that was Bill Gates you spotted. And while Oxford recalls the arts, Cambridge has embraced the sciences. Both Isaac Newton and Stephen Hawking are graduates, joined by thousands of luminaries in every field.

There is much to explore in Cambridge, so give yourself time to wander.

ESSENTIALS

Getting There   Trains depart frequently from London's Liverpool Street and King's Cross stations, arriving an hour later. For inquiries, call **0345/484950** (in the U.K. only) or 01603/764776). An off-peak same-day round-trip is £13.20 ($21). A peak-time same-day round-trip is £15.60 ($25). An off-peak longer stay round-trip (up to a 5-day period) is £17.80 ($28).

National Express buses run hourly between London's Victoria Coach Station for the 2-hour trip to Drummer Street Station in Cambridge. A one-way costs £7 ($11), a same-day round-trip £7.50 ($12). If you'd like to return in a day or two the cost is £9 ($14). Call **0990/808080** for information and schedules.

To drive from London, head north on the M11.

Visitor Information   The **Cambridge Tourist Information Centre,** Wheeler Street (☎ 01223/322640), in back of the Guildhall, offers a wide range of information. From April to September, hours are Monday to Friday 10am to 6pm, Saturday 9am to 5pm, and Sunday 10:30am to 3:30pm; July and August, open daily 9am to 6pm; October to March, Monday to Friday 10am to 6pm and Saturday 9am to 5pm.

A tourist reception center for Cambridge and Cambridgeshire is operated by **Guide Friday Ltd.** on the concourse of Cambridge Railway Station (☎ **01223/362444**). The center sells brochures and maps, and books rooms. Open daily in summer from 9:30am to 6pm; the center closes at 3pm in winter.

Getting Around   The center of Cambridge is made for pedestrians, so park your car at one of the many car parks (they increase in price as you approach the city center) and stroll among the widely dispersed colleges. Follow the courtyards through to the "Backs" (the college lawns) and walk through to Trinity (where Prince Charles studied) and St. John's colleges, which contains the Bridge of Sighs.

Another popular way of getting around is bicycling. **Geoff's Bike Hire,** 65 Devonshire Rd. (☎ **01223/365629**), rents bicycles for £4 ($6) for 3 hours, £6 ($10) per day, or £15 ($24) per week. A deposit of £25 ($40) is required. Open daily in summer from 9am to 6pm; off-season Monday to Saturday from 9am to 5:30pm.

Stagecoach Cambus, 100 Cowley Rd. (☎ **01223/423554**), operates a network of buses, with fares ranging in price from 50p to £1.60 (80¢ to $3). The local tourist office has schedules.

GUIDED TOURS

A good person to know if you're in the Cambridge area is Mrs. Isobel Bryant, who operates **Heritage Tours** from her 200-year-old home, Manor Cottage, Swaffham Prior CB5 0JZ (☎ **01638/741440**). An expert on the region, she will arrange tours starting from your hotel or Cambridge railway station to Lavenham with its thatched and timbered houses, to the fine medieval churches of the Suffolk villages, to Ely Cathedral, or to one of the nearby grand mansions with their many treasures. The charge of £100 ($160) is for the day for up to three or £110 ($176) for four passengers and all travel expenses, including the service of the driver/guide. Lunch in a village pub and admission fees add £3 to £6 ($5 to $10) per person. Mrs. Bryant also offers walking tours around the Cambridge colleges; they cost £35 ($56) for a family-size party and last about 2 hours.

Guide Friday, Ltd., on the concourse of Cambridge Railway Station (☎ **01223/362444**), has daily guided tours of Cambridge via open-top, double-decker buses. In summer, buses depart every 30 minutes from 9:45am to 2:45pm. Departures are curtailed off-season, depending on demand. The tour allows visitors to get off at any of the many stops and rejoin the tour whenever they wish. Tickets are valid all day. The fare is £7.50 ($12) for adults, £6.50 ($10) for senior citizens and students, and £2 ($3) for children 5 to 12, free for children 4 and under. Office hours are 9:30am to 3pm daily.

EXPLORING THE UNIVERSITY

Oxford University predates Cambridge, but by the early 13th century scholars began gathering here, too. Eventually, Cambridge won partial recognition from Henry III, rising or falling with the approval of subsequent English monarchs. Cambridge consists of 31 colleges for both men and women. Colleges are closed for exams from mid-April until the end of June.

The following listing is only a sample of some of the more interesting colleges. If you're planning to be in Cambridge awhile, you might also want to visit **Magdalene College,** on Magdalene Street, founded in 1542; **Pembroke College,** on Trumpington Street, founded in 1347; **Christ's College,** on St. Andrew's Street, founded in 1505; and **Corpus Christi College,** on Trumpington Street, which dates from 1352.

✪ **King's College**   The adolescent Henry VI founded King's College on King's Parade (☎ **01223/331212**) in 1441. Most of its buildings today date from the 19th

Cambridge

0 [======] 400 m
          440 y

N

To Ely ↗

Victoria Rd.

Chesterton Rd.

River Cam

Chesterton Lane

Jesus Green

Castle St.

To Bedford

Northampton St.

Magdalen St.

Portugal Pl.

Park Parade

Park St.

Round Church St.

St. John's St.

Jesus Lane

Midsummer Common

Butts Green To Newmarket →

Victoria Ave.

Green St.

Trinity St.

Market St.

King St.

Christ's Pieces

"The Backs"

River Cam

Queen's Rd.

Sidney St.

Malcolm St.

Hobson St.

St. Andrews St.

Drummer St.

Emmanuel St.

Parker St.

Emmanuel Rd.

Clarendon St.

New Sq.

Fitzroy St.

Eden St.

City Rd.

Petty Curry

Corn Exchange St.

Benet St.

Kings Parade

West Rd.

Mill Lane

Pembroke St.

Little St. Mary's Lane

Downing St.

Downing Pl.

Park Terrace

Parkside

East Rd.

Parkers Piece

Gonville Pl.

Mill Rd.

Sidgwick Ave.

Silver St.

Sheeps Green

The Fen

Tennis Court Rd.

Trumpington St.

Regent St.

Gresham Rd.

Newnham Rd.

The Fen

Botanic Gardens

Causeway

Lensfield Rd.

Hills Rd.

Harvey Rd.

↓ To London

To Colchester

E-0156

"The Backs" ⑩	Jesus College ⑥	Sidney Sussex College ⑦
British Rail Station ㉙	King's College ⑱	
Bus Station ⑬	Magdalene College ④	Swimming Pool ①
Christ's College ⑫	Newnham College ㉓	Trinity College ⑨
Clare College ⑲	Pembroke College ㉕	Westminster College ②
Corpus Christi College ㉔	Peterhouse College ㉖	
Downing College ㉘	Police Station ⑭	
Emmanuel College ⑮	Punts ⑤	
Fitzwilliam Museum ㉗	Queen's College ㉑	
Folk Museum ③	St. Catharine's College ⑳	
General Post Office ⑯	St. John's College ⑧	Information ⓘ
Gonville & Caius College ⑪	Selwyn College ㉒	

311

A Word of Warning

Unfortunately, because of disturbances caused by the influx of tourists to the university, Cambridge has had to limit visitors, or exclude them altogether, from various parts of the university. In some cases, a small entry fee is charged. Small groups of up to six are generally admitted with no problem; you can inquire from the tourist office about visiting hours (see "Essentials").

---

century, but its crowning glory, the perpendicular **King's College Chapel,** was built in the Middle Ages and is one of England's irreplaceable monuments. Owing to whims of royalty, the chapel wasn't completed until the early 16th century.

Henry James called King's College Chapel "the most beautiful in England." Its most striking features are the magnificent fan vaulting, all in stone, and the great windows, most of which were fashioned by Flemish artisans between 1517 and 1531 (the west window dates from the late Victorian period). In hues of red, blue, and amber, the long range of windows around the back of the chapel depicts the Birth of the Virgin; the Annunciation; the Birth of Christ; the Life, Ministry, and Death of Christ; the Resurrection; the Ascension; the Acts of the Apostles; and the Assumption. The upper range contains Old Testament parallels to these New Testament stories. The chapel also boasts Rubens' *Adoration of the Magi* and a rood screen from the early 16th century.

The chapel is open during vacation time Monday to Saturday 9:30am to 4:30pm, and on Sunday 10am to 4:30pm. During term, the public is welcome to attend choral services Tuesday to Saturday at 5:30pm and on Sunday at 10:30am and 3:30pm, and the chapel is open to visitors Monday to Saturday 9:30am to 3:15pm and Sunday 1:15 to 2:15pm and 5 to 5:30pm; it's closed December 23 to January 1. It may be closed at other times for recording sessions, broadcasts, concerts, or other special events. An exhibition in the seven northern side chapels recounts much of the history of the chapel. Admission to the college and chapel, including the exhibition, is £3 ($5) for adults, £2 ($3) for students and children 12 to 17, free for children under 12.

Peterhouse College   On Trumpington Street, Peterhouse College (☎ **01223/ 338200**) attracts visitors largely because it's the oldest Cambridge college, founded in 1284 by Hugh de Balsham, the bishop of Ely. Of the original buildings, only the hall remains. It was restored in the 19th century and now has stained-glass windows by William Morris. Old Court, constructed in the 15th century, was renovated in 1754; the chapel dates from 1632. Ask permission to enter at the porter's lodge.

Trinity College   On Trinity Street, Trinity College (not to be confused with Trinity Hall) is the largest college in Cambridge. It was founded in 1546 by Henry VIII, who consolidated a number of smaller colleges that had existed on the site. The courtyard is the most spacious in Cambridge, built when Thomas Nevile was master. Sir Christopher Wren designed the library. For admission to the college, apply at the porter's lodge, or call ☎ **01223/338400** for information. There's a charge of £1.50 ($2) from March to May 4 and June 21 to November 2.

Emmanuel College   On St. Andrew's Street, Emmanuel (☎ **01223/334274**), was founded in 1584 by Sir Walter Mildmay, a chancellor of the exchequer to Elizabeth I. Harvardians take note: John Harvard, founder of Harvard University, studied here. You can take a scenic stroll around its attractive gardens and visit the chapel designed by Sir Christopher Wren and consecrated in 1677. Both the chapel and college are open daily 9am to 6pm.

Queens' College   On Queens' Lane, Queens' College (☎ **01223/335511**) is the loveliest of Cambridge's colleges. Dating back to 1448, it was founded by two English queens, one the wife of Henry VI, the other the wife of Edward IV. Its second cloister is the most interesting, flanked by the early-16th-century half-timbered President's Lodge. Admission is £1 ($1.60), free for children under 12. A short printed guide is issued. Individual visitors are admitted daily from 1:45 to 4:30pm, but during March to October the college is also open to visitors daily 10:15am to 12:45pm. Entry is by the old porter's lodge in Queens' Lane only. The old hall and chapel are usually open to the public when not in use.

St. John's College   On St. John's Street, this college (☎ **01223/338600**) was founded in 1511 by Lady Margaret Beaufort, mother of Henry VII, who had launched Christ's College a few years earlier. The impressive gateway bears the Tudor coat of arms, and Second Court is a fine example of late Tudor brickwork. Its best-known feature is the **Bridge of Sighs** crossing the Cam. Built in the 19th century, it was patterned after the covered bridge in Venice. It connects the older part of the college with New Court, a Gothic revival on the opposite bank from which there is an outstanding view of the famous "Backs." The Bridge of Sighs is closed to visitors, but can be seen from neighboring Kitchen Bridge. Wordsworth was an alumnus of the college, which is open March to October, daily 10:30am to 5:30pm. Admission is £1.75 ($3) for adults and £1 ($1.60) for children. Visitors are welcome to attend choral services in the chapel.

MORE CAMBRIDGE ATTRACTIONS

✪ Fitzwilliam Museum. Trumpington St., near Peterhouse. ☎ **01223/332900.** Free admission. Tues–Sat 10am–5pm, Sun 2:15–5pm. Guided tours, Sun 2:30pm. Closed Jan 1, Good Friday, May Day, and Dec 24–31.

This is one of Britain's finest museums. Founded by the bequest of the 7th Viscount Fitzwilliam of Merrion to the University of Cambridge in 1816, this museum's permanent collections contain remarkable antiquities from ancient Egypt, Greece, and Rome. Newly created galleries display Roman and Romano-Egyptian art along with Western Asiatic exhibits. The Fitzwilliam's Applied Arts section showcases English and European pottery and glass as well as furniture, clocks, armor, fans, rugs and samplers, Chinese jades, and ceramics from Japan and Korea. The museum also has married a rare ancient and medieval coin collection with a host of medals created from the Renaissance onward. But the Fitzwilliam is best loved for its paintings, which include masterpieces by Simone Martini, Titian, Veronese, Rubens, Van Dyck, Canaletto, Hogarth, Gainsborough, Constable, Monet, Degas, Renoir, Cézanne, and Picasso. There is also a fine collection of other 20th-century art, miniatures, drawings, watercolors, and prints.

Great St. Mary's. King's Parade. ☎ **01223/350914.** Admission to tower £1.50 ($2) adults, 50p ($1) children. Tower Mon–Sat 10am–4:30pm, Sun 12:30–4:30pm. Church daily 9am–6pm.

Insider's Tip

The Fitzwilliam stages occasional musical events, including evening concerts, in Gallery III. Throughout the year, it also plays host to some of the best lectures in England. For more details, call ☎ **01223/332900.**

Closely associated with events of the Reformation, this university church was built mostly in 1478 on the site of an 11th-century church. The cloth that covered the hearse of King Henry VII is on display in the church. A fine view of Cambridge may be seen from the top of the tower.

PUNTING THE CAM

Punting along the Cam in flat-bottomed wooden boats built somewhat like Venetian gondolas is a traditional pursuit here. Downstream, the Cam winds about the ivy-covered "Backs" of the colleges, their lush gardens sweeping riverwards. Two miles upriver lies **Grantchester,** immortalized by Rupert Brooke in the verse cited below. Literary types flock to Grantchester's Green Man pub (see "Pubs," below), which can be reached by punting or by taking the path following the River Granta for less than an hour to Grantchester Meadows. The town lies about a mile from the meadows. When the town clock stopped for repairs in 1985, its hands were left frozen "for all time" at ten to three in honor of Brooke's famed verse.

People sprawled along the banks of the Cam on a summer day wait to judge and ridicule you as you maneuver your punt with a 15-foot-long pole. The river's floor is muddy, and many a student has lost his pole in the riverbed shaded by the willows. If your pole gets stuck, it may be better to leave it sticking in the mud than to risk a plunge (and more ridicule) by trying to claim it too forcefully from the river.

Scudamore's Boatyards, Granta Place (☎ **01223/575431**), by the Anchor Pub, has been in business since 1910. Punts, canoes, and rowboats rent for £10 ($16) per hour. A £40 ($64) cash or credit-card deposit is required. There's a maximum of six persons per punt. They're open from March to late September or October daily from 9am until dusk, depending on the weather and number of clients. You may prefer a chauffeur, in which case there's a minimum charge of £20 ($32) for two people and £5 ($8) per person after that.

Cambridge Punt Company, working out of the Anchor Pub, Silver Street (☎ **01223/327280**), conducts highly recommended 45-minute rowboat tours. A guide (usually a Cambridge student) appropriately dressed in a straw boater hat will simultaneously punt and deliver running commentary to groups of one to six persons. Tours cost £20 ($32) for two, and £5 ($8) per adult after that (£2.50 ($4) for children 5 to 12). Kids 4 and under ride free. The Anchor Pub's service staff can call a guide over to your table. For the independent, "unchauffeured" boats rent for £10 ($16) per hour. The company is open daily from 9am to dusk, though everyone packs up and goes home if it rains or if the winds get too high.

WHERE TO STAY
MODERATE

Gonville Hotel. Gonville Place, Cambridge, Cambridgeshire CB1 1LY. ☎ **800/528-1234** or 01223/366611. Fax 01223/315470. www.hotelnet.co.uk. 62 units. TV TEL. £101 ($162) double. Rates include English breakfast. AE, CB, DC, MC, V.

This comfortable hotel and its grounds are opposite Parker's Piece, only a 5-minute walk from the center of town. The Gonville has been much improved in recent years, and is now better than ever, though not yet the equal of the University Arms (see below). It's not unlike an ivy-covered country house, with shade trees and a formal car entry. The recently refurbished rooms are comfortable and furnished in a modern style. There's central heating throughout and air-conditioning in the restaurant. For extra charges, laundry and dry cleaning, babysitting, and secretarial services are made available.

University Arms Hotel. Regent St., Cambridge, Cambridgeshire CB2 1AD. ☎ **01223/351241.** Fax 01223/315256. 116 units. TV TEL. £120–£135 ($192–$216) double; £250 ($400) suite. Rates include English breakfast. AE, MC, V. Bus: 1.

Built in 1834, this hotel maintains much of its Edwardian charm and many of its original architectural features despite modernization over the years. Near the city center and the university, it offers tastefully decorated bedrooms with central heating and a radio. In addition to trouser presses and hair dryers, suite residents will find fresh flowers, fruits, and chocolates in their rooms. The Octagon Lounge, with its stained-glass domed ceiling and open log fire, is a popular place to meet for tea. The spacious oak-paneled restaurant features both table d'hôte and à la carte menus. The hotel porter arranges guided tours of the city. For a hotel of this price range, the expected amenities are delivered: concierge, room service, dry cleaning/laundry, babysitting, and secretarial services.

INEXPENSIVE

Arundel Hotel. Chesterton Rd., Cambridge, Cambridgeshire CB4 3AN. ☎ **01223/367701.** Fax 01223/367721. 105 units. TV TEL. £60–£90 ($96–$144) double. Rates include continental breakfast. AE, DC, MC, V. Bus: 3 or 5.

Occupying one of the most desirable sites in Cambridge, until recently this hotel consisted of six identical Victorian row houses—each fronted with the same dark-yellow local bricks—which were interconnected many years ago to form a coherent whole. In 1994, after two additional row houses were purchased from the university, the hotel was enlarged, upgraded, and expanded into the well-maintained hostelry you'll see today. Although not as well appointed as the University Arms, it competes successfully with the Gonville. In fact, its cuisine is better than that served at the Gonville or the Arms. Rooms overlooking the River Cam and Jesus Green cost more; and because there's no elevator, rooms on lower floors cost more than those near the roof. Regardless of their location, all accommodations are clean, simple, and comfortable. There's a bar and restaurant (see "Where to Dine," below) on the premises and a garden with outdoor tables for warm-weather drinking. A coin-operated launderette is on the premises.

Regent Hotel. 41 Regent St., Cambridge, Cambridgeshire CB2 1AB. ☎ **01223/351470.** Fax 01223/566562. www.regenthotel.co.uk. 26 units. TV TEL. £80 ($128) double. Rates include English breakfast. AE, DC, MC, V.

This is one of the most desirable of the reasonably priced small hotels in Cambridge. Right in the city center, overlooking Parker's Piece, the house was built in the 1840s as the original site of Newham College. It became a hotel when the college outgrew its quarters. The attractive, comfortable bedrooms have radios, hair dryers, and trouser presses. There's a cocktail bar on the street level, and the coffee bar serves breakfast, late snacks, and afternoon tea.

WHERE TO DINE
MODERATE

Arundel House Restaurant. Chesterton Rd. ☎ **01223/367701.** Reservations recommended. Main courses £9–£13 ($14–$21); 2-course fixed-price lunch £9.75 ($16), 3-course fixed-price lunch £11 ($18), Sun lunch £12 ($19); 2-course fixed-price dinner £13.50 ($22),

3-course dinner £16 ($26). AE, DC, MC, V. Daily 12:15–1:45pm and 6:30–9:30pm. Bus: 3 or 5. FRENCH/BRITISH/VEGETARIAN.

One of the most acclaimed restaurants in Cambridge is in this hotel overlooking the River Cam and Jesus Green, a short walk from the city center. Winner of many awards, the cuisine is not only excellent and fresh, but is also a good value. The warm decor features Louis XV-style chairs and spacious tables. The fare changes frequently, and you may dine à la carte or from the set menu. There's also a children's menu with a maximum price of £2.25 ($4). Appetizers may consist of a homemade golden pea and ham soup, or a white-rum and passion-fruit cocktail. Fish choices are likely to include plaice or salmon, which mightily compete against the marinated venison and seasonal root vegetables in a shortcrust pastry.

Midsummer House. Midsummer Common. ☎ **01223/69299.** Reservations required. 3-course lunch £23 ($37), Sun lunch £25 ($40); 3-course fixed-price dinner £39.50 ($63), 6-course fixed-price dinner £50 ($80). AE, MC, V. Tues–Fri and Sun 12:30–1:45pm; Tues–Sat 7:30–9:30pm. CONTINENTAL.

Located near the River Cam in an Edwardian-era cottage, the Midsummer House is one of the dining discoveries of Cambridge. The preferred dining area is in an elegant conservatory, but you can also find a smartly laid table upstairs. The fixed-price menus are wisely limited, and quality control and high standards are much in evidence despite a frequent change of chefs. The waiters will be glad to assist you as you peruse the menu, which traditionally has offered some of the freshest and best selections of dishes in Cambridge.

✪ **Twenty Two.** 22 Chesterton Rd. ☎ **01223/351880.** Reservations required. Fixed-price menu £28.50 ($46). AE, MC, V. Tues–Sat 7:30–10pm. ENGLISH/CONTINENTAL.

Who would expect to find one of the best restaurants in Cambridge in this quiet residential and hotel district? In the vicinity of Jesus Green, it's an address jealously guarded by locals. This homelike but elegant Victorian dining room offers an ever-changing fixed-price menu based on fresh market produce. Owners David Carter and Louise Crompton meld time-tested recipes with their own inspirations. Typical dishes include a warm squid salad with ginger dressing, and roast chump of lamb with braised white cabbage, best followed by the Grand Marnier parfait.

INEXPENSIVE

Browns. 23 Trumpington St. ☎ **01223/461655.** Main courses £7.45–£15 ($12–$24). AE, MC, V. Mon–Sat 11am–11:30pm; Sun noon–11:30pm. Bus: 2. ENGLISH/CONTINENTAL.

Long a favorite at Oxford, Browns became a sensation at Cambridge some time ago. It was built opposite the Fitzwilliam Museum in 1914 as the outpatient department of a hospital dedicated to Edward VII; that era's grandeur remains most vividly in the building's neoclassical colonnade. Today it's the most lighthearted place for dining in the city, with wicker chairs, high ceilings, pre-World War I woodwork, and a long bar covered with bottles of wine. The extensive bill of fare includes various pastas, scores of fresh salads, several selections of meat and fish (from charcoal-grilled leg of lamb with rosemary to fresh fish in season), hot sandwiches, and the chef's daily specials. If you drop by in the afternoon, you can also order thick milk shakes or natural fruit juices. In fair weather, outdoor seats are prized possessions.

PUBS

Cambridge Arms. 4 King St. ☎ **01223/505515.** Bar snacks £3–£6.50 ($5–$10). AE, V. Mon–Sat noon–5:30pm; Sun noon–2:30pm. Pub Mon–Sat 11am–11pm; Sun noon–10:30pm. ENGLISH.

This no-nonsense pub in the center of town bustles with atmosphere and dispenses endless platters of food to clients over the bar's countertop. Favorites include the chef's daily specials, grilled steaks, lasagna, and an array of both hot and cold dishes. Also on site is a Victorian-style coffee shop open daily 10am to 10pm with not-so-Victorian access to six computers equipped with business software, Internet, and e-mail facilities. The cellar is the site of the old Scarlet Brewery and is rife with rustic beermaking implements. Tours of the cellar, including a brief history of the art of brewing, are free.

✪ **The Green Man.** 59 High St., Grantchester. ☎ **01223/841178.** Lunch main courses £5–£8 ($8–$13); fixed-price dinner £12.25 ($20); Sun lunch £10.75 ($17). AE, MC, V. Daily noon–2pm and 6–9pm; pub Mon–Fri 11am–3pm, Sat 11am–11pm; Sun noon–10:30pm. Bus: 118 from Cambridge. ENGLISH.

Named in honor of Robin Hood, this 400-year-old inn is the most popular pub for outings from Cambridge. It's located on A604, 2 miles south of Cambridge in the hamlet of Grantchester, made famous by Rupert Brooke, the Edwardian-era poet best known for his sonnet "The Soldier." Grantchester is one of the shire's most beautiful villages, with an old church and gardens leading down to a series of peaceful meadows. Even if you haven't heard of Brooke, you might enjoy spending a late afternoon wandering through the old church and then heading, as everybody does, to the Green Man. In winter a crackling fire welcomes the weary inside, but in summer it's more tempting to retreat to the beer garden, from which you can stroll to the edge of the River Cam. Place your order at the counter, after which an employee will bring your food to your table. Your choices include steak-and-Guinness pie and a 7-inch Yorkshire pudding.

4 Canterbury

56 miles SE of London

Under the arch of the ancient West Gate went Chaucer's knight, pardoner, nun, squire, parson, merchant, miller, and others—all spinning tales. They were bound for the shrine of Thomas à Becket, archbishop of Canterbury, who was slain by four knights of Henry II on December 29, 1170 at the cathedral. (In penance, the king was later made to walk barefoot from Harbledown to the tomb of his former friend, and allow himself to be flogged.) The shrine was finally torn down in 1538 by Henry VIII, as part of his campaign to destroy monasteries and graven images; but by then, Canterbury had become inexorably fixed in the pilgrim's imagination.

This Kentish city on the River Stour is the ecclesiastical capital of England. The city was once fully walled, and abundant traces of its old fortifications remain despite enormous damage caused by the Nazi blitz of 1941. Pilgrims to Canterbury continue to arrive today, but are called "daytrippers," and have overrun the city and its monuments. The city has an active university life—mainly students from Kent—and an enormous number of pubs and shops. Canterbury is best seen in the early morning or the early evening, when daytrippers are scarce.

ESSENTIALS

Getting There There's frequent train service from Victoria, Charing Cross, Waterloo, or London Bridge Station. The journey takes 1½ hours. For schedules and information, call ☎ **0345/484950** (U.K. only) or 01603/764776.

The bus from Victoria Coach Station takes 2 to 3 hours and leaves twice daily. For schedules and information, call ☎ **0990/808080.**

To drive from London, take A2, then M2. Canterbury is signposted all the way. The city center is closed to cars, but it's only a short walk from several parking areas to the cathedral.

Visitor Information   The **Visitors Information Centre** is at 34 St. Margaret's St. (☎ 01227/766567), near St. Margaret's Church. Open April to October daily 9:30am to 5:30pm (closes at 5pm from November to March).

SEEING THE SIGHTS

✪ **Canterbury Cathedral.** 11 The Precincts. ☎ **01227/762862.** Admission £2.50 ($4) adults, £1.50 ($2) children, students and seniors. Guided tours (based on demand) £3 ($5) adults, £2 ($3) students and seniors, £1.50 ($2) children. Easter–Sept daily 8:45am–7pm; Oct–Easter daily 8:45am–5pm.

The foundation of this splendid cathedral dates back to the coming of the first archbishop, Augustine, from Rome in A.D. 597, but the earliest part of the present building is the great Romanesque crypt built circa 1100. The monastic "quire" erected on top of this at the same time was destroyed by fire in 1174, only 4 years after the murder of Thomas à Becket on a gloomy December evening in the northwest transept. The quire was immediately replaced by a magnificent Gothic structure, the first major expression of its kind in England.

The cathedral is noteworthy for the medieval royal tombs of King Henry IV and Edward the Black Prince, as well as those of numerous archbishops. The cathedral stands amid the remains of the buildings of the monastery—cloisters, chapter house, and Norman water tower, which have survived intact from Henry VIII's Reformation to the present day.

Though Henry VIII destroyed Becket's shrine, its site is still honored in Trinity Chapel, near the high altar. The saint is said to have worked miracles, which were recounted in a number of panels of rare stained glass. Perhaps the greatest miracle is that, with some guile, the windows escaped both Henry VIII's idol-smashers and Hitler's blitz. Though German bombs blew out windows in the cathedral, wise caretakers had stowed Becket's glass safely away. Behind the high altar stands St. Augustine's Chair, one of the symbols of the archbishop's authority, and of the history of Christianity in England.

The Canterbury Tales. 23 St. Margaret's St. (off High St., near the cathedral). ☎ **01227/454888.** Admission £5 ($8) adults, £4.25 ($7) seniors and students, £4 ($6) children 5–16, free for children 4 and under. Daily 9:30am–5:30pm.

One of the most visited museums in town re-creates the pilgrimages of Chaucerian England through a series of medieval tableaux. Visitors are handed headsets that replay five of Chaucer's *Canterbury Tales* and the story of the murder of St. Thomas à Becket, which occurred in the nearby cathedral. A tour of all exhibits takes about 45 minutes.

GUIDED WALKS & RIVER TOURS

From Easter to early November, daily guided tours of Canterbury are organized by the **Guild of Guides,** Arnett House, Hawks Lane (☎ 01227/459779), costing £3.25 ($5) for adults and £2.75 ($4) for students and children over 14, and £8 ($13) for a family ticket. Leaving daily at 2pm from the end of March to the end of October, tours meet at the Visitors Information Centre, 34 St. Margaret's Street, in the pedestrian zone near the cathedral. From July to August there's also a tour at 11am Monday to Saturday.

From just below the Weavers House, **Weavers River Trip,** Weavers House, 1 St. Peter's St. (☎ 01227/464660), has boats that leave for half-hour trips along the

Canterbury

Canterbury Cathedral **6**
Canterbury Heritage Museum **2**
Canterbury Roman Museum **5**
The Canterbury Tales **4**
St. Augustine's Abbey **7**
The Weaver's House **3**
West Gate Museum **1**

E-0157

319

river with a commentary on the history of the buildings you pass. Boats depart each half-hour from 1pm to sunset from April to September. Tickets are £3.50 ($6) for adults and £2.50 ($4) for children. Umbrellas are available in case of inclement weather.

WHERE TO STAY
MODERATE

County Hotel. High St., Canterbury, Kent CT1 2RX. ☎ **01227/766266.** Fax 01227/451512. 73 units. TV TEL. £103–£118 ($165–$189) double; £185 ($296) suite. AE, DC, MC, V. Parking £2.50 ($4).

This place has been a hotel since the closing years of Victoria's reign, with a recorded history going back to the end of the 12th century. The time-mellowed atmosphere is strongest in the hewn timbers and carved antiques of the residents' lounge on the second floor. The hotel is fully refurbished, and is the finest lodging within Canterbury's central core. Each room has a fully tiled bathroom, and some rooms contain Georgian or Tudor four-poster beds. For fine dining, go to Sully's Restaurant, the hotel's fully air-conditioned dining room (see "Where to Dine," below). For snacks, vegetarian specialties, salads, and hot dishes, the coffee shop is your best bet. There's also the Tudor Bar, where you can have an aperitif or an after-dinner drink.

✪ **Howfield Manor.** Chartham Hatch, Canterbury, Kent CT4 7HQ. ☎ **01227/738294.** Fax 01227/731535. 16 units. TV TEL. £95 ($152) double; £105 ($168) suite. Rates include English breakfast. AE, MC, V. Take the A28 2¼ miles from Canterbury.

The Towns family are the latest innkeepers to operate on this spot, which has held an inn continuously since 1181. Once part of the estate of the Priory of St. Gregory, this is one of the most charming country manors in the vicinity of Canterbury. It's a good and reliable choice, full of beams and nooks, and with enough log fires blazing on a winter's evening to comfort any chilled stranger. Set on 5 acres of rolling meadows, the house offers tastefully furnished bedrooms with such amenities as alarm clocks, trouser presses, and hair dryers. Rooms in the original house have the most character, as reflected in their exposed beams. New-wing bedrooms are larger and furnished with solid oak pieces. The manor's restaurant, Old Well, is excellent (see "Where to Dine," below). Howfield Manor lies 2 miles from Canterbury along the A28 Ashford Road.

INEXPENSIVE

Cathedral Gate Hotel. 36 Burgate, Canterbury, Kent CT1 2HA. ☎ **01227/464381.** Fax 01227/462800. E-mail: cgate@cgate.demon.co.uk. 24 units (12 with bathroom). TV TEL. £50 ($80) double without bathroom, £75 ($120) double with bathroom. Rates include continental breakfast. AE, DC, MC, V. Parking £2 ($3).

Cathedral Gate is for modern-day pilgrims who want to rest their bones at an inn shouldering up to the cathedral's gateway. For those who want to stay close to the cathedral, there's no better choice. Built in 1438, the hotel adjoins Christchurch Gate and overlooks the Buttermarket. The rooms are comfortable and modestly furnished, and betray medieval construction in sloping floors, massive oak beams, and winding corridors. Its menu is like a time warp from the 1960s—good items such as Lancashire hotpot, Cornish pasties, steak-and-kidney pie, and treacle sponge with custard and cream. An in-house bar is licensed to serve residents, and there's a courtyard garden with cathedral views. It's a 10-minute walk from the train station.

✪ **Ebury Hotel.** 65–67 New Dover Rd., Canterbury, Kent CT1 3DX. ☎ **01227/768433.** Fax 01227/459187. 15 units. TV TEL. £65–£68 ($104–$109) double; £75 ($120) triple; £89 ($142) quad. Rates include English breakfast. AE, MC, V. Closed Dec 21–Jan 12. Follow the signs to A2, Dover Rd. on L.H.S. south of the city.

One of the finest B&B hotels in Canterbury, this gabled Victorian house stands at the edge of town set back from the New Dover Road in 2 acres of garden and within easy walking distance of the center. Built in 1850, it's composed of two separate houses that were joined several years ago. It's important to reserve here, since this well-furnished, roomy, family-run hotel is quite popular. The hotel has a heated indoor swimming pool and spa, as well as a spacious lounge and a licensed restaurant serving English meals prepared with fresh vegetables. Char-grills and dishes based on family recipes are especially good, including lamb chops with watercress. They also rent flats on a weekly basis.

✪ **Three Tuns Inn.** 24 Watling St. (just off Castle St.), Canterbury, Kent CT1 2UD. ☎ **01227/767371.** Fax 01227/785962. 6 units. TV TEL. £42.50–£50 ($68–$80) double. AE, DC, MC, V.

In the center of town, this old-fashioned inn derives most of its business from an exceptionally busy pub. However, many appreciate the handful of antique bedrooms upstairs in the 15th-century building, which impart an old-world charm. William and Mary, who later became king and queen of England, stopped here in 1679; you can follow their example, even going so far as to stay in the same room. The pub downstairs serves a buffet-style tavern fare lunch Monday to Saturday noon to 2pm and Sunday noon to 3pm. Crowds from the pub spill into a side room, the Chapel Restaurant, where illegal Catholic masses were held during the Civil War. It still has the entrance to a secret passageway that allowed celebrants to leave quickly in case of a raid.

WHERE TO DINE
MODERATE

Duck Inn. Pett Bottom, near Bridge. ☎ **01227/830354.** Reservations recommended. Main courses £7–£13 ($11–$21); fixed-price 2-course lunch (Mon–Fri) £11–£12 ($18–$19); fixed-price 3-course dinner £14–£20 ($22–$32). AE, DC, MC, V. Drive 5 miles outside Canterbury near the village of Bridge on the road to Dover. ENGLISH.

Once called the Woodsmen Arms, this restaurant became known as the Duck Inn because of its low door: The clientele would shout "duck!" when a new patron arrived. Set in the Pett Bottom valley, this 16th-century place keeps to English fare. During the summer season, waiters serve diners either indoors or out in the English country garden. The menu changes weekly, although there are a few standards. You can start with one of the homemade soups, such as country vegetable or celery and Stilton. For your main course, the menu may include game pies (in season) or mussels marinara; a duck preparation is always on the menu. For dessert, try a local favorite, the homemade date pudding with toffee sauce. Take note, Bond fans: According to the film *You Only Live Twice*, 007 grew up next door to the Duck Inn.

Old Well Restaurant. At Howfield Manor, Chartham Hatch. ☎ **01227/738294.** Reservations recommended. Main courses £13–£17 ($21–$27). AE, DC, MC, V. Daily noon–2pm and 7:30–9pm. CONTINENTAL/FRENCH.

At this country manor (see "Where to Stay," above), meals are served in the manor's chapel, dating back to 1181. Nearby, the old well where monks drew their water is still visible. Head Chef Andrew Leach and his brigade favor a market-fresh cuisine where each dish is prepared daily. Bolstered by a home-like atmosphere, friendly service, and a well-chosen wine list, Leach graces your meal with such dishes as a phyllo pastry basket filled with chicken livers in a wild mushroom and port-wine sauce. Fine main courses abound, such as guinea fowl with apple and Calvados, or confit of duck surrounded by a sauce of black currants and pink peppercorns. Arrive early to enjoy a drink in the Priory Bar, with its trompe l'oeil murals and a real priesthole (the bar staff will be delighted to explain what that means, just to get the conversation rolling).

Sully's. In the County Hotel, High St. ☎ **01227/766266.** Reservations recommended. Fixed-price lunch £17 ($27) for 2 courses, £16 ($26) for 3 courses; fixed-price dinner £23–£27.50 ($37–$44). AE, DC, MC, V. Daily 12:30–2:20pm and 7–10pm. ENGLISH/CONTINENTAL.

The most distinguished restaurant in Canterbury is located in its most distinguished hotel (see "Where to Stay," above). Although the place is without windows and the decor is straight out of the 1960s, the seating and comfort level is first-rate, and the menu offers good value. You can always count on a selection of plain, traditional English dishes, but try one of the more imaginatively conceived platters instead. Look for seasonal specialties as well. A typical menu might begin with fresh rock oysters glazed with a lime sabayon and follow with a roast from the carving trolley, or filet of pork with Rösti and a Madeira sauce. We recommend the boned Dover sole with white wine and chive sauce or pot-roasted guinea fowl served with a puree of parsnip (the most popular vegetable of the Middle Ages).

5 Shakespeare's Stratford-upon-Avon

91 miles NW of London, 40 miles NW of Oxford

Crowds of tourists overrun this market town on the Avon River during the summer months. In fact, Stratford so aggressively hustles its Shakespeare connection that it seems at times everybody here is in business to make a buck off the Bard. If he could return today, Shakespeare would be faced with Bard T-shirts, china models of Anne Hathaway's cottage, and Big Macs, before looking for a less trampled town to live out his final days.

Actor David Garrick launched the shrine in 1769 when he organized the first of the Bard's commemorative birthday celebrations. Little is known about Shakespeare's early life; many of the stories connected with his days in Stratford are largely fanciful, invented to amuse and entertain the vast number of pilgrims to his birthplace.

A magnet for visitors today is the Royal Shakespeare Theatre, where Britain's foremost actors perform during a long season that lasts from November until September. Other than the theater, Stratford is nearly devoid of any rich cultural life, and you may want to rush back to London after you've seen the literary pilgrimage sights and watched a production. If you can, visit in winter, when the throngs dwindle.

ESSENTIALS

Getting There   Amazingly, there are no direct trains from London. From London's Paddington Station, you can take a train to Leamington Spa, where you pick up a connection for Stratford-upon-Avon. The journey takes about 3 hours at the cost of £20 ($32) for a round-trip ticket. Call ☎ **0345/484950** (in the U.K. only) or 01603/764776 for information and schedules. The train station at Stratford is on Alcester Road (☎ **01203/555211**). It's closed on Sundays from October to May, so you'll have to rely on the bus.

Eight **National Express** buses (☎ **0990/808080**) leave daily from Victoria Station, with a trip time of 3¼ hours. A single-day round-trip ticket costs £13.50 ($22) except Friday when the price is £16 ($26).

To drive from London, take the M40 toward Oxford and continue to Stratford-upon-Avon on A34.

Stratford–upon–Avon

Anne Hathaway's Cottage **7**
Hall's Croft **8**
Harvard House **3**
Holy Trinity Church **9**
Mary Arden's House and the
    Shakespeare Countryside Museum **1**

New Place/Nash's House **4**
Royal Shakespeare Theatre **5**
Shakespeare's Birthplace **2**
Swan Theatre **6**

Visitor Information The **Tourist Information Centre,** Bridgefoot, Stratford-upon-Avon, Warwickshire CV37 6GW (☎ **01789/293127**), provides all the information you'll need. It's open March to October Monday to Saturday 9am to 6pm, Sunday 11am to 5pm. From November to February, the hours are Monday to Saturday 9am to 5pm.

To contact the **Shakespeare Birthplace Trust,** which administers many of the attractions, send a self-addressed envelope and International Reply Coupon to the Director, the Shakespeare Centre, Henley Street, Stratford-upon-Avon, Warwickshire CV37 6QW (☎ **01789/204016**).

VISITING THE SHRINES

Besides the attractions on Stratford's periphery, there are many Elizabethan and Jacobean buildings in town—many of them administered by the Shakespeare Birthplace Trust. One ticket—costing £10 ($16) for adults, £5 ($8) for children, or £26 ($42) family ticket (2 adults, 3 children)—will permit you to visit the five major Shakespeare Birthplace Trust sights: Shakespeare's Birthplace, Anne Hathaway's Cottage, New Place/Nash's House, Mary Arden's House, and Hall's Croft. Seniors and students pay £9 ($14). Pick up the ticket if you're planning to do much sightseeing (obtainable at your first stopover at any one of the Trust properties).

✪ **Shakespeare's Birthplace.** Henley St. ☎ **01789/204016.** Admission £4.50 ($7) adults, £2 ($3) children. Mar 20–Oct 19 Mon–Sat 9am–5pm, Sun 9:30am–5pm; off-season Mon–Sat 9:30am–4pm, Sun 10am–4pm. Closed Dec 24–26.

The son of a glover and whittawer (leather worker), the Bard was born on St. George's Day, April 23, 1564, and died on the same date 52 years later. Filled with Shakespeare memorabilia, this Trust property is a half-timbered structure, dating from the first part of the 16th century. It was bought by public donors in 1847 and preserved as a national shrine. You can visit the bedroom where Shakespeare was probably born, a fully equipped kitchen of the period (look for the "babyminder"), and a Shakespeare Museum, illustrating his life and times. Later, you can walk through the garden. You won't be alone: it's estimated that some 660,000 visitors pass through the house annually.

Built next door to commemorate the 400th anniversary of the Bard's birth, the **Shakespeare Centre** serves both as the administrative headquarters of the Trust and as a library and study center. An extension houses a visitors' center, which acts as a reception area for all those coming to the birthplace. It's in the town center near the post office close to Union Street.

✪ **Anne Hathaway's Cottage.** Cottage Lane, Shottery. ☎ **01789/292100.** Admission £3.50 ($6) adults, £1.50 ($2) children. Mar 20–Oct 19 Mon–Sat 9:30am–5pm, Sun 9:30am–5pm; off-season Mon–Sat 9:30am–4pm, Sun 10am–4pm. Closed Jan 1, Good Friday, and Dec 24–26. Take a bus from Bridge St. or walk via a marked pathway from Evesham Place in Stratford across the meadow to Shottery.

Before she married Shakespeare, Anne Hathaway lived in this thatched, wattle-and-daub cottage in the hamlet of Shottery, a mile from Stratford. It's the most interesting and the most photographed of the Trust properties. The Hathaways were yeoman farmers, and the cottage provides a rare insight into the life of a family in Shakespearean times. The Bard was only 18 when he married Anne, who was much older. Many of the original furnishings, including the courting settle and utensils, are preserved inside the house, which was occupied by descendants of Shakespeare's wife's family until 1892. After visiting the house, take time to linger in the garden and orchard.

New Place/Nash's House. Chapel St. ☎ **01789/204016.** Admission £3 ($5) adults, £1.50 ($2) children. Mar 20–Oct 19 Mon–Sat 9:30am–5pm, Sun 10am–5pm; off-season Mon–Sat 10am–4pm, Sun 10:30am–4pm. Open at 1:30pm Jan 1 and Good Friday; closed Dec 24–26. Walk west down High St.; Chapel St. is a continuation of High St.

Shakespeare retired to New Place in 1610, a prosperous man by the standards of his day, and died here 6 years later. Regrettably, the house was torn down, so only the garden remains. A mulberry tree planted by the Bard was so popular with latter-day visitors to Stratford that the garden's cantankerous owner chopped it down. The mulberry tree that grows here today is said to have been planted from a cutting of the original tree. You enter the gardens through Nash's House (Thomas Nash married Elizabeth Hall, a granddaughter of Shakespeare). Nash's House has 16th-century period rooms and an exhibition illustrating the history of Stratford. The popular Knott Garden adjoins the site and represents the style of a fashionable Elizabethan garden.

Mary Arden's House & the Shakespeare Countryside Museum. Wilmcote. ☎ **01789/204016.** Admission £4 ($6) adults, £2 ($3) children. Mar 20–Oct 19 Mon–Sat 9:30am–5pm, Sun 10am–5pm; off-season Mon–Sat 10am–4pm, Sun 10:30am–4pm. Open at 1:30pm Jan 1 and Good Friday; closed Dec 24–26. Take the A34 (Birmingham) road for 3½ miles.

Reputedly this Tudor farmstead, with its old stone dovecote and various outbuildings, was the girlhood home of Shakespeare's mother—or so claimed an 18th-century entrepreneur. The house contains country furniture and domestic utensils, and in the barns, stable, cowshed, and farmyard you'll find an extensive collection of farming implements illustrating life and work in the local countryside from Shakespeare's time to the present.

Hall's Croft. Old Town. ☎ **01789/292107.** Admission £3 ($5) adults, £1.50 ($2) children and £18 ($29) family ticket for the 3 houses in town. Mar 20–Oct 19 Mon–Sat 9:30am–5pm, Sun 10am–5pm; off-season Mon–Sat 10am–4pm, Sun 10:30am–4pm. Open at 1:30pm Jan 1 and Good Friday; closed Dec 24–26. Walk west from High St., which becomes Chapel St. and Church St. At the intersection with Old Town, go left.

This house is on Old Town street, not far from the parish church, Holy Trinity. It was here that Shakespeare's daughter Susanna probably lived with her husband, Dr. John Hall. Hall's Croft is an outstanding Tudor house with a walled garden, furnished in the style of a middle-class home of the time. Dr. Hall was widely respected and he built up a large medical practice in the area. Exhibits illustrating the theory and practice of medicine in Dr. Hall's time are on view.

Holy Trinity Church (Shakespeare's Tomb). Old Town. ☎ **01789/266316.** Church, free; Shakespeare's tomb, donation 60p ($1) adults, 40p (65¢) students. Mar–Oct Mon–Sat 8:30am–6pm, Sun 2–5pm; Nov–Feb Mon–Sat 8:30am–4pm, Sun 2–5pm. Walk 4 minutes past the Royal Shakespeare Theatre with the river on your left.

In an attractive setting near the Avon River is the parish church where Shakespeare is buried ("and curst be he who moves my bones"). The church is one of the most beautiful parish churches in England.

Impressions

It is something, I thought, to have seen the dust of Shakespeare.
    —Washington Irving, _The Sketch Book_ (1820)

Harvard House. High St. ☎ **01789/204507.** Admission free. Mar–Oct Tues–Sat 10am–4pm, Sun 10:30am–4pm. Closed Monday.

The most ornate home in Stratford, Harvard House is a fine example of an Elizabethan town house. Rebuilt in 1596, it was once the home of Katherine Rogers, mother of John Harvard, founder of Harvard College. In 1909 the house was purchased by a Chicago millionaire, Edward Morris, who presented it as a gift to the famous American university. The rooms are filled with period furniture, and the floors are made of local flagstone. Look for the Bible Chair, used for hiding the Bible during the days of Tudor persecution.

GUIDED TOURS

Guided tours of Stratford-upon-Avon leave from near the **Guide Friday Tourism Center,** Civic Hall, Rother Street (☎ **01789/294466**). In summer, open-top double-decker buses depart every 15 minutes daily from 9:30am to 5:30pm. You can take a 1-hour ride without stops, or you can get off at any or all of the town's five Shakespeare Properties. Although the bus stops are clearly marked along the historic route, the most logical starting point is on the sidewalk in front of the Pen & Parchment Pub, at Bridgefoot, at the bottom of Bridge Street. Tour tickets are valid all day, so you can hop on and off the buses wherever you want. The tours are £8 ($13) for adults, £6 ($10) for senior citizens or students, and £2.50 ($4) for children under 12.

✪ SEEING THE PLAYS

On the banks of the Avon, the **Royal Shakespeare Theatre,** Waterside, Stratford-upon-Avon CV37 6BB (☎ **01789/295623**), is a major showcase for the Royal Shakespeare Company. Seating 1,500 people, the theater's season runs from November until September. The company includes some of the finest actors on the British stage. In an average season, five Shakespearean plays are staged.

You'll usually need reservations. There are two successive booking periods, each one opening about 2 months in advance. You can make reservations from a North American or an English travel agent. A small number of tickets are always held for sale on the day of a performance, but it may be too late for a good seat if you wait until you arrive in Stratford. Tickets can be booked through New York agents **Edwards and Edwards** or **Keith Prowse** (who will add a service charge) or directly with the theater box office by major credit card; for both U.K. and U.S. contact information for both agents, see p. 278 in chapter 9. The box office is open Monday to Saturday from 9am to 8pm, but closes at 6pm on days when there are no performances. The price of seats ranges from £6.50 to £46 ($10 to $74). You can make a credit-card reservation and pick up your tickets on the performance day, but you must cancel at least 2 full weeks in advance to get a refund.

Opened in 1986, the **Swan Theatre** is architecturally connected to the back of its older counterpart and shares the same box office, address, and phone number. It seats 430 on three sides of the stage, much as it would be in an Elizabethan playhouse. The Swan presents a repertoire of about five plays per season, with tickets ranging from £9 to £30 ($14 to $48).

The most recent addition to the Royal Shakespeare complex is **The Other Place,** a small, starkly minimalist theater located on Southern Lane, about 300 yards from its better-established counterparts. It was redesigned in 1996 as an experimental workshop theater without a permanent stage; seats can be radically repositioned (or removed completely) throughout the theater. Examples of recent presentations include a "promenade production" of *Julius Caesar*, in which the actors spent the whole play moving freely among a stand-up audience. Tickets are sold at the complex's main box office and generally range from £12 to £18 ($19 to $29), though this is subject to change.

The Swan Theatre has a **painting gallery** (☎ 01789/412602) with a basic collection of portraits of famous actors and scenes from Shakespeare's plays by 18th- and 19th-century artists. The gallery also houses occasional small exhibitions. It also operates as a base for guided tours with lively running commentary through the world-famous theaters. Guided tours are conducted Monday to Wednesday and Friday at 1:30 and 5:30pm, and four times every Sunday afternoon, production schedules permitting. Tours, which include stopovers at the souvenir shop, cost £4 ($6) for adults, £3 ($5) for students or senior citizens. Call ahead for tour times.

WHERE TO STAY

During the long theater season, it's best to reserve in advance. However, the **Tourist Information Center** (part of the national "Book-a-Bed-Ahead" service, which enables visitors to make reservations in advance) will help find accommodations in all ranges. The fee for room reservations made is 10% of the first night's stay (bed-and-breakfast rate only), deductible from the visitor's final bill.

VERY EXPENSIVE

✪ **Welcombe Hotel.** Warwick Rd., Stratford-upon-Avon, Warwickshire CV37 ONR. ☎ **01789/295252.** Fax 01789/414666. www.welcombe.co.uk. 68 units. TV TEL. £150–£160 ($240–$256) double; from £225–£275 ($360–$440) suite. Rates include English breakfast. AE, DC, MC, V. Take A439 1½ miles northeast of the town center.

For a formal, historic hotel in Stratford, there's none better. One of England's great Jacobean country houses, this hotel is a 10-minute ride from the heart of Stratford-upon-Avon. Its keynote feature is an 18-hole golf course. It's surrounded by 157 acres of grounds and has a formal entrance on Warwick Road, a winding driveway leading to the main hall. Guests gather for afternoon tea or drinks on the rear terrace, with its Italian-style garden and steps leading down to flower beds. The public rooms are heroic in size, with high mullioned windows providing views of the park. Regular bedrooms—some seemingly big enough for tennis matches—are luxuriously furnished; those in the garden wing, although comfortable, are small.

Dining: The hotel's restaurant offers a traditional mix of French and English dishes, although cuisine is not the major reason to check in here.

Amenities: 24-hour room service, laundry service and dry cleaning; babysitting, secretarial services, courtesy car; 18-hole 6,202-yard golf course, tennis courts, putting green.

EXPENSIVE

Alveston Manor Hotel. Clopton Bridge, Stratford-upon-Avon, Warwickshire CV37 7HP. ☎ **800/225-5843** or 01789/204581. Fax 01789/414095. 120 units. TV TEL. £120–£145 ($192–$232) double; £165–£225 ($264–$360) suite. AE, DC, MC, V.

This Tudor manor is perfect for theatergoers—it's just a 2-minute walk from the Avon off B4066. The Alveston is one of the most atmospheric choices within the town itself. The hotel has a wealth of chimneys and gables, and everything from an Elizabethan gazebo to Queen Anne windows. Mentioned in the *Domesday Book*, the building predates the arrival of William the Conqueror. The rooms in the manor house will appeal to those who appreciate the old-world charm of slanted floors, overhead beams, and antique furnishings. Some triples or quads are available in the modern section, which is connected by a covered walk through the rear garden. The rooms here have built-in pieces and a color-coordinated decor; 15 are set aside for non-smokers. The lounges are in the manor; there's a view of the centuries-old tree at the top of the garden—said to have been the background for the first presentation of *A Midsummer Night's Dream.* Logs burn in the Tudor fireplace in the main living room, with its linen-fold paneling.

Dining: Meals are served amid oak beams and leaded-glass windows in the softly lit **Manor Restaurant.** This isn't, however, fine or intimate dining (bus tours stop here). But the bar, paneled in 16th-century oak, never closes, and is the best place in Stratford for a drink at any time.

Amenities: Room service, concierge, babysitting, laundry service, conference room. A health club and massage service is nearby for an additional fee.

Stratford Moat House. Bridgefoot, Stratford-upon-Avon, Warwickshire CV37 6YR. ☎ **01789/279988.** Fax 01789/298589. 249 units. TV TEL. £140 ($224) double; £210 ($336) suite. AE, DC, MC, V.

Moat House stands on 5 acres of landscaped lawns on the banks of the River Avon near Clopton Bridge. Although lacking the charm of the Alveston Manor, as far as amenities go, this modern hotel is just as highly rated as the Welcombe. It's one of the flagships of Queens Moat Houses, a British hotel chain, and was built in the early 1970s and last renovated in 1995. The hotel hosts many conferences, so don't expect to have the place to yourself. Every bedroom has a high standard of comfort, with bathrooms with generous shelf space, large mirrors, coffeemakers, and hair dryers.

Dining: The restaurant features a standard British and continental menu, as well as a carvery of hot and cold roasts. You can drink in the **Tavern Pub** and in the **Terrace Nightspot,** a disco open Friday and Saturday from 9pm to 2am. There's no cover charge for hotel guests; nonresidents pay £10 ($16) after 10:30pm.

Amenities: 24-hour room service, laundry service, and a leisure complex with a swimming pool.

MODERATE

The Arden Thistle Hotel. 44 Waterside, Stratford-upon-Avon, Warwickshire CV37 6BA. ☎ **01789/294949.** Fax 01789/415874. www.stratforduponavon.co.uk/arden.html. 62 units. TV TEL. £112 ($179) double. AE, DC, MC, V.

Theater-goers flock to this hotel across the street from the main entrance of the Royal Shakespeare and Swan theatres. The Thistle chain completely refurbished the interior after buying the Arden in 1993. Its red-brick main section dates from the Regency period, although over the years a handful of adjacent buildings were included and an uninspired modern extension added. Today, the interior has a well-upholstered lounge and bar; a dining room with bay windows; a covered garden terrace; and comfortable but narrow bedrooms with trouser presses, hair dryers, and hot-beverage facilities. A standard fixed-price dinner for £25 ($40) is served in the restaurant. Both continental and English dishes are served, but don't expect much.

Dukes. Payton St., Stratford-upon-Avon, Warwickshire CV37 6UA. ☎ **01789/269300.** Fax 01789/414700. www.astanet.com/get/dukeshtl. 22 units. TV TEL. £70–£115 ($112–$184) double. Rates include English breakfast. AE, DC, MC, V.

Located north of Guild Street in the center of Stratford, this little charmer was formed when two Georgian town houses were united and restored. It's a good place to escape the crowds that overrun such properties as the Falcon. The family-operated inn has a large garden and is close to Shakespeare's birthplace. The public areas and bedrooms are attractive, having been restored to an impressive degree of comfort and coziness. The furniture is tasteful, much of it antique. Dukes also serves a good English and continental cuisine. No children under 12 are accepted here. Despite the reasonable rates (for England, anyway), the hotel offers many amenities that you would find in a more expensive hotel: room service, concierge, dry cleaning and laundry service.

Falcon. Chapel St., Stratford-upon-Avon, Warwickshire CV37 6HA. ☎ **01789/279953.** Fax 01789/414260. 73 units. TV TEL. £105 ($168) double; £125 ($200) suite. AE, DC, MC, V.

Falcon is a blend of the very old and the very new. The black-and-white timbered inn was licensed a quarter of a century after Shakespeare's death; connected to its rear by a glass passageway is a more sterile bedroom extension added in 1970. In the heart of Stratford, the inn faces the Guild Chapel and the New Place Gardens. You arrive at the rear portion to unload luggage, just as horse-drawn coaches once dispatched their passengers—except that today you might be jostled by a tour group checking in. The recently upgraded rooms in the mellowed part have oak beams, diamond leaded-glass windows, some antiques, good reproductions, and such extras as radios, electric trouser presses, and coffeemakers, but not enough soundproofing to drown out the BBC on your next-door neighbor's telly.

The comfortable lounges, also recently upgraded, are some of the finest in the Midlands. In the intimate Merlin Lounge is an open copper-hooded fireplace where coal and log fires are kept burning under beams salvaged from old ships (the walls are a good example of wattle and daub, typical of Shakespeare's day). The Oak Bar is a forest of weathered beams, and on either side of the stone fireplace is paneling removed from the poet's last home, New Place. Most meals are à la carte, unless you prefer to eat in the bar, where platters are offered.

✪ **Stratford House.** 18 Sheep St., Stratford-upon-Avon, Warwickshire CV37 6EF. ☎ **01789/268288.** Fax 01789/295580. 12 units. TV TEL. £84–£90 ($134–$144) double; £125 ($200) suite. Rates include English breakfast. AE, DC, MC, V. Parking £3 ($5).

The staff at this Georgian house 100 yards from the River Avon and the Royal Shakespeare Theatre extends a warm welcome to guests. The house is furnished tastefully, somewhat like a private home, with books and pictures along with a scattering of antiques. Everything is spotlessly maintained. There is a walled courtyard on the side with flowering plants. All bedrooms have tea and coffeemakers. Both hotel guests and outsiders can dine in the garden restaurant, Shepherd's.

White Swan. Rother St., Stratford-upon-Avon, Warwickshire CV37 6NH. ☎ **800/225-5843** in the U.S. and Canada, or 01789/297022. Fax 01789/268773. 39 units. TV TEL. £80 ($128) double; £119 ($190) suite. Children up to 16 stay free in parents' room. Rates include English breakfast. AE, DC, MC, V.

This cozy, intimate hotel is one of the most atmospheric in Stratford and is, in fact, its oldest building. In business for more than a century before Shakespeare appeared on the scene, it competes successfully with the Falcon in offering an ancient atmosphere. The gabled medieval front would present the Bard with no surprises, but the modern comforts inside would surely astonish him, even though many of the rooms have been preserved. Paintings dating from 1550 hang on the lounge walls. All bedrooms are well appointed; amenities include a radio, trouser press, and hair dryer. The hostelry has a spacious restaurant where good food is served. The oak-beamed bar is a popular meeting place (see "Pubs," below).

INEXPENSIVE

Sequoia House. 51–53 Shipston Rd., Stratford-upon-Avon, Warwickshire CV37 7LN. ☎ 01789/268852. Fax 01789/414559. www.stratforduponavon.co.uk/sequoiahouse.html. 24 units (20 with bath or shower). TV TEL. £42 ($67) double without bath, £59–£74 ($94–$118) double with bath. Rates include English breakfast. AE, DC, MC, V.

This privately run hotel has its own beautiful garden on three-quarters of an acre across the Avon opposite the theater, conveniently located for visiting the major Shakespeare sites. Renovation has vastly improved the house, which was created from two late-Victorian buildings. Today it offers rooms with coffeemakers and hot and cold running water. Guests gather in a lounge that has a licensed bar and an open Victorian fireplace.

✪ **Stratheden Hotel.** 5 Chapel St., Stratford-upon-Avon, Warwickshire CV37 6EP. ☎ **01789/297119.** Fax 01789/297119. 9 units. TV TEL. £58–£64 ($93–$102) double. Rates include English breakfast. MC, V.

A short walk north of the Royal Shakespeare Theatre, this hotel is tucked away in a desirable position on a plot of land that was first mentioned in a property deed in 1333. Built in 1673 and today the oldest-remaining brick building in the town center, it has a tiny rear garden and top-floor rooms with slanted, beamed ceilings. Under the ownership of the Wells family for the past quarter century, it has improved again in both decor and comfort with the addition of fresh paint, new curtains, and good beds. Tea and coffeemakers allow you to have a "cuppa" any time of the day or night. The dining room, with a bay window, has an overscale sideboard that once belonged to the "insanely vain" Marie Corelli, an eccentric novelist, poet, and mystic, and a favorite author of Queen Victoria. Corelli was noted for her passion for pastoral settings and objets d'art. You can see an example of her taste: a massive mahogany tester bed in Room 4.

WHERE TO DINE
MODERATE

The Box Tree Restaurant. In the Royal Shakespeare Theatre, Waterside. ☎ **01789/ 293226.** Reservations required. Matinee lunch £16.50 ($26); dinner £25.50–£26.50 ($41–$42). AE, MC, V. Thurs–Sat noon–2:30pm; Mon–Sat 5:45pm–midnight. FRENCH/ITALIAN/ENGLISH.

This restaurant enjoys the best location in town—in the theater itself—with its glass walls providing an unobstructed view of swans on the Avon. You can partake of an intermission snack of smoked salmon and champagne, or dine by flickering candlelight after the performance. Many dishes such as apple and parsnip soup are definitely old English; others reflect a continental touch, such as fried polenta with filets of pigeon and bacon. For your main course, you might select Dover sole, salmi of wild boar, pheasant, or roast pork loin. Homemade desserts are likely to include crème brûlée, an old-time favorite at The Box Tree. There's a special phone for reservations in the theater lobby.

Greek Connection. 1 Shakespeare St. ☎ **01789/292214.** Reservations recommended. Main courses £8.25–£16 ($13–$26); 3-course early evening, fixed-price dinner £9.75 ($16) from 5:30–7pm only. MC, V. Summer daily noon–2:30pm; year-round daily 5:30–10:30pm. GREEK/INTERNATIONAL.

Situated in the heart of Stratford within a 3-minute walk of Shakespeare's birthplace, the Greek Connection occupies the vaulted premises of what was formerly a Methodist chapel built in 1854, which also put in service for a time as an automobile museum. The restaurant serves authentic Greek cuisine, accompanied by live Greek music and dancing nightly. Chefs Spiros and George serve a variety of Greek and international dishes from an à la carte menu. Their moussaka is especially inspiring; the chefs piquantly season freshly minced meat between layers of sliced eggplant, zucchini, and potato, crowning the layers with a creamy dome of béchamel and sprinkled parmesan cheese, swelled like a soufflé through baking (they also offer a vegetarian version). The kebab charcoal grill holds a prime place in the kitchen, where lamb, pork, and chicken are barbecued over wood embers. Appetizers range from stuffed vine leaves to the famed *avgolemono* (chicken and rice soup creamed with beaten eggs and flavored with lemon). Many prefer the *Mezedakia*, a sampling of Greek hors d'oeuvres.

INEXPENSIVE

✪ **Hussain's.** 6A Chapel St. (across from the Shakespeare Hotel and historic New Place). ☎ **01789/267506.** Reservations recommended. Main courses £6.75–£12 ($11–$19). AE, DC, MC, V. Daily noon–2:30pm and 5pm–midnight. INDIAN.

Compared to a private Indian home, this restaurant has many admirers—some consider it one of the brighter spots on the bleak culinary landscape hereabouts. The owner has chosen a well-trained, welcoming, alert staff. You can select from an array of northern Indian tandooris plus various curries with lamb or prawn. There is a three-course lunch from 12:30 to 2:30pm for £6 ($10). Fixed-price pre- and post-theater dinners are also available.

The Opposition. 13 Sheep St. ☎ **01789/269980.** Reservations recommended. Main courses £6–£15 ($10–$24). MC, V. Daily noon–2pm and 5:30–11pm. INTERNATIONAL.

Located in the heart of Stratford, in a 16th-century building, this is a refreshingly unpretentious restaurant with a high turnover of loyal clients drawn to the good bistro cookery at reasonable prices. Morning coffee, tea cakes, and croissants are sold Monday to Saturday from 11am to noon, but most people come for a meal. Choices include chicken cooked with spinach, stuffed with mango and curry, or prepared Cajun-style; salmon either grilled or poached and served with hollandaise; and grilled sirloin or filet of beef. In case you wondered what Banoffi pie is (a specialty here), it's made with toffee, bananas, biscuits, and whipped cream.

PUBS

The Black Swan ("The Dirty Duck"). Waterside. ☎ **01789/297312.** Reservations required for dining. Main courses £7–£15 ($11–$24); bar snacks £1.50–£4 ($2–$6). MC, V (restaurant only). Pub Mon–Sat 11am–11pm; Sun noon–3pm and 7–10:30pm. Restaurant Tues–Sun noon–2pm; Mon–Sat 6–11:30pm. ENGLISH.

Affectionately known as "The Dirty Duck," this has been a popular hangout for Stratford players since the 18th century. The wall is lined with autographed photos of its patrons such as Sir Laurence Olivier. The front lounge and bar crackles with intense conversation; in the spring and fall, an open fire blazes. Typical English grills are featured in the Grill Room, never accused of serving the best food in Stratford. You'll be faced with a choice of a dozen appetizers, most of which would make a meal in themselves. Main dishes include braised kidneys or oxtails, roast chicken, or honey-roasted duck. In fair weather, you can have drinks in the front garden and watch the swans glide by on the Avon.

The Garrick Inn. 25 High St. ☎ **01789/292186.** Main courses £5–£9 ($8–$14). MC, V. Meals daily noon–8:30pm. Pub Mon–Sat 11am–11pm; Sun noon–10:30pm. ENGLISH.

Near Harvard House, this black-and-white timbered Elizabethan pub dating from 1595 has an unpretentious charm. The front bar is decorated with tapestry-covered settles, an old oak refectory table, and an open fireplace which attracts the locals. The black bar has a circular fireplace with a copper hood and mementos of the triumphs of the English stage. The specialty is homemade pies such as steak and ale, steak and kidney, or chicken and mushroom.

White Swan. In the White Swan Hotel, Rother St. ☎ **01789/297022.** Dinner reservations recommended. Bar snacks £2–£6 ($3–$10); fixed-price 3-course dinner £20 ($32). AE, DC, MC, V. Morning coffee daily 10am–noon; self-service bar snacks daily 12:30–2pm; afternoon tea daily 2–5:30pm; dinner Mon–Thurs 6–9pm, Fri–Sat 6–9:30pm, Sun 7–9pm. ENGLISH.

Housed in the town's oldest building, this is one of the most atmospheric pubs in Stratford. Once you step inside, you're drawn into a world of cushioned leather arm-chairs, old oak settles, oak paneling, and fireplaces. You're likely to meet a worthy cross-section of amiable drinkers in a setting once enjoyed by Shakespeare himself, when it was known as the Kings Head. At lunch you can partake of the hot dishes of the day, along with fresh salads and sandwiches.

6 Salisbury & Stonehenge

90 miles SW of London

Long before you've even entered Salisbury, the spire of Salisbury Cathedral will come into view—just as John Constable painted it so many times. The 404-foot pinnacle of the early English and Gothic cathedral is the tallest in England. Salisbury, or New Sarum, lies in the valley of the Avon River, and is a fine base for touring such sights as Stonehenge. Filled with Tudor inns and tearooms, it's known to readers of Thomas Hardy as Melchester and to fans of Anthony Trollope as Barchester.

Salisbury today is often viewed as only a "refueling stop" or overnight stopover for visitors anxious to explore Stonehenge. However, the old market town is an interesting destination in its own right. There's another reason some visitors like to drop off at Salisbury, the only true city in Wiltshire: Its pub-to-citizen ratio is said to be the highest in the country.

ESSENTIALS

Getting There A **Network Express** train departs hourly from Waterloo Station in London bound for Salisbury (trip time: 2 hours). For information, call ☎ **0345/484950** (U.K. only) or 01603/764776.

Five **National Express** buses per day run from London Monday to Friday. On Saturday and Sunday, four buses depart Victoria Coach Station for Salisbury (trip time: 2½ hours). For information, call ☎ **0990/808080.**

To drive from London, head west on M3 to the end of the run, continuing the rest of the way on A30.

Visitor Information The **Tourist Information Centre** is at Fish Row (☎ **01722/334956,** fax 01722/422059). From October to April, it's open Monday to Saturday 9:30am to 5pm; in May, Monday to Saturday 9:30am to 5pm and Sunday 10:30am to 4:30pm; in June and September, Monday to Saturday 9:30am to 6pm and Sunday 10:30am to 4:30pm; and in July and August, Monday to Saturday 9:30am to 7pm and on Sunday from 10:30am to 5pm.

SEEING THE SIGHTS

✪ **Salisbury Cathedral.** The Close. ☎ **01722/323279.** Suggested donation £2.50 ($4); chapter house 30p (50¢). May–Aug daily 8:30am–8:30pm; Sept–Apr daily 8am–6:30pm.

You can search all of England, but you'll find no better example of the early English, or pointed, style than Salisbury Cathedral. Construction was begun as early as 1220 and took 38 years to complete; this was considered rather fast in those days since it was customary for the building of a cathedral to last at least three centuries. In spite of an ill-conceived renovation in the 18th century, Salisbury Cathedral's architectural integrity remains.

The cathedral's especially attractive 13th-century octagonal chapter house possesses one of the four surviving original texts of the Magna Carta, along with treasures from the diocese of Salisbury and manuscripts and artifacts belonging to the cathedral. The cloisters enhance the beauty of the cathedral, and its exceptionally large close, comprising at least 75 buildings, sets off the cathedral effectively.

In the Cathedral Cloisters is a **Brass Rubbing Centre** (☎ **01722/323279**). It's open mid-June to September Monday to Saturday from 10am to 6pm, Sunday 11:15am to 4pm. A helpful staff will guide you to choose from a variety of exact replicas molded from the original brasses: local medieval and Tudor knights and ladies, famous historical faces, even Celtic designs. The £3 ($5) average charge made for each rubbing includes materials and instructions. You can also buy ready-made rubbings and historical gift items.

✪ **Wilton House.** 3 miles west of Salisbury on A30. ☎ **01722/746729.** Admission £6.75 ($11) adults, £4 ($6) children 5–15, free for children under 5. Easter–Oct daily 11am–6pm. Last admission at 5pm. *Not open in Spring*

In the town of Wilton is one of England's great country estates, the home of the earls of Pembroke. Wilton House dates from the 16th century, but it's most noted for its 17th-century staterooms by the celebrated architect Inigo Jones. Many famous people have either lived at or visited Wilton; it's also believed that Shakespeare's troupe entertained here. Preparations for the D-day landings at Normandy were laid out here by Eisenhower and his advisers, with only the silent Van Dyck paintings in the Double Cube room as witnesses.

The house is filled with beautifully maintained furnishings and world-class art, including paintings by Van Dyck, Rubens, Brueghel, and Reynolds. A dynamic film introduced and narrated by Anna Massey brings to life the history of the family since 1544, the year they were granted the land by Henry VIII. You can then visit a reconstructed Tudor kitchen and Victorian laundry plus "The Wareham Bears," a collection of some 200 miniature dressed teddy bears.

Growing on the 21-acre estate are giant Cedars of Lebanon, the oldest of which were planted in 1630. The Palladian Bridge was built in 1737 by the ninth earl of Pembroke and Roger Morris. The grounds include rose and water gardens, riverside and woodland walks, and a huge adventure playground for children.

✪ **Stonehenge.** Junction of A303 and A344/A360. ☎ **01980/623108.** Admission £3.90 ($6) adults, £2.90 ($5) students and seniors, £2 ($3) children. Mar 16–May and Sept–Oct 15 daily 9:30am–6pm; June–Aug daily 9am–7pm; Oct 16–Mar 15 daily 9:30am–4pm. Bus: Stonehenge.

Two miles west of Amesbury and about 9 miles north of Salisbury is the renowned Stonehenge stone circle, believed to be anywhere from 3,500 to 5,000 years old. This huge circle of lintels and megalithic pillars is the most important prehistoric monument in Britain. Some are disappointed when they see that Stonehenge is nothing more than concentric circles of stones surrounded by a fence. Keep in mind, however, what a dedication of love the design represents. Many of the boulders—the bluestones in particular—were quarried and moved from sites as far away as southern Wales in a time before forklifts, lorries, and dynamite.

The widely held view of the 18th- and 19th-century romantics that Stonehenge was the work of the Druids is without foundation. The boulders, many weighing several tons, are believed to have predated the arrival in Britain of the Celtic cult. Recent excavations continue to bring new evidence to bear on the origin and purpose of Stonehenge. *Stonehenge Decoded,* by Gerald S. Hawkins and John B. White, maintains that the site was an astronomical observatory—that is, a Neolithic "computing machine" capable of predicting eclipses.

Your ticket permits you to go inside the fence surrounding the site that protects the stones from vandals and souvenir hunters. You can go all the way up to a short rope barrier about 50 feet from the stones. A modular walkway has been introduced to cross the archeologically important avenue, the area that runs between the Heel Stone and the main circle of stones. This enables visitors to complete a full circuit of the stones and to see one of the best views of a completed section of Stonehenge as they pass by. This is an excellent addition to the well-received audio tour introduced in 1995.

WHERE TO STAY
MODERATE
✪ **The Rose and Crown.** Harnham Rd., Salisbury, Wiltshire SP2 8JQ. ☎ **01722/399955.** Fax 01722/339816. 28 units. TV TEL. £114–£129 ($182–$206) double; £159 ($254) suite. AE, DC, MC, V. Take A3094 1½ miles from the center of town.

This half-timbered, 13th-century inn stands with its feet almost in the Avon River; beyond the water you can see the tall spire of the cathedral. Because of its more tranquil location, we prefer it to either the White Hart or the Red Lion; you can easily walk over the arched stone bridge to the center of Salisbury from here in 10 minutes or so. The lawns and gardens between the inn and the river are shaded by old trees, and chairs are set out so you can enjoy the view and count the swans. The inn, part of the Queens Moat House Hotels chain, has both an old wing and a modern new one. The old wing has more appeal, with sloping ceilings and antique fireplaces and furniture. Each room has a radio, coffeemaker, hair dryer, and trouser press. You can dine on English fare while overlooking the river. Across the courtyard are two taverns; you can choose either of two bars with oak beams and log fires. Services include room service and laundry.

White Hart. 1 St. John St., Salisbury, Wiltshire SP1 2SD. ☎ **01722/327476.** Fax 01722/412761. 68 units. TV TEL. £110–£140 ($176–$224) double. AE, DC, MC, V.

Combining the best of old and new, the White Hart has been a Salisbury landmark since Georgian times. Its classic facade is intact, with tall columns crowning a life-size effigy of a hart. The older accommodations are traditional, and a new section has been added in the rear, opening onto a large parking area—like a motel. New-wing units are tastefully conceived and decorated. The hotel was completely refurbished in 1995. You can enjoy a before-dinner drink in White Hart, followed by a meal in the White Hart Restaurant for £19 to £23 ($30 to $37).

INEXPENSIVE
✪ **Grasmere House.** 70 Harnham Rd., Salisbury, Wiltshire SP2 8JN. ☎ **01722/338388.** Fax 01722/333710. 20 units. TV TEL. £95–£125 ($152–$200) double. Rates include English breakfast. AE, DC, MC, V. Take A3094 1½ miles from the center of town.

Grasmere stands near the confluence of the Nadder and Avon rivers on 1½ acres of grounds. Constructed in 1896 for Salisbury merchants, the house still resembles a family home. Many of the old features were retained, including a "calling box" for servants in the dining room. Three luxurious bedrooms overlook the cathedral, as does a new conservatory bar. The original house holds four bedrooms; the rest are in the new wing. All rooms have a trouser press and a hair dryer. The house operates a restaurant popular with locals and residents alike. Steaks are a specialty, ranging from flambéed to au poivre.

✪ **The New Inn & Old House.** 39–47 New St., Salisbury, Wiltshire SP1 2PH. ☎ **01722/327679.** 8 units. TV. £50–£70 ($80–$112) double. Rates include continental breakfast. AE, MC, V. Free parking.

This upscale B&B is one of the finest in Salisbury but, despite its name, isn't new at all. It's a 15th-century building with a walled garden backing up to the Cathedral Close Wall. Its bedrooms are well appointed, oak beamed, and evocative of an earlier century. The inn's center is the serving bar, which adjoins onto three outer rooms: one, a tiny sitting area, another, a tavern with high-backed settles and a fireplace, and the third, a lounge. In the Inn, main courses are reasonably priced. Adjacent to the main building is a coffee house and gift shop. This is a non-smoking facility.

WHERE TO DINE

The best restaurants are found not in the core of Salisbury itself but on the outskirts—at either the Silver Plough at Pitton or Howard's House at Teffont Evias.

Harper's Restaurant. 7–9 Ox Row, Market Sq. ☎ **01722/333118.** Reservations recommended. Main courses £8.50–£12.50 ($14–$20); fixed-price 3-course meals £8 ($13) at lunch, £13 ($21) at dinner. AE, DC, MC, V. Mon–Sat noon–2pm and 6:30–9:30pm; Sun 6–9:30pm. Closed Sun Oct–May. ENGLISH/INTERNATIONAL.

The chef-owner of this place prides himself on specializing in "real food"—homemade, uncomplicated, and wholesome. The pleasantly decorated restaurant is on the second floor of a red-brick building at the back side of Salisbury's largest parking lot, in the center of town. Within the same all-purpose dining room, you can order from two different menus, one featuring cost-conscious bistro-style platters, including beefsteak casserole with "herbey dumplings." A longer menu, listing items that take a bit more time to prepare, includes all-vegetarian pasta diavolo or spareribs with french fries and rice.

Salisbury Haunch of Venison. 1 Minster St. ☎ **01722/322024.** Main courses £9–£12 ($14–$19); bar platters for lunches, light suppers, and snacks £4–£6 ($6.30–$10). AE, DC, MC, V. Restaurant daily noon–3pm; Mon–Sat 7–9:30pm. Pub Mon–Sat 11am–11pm; Sun noon–3pm and 7–11pm. Closed Christmas–Easter. ENGLISH.

Right in the heart of Salisbury, this creaky-timbered, 1320 chophouse serves excellent dishes, especially English roasts and grills. Stick to its specialties and you'll rarely go wrong. Begin perhaps with tasty warm salad of venison sausages with garlic croutons, then follow with the house specialty: roast haunch of venison with garlic and juniper berries. Many other classic English dishes are served as well including a medley of fish and shellfish or else grilled Barnsley lamb chops with "bubble & squeak" (cabbage and potatoes).

The centuries have given a gleam to the oak furnishings, and years of polishing have worn down the brass. Tortuous steps lead to tiny, cozy rooms (there is one small room with space for about four to sit, where you can revel in England's past, present, and future). Two of the restaurant windows overlook St. Thomas's cloisters.

IN NEARBY PITTON

Silver Plough. White Hill, Pitton, near Salisbury. ☎ **01722/712266.** Reservations recommended. Main courses £8–£13 ($13–$21); bar platters £3.50–£8 ($6–$13). AE, DC, MC, V. Restaurant daily noon–2pm; Mon–Sat 7–10pm, Sun 7–10pm. Pub Mon–Sat 11am–3pm and 6–11pm; Sun noon–3pm and 7–10:30pm. Closed for some meals Dec 25–26 and Jan 1. Take A30 5 miles east of Salisbury; it's at the southern end of the hamlet of Pitton. ENGLISH.

Built as a stone-sided farmhouse 150 years ago, the Silver Plough is now a charming and accommodating country pub with a restaurant. Specializing in fish and game dishes, it contains heavily beamed ceilings hung with tankards, coach horns, and other country-inspired memorabilia. Snacks are available in the bar. In the somewhat more formal dining room, the chef prepares such dishes as fresh Dorset mussels in a white wine, garlic, and cream sauce, sliced breast of duck in cracked pepper or orange sauce, and roast guinea fowl in a sharp strawberry sauce. The Silver Plough has known many famous visitors, but apart from displaying a signed letter from Queen Victoria thanking the women of England for their concern after the death of her husband, Albert, the management prefers to stick to its quiet, country atmosphere and to concentrate on making its guests feel at home.

Index

See also separate Accommodations, Restaurant, and Afternoon Tea indexes, below. Page numbers in italics refer to maps.

RESTAURANTS

AFTERNOON TEA

FROMMER'S® COMPLETE TRAVEL GUIDES
(Comprehensive guides with selections in all price ranges—from deluxe to budget)

Alaska
Amsterdam
Arizona
Atlanta
Australia
Austria
Bahamas
Barcelona, Madrid & Seville
Belgium, Holland & Luxembourg
Bermuda
Boston
Budapest & the Best of Hungary
California
Canada
Cancún, Cozumel & the Yucatán
Cape Cod, Nantucket & Martha's Vineyard
Caribbean
Caribbean Cruises & Ports of Call
Caribbean Ports of Call
Carolinas & Georgia
Chicago
China
Colorado
Costa Rica
Denver, Boulder & Colorado Springs
England
Europe
Florida

France
Germany
Greece
Hawaii
Hong Kong
Honolulu, Waikiki & Oahu
Ireland
Israel
Italy
Jamaica & Barbados
Japan
Las Vegas
London
Los Angeles
Maryland & Delaware
Maui
Mexico
Miami & the Keys
Montana & Wyoming
Montréal & Québec City
Munich & the Bavarian Alps
Nashville & Memphis
Nepal
New England
New Mexico
New Orleans
New York City
Nova Scotia, New Brunswick & Prince Edward Island
Oregon
Paris
Philadelphia & the Amish Country

Portugal
Prague & the Best of the Czech Republic
Provence & the Riviera
Puerto Rico
Rome
San Antonio & Austin
San Diego
San Francisco
Santa Fe, Taos & Albuquerque
Scandinavia
Scotland
Seattle & Portland
Singapore & Malaysia
South Pacific
Spain
Switzerland
Thailand
Tokyo
Toronto
Tuscany & Umbria
USA
Utah
Vancouver & Victoria
Vermont, New Hampshire & Maine
Vienna & the Danube Valley
Virgin Islands
Virginia
Walt Disney World & Orlando
Washington, D.C.
Washington State

FROMMER'S® DOLLAR-A-DAY GUIDES
(The ultimate guides to comfortable low-cost travel)

Australia from $50 a Day
California from $60 a Day
Caribbean from $60 a Day
England from $60 a Day
Europe from $50 a Day
Florida from $60 a Day
Greece from $50 a Day
Hawaii from $60 a Day
Ireland from $50 a Day

Israel from $45 a Day
Italy from $50 a Day
London from $70 a Day
New York from $75 a Day
New Zealand from $50 a Day
Paris from $70 a Day
San Francisco from $60 a Day
Washington, D.C., from $60 a Day

FROMMER'S® MEMORABLE WALKS

Chicago
London

New York
Paris

San Francisco

FROMMER'S® PORTABLE GUIDES

Acapulco, Ixtapa/ Zihuatenejo	Dublin	Puerto Vallarta, Manzanillo & Guadalajara
Bahamas	Las Vegas	San Francisco
California Wine Country	London	Sydney
Charleston & Savannah	Maine Coast	Tampa Bay & St. Petersburg
Chicago	New Orleans	Venice
	New York City	Washington, D.C.
	Paris	

FROMMER'S® NATIONAL PARK GUIDES

Grand Canyon
National Parks of the American West
Yellowstone & Grand Teton

Yosemite & Sequoia/ Kings Canyon
Zion & Bryce Canyon

THE COMPLETE IDIOT'S TRAVEL GUIDES
(The ultimate user-friendly trip planners)

Cruise Vacations	Las Vegas	New York City
Planning Your Trip to Europe	Mexico's Beach Resorts	San Francisco
Hawaii	New Orleans	Walt Disney World

SPECIAL-INTEREST TITLES

The Civil War Trust's Official Guide to the Civil War Discovery Trail
Frommer's Caribbean Hideaways
Israel Past & Present
New York City with Kids
New York Times Weekends
Outside Magazine's Adventure Guide to New England
Outside Magazine's Adventure Guide to Northern California

Outside Magazine's Adventure Guide to the Pacific Northwest
Outside Magazine's Guide to Family Vacations
Places Rated Almanac
Retirement Places Rated
Washington, D.C., with Kids
Wonderful Weekends from Boston
Wonderful Weekends from New York City
Wonderful Weekends from San Francisco
Wonderful Weekends from Los Angeles

THE UNOFFICIAL GUIDES®
(Get the unbiased truth from these candid, value-conscious guides)

Atlanta	Florida with Kids	Miami & the Keys	Skiing in the West
Branson, Missouri	The Great Smoky & Blue Ridge Mountains	Mini-Mickey	Walt Disney World
Chicago		New Orleans	Walt Disney World Companion
Cruises		New York City	
Disneyland	Las Vegas	San Francisco	Washington, D.C.

FROMMER'S® IRREVERENT GUIDES
(Wickedly honest guides for sophisticated travelers)

Amsterdam	London	New Orleans	San Francisco
Boston	Manhattan	Paris	Walt Disney World
Chicago			Washington, D.C.

FROMMER'S® DRIVING TOURS

America	Florida	Ireland	Scotland
Britain	France	Italy	Spain
California	Germany	New England	Western Europe

www.frommers.com

Arthur Frommer's OUTSPOKEN ENCYCLOPEDIA OF TRAVEL

You've Read our Books, Now Visit our Website...

With more than 6,000 pages of the most up-to-date travel bargains and information from the name you trust the most, Arthur Frommer's Outspoken Encyclopedia of Travel brings you all the information you need to plan your next trip.

Register to Win free tickets, accommodations and more!

Arthur Frommer's Daily Newsletter

Bookmark the daily newsletter to read about the hottest travel news and bargains in the industry or subscribe and receive it daily on your own desktop.

Hot Spot of the Month

Check out the Hot Spot each month to get the best information and hottest deals for your favorite vacation destinations.

200 Foreign & Domestic Destinations

Choose from more than 200 destinations and get the latest information on accommodations, airfare, restaurants, and more.

Frommer's Travel Guides

Shop our online bookstore and choose from more than 200 current Frommer's travel guides. Secure transactions guaranteed!

Bookmark www.frommers.com for the most up-to-date travel bargains and information—updated daily!

WHEREVER YOU TRAVEL, *H*ELP IS NEVER FAR AWAY.

From planning your trip to providing travel assistance along the way, American Express® Travel Service Offices are always there to help.

London

American Express Travel Service
1 Savoy Court ·
0171/240-1521

American Express Travel Service
78 Brompton Road
0171/584-6182

American Express Travel Service
111 Cheapside
0171/600-5522

American Express Travel Service
6 Haymarket
01·71/930-4411

American Express Travel Service
89 Mount Street Mayfair
0171/499-4436

American Express Travel Service
102 Victoria Steet
0171/828-7411

Travel

http://www.americanexpress.com/travel

**American Express Travel Service Offices are found
in central locations throughout the United Kingdom.**